Sexual Assault Kits and Reforming the Response to Rape

Sexual Assault Kits and Reforming the Response to Rape curates the current state of untested sexual assault kit research and highlights emerging best practices by exploring the past, the present, and the future of our collective response to rape.

This book is the first to address the most critical topics related to untested sexual assault kits and the Department of Justice's Sexual Assault Kit Initiative, bringing together leading US scholars, practitioners, policy makers, and survivors. In a series of well-researched and thoughtful thematic chapters, the book explores the current state of knowledge related to untested kits, survivors, and perpetrators, while also documenting fundamental and necessary changes in how societal systems respond to rape. It provides an opportunity to learn from our past, highlight what we could do differently now, and envision a better future for victims of rape and those tasked with ensuring justice. It may also serve as a cautionary tale for those jurisdictions that have yet to face their backlog or who have failed to embrace the practice and policy changes that have emerged from the Sexual Assault Kit Initiative.

Sexual Assault Kits and Reforming the Response to Rape is essential reading for practitioners (including law enforcement, prosecutors, victim advocates, mental health providers, forensic nurses, and forensic scientists), stakeholders, legislators, and policy makers. It will also be of interest to upper-level students and scholars working on interpersonal violence, gender-based violence, and forensic nursing in social/behavioral science fields.

Rachel E. Lovell (PhD, Sociology, The Ohio State University) is an Assistant Professor of Criminology and Director of the Criminology Research Center at Cleveland State University in Cleveland, Ohio. She is an applied criminologist and methodologist whose research focuses on gender-based violence and victimization, particularly sexual assault, human trafficking, and intimate partner violence. Since 2015, Dr. Lovell has been the Principal Investigator on several large action research projects on untested sexual assault kits in collaboration with the Cuyahoga County Prosecutor's Office and the Akron Police Department, with funding provided by the Department of Justice's Sexual Assault Kit Initiative. As an extension of the Sexual Assault Kit Initiative, she serves as the lead researcher on the Cuyahoga County Prosecutor's Office's Lawfully "Owed" DNA Initiative. Dr. Lovell is also the Principal Investigator on a National Institute of Justice grant to employ machine learning technology to analyze the narratives of thousands of sexual assault police reports for "signaling" language regarding a victim's credibility. She is an established scholar with over $5.5 million in external funding in the last nine years and several dozen peer-reviewed publications and book chapters.

Jennifer Langhinrichsen-Rohling (PhD, Clinical-Community Psychology, University of Oregon) is a Professor in the Department of Psychological Science at the University of North Carolina—Charlotte. She is core faculty in the Clinical Health concentration of the Health Psychology PhD program and a licensed clinical psychologist in North Carolina. Dr. Langhinrichsen-Rohling's research focuses on individual, couple, family, and system-level factors associated with prevention and response to intimate partner violence, sexual assault, and self-harming behaviors. Dr. Langhinrichsen-Rohling has recently been working at the system level to promote trauma-informed care and prevent and repair institutional betrayal. Across her career, Dr. Langhinrichsen-Rohling directed the Gulf Coast Behavioural Health and Resiliency Center and the Youth Violence Prevention Program at the University of South Alabama. Currently, she routinely consults with integrated health-care settings, WIC clinics, domestic violence batterer intervention programs, service providers, and community advocacy groups to enhance access to evidence-based services for under-resourced populations. For four years, Dr. Langhinrichsen-Rohling served as the Primary Investigator on the Mobile Police Department's Sexual Assault Kit Initiative, which successfully tested the backlog of sexual assault kits (SAKs) in Mobile, changed police policies and practices around SAK submission, established the Promise Initiative, and started a Family Justice Center. Dr. Langhinrichsen-Rohling is an established scholar with over 200 peer-reviewed publications and book chapters. She also has experience as both a journal and book section editor. Most recently, she served as a section editor of the intimate partner violence component of the five-volume Handbook of Interpersonal Violence.

Sexual Assault Kits and Reforming the Response to Rape

Edited by Rachel E. Lovell and Jennifer Langhinrichsen-Rohling

LONDON AND NEW YORK

Cover image: John J. Lawrence

First published 2023
by Routledge
4 Park Square, Milton Park, Abingdon, Oxon OX14 4RN

and by Routledge
605 Third Avenue, New York, NY 10158

Routledge is an imprint of the Taylor & Francis Group, an informa business

British Library Cataloguing-in-Publication Data
A catalogue record for this book is available from the British Library

Library of Congress Cataloging-in-Publication Data
Names: Lovell, Rachel E., editor. | Langhinrichsen-Rohling, Jennifer, editor.
Title: Sexual assault kits and reforming the response to rape / edited by
Rachel Lovell and Jennifer Langhinrichsen-Rohling.
Description: New York : Routledge, 2022. | Includes bibliographical
references and index.
Identifiers: LCCN 2022023939 (print) | LCCN 2022023940 (ebook) |
ISBN 9781032033433 (hbk) | ISBN 9781032033396 (pbk) | ISBN
9781003186816 (ebk)
Subjects: LCSH: Rape. | Rape kits. | Rape victims.
Classification: LCC HV6558 .S492 2022 (print) | LCC HV6558 (ebook) |
DDC 362.88392--dc23/eng/20220628
LC record available at https://lccn.loc.gov/2022023939
LC ebook record available at https://lccn.loc.gov/2022023940

ISBN: 978-1-032-03343-3 (hbk)
ISBN: 978-1-032-03339-6 (pbk)
ISBN: 978-1-003-18681-6 (ebk)

DOI: 10.4324/9781003186816

Typeset in Sabon
by KnowledgeWorks Global Ltd.

Dedication

Cleveland—mid-1990s, a 13-year-old female was walking home from middle school when she saw a car moving slowly toward her with two males in it. The car stopped and she crossed to the other side of the street. She continues walking and the car follows her. The car stops again. One of the males exited the vehicle and asked her age. She shrugs and keeps walking. The male grabs her, forces her into the backseat of a car where another male is seated, gets back into the car, and starts driving. The second male in the backseat begins to fondle her breast and genital area over her clothes. He then unbuttons her pants, removing her underwear with them. He slaps her several times, telling her to shut up as she struggles, kicks, cries, and screams. He then rapes her vaginally while the first male drives. She is driven to a white house. The second male carries her into the house while the first male holds the door open. Once inside the house, she is left in a room with a mattress on the floor while the suspects stand watch. While being held captive, the second male rapes her vaginally again. She is held captive until 4:30 the next morning, when the second male wakes her and forces her into the car. She is forced out of the car at a nearby convenience store. The suspects drive off. She walks home and when no one answers, she walks to a friend's house and calls the police. Police respond to the call. The victim is taken to the hospital, where she has a sexual assault kit (SAK), also known as a rape kit, collected. Police take an incident report from the victim. The case is forwarded for investigative follow-up by detectives.

The investigative report, in its entirety, reads: Victim is a habitual runaway and has run away three times prior and each time has been located in an apt above store on [street name] and [street name] (tenant unknown). Mother filed unruly on the victim. ER doctor said there was no evidence of trauma to the vaginal area. *Three sentences*. That's it. That's where the investigation for this case ended.

This was the first case I (RL) read when I began working as a research partner for the Cuyahoga County SAK Task Force, led by the Cuyahoga County Prosecutor's Office in late 2014. I knew that the sexual assault kit associated with this file was only recently submitted for DNA testing, but how could this case end like this? Victim is a habitual runaway. What happened with this case? I searched the case files for more information. Where was her formal statement (investigative interview) with detectives? Had the detectives even talked to her? Did the police conduct interviews with any potential witnesses? Did they try to locate the house where she was held captive and collect evidence? This critical information and the expected documentation of police effort just did not exist. In fact, the case file indicated that the police did little-to-no investigative work on this case. Reading about the gang and captivity rape of a 13-year-old girl snatched off the street while walking home from middle school was bad enough, but to have this terrible event end with the notation that the "victim is a habitual runaway" was a gut punch.

This case file, along with numerous others we have read across our many years of working on the SAK Initiative (JLR, RL), still haunts us. The lack of criminal justice response for this child and the thousands of other sexual assault victims with shelved, under, or non-investigated SAKs, highlights the insidious impact of rape myths and cultural biases, the prevalence of the secondary (institutional) rape too often experienced by vulnerable victims, our dangerous misunderstanding of sexual assault predators, their criminal proclivities, and their tendency to exploit victim vulnerabilities, and the sometimes callous lack of response by some of those charged with obtaining justice and preventing other rapes in an equitable fashion.

Thus, with these shelved SAK victims in mind and heart, we dedicate this book to survivors and their recovery journey. We dedicate this book to the no-longer 13-year-old survivor whose horrific rape was ignored and the many other survivors whose kits remained shelved. We remember that each kit is more than a box of evidence. Each lab report is more than a piece of paper. These came from your body and represent your intimate trauma.

The SAKs that you shared with us, directly or indirectly, are changing our collective response to rape. These reforms include evidence-based trauma responses, advocate agency, police culture, lab policy, prosecutor strategy, prevention efforts, and state, regional, and national movements, policies, laws, and mandates. As such and in keeping with this dedication, the phoenix on the front cover was designed specifically for this book by John Lawrence. The phoenix symbolizes rebirth, reform, and triumph over adversity. Teal (the color for sexual violence awareness) gives rise to red (the color symbolizing the fire of courage as well as a passion for truth, healing, and post-traumatic growth). We can think of no better way to describe survivors of sexual assault. These phoenixes are galvanizing change and, along the way, reforming how organizations, institutions, and the public respond to sexual assault.

Alongside survivors are many others who are reforming our response to sexual assault; many noteworthy change agents contributed to this book as part of their effort. We thank you and are excited to give voice to your efforts in this book. We also acknowledge that our contributions (JLR, RL) over the years were made possible through collaborations with colleagues, community stakeholders, graduate and undergraduate students, and the unwavering support of our families and friends. In particular,

JLR would like to thank her family—Marty, Ali, Rosy, Frank, Ryan, and Ruth Langhinrichsen-Rohling, dear friends—especially Brenda and Kathy, the Mobile SAKI Promise initiative team members, Lifelines Counseling Center and the Mobile Police Department, and key graduate students who have contributed to this work, including Emma Lathan, Jessica Duncan, Fallon Richie, and Bridget Jules. RL would like to thank John, Olivia, and Samantha Lawrence, numerous supporters and change agents in the community including Mary Weston, Timothy McGinty, Michael O'Malley, Melissa Riley, and many others from the Sexual Assault Kit Task Force, Teresa Stafford, and many others from the Cleveland Rape Crisis Center, the Akron SAKI team, and our team of SAKI researchers including Daniel Flannery, Laura Overman, Margaret McGuire, Joanna Klingenstein, Duoduo Huang, Wenxuan Huang, Danielle Sabo, and several graduate and undergraduate students.

And so many more.

Contents

SECTION II
Where are we now? Present reform efforts

Figures

Tables

Contributors

Natasha Simone Alexenko is a victim and survivor of sexual assault. In 1993, she was a 20-year-old college student living in New York City when she was violently raped at gunpoint. She reported the rape to police and had a kit collected. After nearly a decade, Alexenko's untested rape kit was finally processed, and her rapist, who roamed free for nearly 15 years, was brought to justice. In 2011, she founded Natasha's Justice Project to help end the national rape kit backlog and empower and assist survivors of sexual assault. She is the author of the book *A survivor's journey from victim to advocate*, where she shares the arduous healing journey from victim to a national and international advocate for survivors.

Margaret Bassett, MS Ed, LPC-S, is the Director of Applied Research & Innovative Instruction at the UT Austin Steve Hicks School of Social Work, the Institute on Domestic Violence & Sexual Assault. She directs the Expert Witness training. Ms. Bassett has 35 years of experience working in the field of interpersonal violence. She is currently pursuing an Executive EdD in Higher Education Leadership at The University of Texas at Austin.

Antoinette Bonsignore, JD, is a Seattle-based rape kit reform advocate as well as an advocate for domestic and sexual violence survivors. She has a law degree and is currently serving as a legal and prosecutorial analyst for the Washington State Criminal Justice Training Commission. She is working to reform the law enforcement and prosecutorial response to sexual assault cases.

Noël Busch-Armendariz, PhD, is a nationally recognized expert in gender-based violence. She is a University Presidential Professor at the UT Austin Steve Hicks School of Social Work and previously served as UT Austin's Associate Vice President for Research and SHSSW's Associate Dean for Research. She is the founding and current director of IDVSA, a collaboration of the Schools of Social Work, Nursing, and Law, and the Bureau for Business Research. Since joining UT Austin, Dr. Busch-Armendariz has been awarded $13 million to direct more than 90 projects from funders such as NSF, NIJ, OVW, and OVC.

Bradley A. Campbell, PhD, is an Associate Professor in the Department of Criminal Justice at the University of Louisville. His research focuses on police investigations, decision-making, training evaluation, and response to victims. Currently, Campbell is the lead researcher on two federally funded projects—The Kentucky Sexual Assault

Kit Backlog Action Research Project and a National Institute of Justice-funded experiment to implement and evaluate victim-centered, trauma-informed interview training for sexual assault investigators. Campbell's recent work has been published in the *Journal of Experimental Criminology, Journal of Criminal Justice*, and *Criminal Justice & Behavior*.

Rebecca Campbell, PhD, is a Professor of Psychology at Michigan State University. Dr. Campbell's research examines how contact with the legal and medical systems affects sexual assault survivors' well-being. She was the lead researcher for the National Institute of Justice-funded Detroit Sexual Assault Kit Action Research Project, which was designated as an Exemplary Project by the Association of Public & Land Grant Universities (APLU) and the W.K. Kellogg Foundation. Dr. Campbell is the author of *Emotionally Involved: The Impact of Researching Rape* (2002, Routledge).

Mateo Cello, MPA, is a Policy Associate at the Joyful Heart Foundation. He studies how sexual assault evidence laws are being implemented throughout the nation. He also works with state legislators and local stakeholders to push for sexual assault evidence legislation in their jurisdiction. Mateo holds a masters' degree in Public Administration from Baruch College.

Deborah M. Clubb is an award-winning advocate for women and survivors of violence, executive director of the Memphis Area Women's Council, and coordinator of the Memphis Says NO MORE campaign. Deborah joined the Women's Council as founding executive director in 2004 after 25 years as a daily newspaper reporter and editor at *The Commercial Appeal* (Memphis).

C. Austin Coates is a Clinical Health Psychology doctoral student at the University of North Carolina, Charlotte. Her research interests include childhood trauma, abuse, neglect, and interpersonal violence. Her current research focuses on interpersonal violence and ways in which systems can support survivors of violence.

Rachel Crisler is an undergraduate student at the University of North Carolina, Charlotte. She is majoring in Psychology and History. Her research and clinical interests center on abnormal, alternative, and cognitive psychology. She also studies Victorian Women writers of science and technology. She has been published on this topic.

Bridget Diamond-Welch, PhD, is the Director for Research & Innovation for the School of Health Sciences and Associate Professor of Research at the University of South Dakota. She is the researcher who is associated with South Dakota's 2019 Sexual Assault Kit Initiative (SAKI) grant from the Bureau of Justice Assistance. She is also the evaluator on a telehealth sexual assault medical forensic exam grant and works extensively on sexual assault issues across the state of South Dakota.

Carolyn Dolan, MSN, JD, is the Clinical Director of HEART, a nurse practitioner, and the Project Director for an HRSA continuation grant under the project title, "SOUTH SANES-South Alabama Sexual Assault Nursing Empowerment and

Support." She is also a subrecipient of the International Association of Forensic Nursing's HRSA-funded technical assistance project, which seeks to provide support to all OVC campus-based projects. Her SANE experience spans over 20 years and includes SANE-Pediatric (2021) and SANE-Adult certification (2019). She is also an attorney and a past president (2018) of The American Association of Nurse Attorneys (TAANA) and a current officer of The American Association of Nurse Attorneys Foundation.

Thomas Dover, PhD, is a Crime Analyst with the FBI's Behavioral Analysis Unit-5 and instructs on topics pertaining to behavioral analysis for the FBI National Academy in Quantico, Virginia. He has over 25 years of experience providing analytical assistance to local, state, and federal agencies in investigating and prosecuting violent crimes. Dover's research focuses on modeling criminal behavior and offender decision-making, case-linkage analysis, identifying and reducing analytical and investigative bias, and developing methods to structure and automate case analysis techniques. He has a PhD in Computational Criminology.

Nancy R. Downing, PhD, RN, SANE-A, SANE-P, FAAN, is an Associate Professor in the Center of Excellence in Forensic Nursing at Texas A&M University in Bryan-College Station, TX. She has been a certified sexual assault nurse examiner since 2004, providing care to patients across the lifespan impacted by interpersonal violence. She teaches in the forensic nursing master's degree program and conducts research focused on intersections of trauma, abuse, substance use, and associated health outcomes. She is the Principal Investigator of an Office for Victims of Crime grant to develop and implement Tex-TRAC, a telehealth sexual assault nurse examiner (SANEs) program that connects rural nurses with expert SANEs to guide them through medical forensic examinations.

Jessica Duncan, PhD, completed her graduate degree in Clinical and Counseling Psychology at the University of South Alabama. She worked for four years as a research assistant on the Mobile, AL Sexual Assault Kit Initiative. She completed her APA-accredited internship at Atascadero State Hospital, and she is currently employed in a private practice setting completing comprehensive psychological evaluations for adolescents and adults. Her research focuses on exploring the factors that influence sexual assault investigations and examining public attitudes toward victims of crime and criminal behavior.

Mary Faulkner is the Sexual Assault Kit Initiative (SAKI) Site Coordinator for the City of Duluth Police Department (DPD). She is a sexual assault advocate with the Program for Aid to Victims of Sexual Assault (PAVSA). She has a master's degree from Pennsylvania State University in History and Women's Studies.

Hannah Feeney, PhD, is a Community Psychologist in RTI International's Division of Applied Justice Research. Dr. Feeney has a decade of experience conducting research on the violence and victimization of marginalized communities. Her areas of expertise include community and systems' response to victimization, help-seeking behavior in survivors, and untested sexual assault kits. Dr. Feeney supports the Sexual Assault Kit Initiative and various dissemination activities on projects related to sexual victimization.

Holly Fuhrman, MA, JD, is a Senior Associate Attorney Advisor at AEquitas. Holly manages all resource development, conducts extensive legal research, and co-manages programmatic activities under several AEquitas initiatives. She has co-authored numerous resources for AE, including the Model Response to Sexual Violence for Prosecutors (RSVP Model), as well as resources on combatting racial bias in the prosecution of violence against women, strategies for prosecuting domestic violence amid the COVID-19 pandemic, charging considerations in the prosecution of marital rape, and strategies for combatting witness intimidation. Prior to AEquitas, Holly served as the 2016-17 Hillary Rodham Clinton Law Fellow at the Georgetown Institute for Women, Peace, and Security, where she conducted international field research on women's involvement in peace and transitional justice processes in conflict-affected areas, including Ukraine and Myanmar.

Mattie Jones is an undergraduate at the University of South Dakota with a double major in psychology and criminal justice. She is an undergraduate researcher on the SAKI grant. She is interested in pursuing a career in law enforcement with a focus on forensic psychology and victim advocacy.

Bridget Jules is a doctoral student in Clinical Health Psychology at the University of North Carolina, Charlotte. Her research is focused on the development of healthy relationships. She conducts research to determine how to mitigate the risk of interpersonal violence, relational distress, and infidelity.

Timothy G. Keel, MS, is a Major Case Specialist with the FBI's Behavioral Analysis Unit in Quantico, Virginia. He is a certified behavioral analyst (Profiler) who assists local police departments with serial offender cases, as well as odd and unusual homicides. He has over 40 years of law enforcement experience and is a former Detective Lieutenant in the Baltimore Police Department, Homicide Unit. He has an MS in Management and Leadership.

Joanna Klingenstein, MA, is a Research Associate at the Begun Center for Violence Prevention Research and Education at Case Western Reserve University. She serves on research projects related to gender-based violence and criminal justice, and she has experience in social work. Her educational background is in religious studies, counseling, and the arts.

Ilse Knecht has 20 years invested in victim advocacy and is a nationally recognized expert on the rape kit backlog. She leads Joyful Heart's End the Backlog campaign, which is at the forefront of identifying untested rape kits across the country, appealing for laws and policies to improve criminal justice responses to sexual violence; and working with jurisdictions to assist them to develop and implement survivor-centered reforms. Previously, Ilse spent 16 years at the National Center for Victims of Crime, where she created the DNA Resource Center and led the center's efforts to reform policies and practices related to testing rape kits. She credits her mother with instilling a duty in her to "do unto others as you would have them do unto you."

Sarah Koon-Magnin, PhD, has published extensively in the area of sexual assault, with work appearing in *Violence Against Women, Violence & Victims, the Journal* *of Interpersonal Violence,* and *Sex Roles.* Dr. Koon-Magnin co-authored a book on *Gender Identity, Sexual Orientation, and Sexual Assault: Challenging the Myths* (with Corina Schulze and Valerie Bryan) and is the sole author of the book *Sexual Assault and Harassment in America: Examining the Facts.* She is particularly interested in the disclosure experience for victims, those receiving the disclosures, and promoting trauma-informed responses.

Jennifer Langhinrichsen-Rohling, PhD, is a Professor in the Department of Psychological Sciences at the University of North Carolina, Charlotte. She is core faculty in the Clinical Health concentration of the Health Psychology PhD program and a licensed clinical psychologist in NC. Dr. Langhinrichsen-Rohling's research focuses on individual, couple, family, and system-level factors associated with the prevention of and response to intimate partner violence, sexual assault, and self-harming behaviors. She was one of the lead research partners with the Mobile, Alabama Sexual Assault Kit Initiative and is now working with the Charlotte SAKI project.

Emma C. Lathan, PhD, is a postdoctoral fellow at the Grady Trauma Project, Department of Psychiatry and Behavioral Sciences, Emory University. Dr. Lathan's program of research primarily investigates how post-trauma interaction with the criminal justice and health-care systems impacts sexual assault victims' health and system engagement. She also brings a unique perspective through her focus on enhancing patient and professionals' outcomes via system-wide adoption and evaluation of trauma-informed care. Dr. Lathan has worked on Mobile, Alabama's Sexual Assault Kit Initiative under the mentorship of Jennifer Langhinrichsen-Rohling, PhD, and Tres Stefurak, PhD, since 2016.

Jennifer Gentile Long, MGA, JD, is the Chief Executive Officer at AEquitas, which she co-founded in April 2009 to provide prosecutors and allied professionals in the field with customized expertise and support in the prosecution of gender-based violence and human trafficking. Jennifer currently serves as an Advisory Committee Member with the American Law Institute, an Editorial Board Member with the Civic Research Institute for the Sexual Assault and Domestic Violence Reports, and an adjunct professor at Georgetown University Law Center. Prior to AEquitas, Jennifer served as the Director of the National Center for the Prosecution of Violence Against Women at the National District Attorneys Association; she also served as an advocate for victims of domestic violence and child abuse in Philadelphia and Bermuda, respectively.

Charlotte Lopez-Jauffret, MS, is a forensic scientist, criminologist, and research scientist. She received her master's in forensic science with a concentration in forensic molecular biology from George Washington University and is also pursuing her doctoral degree in Justice, Law and Criminology at American University. Charlotte has worked both inside and outside forensic laboratories testing Sexual Assault Kits, processing firearms for DNA and/or fingerprints, and analyzing data for intelligence distribution. Her research focuses on the intersection of criminal justice and forensic science including sexual assault legislation, DNA privacy, and standards of evidence. She currently works as a senior research scientist on state and federal criminal justice projects.

Rachel E. Lovell, PhD, is an Assistant Professor of Criminology and Director of the Criminology Research Center at Cleveland State University. She is an applied criminologist and methodologist whose research focuses on gender-based violence and victimization, particularly sexual assault, human trafficking, and intimate partner violence.

Jim Markey, MEd, is retired as a detective sergeant overseeing the adult sex crime unit, which investigated more than 7,000 sexual assault investigations including over 100 serial rape suspects. He developed and implemented the Phoenix Police Department Sexual Assault Cold Case Team in 2001 resulting in the re-investigation and resolution of over 4,000 old rape cases. He currently works with Research Triangle Institute, International in Raleigh, NC, as a Senior Law Enforcement Specialist.

Yulanda McCarty-Harris is the Director of Culture, Employee Engagement and Diversity Engagement Inclusion and Belonging at the University of Texas Development Office. She is an accomplished senior leader and attorney with 21 years in the public/private sector, including 14 years in higher education. She has successfully led compliance efforts, including preventing all forms of discrimination, including sexual harassment, and is an expert in diversity, equity, and inclusion concepts. She is currently a doctoral candidate in UT's Higher Education Leadership Program.

Kathryn A. McGill, MA, is a current doctoral student in the combined integrated Clinical and Counseling Psychology PhD program at the University of South Alabama in Mobile, AL. Additionally, she has served as a graduate researcher in partnership with the Mobile Police Department and the University of South Alabama under the DOJ's Sexual Assault Kit Initiative (SAKI). Her research interests lie within the intersection of Psychology, specifically trauma, and the Criminal Justice System, with a focus on the offender and the victim.

Margaret J. McGuire, MPH, CPH, is an independent public health researcher based in Cleveland, Ohio. As a former Research Associate at Begun Center for Violence Prevention Research and Education at Case Western Reserve University, she served on the Cuyahoga County Sexual Assault Kit Initiative research team and other projects related to gender-based violence. She also previously worked in the anti-sexual violence field with Ohio's statewide coalition, the Ohio Alliance to End Sexual Violence. Her current research draws on these previous experiences, and she specializes in systems advocacy, prevention, and evaluation within the public health field to increase access to services by underserved populations.

Heather C. Melton, PhD, is an Associate Professor of Sociology and the Director of Criminology at the University of Utah. Her research focuses on gender-based abuse, including intimate partner abuse, stalking, and sexual assault, and the criminal justice system's response to those issues. She participated as a researcher on the Sexual Assault Kit Initiative for the state of Utah.

Patricia A. Melton, PhD, is a Senior Research Forensic Scientist at RTI International and a Director of the National Sexual Assault Kit Initiative (SAKI) Training and Technical Assistance project. In this capacity, she authors, coordinates, and directs the activities that assist grantees currently awarded under the SAKI project. She also directs the implementation of the SAKI vision in additional jurisdictions to address sexual assault response reform through a nationwide promotion and education platform.

Jennifer Newman, JD, is an Associate Attorney Advisor at AEquitas. She began her career as an Assistant District Attorney in Philadelphia, where she handled cases in the Municipal Court, and later became a specialized prosecutor in the Juvenile Unit and Family Violence and Sexual Assault Unit. As an ADA, Jennifer sought justice for victims of intimate partner violence, sexual violence, child abuse, and child sexual abuse and regularly litigated complex motions to protect victims and hold offenders accountable. Prior to her work at the Philadelphia District Attorney's Office, Jennifer was a student at Georgetown University Law Center. During law school, Jennifer interned for the Montgomery County State's Attorney's Office in Montgomery County, Maryland, as well as the US Attorney's Office for the District of Columbia.

Patricia "Patti" Powers, JD, is an Attorney Advisor at AEquitas. Prior to AEquitas, Patti served as a prosecutor for 27 years in Washington State, where she specialized in the prosecution of sexual violence, domestic violence, child sexual and physical abuse, homicide, and cold cases. As a prosecutor, Patti developed a reputation as a tireless advocate for justice by bringing even the most complex cases to trial, including two cold case homicides that were later featured on the docuseries On the Case with Paula Zahn. Patti was also appointed as a Highly Qualified Expert on an intermittent basis for the US Army Criminal Investigative Division. During her tenure as a Highly Qualified Expert, Patti consulted on sexual assault and domestic violence cases involving members of the armed forces and provided specialized training for Criminal Investigations (CID) Special Agents and members of the Judge Advocate General's Corps.

Kimberly Pusey, MS, is a doctoral student in the combined integrated Clinical and Counseling Psychology PhD program at the University of South Alabama in Mobile, Alabama. While at the University of South Alabama, she has served in many roles in the community including as a graduate research assistant on the Mobile, Alabama Sexual Assault Kit Initiative Grant. She has also provided therapeutic services at Child Welfare and at the local juvenile detention center. Post-graduation, she plans to focus her research and clinical work on the etiological factors leading to antisocial behavior as well as on providing treatment geared toward reducing recidivism.

Alison Rudd, EdD, FNP-C, serves as Training Coordinator for HEART. In the United States, she is an Associate Professor of Simulation and a Certified Healthcare Simulation Educator (CHSE). She also has an active clinical practice with the USA Department of Emergency Medicine as a board-certified family nurse practitioner and certified SANE. For the past 12 years, Dr. Rudd has worked with health professions faculty to design and implement objective-driven, simulation-based training experiences for students and clinicians. Dr. Rudd has coordinated multiple SANE clinical skills labs at the University of South Alabama's state-of-the-art simulation center, now an approved training site by the International Association of Forensic Nurses (IAFN).

Danielle B. Sabo, PhD, is a Research Associate at Begun Center for Violence Prevention Research and Education at Case Western Reserve University. She has a PhD in Sociology. Her mixed-methods research focuses on the lived experience of sexual trauma and its impact on health outcomes over the life course. In particular, her work strives to amplify the voices of queer-identified, gender-diverse individuals and those with an intersection of marginalized identities.

Burcu Sagiroglu, MPP, is the Policy and Advocacy Associate at the Joyful Heart Foundation. In line with the organization's goal to end the sexual assault kit backlog and to advance survivors' access to justice, Burcu takes part in formulating and implementing policy data and advocacy strategies. She holds a masters in public policy degree from the University of Maryland, College Park, and a bachelor's degree in government from Colby College. Prior to this role, she worked on policy and implementation solutions concerning systemic barriers to equal access to resources for vulnerable groups, including street children with disabilities in India, refugees in the United States and West Asia, and victims of femicides and gender-based violence in Turkey.

Tom Scott, MA, is a Social Scientist in RTI International's Division of Applied Justice Research. His work uses science to improve both violent crime investigations and crime data in the United States. He also researches gun violence and has conducted an evaluation of gun control legislation and a study on the underground gun market.

Candice N. Selwyn, PhD, is the Project Director of HEART: promoting Health, Empowerment, and Recovery from Trauma and a Research Assistant Professor in the College of Nursing with a PhD in Clinical-Counseling Psychology. Her work focuses on the ways in which health-care provision can support or impede victim-survivors' recovery from interpersonal trauma, such as childhood abuse, intimate partner violence, and sexual assault. With an expertise in the provision of trauma-informed health care, Dr. Selwyn oversees all aspects of the OVC-funded HEART Project to ensure the program adheres to principles and practices of trauma-informed care.

Paul J. Speaker, PhD, is a finance professor in the John Chambers College of Business & Economics at West Virginia University. Dr. Speaker is the Principal Investigator for Project FORESIGHT, a business-guided analysis of Forensic Science Laboratories. He works closely with the Office of Justice Programs and the Forensic Technology Center of Excellence at RTI International with projects ranging from sexual assault kit testing to costs of the opioid crisis to optimal staffing at forensic laboratories. Dr. Speaker's research activity includes numerous studies in the business of forensics, including the estimation of the return on investment from testing sexual assault kits.

Teresa M. Stafford, MSCJ, is the Chief Executive Officer at Hope and Healing Survivor Resources Center overseeing the Battered Women's Shelter and Rape Crisis Center of Medina and Summit Counties. Teresa has over 25 years of experience providing programmatic oversight and direct service to offenders and survivors, specializing in sexual violence, domestic violence, human trafficking, and families of homicide victims. Teresa advocates for the systemic change needed to create a trauma-informed and culturally responsive climate for all survivors and staff.

Tres Stefurak, PhD, is the Associate Dean and Professor of Counseling Psychology in the College of Education & Professional Studies at the University of South Alabama. Dr. Stefurak has previously worked on research and evaluation projects aimed at implementing evidence-based and trauma-informed practices in juvenile justice, child and adolescent mental health, child welfare, and law enforcement settings. Most recently, he has been one of the research partners for the City of Mobile, AL's SAKI grants funded by the Department of Justice. This series of grants cataloged, reinvestigated, and pursued convictions for hundreds of victims whose DNA evidence was never submitted. As part of this work, new trauma-informed policing practices were implemented, and the police adopted a policy to "submit all kits."

Kevin J. Strom, PhD, has led the National SAKI TTA project since its inception in 2015 and directs the Center for Policing Research and Investigative Science at RTI International. He is a Criminologist who has focused his work on understanding the size and nature of the problem of unsubmitted SAK's and on improving the quality and consistency of victim-focused responses and investigations. As part of his work, he has collaborated on numerous investigative unit assessments that utilized a structured process for supporting agencies in implementing recommended practices and for helping to build out the evidence based on what works in sexual assault investigations.

Caitlin Sulley, LMSW, is the Director of Scientific Opportunities, Operations, & Sustainability at the Steve Hicks School of Social Work's Institute on Domestic Violence & Sexual Assault (IDVSA). She directs research and training initiatives focused on institutional response to sexual assault, gender-based violence among college populations, and victim engagement in the criminal justice system. She served survivors of sexual assault and family violence in law enforcement and community-based settings.

Melanie Susswein, MSW, is an award-winning social marketing communicator and project director. She joined The University of Texas at Austin in 2018 as the Director of Marketing and Communications for the Institute on Domestic Violence & Sexual Assault and is now affiliated with the Center for Health Communication at the Moody School of Communication. Melanie's portfolio includes extensive work on violence prevention, women's health, work with and on behalf of children with special health-care needs and disabilities, and a wide array of diverse populations in Texas and around the country. She earned her MSW at the University of Pennsylvania and completed a year of service in Israel for a domestic violence prevention program.

Julie L. Valentine, PhD, RN, CNE, SANE-A, is the Associate Dean of Undergraduate Studies and Research and an Associate Professor at Brigham Young University College of Nursing and a certified adult/adolescent sexual assault nurse with Wasatch Forensic Nurses. Her clinical specialty and research focus areas are sexual violence, intimate partner violence, and criminal justice system response to sexual violence. Dr. Valentine is the primary author of three awarded federal grants since 2015 totaling 3.45 million dollars. She is the primary investigator on several studies related to sexual assault.

Veronique N. Valliere, PsyD, is a licensed psychologist and has her doctorate in Clinical Psychology from the Graduate School of Applied and Professional Psychology of Rutgers University. She has over 30 years of experience in the field and has worked clinically with violent offenders and their victims, adult and child. She also serves on the Pennsylvania Sexual Offender Assessment Board and has been reappointed continuously since 1997. She has trained for the FBI, DOJ, DOD, Bureau of Indian Affairs, Ontario Police, Alberta Crown Prosecutor's Office, Amber Alert, Army JAG Office, National Center for the Prosecution of Violence Against Women, and other agencies. She is recognized as an expert on victim behavior and has testified nationally and internationally. Dr. Valliere is the author of *Understanding Victims of Interpersonal Violence: A Guide for Investigators and Prosecutors,* published by Routledge Press.

Mary Weston, JD, is an Assistant Prosecuting Attorney and Supervisor of the Cuyahoga County Prosecutor's Office's Cold Case/GOLD Unit. The Unit focuses on reviewing cold case sexual assaults and homicides for new leads (including the applicability of advanced DNA methodologies), and the collection of Lawfully Owed DNA. Mary has been an Assistant Prosecuting Attorney since 2006 and joined the Cuyahoga County Sexual Assault Kit Taskforce when it was formed in 2013. She is a Project Manager for the Taskforce, overseeing all aspects of cold case sexual assault and homicide investigations.

Angela Williamson, PhD, is the Supervisor of the Forensics Unit/FBI ViCAP Liaison at The United States Department of Justice, Bureau of Justice Assistance. Angela also serves as the Forensic Subject Matter Expert for BJA and FBI ViCAP/BAU and assists Law Enforcement agencies across the United States. She developed and oversees the Sexual Assault Kit Initiative (SAKI), along with other forensic-based programs at BJA. She has over 16 years of experience as a forensic specialist working on complex criminal cases and missing/unidentified persons' investigations. In 2018 and 2020, Angela received the United States Department of Justice Assistant Attorney General's Distinguished Service Award for outstanding contributions to the mission and goals of the Office of Justice Programs. In 2019, Angela received the International Homicide Investigators Association Award for Excellence for her role in the Samuel Little serial killer investigation.

Amanda R. Young, MPA, is a research public health analyst at RTI International and serves as the training director for the National Sexual Assault Kit Initiative Training and Technical Assistance team. Ms. Young is responsible for the development and execution of training events for SAKI grantees, including national meetings, regional events, and webinars. Ms. Young previously worked in a police department, where she assisted victims of crimes in navigating the court system and finding available community services.

Brianna Zimmer is an undergraduate at the University of South Dakota with a double major in Criminal Justice and Political Science. She is an undergraduate researcher on the SAKI grant. She is interested in pursuing a career in law enforcement with a focus on sexual assault and domestic violence.

Introduction

Rachel E. Lovell and Jennifer Langhinrichsen-Rohling

The chapter details the problems of untested (or "backlogged") sexual assault kits (SAKs), also known as rape kits, and the legislative and funding advancements in rape kit reform (#EndtheBacklog) accelerated through the national #MeToo and #TimesUp viral social movements. The chapter summarizes the overall aims and organizational structure of the book as well as the intended audiences—students, educators, academics, scholars, law enforcement officers, prosecutors, sexual assault advocates, nurses, and policy makers. The chapter closes by introducing the readers to the coeditors of the book.

A massive initiative to test hundreds of thousands of SAKs, also known as rape kits, in the United States—the U.S. Department of Justice's (DOJ) Sexual Assault Kit Initiative (or SAKI)—has unearthed failed practices while shining a bright light on thousands of shelved stories. These are stories of interpersonal victimization (often of the most vulnerable) and systemic victimization by institutions designed to support, protect, and serve. Since being unearthed, stories connected to previously untested SAKs and under- or completely non-investigated rapes are now providing a once-in-a-lifetime opportunity for redemption. These kits are a pathway for us to learn from past mistakes, improve the present response, and reform the future.

This edited book details results from the first major leg of this journey: from shelved kits to a reformed response to rape. This book seeks to further advance the journey of rape reform by compiling information related to the historical accumulation of kits and failed disclosure and response processes. In the process, this work highlights critical lessons learned by the multiple disciplines involved in the rape response and generates recommendations related to the promise of ongoing and future best practices.

The Problem of Untested Sexual Assaults Kits

Hundreds of thousands of kits have languished, untested in evidence storage facilities across the United States. An SAK consists of a set of items used by medical professionals to collect and preserve evidence (e.g., vaginal swabs, fingernail clippings) from a victim of rape. This kit contains, at times, the only evidence that links a suspected perpetrator to the rape; this linkage, however, requires testing of the DNA potentially contained within the kit. Yet, many of these kits had been shelved—in decrepit, non-air-conditioned warehouses, bathrooms, closets, and backspaces of evidence rooms—and forgotten about for decades. Lack of attention to these kits has continued even as DNA testing advances have blossomed and societal attitudes toward the

DOI: 10.4324/9781003186816-1

crime of rape have evolved. Moreover, while these SAKs sat, many of the suspected rapists remained free and continued to rape. Thus, these untested kits represent both potentially actionable evidence of a crime and are simultaneously a physical reminder of a failed criminal justice response and the institutionalized betrayal of multiple generations of rape survivors.

To right this wrong, there has been a dramatic increase in efforts to systematically address large numbers of untested (often referred to as "backlogged") kits in numerous jurisdictions across the United States. The purpose is to forever #EndTheBackLog. To their credit, state legislators (in alignment with public outrage) quickly heeded calls for reform. As a result, in a decade, the number of US states that passed some type of SAK testing reform increased from just one state in 2010 to almost all states by 2022. In other words, nearly all US residents have been impacted directly or indirectly by some form of legislatively mandated SAK reform.

Contemporaneously, the availability of federal funding to address untested kits has also increased dramatically, most notably from hundreds of millions (and counting) in funding provided by the DOJ's SAKI. While this money has primarily been directed toward police departments, prosecutors, forensic labs, and governmental bodies, several funded sites have also embedded action-oriented social and behavioral science researchers within their multidisciplinary teams. These scientists have utilized their inclusion to learn as much as possible from the testing of these kits.

These legislative and funding advancements have been accelerated even further by demands for accountability for sexual perpetration, as exemplified by the national #MeToo and #TimesUp viral social movements—bringing to the forefront the atrocities committed by men like Harvey Weinstein, Bill Cosby, and Larry Nassar. These movements demonstrate that sexual misconduct and violence are common, most often directed against women and girls, and have been an open and tolerated secret.

In many ways, as atrocious as these crimes are, decades of sexual abuse denials and cover-ups by organizations and institutions that were supposed to support, protect, and serve like Catholic dioceses across the United States and the Boy Scouts of America have laid bare a different kind of betrayal—institutional betrayal (Smith & Freyd, 2014). These organizations colluded to shield offenders from accountability, and as a result, their actions (and/or inactions) further exploited the victims and made our communities more dangerous. These scandals and the backlash they have engendered have also helped spur long-needed momentum to fundamentally reform how the criminal justice system responds to sex crimes.

The amount of progress in the area of untested kits is truly monumental. Less than ten years ago, most jurisdictions in the United States saw little value in efforts to test all currently collected kits, much less testing "old" kits. However, as detailed in the included chapters, a decade later, we are now at a place where the value-added of "test-all" is irrefutable in terms of criminal justice outcomes–for identifying unknown rapists, better understanding perpetrators' offending patterns and behaviors, and solving past, current, and even future crimes. Meanwhile, hearing the voices of survivors and listening to the wisdom of change agents has solidified public support for kit testing as the morally right thing to do for victims—past, present, and future.

The most common question asked about the kits: How could this have happened? How could there be hundreds of thousands of SAKs across the United States just gathering dust while offenders remained free? The nuance of the answer to this question is discussed in more detail in Chapter 1. But, the short answer is *the problem is so much larger than just the kits*. The kits are a symptom of a systemic issue. Kits were not tested, but guess what? Many other investigative and prosecutorial tasks were also not accomplished. Victims were not called. Suspects and eyewitnesses were not interviewed. Evidence was not collected. Cases were not reviewed or charged by prosecutors. And most importantly, victims were not believed, supported, or taken seriously.

As you will read in these chapters, the story of untested SAKs is largely the story of forgotten rape victims—as rape is a crime that primarily affects women and girls, the most vulnerable among us, and/or the marginalized. This includes children and adolescents (girls and boys), women and girls of color, LGBTQ+ individuals, those with limited economic means, those with disabilities, those with substance use issues, those under the influence of drugs and alcohol, and especially those at the intersection of these vulnerabilities or who hold multiple marginalized identities.

In sum, these kits are so much more than just kits. They are a symbol of our failed response to rape—a habitual institutional response that we cannot test our way out of. In this process of transformation, now the kits are also a symbol of change—and an opportunity for redemption. It is in keeping with this opportunity that we chose to write and edit this book.

Overall Aims and Intended Audience of the Book

This book is the first to address the most critical topics related to DOJ's SAKI and untested kits more broadly. It brings together leading scholars, practitioners, policy makers, and advocates located in diverse communities across the United States. In a series of well-researched and thoughtful chapters, it showcases key themes in reforming a rape response by curating the current state of knowledge and highlighting emerging, innovative practices.

Given the nascent nature of SAK reform initiatives, the knowledge we are gaining is not readily located in one place nor confined to one field or discipline. Therefore, the chapters have been structured to be accessible to a broad audience from various disciplines, emphasizing readability and (when possible) lack of technical or discipline-specific jargon. We stressed to contributors the need to keep the *so why does this matter?* and *why should I be writing this chapter?* at the forefront.

Although there are undoubtedly other potential audiences, we specifically envisioned two primary audiences for this book. First, for students and educators, each chapter includes key points, discussion questions, and a recommended or further reading section to facilitate the book's usage in a seminar-like environment. Second, for practitioners, stakeholders, and policy makers, we have organized the book so that practitioners from one discipline (e.g., law enforcement) could learn about another discipline (e.g., forensic nursing). To this end, we expect the key points sections to be especially useful to those seeking takeaway messages from each chapter.

The chapters are almost exclusively US-focused—an artifact of the sexual kit testing initiatives being US-based. Nevertheless, several cross-national takeaways exist, especially for more economically developed countries that have yet to adopt nationwide "test all" approaches to SAKs. The lessons learned that are detailed in this book could serve as a valuable guide to implementing large-scale international reform.

Across the United States, sex crimes are named and defined differently. The criminal acts range from sexual penetration to sexual contact to exposure, with additional elements ranging from physical force to lack of consent. Contributors use the terms rape and sexual assault somewhat interchangeably when referring to any of these crimes, which might or might not align with specific state statutes. *Sexual assault* is a more general term to refer to sexual contact that is not consensual. *Rape* is most often associated with non-consensual penetration. *Victim* is most often used by the criminal justice system to refer to a person who has been wronged in a crime. *Survivor* is a term used to describe the person who has been wronged outside of the criminal justice system—indicating that they are more than what happened to them, and acknowledging their journey toward surviving and thriving. Establishing a widely accepted and utilized nomenclature will be important as advances continue.

The Organizational Structure of the Book

Figure 0.1 illustrates the general path of a rape case in the criminal justice system, particularly when there is an associated SAK. The process is a complicated and convoluted one, with many decision points. The chapters in this book highlight many of these and are organized primarily around these key phases and decision points.

Specifically, the book is divided into three sections. Section I revisits the past and contains the *how did we get here* chapters. These chapters include background on untested kits and SAKI, attrition in rape cases, victim disclosure, the rape of women of color, and a survivor's journey from being a victim with an untested kit to an advocate for change.

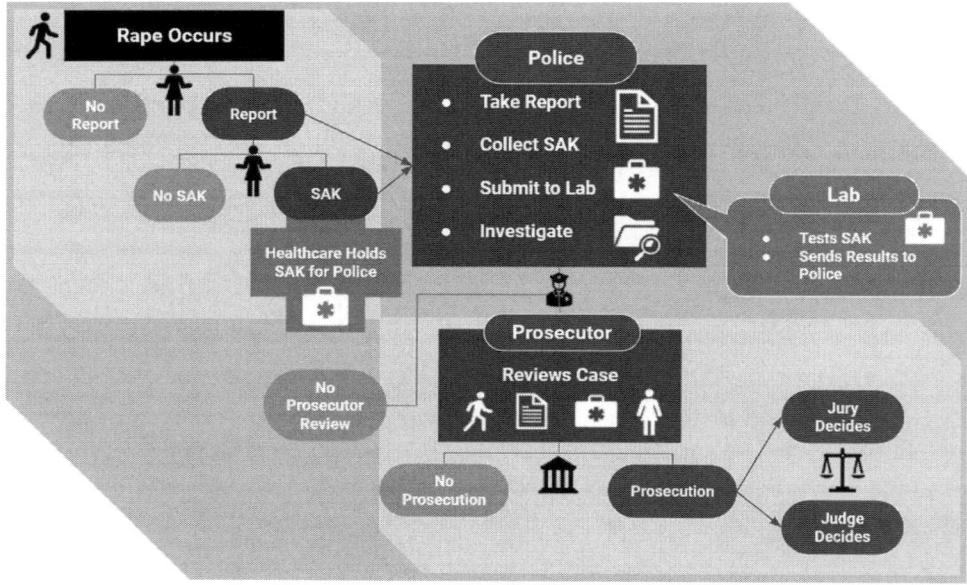

Figure 0.1 General Path of a Rape Case in the Criminal Justice System

Source: Joanna Klingenstein for visualization.

Section II visits the present and contains the *where we are now* chapters, detailing current reform efforts and how SAKI is advancing what we know. These chapters include lessons learned in how jurisdictions can successfully address their untested kits; advancing our understanding of sexual assault offending, sexual victimization, victim notification, and prosecution; a case study of one SAKI jurisdiction's journey toward reform; improving the sexual assault forensic exam collection processes, testing protocols at the lab, the cost-effectiveness of testing kits; and the legislative journey in eliminating the SAK backlog.

The final section, Section III, envisions a future reformed response and contains the *where we want to be* chapters. These chapters include innovative reform and prevention efforts currently being implemented across several jurisdictions, like trauma-informed training for law enforcement, best practices in victim notification, a multidisciplinary rape response, accountability via legislated case reviews, public awareness and prevention efforts, and imagining a better victim response. This section ends with a concluding chapter that highlights key themes throughout the book and paves the way toward a reformed path going forward.

The Contributors

The book's chapters have been written by dedicated scientists who are connected to untested kits, SAKI, and rape reform; other contributors are leading sexual assault advocates, nurses, policy makers, law enforcement officers, and prosecutors; and lastly, some contributors are survivors of sexual violence whose efforts to make positive change in the lives of many have been a part of their post-traumatic growth and healing process. As editors, we wanted you to know more about these remarkable agents of change. They are working in this area because they are passionate about reforming the systemic response to rape. This includes people who are: championing the cause at the federal level; sharing their rape experience with thousands to help secure funding; reading rape report after rape report to distill generalizable knowledge; helping obtain a DNA profile; or securing a long-delayed prosecution. This also includes people who are: assisting victims in feeling safer by securing justice in the police station and the courtroom and those who are working with legislators to change minds and formalize sustainability processes.

Standard practice in academic writing is to exclude personalized details. We took a different approach. We sought to center our contributors' voices to allow readers to understand why these contributors were chosen to write their respective chapters. Thus, each chapter includes a brief section on the contributors–to situate their experiences and expertise within the larger reform framework. As editors, we continue to be inspired by these contributors. We hope, as readers, you are as well.

Who We Are and Why We Wrote This Book

We also would like to situate ourselves within this revolution of change. Both of us (RL and JLR) are researchers who have been working in SAKI for many years. Since SAKI's inception, we have been (and continue to be) embedded research partners for jurisdictions addressing their untested kits.

I (RL) began working in this area starting in Fall 2014, when then Cuyahoga County (Cleveland, Ohio, the United States) Prosecutor Timothy J. McGinty reached out to the Begun Center for Violence Prevention Research and Education at Case Western Reserve University in Cleveland, Ohio, where I was working as a senior-level researcher (but have since accepted a position at Cleveland State University). A year prior, McGinty had formed the multidisciplinary team now known as the Cuyahoga County SAK Task Force, led by the Cuyahoga County Prosecutor's Office, to follow up (via investigation and prosecution) on the testing of what ended up being over 7,000 untested kits in the county (primarily within the city of Cleveland). McGinty reached out to the Begun Center to potentially fund an applied research project on the Task Force's efforts, which began in early 2015. This was the start of what was to become a long-standing (seven years and counting) collaborative partnership with the Cuyahoga County Prosecutor's Office, with funding provided by DOJ's SAKI. This expanded in 2019 to include a collaboration with the Akron Police Department as part of the Akron SAKI.

Likewise, I (JRL) was approached by the Mobile Alabama Police Department after being recommended for inclusion by Lifelines Counseling Center, which functions as the local Rape Crisis Agency. The Mobile Police Department had received DOJ's SAKI funding and wanted a research partner to help them design a database to catalog and trace the testing results of 1,412 kits that were certified as part of their "backlog." At the time, I was working as a Professor in the Department of Psychology at the University of South Alabama (South), and I had a long history of community-engaged scholarship focused on intimate partner violence, stalking, rape, post-traumatic stress disorder, and institutional betrayal. As I joined the SAKI work in Mobile (which subsequently included multiple rounds of funding), I helped South put together an academic team that originally included Drs. Tres Stefurak and graduate students Emma Lathan and Jessica Duncan (now Drs. Lathan and Duncan). Over time, the South team has expanded and evolved to include many others, some of whom have contributed to this book. Many participated in a trauma-informed care collaborative I launched at South. In 2019, I accepted a position in the Department of Psychological Science at the University of North Carolina Charlotte. I have recently been officially asked to join the Charlotte, North Carolina SAKI team as their academic partner and expect to continue this work at my new SAKI site.

Thus, we are experts in untested kits and have strong records of SAKI-related scholarly publications. In addition, we are actively engaged in disseminating key findings from SAKI research to practitioners and general audiences. While we are well-versed in the field of SAKs, we are not experts in all the disciplines that SAKI encompasses. Thus, we chose to have an edited book with noted experts representing key fields. We believe this approach has generated a book with the broadest possible interest and the latest discipline-specific knowledge. We believe there is essential information for all those involved in responding to rape cases. We are also excited to note that this approach showcases the groundbreaking interdisciplinary reforms being implemented across jurisdictions throughout the United States.

Reference

Smith, C. P., & Freyd, J. J. (2014). Institutional betrayal. *American Psychologist*, 69(6), 575–587. https://doi.org/10.1037/a0037564

Section I

How did we get here?

Revisiting the past

1 "On the shelves, covered in dust"

The history of untested sexual assault kits in the United States

Rebecca Campbell and Hannah Feeney

Author Note

Research described in this chapter was supported by grants awarded to the first author by the National Institute of Justice (2011-DN-BX-0001, 2014-NE-BX-0006) and by a grant awarded to the Michigan State Police by the Sexual Assault Kit Initiative Bureau of Justice Assistance, Office of Justice Programs, U.S. Department of Justice (#2015-AK-BX-K0155). The opinions or points of view expressed in this document are solely those of the authors and do not reflect the official positions of any participating organization or the U.S. Department of Justice.

In 2009, an assistant prosecuting attorney saw something unimaginable. It was not at a crime scene but rather in a police property storage facility: thousands and thousands of boxes of medical forensic evidence collected from sexual assault victims—thousands of blood, semen, skin, and saliva samples—were sitting on shelves. The boxes were sexual assault kits (SAKs), also known as rape kits, and they were supposed to be at a crime laboratory for testing. But they were not at the lab, and they had never been submitted to a lab for testing. Instead, they were just sitting there, in a warehouse, *on the shelves, covered in dust* (Campbell et al., 2015). As the prosecutors grappled with their discovery, they assumed this miscarriage of justice was unique to their city, a horrible catastrophe that would take years to fix. They would quickly learn that it was not just this city. Large stockpiles of untested SAKs have been found in police property storage facilities in jurisdictions throughout the United States (Campbell et al., 2017; Human Rights Watch, 2009, 2010; Pinchevsky, 2018; Strom & Hickman, 2010; Strom et al., 2021).

Sexual assault victims have reported their violent crimes to the police; they have endured lengthy, invasive medical exams for the collection of trace evidence from their bodies; they have released their kits to police with the understanding that the evidence would be submitted for forensic testing, and instead, the kits were shelved.

This has been happening for decades, well before this one city's discovery in 2009 and well since in countless more cities. For many jurisdictions, it has been routine practice to put unsubmitted rape kits in storage, and as these piles of SAKs have been discovered, victims, advocates, and policy makers have asked, why? Why did this happen? What do we do with these kits now? And how can we prevent this from happening again?

In this chapter, we will examine these questions by tracing the history of how the national problem of untested SAKs developed over time. The authors of this

DOI: 10.4324/9781003186816-3

chapter had the opportunity to conduct long-term formative research in one such city, Detroit, MI, just as this issue was coming to light and news stories were starting to break. Over the course of five years of study (2010–2015), and five additional years of collaboration and consultation (2016–2020), we helped elevate the problem of untested SAKs as an issue meriting further study and policy reform. This early research conducted in Detroit and other key cities (e.g., New York, Los Angeles, and Houston) elicited national attention to this critical issue and revealed some of the underlying causes for untested SAKs. As such, this chapter will review how numerous stockpiles of untested SAKs are the result of a complex interaction of multiple problems, including long-standing resource constraints, deeply held biases about victims of sexual assault, and organizational priorities that did not value the safety and well-being of survivors. It is not a simple problem to fix, but this chapter will detail new policy programs and empirical research that have identified promising practices for finding untested kits, moving them through testing, and utilizing the findings to improve investigations, prosecutions, and response to survivors.

In this chapter, our focus will be on SAKs in police storage that have never been submitted to a forensic laboratory for DNA analysis, which the Department of Justice refers to as "untested/unsubmitted" SAKs; by contrast, "backlogged" SAKs are those that have been submitted to a lab, but still await testing (Nelson, 2010; Ritter, 2011). Media and advocacy groups often use the term "backlog" to refer to SAKs in police property that have not been submitted for testing, and this term certainly has intuitive meaning and appeal, but we will be using the nomenclature recommended by the Department of Justice as it distinguishes kits not tested because police never submitted them to a lab for analysis ("unsubmitted") from kits that have been submitted but await testing in a lab ("backlogged"). The third category of kits represents those that were tested at the time of their original collection but may benefit from additional testing given recent advances in forensic testing technology (often referred to as partially tested kits). In this chapter, our aim is to discuss *unsubmitted* kits and to document the reasons why so many kits were never even submitted for forensic DNA analysis.

Creating Supply: The Practice of Collecting Sexual Assault Medical Forensic Evidence

The practice of post-assault medical forensic exams (MFEs) began in the 1980s to systematize the collection of physical evidence from victims' bodies (Martin, 2005). In this early era, these exams were focused primarily on evidence collection and included plucking head and pubic hairs; obtaining fingernail scrapings in the event the assailant was scratched during the attack; swabbing the genitals, anus, mouth, breasts, and/or other body areas to collect semen, blood, or saliva; and photographing injuries. These exams might also include post-assault health care, including injury assessment, emergency contraception to prevent pregnancy (if applicable), and prophylaxis for sexually transmitted infections that might have been contracted during the assault. Unfortunately, a common practice at this time prioritized forensic evidence collection over patient health care to the degree that victims often characterized their post-assault medical experiences as retraumatizing and so emotionally distressing that some survivors have referred to the exams as a "second rape" (Campbell & Raja, 2005; Campbell et al., 2001).

In the 1990s, the nursing profession sought to address these problems by creating sexual assault nurse examiner (SANE) programs, which redefined the purpose of these exams as providing comprehensive health-care and supporting survivors' emotional well-being (Lynch, 1993). Staffed by specially trained forensic nurses (rather than emergency department [ED] physicians), SANEs were trained in forensic evidence collection techniques, court testimony preparation, and victim-centered, trauma-informed care. This new model of post-assault health-care was effective in addressing gaps in service delivery. Patients treated in these programs were significantly more likely to experience shorter wait times, receive comprehensive health-care, and have overall better experiences with post-assault medical providers (Campbell et al., 2006). Victims treated by SANE are also more likely to receive crisis intervention, advocacy, and emotional support (Campbell et al., 2008; DuMont et al., 2009; Ericksen et al., 2002). This emphasis on holistic care did not detract from the forensic evidence collection components of the examination as comparative studies have found that SANEs are more skilled in forensic evidence collection relative to non-SANE health-care providers (Ledray, 1999; Ledray & Simmelink, 1997; Sievers et al., 2003). SANE programs have also been shown to work more collaboratively with law enforcement personnel and prosecutors (Campbell et al., 2007, 2010).

In the 2000s and 2010s, practitioners and policy makers recognized the demonstrated success of SANE and sought to prioritize the national expansion of SANE programs (Government Accountability Office, 2019; Zweig et al., 2014). In 2004, the Department of Justice developed the first standardized national protocol for post-assault MFEs to guide SANEs and ED staff regarding best practice, which was revised and expanded in 2013 (Department of Justice, 2004). To encourage medical professionals to implement the protocol as intended, the Office of Violence Against Women funded the International Association of Forensic Nurses (IAFN) with a multi-year training and technical assistance (TTA) project to teach the national protocol to health-care practitioners throughout the United States and in Indian country. Also, in this era, the re-authorization of the federal Violence Against Women Act (VAWA) sought to address two key barriers to victims' access to MFEs. First, this legislation allowed victims to obtain MFEs at no charge, so hospitals could no longer bill survivors for their care; second, this law allowed survivors to obtain MFEs without authorization of law enforcement, so victims could receive exams without the requirement of reporting to the police (Zweig et al., 2014).

Taken together, post-assault medical care has seen consistent and steady progress throughout the past 40 years, such that now it is common practice for sexual assault survivors seeking medical care to have comprehensive post-assault exams *and* obtain trauma-informed forensic evidence collection kits. What that also means is that a great many kits have been collected over the past 40 years, particularly with the advent of SANEs and the increased availability of MFEs without reporting mandates. This, in turn, raises a critical question: *What was done with all those kits?*

Increasing Demand: The Emergence of Forensic DNA Testing

After a SAK has been collected by a SANE or other medical provider, it is taken into legal custody by the police, who are responsible for submitting the rape kit to a forensic laboratory for testing. When the collection of rape kits became a standardized practice in the 1980s, forensic crime laboratories did not yet have many options for how to analyze the biological samples in those kits, which limited what could be learned from the evidence. For example, at that time, kit specimens were tested using discriminating protein markers, such as ABO blood typing; however, proteins degrade quickly, so the kits had to be tested promptly for maximum gain (Butler, 2015). Once tested, ABO blood typing could determine, for example, whether a suspect had the same blood type as the crime suspect/kit sample; however, given that millions of people may also have the same blood type, this testing approach could not concretely identify a suspect. Overall, the investigative utility of kit testing was limited for identifying suspects, and its use in court was likewise limited for confirming the identity of the accused (Lander, 1991).

In the early 1990s, technological advances made it possible to extract DNA from biological forensic samples, but initially, DNA testing still had limited practical utility to police and prosecutors because there was no organized database of reference samples to which DNA profiles could be compared (Butler, 2015). The importance of DNA evidence to the criminal justice system radically changed with the development of a national criminal DNA database, Combined DNA Index System (CODIS), which was authorized by the federal DNA Identification Act of 1994 and implemented in 1999. With the advent of CODIS, a forensic evidence sample included in a SAK could be analyzed for DNA, and if the obtained profile met biological quality standards for the number of core loci, it could be uploaded to the national database and compared to reference samples in CODIS's two indexing systems (Butler, 2015).

First, the offender index contains known DNA reference samples from offenders collected at the time they were arrested or convicted for a prior crime (i.e., a CODIS "qualifying offense"). State laws vary as to which crimes qualify for mandatory DNA collection, but typically being arrested or convicted of a felony requires an offender to give a buccal swab sample (Mukasey, 2008). These reference DNA samples are linked to offenders' names, so when new profiles are entered into CODIS, they are compared to these reference specimens, and if there is a match—termed a "hit," or more specifically, an "offender hit"—then law enforcement personnel have a promising investigative lead as to the identity of the offender or confirmation of the offender's identity.

Second, the forensic index contains unknown/unidentified DNA profiles obtained at crime scenes. For example, a blood sample at an unsolved homicide crime scene could be analyzed for DNA and entered into the forensic index; likewise, semen samples from a rape kit collected for stranger assault could be analyzed and identified DNA could be entered into the forensic index. When profiles are loaded to this index, they are searched against the reference samples in the offender index to determine if there is a match to a known profile, revealing or confirming the identity of the offender. It is also possible that samples within the forensic index will match to each other, revealing associations between unsolved cases, which in itself might provide useful investigative information for law enforcement personnel. CODIS hits (either offender hits or forensic hits) may occur in other sexual assault cases or in other types of crimes (e.g., homicide, assault, robbery, etc.), which can provide more insight into offenders' criminal behavior. CODIS hits may also be instrumental in clearing or exonerating individuals who have been wrongly accused if the DNA match is not the accused/convicted individual.

Forensic DNA testing and CODIS were game changers for how the criminal justice system could approach the investigation and prosecution of reported crimes, but unfortunately, US forensic crime labs did not have sufficient capacity to meet increasing demand for this powerful new tool. The Department of Justice's Bureau of Justice Statistics (BJS) began conducting censuses of publicly funded US crime laboratories in 2002 to track the country's testing capacity. While the number of public labs did increase over time, from 351 in 2002 to 409 in 2014 (the most recent census), the number of requests for DNA testing increased exponentially. As a result, labs have not been able to keep pace, which has created substantial backlogs of evidence awaiting testing.

Testing capacity has been a growing concern for years, and in 2009, the National Academy of Sciences issued a report stating that: "Forensic laboratories are under resourced and understaffed, which contributes to case backlogs and likely makes it difficult for laboratories to do as much as they could to: (1) inform investigations, (2) provide strong evidence for prosecutions, and (3) avoid errors that could lead to imperfect justice" (2009, p. 14). Ten years later, the Government Accountability Office (GAO, 2019) found that state and local government crime labs continue to have backlogs of requests for crime scene DNA analysis.

These forensic evidence backlogs started to affect how police prioritized which evidence should be submitted for testing in the first place (Campbell et al., 2015). *There were growing indications that the police had simply stopped submitting some types of crime evidence for forensic DNA testing altogether.* In these instances, the problem was not *backlogged* evidence sitting in the crime lab awaiting testing but rather evidence that was never given the opportunity to be tested (*unsubmitted*). Instead, crime scene evidence was being stored—untested—in police property facilities throughout the United States, and rape kit evidence appeared to be particularly impacted by this unofficial approach to prioritization.

Discovering Surplus: The Accumulation of Unsubmitted SAKs

In the late 1990s, the first known case of widespread stockpiling of untested rape kits in the United States was discovered in New York City. New York Police Department (NYPD) conducted a massive reorganization of its crime scene property storage facilities, and in doing so, rape kits that had been previously dispersed throughout different bins and boxes were located and inventoried, which revealed that they had approximately 16,000 unsubmitted rape kits in storage. Police officials informed the Mayor's Office and the Prosecutor's Office about the discovery, and subsequent media attention and congressional review (see the Weiner Report, 2002) prompted the Mayor's Office to allocate $12 million to test all of these kits.

As the NYC situation was unfolding, media outlets began reporting that there may also be thousands of untested rape kits in the Los Angeles Police Department and the Los Angeles Sheriff's Department storage facilities, which garnered the attention of Human Rights Watch (HRW). HRW pressured Los Angeles officials for an exhaustive count of all untested SAKs, and in 2009, HRW issued a report indicating 12,669 untested SAKs were found in LA-area police departments. With funding from federal, state, public, and private sources, all Los Angeles SAKs were tested by 2011 (Peterson et al., 2012). In 2004, the State of Illinois disclosed that there may be thousands of untested SAKs in police property facilities throughout the state, so HRW initiated an investigative project there as well, which revealed that only 1,474 of 7,494 SAKs in Illinois booked into evidence from 1995 to 2009 had been confirmed as tested (Human Rights Watch, 2010). Through federal grant funding and the passage of new laws requiring kit testing, all previously unsubmitted SAKs in Illinois were tested by 2013 (Sweeney, 2013).

The high-profile cases in New York City, Los Angeles, and Illinois prompted victim advocacy organizations across the country to begin systematically tracking US cities with large numbers of untested rape kits. The Joyful Heart Foundation's (JHF) "endthebacklog.org" sought to document the number of unsubmitted SAKs in major US cities through media reports and Freedom of Information Act (FOIA)/public records requests (as was done in the HRW projects). Their initial work identified nearly 40 cities with large numbers of untested SAKs, spanning all regions of the county. Most of these were larger urban communities with populations over 300,000 (ranging to several million), and the number of unsubmitted kits varied from several hundred (e.g., 200 in Nashville) to over 10,000 (e.g., Memphis, Detroit). Kits had been accumulating for decades, dating back to the 1980s when rape kit collection was first instituted in hospital EDs. For more information on the JHF and its impact on policies and procedures related to rape kit testing, see Chapter 18.

These city-by-city census projects identified a surprising number of local jurisdictions with large numbers of unsubmitted kits, which suggested that this may indeed be a national-scale problem. In an effort to capture the true national scope of the issue, Lovrich et al. (2004) surveyed a national random sample of 3,400 law enforcement regarding their *estimated number* of unsolved homicide, rape, and property cases that contained unsubmitted forensic evidence. Lovrich et al. (2004) found that there were 169,000 rape cases dating from 1982 to 2002 containing untested biological evidence (presumably, an untested rape kit). Strom and Hickman (2010) revised and expanded the Lovrich et al. (2004) survey to assess law enforcement agencies' evidence submission practices for the years 2003 through 2007 (i.e., the five years after the Lovrich et al., 2004 project) and found that there were 27,595 unsolved rape cases from 2003 to 2007 that had unsubmitted forensic evidence. Notably, neither Lovrich et al. (2004) nor Strom and Hickman (2010) asked law enforcement agencies to conduct actual censuses of their untested kits, but their estimated counts suggested that for crimes committed between the years 1982 and 2007, there may have been upward of 200,000 untested SAKs in police property in the jurisdictions studied. Strom and Hickman (2010) aptly referred to this phenomenon as "justice denied" (p. 382), as the hundreds of thousands of unsubmitted rape kits represented just as many victims whose MFEs had been for naught. This raises another critical question: *Why weren't these rape kits submitted for forensic testing?*

Identifying Causes: The Underlying Reasons Why SAKs Are Not Submitted for Testing

With the discovery of more and more cities throughout the United States with large stockpiles of untested SAKs, researchers started exploring why police personnel were not submitting rape kits to crime laboratories for DNA testing. The answer to that key question turned out to be more complicated than a simple imbalance of supply and demand.

First, several studies found that law enforcement personnel did not submit SAKs for forensic DNA testing because they did not think that DNA testing would be necessary or helpful to their task of investigating a reported crime. In national surveys conducted by Lovrich et al. (2004) and Strom and Hickman (2010), the most commonly cited reason for not submitting forensic evidence for testing was that a suspect had not yet been identified in the case. This finding may seem counterintuitive given that DNA testing can be used to *reveal* the offender's identity in stranger cases but recall that when forensic DNA technology first emerged in the mid-1990s, it had limited utility for suspect identification. It was not until the creation and population of the CODIS database that effective suspect identification could be completed through forensic testing. However, changes in technology outpaced changes in practice, and police did not change their forensic evidence submission practices even with the emergence of CODIS.

Police also indicated that they did not submit evidence for testing in circumstances where: (a) no charges were expected to be filed against the offender, (b) a suspect had already been or would already be adjudicated, or (c) if prosecutors did not specifically request they test the evidence (Lovrich et al., 2004; Strom & Hickman, 2010). These findings suggest that police did not view forensic evidence testing as an investigatory resource that could support them in building a case but rather as a confirmatory check only for those cases already referred for prosecution.

Second, police did not submit kits for forensic DNA analysis because they knew their local crime labs had limited testing capacity. In most communities, submitting, testing, and receiving results regarding forensic testing outcomes was a lengthy process, and police often did not get the results back in time for that information to be helpful to their investigation (Lovrich et al., 2004; Peterson et al., 2012; Strom & Hickman, 2010; Tasca et al., 2013). To counteract these capacity issues, law enforcement limited their requests and prioritized which cases should benefit from these highly limited resources (Campbell & Fehler-Cabral, 2021; Lovrich et al., 2004; Strom & Hickman, 2010). For decades, decisions regarding which cases and what evidence would be submitted for testing were left to police discretion, without much organizational review or oversight (Campbell & Fehler-Cabral, 2021). Given that sexual assault cases are often not organizational priorities in many law enforcement agencies (Spohn, 2020), it is perhaps not surprising that SAK evidence continued to accumulate in police storage.

Third, sexual assault cases were often not top priorities for the police because of long-standing, deeply held beliefs about victims' credibility and widespread erroneous beliefs among law enforcement personnel that victims lie about reported rapes (Morabito et al., 2019; Spohn et al., 2014; Venema, 2016). Research findings indicate that law enforcement determines victim credibility on an expansive set of factors that encompass:

- who they are (gender, age, race/ethnicity, socioeconomic status, sexual orientation); who assaulted them (a stranger or someone known them);
- where the assault occurred (neighborhood and time of day);
- motivations for making a report (altruistic or revenge motives);
- how they behaved prior to the assault (engagement in "risky behaviors," such as alcohol/drug use);
- how they behaved during the assault (physical resistance); and
- how they behaved after the assault (prompt reporting to the police, visible signs of distress) (Frohmann, 1997; Jordan, 2004; Kaiser et al., 2017; Kelley & Campbell, 2013; Morabito et al., in press; Murphy et al., 2014; Schwartz, 2010; Spohn & Tellis, 2010; Spohn et al., 2014; Tasca et al., 2013; Venema, 2016).

It would be impossible for any singular victim to meet all of these implicit and explicit criteria to be deemed "credible." But unfortunately, police perceptions of victims' credibility do affect their approach to sexual assault investigations, including:

- how harshly they interview victims (Greeson et al., 2016; Jordan, 2004; Kaiser et al., 2017; Patterson, 2011a, 2011b);
- how they frame the incident in the official police report (Murphy et al., 2014; Shaw et al., 2016; Spohn & Tellis, 2010; Tasca et al., 2013);
- how thoroughly they conduct the investigation (Murphy et al., 2014; Shaw et al., 2017; Spohn & Tellis, 2010; Tasca et al., 2013); and
- whether they submit the SAK for testing (Campbell & Fehler-Cabral, 2018).

Campbell and Fehler-Cabral's (2018) review of Detroit police reports associated with unsubmitted SAKs revealed that police did not submit kits:

- if the victim knew the offender (in which case police believed the incident was consensual);
- if they thought the victim might have been engaged in sex work/prostitution (in which case the police believed the victim was alleging rape because of lack of payment); or
- if the victim was an adolescent (in which case the police believed the victim was lying to cover up "bad" behavior).

These victim blaming approaches to decision-making are likely to have impacted a large number of rapes given that many assaults are between known parties (Jones et al., 2003; Kilpatrick et al., 2003; Morgan & Kena, 2018), and adolescents and young adults are at high risk for sexual assault (Breiding, 2014; Planty et al., 2013). Taken together, these data suggest that thousands of rape kits were never submitted for DNA testing because of biased beliefs among police.

Research on the underlying reasons why police do not submit SAKs for DNA testing indicates the root causes of this national-scale problem are more complicated than a simple lack of resources. Many agencies did not understand how to leverage forensic testing, even after the advent of CODIS. While lab resource constraints and rapid technology advancements are a factor, law enforcement agencies have shown, through their actions and inactions, how they define their organizational priorities and how they allocate scarce resources. Police often made assumptions about victims' credibility, and they decided they would not allocate limited testing resources to cases they thought had no merit. This raises yet another critical question: *what would happen if these previously unsubmitted SAKs were finally tested? Would the evidence suggest that these cases did indeed have merit?*

Determining Value: The Return on Investment (ROI) for Testing SAKs

In many cities, when large stockpiles of untested SAKs have been discovered, media coverage and public outcry have pressured criminal justice personnel to submit all kits for testing (Strom et al., 2021), which has provided an opportunity to study what can be gleaned from this evidence and evaluate whether police assumptions about these cases are founded. For example, Peterson et al. (2012) tracked the outcomes of 1,320 SAKs randomly sampled from 10,895 untested rape kits from Los Angeles. In this sample, more than half of all samples tested had DNA profiles that were entered into CODIS ($n = 699$). These CODIS uploads resulted in 347 CODIS hits (50% of profiles uploaded to CODIS; 26% of the total sample tested).

Criminal justice policy makers were encouraged by these findings, and in 2010, the National Institute of Justice funded two action research projects to document the outcomes of additional kit testing.

- In Detroit, Campbell et al. (2015) tested a stratified random sample of 1,595 previously unsubmitted SAKs from approximately 11,000 previously untested kits. Testing results were similar to those reported in Los Angeles, with nearly half of all samples tested yielding DNA profiles suitable for upload to CODIS (49% of the total sample tested, $n = 795$), which ultimately resulted in 455 CODIS hits (58% of profiles uploaded to CODIS; 28.5% of the total sample tested).
- In a follow-up study, Campbell et al. (2020) reviewed the testing results of the remaining 7,287 previously unsubmitted SAKs in Detroit. Results indicated 2,938 SAKs had a DNA profile that met eligibility for upload into CODIS (40% of the total sample tested), and 1,675 SAKs yielded a CODIS Hit (57% of profiles uploaded to CODIS; 23% of the total sample tested).
- In Houston, Wells et al. (2016) tracked the outcomes of 493 SAKs sampled from their inventory of 6,663 previously unsubmitted kits. These kits yielded slightly fewer DNA profiles suitable for CODIS upload (43% of the total sample tested, $n = 203$) and 104 CODIS hits (51% of profiles uploaded; 21% of the total sample tested).
- Other cities, such as Cleveland, also began testing their unsubmitted SAKs (Lovell et al., 2018) and found that from a sample of 4,966 SAKs, there were 2,943 DNA profiles eligible for CODIS upload (59% of the total sample tested) and 1,935 CODIS hits (66% of profiles uploaded; 39% of the total sample tested).

Delving deeper into these testing results, a substantial proportion of CODIS hits associated with previously unsubmitted SAKs had associations to other sexual assault cases, indicating a pattern of suspected serial sexual offending.

- For example, Campbell et al. (2020) found that as many as 40% of sexual offenders identified through the testing of previously unsubmitted SAKs were linked to two or more sexual assaults via DNA and/or criminal history records. Among these suspected serial sexual offenders, 76% continued to commit sexual assaults across the lifespan and well into later adulthood (Campbell et al., 2019).
- Findings from Cleveland indicate that serial sexual offending rates may be even higher, with Lovell et al. (2017) documenting that 56% of the offenders identified through SAK testing in their sample were linked to other sexual assault cases by DNA or criminal history records.

Importantly, these studies suggest that these serial offenders are often linked to other serious crimes in addition to sexual assaults. For example, Lovell et al. (2020)

found that offenders identified through SAK testing are also linked to burglary, theft, drug crimes, domestic violence, and felony weapon charges. For more information on how the SAK initiatives are changing what we know about sexual offenders, see Chapter 7.

These findings make clear there is valuable evidence in SAKs that may help identify offenders, and cost-benefit analysis studies have taken this a step further by evaluating potential returns on investment (ROI) for testing previously unsubmitted SAKs. Beneficial ROIs have been identified in regard to survivors seeking resolution of their cases, improved public safety through prevention of repeat assaults from serial sexual offenders, and prevention of societal costs and strains to health systems that treat victims of violence (Speaker, 2019; Wang & Wein, 2018; Wang et al., 2020). Speaker's (2019) analysis quantified these ROIs and indicated that testing previously unsubmitted SAKs yields an 81:1 return on investment, emphasizing that timely submission and testing puts valuable information in the hands of police and prosecutors much more quickly, thus increasing ROI gains: "If the SAK is submitted immediately to the laboratory, then the statute of limitations would not have come into play, nor is it likely that the perpetrator of the sexual assault has already been arrested" (p. 22). Speaker noted that his estimates were likely conservative given that prosecution possibilities are limited for older kits, and that timely testing can help police and prosecutors act more quickly to prosecute offenders and thereby protect public safety. For more information on cost-benefit and ROI studies, see Chapter 17.

Developing Solutions: Changing the Criminal Justice System Response to Sexual Assault

Prior research on unsubmitted SAKs has indicated that there are good reasons to test rape kits as this evidence may serve a preventive role in protecting public safety. As these data have gradually emerged over the last two decades and the benefits of testing have become clearer, multiple federal programs were created to help remedy this problem. For example, the Debbie Smith Act (2004, 2008, 2014) and the Sexual Assault Forensic Evidence Reporting (SAFER) Act (2013) (an expansion of the use of Debbie Smith Act) fund crime labs to test previously unsubmitted DNA evidence and allow jurisdictions to proactively audit their untested sexual assault DNA evidence and develop plans for testing previously unsubmitted rape kits.

However, testing previously unsubmitted kits is only meaningful if the findings are used to inform investigations, facilitate prosecutions, and support victim advocacy. The Department of Justice's Bureau of Justice Assistance created the National Sexual Assault Kit Initiative (SAKI) in 2015 to encourage local, regional, and state-level agencies to do just that. SAKI supports agencies as they seek to understand the scope of their unsubmitted SAKs through the inventorying and testing of previously untested SAKs, *and* encourages agencies to then act on testing results through investigation, prosecution, and victim advocacy. As of December 2021, SAKI was funding 71 sites, including states, cities, and counties, to inventory and test previously unsubmitted SAKs and to investigate and prosecute leads from these unsolved cases. A major goal for the initiative is also to support sexual assault reform including the development and implementation of effective policies and practices that will prevent the re-accumulation of unsubmitted kits in the future.

Research on unsubmitted kits is ever evolving, and SAKI has been instrumental in expanding national-scale and regional studies, as well as site-specific projects. For example, Strom et al. (2021) developed an updated national estimate of the number of unsubmitted SAKs in US law enforcement agencies between 2014 and 2018. Using county-level information on inventories of unsubmitted SAK across 15 states, the study utilized imputation models to determine there were 300,000–400,000 unsubmitted SAKs in police storage during this timeframe (Strom et al., 2021).

SAKI has also supported recent research on forensic testing outcomes across a variety of community contexts to determine whether CODIS hit rates and potential ROI applies in smaller communities with smaller numbers of untested SAKs. For instance, Campbell et al. (2020) evaluated forensic testing outcomes in a state-wide sample of 3,422 previously unsubmitted SAKs, and testing revealed $n = 1,239$ of these SAKs contained a DNA profile that met eligibility for upload into CODIS (36% of the total sample tested). Once uploaded, $n = 585$ SAKs yielded a CODIS Hit (47% of profiles uploaded to CODIS; 17% of the total sample tested).

Despite being sourced from areas of varied geographic size and population densities, these rates are consistent with studies representing exclusively urban populations, suggesting approximately half of SAKs tested will yield a CODIS profile, and approximately half of those uploaded profiles will yield a hit. While hit rates were often higher in larger metropolitan areas, Campbell et al. (2020) found that hit rates in micropolitan and rural areas were still high enough to warrant consistent SAK testing in smaller jurisdictions as well.

As communities across the country continue to reduce their numbers of previously unsubmitted kits, policy makers are working to ensure that stockpiles of untested kits can never start accumulating again. To stay abreast of ever evolving legislative efforts, the advocacy organization End the Backlog tracks rape kit reform legislation. To date, as described in Chapter 18, 45 states have passed some SAK reform legislation. In 2019 alone, End the Backlog identified 103 relevant bills introduced in 35 states. The purpose of such legislation is typically to remove police discretion in SAK testing practices and require that all kits released by victims be submitted to crime laboratories for DNA testing, often with legislatively mandated timelines to ensure timely testing.

Evaluations of these mandatory testing laws have thus far yielded mixed results. On the one hand, they have been effective in finding older SAKs, testing these SAKs, and uploading eligible profiles to CODIS; on the other hand, jurisdictions mandating testing laws have yet to see significant changes in sexual assault arrest rates, suggesting that law enforcement personnel may not be consistently acting upon the testing results (Davis et al., 2020, 2021; Mourtgos et al., 2021). However, as noted previously, kit testing is only as impactful as the efforts taken to use the forensic results, and some studies have shown that this is indeed possible. In Denver, CO, Davis and Wells (2019) found that nearly 60% of SAK cases with a CODIS hit resulted in arrest and filing charges. In Cuyahoga County, OH, Lovell et al. (2018) reported that as many as 25% of completed investigations related to previously untested SAKs yielded indictments. These studies suggest high utilization of SAK forensic evidence is possible when acted upon intentionally.

As jurisdictions across the United States continue to improve their response to sexual assault victims by testing previously unsubmitted and newly collected forensic evidence kits, criminal justice professionals and policy makers must find ways to ensure mandatory testing practices realize their full potential. Forensic evidence should be collected with the intention of testing that evidence (with survivors' consent), and testing should be completed with the intention to act upon the findings to hold perpetrators accountable and protect public safety.

Key Points

- The need for forensic evidence collection and testing has evolved over the past four decades due to developments in forensic medical exams and forensic testing technology.
- The ways in which forensic evidence can be used to support investigations have evolved significantly, particularly with the advent of CODIS.
- Stockpiles of previously unsubmitted SAKs developed across the United States as a result of multiple interrelated factors, including resource scarcity, misunderstanding of the investigative utility of forensic evidence, and long-standing victim blaming beliefs held by law enforcement.
- Legislative reform has contributed to the reduction of the SAK backlog in jurisdictions across the country.

Discussion Questions

1 In media stories, the problem of untested SAKs is often described in terms of resource constraints in crime laboratories—how does that framing impede our understanding of this problem?
2 How might victims whose SAKs were not submitted for testing be impacted by recent legislative reform?
3 Rapid advancements in forensic technology contributed to police failing to submit SAKs for testing. As technology continues to evolve, how can this communication gap be prevented in the future?

Further Reading

Campbell, R., & Fehler-Cabral, G. (2018). Why police "couldn't or wouldn't" submit sexual assault kits (SAKs) for forensic DNA testing: A focal concerns theory analysis of untested rape kits. *Law & Society Review, 52*(1), 73–105. https://doi.org/10.1111/lasr.12310

Spohn, C. (2020). Sexual assault case processing: The more things change, the more they stay the same. *International Journal for Crime, Justice, and Social Democracy, 9*(1), 86–94. https://doi.org/10.5204/ijcjsd.v9i1.1454

Strom, K., Scott, T., Feeney, H., Young, A., Couzens, L., & Berzofsky, M. (2021). How much justice is denied? An estimate of unsubmitted sexual assault kits in the United States. *Journal of Criminal Justice, 73*, 1–9. https://doi.org/10.1016/j.jcrimjus.2020.101746

References

Breiding, M. J. (2014). Prevalence and characteristics of sexual violence, stalking, and intimate partner violence victimization—National intimate partner and sexual violence survey, United States, 2011. *Morbidity and Mortality Weekly Report. Surveillance Summaries* (Washington, DC: 2002), 63(8).

Butler, J. M. (2015). *Advanced topics in forensic DNA typing: Interpretation.* Academic Press.

Campbell, R., Feeney, H., Fehler-Cabral, G., Shaw, J., & Horsford, S. (2017). The national problem of untested sexual assault kits (SAKs): Scope, causes, and future directions for research, policy, and practice. *Trauma, Violence, & Abuse, 18*(4), 363–376. https://doi.org/10.1177/1524838015622436

Campbell, R., & Fehler-Cabral, G. (2018). Why police "couldn't or wouldn't" submit sexual assault kits (SAKs) for forensic DNA testing: A focal concerns theory analysis of untested rape kits. *Law & Society Review, 52*(1), 73–105. https://doi.org/10.1111/lasr.12310

Campbell, R., & Fehler-Cabral, G. (2022). "Just bring us the real ones:" The role of forensic crime laboratories in guarding the gateway to justice for sexual assault victims. *Journal of Interpersonal Violence, 37,* NP3675–NP3702.

Campbell, R., Feeney, H., Goodman-Williams, R., Sharma, D. B., & Pierce, S. J. (2020). Connecting the dots: Identifying suspected serial sexual offenders through forensic DNA evidence. *Psychology of Violence, 10,* 255–267.

Campbell, R., Fehler-Cabral, G., Pierce, S. J., Sharma, D. B., Bybee, D., Shaw, J., Horsford, S., & Feeney, H. (2015). *The Detroit sexual assault kit (SAK) action research project (ARP), final report.* National Institute of Justice. https://www.ncjrs.gov/pdffiles1/nij/grants/248680.pdf

Campbell, R., Long, S. M., Townsend, S. M., Kinnison, K. E., Pulley, E. M., Adames, S. B., & Wasco, S. M. (2007). Sexual assault nurse examiners' (SANEs) experiences providing expert witness court testimony. *Journal of Forensic Nursing, 3,* 7–14.

Campbell, R., Patterson, D., Adams, A. E., Diegel, R., & Coats, S. (2008). A participatory evaluation project to measure SANE nursing practice and adult sexual assault patients' psychological well-being. *Journal of Forensic Nursing, 4,* 19–28.

Campbell, R., Patterson, D., & Fehler-Cabral, G. (2010). Using ecological theory to evaluate the effectiveness of an indigenous community intervention: A study of sexual assault nurse examiner (SANE) programs. *American Journal of Community Psychology, 46,* 263–276.

Campbell, R., & Raja, S. (2005). The sexual assault and secondary victimization of female veterans: Help-seeking experiences in military and civilian social systems. *Psychology of Women Quarterly, 29,* 97–106.

Campbell, R., Townsend, S. M., Long, S. M., Kinnison, K. E., Pulley, E. M., Adames, S. B., & Wasco, S. M. (2006). Responding to sexual assault victims' medical and emotional needs: A national study of the services provided by SANE programs. *Research in Nursing & Health, 29,* 384–398.

Campbell, R., Wasco, S. M., Ahrens, C. E., Sefl, T., & Barnes, H. E. (2001). Preventing the "second rape:" Rape survivors' experiences with community service providers. *Journal of Interpersonal Violence, 16,* 1239–1259.

Davis, R. C., Auchter, B., Wells, W., Camp, T., & Howley, S. (2020). The effects of legislation mandating DNA testing in sexual assault cases: Results in Texas. *Violence Against Women, 26*(5), 417–437. https://doi.org/10.1177%2F1077801219838330.

Davis, R. C., Jurek, A., Wells, W., & Shadwick, J. (2021). Investigative outcomes of CODIS matches in previously untested sexual assault kits. *Criminal Justice Policy Review.* Advance online publication. https://doi.org/10.1177%2F0887403421990723

Davis, R. C., & Wells, W. (2019). DNA testing in sexual assault cases: When do the benefits outweigh the costs? *Forensic Science International, 299,* 44–48. https://doi.org/10.1016/j.forsciint.2019.03.031

Department of Justice. (2004). *A national protocol for sexual assault medical forensic examinations: Adults & adolescents* (1st ed.). Author.

DuMont, J., White, D., & McGregor, M. J. (2009). Investigating the medical forensic examination from the perspectives of sexually assaulted women. *Social Science & Medicine, 68,* 774–780.

Ericksen, J., Dudley, C., McIntosh, G., Ritch, L., Shumay, S. & Simpson, M. (2002). Client's experiences with a specialized sexual assault service. *Journal of Emergency Nursing, 28,* 86–90.

Frohmann, L. (1997). Convictability and discordant locales: Reproducing race, class, and gender ideologies in prosecutorial decision making. *Law & Society Review, 31,* 531–556.

Government Accountability Office (GAO). (2019). *DNA evidence: DOJ should improve performance measurement and properly design controls for national wide grant program.* https://www.gao.gov/assets/gao-19-216.pdf

Greeson, M. R., Campbell, R., & Fehler-Cabral, G. (2016). "Nobody deserves this:" Adolescent sexual assault victims' perceptions of disbelief and victim-blame from police. *Journal of Community Psychology, 44,* 90–110.

Human Rights Watch. (2009). *Testing justice: The rape kit backlog in Los Angeles city and county.* Author.

Human Rights Watch. (2010). *"I used to think the law would protect me" Illinois's failure to test rape kits.* Author.

Jones, J. S., Rossman, L., Wynn, B. N., Dunnuck, C., & Schwartz, N. (2003). Comparative analysis of adult versus adolescent sexual assault: Epidemiology and patterns of anogenital injury. *Academic Emergency Medicine, 10*(8), 872–877.

Jordan, J. (2004). Beyond belief? Police, rape, and women's credibility. *Criminal Justice, 4,* 29–59.

Kaiser, K. A., O'Neal, E. N., & Spohn, C. (2017). "Victim refuses to cooperate:" A focal concerns analysis of victim cooperation in sexual assault cases. *Victims & Offenders, 12,* 297–322.

Kelley, K. D., & Campbell, R. (2013). Moving on or dropping out: Police processing of adult sexual assault cases. *Women & Criminal Justice, 23,* 1–18.

Lander, E. S. (1991). Research on DNA typing catching up with courtroom application. *American Journal of Human Genetics, 48*(5), 819–823.

Ledray, L. (1999). *Sexual assault nurse examiner (SANE) development & operations guide.* Office for Victims of Crime, U.S. Department of Justice.

Ledray, L., & Simmelink, K. (1997). Efficacy of SANE evidence collection: A Minnesota study. *Journal of Emergency Nursing, 23,* 75–77.

Lovell, R., Huang, W., Overman, L., Flannery, D., & Klingenstein, J. (2020). Offending histories and typologies of suspected sexual offenders identified via untested sexual assault kits. *Criminal Justice and Behavior, 47*(4), 470–486. https://doi.org/10.1177%2F0093854819896385

Lovrich, N. P., Pratt, T. C., Gaffney, M. J., Johnson, C. L., Asplen, C. H., Hurst, L. H., & Schellberg, T. M. (2004). *National Forensic DNA study report.* National Institute of Justice.

Lynch, V. A. (1993). Forensic nursing: Diversity in education and practice. *Journal of Psychosocial Nursing and Mental Health Services, 31,* 7–9.

Martin, P. Y. (2005). *Rape work: Victims, gender, and emotions in organization and community context.* Routledge.

Morgan, R. E., & Kena, G. (2018). *Criminal victimization, 2016: Revised.* Bureau of Justice Statistics (BJS), US Department of Justice, Office of Justice Programs & United States of America.

Mourtgos, S. M., Adams, I. T., Nix, J., & Richards, T. (2021). Mandatory sexual assault kit testing policies and arrest trends: A natural experiment. *Justice Evaluation Journal, 4*(1), 145–162. https://doi.org/10.1080/24751979.2021.1881410

Mukasey, M. B. (2008). *DNA-sample collection and biological evidence preservation in the federal jurisdiction.* Department of Justice, Federal Register.

Murphy, S. B., Edwards, K. M., Bennett, S., Bibeau, S. J., & Sichelstiel, J. (2014). Police reporting practices for sexual assault cases in which "the victim does not wish to pursue charges." *Journal of Interpersonal Violence, 29,* 144–156.

National Academy of Sciences. (2009). *Strengthening forensic science in the United States: A path forward.* Author.

Nelson, M. S. (2010). *Making sense of DNA backlogs, 2010-myths vs. reality.* Washington, DC: The National Institute of Justice.

Patterson, D. (2011a). The linkage between secondary victimization by law enforcement and rape case outcomes. *Journal of Interpersonal Violence, 26,* 328–347.

Patterson, D. (2011b). The impact of detectives' manner of questioning on rape victims' disclosure. *Violence Against Women, 17,* 1349–1373.

Peterson, J., Johnson, D., Herz, D., Graziano, L., & Oehler, T. (2012). *Sexual assault kit backlog study.* The National Institute of Justice.

Pinchevsky, G. M. (2018). Criminal justice considerations for unsubmitted and untested sexual assault kits: A review of the literature and suggestions for moving forward. *Criminal Justice Policy Review, 29*(9), 925–945. https://doi.org/10.1177%2F0887403416662899

Planty, M., Langton, L., Krebs, C., Berzofsky, M., & Smiley-McDonald, H. (2013). *Female victims of sexual violence, 1994–2010. Special Report* (No. NCJ 240655). Bureau of Justice Statistics, US Department of Justice.

Ritter, N. (2011). *The road ahead: Unanalyzed evidence in sexual assault cases.* Washington, DC: The National Institute of Justice.

Schwartz, M. D. (2010). *Police investigation of rape: Roadblocks and solutions.* National Institute of Justice.

Shaw, J. L., Campbell, R., & Cain, D. (2016). The view from within the system: How police explain their response to sexual assault. *American Journal of Community Psychology, 58*(3–4), 446–462. https://doi.org/10.1002/ajcp.12096

Sievers, V., Murphy, S., & Miller, J. (2003). Sexual assault evidence collection more accurate when completed by sexual assault nurse examiners: Colorado's experience. *Journal of Emergency Nursing, 29,* 511–514.

Spohn, C. (2020). Sexual assault case processing: The more things change, the more they stay the same. *International Journal for Crime, Justice, and Social Democracy, 9*(1), 86–94. https://doi.org/10.5204/ijcjsd.v9i1.1454

Spohn, C., & Tellis, K. (2010). Justice denied? The exceptional clearance of rape cases in Los Angeles. *Albany Law Review, 74,* 1379–1421.

Spohn, C., White, C., & Tellis, K. (2014). Unfounding sexual assault: Examining the decision to unfound and identifying false reports. *Law and Society Review, 48,* 161–192.

Strom, K. J., & Hickman, M. J. (2010). Unanalyzed evidence in law-enforcement agencies: A national examination of forensic processing in police departments. *Criminology & Public Policy, 9*(2), 381–404. https://doi.org/10.1111/j.1745-9133.2010.00635.x

Tasca, M., Rodriguez, N., Spohn, C., & Koss, M. P. (2013). Police decision making in sexual assault cases: Predictors of suspect identification and arrest. *Journal of Interpersonal Violence, 28,* 1157–1177.

Venema, R. M. (2016). Police officer schema of sexual assault reports: Real rape, ambiguous cases, and false reports. *Journal of Interpersonal Violence, 31,* 872–899.

Wang, Z., MacMillan, K., Powell, M., & Wein, L. M. (2020). A cost-effectiveness analysis of the number of samples to collect and test from a sexual assault. *Proceedings of the National Academy of Sciences, 117*(24), 13421–13427. https://doi.org/10.1073/pnas.2001103117

Wang, C., & Wein, L. M. (2018). Analyzing approaches to the backlog of untested sexual assault kits in the USA. *Journal of Forensic Sciences, 63*(4), 1110–1121. https://doi.org/10.1111/1556-4029.13739

2 Where's my kit? An overview of attrition in sexual assault cases

Kathryn A. McGill, Kimberly Pusey, and Sarah Koon-Magnin

Author Note

The opinions or points of view expressed in this document are solely those of the authors and do not reflect the official positions of any participating organization or the U.S. Department of Justice.

Consider a crime, whether featured in the news or discussed by word-of-mouth, that has recently been a topic of conversation. Chances are it was a violent crime and that initial, and sometimes numerous, contact(s) with the criminal justice (CJ) system have already occurred. Public interest and corresponding news coverage in crime are biased toward the most serious types of offenses, which are often those that progress further in the CJ system (Greer, 2007). However, these crimes are not representative of most crimes in the United States (Morgan & Thompson, 2021). Approximately half of all crimes are never reported, and the rates of reporting are dramatically lower in cases of sexual assault (SA; Morgan & Thompson, 2021; Sinozich & Langton, 2014). Moreover, even if a SA case is reported to law enforcement, it is unlikely to progress throughout the entire CJ system, a process known as "case attrition" (Frazier & Haney, 1996; Lovell et al., 2021). Specifically, a case that fails to progress through all stages of the CJ system has experienced case attrition. Given this phenomenon, the CJ system is frequently compared to a funnel in which a large number of cases at the top (i.e., all reported cases) gradually narrow, and only a small fraction moves through the bottom of the funnel (i.e., incarceration; Morabito et al., 2019; see Figure 2.1).

Below we detail the key stages in the CJ system.

Reporting—Take as an example a vehicle is stolen from a neighborhood street and there are no witnesses. When the owner notices their vehicle missing, they may call the police, initiating contact with the CJ system. Reporting a crime is a particular type of disclosure, as described in Chapter 3. *Not all cases are reported to law enforcement.*

Arresting—Law enforcement, upon receiving a report, will respond to the scene and gather information from the vehicle owner. *If there is not sufficient evidence to demonstrate that a crime occurred or determine who committed it, law enforcement will not make an arrest.*

Charging—If law enforcement, through investigation, can demonstrate probable cause that a vehicle was stolen and identify a suspect, they are able to make an arrest. The case would then be handed to the prosecutor, who would determine whether the evidence is strong enough to justify charges. *If the prosecutor does not view the evidence as sufficient, they will not file charges.*

DOI: 10.4324/9781003186816-4

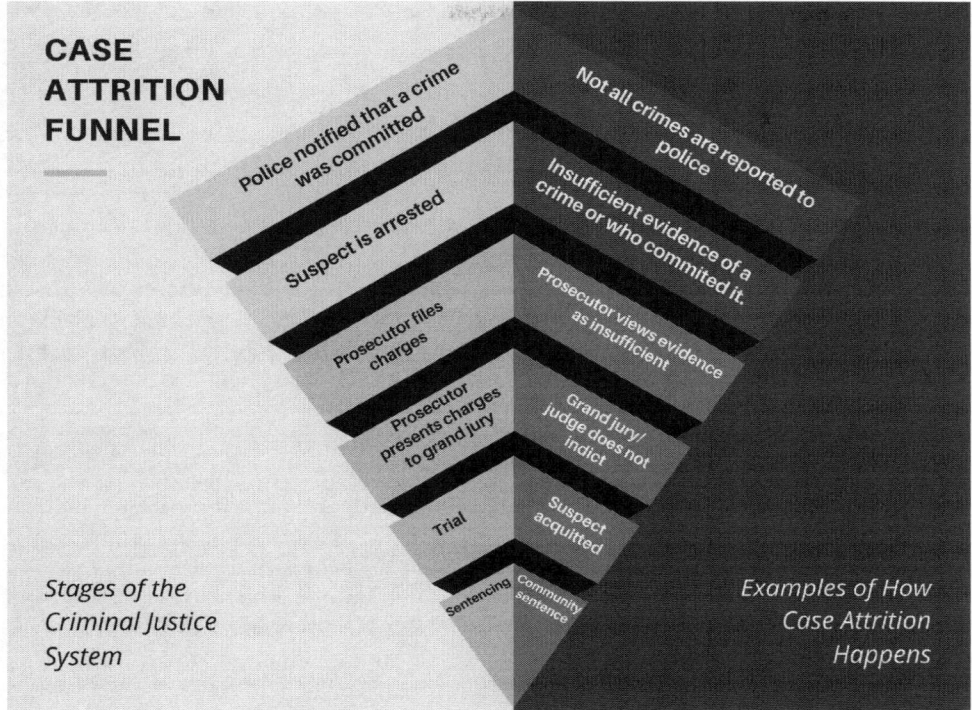

Figure 2.1 Stages of Criminal Justice System

Presenting to a grand jury—If there is sufficient evidence to move forward with charges of car theft, the prosecutor will file them and present the case to a grand jury or at a preliminary hearing (depending on the jurisdiction). *If a grand jury or judge does not agree that there is probable cause that the suspect committed the crime, the charges will be dismissed.*

Disposing—Given that a finding of probable cause that a vehicle was stolen is issued (whether through an indictment by the grand jury or a finding by a judge), the prosecutor will move toward trial. *If at the trial, the jury does not find beyond a reasonable doubt that the suspect committed the crime of which they are accused, they will be acquitted.*

Sentencing and incarcerating—Given a conviction, the offender will face sentencing. *Most convicted offenders are sentenced to a community sentence (e.g., probation, restitution, community service;* Jones, 2018). However, some offenders, particularly those convicted of violent or repeat offenses, are sentenced to a period of incarceration (Jones, 2018).

The preceding example of a car theft highlights the complexity of the CJ system and the potential for case attrition at various stages. Most cases do not move through the full CJ system and all its stages (Morgan & Thompson, 2021). Furthermore, the example used above, car theft, is generally not a crime that is highly politicized. For example, there is rarely a requirement of victim cooperation or a need for other forms of corroboration when a car is stolen; instead, a victim is generally believed when they report that their car has been stolen. Case attrition is more common, complex, and nuanced in cases of SA, a crime which is highly gendered, racialized, and historically focused on victim credibility (O'Neal, 2019; Sorenson & Siegel, 1998; Spohn & Tellis, 2014; see Chapter 3).

This chapter seeks to situate the SAK backlog within the broader context of how SA investigations generally proceed and where they often stop in order to provide a better understanding of SA investigation and case processing. This topic is important because it provides insight into the experience of reporting a case to law enforcement and how it may (or may not) progress after that. It also gives a sense of the barriers that exist in the CJ system and what factors predict a case's likelihood of moving forward. In the sections that follow, we discuss how case attrition is measured and what this line of inquiry reveals. Specifically, we discuss legal and extralegal factors that are associated with whether cases proceed or fall out of the CJ system; thus, experiencing attrition.

As a team, the authors have extensive clinical and research experiences related to SA. Two of the authors are doctoral-level clinicians in training with experiences treating trauma and stressor-related disorders within the community and justice-involved populations (McGill & Pusey), and the third author is a criminologist and associate professor (Koon-Magnin). Specifically, as graduate assistants (McGill & Pusey), on the Mobile Alabama SAKI Grant—Mobile Police Department and University of South Alabama (Drs. Langhinrichsen-Rohling and Stefurak, PI's), the authors were immersed in SA literature, aided in the implementation and execution of the grant, and collaborated with other stakeholders, including police officers, assistant district attorneys, and rape crisis advocates. Dr. Koon-Magnin is an advisor on the HEART project (see Chapter 15) and has collaborated with Lifelines Rape Crisis Center. Also, Dr. Koon-Magnin has published a book on SA within the LGBTQ community.

Revealing and Documenting the Problem

In the late 1980s and 1990s, there were three parallel processes occurring which altered the landscape of investigating SA cases: (1) the United States became more invested in response to sex offenders, (2) DNA technology improved, and (3) police were increasingly community-oriented. During this period, a series of especially violent sexual crimes received substantial media coverage and legislative attention (i.e., Jacob Wetterling, Megan Kanka; Wright, 2014). Public sentiment against sex offenders fortified, leading to enactments of hundreds of new laws intended to control sexual offending throughout the United States (Levenson et al., 2007; Wright, 2014). These laws required registration of convicted sexual offenders, community notification of local offenders, and restricted sex offenders from living near places children regularly congregate (e.g., schools, playgrounds, childcare facilities; Wright, 2014). These laws ostensibly indicated to the public that SA was a serious offense that would be vigorously responded to by the CJ system.

Simultaneously, understanding of DNA technology had started to improve, making it possible to scientifically demonstrate sexual contact in some cases (see Chapter 16). The power of DNA evidence increased in 1994 with the advent of Combined DNA Index System (CODIS), a database of DNA samples which aided law enforcement in the identification and exclusion of suspects. It also broke down the barriers of jurisdictional communication by conducting comparisons across time and place and identifying previously unknown patterns of offending through forensic hits (R. Campbell et al., 2020).

Another change during this period was the rise in community-oriented policing, which emphasizes transparency and partnership between law enforcement and the communities they serve (Gill et al., 2014). Generally, community-oriented policing aims to drastically alter the relationship between law enforcement and the community via transparency and collaboration (Campbell et al., 2017a; Lee, 2019). Jurisdictions displayed increased openness to sharing data with researchers for evaluation, which promoted a broader research agenda on case attrition (Campbell et al., 2017b). Community-oriented policing also connected stakeholders in the community and facilitated interdisciplinary collaboration.

Despite these changes, there was an unknown parallel process occurring, thwarting the efforts to reduce case attrition in SA—the discovery of very large numbers of untested SA kits languishing in evidence storage facilities in cities across the United States. This overshadowed prior efforts at improving SA case outcomes introducing the perception that these steps were merely performative in nature (Campbell et al., 2017a; Koon-Magnin, 2022).

However, because of these changes, researchers were able to assist with understanding case attrition, including factors that led to the backlog. Their work revealed that investigative steps were routinely omitted during SA cases and that the norm was failure to progress through the system to an arrest, charge, or conviction (see Figure 2.2; Campbell et al., 2017a; Frazier & Haney, 1996; Spohn & Tellis, 2010). The discovery of thousands of untested SAKs across the nation was more than a failure of testing kits. Rather, untested SAKs were evidence of a larger problem in SA case processing—case attrition.

Methods of Understanding Factors of Case Attrition

To systematically evaluate the presence and nature of case attrition within the CJ system, researchers in many communities formed partnerships with the CJ agencies. For example, these partnerships have developed in Wayne County (Detroit), Michigan (Campbell, R. et al., 2017b); Cuyahoga County (Cleveland), Ohio (Lovell et al., 2018); Mobile, Alabama (Langhinrichsen-Rohling et al., 2019; Lathan et al., 2019), Los Angeles County, California (Spohn & Tellis, 2010; Spohn & Tellis, 2014), and Harris County (Houston), Texas (Campbell, B. & Wells, 2014). Through such partnerships, CJ agencies shared confidential resources with researchers, including case files and their own experiences working with SA victims. Quantitative studies often include case file review; qualitative studies generally rely upon interviews with stakeholders (e.g., law enforcement, prosecutors, victims); mixed methods studies utilize quantitative and qualitative research techniques. These data sources allowed researchers to quantify the rates of attrition as well as determine where attrition is most likely to take place within the CJ system.

When researchers engage in case file review, the most common method is quantitatively *coding case files* for various factors that lead to case attrition (Shaw & Campbell, 2013). All cases should have an original police report from the responding officer, but the content of those reports varied significantly over time, by the responding police officer, and by jurisdiction. This led to investigative steps being carried

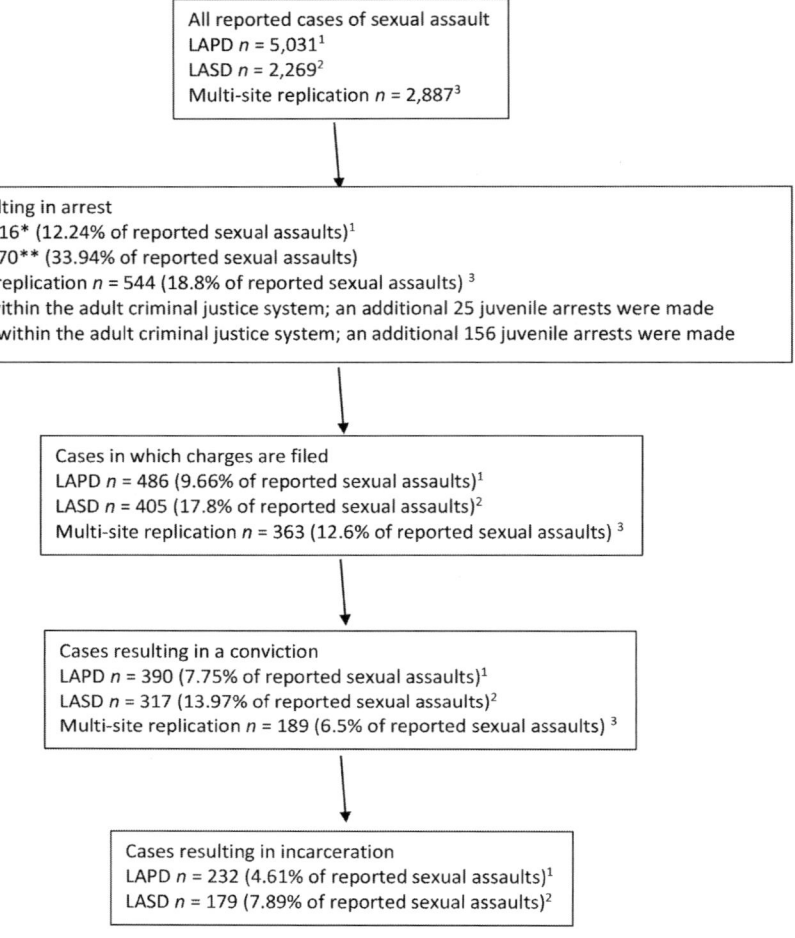

All reported cases of sexual assault
LAPD *n* = 5,031[1]
LASD *n* = 2,269[2]
Multi-site replication *n* = 2,887[3]

Cases resulting in arrest
LAPD *n* = 616* (12.24% of reported sexual assaults)[1]
LASD *n* = 770** (33.94% of reported sexual assaults)
Multi-site replication *n* = 544 (18.8% of reported sexual assaults) [3]
* arrests within the adult criminal justice system; an additional 25 juvenile arrests were made
** arrests within the adult criminal justice system; an additional 156 juvenile arrests were made

Cases in which charges are filed
LAPD *n* = 486 (9.66% of reported sexual assaults)[1]
LASD *n* = 405 (17.8% of reported sexual assaults)[2]
Multi-site replication *n* = 363 (12.6% of reported sexual assaults) [3]

Cases resulting in a conviction
LAPD *n* = 390 (7.75% of reported sexual assaults)[1]
LASD *n* = 317 (13.97% of reported sexual assaults)[2]
Multi-site replication *n* = 189 (6.5% of reported sexual assaults) [3]

Cases resulting in incarceration
LAPD *n* = 232 (4.61% of reported sexual assaults)[1]
LASD *n* = 179 (7.89% of reported sexual assaults)[2]

[1] Spohn & Tellis (2014)
[2] Spohn & Tellis (2014)
[3] Morabito et al. (2019)

Figure 2.2 A Depiction of Sexual Assault Case Attrition as Reported across Several Major Studies

out or omitted; thus, subjective codes characterizing their content were also recorded (see Box 2.1 for a fictionalized example). In short, the content of the initial report impacted how the case was processed.

Researchers also conducted qualitative interviews or focused groups with the CJ practitioners who made decisions regarding cases to identify factors that might not explicitly be stated in a case file. By interviewing victims, victim advocates, or SANEs, researchers sought to better understand a perspective often absent from case files or law enforcement (Campbell & Fehler-Cabral, 2018). These varied sources of data, when triangulated, revealed patterns of case attrition that are discussed in this chapter.

Box 2.1

Example of two case reports: One with and without subjective content

Case 1 Example: At 1:32 A.M., the victim (Black female) reported she was walking to her car when a suspect (unknown black male) approached her. Victim reported that the suspect forced her into her vehicle and sexually assaulted her. Detectives responded.

Case 2 Example: At 01:32 A.M., a Black female prostitute (known to police) reported she was walking to her car when an unknown black male suspect approached her. Victim reported that the suspect forced her into her vehicle and sexually assaulted her. Victim appeared to be high on crack cocaine and was noncompliant when responding to questions. Detectives responded.

Although both examples include a report of a specific offense to police, the second example includes more data regarding the responding officer's thoughts about the crime, factors which may impact whether the case moves forward. For example, if an officer includes statements such as "prostitute," "high," or "noncompliant" without citing evidence, this language may signal to police officers not to continue with the case.

Research on SA Case Attrition

Generally, researchers categorize the factors that impact case attrition as legal and extralegal (Frazier & Haney, 1996; Lovell et al., 2021). Although legal and extralegal factors are often discussed and tested as separate concepts, these factors overlap in complex and important ways and can reciprocally influence each other.

For context, it is important to note that for both factors, law enforcement and prosecutors make their decisions based on "downstream orientation," which refers to the ultimate anticipated outcome of the case by a jury (Spohn et al., 2001). For example, if law enforcement believes that prosecutors will not file charges, they often choose not to make an arrest in that specific case or future cases of a similar nature. Additionally, if prosecutors do not believe they can obtain a conviction, even if they believe a crime occurred, they may not pursue charges (Spohn & Tellis, 2014).

Legal Factors

Legal factors are defined as characteristics of a case that are explicitly mentioned as elements of the crime, such as use of a weapon, type of assault/penetration, number of assailants, and presence or absence of physical evidence (Frazier & Haney, 1996; Lovell et al., 2021). These factors are legally relevant because the crime being charged depends on the type or combinations of penetrations committed (e.g., oral, anal, vaginal), and the severity of the crime (as defined by number of assailants, whether a weapon was used, etc.) under the law. Such characteristics are written into state statutes defining the crime and are thus a major determinant for how cases are charged (or not). The strength of the evidence, which is a key downstream consideration, is another important predictor of case attrition.

Characteristics of the assault

SA can be classified into different types or degrees, with penetrative assaults generally treated as more serious than contact offenses and assaults that result in physical injury as more serious than assaults that do not. For example, the most severe crimes (sometimes called "Rape in the First Degree") often includes use of weapon, significant physical injury to the victim, and evidence of penetration, whereas a lesser degree of the same crime ("Rape in the Second Degree") may not include the same components (e.g., contact vs. penetration). Legally, higher degrees of crime is associated with longer and/or harsher sentences, indicative of a more severe crime.

Typically, the more severe the assault, the more likely that the crime will progress through the CJ system. For example, evidence of bodily injury to the victim (vs. no bodily injury) is more often associated with referral to the next step in the judicial process (Campbell et al., 2009; Frazier & Haney, 1996) and having a higher likelihood of a suspect being questioned (Frazier & Haney, 1996) or arrested (Shaw & Campbell, 2013). Additionally, the presence of bodily injury (Patterson & Campbell, 2012) and anogenital injury (Valentine et al., 2019) result in a higher likelihood of the SAK being submitted.

The strength of this relationship is both significant and substantial. In one study, cases involving bodily injury were eight times more likely to be referred for felony charges than cases without bodily injury (Alderden & Ullman, 2012). Although documented physical injury may be a necessary component of a more severe degree/ charge, physical violence and bodily injury are not required components for many charges of SA. Regardless of the legal requirement, the absence of physical injury is significantly associated with an increase in case attrition, including SAKs not being tested.

Other legal factors relating to the severity of the crime include the nature of the assault, the number of charges, and the presence or absence of a weapon. According to one major study, when penetration occurred, a suspect was more likely to be interviewed (Frazier & Haney, 1996). In another study, when penetration of any type occurred, the case was six times more likely to continue in the criminal process compared to cases without penetration (i.e., fondling), though the authors found no significant impact on the number of types of acts on case processing (Campbell et al., 2009). In a more recent study, when a criminal case included multiple charges or types of acts, it was more likely to progress through the CJ system (Valentine et al., 2019). Finally, many states specify higher degrees of severity (and corresponding punishment) if a weapon was used in the crime. The likelihood of a case being referred for prosecution increases when a case involves a weapon (Murphy et al., 2013; Shaw & Campbell, 2013). The victim does not need to see the weapon or be physically harmed for these factors to have an impact; simply presenting the threat of a weapon or bodily injury can result in a higher likelihood of case processing (Frazier & Haney, 1996; Spohn & Tellis, 2014). In a qualitative study, the bodily injury seems to have a significant effect on case attrition, as an injured victim is perceived as more impactful to a jury, resulting in a stronger downstream orientation (Menaker et al., 2017). The perception of crime severity can result in the process ceasing (e.g., a kit not being submitted, arrest not being made, charges not being filed) if there is an idea that a serious crime did not occur.

Evidentiary characteristics

Another legal area that is consistently related to case attrition is evidentiary characteristics of the crime, such as the number of suspects or presence of eyewitnesses, as well as the absence or presence of physical evidence (e.g., SAK). Often, a higher number of suspects increases the likelihood that a case will continue to be processed (Campbell et al., 2017b; Shaw & Campbell, 2013). However, a study of adolescent assault victims found that a single suspect, rather than multiple, increased the likelihood of a kit being submitted (Shaw & Campbell, 2013). The authors speculate that this counterintuitive finding may reflect the rarity of cases involving multiple suspects unknown to the victim (Shaw & Campbell, 2013), as most assaults involve a single suspect (Sinozich & Langton, 2014).

Additionally, when there are eyewitnesses, a suspect is more likely to be interviewed as well as continue through the CJ process (Frazier & Haney, 1996). Qualitatively, this idea is supported as well, that more witnesses to a crime will increase the chance of arrest (Menaker et al., 2017). Physical evidence, especially SAKs, results in a higher likelihood of an arrest and referral to prosecution (Lovell et al., 2021; Wentz & Keimig, 2019). This most likely comes from the idea that the lack of physical evidence will not be received favorably by a jury, resulting in prosecution not taking the case (Murphy et al., 2013). The importance of physical evidence as a predictor of case attrition makes the backlog even more significant because SAKs are a central method of acquiring essential evidence. Although physical evidence can facilitate the progress of a case through the CJ system, such as through arrest or prosecution, physical evidence alone is not enough to have a successful case (Menaker et al., 2017).

Extralegal Factors

Extralegal factors are not sanctioned by law and, as a result, are not legally relevant but can be more impactful than legal factors in predicting case attrition (Frazier & Haney, 1996). In one study, "most of the factors that significantly predicted whether cases were founded, resulted in arrest, were presented to the prosecution, or resulted in felony charges were extralegal in nature. In other words, factors that mattered most were those that should not matter when determining if a crime occurred" (Alderden & Ullman, 2012, p. 541).

Report characteristics

The mechanisms of how a crime was reported, specifically the nature of when and how it was reported (i.e., whether it was delayed), can result in attrition. Less timely reports are less likely to lead to an arrest (Menaker et al., 2017) or even have an initial report filed (Morabito et al., 2019). There has also been a link between attrition and the time between the assault and the exam, with longer time frames resulting in higher attrition (Campbell et al., 2009). This may be the result of reduced physical evidence following post-assault activities, such as bathing or changing clothes, but Thompson and Schmidt (2018) found no significant difference in the likelihood of a CODIS hit following such activities. Regardless, a SA that was reported in a delayed manner is less likely to be referred for testing (Patterson & Campbell, 2012; Valentine et al., 2019). A delayed report may impact law enforcement's perceptions of the victim's credibility and undermine their belief that a crime occurred.

Victim credibility

Although there is no agreed upon definition of "victim credibility," broadly, this term refers to the perceived sense of faith or belief in this victim's account of the SA and is a critical factor in predicting case attrition (Kaiser et al., 2017). Victim credibility can be shaped by legal factors, such as the presence of bodily injury, which is often interpreted as evidence of physical resistance and lack of consent to the assault. This relationship persists, even though requirements that the victim physically fight back have been removed from SA legislation. However, many extralegal factors have been shown to shape perceptions of victim credibility, including *victim characteristics* (age, race) and *victim behaviors* (engaging in any so-called "risky" behaviors preceding the assault; Alderden & Ullman, 2012; see Chapter 3).

To best understand the impact of SA victim credibility on case attrition, it is important to recognize the influence of "rape culture"—a common set of beliefs held at a societal level that normalize and promote sexual violence (Herman, 1988). Rape culture perpetuates rape myths—widely held societal beliefs about rape that are inaccurate or misleading (McMahon & Farmer, 2011). Examples of rape myths are "healthy women can resist all sexual attacks," "victims are attacked by strangers," "if a girl acts like a slut, eventually she is going to get into trouble," and "false reports of rape are common" (Cuklanz, 2000; McMahon & Farmer, 2011).

Rape myth acceptance can lead to disbelief of SA victims that have experiences or engage in behavior that is contradictory to the myths (Du Mont et al., 2003). Rape myth acceptance is also associated with increased culpability on the victim and decreased responsibility on the perpetrator. As police officers are a part of society, they can often hold myth-related beliefs about SA, which becomes problematic as police officers serve as gatekeepers of the CJ system (O'Neal, 2019). That is, if law enforcement does not work diligently to investigate a reported SA, the case stands little chance of moving forward. Whereas rape culture and rape myth acceptance impact perceptions of victim credibility at a societal level, which is problematic in itself, disbelief of a victim, specifically by a police officer, can result in reduced investigative practices and subsequent early case attrition.

Studies of the backlog in Detroit, Michigan, demonstrated that law enforcement attitudes impacted case processing, particularly noting a trend of disbelief in victims' accounts of their assaults (Campbell et al. 2017b). The impact of law enforcement attitudes on the experience of secondary victimization has been well documented (O'Neal, 2019), but given the strong relationship between victim cooperation and case attrition (see Kaiser et al., 2017), these attitudes may be impacting case attrition in two ways. First, disbelief in victim accounts may directly reduce the likelihood that law enforcement will pursue a quality investigation of the case, leading to early case closure. Second, if the victim senses that law enforcement does not believe their account, they may reduce or withdraw their participation in the investigation, indirectly leading to case attrition through a reduction in victim cooperation. This withdrawal can be interpreted as deception or a lack of commitment to pursuing the case, both of which further undermine victim credibility, creating a cycle that exacerbates case attrition.

VICTIM CHARACTERISTICS

Victim demographic characteristics, such as age, race, gender identity, and sexual orientation, have been found to affect victim credibility (George & Martínez, 2002; Walker et al., 2005). Specifically, youth, individuals of color, males, and members of LGBTQ+ groups face more disbelief than adult, white, cisgender female, and heterosexual victims.

Age is a complex factor in contributing to victim credibility. Young children may be viewed as dishonest and potentially coached by an adult (e.g., in the context of a divorce), and teenagers are frequently perceived to be lying for attention or to get out of trouble (Greeson et al., 2016). More so, in cases of child SA, a victim who is "credible" is one who "gives consistent, detailed, and descriptive statements"—a strong qualitative predictor of case resolution (Menaker et al., 2017). Younger adolescents, ages 13–15, were more likely to have kits submitted than older adolescents, ages 16–17 (Shaw & Campbell, 2013). The older a victim was, the less likely that a case would result in a charge, specifically, "for an increase of ten years in age, a woman was 45% less likely to have her case result in a charge" (Du Mont & Myhr, 2000, p. 1122).

Prevalent, harmful, and inaccurate stereotypes about people of color influence the believability of reports. For example, societal beliefs about hyper-sexuality may lead to perceptions that undermine a Black woman's ability to withhold consent (George & Martínez, 2002). Race is commonly identified as a contributor to the experiences of secondary victimization and case attrition. When interviewing members of the multidisciplinary team who responded to the rape kit backlog in Detroit, representatives of all agencies other than law enforcement specifically noted the impact of the extralegal factors of gender, race, and socioeconomic status as drivers of case attrition (Campbell & Fehler-Cabral, 2018). According to one interview participant, "'It's not that complicated to figure out … this is a crime that affects women, and in this city, that means Black women, poor Black women … there's a good chunk of the explanation'" for case attrition (Campbell & Fehler-Cabral, 2018, p. 90). Regarding victims of SA, another participant noted, "'Many of them are poor … many of them are living not only a legacy of racism but active racism, active misogyny … and the criminal justice system [is just going to] exacerbate [that,]'" (Campbell & Fehler-Cabral, 2018, p. 90). Although qualitative accounts from first responders indicate that racism, sexism, and classism impact SA case attrition, due to the lack of valid and reliable measures, quantitative work assessing these impacts is less definitive at this point.

Gender and sexual orientation also impact perceived victim credibility. Because SA has historically been a female-focused crime (Brownmiller, 1975), rape myths often perpetrate the societal belief that men cannot be raped (O'Neal, 2019; Schulze et al., 2019). Arrest is less likely when a victim is a male (Peterson et al., 2013), but other studies have found that kit submission is more likely for a male than a female victim (Valentine et al., 2019). This may also reflect a dynamic in which male victims are more likely to pursue a SAK only if there is a physical injury requiring medical attention, whereas female victims may undergo a SAK regardless of physical injury. Male victims often experience more homophobic treatment and disinterest from police when compared to female victims, which poses a significant barrier to reporting (Walker et al., 2005).

Many victims of the LGBTQ+ community decide not to report at all, given concerns that they will be stigmatized, judged, or disbelieved (Schulze et al., 2019). The past decade has seen substantial growth in the literature focused on SA within the LGBTQ+ community and attempts to address barriers to service provision and enhance the likelihood of reporting (Du Mont et al., 2020). The complex and intersectional nature of these variables with race, age, and gender are difficult to measure but essential to a complete understanding of CJ processing of SA. Thus, additional complex quantitative designs are needed to measure the impact of demographic characteristics on case attrition.

Furthermore, victims of lower socioeconomic status, with impaired cognitive functioning, suffering from mental illness, or involved in sex work are less likely to be believed (Spohn & Tellis, 2014; Valentine et al., 2019), perhaps due to societal ideas about rape seeped in racism and classism. Moreover, "Prosecutors, victim advocates, forensic nurses, and forensic scientists argued that intersectional sexism, racism, and classism was fundamental to why the police would not help so many rape victims" (Campbell & Fehler-Cabral, 2018, p. 90). For example, as an explanation as to why SAKs were not submitted, interviewed key stakeholders in Detroit expressed the sentiment: "'She was prostituting, and she agreed to the money, and he didn't pay her ... she says it's rape. It's not, it's a deal gone bad'" (2018. p. 91). In Los Angeles, cases involving "questions about character/reputation" and "mental illness or mental health issues" were significantly and substantially more likely to be unfounded, which means it was determined that a crime did not occur and, therefore, law enforcement would not pursue further investigation (Spohn & Tellis, 2014). This is often due to the downstream prosecutorial effect that a jury would not believe the victim (Campbell & Fehler-Cabrel, 2018).

VICTIM BEHAVIORS

Consistent with the importance of victim credibility discussed earlier, victims of SA are often scrutinized and judged for their behaviors before, during, and after the SA to assess their credibility. Specifically, victims who engage in "risk-taking" behavior prior to a SA, such as drinking alcohol, using illicit drugs, or going out alone, are more likely to have their accounts of the assault questioned or doubted (Du Mont et al., 2003). Although there are neurobiological reasons for freezing or not fighting back during a SA (Hopper & Archambault, 2020), SA victims who do not physically fight back during an assault are often questioned or doubted (Hopper & Archambault, 2020). Even actions taken after the SA are sometimes used to undermine victim credibility, particularly if they appear to have a low affect when reporting (i.e., not crying, which is a normal response following an experience of trauma) or wait more than a couple of hours to seek assistance from medical or law enforcement.

Additionally, victims of SA may choose to pull back from an investigation (e.g., not respond to phone messages, skip a scheduled interview), a common trauma response, which police officers may interpret as the victim being uncooperative. An "uncooperative victim" is often perceived as less credible, as scripts around SA depict "true" victims as fully participatory in the CJ process (Kaiser et al., 2017). All these factors which enhance the judgment of victims and undermine their credibility are important because of their likely indirect influence on case attrition. If the decision-makers (i.e., police officers, prosecutors) do not perceive the victim as credible based on their behaviors, they are less likely to move forward with a case. Even if they believe the victim's account of the crime, their downstream orientation (i.e., toward obtaining a conviction) may lead them to drop a case if the victim is viewed as uncooperative.

Relationship context

Another important extralegal factor in cases is the relationship between a victim and a perpetrator. Although a known perpetrator is more likely to be questioned than an unknown perpetrator (as law enforcement already has an identified suspect) when a victim knows the suspect, their report might be taken less seriously. If a stranger offender can be identified, the case is more likely to proceed than cases involving an acquaintance (Frazier & Haney, 1996). This is particularly important if it is a romantic or familial relationship. If a SA takes place following the dissolution of a romantic relationship, the victim may be depicted as having a high motivation to lie to get even with the accused assailant. Within the context of a divorce, a child may be accused of lying about sexual abuse to give one parent leverage over the other in child custody or other decisions. If a victim is viewed as having reason to be dishonest, their credibility may be undermined, leading to an increased risk of case attrition following the initial investigation. Even if the suspect and victim are not in a romantic relationship (e.g., classmates, coworkers, acquaintances), the case may be less likely to proceed than a case involving strangers (Frazier & Haney, 1996; Lovell et al., 2021).

If a SA takes place within the context of intimate partner violence (IPV), some research finds that an arrest is more likely to take place compared to cases involving strangers (Spohn & Tellis, 2014). However, once again, this effect may be driven by the fact that an intimate partner can be more easily identified and located than a stranger, making an arrest possible. Within IPV SA, the strongest predictors of an arrest being made are use of a weapon and physical injury to the victim (Spohn & Tellis, 2014). Despite their increased likelihood of arrest compared to a stranger assault, other research indicates that IPV SAs are less likely to result in felony charges than other cases (Alderden & Ullman, 2012). A recent study of previously unsubmitted or untested SAKs from IPV SA cases found that the DNA profiles associated with these kits were more likely than those found in non-IPV cases to be serial offenders with cases against multiple victims (Lovell et al., 2019), a finding which certainly warrants further study and demonstrates the utility of testing SAKs.

Societal context

Societal context has been identified as another extralegal factor that can impact case attrition. Adding to the complexity of societal issues is the fact that they exist at many levels. That is, rape myths are prevalent within society, impact institutional policies and practices, and are reflected in the behaviors and words of individuals. Racism is another phenomenon that exists at multiple levels and in multiple ways. Given its varied manifestations and omnipresence, the impact of racism on case attrition remains unclear. While early work suggested that SAs against white victims may move farther in the CJ system than cases against victims of other races (Wolfgang & Reidel, 1973; Brownmiller, 1975), more recent work has found that race did not have a significant impact on case attrition after controlling for other relevant variables, such as assault characteristics and strength of evidence (Alderden & Ullman, 2012; Spohn & Tellis, 2014). However, this may reflect more thorough or persistent investigation into cases with a white victim. A study of unsubmitted SAKs found that the SAKs collected relating to crimes against non-white victims were more likely to be tested than SAKs collected relating to crimes against white victims (Shaw & Campbell, 2013). These researchers speculated that perhaps this finding was driven by the unmeasured effect of the perpetrator's race, though they could not capture such data. There is also strong theoretical and qualitative evidence that reporting of SA to law enforcement is lower in non-white communities (Tillman et al., 2010). Overall, race seems to impact decision-making at all levels of case processing. A multi-site study found that race was a significant predictor of arrest in "small sites" (jurisdictions with populations of approximately 100,000) when the SA was committed against a Black victim. Specifically, "in small jurisdictions, incidents involving Black victims are more than three times more likely to end in an arrest than those involving white victims" (Morabito et al., 2019, p. 40). In addition to the fact that race and racism seem to matter at different stages of the CJ system, they may have different impacts in different jurisdictions.

Jurisdiction context

Another set of extralegal factors that have been shown to impact case processing and, ultimately, attrition are characteristics of the jurisdiction. In their 6-site study, Morabito et al. (2019) found that law enforcement in larger jurisdictions utilized exceptional clearances (a status reserved for cases that an arrest cannot be made due to extenuating circumstances, such as death or extradition) to close cases more frequently than smaller jurisdictions. In a study of the presence of SAKs in 911 counties across 15 states, Strom et al. (2021) found that counties with larger populations were more likely to report having unsubmitted SAKs than counties with smaller populations. Though the authors caution against reading too much into these emerging findings, the relationship between population and SA case handling warrants further investigation.

An emerging theme in multiple studies is the impact of resource availability on attrition. As previously mentioned, DNA technology is a somewhat recent development and was not consistently available for all jurisdictions even after its development (Campbell et al., 2017b). Prior to the widespread use of CODIS, many agencies only regularly tested kits when they had a known suspect for comparison and would only submit a kit without a known suspect about half the time (Strom & Hickman, 2010). Other agencies chose not to submit SAKs for testing when there was a known assailant, as they assumed that a DNA confirmation of the identification would not add to the evidence (Strom & Hickman, 2010). The framework that testing the kit would not benefit the case (e.g., because a suspect was already identified or there were no possible leads) is problematic because it leads to failure to identify a suspect or match for prosecution, failure to build the CODIS database, and reduced likelihood of identifying an unknown suspect (Campbell et al., 2017b).

In their work on the causes of the SAK backlog in Kansas, Whisman and Roberts (2017) noted that substantial deficits in both resources and training contributed to the development of the backlog. Findings relating to the SAK backlog in Detroit also suggested that resources (including the need for more personnel) were a substantial contributor (Campbell et al., 2017b). A growing body of literature on the influence of training law enforcement on items such as trauma-informed policies and rape myths shows that training can improve attitudes toward SA victims and knowledge of trauma-informed approaches (B.A. Campbell et al., 2020; see also Chapter 19). Such knowledge should reduce the occurrence of victim blaming and, in turn, secondary victimization. It should also improve outcomes by enhancing trauma-informed, victim-centered approaches that may increase the likelihood of victim cooperation in the CJ process (B.A. Campbell et al., 2020).

A major review of case attrition and what new research into SAKs contributes to understanding this phenomenon describes the problematic impact of SA case handling as a "bureaucratic burden" (Lovell et al., 2021). The authors propose that "SA attrition might function more like a bureaucratic burden—where the onus to 'solve' the case is heavily placed on victims, which is a more passive way to (mis)handle SA but one that can still serve to further harm victims (e.g., institutional betrayal)" (Lovell et al., 2021, pp. 545–546). In other words, in addition to the fact that data show that few cases progress through the CJ system (see Figure 2.1), which is difficult for victims seeking justice, when cases experience attrition, there may be a tendency to blame that occurrence on victims (i.e., they did not collect sufficient evidence or remember the assault accurately, they did not cooperate fully or consistently "enough" in the eyes of the CJ system).

Legal and Extralegal Factors in Summary

Although we discuss legal and extralegal factors as separate concepts, they often interact. The factors that may lead to case attrition may not have the same impact on every case. Furthermore, there are factors that may be both legally and extralegally relevant. As an example, if a prosecutor strongly believes that a victim has filed a false report and is being dishonest, they cannot move forward with that case, and their reasoning would be legally relevant. However, many honest victims experience doubt, disbelief, and skepticism in the CJ system due to extralegal factors (e.g., delayed reporting, perceived "high risk" behaviors). In both cases, the decision is based on victim credibility, but a demonstrable false report (legal) differs substantially from perceived belief in victim's truthfulness (extralegal).

The interaction between different legal and extralegal factors is not always clear, may overlap, and may not be well defined yet (e.g., victim credibility) despite their clear significance. This results in researchers having difficulty parsing out the direct and indirect effects of different factors, requires complex statistical methodology, and calls attention to measures not yet developed. Because researchers rely on law enforcement records to accomplish this type of study, it is difficult for researchers to gather more details or responses. Specifically, most information taken from case files has already been interpreted or subject to the potential biases of the police officer recording the information. A potential solution for this would be a collaboration between law enforcement and researchers, such that through longitudinal study, they could mutually determine what factors to examine and how to receive more complete data.

Looking Forward

The discovery of thousands of untested SA kits, although devastating to survivors of SA, allowed for substantial change and transparency in SA cases. Specific communities have been particularly impacted and undergone substantial policy development and change to make sure that another backlog does not occur. For example, Mobile, AL, a recipient of multiple Department of Justice SA Kit Initiative Grants, has enacted significant change through "The Promise Initiative" (Lathan et al., 2019; see Chapter 10). In addition to a complete review and revision of policies and procedures relating to SA, a policy was implemented to test all SA kits, thus removing police officer discretion from this crucial stage of case attrition. As part of The Promise Initiative, the Mobile Police Department also implemented training for all patrol officers (both as part of the academy and recurring) which led to reduced rape myth adherence and improved attitudes toward victims of SA (Lathan et al., 2021). These concrete policies and actions, if enacted nationwide, could potentially reduce SA case attrition at the investigative stage and reduce the risk of developing another SAK backlog in the future.

Key Points

- Case attrition refers to the failure of a case to move through the formal CJ process and may occur at various stages, including failure to test a SAK, investigation, arrest, referral to prosecution, charges, conviction, and incarceration.
- Case attrition is a substantial problem in the United States, as approximately 20% of cases result in an arrest and 5% of cases result in a conviction.
- Legal factors, including characteristics of the assault and strength of evidence, significantly impact case attrition.
- Extralegal factors, including report characteristics, victim credibility, relationship context, societal context, and jurisdiction context, significantly impact case attrition.

Discussion Questions

1 Does the current level of case attrition send a message about the way that SA is processed in the United States?
2 How does an understanding of case attrition inform our understanding of how the backlog came to be?
3 What factors discussed here do you think have the most substantial impact on the high rate of SA case attrition in the United States?
4 Should extralegal factors be considered in case processing? If so, to what degree? If not, how might their impact be minimized?

References

Alderden, M. A., & Ullman, S. E. (2012). Creating a more complete and current picture: Examining police and prosecutor decision-making when processing sexual assault cases. *Violence Against Women, 18*(5), 525–551. https://doi.org/10.1177/1077801212453867.
Brownmiller, S. (1975). *Against our will: Men, women, and rape.* Ballantine Books.

Campbell, R., Feeney, H., Fehler-Cabral, G., Shaw, J., & Horsford, S. (2017a). The national problem of untested sexual assault kits (SAKs): Scope, causes, and future directions for research, policy, and practice. *Trauma, Violence, & Abuse, 18*(4), 363–376. https://doi.org/10.1177/1524838015622436.

Campbell, R., Fehler-Cabral, G., Bybee, D., & Shaw, J. (2017b). Forgotten evidence: A mixed methods study of why sexual assault kits (SAKs) are not submitted for DNA forensic testing. *Law and Human Behavior, 41*(5), 454–467. https://doi.org/10.1037/lhb0000252

Campbell, R., Feeney, H., Goodman-Williams, R., Sharma, D. B., & Pierce, S. J. (2020). Connecting the dots: Identifying suspected serial sexual offenders through forensic DNA evidence. *Psychology of Violence, 10*(3), 255–267. https://doi.org/10.1037/vio0000243.

Campbell, R., & Fehler-Cabral, G. (2018). Why police "couldn't or wouldn't" submit sexual assault kits for forensic DNA testing: A focal concerns theory analysis of untested rape kits. *Law & Society Review, 52*(1), 73–105. https://doi.org/10.1111/lasr.12310.

Campbell, B. A., Lapsey, D. S., & Wells, W. (2020). An evaluation of Kentucky's sexual assault investigator training: Results from a randomized three-group experiment. *Journal of Experimental Criminology, 16*(4), 625–647. https://doi.org/10.1007/s11292-019-09391-0

Campbell, R., Patterson, D., Bybee, D., & Dworkin, E. R. (2009). Predicting sexual assault prosecution outcomes: The role of medical forensic evidence collected by sexual assault nurse examiners. *Criminal Justice and Behavior, 36*(7), 712–727. https://doi.org/10.1177/0093854809335054

Campbell, B. A., & Wells, W. (2014). Testing sexual assault kits in cold cases and follow-up investigations: Practices used in agencies in the United States. A Report to the Houston, TX Sexual Assault Kit Action-Research Working Group. https://doi.org/10.13140/2.1.4526.1603

Cuklanz, L. M. (2000). *Rape on prime time: Television, masculinity, and sexual behavior.* University of Pennsylvania Press.

Du Mont, J., Hemalal, S., Kosa, S. D., Cameron, L., & Macdonald, S. (2020). The promise of an intersectoral network in enhancing the response to transgender survivors of sexual assault. *PLoS One, 15*(11), e0241563. https://doi.org/10.1371/journal.pone.0241563

Du Mont, J., Miller, K. L., & Myhr, T. L. (2003). The role of "real rape" and "real victim" stereotypes in the police reporting practices of sexually assaulted women. *Violence Against Women, 9*(4), 466–486. https://doi.org/10.1177/1077801202250960

Du Mont, J., & Myhr, T. L. (2000). So few convictions: The role of client-related characteristics in the legal processing of sexual assaults. *Violence Against Women, 6*(10), 1109–1136. https://doi.org/10.1177/10778010022183541

Frazier, P. A., & Haney, B. (1996). Sexual assault cases in the legal system: Police, prosecutor, and victim perspectives. *Law and Human Behavior, 20*(6), 607–628. https://doi.org/10.1007/BF01499234

George, W. H., & Martínez, L. J. (2002). Victim blaming in rape: Effects of victim and perpetrator race, type of rape, and participant racism. *Psychology of Women Quarterly, 26*(2), 110–119. https://doi.org/10.1111/1471-6402.00049

Gill, C., Weisburd, D., Telep, C. W., Vitter, Z., & Bennett, T. (2014). Community-oriented policing to reduce crime, disorder and fear and increase satisfaction and legitimacy among citizens: A systematic review. *Journal of Experimental Criminology, 10*(4), 399–428. https://doi.org/10.1007/s11292-014-9210-y

Greer, C. R. (2007). *News media, victims and crime* (pp. 21–49). London: Sage.

Greeson, M. R., Campbell, R., & Fehler-Cabral, G. (2016). "Nobody deserves this": Adolescent sexual assault victims perceptions of disbelief and victim blame from police. *Journal of Community Psychology, 44*(1), 90–110. https://doi.org/10.1002/jcop.21744

Herman, D. (1988). The rape culture. *Culture*, 1(10), 45–53.

Hopper, J., & Archambault, S. J. (2020). *Important Things to Get Right About the "Neurobiology of Trauma."* End Violence Against Women International. https://evawintl.org/wp-content/uploads/TB-Trauma-Informed-Combined-1-3.pdf

Jones, A. (2018). Correctional control 2018: Incarceration and supervision by state. *Prison Policy Initiative*, 12(11). https://www.prisonpolicy.org/reports/correctionalcontrol2018.html.

Kaiser, K. A., O'Neal, E. N., & Spohn, C. (2017). "Victim refuses to cooperate": A focal concerns analysis of victim cooperation in sexual assault cases. *Victims & Offenders*, 12(2), 297–322. https://doi.org/10.1080/15564886.2015.1078864

Koon-Magnin, S. (2022). *Sexual Assault and Harassment in America: Examining the Facts.* ABC-CLIO.

Langhinrichsen-Rohling, J., Lathan, E., Duncan, J., McGill, K., & Stefurak, J. T. (2019, June). *Incorporating the principles of trauma-informed care as a pathway to creating and sustaining a coordinated community response to sexual assault.* Symposium presentation at the 4th Annual National SAKI Grantees Meeting, Arlington, VA.

Lathan, E., Langhinrichsen-Rohling, J., Duncan, J., & Stefurak, J. T. (2019). The promise initiative: Promoting a trauma-informed police response to sexual assault in a mid-size Southern community. *Journal of Community Psychology*, 47(7), 1733–1749. https://doi.org/10.1002/jcop.22223

Lathan, E. C., Langhinrichsen-Rohling, J., Stefurak, J., & Duncan, J. (2021). Using collaborative, mixed-methods research to determine professional self-care's relation to burnout among police officers at a sexual assault kit initiative site. *Journal of Police and Criminal Psychology*, 1–13. https://doi.org/10.1007/s11896-020-09423-w

Lee, S. (2019). Crime victim awareness and assistance through the decades. *National Institute of Justice Journal*, 281, 1–10. https://www.ojp.gov/pdffiles1/nij/252733.pdf

Levenson, J. S., Brannon, Y. N., Fortney, T., & Baker, J. (2007). Public perceptions about sex offenders and community protection policies. *Analyses of Social Issues and Public Policy*, 7(1), 137–161. https://doi.org/10.1111/j.1530-2415.2007.00119.x

Lovell, R. E., Collins, C. C., McGuire, M. J., Overman, L. T., Luminais, M. N., & Flannery, D. J. (2019). Understanding intimate partner sexual assaults: Findings from sexual assault kits. *Journal of Aggression, Maltreatment & Trauma*, 28(1), 8–24. https://doi.org/10.1080/10926771.2018.1494234

Lovell, R., Luminais, M., Flannery, D. J., Bell, R., & Kyker, B. (2018). Describing the process and quantifying the outcomes of the Cuyahoga County sexual assault kit initiative. *Journal of Criminal Justice*, 57, 106–115. https://doi.org/10.1016/j.jcrimjus.2018.05.012

Lovell, R., Overman, L., Huang, D., & Flannery, D. J. (2021). The bureaucratic burden of identifying your rapist and remaining "cooperative": What the sexual assault kit initiative tells us about sexual assault case attrition and outcomes. *American Journal of Criminal Justice*, 46(3), 528–553. https://doi.org/10.1007/s12103-020-09573-x

McMahon, S., & Farmer, G. L. (2011). An updated measure for assessing subtle rape myths. *Social Work Research*, 35(2), 71–81. https://doi.org/10.1093/swr/35.2.71

Menaker, T. A., Campbell, B. A., & Wells, W. (2017). The use of forensic evidence in sexual assault investigations: Perceptions of sex crimes investigators. *Violence Against Women*, 23(4), 399–425. https://doi.org/10.1177/1077801216641519

Morabito, M. S., Williams, L. M., & Pattavina, A. (2019). *Decision making in sexual assault cases: Replication research on sexual violence case attrition in the US.* Office of Justice Programs, National Criminal Justice Reference Service. https://www.ojp.gov/pdffiles1/nij/grants/252689.pdf

Morgan, R. E., & Thompson, A. (2021). *Criminal victimization, 2020.* Bureau of Justice Statistics. https://bjs.ojp.gov/sites/g/files/xyckuh236/files/media/document/cv20.pdf

Murphy, S. B., Banyard, V. L., & Fennessey, E. D. (2013). Exploring stakeholders' perceptions of adult female sexual assault case attrition. *Psychology of Violence, 3*(2), 172–184. https://doi.org/10.1037/a0029362

O'Neal, E. N. (2019). "Victim is not credible": The influence of rape culture on police perceptions of sexual assault complainants. *Justice Quarterly, 36*(1), 127–160. https://doi.org/10.1080/07418825.2017.1406977

Patterson, D., & Campbell, R. (2012). The problem of untested sexual assault kits: Why are some kits never submitted to a crime laboratory? *Journal of Interpersonal Violence, 27*(11), 2259–2275. https://doi.org/10.1177/0886260511432155

Peterson, J. L., Hickman, M. J., Strom, K. J., & Johnson, D. J. (2013). Effect of forensic evidence on criminal justice case processing. *Journal of Forensic Sciences, 58*, S78–S90. https://doi.org/10.1111/1556-4029.12020

Schulze, C., Koon-Magnin, S., & Bryan, V. (2019). *Gender identity, sexual orientation, and sexual assault: Challenging the myths.* Lynne Rienner Publishers, Inc.

Shaw, J., & Campbell, R. (2013). Predicting sexual assault kit submission among adolescent rape cases treated in forensic nurse examiner programs. *Journal of Interpersonal Violence, 28*(18), 3400–3417. https://doi.org/10.1177/0886260513504496

Sinozich, S., & Langton, L. (2014). *Rape and sexual assault victimization among college-age females, 1995–2013.* Bureau of Justice Statistics. https://bjs.ojp.gov/content/pub/pdf/rsavcaf9513.pdf

Sorenson, S. B., & Siegel, J. M. (1998). Gender, ethnicity, and sexual assault: Findings from a Los Angeles study. In M. E. Odem, & J. Clay-Warner (Eds.), *Confronting rape and sexual assault* (pp. 211–222). SR Books.

Spohn, C., Beichner, D., & Davis-Frenzel, E. (2001). Prosecutorial justifications for sexual assault case rejection: Guarding the "gateway to justice." *Social Problems, 48*(2), 206–235. https://doi.org/10.1525/sp.2001.48.2.206

Spohn, C., & Tellis, K. (2010). Justice denied: The exceptional clearance of rape cases in Los Angeles. *Albany Law Review, 74*(3), 1379–1422.

Spohn, C., & Tellis, K. (2014). *Policing and prosecuting sexual assault: Inside the criminal justice system.* Lynne Rienner Publishers, Inc.

Strom, K. J., & Hickman, M. J. (2010). Unanalyzed evidence in law-enforcement agencies: A national examination of forensic processing in police departments. *Criminology & Public Policy, 9*(2), 381–404. https://doi.org/10.1111/j.1745-9133.2010.00635.x

Strom, K., Scott, T., Feeney, H., Young, A., Couzens, L., & Berzofsky, M. (2021). How much justice is denied? An estimate of unsubmitted sexual assault kits in the United States. *Journal of Criminal Justice, 73*, 101746. https://doi.org/10.1016/j.jcrimjus.2020.101746

Thompson, K., & Schmidt, D. (2018). Executive Summary: The Kansas Sexual Assault Kit Initiative (SAKI) Law Enforcement Survey Analysis of the Cross-Sectional Sample. https://www.kansas.gov/kbi/docs/media%20releases/KS%20SAKI%20Exec%20Summary%204%20-%20Forensic%20Results%20of%20Cross%20Sectional%20Sample.pdf

Tillman, S., Bryant-Davis, T., Smith, K., & Marks, A. (2010). Shattering silence: Exploring barriers to disclosure for African American sexual assault survivors. *Trauma, Violence, & Abuse, 11*(2), 59–70. https://doi.org/10.1177/1524838010363717

Valentine, J. L., Sekula, L. K., Cook, L. J., Campbell, R., Colbert, A., & Weedn, V. W. (2019). Justice denied: Low submission rates of sexual assault kits and the predicting variables. *Journal of Interpersonal Violence, 34*(17), 3547–3573. https://doi.org/10.1177/0886260516681881

Walker, J., Archer, J., & Davies, M. (2005). Effects of rape on men: A descriptive analysis. *Archives of Sexual Behavior, 34*(1), 69–80. https://doi.org/10.1007/s10508-005-1001-0

Wentz, E., & Keimig, K. (2019). Arrest and referral decisions in sexual assault cases: The influence of police discretion on case attrition. *Social Sciences*, 8(6), 180. https://doi.org/10.3390/socsci8060180

Whisman, K., & Roberts, M. (2017). The Kansas Sexual Assault Kit Initiative: Underlying Factors Contributing to the Accumulation of Unsubmitted Sexual Assault Kits in Kansas. https://www.kansas.gov/kbi/news/docs/Underlying%20Factors%20Contributing%20to%20the%20Accumulation%20of%20Unsubmitted%20SAKs.pdf

Wolfgang, M., & Reidel, M. (1973). Race, judicial discretion and the death penalty. *Annals*, *407*,119–133. https://doi.org/10.1177/000271627340700110

Wright, R. (Ed.). (2014). *Sex offender laws: Failed policies, new directions*. Springer Publishing Company.

3 Understanding sexual assault disclosure

Victim decision-making processes underlying the National Sexual Assault Kit Initiative

Jennifer Langhinrichsen-Rohling, Bridget Jules, Emma C. Lathan, C. Austin Coates, and Rachel Crisler

Author Note

The opinions or points of view expressed in this document are solely those of the authors and do not reflect the official positions of any participating organization or the U.S. Department of Justice.

Obtaining, submitting, and testing sexual assault kits (SAKs) from engaged survivors is essential to the justice process. Consequently, timely and inclusive submission of SAKs is now becoming a matter of law (see Chapter 18). However, addressing cultural, organizational, and professional barriers to victim engagement continues to be essential, as there are multiple junctures at which the sexual assault criminal justice process relies on survivors' choices. For example, for a survivor to obtain a SAK and initiate the forensic process, they must first choose to disclose the sexual assault, often to multiple informal (friends, family) and formal recipients, including medical and criminal justice professionals (e.g., advocates, resident advisors, responding police officers and assigned sex crimes detective(s), emergency department personnel, a sexual assault nurse examiner (SANE)). Typically, the survivor soon faces another decision, whether to formally engage with the justice system. A hypothetical timeline of these decision processes and the factors influencing the victim's disclosure-related decisions is presented in Figure 3.1. Formal engagement with the criminal justice system only occurs if the survivor chooses to make an official sexual assault report, as this step links the SAK, the victim, and the case together for investigative purposes. Given the time-intensive requirements of a sexual assault investigation, forensic testing, and potential prosecution, the sexual assault victim may need to revisit their choice to engage with the criminal justice system at multiple points. This is certainly the case for victims whose SAK was shelved in the SAK backlog.

Many survivors consider the potential short-term and long-term impacts on themselves and others when making these decisions. While the benefits of disclosure might include greater access to services, support, and care, in conjunction with an increased possibility of justice and prevention of harm to others, victims also imagine and anticipate negative social reactions to their disclosure (e.g., Ullman & Peter-Hagene, 2010), including from their family and friends (informal disclosure),

DOI: 10.4324/9781003186816-5

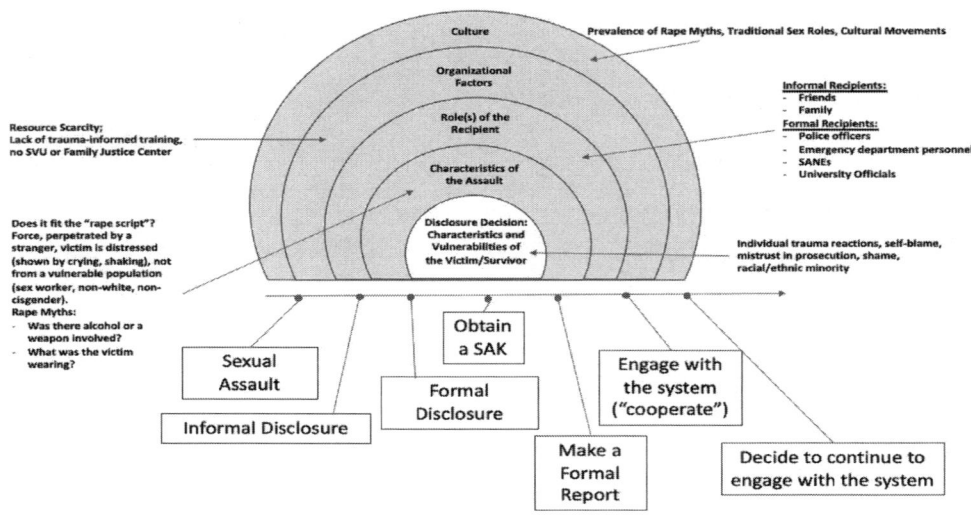

Figure 3.1 Factors Influencing Sexual Assault Disclosure and Victim Case Decisions across Time

medical and criminal justice personnel, their community, and the public (formal and public disclosure). Based on historical law enforcement responses, many expect their credibility to be challenged (Tuerkheimer, 2021). Some also consider the impact of these decisions on their perpetrator, who may be known to them, a public figure, dangerous, and/or embedded within their community (e.g., priest, coach, teacher). Potential negative impacts of the disclosure might include retribution, gaslighting and/or institutional betrayal, and secondary trauma or revictimization by the system. Supporting the importance of considering disclosure impacts, Campbell and Raja (1999) referred to the experience of secondary victimization by the criminal justice system as a survivor's second rape.

Given the risks and benefits of disclosure it is perhaps unsurprising that low rates of formal (e.g., healthcare providers, law enforcement officers) disclosure of sexual assault have been consistently documented (1% to 36%; Demers et al., 2018). Informal disclosure rates, while generally higher, are also low; these vary substantially by survivor and assault characteristics. Male victims have lower rates of disclosure than female victims across all forms of sexual violence (Mennicke et al., 2021). Significant differences in disclosure rates by race and ethnicity also occur, with ethnic minorities being less likely to disclose (Spencer et al., 2020). Additionally, assaults perpetrated by an acquaintance, friend, or dating partner are less likely to be disclosed than those perpetrated by a stranger (Spencer et al., 2020).

Moreover, even among survivors who do choose to disclose their assault, few move beyond informal disclosure to make a formal report to an investigative authority (Orchowski & Gidycz, 2012). In the United States, only 15–32% of sexual assaults are reported to authorities (Planty et al., 2016). In fact, sexual assault is the most underreported violent crime (Bureau of Justice Statistics, 2017). Similar reporting patterns for rape have been noted in several other countries, with the mean rate of reporting hovering around 14% across Canada, New Zealand, Australia, the United States, England, and Wales (Daly & Bouhours, 2010).

An even smaller number of sexual assault survivors make the decision to obtain a SAK. Fewer still link their SAK with an official police report. Consequently, many cities (or their urban hospitals) have an accumulation of SAKs where the victim has decided not to submit their SAK to police, make an official report, or open an official investigation. These "anonymous" or "restricted" SAKs are sometimes referred to as Jane Doe kits, reflecting the reality that many are obtained from female victims (see Chapter 13). *Taken together, these findings suggest that only a tiny fraction of the sexually victimized population is represented by survivors who choose to obtain a SAK and formally report their assault to the police.*

Yet, even individuals drawn from this small subgroup of survivors face considerable scrutiny as others judge the credibility of their disclosure. Judgments that the victim lacks credibility are one of the many reasons for the accumulation of SAKs in the backlog (Campbell et al., 2015). Judgments, gaslighting, and stigma are linked with survivor disengagement from the process. Thus, responses to the survivor's initial disclosure are critical. Positive, trauma-informed responses to disclosure can foster healing and potentially promote sustained engagement with the legal system (Ahrens et al., 2010). Conversely, negative responses to a survivor's disclosure are associated with secondary trauma and adverse outcomes including post-traumatic stress disorder and depression. In addition, unsupportive responses to a survivor's sexual assault disclosure can have a ripple effect, making it harder for other victims to come forward as they too anticipate experiencing negative, harmful, or disbelieving responses.

Low rates of disclosing and reporting sexual assault have consequences for the survivor, the perpetrator, and the community. At the community level, there is emerging evidence that many sexual offenders continue to perpetrate both general and sexual crimes after their initial sexual assault (see Chapter 7). Consequently, low rates of reporting thwart efforts to identify and incarcerate rapists, many of whom continue to offend (Lovell et al., 2020). Low rates of reporting also prevent a full understanding of the scope of the problem, which in turn, is an impediment to needed societal change. Lack of disclosing and reporting reduces the likelihood that adequate resources will be allocated for sexual assault prevention and intervention efforts. However, *disclosure rates will only increase if we prevent harmful responses to disclosure. Thus, we need to promote enhanced cultural, institutional, professional, and interpersonal disclosure responses to advance sexual assault reform. Responses to sexual assault disclosure need to be trauma-informed.* This sentiment is captured in the global campaign, Start by Believing (2020), launched by End Violence Against Women International.

To advance the reform effort, the current chapter will focus on factors that influence both the decision to disclose (informal/formal recipients) and/or officially report and engage, as well as factors underlying the harmful responses survivors have received to their disclosures. Existing models of the disclosure decision process will be briefly summarized. Overarching cultural factors, which include widespread acceptance of rape myths, adherence to stereotypical sex and gender roles, and stigmatization of marginalized individuals, are posited as foundational to our understanding of the disclosure process. Current cultural movements impacting disclosure decisions will be noted (#MeToo; #timesup; establishment of family justice centers). Finally, this chapter will explore factors associated with disclosure at the level of the professional recipient (e.g., attitudes, knowledge and beliefs of police officers, prosecutors) and organizations and systems (e.g., *Does this police department follow trauma-informed practices? Is there a history of institutional betrayal by the police department? Does this hospital have a trained sexual assault nurse examiner?*). We then describe how these factors work in concert to impact a survivor's decision to self-disclose their assault, document their victimization, collect evidence from their own body via obtaining a SAK, make a formal police report, and choose to engage and/or re-engage with the justice system. *See Figure 3.1 for a visual summary of the processes facing survivors who are taking action with hopes of obtaining justice, preventing others from being assaulted, and/or increasing their own likelihood of healing and closure.*

The authors of this chapter are well-positioned to contribute a chapter on sexual assault disclosure. The first author is a Professor in the Department of Psychological Science at the University of North Carolina Charlotte. Dr. Langhinrichsen-Rohling has over thirty-five years of research on victims and perpetrators of sexual assault, trauma, intimate partner violence, and stalking. She currently directs the THRIVE research lab (Trauma, Healing, and Resilience in a Violence-Free Environment), which has ongoing projects with the UNC Charlotte BHealthier Clinic, the UNC Charlotte Title IX office, and the Charlotte-Mecklenburg Police Department. The THRIVE team, which includes Emma Lathan (currently a post-doctoral fellow with the Grady Trauma Project at Emory University School of Medicine), Bridget Jules and Austin Coates (Clinical Health Psychology doctoral students at UNC Charlotte), and Rachel Crisler (a current undergraduate student majoring in Psychology and History at UNC Charlotte) has studied victim disclosure, judgments of victim credibility, and institutional betrayal/secondary trauma related to sexual assault reporting among college students via university-wide climate surveys (Mennicke et al., 2021), Title IX case reports, and through coding more than one thousand SAKI case files (Lathan et al., 2019).

Disclosure Decisions: Models and Theories

Existing models of disclosure have primarily focused on describing the process of *informal disclosure,* which consists of sharing your sexual assault experience with friends, family, and loved ones, so these theories may not fully generalize to disclosure to formal sources, the process of deciding to obtain a SAK, or to the decision to officially report the crime of rape. However, they offer valuable scaffolding. Three main theories to consider are Derlega and Grzelak's (1979) Functional Theory of Disclosure and the Disclosure Process Model (Chaudoir & Fisher, 2010).

Derlega and Grzelak's (1979) Functional Theory of Disclosure describes victims' motivations to disclose. Individuals choose to disclose to achieve one or more of five basic functions: self-expression, self-clarification, social validation, relationship development, or social control. *Self-expression disclosure* seeks distress relief through sharing negative emotions and disclosing personal problems. *Self-clarification disclosure* conveys information about one's identity and defines one's position for self and others. *Social validation disclosure* seeks to validate one's self-concept and self-value through increased social approval and social acceptance. *Relationship development disclosure* seeks to increase relational intimacy and closeness with another person through the sharing of private or vulnerable information. Finally, *social control disclosure* is utilized to strategically share personal information to control social outcomes and resources (i.e., social benefits, information). Similar to the

Functional Theory of Disclosure (Derlega & Grzelak, 1979), the Disclosure Decision Model (Omarzu, 2000) proposes that the disclosure decision process is activated by the increased accessibility of the social rewards. In this model, the rewards are: social approval, intimacy, relief of distress, social control, and identity clarification. According to these theories, the utility of disclosing is weighed against the risks with these goals in mind. First, the survivor must view disclosure as a reasonable strategy for reaching the identified goal. Next, a target for disclosure must be selected (i.e., the disclosure recipient). Finally, the survivor must evaluate the subjective utility against the risk of disclosure in reference to the chosen disclosure recipient and the imagined social exchange (e.g., How will my mother react? Will police officers believe me?) Theoretically, this evaluation informs both the choice to disclose and the breadth of disclosure undertaken in any given situation. A case example of the disclosure decision is presented in Box 3.1.

The Disclosure Process Model (Chaudoir & Fisher, 2010) expands the conversation by identifying when and why disclosure may be judged as particularly beneficial versus risky. Theoretically, as depicted in Figure 3.1, the disclosure process contains multiple decision points. Approach (i.e., obtaining a reward or desired end state) and avoidance (i.e., avoiding an undesirable end state) motivations are thought to shape each juncture. According to this theory, a survivor's decision begins with a judgment related to the accessibility of their approach goals. Disclosure approach goals might include receiving social support, gaining access to health or mental health services, gaining access to resources and accommodations, ensuring safety against perpetrators, and gaining justice. Conversely, survivors then consider the likelihood of achieving their avoidance goals. Avoidance goals may include wanting to keep the details of their assault private and/or a desire to avoid others' judgments. Avoidance goals might also include practical considerations such as the need to avoid losing time, resources, and energy pursuing justice that is perceived as unlikely to materialize. *According to theory, disclosure, reporting, and engagement decisions are best understood when the interplay of approach and avoidance goals is considered.*

Survivor Barriers to Making an Official Report: Approach and Avoidance Goals

Given the intersection of approach and avoidance goals, it is not surprising that many survivors are hesitant to report their sexual assault. According to the 2005-2010 National Crime Victimization Survey, survivors' most common reasons for non-reporting were: 20% feared retaliation, 13% believed it was a personal matter, 8% thought their assault was not important enough to warrant a report, and 7% did not want to get the perpetrator in trouble (Planty et al., 2016). Other reasons for victims not reporting their sexual assault include shame, self-blame, fear for safety, confusion, embarrassment, length of time between assault and report, having a close relationship with the perpetrator, and being worried about responses from family and friends (Wolitzky-Taylor et al., 2011). Survivors also worry about other people's judgments of their behavior. In a recent study of victims' self-reported barriers to reporting, the most common barriers were fear of not being believed (78% endorsed), shame (73%), stigma (59%), lack of confidence in prosecution (50%) and fear of retaliation (48%). When the responses of victims were compared with non-victims, victims endorsed more concerns about the confidentiality of their reports and greater

---

Box 3.1

Case example of disclosure decision

Renee is a 26-year-old married woman. Last week, she went out to a nightclub with several of her friends to celebrate a birthday. During the evening, Renee began dancing with a mutual friend who was also invited to the birthday celebration. Throughout the night, Renee and her male friend danced together, laughed, and bought each other drinks. However, when Renee went to use the restroom, her male friend followed her into the bathroom and began touching her. Renee asked him to leave, but he assured her that she "wanted it" since they had been dancing together all night. He then raped Renee. Renee repeatedly told him to stop, but she did not physically fight him because she feared how he might react. Throughout the rape, she felt frozen from action and just prayed it would be over quickly.

Renee's decision about whether or not to disclose her assault is now informed by multiple factors. Renee felt confused and shocked; she blamed herself for this assault. She had thoughts like she shouldn't have been dancing with or buying this man drinks. Renee considered telling her female friends at the party what had happened but felt fearful of ruining their night and telling on their friends. Renee also worried about the responses she would get from friends and family if she told them what happened. At the same time, she feels strongly that her male friend should not be allowed to think his behavior was acceptable. Renee is shaking and unsteady and knows that she really does not want this to happen to anyone else.

Renee's decision to formally disclose this assault could serve many purposes including relieving her own distress and getting support, helping protect others, and gaining access to post-assault services or justice within the legal system. However, Renee is aware of the risks and barriers to the disclosure of her assault. These same factors are also influencing her decision of whether to obtain a SAK. For example, Renee knows her experience does not fit the stereotypical "script" of sexual assault. She was assaulted by a man who she knew, and she had consensually engaged in dancing prior to the assault. Renee was also drinking alcohol before the rape, which she worries will impact her ability to appear credible before the legal system and may lead others to think she consented to the assault or that her memory of the event is faulty. With these thoughts in mind, Renee considers the potential benefits of disclosure (i.e., access to resources, legal justice, social support, protection of future women) versus the risks (i.e., potential anger and/or loss of her husband, disruptions in friendships, disbelief and judgment from the legal system due to credibility factors, fear of re-traumatization from getting a SAK, and she worries about the stigma, shame and lack of privacy she might experience with disclosure). As all of this is going through her mind, her closest friend asks her if she is okay. What do you think Renee decided to say and do?

---

distrust of the police/legal system (Mills et al., 2021). These victim-generated reasons have been collapsed across studies to generate a word cloud (see Figure 3.2).

There is also considerable variability in trauma reactions among victims (see Chapter 8). These might also influence willingness to disclose and officially report. For example, a victim might retrospectively view their thoughts, feelings, and behaviors during the rape with shame, blame, concern, suspicion, or doubt. During the assault, it is common for victims to freeze (Galliano et al., 1993). Afterward, they may unfairly blame themselves for being frozen, not understanding their behavior

Figure 3.2 Victim Reasons for Choosing Not to Disclose

as a survival response. They may question themselves and wonder why they did not fight or flee. They may have trouble remembering the order of events, which is a stark mismatch with police expectations for a clear timeline (see Chapter 5 for a survivor account of these experiences). Victims may experience their memory as fragmented or have narrowed their attention to one detail or sensory experience to mentally survive the attack; these common trauma reactions can also be confusing and disclosure-inhibiting for victims (Campbell, 2022).

Some victims are surprised and dismayed that their bodies had physiological reactions to the rape (e.g., registering some level of physical response, up to and perhaps including orgasm). These wide-ranging and disparate physical responses are trauma-normative but can be upsetting to disclosure recipients. Furthermore, there may have been consensual parts of the early experience between the victim and the perpetrator (e.g., agreed to share a ride or a kiss). Or, the victim and perpetrator may have shared engagement in a risky or illegal activity prior to the rape. Disclosure of the entirety of the rape experience is substantially less likely when the victim's actions, reactions, and recollections fail to conform to their own or others' rape expectations or the stereotypical rape script. Finally, according to the stereotypical assault script, rape is expected to include overt signs of physical trauma (e.g., bruising) and result in victim distress (e.g., crying, shaking, fear). Victims whose trauma reactions include numbness or other unexpected emotions may be less likely to acknowledge their experience as rape and subsequently be less likely to disclose and report (Cleere & Lynn, 2013). *Unexpected, while normative, trauma responses reduce the likelihood of disclosure and increase the likelihood of negative or non-supportive reactions to disclosure from others.*

Ongoing and Emerging Cultural Contexts: Widespread Acceptance of Rape Myths

Perceptions of sexual assault and responses to sexual assault victims are often informed by deeply embedded culturally specific rape myths (McMahon & Farmer, 2011). Rape myths are false beliefs about rape that are shaped by prejudicial beliefs that justify violence against women and shift the blame from the perpetrator to the victim (McMahon & Farmer, 2011). These myths include beliefs that the assault was a consensual experience; disbelief in some or all details of the event; beliefs that survivors wanted the assault to occur; or beliefs that the assault was justified given characteristics of the victim (i.e., clothing worn, prior sexual experiences, initial flirtation, use of alcohol/substances). Biased beliefs about what constitutes sexual assault and what motivates perpetrators to rape can influence the disclosure responses of friends, family, professionals, and the institutions with which victims interact.

Some myths have been reified into a prototypical rape stereotype. According to this script, rape is characterized by violent and forceful penetration, perpetrated by a stranger in a public but deserted place, to a moral and well-behaved woman, who is often presumed to be white and young, and who becomes physically injured while resisting the perpetrator (Stirling et al., 2020). Though this scenario is far from the norm of sexual assault experiences (Planty et al., 2016), instances that do not fit this "script" enhance the likelihood of non-disclosure because they increase the probability that the sexual assault will not be understood, labeled, and subsequently investigated as "rape." *Deviations from this prototypical rape script will also be viewed as more problematic by prosecutors who rely on jurors to hold perpetrators accountable.*

Sexual assault survivors can also hold rape myths. This can lead some victims to conclude that their experience was not serious enough to warrant reporting. They also may not judge their experience to be a sexual assault (Krebs et al., 2011; Smith & Freyd, 2014). In a 2016 study of 276 female college students, survivors with greater endorsement of rape myths were less likely to label their past sexual assault experience as rape (LeMaire et al., 2016). Unacknowledged rape is the term used to define events that meet legal or empirical definitions of rape but are not labeled as such by survivors (Wilson & Miller, 2016). For example, instead of rape, a survivor may label their experience as a "miscommunication," a "drunken hook-up," or a "bad decision." A 2016 meta-analysis indicated that, on average, 60% of rape survivors meet the criteria of unacknowledged rape (Wilson & Miller, 2016). Similarly, a study of 178 female college students indicated that 77.5% of rape survivors did not acknowledge their experiences as rape (Wilson & Scarpa, 2017). Sexual assaults that do not fit the stereotypical "script" of rape (i.e., rape by acquaintance rather than stranger, rapes that do not include overt violence and victim injury) are more likely to be unacknowledged by survivors (Cleere & Lynn, 2013). Survivors of unacknowledged rapes are less likely to disclose their experience to friends and family, seek medical care, and formally disclose or report the incident to the police (Wilson & Miller, 2016). They are also more likely to experience revictimization (Littleton et al., 2009). Thus, rape scripts detrimentally impact both survivor health and justice outcomes.

Rape myths also impact the reactions of those asked to judge a legal trial. Greater endorsement of culturally held rape myths is associated with jury members who are pre-disposed to a not-guilty verdict (Dinos et al., 2015). Negative attitudes toward rape victims by jurors have been identified as a barrier to convictions (Temkin, 2010). One pernicious rape myth is that false reports of rape are common. *For example, in a recent study, 40.2% of participants endorsed the myth that accusations of rape are often false (McGee et al., 2011). However, the evidence suggests that less than 10%*

of reported rapes are false or unfounded (Lisak et al., 2010). *Jurors who believe in high rates of false accusations are more likely to look for ulterior motives for victim disclosure and to perceive a lack of victim credibility.*

The perception that women are falsely accusing men of rape underlies #HimToo, a viral social movement fueled by a tweet ruing the "current climate of false sexual accusations by radical feminists with an axe to grind" (Tuerkheimer, 2021). Stereotypes of lying accusers include the "gold digger" who has a financial reason underlying her accusation; the "attention seeker" who is reporting rape to garner the spotlight; the "regretful woman" who wishes she had not had consensual sex, and thus, calls it rape afterward; and the "woman scorned" who is making an accusation of rape to get retribution (Tuerkheimer, 2021). *Unfortunately, the drive to uncover the "true" motivation underlying a woman's potentially false rape disclosure unfairly flips the script from a focus on the perpetrator's behavior to a focus on the victim's credibility. This serves to silence survivors.*

Historic Cultural Contexts: Adherence to Stereotypical Sex and Gender Roles

Sex and gender roles influence the culturally understood narrative around sexual encounters, including who is expected to initiate sex and with what persistence (men), and who is expected to say no but potentially not mean it (women). Sex roles also underlie perceptions about the loss of virginity, and they prescribe the expected number of sexual partners for males (many) versus females (few to none). These beliefs, in turn, impact attributions about rape.

Traditional gender roles characterize the behaviors and traits that men and women should exhibit to exemplify socially defined masculine and feminine ideals. Traditional gender roles for men include being assertive, head of household, and lacking emotion, while traditional gender roles for women include being passive, domestic, and emotional. Endorsement of these roles is linked with rape attributions. For example, masculine sex-typed males typically endorse more rape-supportive attitudes than androgynous males; gender-stereotypical males also consider stranger rape as more serious than acquaintance rape (Quackenbush, 1989). Likewise, among college students, males and those holding traditional gender role beliefs consistently endorse more rape supportive attitudes and hold negative stereotypes about rape (Talbot et al., 2010).

Gender roles inform sexual activity. According to sexual script theory (Simon & Gagnon, 2003), sexual initiation should follow traditional gender roles in which men initiate sexual activity while women restrict access. Strict adherence to traditional gender roles has been shown to promote sexually coercive behaviors like sexual assault (Byers, 1996), use of violent and/or rape-supportive pornography, and the development of rape scripts among men. Conversely, these beliefs contribute to occurrences of unrecognized rape and lack of disclosure and reporting among victims (Clark & Carroll, 2008). Overall, male sex, masculine gender ideology, and heterosexual orientation predict greater victim blame, lower perpetrator blame, and a reduced likelihood of disclosure and/or reporting to authorities (Seibold-Simpson et al., 2021).

Female virginity prior to marriage is viewed as essential in certain cultural groups (Boudreau et al., 2018). When virginity is highly valued, unmarried female rape victims may experience cultural and familial pressure not to disclose their sexual assault. Historically, unmarried women who have been raped have been ostracized by their families and community or forced to marry an abusive partner (Kim et al., 2017). Similarly, when monogamy and sexual purity are culturally required, women may withhold disclosing their experiences of sexual assault so as not to be seen as sexually promiscuous by their partners, families, or communities. Conversely, in many countries, rape victims who are known to be sex workers and thus in clear violation of sexual purity norms are the most vulnerable to negative or dismissive reactions from others upon disclosure of rape (e.g., Muganyizi et al., 2009).

The dynamics of sexual violence disclosure are further complicated among male victims due to the elevated levels of disbelief, discrimination, and social invisibility they face upon disclosure (Von Hohendorff et al., 2017). In cultures in which masculine agency in sexual interactions is valued, men may fail to disclose their sexual assault to preserve their masculine agency/power and highlight their rejection of feminine vulnerability (Dworkin & Weaver, 2021). Moreover, since women experience higher rates of sexual victimization than men (Hines et al., 2012); sexual assault resources are often directed toward female victims (Allen et al., 2015). This further inhibits disclosure for men as they do not fit the "stereotypical rape victim" (Donne et al., 2018) and they do not see themselves represented in response and recovery efforts. Lastly, social judgments differ when directed to male versus female rape victims. *Male victims of sexual assault are judged as more likely to have initiated or encouraged the sex act and enjoyed it; they are also perceived to be less likely to be stressed afterward (Smith et al., 2010).*

Historical Cultural Context: Discrimination and Stigmatization of Marginalized Victims

Barriers to reporting may also differ in line with existing social hierarchies and power dynamics. *Individuals belonging to certain socio-demographic groups encounter greater hardship in making reports due to their historical and systemic experiences of prejudice and discrimination* (Franklin & Garza, 2021). Minority stress theory (MST; Meyer, 2003) explains this by specifying that the stigma, prejudice, and discrimination that can arise from belonging to a marginalized group can create ongoing hostile social environments, which include experiences of invisibility and dismissal from those in power. This is the inequitable starting point from which individuals who regularly experience prejudice and discrimination must initiate their disclosure of sexual assault. Consistent with the tenets of MST, sexual assault reporting, especially to police, is lower for Black women than their white counterparts (Fisher et al., 2003).

Additional barriers to disclosure have been documented across many marginalized populations including racial minority groups and LGBTQIA+ communities. Specifically, victims' expectations of encountering bias are coupled with historically negative interactions with service and legal systems for BIPOC survivors. The result among BIPOC survivors and other historically marginalized populations (e.g., immigrants, LGBTQIA+ community members) is a greater fear of discriminatory treatment by agencies who serve victimized individuals (Binion & Gray, 2020) and correspondingly low rates of disclosure to formal resources (Taylor et al., 2009). See Chapter 4 for more about establishing an equitable response to BIPOC survivors.

In general, victims from vulnerable and marginalized populations also face judgments that they are less credible in their accounts of assault (O'Neal, 2019). This is concerning because, in the absence of corroborating evidence, police judgments about victim credibility are the most critical factor in determining arrest decisions as well as whether the case is ever presented to prosecutors (Campbell et al., 2015). For example, sex workers are often denied victim status as they are seen as "irresponsible citizens" who should be blamed (Stardust et al., 2021). There are similar attributions for those who are young, living in social housing, in poor health, or single (Long & Butler, 2018). Unfortunately, these individuals are also seen as vulnerable targets by perpetrators of assault. *Thus, victims from vulnerable or marginalized populations are doubly victimized as they face both increased risk of assault and increased risk of system failure upon disclosure.*

Of grave concern, perpetrators are also familiar with existing barriers to victim disclosure and reporting, which they too frequently use to their advantage. For example, many perpetrators deliberately target victims who belong to vulnerable, marginalized, or stigmatized groups (e.g., sex workers, women of color, children, students, those of lower SES, individuals who are developmentally delayed) or who have a consensual role a risky situation (e.g., engaged in substance use, sharing a ride with a stranger). These victims are more likely to blame themselves for the assault, less likely to disclose and report, and if reported, their experiences are less likely to be judged as credible (Tuerkheimer, 2021). This is akin to the advantage obtained by predators who deliberately target vulnerable prey (e.g., those injured, weakened, or separated from the herd). *Since vulnerable victims are disproportionately targeted by perpetrators, these victims have a particular need for skilled trauma-informed care and support when disclosing and moving through the post-assault process.*

Emerging Cultural Dynamics: Social Movements Promoting Disclosure (#MeToo; #timesup)

The #MeToo movement was founded in 2006 to help survivors of sexual violence, particularly Black women and girls, find pathways to healing. Following the #MeToo movement's launch, thousands of women publicly disclosed their experiences of sexual assault via social media. This movement was designed to quash the stigma surrounding victimization and demonstrate how survivors' collective public disclosure can hold perpetrators accountable and produce systematic change. The Time's Up movement shares a similar vision for women's empowerment, with specific solution-based steps. Specifically, the Time's Up movement was developed by over three hundred women in Hollywood, and it focuses on sexual assault in professional realms. This movement included the development of a legal defense fund to support survivors whose assault was tied to the workplace (TIMESUP, 2022).

Despite the positive intentions of these movements, one recent qualitative study exploring survivor perceptions of the #MeToo movement demonstrated that the movement's potential benefits (e.g., providing a voice, empowerment) may be mitigated in survivors who experience a backlash to their disclosure (Coates, 2021). Specifically, all survivors within a small qualitative study ($n = 8$) described receiving negative reactions to their social media disclosure of being raped. Of concern, they reported that contributing to #MeToo was frequently judged by others as a ploy to garner attention rather than a legitimate disclosure of trauma (Coates, 2021).

Emerging Cultural Dynamics: Family Justice Centers, Advocates, Increased University Response and Prevention Efforts

The emergence and proliferation of rape crisis centers (RCCs), Special Victim Units (SVUs), and off-site Family Justice Centers throughout the United States, in conjunction with the greater incorporation of sexual assault advocates into healthcare, educational, and criminal justice systems, has also impacted disclosure and reporting experiences. These advances are promising as survivors who are paired with an RCC advocate experience significantly less secondary victimization (i.e., distressing experiences with agencies following the assault that increase distress) and reduced emotional distress in response to their involvement with the justice system (see Chapter 24). *Advocates who are trained to be victim-centered and to provide trauma-informed responses can model these behaviors to other professionals while providing needed support for survivors.*

Educational systems have been increasingly tasked with prevention, early intervention, and trauma-informed responses to sexual assault (see Chapter 15), as college is a high-risk environment for violent victimization. Consequently, Resident Assistants (RAs) often serve as the first recipients of sexual disclosure in the university environment. Generally, university mandates require RAs to respond by providing both emotional and material support; in essence, RAs are expected to function as both advocates and resource officers who can be mandated to provide a referral to the campus Title IX office, the on-site campus counseling center, the university police, and/or the student health center. However, in a recent study of 300 undergraduate RAs located at US campuses, RA disclosure responses varied substantially in spite of mandated policies. Sex of the RA (male/female), endorsement of rape myths, and adherence to feminist beliefs were all associated with differential responses (Holland et al., 2020). *Increasing the ability to RAs to function as trauma-informed and victim-centered advocates when receiving a sexual assault disclosure is critical to changing rape culture in a high-risk environment (i.e., college campuses).*

It is within these long-standing, larger, and yet dynamic cultural contexts that the disclosure decisions (informal, formal) and choices to engage in other sexual assault-related processes (obtaining a SAK, making an official report) are made. Adding to the complexity of these decisions, other ongoing professional and organizational/systemic factors that function as barriers to disclosure are prevalent.

Professional-Level Factors That Function as Recipient Barriers to Disclosure

Survivors who chose to report their sexual assault often recount their story to several professionals across multiple systems (e.g., responding officers and sex crime detectives from the police department; front desk staff in various locations, a SANE, healthcare providers and rape crisis advocates at the hospital; and/or paralegals and prosecutors within the district attorney's office). Survivors' anticipation of suspicious, dismissive, or inadequate responses from one or more of these individuals, including not being believed or being blamed for the assault, discourages reporting (Patterson & Campbell, 2010). For example, Planty et al. (2016) indicated that 13% of survivors chose not to report because they believed that the police would be unhelpful in their case. *This highlights the need to train all professionals who may potentially interact with a sexual assault survivor in trauma-informed care.*

Survivors may also experience additional trauma when disclosing to legal and medical professionals. Roughly one-third of rape victims consider their involvement with the criminal justice system to be harmful (Campbell et al., 2001); 84% of mental health professionals believe that system involvement will be retraumatizing (Campbell & Raja, 1999). With regard to psychological health, survivors indicated that, as a result of their contact with the legal system, they felt violated (89%), bad about themselves (87%), reluctant to seek further help (80%), guilty/self-blaming (73%), depressed (71%), and distrustful (53%; Campbell & Raja, 2005).

What Factors Influence Professionals to Respond Negatively to Sexual Assault Disclosures?

Professionals are, of course, people who are raised in a culture. If that culture promotes the endorsement of rape myths, promulgates stereotypical sex and gender roles that influence the choice of occupations (e.g., police officer is a masculine profession; victim advocate is a feminine profession), dictates the scripts by which sexual encounters are enacted, and predetermines relative positions of power (i.e., patriarchy leaves all women vulnerable to abuse and subjugation to maintain dominance and control by men), professionals will be primed to respond negatively to rape disclosures. Biases are also more likely to be enacted in climates with low resources and in which individuals respond to events on a case-by-case basis rather than by enacting standard operating procedures. Biases are more present in climates that fail to require evidence-based training and have an overall lack of accountability. Thus, we assert that negative responses and biased reactions by professionals can be prevented with ongoing training, bias-reducing standard operating policies and procedures (e.g., submit all kits, fully investigate all reported assaults, start by believing), and enhanced individual accountability for negative reactions to victims. Including a provision that outcome and process data are routinely disaggregated by vulnerable populations, and particular workgroups may be particularly important to enact an equitable response. *These efforts require organizational and systemic change in response to sexual assault disclosures and reports.*

Organizational and System-Level Barriers to Disclosure

Persistent utilization of traditional police interview techniques and an organizational lack of training about how to conduct a trauma-informed sexual assault investigation are system-level barriers to victim disclosure. Most police officers in the United States are trained in the Reid Technique (Kozinski, 2018), a commercially marketed method of suspect interrogation, which promises an 80% interrogation to confession rate (Inbau et al., 2013). To detect deception, the Reid technique uses the following three components: factual analysis (e.g., estimates an individual's probable guilt based on demographics, motivation, and evidence), interviewing (e.g., determines whether an individual is being deceptive), and interrogation (e.g., seeks to elicit a confession). However, even with training, police officers cannot successfully identify truthful versus false denials of guilt at rates greater than chance, making them no more accurate than lay people at detecting deception (Aamodt & Custer, 2006; Bogaard et al., 2016).

Unfortunately, deception detection methods, designed for perpetrators, are sometimes used to interview sexual assault victims. Police officers disbelieve a greater number of sexual assault victims than victims of any other crime (End the Backlog, 2019). For example, officers in Venema's (2016) qualitative study indicated they used a "light interrogation" when they questioned whether a sexual assault report is legitimate. Interrogation/cross-examination of survivors is particularly problematic due to the nature of traumatic memories. Changes in brain activation and the release of stress hormones during traumatic events affect memory encoding, consolidation, and retrieval (Cuevas et al., 2018). Survivors' memories may be fragmented, which may be perceived by officers as not being credible. Further, research on traumatic memories demonstrates that cross-examination may increase errors in traumatic memory reports, regardless of initial accuracy; this technique may lead to genuine memory distortion (Segovia et al., 2017; Chapter 8). *Thus, a lack of understanding of trauma increases the likelihood of institutional betrayal by reducing the perceived credibility of survivors.*

In response, police departments have put policies and procedures in place to encourage better responses to disclosure and sexual assault reports. These include standard operating procedures (submit all kits, investigate all reports) and greater access to systematic trauma-informed sexual assault investigations training (Lathan et al., 2019, see Chapter 10). Research confirms that officers who use a "gentle manner" of questioning with victims obtain better victim statements, which in turn, produces stronger evidence for prosecution (Patterson, 2011).

Other system-wide and organizational factors that discourage disclosure and continued engagement include lack of resources. Hospitals with SANEs are poised to respond to victims with trauma-informed care and up-to-date forensic techniques. However, many hospitals (particularly those located in rural areas) and university student health centers lack SANEs (see Chapters 14 and 15). Police departments struggle with a lack of resources as well. We assert that organizational difficulties may manifest in the absence of an SVU or Family Justice Center, in a continual push to close cases quickly, or in the absence of thorough investigations of sexual assaults due to lack of personnel time, energy, or experience. Under-resourced departments may also move officers to different positions more frequently. This may mean that incoming officers have less specialized training or experience in sexual assault response or investigation than is needed. Lack of resources further downstream in the criminal justice system may also discourage officers from offering hopeful responses to sexual assault victims. This may be due to an officer's awareness that the forensic lab may have limited testing available and/or that local prosecution may decline to prosecute sexual assault cases that they judge to be unwinnable or they perceive will command too large a share of limited resources.

Conclusion

The criminal justice system is designed to punish offenders. Threat of punishment is also expected to deter crime. However, sexual assault is one of the least reported, investigated, and successfully prosecuted crimes. This stark reality was highlighted with the discovery of hundreds of thousands of unsubmitted SAKs across the United States. In this chapter, the process of obtaining justice, in conjunction with healing post-assault, typically begins with disclosure of the assault. Models of disclosure highlight the many functions of disclosure for the victim including self-expression, self-clarification, social validation, relationship development, social control, safety, and survival. Prevailing cultural factors such as endorsement of rape myths, holding traditional sex and gender roles, and systemic discrimination and/or prejudice toward vulnerable populations influence the decision to disclose as well as responses to disclosure. Offenders also use these factors to target vulnerable victims. Currently, there are cultural movements (#MeToo, Start By Believing) that are encouraging victims to disclose while simultaneously addressing barriers to providing a healing response to a disclosure. Figure 3.1 demonstrates how a victim's disclosure and decision-making process is influenced by intersecting factors at the individual, assault, recipient, organizational, and cultural levels. We argue that negative responses to disclosure will diminish with cultural challenges to rape myths and stereotypical sex roles, greater dedication of resources to trauma informed training, and the development of specialized competencies among disclosure recipients including resident advisors, police officers, advocates, and prosecutors. We also need systemic investment in the accountable use of standardized operating procedures for sexual assault investigations to reduce the influence of implicit and explicit rape biases (Strom & Hickman, 2016).

Key Points

- Official disclosures of sexual assault and the choice to obtain a SAK are made with the hope of obtaining justice, preventing others from being assaulted, and increasing a survivor's likelihood of healing and closure.
- Disclosure of sexual violence is a complex process that is informed by the characteristics of the survivor, the perpetrator, the assault, and the system in which the survivor is embedded.
- Theories of disclosure highlight the multiple motivations that may underlie victim disclosure including *self-expression, self-clarification, social validation, relationship development, and social control.* Survivors have reasons to approach and avoid informal and formal disclosure and reporting of their sexual assault.
- Reactions to disclosure influence survivor engagement within the legal system and may have long-term implications for survivor well-being. Formal disclosure rates will remain low unless and until we prevent harmful responses to disclosure and victim decision-making.
- Unlike victims of other crimes, survivors of sexual assault are often revictimized within the legal system through the disbelief of their disclosure and the use of processes to assess victim credibility (i.e., interrogation, cross-examination).
- Survivors who experience sexual assaults that do not fit the "script" for stereotypical sexual assault or who belong to a vulnerable group face additional challenges in their interactions with the legal system and in their pursuit of perpetrator accountability.
- Social media movements that encourage disclosure and seek to empower victims may also generate mixed public reactions.
- Rape myths and stereotypical sex roles influence the likelihood of disclosure at each point of the process. These also influence recipient responses to disclosure.

- To reduce the influence of these biases, we recommend that police departments, universities, and healthcare centers develop and consistently utilize standardized operating procedures in response to sexual assault disclosures (Strom et al., 2016).
- Professionals, as well as advocates, RAs, and others who could interact with rape survivors, should receive training in the diversity of victim responses to trauma, learn evidence that challenges existing rape myths and stereotypical rape scripts, and be supported to provide trauma-informed services with consistency and skill throughout the process.

Discussion Questions

1 What factors influence a survivor's decision to disclose an experience of sexual assault? How do these factors change in the context of informal disclosure, formal disclosure, and reporting of sexual assault?
2 Do you think our culture promotes doubt against accusers while protecting abusers? What factors are involved? How can this be addressed?
3 Under what conditions do you think you would or would not report a sexual assault you experienced to police?
4 What changes could be implemented within the criminal justice or legal systems to enhance trauma-informed responses to survivors of sexual violence?
5 This chapter describes some of the processes occurring before the decision to report the sexual assault is made and some processes that are occurring in response to reports of sexual assault. How should this information be used to strengthen the National Sexual Assault Kit Initiative?

Further Reading or Recommended Sources

Tuerkheimer, D. (2021). *Credible: Why we doubt accusers and protect abusers.* HarperCollins Publishers.

References

Aamodt, M. G., & Custer, H. (2006). Who can best catch a liar? A meta-analysis of individual differences in detecting deception. *Forensic Examiner, 15*(1), 6–11.

Ahrens, C. E., Stansell, J., & Jennings, A. (2010). To tell or not to tell: The impact of disclosure on sexual assault survivors' recovery. *Violence and Victims, 25*(5), 631–648.

Allen, C. T., Ridgeway, R., & Swan, S. C. (2015). College students' beliefs regarding help seeking for male and female sexual assault survivors: Even less support for male survivors. *Journal of Aggression, Maltreatment & Trauma, 24*(1), 102–115.

Binion, K., & Gray, M. J. (2020). Minority stress theory and internalized homophobia among LGB sexual assault survivors: Implications for posttraumatic adjustment. *Journal of Loss and Trauma, 25*(5), 454–471. https://doi.org/10.1080/15325024.2019.1707987

Bogaard, G., Meijer, E. H., Vrij, A., & Merckelbach, H. (2016). Strong, but wrong: Lay people's and police officers' beliefs about verbal and nonverbal cues to deception. *PLoS ONE, 11*(6), Article e0156615.

Bureau of Justice Statistics. (2017). *National crime victimization survey, 2010-2016.* Department of Justice, Office of Justice Programs.

Byers, E. S. (1996). How well does the traditional sexual script explain sexual coercion? *Journal of Psychology and Human Sexuality, 8*(1), 7–25.

Campbell, B., Menaker, T. A., & King, W. R. (2015). The determination of victim credibility by adult and juvenile sexual assault investigators. *Journal of Criminal Justice, 43*, 29–39.

Campbell, R., & Raja, S. (1999). Secondary victimization of rape victims: Insights from mental health professionals who treat survivors of violence. *Violence and Victims, 14*(3), 261–275. https://doi.org/10.1891/0886-6708.14.3.261

Campbell, R., & Raja, S. (2005). The sexual assault and secondary victimization of female veterans: Help-seeking experiences with military and civilian social systems. *Psychology of Women Quarterly, 29*(1), 97–106. https://doi.org/10.1111/j.1471-6402.2005.00171.x.

Campbell, R., Wasco, S. M., Ahrens, C. E., Sefl, T., & Barnes, H. E. (2001). Preventing the "second rape": Rape survivors' experiences with community service providers. *Journal of Interpersonal Violence, 16*(2), 1239–1259. https://doi.org/10.1177/0886260010 16012002

Chaudoir, S. R., & Fisher, J. D. (2010). The disclosure processes model: Understanding disclosure decision making and post disclosure outcomes among people living with a concealable stigmatized identity. *Psychological Bulletin, 136*(2), 236–256. doi: 10.1037/ a0018193

Cleere, C., & Lynn, S. J. (2013). Acknowledged versus unacknowledged sexual assault among college women. *Journal of Interpersonal Violence, 28*(12), 2593–2611. https://doi. org/10.1177/0886260513479033

Coates, C. A. (2021, November). *Two sides to #MeToo: A qualitative analysis of college sexual assault survivors' experiences of the #MeToo movement* [Poster presentation]. International Society for Traumatic Stress Studies.

Cuevas, K. M., Balbo, J., Duval, K., & Beverly, E. A. (2018). Neurobiology of sexual assault and osteopathic considerations for trauma-informed care and practice. *The Journal of the American Osteopathic Association, 118*(2), e2–e10. https://doi.org/10.7556/jaoa. 2018.018

Daly, K., & Bouhours, B. (2010). Rape and attrition in the legal process: A comparative analysis of five countries. *Crimes and Justice, 39*(1), 565–650. https://doi.org/10.1086/ 653101

Demers, J. M., Ward, S. K., Walsh, W. A., Banyard, V. L., Cohn, E. S., Edwards, K. M., & Moynihan, M. M. (2018). Disclosure on campus: Students' decisions to tell others about unwanted sexual experiences, intimate partner violence, and stalking. *Journal of Aggression, Maltreatment & Trauma, 27*(1), 54–75. https://doi.org/10.1080/10926771.20 17.1382631

Derlega, V. J., & Grzelak, J. (1979). Appropriateness of self-disclosure. In G. J. Chelune (Ed.), *Origins, patterns, and implications of openness in interpersonal relationships* (pp. 151–176). Jossey-Bass.

Dinos, S., Burrowes, N., Hammond, K., & Cunliffe, C. (2015). A systematic review of juries' assessment of rape victims: Do rape myths impact on juror decision-making? *International Journal of Law, Crime and Justice, 43*(1), 36–49.

Dworkin, E. R., & Weaver, T. L. (2021). The impact of sociocultural contexts on mental health following sexual violence: A conceptual model. *Psychology of Violence, 11*(5), 476–487. https://doi.org/10.1037/vio0000350

Fisher, B. S., Daigle, L. E., Cullen, F. T., & Turner, M. G. (2003). Reporting sexual victimization to the police and others: Results from a national-level study of college women. *Criminal Justice and Behavior, 30*, 6–38. https://doi.org/10.1177/0093854802239161

Franklin, C. A., & Garza, A. D. (2021). Sexual assault disclosure: The effect of victim race and perpetrator type on empathy, culpability, and service referral for survivors in a hypothetical scenario. *Journal of Interpersonal Violence, 36*(5–6), 2327–2352.

Galliano, G., Noble, L. M., Travis, L. A., & Puechl, C. (1993). Victim reactions during rape/ sexual assault: A preliminary study of the immobility response and its correlates. *Journal of Interpersonal Violence, 8*(1), 109–114. https://doi.org/10.1177/088626093008001008

Hines, D. A., Armstrong, J. L., Reed, K. P., & Cameron, A. Y. (2012). Gender differences in sexual assault victimization among college students. *Violence and Victims*, 27(6), 922–940.

Inbau, F. E., Reid, J. E., Buckley, J. P., & Jayne, B. C. (2013). *Criminal interrogation and confessions* (5th ed.). Jones and Bartlett Learning.

Kim, T., Draucker, C. B., Bradway, C., Grisso, J. A., & Sommers, M. S. (2017). Somos Hermanas Del Mismo Dolor (We Are Sisters of the Same Pain): Intimate partner sexual violence narratives among Mexican immigrant women in the United States. *Violence Against Women*, 23(5), 623–642. https://doi.org/10.1177/1077801216646224

Kozinski, W. (2018). The Reid interrogation technique and false confessions: A time for change. *Seattle Journal for Social Justice*, 16(2), 301–345.

Krebs, C. P., Barrick, K., Lindquist, C. H., Crosby, C. M., Boyd, C., & Bogan, Y. (2011). The sexual assault of undergraduate women at historically Black colleges and universities (HBCUs). *Journal of Interpersonal Violence*, 26(18), 3640–3666. https://doi.org/10.1177/0886260511403759

LeMaire, K. L., Oswald, D. L., & Russell, B. L. (2016). Labeling sexual victimization experiences: The role of sexism, rape myth acceptance, and tolerance for sexual harassment. *Violence and Victims*, 31(2), 332–346. https://doi.org/10.1891/0886-6708.VV-D-13-00148

Lisak, D., Gardinier, L., Nicksa, S. C., & Cote, A. M. (2010). False allegations of sexual assault: An analysis of ten years of reported cases. *Violence Against Women*, 16(12), 1318–1334. https://doi.org/10.1177/1077801210387747

Littleton, H. L., Axsom, D., & Grills-Taquechel, A. (2009). Sexual assault victims' acknowledgement status and revictimization risk. *Psychology of Women Quarterly*, 33(1), 34–42. https://doi.org/10.1111/j.1471-6402.2008.01472.x

Long, L., & Butler, B. (2018). Sexual assault. *The Obstetrician and Gynecologist*, 20(2), 87–93. https://doi.org/10.1111/tog.12474

Lovell, R., Huang, W., Overman, L., Flannery, D. J., & Klingenstein, J. (2020). Offending histories and typologies of suspected sexual offenders identified via untested sexual assault kits. *Criminal Justice and Behavior*, 47(4), 470–486. https://doi.org/10.1177/0093854819896385

McGee, H., O'Higgins, M., Garavan, R., & Conroy, R. (2011). Rape and child sexual abuse: What beliefs persist about motives, perpetrators, and survivors? *Journal of Interpersonal Violence*, 26(17), 3580–3593.

McMahon, S., & Farmer, G. L. (2011). An updated measure for assessing subtle rape myths. *Social Work Research*, 35(1), 71–81. https://doi.org/10.1093/swr/35.2.71

Mennicke, A., Bowling, J., Gromer, J., & Ryan, C. (2021). Factors associated with and barriers to disclosure of a sexual assault to formal on-campus resources among college students. *Violence Against Women*, 27(2), 255–273. https://doi.org/10.1177/1077801219889173

Mennicke, A., Coates, C. A., Jules, B., & Langhinrichsen-Rohling, J. (2021). Who do they tell? College students' formal and informal disclosure of sexual violence, sexual harassment, stalking, and dating violence by gender, sexual identity, and race. *Journal of Interpersonal Violence*, 1–28. https://doi.org/10.1177/08862605211050107

Meyer, I. H. (2003). Prejudice, social stress, and mental health in lesbian, gay, and bisexual populations: Conceptual issues and research evidence. *Psychological Bulletin*, 129(5), 674–697. https://doi.org/10.1037/0033-2909.129.5.674

Mills, K. J., Mongene, N. G., Taylor, S. E., Ansari, N. F., & Parkhill, M. R. (2021). Victims of sexual assault report different barriers preventing them from reporting than nonvictims. *The Behavior Therapist*, 44(8), 399–411.

Muganyizi, P. S., Hogan, N., Emmelin, M., Lindmark, G., Massawe, S., Nystrom, L., & Axemo, P. (2009). Social reactions to rape: Experiences and perceptions of women rape survivors and the potential support providers in Dar es Salaam, Tanzania. *Violence and Victims*, 24(5), 607–626. https://doi.org/10.1891/0886-6708.24.5.607

O'Neal, E. N. (2019). "Victim is not credible": The influence of rape culture on police perceptions of sexual assault complainants. *Justice Quarterly, 36*(1), 127–160.

Omarzu, J. (2000). A disclosure decision model: Determining how and when individuals will self-disclose. *Personality and Social Psychology Review, 4*(2), 174–185. https://doi.org/10.1207/S15327957PSPR0402_05

Orchowski, L. M., & Gidycz, C. A. (2012). To whom do college women confide following sexual assault? A prospective study of predictors of sexual assault disclosure and social reactions. *Violence Against Women, 18*(3), 264–288. https://doi.org/10.1177/1077801212442917

Patterson, D. (2011). The impact of detectives' manner of questioning on rape victims' disclosure. *Violence Against Women, 17*(11), 1349–1373. https://doi.org/10.1177/1077801211434725

Patterson, D., & Campbell, R. (2010). Why rape survivors participate in the criminal justice system. *Journal of Community Psychology, 38*(2), 191–205. https://doi.org/10.1002/jcop.20359

Planty, M., Langton, L., Berzofsky, M., Krebs, C., & Smiley-McDonald, H. (2016). *Female victims of sexual violence, 1994–2010.* Department of Justice, Office of Justice Programs, Bureau of Justice Statistics.

Quackenbush, R. L. (1989). A comparison of androgynous, masculine sex-typed, and undifferentiated males on dimensions of attitudes toward rape. *Journal of Research in Personality, 23*(3), 318–342.

Segovia, D. A., Strange, D., & Takarangi, M. K. T. (2017). Trauma memories on trial: Is cross-examination a safeguard against distorted analogue traumatic memories? *Memory, 25*(1), 95–106. https://doi.org/10.1080/09658211.2015.1126608

Seibold-Simpson, S. M., McKinnon, A. M., Mattson, R. E., Ortiz, E., Merriwether, A. M., Massey, S. G., & Chiu, I. (2021). Person and incident-level predictors of blame, disclosure, and reporting to authorities in rape scenarios. *Journal of Interpersonal Violence, 36,* NP4788–NP4814.

Smith, C. P., & Freyd, J. J. (2014). Institutional betrayal. *American Psychologist, 69*(6), 575–587. https://doi.org/10.1037/a0037564

Smith, R. E., Pine, C. J., & Hawley, M. E. (1988). Social cognitions about adult male victims of female sexual assault. *The Journal of Sex Research, 24*(1), 101–112. https://doi.org/10.1080/00224498809551401

Spencer, C., Stith, S., Durtschi, J., & Toews, M. (2020). Factors related to college students' decisions to report sexual assault. *Journal of Interpersonal Violence, 35*(21–22), 4666–4685. https://doi.org/10.1177/0886260517717490

Stardust, Z., Treloar, C., Cama, E., & Kim, J. (2021). "I wouldn't call the cops if I was being bashed to death": Sex work, whore stigma and the criminal legal system. *International Journal for Crime, Justice, and Social Democracy, 10*(3), 142–157.

Stirling, J. L., Hills, P. J., & Wignall, L. (2020). Narrative approach to understanding people's comprehension of acquaintance rape: The role of sex role stereotyping. *Psychology and Sexuality.* https://doi.org/10.1080/19419899.2020.1745873

Strom, K. J., & Hickman, M. J. (2016). Untested sexual assault kits: Searching for an empirical foundation to guide forensic case processing decisions. *American Society of Criminology, 15*(2), 593–601. https://doi.org/10.1111/1745-9133.12213

Talbot, K. K., Neill, K. S., & Rankin, L. L. (2010). Rape-accepting attitudes of university undergraduate students. *Journal of Forensic Nursing, 6*(4), 170–179.

Taylor, T. J., Holleran, D., & Topalli, V. (2009). Racial bias in case processing: Does victim race affect police clearance of violent crime incidents? *Justice Quarterly, 26*(3), 562–591.

Temkin, J. (2010). "And always keep a-hold of nurse, for fear of finding something worse": Challenging rape myths in the courtroom. *New Criminal Law Review, 13*(4), 710–734.

TIME'S UP. (2022). *We are resetting to rebuild for the future of TIME'S UP.* Accessed on July 11, 2022 at www.timesupnow.org.

Tuerkheimer, D. (2021). *Credible: Why we doubt accusers and protect abusers.* Harper Collins Publishers.

Ullman, S. E., & Peter-Hagene, L. (2010). Social reactions to sexual assault disclosure, coping, perceived control and PTSD symptoms in sexual assault victims. *Journal of Community Psychology, 42*(4), 495–508. https://doi.org/10.1002/jcop.21624

Venema, R. M. (2016). Police officer schema of sexual assault reports: Real rape, ambiguous cases, and false reports. *Journal of Interpersonal Violence, 31*(5), 872–899. https://doi.org/10.1177/0886260514556765

Von Hohendorff, J., Habigzang, L. F., & Koller, S. H. (2017). "A boy, being a victim, nobody really buys that, you know?": Dynamics of sexual violence against boys. *Child Abuse and Neglect, 70*, 53–64.

Wilson, L. C., & Miller, K. E. (2016). Meta-analysis of the prevalence of unacknowledged rape. *Trauma, Violence, and Abuse, 17*(2), 149–159. https://doi.org/10.1177/1524838015576391

Wolitzky-Taylor, K., Resnick, H., McCauley, J., Amstader, A., Kilpatrick, D., & Ruggiero, K. (2011). Is reporting of rape on the rise? A comparison of women with reported versus unreported rape experiences in the National Women's Study Replication. *Journal of Interpersonal Violence, 26*(4), 807–832. https://doi.org/10.11.77/0886260510365869

4 Sexual assault of women of color

Establishing an equitable and culturally specific response

Teresa M. Stafford

Author Note

The opinions or points of view expressed in this document are solely those of the author and do not reflect the official positions of any participating organization or the U.S. Department of Justice.

Sexual assault for women of color has historically been an intersectional attack against their gender and racial identities. These circumstances account for many of the barriers that survivors of color face as they seek help post-victimization. The barriers include but are not limited to:

Experiences of generational and historical trauma
Distrust of the criminal justice system and social services demonstrated by low reporting levels and frequent disengagement from services
Lack of culturally appropriate services
Strong allegiance to race
Lack of service providers who look like the survivor or share the survivor's everyday experiences
Fear of reinforcing negative stereotypes associated with their race or ethnicity

Survivors of color are often stereotyped by individuals working within criminal justice and community-based social service agencies. Examples of stereotypes include: Black and Latina women are promiscuous and manipulative. Asian women are submissive. Men of color, particularly Black men, are sexual predators or hypersexual. These stereotypes perpetuate the notion that survivors of color may have been willing participants in their victimization. They further serve to demean, victim blame, and minimize the seriousness of sexual violence perpetrated against individuals of color, and they reduce the likelihood of legal sanctions and actions for these survivors. Often survivors of color must confront not only their sexual victimization but also other race or ethnic-related issues, such as protecting their perpetrator, family, or community from further discrimination/harm, preventing their own and others' mistreatment by the criminal justice, medical, and social service systems, and conforming to the cultural values and norms of the dominant culture.

This chapter highlights the importance of providing a culturally specific response to survivors of sexual violence, in particular survivors who are women and girls of color. I aim to provide guidance and detail lessons learned to aid in a broad and shared

DOI: 10.4324/9781003186816-6

understanding how inequitable practices in programs and systems, in conjunction with the increased vulnerabilities to sexual violence, combine to impact survivors of color on a personal and intrapersonal level. Recommendations are provided to improve our ability to respond in a trauma-informed, culturally specific, and inclusive manner.

I begin by exploring our current response to rape through the lens of historical trauma for individuals and communities of color in the United States and I provide examples of how the vestiges of this historical trauma are still apparent today. I draw heavily upon my experiences as an advocate of color with over 15 years of work within the social services. This chapter also considers what culturally responsive services look like and how to implement them, based upon my leadership in the largest rape crisis center in the United States. Lastly, I posit a path forward to achieve systemic change and a reformed, equitable, and culturally specific response to rape.

The Impact of Historical Trauma

To understand where we are in terms of our response to rape, we first must understand how we got here. Traumatic experiences shared by communities can result in cumulative emotional and psychological wounds that are passed down through generations. This concept is called *historical trauma*. As a result, people within these same historically traumatized communities experience higher rates of mental and physical illness, substance abuse, and current victimization (SAMHSA, 2014). Historical trauma extends beyond what happened in the past—to what is still happening today. Professionals striving to establish a more equitable response to sexual violence must first understand the impact of historical trauma and recognize how we as a society respond differently to the sexual assault of women and girls of color compared to their white counterparts.

Sexual violence in the United States was historically used to control and exert power over groups that were not part of the dominant culture. For women of color, this started with the colonization of Native land. Native Indigenous women experienced sexual violence as a means to depower and dehumanize them during colonization. Native children were forced into boarding schools to assimilate to European culture under the concept of *kill the Indian and save the man* (Simonson & Nadeau, 2016). They often experienced sexual violence as a result. Native women were reduced to sexual conquests, as a means to establish a patriarchal system. This is most notable as written in the diary of Michele de Cuneo, who came to North America with Christopher Columbus. Michele de Cuneo wrote:

> When I was in the boat, I captured a very beautiful Carib woman … Having brought her into my cabin, and she being naked as is their custom, I conceived desire to take my pleasure. I wanted to put my desire to execution, but she was unwilling for me to do so, and treated me with her nails in such wise that I would have preferred never to have begun. But seeing this … I took a rope-end and thrashed her well, following which she produced such screaming and wailing as would cause you not to believe your ears. Finally we reached an agreement such that, I can tell you, she seemed to have been raised in a veritable school of harlots.
>
> (as cited in Deer, 2015)

Michele de Cuneo's diary excerpt details a sexual assault that disregards Native culture and promotes the establishment of systemic sexual victimization against women of color in the United States. The colonization of Native land established a complex system in which holding non-native offenders of sexual violence accountable for their actions was nonexistent.

The vestiges of this are still seen today. The loss of tribal sovereignty impacts tribal governments' ability to hold non-natives responsible when they commit crimes on Native land. While the majority of victims of sexual violence are sexually assaulted by someone from their own racial or ethnic identity, this is not true for American Indians. According to the U.S. Department of Justice, Office of Justice Programs (2018), at least 70% of the violent victimizations experienced by American Indians are committed by persons not of the same race—a substantially higher rate of interracial violence than experienced by either white or Black victims. These dynamics play a significant role in Native American women having the highest rate of sexual victimization compared to their counterparts. Native women are targeted because of the intersection of race and gender.

Systemic sexual violence for women of color continued during the enslavement of Black/African-Americans. Sexual violence was once again used as a tool to exert power and control while establishing a system with no accountability for male perpetrators. During the transatlantic slave trade, Black girls' and women's bodies were seen as capital, as they had the ability to produce more slaves. Black girls and women had value beyond their ability to work in the fields—as they could birth children who would, in turn, become slaves. Up until puberty, enslaved females were sold at a higher rate compared to their counterparts (Mintz, n.d.) The enslavement of Black bodies forced Africans to lose connection to self and their culture, and in many cases, led to the forced separation of families. The sexual assault of Black women was prevalent throughout slavery. This often overshadowed the sexual abuse of Black men, which was also occurring during this same time period. *Buck breaking* was the act of forcing an enslaved Black man to lower his pants and bend over a tree stump to be flogged severely. This would weaken him so that he would not resist the rape that followed. Rape was also used as a weapon to break down Black enslaved men (Johnson, 2018).

Enslaved people were seen as less than human and forced to reproduce to generate more slaves. Generations of Black people were born into a society that only saw them as chattel and sex objects. The bodies of enslaved Black women were parallel to what may be considered community property. The 1859 case of George v. the State of Mississippi outlines this concept. George, a slave, was actually found guilty of raping an enslaved Black girl in 1859. However, during his appeals hearing, George's attorney argued to the court,

> The crime of rape does not exist in this State between African Slaves, our laws recognize no marital status as between slaves, their sexual intercourse is left to be regulated by their owners. The regulations of law, as to the white race, on the subject of sexual intercourse, do not and cannot, for obvious reasons, apply to slaves; their intercourse is promiscuous, and the violation of a female slave by a male slave would be a mere assault and battery.

The judge agreed with George's attorney and reversed his conviction (Tushnet, 1975)

Vestiges of this thinking are still apparent today. As a victim advocate, I became accustomed to the fact that many Black and Hispanic survivors would have their cases pled down to a non-sex offense, in essence mirroring the outcome of the 1859 case George v. the State of Mississippi. These plea deals demonstrate the minimization of these women's sexual assault by the same system 150+ years post-George v. the State of Mississippi.

The unchecked sexual assault against enslaved Black girls and women also established a toxic and violent dynamic between Black women and white women. White women often saw the enslaved Black woman as their husband's mistress rather than a victim of his actions. In the biography *Twelve Years a Slave: The Narrative of Solomon Northup*, the story of Patsey, an enslaved Black woman, highlights the victimization occurring at the hands of the slaveowner and his wife. Patsey was raped by her slave owner and physically abused by his jealous wife. The wife blamed Patsy for what she saw as her husband's betrayal of their marriage (National Humanities Center Resource Toolbox, 2009).

Vestiges of Patsy's experience—not being seen as a victim but rather as a willing participant in her victimization—are still apparent today, unfortunately. Katz et al. (2017) found that white female bystanders were less likely to intervene when a Black woman was at risk for incapacitated sexual assault. In their experiment, white women in the study who were assigned to the Black victim condition reported less intent to intervene, less personal responsibility to intervene, and greater perceived victim pleasure than participants assigned to the control condition—indicating support for the reinforced stereotype that Black women are sexually promiscuous, lack ownership of their bodies, and need less protection.

Offenders of sexual assault and human trafficking frequently know that the penalties for sexually assaulting women of color are historically lower and remain so. Traffickers intentionally target their victims due to a lack of sanctions. The Urban Institute interviewed traffickers, many of whom knew that trafficking Black women would land them less jail time than trafficking white women if caught (as cited in Davey, 2020). These inequitable dynamics increase the victimization that Black and Hispanic women and girls experience. In 2012, African-American children comprised 59% of all prostitution arrests for those under 18—more than any other racial group (Federal Bureau of Investigation (FBI), Uniform Crime Report, 2012). In a two-year review of all suspected human trafficking incidents, 94% of victims were identified as female, 40% of victims were African-American and 24% were Hispanic (U.S. Department of Justice, 2011). When systems fail to hold offenders accountable, two things happen. There is an increase in victimization and there is a decrease in reporting rates among survivors.

Distrust of systems

Communities of color show greater distrust in systems such as the criminal justice system, child protective services, and the healthcare system. This distrust impacts disclosure rates, the reporting process, and accessing services post victimization (see Chapter 3 for more on disclosure). Between the 1930s and the 1970s, approximately one-third of the female population of Puerto Rico was sterilized, making it the highest rate of sterilization in the world. Eugenic sterilization laws were disproportionately applied to Hispanic women and girls (Krase, 2014).

Vestiges of these systemic abuses are still apparent today. The historical trauma connected to forced sterilization impacts Hispanic women seeking medical treatment and undergoing forensic medical exams post-victimization. One of my first sex trafficking cases as an advocate involved a foreign-born survivor from Guatemala. I supported the survivor at the hospital along with the Sexual Assault Nurse Examiner (SANE) and an interpreter (see Chapter 12). When the SANE started to explain the vaginal exam, the survivor adamantly denied that step in the process. The nurse took the time to explain everything she would do. The interpreter explained to us that because of the forced sterilizations that have taken place in the United States, many Hispanic women will forgo a pelvic exam until they have given birth. Should a case like this be encountered, it is recommended that when the professional explains the forensic exam to a Hispanic survivor, the professional should slow down, provide additional details, and answer all questions to build trust with the survivor.

Distrust of systems also impacts willingness to report sexual violence. For every Black woman who reports a sexual assault, an estimated 15 do not (Hart & Rennison, 2003). While I am an advocate for survivors of sexual violence, I am also a survivor of childhood sexual abuse. I was engaged with the juvenile justice system and child protective services due to fighting at school during the time period of my victimization. I intentionally chose to remain silent and not report my sexual abuse for several reasons, but mostly because of a lack of trust. How could I trust a system that failed to recognize my trauma response and instead treated me like a criminal? How could I trust a system that never asked me why I was behaving the way I was? How could I trust a system that historically did not protect Black women and girls?

Before the age of 18, roughly one in four Black girls will be sexually abused (Black et al., 2011). Girls of color are pushed out of school and into the criminal justice system at a high rate because of their victimization—sometimes referred to as the sexual abuse to prison pipeline (Saar et al., 2019). Research conducted by Georgetown Law's Center on Poverty and Inequality examined the *adultification* of Black girls. Survey participants perceived Black girls as needing less protection, less support, and less comfort, but also knowing more about sex and having more familiarity with adult topics compared to white girls of the same age (Saar et al., 2019). Girls of color account for approximately 66% of incarcerated girls but make up about 22% of the youth population (Saar et al., 2019).

As a former member of a multidisciplinary team that met regularly to discuss treatment plans for trafficked girls who are engaged with the criminal justice system, I would often hear professionals project the same beliefs that fostered the adultification of girls of color. These negative perceptions impacted the decision-making process and influenced who some members of the team saw as victims. This adultified perception of Black girls parallels the stereotyping of Black women and girls that were birthed from slavery.

Stereotyping survivors of color shifts the blame from institutions and perpetrators to the victim. This dynamic is evident in how society has responded to the survivors of R. Kelly, who was recently convicted of racketeering, sexual exploitation of a child, kidnapping, bribery, and sex trafficking. Accusations against R&B singer R. Kelly by Black women and girls have been reported to law enforcement since the early 1990s. Many of these victims were stereotyped and not believed. Even today—post-#MeToo—across social media platforms, people blame teenage girls for their victimization, stating they were "fast," which is modern-day terminology for the stereotype of the sexually permissive woman, a Jezebel, who knew what she were getting into by dealing with R. Kelly. Victims have also been described as money hungry-groupies or women engaged in a setup to take a Black man down—all of which put his artistic worth over that of Black girls and women's bodies. It took the grassroots activism of #muterkelly co-founders Kenyette Barnes and Oronike Odeleye to bring national attention to R. Kelly's offending behavior, which eventually opened criminal cases against him in two states.

The efforts of Barnes and Odeleye are similar to those of Civil Rights activist Rosa Parks, who investigated and brought national attention to authorities regarding the rape of Recy Taylor while working for the National Association for the Advancement of Colored People (McGuire, 2011). Recy Taylor was sexually assaulted in 1944 by six white men. Three-quarters of a century later, Black women are still advocating for themselves to be seen as victims of sexual violence by systems that are charged with doing such and, at times, even tasked with investigating their own cases of perpetration (Lovell et al., 2020).

The disparities in sentencing between offenders of color and white offenders discourage survivors of color from reporting to law enforcement or from experiencing the community's support when they do make a report. Brock Turner, a white freshman athlete from Stanford University, sexually assaulted an unconscious woman and was sentenced to six months in jail. The sentencing judge feared that a longer sentence would have a *severe impact on him*. Brock Turner's case set up a dynamic such that survivors of color, who are typically assaulted by someone from their own racial or ethnic identity (except for Native women [Black et al., 2011]) may have a strong allegiance to protecting offenders who look like them, from an unjust system when punishment is not equal. Some survivors of color face backlash from their families and communities due to racial disparities in the sentencing of offenders. Expectations from communities of color have caused some women of color to feel that they should put their communities' needs over their own and hold a racial allegiance to their offender. This concept further highlights the intersectional experience of sexual assault for women of color.

Among the survivors of color with whom I worked, recantation and disengagement happened repeatedly. Too often, when survivors of color disengaged, or if they were not completely truthful about some aspect of the incident but not the incident itself (e.g., lying about being at the location to buy drugs but not about being raped after attempting to buy drugs), some professionals would automatically assume they lied about the sexual assault and they would threaten to charge them with making a false report. Both of these approaches further highlight why victims of color do not trust the criminal justice system.

While working for the county prosecutor's office, I witnessed firsthand a sexual assault case that retraumatized the survivor of color. The case was scheduled for trial, but the survivor was not returning the prosecutor's phone calls. The survivor informed me that she could not handle the pressure and was not doing well. *However, the prosecutor's decision to move forward with the trial outweighed the victim's mental state.* Consequently, a bench warrant was issued for her arrest. She was arrested and the victim was held in the county jail until she testified in court.

Imagine being a victim of sexual assault and being locked up in jail solely because the trauma from the assault impacted your mental health.

Black women with lower socioeconomic statuses (Bryant-Davis et al., 2011) and Black women who have experienced multiple forms of sexual victimization (Campbell et al., 2008) are particularly vulnerable to post-traumatic stress disorder, depression, suicidal ideation, pain-related health problems, fatigue, and nausea. I never witnessed a bench warrant being issued for a white victim to compel testimony. Utilizing bench warrants to make victims testify is not trauma-informed. It projects the *strong women* stereotype where it is perceived that Black women can handle enormous amounts of pain and trauma. Threatening victims to participate in the criminal justice system process is repeat traumatization in that another entity— the state—is exerting their power over the victim and giving them no choice in their healing process. *In creating an equitable response to sexual violence, professionals must stop practices that penalize survivors of color for their trauma response.*

Survivors of color disengage during the criminal justice system process for numerous reasons. Upon speaking with the victims, I would learn they were either scared to testify in front of their perpetrators, pressured by family and friends not to put another Black or brown man in prison, caught between loyalty to their race and a system that disenfranchises people that look like them, and/or finding that the trauma associated with their victimization overwhelmed them. Some survivors found it easier to disconnect than stay engaged; others became frustrated with comments from professionals that demeaned their cultural identities (see Chapter 2 on attrition in the criminal justice system). Instead of projecting the "strong women" phenomenon onto women of color survivors, professionals must take the time to understand the complexities of what it means to be a survivor of sexual assault for women and girls of color.

Culturally responsive services

Knowing that the majority of survivors of color never engage in the criminal justice system, community-based advocacy organizations such as rape crisis centers, child advocacy, and family justice centers play a crucial role for survivors. They can be a form of radical healing for survivors seeking justice outside of the criminal justice system. However, like the criminal justice system, victim advocacy organizations often lack diverse representation. The lack of service providers who look like survivors or share survivor's everyday experiences can establish a dynamic where trust and comfort are nonexistent. In 2014, the Ohio Alliance to End Sexual Violence conducted a survey to identify the number of women of color who were staffing rape crisis centers across Ohio. The survey identified 104 white individuals compared to 10 African-American/Black, two Hispanic, and three biracial paid employees. Women of color during this time period held two manager/coordinator positions, and two were identified as program directors (Ohio Alliance to End Sexual Violence, 2014). At the time of the writing of this chapter, I was one of the two women of color at the director level working at a rape crisis center in Cleveland, Ohio—a city that is majority residents of color.

In 2018, Cleveland Rape Crisis Center partnered with the Begun Center for Violence Prevention Research and Education at Case Western Reserve University to identify program outcomes for the victim advocacy program and to examine client engagement across programs. As a program director at the time, two things stood out for me—(a) survivors of color want to work with professionals with similar cultural backgrounds and (b) there is a need to develop culturally responsive programming. The data from the evaluation showed that Black survivors disconnected from services at a higher rate than other survivors. I would often hear from clinicians representing the dominant culture that *Black survivors were not ready for counseling or services, dealing with their trauma was just too hard.*

These words resonated with me as victim-blaming. The data highlighted that some survivors felt that the service provider did not respect their racial identity, socioeconomic status, and sexual or gender identity. Professionals must be willing to ask themselves the challenging questions, *What are we doing that causes a survivor to disengage in services? How am I showing up as a professional? What barriers are we creating that impact survivors?*

As a result of this survey and other conversations, Cleveland Rape Crisis Center became more intentional about whom they serve and how they serve survivors. This journey included a three-year strategic plan that focused on enhancing relationships and engagement with the Hispanic, African-American, and LGBTQI+ communities and increasing diversity at every level in the organization, including its board of directors. Increasing diversity was one of the first steps to becoming a more inclusive organization where staff members could bring their whole selves to work. A diverse and inclusive workforce means diversity of thought is appreciated while innovation and productivity are increased. However, before diving into enhancing relationships with these communities, the agency did some self-reflection and education at the individual level. We engaged with outside consultants to assist in delivering educational learning series to staff. This learning is now included in all new staff orientations.

Systematic change: A path forward

Systemic change requires a three-step process—individual work, interpersonal work, and institutional work. This three-step process will assist in ensuring that systemic change is accomplished through the lens of equity and inclusion. Individual or micro-level work includes examining one's own culture, morals and values, and biases. Individuals must take the time to educate themselves regarding the historical trauma that exists for survivors of sexual violence and how it manifests today. This chapter is only a snapshot! Leaders within organizations must understand what it means to lead a trauma-informed and culturally inclusive organization. Leadership readiness is paramount to fostering an equitable and inclusive culture. At the interpersonal level, one must examine how our beliefs and cultural norms manifest when engaging with people from various cultures. *What stereotypes have you internalized regarding your own identities? What stereotypes might you unconsciously project when engaging with survivors or even colleagues? What biases might be present during your decision-making process?*

It is not just about pointing fingers. We ALL have biases. Our biases do not necessarily make us flawed individuals. It just means that we are paying attention to the world that we are socialized in both personally and professionally. If we slow down to engage in self-reflection and be open to feedback, we are able to identify where we might have biases. Therefore, our biases can be predictable and can become preventable.

At an institutional or macro level, we need to examine policies that might impact survivors of color from reporting or engaging in services. *Are you using evidence-based programming designed for survivors of color or programming designed for the dominant groups in society?* During the racial uprising that started after the death of George Floyd, the Cleveland Rape Crisis Center saw a decrease in the number of Black survivors reporting and accessing advocacy services. As a result, we now facilitate a support group specifically for Black women called *Sister Circle* to address the unique challenges Black women survivors might face while engaging in the criminal justice system. We sought outside expertise from Dr. Tyffani Monford-Dent, a Black psychologist specializing in working with survivors of color. She created the curriculum for Sister Circle. Black women at Cleveland Rape Crisis Center facilitate Sister Circle to create a trauma-informed and culturally responsive space. Many rape crisis centers and other advocacy groups rely heavily on evidence-based programming. Unfortunately, much of the evidence-based programming has been designed for and is centered on the dominant group in our society and may not adequately address the unique needs of survivors of color. Programs must go beyond a cookie-cutter approach to supporting survivors and develop culturally specific programming that will meet the needs of diverse survivors. This should enhance engagement and promote healing.

The Cleveland Rape Crisis Center also worked to ensure that our spaces, located throughout our service areas, were culturally appropriate and that survivors would see aspects of their culture reflected throughout the offices. A couple of years ago, the agency established an *Access to Care* team. The team's purpose was to ensure that all survivors had access to services in a timely manner and that our decision-making process was equitable. The organization developed equity primes to assist with pushing beyond maintaining the status quo and making decisions that might further marginalize survivors of color. Equity primes help make the decision-making process conscious. Conversely, these primes minimize the opportunity for implicit bias to be present. For example, during an Access to Care meeting, a team member suggested a new protocol to manage clients accessing our transportation services for appointments. Members of the team identified areas where the new protocol actually created barriers for survivors instead of eliminating barriers. A team member utilized an equity prime asking, *How is this new protocol isolating others who are often marginalized?* The question assisted the team with identifying the actual barriers in the new protocol that was not equitable. As a result of this discussion, we developed a new protocol that was more equitable. See Figure 4.1 for an example of the equity primes utilized at the Cleveland Rape Crisis Center.

The steps to establishing a trauma-informed, culturally inclusive response to sexual violence

Establishing a multidisciplinary response to sexual violence is one way to reduce some of the inequities that exist for survivors. When establishing a multidisciplinary response team (MDT), communities must go beyond the traditional key players, especially when existing organizations lack cultural diversity. MDTs should seek out culturally specific advocacy organizations or non-traditional community-based organizations that serve diverse populations. These organizations tend to be the

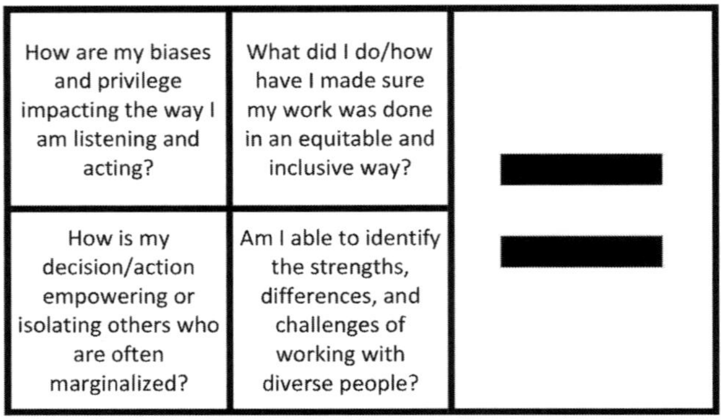

| How are my biases and privilege impacting the way I am listening and acting? | What did I do/how have I made sure my work was done in an equitable and inclusive way? | ▬▬▬ |
| How is my decision/action empowering or isolating others who are often marginalized? | Am I able to identify the strengths, differences, and challenges of working with diverse people? | ▬▬▬ |

Figure 4.1 Equity Primes Utilized at Cleveland Rape Crisis Center

gatekeepers for communities of color; they can assist with relationship building and educating the MDT on challenges that might impact survivor engagement.

MDTs should conduct active case reviews, file audits, survivor surveys, and routinely analyze organizational data to assist with establishing and maintaining a trauma-informed, culturally inclusive response to sexual violence (see Chapter 21 for more information on MDTs in SAKI). Facilitating active case reviews with the MDT will identify any gaps in service, reporting barriers, or inequitable practices. Active case reviews are an opportunity to not only identify challenges but showcase successes as well. Data should be analyzed consistently, yearly at a minimum. For instance, if a community is 40% Hispanic, but only 2% of Hispanic survivors represent the data for reported sexual assault, the MDT must address this immediately. The lower reporting can mean there is a lack of trust, lack of understanding regarding the reporting process, or signal that community members have experienced psychological harm in the past when reporting sexual violence.

Survivor surveys are another method to examine the experience of victims as they engage in services or the criminal justice system. Often, we tend to think of distributing satisfaction surveys at the end of a case or the closing of the service. As previously discussed, survivors of color disengage throughout the process for various reasons. To course-correct, survivors should be surveyed at different points in the process. For example, at Cleveland Rape Crisis Center, we implemented a client satisfaction survey to distribute quarterly. If there are any issues throughout the engagement, we can catch them before a client disengages.

Supervision is another critical way to examine if professionals are approaching survivors in a trauma-informed and culturally inclusive manner. Supervisors must engage in conversations with their staff regarding their caseloads and listen for language that is biased and/or that feeds into negative stereotypes. *As a supervisor, are you noticing a pattern of victims who disengage with your supervisees? Are you identifying cases that are closed and not forwarded to prosecution? Do you have a process in place for handling complaints?*

In 2021, I became the Clients Rights Officer as part of the responsibilities of the Chief Program Officer at the Cleveland Rape Crisis Center. One of my responsibilities includes responding to client complaints and responding to their issues with services. The previous Clients Rights Officer would investigate the complaint and make a final decision regarding the complaint. Instead, I established a diverse team of staff to process client complaints to ensure diverse perspectives are part of the decision-making process. The team includes someone from the advocacy, therapeutic services, intake, and case management teams from various cultural backgrounds. Although this slows the process down slightly, it ensures implicit or explicit biases are minimized. *And, yes, even I have biases that might impact the decision-making process.*

Conclusion

All survivors of sexual violence deserve a response that minimizes revictimization. When survivors of color do not disclose their sexual assaults, it is often because of the fear of not being believed, worries about enforcing negative stereotypes associated with their racial and ethnic identities, and lack of trust with those charged with responding to their victimization. Professionals responding to sexual violence have the opportunity to change this narrative by creating a culture where all survivors are met with a response that starts by believing, validating, affirming, and protecting survivors. One of the bravest things a victim of sexual violence will do is disclose their victimization to helping systems. We must be prepared when they do!

Key Points

- The historical trauma that women of color have experienced in the United States currently impacts how society, systems, and advocacy organizations respond to their survivorship.
- The response often contains stereotypes, projects biases, and includes victim-blaming.
- Until this dynamic is changed, survivors of color will continue to be sexually assaulted at a higher rate compared to their counterparts and they will receive inequitable responses to their disclosures of assault.
- This chapter examines what culturally responsive services look like and how to implement them and posits a path forward to systemic change and a reformed response to rape.

Discussion Questions

1 What policies or practices exist within your organization that might establish barriers for survivors of color seeking services?
2 How can your organization create more equitable practices?
3 What are some biases you have that might impact how you engage with survivors of color?

Further Reading

Burke, T. (2022). *Unbound: My story of liberation and birth of the Me Too Movement.* Flatiron Books.

McGuire, D. R. L. (2011). *At the dark end of the Street: Black women, rape, and resistance— A new history of the civil rights movement from Rosa Parks to the rise of Black power.* Vintage Books.

Listening to Black women and girls. Retrieved from https://www.law.georgetown.edu/poverty-inequality-center/wp-content/uploads/sites/14/2019/05/Listening-to-Black-Women-and-Girls.pdf

References

Black, M. C., Basile, K. C., Breiding, M. J., Smith, S. G., Walters, M. L., Merrick, M. T., Chen, J., & Stevens, M. R. (2011). *The National Intimate Partner and Sexual Violence Survey (NISVS): 2010 Summary Report*. National Center for Injury Prevention and Control, Centers for Disease Control and Prevention.

Bryant-Davis, T., Ullman, S. E., Tsong, Y., & Gobin, R. (2011). Surviving the storm: The role of social support and religious coping in sexual assault recovery of African American women. *Violence Against Women, 17*, 1601–1618. doi:10.1177/1077801211436138

Campbell, R., Greeson, M. R., Bybee, D., & Raja, S. (2008). The co-occurrence of childhood sexual abuse, adult sexual assault, intimate partner violence, and sexual harassment: A mediational model of post-traumatic stress disorder and physical health outcomes. *Journal of Consulting and Clinical Psychology, 76*, 194–207. doi:10.1037/0022-006X.76.2.194

Davey, S. (2020). Snapshot of the state of black women and girls: Sex trafficking in the U.S. Congressional Black Caucus Foundation. Retrieved January 31, 2022 from https://www.cbcfinc.org/wp-content/uploads/2020/05/SexTraffickingReport3.pdf

Deer, S. (2015). *The beginning and end of rape: Confronting sexual violence in Native America*. University of Minnesota Press.

FBI, Uniform Crime Report. (2012). *Crime in the United States 2012*. Retrieved January 31, 2022 from https://ucr.fbi.gov/crime-in-the-u.s/2012/crime-in-the-u.s.-2012/tables/43table datadecoverviewpdf

Hart, T. C., & Rennison, C. (2003). *Reporting crime to the police: 1992–2000*. Bureau of Justice Statistics Special Report. U.S. Department of Justice.

Johnson, E. (2018). *5 horrifying ways enslaved African men were sexually exploited and abused by their white masters*. Retrieved from https://face2faceafrica.com/article/5-horrifying-ways-enslaved-african-men-were-sexually-exploited-and-abused-by-their-white-masters/3

Katz, J., Merrilees, C., Hoxmeier, J. C., & Motisi, M. (2017). White female bystanders' responses to a Black woman at risk for incapacitated sexual assault. *Psychology of Women Quarterly, 41*(2), 273–285. doi: https://doi.org/10.1177/0361684316689367

Krase, K. (2014). *History of forced sterilization and current U.S. abuses. Our Bodies Ourselves*. Retrieved January 31, 2022 from https://www.ourbodiesourselves.org/book-excerpts/health-article/forced-sterilization/

Lovell, R., Overman, L., Huang, D., & Flannery, D. J. (2020). The bureaucratic burden of identifying your rapist and remaining "cooperative": What the sexual assault kit initiative tells us about sexual assault case attrition and outcomes. *American Journal of Criminal Justice*. https://doi.org/10.1007/s12103-020-09573-x

Mintz, S. (n.d.). *Historical context: Facts about the slave trade and slavery*. Retrieved January 31, 2022 from https://www.gilderlehrman.org/history-resources/teaching-resource/historical-context-facts-about-slave-trade-and-slavery

McGuire, D. (2011). *At the dark end of the street: Black women, rape, and resistance—A new history of the civil rights movement from Rosa Parks to the rise of Black power*. Vintage Books.

Saar, M., Epstein, R., Rosenthal, L., & Vafa, Y. (2019). *The sexual abuse to prison pipeline: The girls' story*. Retrieved from https://www.law.georgetown.edu/poverty-inequality-center/wp-content/uploads/sites/14/2019/02/The-Sexual-Abuse-To-Prison-Pipeline-The-Girls%E2%80%99-Story.pdf

SAMHSA. (2014). *Understanding historical trauma when responding to an event in Indian Country.* Retrieved from https://store.samhsa.gov/sites/default/files/d7/priv/sma14-4866.pdf

Simonson, K. L., & Nadeau, G. M. (2016). *Truth and reconciliation: "Kill the Indian, and save the man."* Retrieved on January 31, 2022 from https://www.nativetimes.com/archives/46-life/commentary/14059-truth-and-reconciliationkill-the-indian-and-save-the-man

Tushnet, M. (1975). The American Law of Slavery, 1810–1860: A study in the persistence of legal autonomy. *Law & Society Review, 10*(1), 119–184. https://doi.org/10.2307/3053160

U.S. Department of Justice. (2011). *Characteristics of suspected human trafficking incidents, 2008–2010.* Retrieved from https://bjs.ojp.gov/content/pub/pdf/cshti0810.pdf

U.S. Department of Justice, Office of Justice Programs. (2018). *Criminal victimization, 2018.* Retrieved from https://bjs.ojp.gov/content/pub/pdf/cv18.pdf

5 A survivor's perspective

My sexual assault kit was part of the backlog

Natasha Simone Alexenko

Author Note

The opinions or points of view expressed in this document are solely those of the author and do not reflect the official positions of any participating organization nor the U.S. Department of Justice.

I have learned a great deal since my journey as a survivor began in August of 1992. Today, I exist in a mindset of boundless gratitude and humility. To say that this was always the case would be a cruel exaggeration. When I first went public as a survivor, I shared all the gruesome details of my story with anyone that asked. It was cathartic in a sense for me. However, as time went on, I discovered how important it was to discern the impetus for me to share the details of my assault. Was it to arouse shock or fear? Most importantly, did my telling it serve survivors and advocates and even myself? I am far more discerning now. My advocacy for myself and others continues to evolve, and through missteps and pain, I continue to grow in this respect.

When I was initially approached to write this chapter, I was given complete discretion as to whether or not to share the details of my story. I understand the value this book offers to the public, and I trust its creators implicitly. For these reasons, I am happy to share the details so that this work—and the importance of the larger SAKI movement—is better understood. I also would like to preface the specifics of my assault with an acknowledgment of the many survivors whose perspectives, experiences, and emotions differ from my own. No story or experience will ever invalidate another's journey, we each have our own truth to share and path to follow.

I also want to acknowledge that I am very fortunate to be regularly surrounded by academics, advocates, and survivors with whom I know my story will be safe. I recognize the position of privilege this places me in. I am all too aware that many of my fellow survivors are unable to share, unable to heal, and are not surrounded by the resources I am fortunate enough to be given. I am constantly learning to listen and recognize when I've said too much or not said enough. There are others out there whose voices are equally important. I attempt to approach the telling of my story today with a renewed sense of reverence and respect for others. Having said this, it is a necessary part of this important conversation to include the details of my journey. I can only hope that my point of view can bring some pieces together for others in a meaningful way and can reaffirm for others the importance of centering survivor's voices in the National Sexual Assault Kit Initiative (SAKI) while creating policies that ensure that all sexual assault kits (SAKs) get tested today, tomorrow, and into the foreseeable future.

DOI: 10.4324/9781003186816-7

My Story

I grew up in a small town just outside of Toronto, Ontario. Ever since I could remember, I dreamed of moving to New York City for college, and in 1992, I did just that. Both my parents were immigrants from countries besieged by conflict, and while I felt isolated and protected throughout my childhood, I was all too aware of what violence and trauma looked like.

I enjoyed every moment of my new life as a student and resident of Manhattan's Upper West Side. I lived in a lovely pre-war building nestled near a park that welcomed my dog Savannah and me every day. I felt safe and embraced by my community. After school, I worked at a veterinary hospital a few blocks north of my apartment. It was a bit of a hike, but I enjoyed taking in life around me, so I often walked home. After enjoying a cathartic conversation with a colleague after work on an evening in August of 1993, I walked three blocks from the corner of Broadway to my apartment on West 95th Street. My guard was completely down. I felt safe—I had done this so often that I would take my keys out at the same crack in the sidewalk each time. Yet, this night, I barely had time to take the keys out of my pocket when a man emerged like an apparition before me. He had a gun.

At gunpoint, I was forced to lead him into the building's elevator, which we took to the top floor of my apartment, up a final set of stairs to a landing right before a locked rooftop door. It was there that I was violently raped, robbed, and left naked, but thankfully, still alive.

Afterward, I gathered my belongings and ran to my apartment. I have no memory of how I even got to my door. To this day, I cannot remember whether the memories I have of the aftermath are my own or come from others relaying this portion of my experience to me. I banged on our door, and my roommates came to my rescue as I collapsed on the floor screaming. My immediate instinct was to take a shower, but my roommate, Celia, convinced me to have a SAK done at the hospital. And that is what I did. It was grueling, long, and humiliating. The last thing I wanted was to be naked once more in front of a stranger. When it was over, I just wanted to return home and pretend the horror had never occurred.

But I didn't do that. Instead, I met with law enforcement in the days following my rape on several occasions. I looked at mugshots and retold the events in as much detail as I could recall. My memories were fragmented, and I felt betrayed by them. I couldn't recall any distinguishing features of the man who had raped me. Oddly enough, I could recall with great clarity every inch of the gun he held against me.

The detectives held several interviews with me over the next few weeks, and they were truly kind and patient. I felt that I was believed the entire time. I did not feel that I was being interrogated or that finding the man who raped me was hopeless.

Despite my best efforts to remain in New York and pretend the rape had never occurred, my mother felt it was best for me to return to Canada, where I could heal surrounded by friends and family. I remained in contact with the NYPD for the year after I moved back home to Canada. We communicated regularly, and photos were sent in the hopes that I would recognize a face or recall a detail that I perhaps had missed before. I did not think of my rape kit—not even once. I was under the assumption that it had been sent to the lab and tested for DNA. Why would I think otherwise? Why would I be put through such an ordeal for no reason?

Time passed. About one year after my assault, the NYPD informed me that my case was now "cold." All leads had been exhausted, and nothing more was to be done. In retrospect, I think this is when my life fell apart, as I began to descend further into despair and self-hatred. They could not find the man who raped me, and I felt I was to blame. My foggy memory and my inability to relay vital details were the reasons why a violent, raging human being was still on the streets harming others.

Being isolated in self-hatred and loathing is not a fun place to exist. I had regular conversations in my head that somehow always ended with me questioning why I didn't pay better attention to details during my rape or thinking if only I had not let my guard down, this would not be my reality. It was all my fault—the rape, the foggy recollections, the inability to apprehend a violent criminal.

After several years had passed, I moved back to the United States, where I initially landed in Florida and later relocated to Virginia. During this time period, outwardly, I was doing quite well. I had a successful career, and I was surrounded by friends. However, those closest to me were all too aware of the chaos that enveloped me. My nightmares kept me from sleeping, and I was engaging in destructive behavior by self-medicating my anxiety and depression with alcohol.

While living in Virginia, I received a phone call from the Manhattan District Attorney's office. It was 2003, and nearly a decade had elapsed since I was assaulted. Melissa Mourges, an Assistant District Attorney with the sex crimes unit, patiently explained to me that they had just gotten around to testing my sexual assault evidence kit and that I would need to go to New York to testify before a Grand Jury. Since 9½ years had elapsed, we were nearing the expiration of the statute of limitations of my case (which at that time in New York was 10 years for rape), and she was hoping to indict the DNA profile contained in my rape kit to "stop the clock." This means that although my suspect's identity was still unknown, that person's DNA sequence is unique. So, we could charge that DNA sequence with the crime and later amend the charge if the person's identity became known. I would later learn that this was called a John Doe Indictment—a way to keep my case prosecutable.

Learning new details about my rape kit, including that it had been collecting dust for nearly a decade, did not make me angry. That is not to say I should not have been angry—I think that would be a natural emotion to feel. Instead, I felt relief. I was relieved for reasons that contradicted themselves. On the one hand, I felt that everyone in the New York Police Department (NYPD) would surely be angry with me for not being a better complaining witness (I was, after all, angry at myself). On the other hand, I felt that the entire ordeal could have been a figment of my imagination—like maybe it happened to someone else entirely. This new bit of information helped me process a lot of my emotions and confirmed that this experience, which continued to haunt me, had, in fact, occurred. This outside confirmation of my inner reality was validating.

I traveled to New York to testify before a grand jury. For the first time outside of therapy, I shared the gruesome details of the events that took place in August of 1993. The jury listened intently while I tried my best to choke out every detail. The grand jury was even emotional at times. The DNA in my rape kit was indicted, and just like that, the clock on the statute of limitations was halted (New York has recently eliminated its statute of limitations on rape).

The "win" (the indictment) in 2003 was by no means an assurance that the man who raped me would be charged, apprehended, and successfully prosecuted. There were still obstacles in the way. The Combined DNA Index System (CODIS), the federal DNA database, was not nearly as populated with DNA profiles as it is today. At this time, I was only assured that my rapist would be held responsible for his crimes if he ever entered the system. At that time, it was enough for me that someone still cared about my case, and everything was moving forward as best it could. I was grateful, and this was truly the catalyst for the next stage of my healing process.

During the grand jury process, I learned that my SAK was one of ~11,000 kits that sat collecting dust in a storage facility in New York City. Once the Medical Examiner's Office began being able to upload profiles from now tested kits into CODIS, Robert Morgenthau, New York County's District Attorney at the time, made a point to test and process every single rape kit in the city's possession, regardless of whether the perpetrator was known to the victim. This was unique at the time because the common practice was to only test kits connected to sexual assaults perpetrated by strangers. However, this prevented all of us from learning that one person's stranger rapist was another's known perpetrator. The DNA from these kits could connect the dots. Once this decision was made, SAKs from NYC were processed at the Medical Examiner's Office and sent out on pallets to private labs all across the country. One of those sexual assault evidence kits was mine.

Life continued for me with a renewed sense of hope. That is not to say that the darkness ever left me. Nightmares still plagued me, and while the self-loathing had dissipated to a degree, it still emerged in all its ugliness now and again. In 2004, I moved back to New York to care for my ailing paternal grandmother. I continued to work and expand my life in ways I did not have the courage to do in the past. I still felt I was flawed and broken in some key ways, but there was a light at the end of the tunnel that I could finally begin to make out. My journey was in progress.

The Hit Notification

In 2007, while living on Long Island, New York, a plain-clothed detective greeted me at my door. I had heard musings from neighbors that a car had been spotted parked in front of my home over the course of a few days. So it came as no surprise to me when he approached me at my door. He handed me his card and identified himself as law enforcement. He was sheepish and awkward yet genuine in a way I cannot put into words. For some reason, his obvious discomfort put me at ease. He was only able to muster: *I'm here about the really bad thing that happened to you years ago in New York City.*

Of course, I knew precisely what he was talking about. I nodded my head in acknowledgment and accepted another card he handed me. He explained that this card was from the New York County Sex Crimes Unit and that I was to call them as soon as possible.

Now that I know how victim notifications should properly be administered (see Chapters 9 and 20), I recognize that mine did not follow the recommended script. We are now all too aware of the importance of having an advocate present when a victim is notified. An advocate is essential should the victim require resources to help them process the new information given to them. I can only share my personal experience while emphasizing that it very well could have gone badly. At the time, I was just struck at how awkward the interaction was for both the detective and me. There was a level of humanity in that contact—a sense that he and I were both flawed human beings that had seen heartbreaking things. I took comfort in this. Luckily, I had resources at my disposal that other survivors may not have had access to. I had family and friends to immediately call after the notification and share this new turn of events with and to speculate about what might happen next. I had been open with family and friends about my rape, so there was no issue when it came to sharing this news. Not every survivor shares this luxury.

After playing phone tag for several days, I spoke directly to Melissa Mourgess in Manhattan. My speculations were indeed true—they had found the man who had raped and robbed me in 1992. For some reason, *I immediately wanted to know his name.* I felt that knowing his name would somehow empower me and take away some of the fear he held over me through the years. She told me. His name was Victor Rondon.

I later learned that Rondon had been arrested for possession of an illegal firearm shortly after he assaulted me in 1993. He served time in prison and was released several years later and placed on probation. After living in several states and committing a host of crimes, Victor assaulted a law enforcement official who gave him a citation for jaywalking in Las Vegas, Nevada. After he was arrested, it was noted that he was still on probation in New York. He was extradited to New York City for violating his probation, swabbed for DNA and had his profile uploaded into CODIS. A match was made to the sexual assault evidence kit in my rape case.

I had several meetings with Melissa Mourgess after her initial disclosure to me. She was kind yet stern, matter of fact, but compassionate. I trusted her implicitly. I trusted her because she always made me feel like I was important and that I mattered. She never coddled me or made me feel like a "victim." Instead, Melissa made certain I felt empowered and that I was part of a well-oiled machine that would ensure justice prevailed. She also was careful to be sure I had resources and support at my fingertips should I need them. I felt encouraged.

The 2008 trial was swift but certainly not without intense emotions and upheaval. For me, seeing Victor Rondon in the courtroom was startling. What I still find fascinating is how my brain comprehended our encounter in the courtroom. While intellectually, I was aware that I was safe and that no harm would come to me, my brain's response was to release fire and fury as I found myself hyperventilating and nearly fainting on the witness stand. Because of the level of trust developed between the prosecutors and me, and the fact that my friends were in the courtroom, I was able to muster up the courage to testify. I relayed my story to the jury in as much detail as possible, and Victor Rondon was convicted, sentenced, and put behind bars for many decades. He remains behind bars to this day.

Carrying the Work Forward

I recall the exact moment after my case when I decided to become an advocate. Melissa Mourgess and I were standing together triumphantly on the courthouse steps, and I felt such a sense of elation. Nearly 15 years had elapsed since I had been raped and robbed, and somehow, against all odds, the man who raped me had been apprehended and convicted. I knew so little about unprocessed rape kits and survivors of sexual assault at that time. However, I did know what it was like to be believed, and I wanted so badly to have other survivors experience some of the empowerment I felt. I was compelled to do more.

I turned to Mellissa to ask for suggestions on what I could do with my experience in order to help others. She asked if I would feel comfortable sharing my story with others, as so many survivors of sexual assault at the time were reluctant to go forward.

The groundswell of support we currently are experiencing—thanks in large part to movements like #MeToo—had yet to reach the mainstream in 2008. I feel it's important here to make a note of the fact that I was able to openly discuss my case, as the man who raped me was behind bars. I was surrounded by a supportive family and peer group. My interaction with law enforcement and prosecutors had been positive and, thus, had left me feeling emboldened. This is certainly not always the case, and it's important to recognize how unique of a position I was in. I enthusiastically agreed to go public and share my story in any way that would benefit survivors across the country.

The Beginnings of My Advocacy

In 2011, after several media appearances and my participation in the HBO Documentary *Sex Crimes Unit,* I left my job as the executive director of a maritime museum to pursue advocacy full-time. During my journey as an "open" survivor, I had learned that thousands and thousands of SAKs, just like mine, were sitting on shelves across the country collecting dust. I felt compelled to use my story to help others and make certain these kits were processed so that victims could have the closure I experienced. I did not feel that it was fair to be the anomaly. I started Natasha's Justice Project, an organization dedicated to exposing and eliminating what we were calling the rape kit backlog at that time. I was overwhelmed by the support I received from survivors across the country, and I was grateful to find additional healing through the friendships I made with them throughout the years. What began as a service to others truly ended up bringing me more joy and peace with myself than I ever dreamed possible.

In the early days, I partnered with several organizations to work on legislative measures that would mandate the processing of rape kits (see Chapter 18 for details on legislative measures). There were more visits to lawmakers in Washington, DC than I can count and research projects and a slew of phone calls. The media began reporting on the backlog of unprocessed rape kits as well. It was challenging to precisely describe why the "backlog" occurred. No one could offer a one-size-fits-all solution to a complicated problem.

I was just a layman at the time, and my experiences were particular to my case. As I was beginning to forge relationships with survivors across the nation, it was becoming glaringly obvious that not everyone had received the care and consideration that I did from those who had worked on my case. I know this sounds naïve to say, but I had assumed that everyone was treated with the same level of respect that I was. How could approaches differ to such a degree? It was devastating to hear from other survivors and learn of their struggles. It was humbling to recognize that I was treated far differently than others (see Chapter 3 on disclosure reactions). I learned that regardless of the outcome of a case, survivors who were not treated with reverence or who were even dismissed altogether felt revictimized by the very process that was supposed to support them.

As I developed these relationships and learned about the process, I traveled around the country speaking at college campuses and symposiums. I was invited to share my story and relay my thoughts before members of the Senate and Congress. I met with law enforcement officials and prosecutors in states that were gearing up their efforts to process rape kits. Each encounter filled me with deep reverence and expanded my knowledge on the topic.

Throughout this part of the process, I was a lone survivor without the resources of a large organization or connections to powerful entities. I often pushed my way into conversations to ensure that the voices of survivors were included in the messaging and in the enacted solutions. I was insistent and arrogant—I had to be taken seriously. I felt if I were to shoot for the moon, I would at least be met somewhere halfway in between. I was perhaps naïve in some of my approaches, but my intentions were always sincere.

I couldn't get discouraged with the entire justice system because I began meeting people I continue to have a deep reverence for to this day. I cannot begin to count how many law enforcement members approached me to give me hope and encouragement. Police officers and detectives truly wanted to find a solution and were dedicated to finding justice for survivors. They certainly could have dismissed me and my concerns. Instead, they reached out to me on their own to discuss solutions and share their frustrations with what was occurring, or NOT occurring, with unprocessed sexual assault evidence kits across the country. They treated me as a colleague rather than just another victim with lofty goals. I wish I could share how kind and dedicated these law enforcement officials are to the world. That is not to say I am blind to the realities that exist. If we could somehow replicate the group of police officers and detectives I met with over the years and scatter them across the country, I believe we would find ourselves in a different place today.

There were prosecutors, too, who were opening their doors to me. Kym Worthy, the current Wayne County, Michigan prosecutor and home to Detroit, is one of the most inspiring women I have ever met. Detroit's backlog was notorious for its sheer number of unprocessed kits, and the stories I was hearing from survivors in the area were devastating. Kym refused to give up. All of us watched in awe as she fought harder than anyone I had ever seen.

Nancy O'Malley, District Attorney for Alameda County, California, is another inspiring prosecutor who kindly opened her doors and heart to me. Nancy had been working diligently for decades on meticulously counting every unprocessed rape kit in her jurisdiction, which was no small task. Her approaches and rationale were altruistic and inspiring. She would not take no for an answer. Counting unprocessed rape kits was no easy task, and her methodology was replicated elsewhere.

In addition to being humbled by the company I was keeping, I was met with messages and phone calls from forensic scientists across the country. Seeing boxes cross their workspace that contained vital evidence was moving to them. They recognized that each kit contained the hopes and fears of victims whose bodies had become the crime scene. My kit had crossed the desk of such a person at one time.

While I had initially met with individuals who were a part of the criminal justice process, I later began to meet with academics trying to come up with a solution to the problem at hand. Some people dedicated their careers to understanding what trauma looked like and how the brain processes sexual assault. It was becoming abundantly clear that some members of law enforcement did not recognize that memories of a traumatic event are often fragmented and disjointed. Survivors were often dismissed for their inability to recall details. Sometimes, survivors were outright rejected for not acting in a manner aligned with assumptions of what "being upset" looked like. This was something I knew firsthand. To have a learned expert acknowledge the validity of my own experiences was liberating (see Chapter 8 for a review of the trauma response).

For a person like me who often still felt flawed and haunted by demons, these encounters frequently moved me to tears. Regardless of our disciplines, we all had a common goal—to process rape kits and offer survivors justice. No one expected every case to be solved. We all agreed that we were doing an injustice to survivors by not acknowledging them or by dismissing them outright by not processing their kits. We were also doing an injustice to the public's safety at large by letting these kits languish. It felt as though, at times, we were acting as if rape wasn't a crime at all.

It might seem to someone on the outside that nothing was happening, and I recognize that there are survivors out there who rightfully feel nothing was or is taking place during that time and even today. If you never had the opportunity to meet these individuals, you would justly assume that no one was fighting for you. If your tears and frustration had only been met by doors slamming in your face or, even worse, complete apathy, why would you feel otherwise? Even now, it is easy to forget while working in this field that there are people out there suffering, that have no idea you exist or that you are fighting for them.

I take solace in the hope that all unprocessed kits will be tested. While we may never be able to bring closure to someone who has been suffering for such a long time, they will at least know that someone continued to fight for them.

Beginnings of the Sexual Assault Kit Initiative

In September of 2015, the culmination of some of our efforts was finally realized. While we all acknowledged that while funding would not solve every issue surrounding the rationale for not testing rape kits, it would certainly go a long way toward solving many of the issues. For years the people I had met along my journey had been lobbying diligently to procure funding for testing unprocessed rape kits. Now, over $100 million dollars has been pledged by the Department of Justice's SAKI to process them. Initially, in 2015, a $41 million congressional allocation funded the initiative to the Justice Department and another $38 million in civil forfeitures seized by the Office of Manhattan District Attorney Cyrus Vance. Joseph Biden, then Vice President of the United States, spearheaded these efforts and promised no survivor would be forgotten.

I was elated to be a part of the press conference announcing this project. I shared the podium with all the individuals who had been tirelessly trying to push efforts to bring funding to process sexual assault evidence kits. It was an amazing culmination for me, on a personal level, to stand before everyone who had fought for me during my case, including Melissa Mourgess, Martha Bashford, and Cyrus Vance. Hearing Joe Biden acknowledge what happened to me from the podium moved me to tears. See Figure 5.1.

Figure 5.1 Photo of Natasha Alexenko with Then Vice President Joe Biden in 2015

This event would mark the beginning of the SAKI (see Chapter 1 for a history of SAKI). What I found most moving about the project was that all perspectives were being united to tackle this. It was well understood that advocates, academics, prosecutors, and law enforcement would all need to be brought to the table to form an interdisciplinary team that could dedicate themselves to solving the issue at hand and ensure it would never occur in the future. Initially, however, survivors were not expected to be part of the interdisciplinary teams.

Yet, I had learned throughout my encounters how vital all cogs in the machine were to this process. If one discipline was not present at the table, an important part of the mission would be missing. I hoped that survivors would be included in these discussions as our voices were essential. No successful movement has ever existed where the people directly being affected are not included in conversations. Our perspectives and unique viewpoints are crucial to bringing solutions to the table. No one else can offer the sort of first-hand, experiential information necessary, and our stories validate and confirm the ideas being laid forth by all the disciplines.

It wasn't easy convincing everyone of the necessity of our inclusion. Some thought that perhaps we were too fragile to share our beliefs or that our emotions were too raw to make sense of such a complex issue. I will not deny that there have been moments where my emotions have overtaken me. But emotion and passion are a vital part of how things can move forward. Without them, we cannot continue pushing or inspiring movements. I felt that in order for survivors to understand how crucial they are in the push to process rape kits, others needed to see that we are a part of the solution.

I was honored to officially join SAKI in 2016, and I now work alongside so many of the individuals who inspired and gave me hope along the way. These relationships are a fundamental part of who I am today.

It's so easy to become comfortable in our narratives and forget about other perspectives on an issue you are passionate about. I am trying to be a better listener and absorb all that others must teach me. The luxury of working with such an esteemed group of people is not lost on me. I hope that other survivors will continue to join these discussions as my perspective should never be the only one considered. My experiences are unique to me, and so many others see life through a different lens and have had markedly different experiences from my own.

Progress and the Journey Forward

Part of how I continue to evolve is by recognizing how important it is for me to make sure I do not drown out the voices of others who have not yet had a chance to speak about their journeys. I do want to make it a point to highlight what it looks like when a survivor is treated with respect and encouragement. I want every survivor to be given the same opportunities I have been granted. I think this is the most important message I must relay—supporting us not only helps us heal, but it can make us allies. And we need all the allies we can get.

I have personally witnessed SAKI make tremendous advances since 2016. One of the most fascinating things about SAKI is that the people who were a part of the process during its inception are still a part of it today. They have continued to be a part of this multidisciplinary team because they are dedicated to seeing its mission through. I say this with all sincerity—they are dedicated to ensuring its success because survivors and sexual assault evidence kits matter to them. They also remain because they see the successes and have been able to witness tangible results. I have seen new experts join, and they too are equally as committed to our mission. It is inspiring and leaves me with a great deal of hope.

In addition to physically testing sexual assault evidence kits, we have fundamentally and forever changed the way victims are interviewed after an assault and how they are notified if their languishing kit has finally been tested. It was terrific to watch law enforcement join forces with academics and advocates to establish robust victim-centered and trauma-informed approaches to interviewing survivors. It was abundantly clear that merely testing rape kits would only lead to the problem rearing its ugly head in the future. Measures have been put into place to train all the players involved to be keenly aware of the rationale behind ensuring rape kits are tested and to understand why survivors need to be treated justly. I have traveled across the country to be a part of these training sessions, and I've seen this paradigm shift occur before my very eyes.

Sometimes, it's hard to convey this without sounding as though I am overly optimistic. I have truly witnessed significant changes that have to be seen to be believed. That does not mean we can rest upon our laurels assuming that this problem has been solved because that is far from true. We must continue to be open to learning more as the process moves forward. We must take the lessons we have learned and make certain all jurisdictions across the country are following suit. This is not only a matter of supporting survivors—but it is an issue of public safety. And safety is a right that is essential to all of us.

The work and the people I have met along this journey have brought me to places I never felt worthy of exploring. In 2018, I published my memoirs, and I have cosponsored a host of legislation across the country that addresses rape kit reform. I'm always in awe of the fact that a first-generation American has been included in so many things and that my voice is uplifted and respected. I will continue to value what I have been offered and never lose sight of the mission I set out to accomplish.

Beyond the United States

Presently, my work with SAKI has inspired me to take my work globally. In October 2019, I visited Brazil to share my story and encourage the use of their newly adopted CODIS system. Today, I work for an organization called VOICE that amplifies the voices of women and girls in conflict areas across the globe. I take everything I've learned in the United States and pass it along so that I might cross-pollinate ideas and perspectives. These women have much to teach us as well.

Regardless of where they live, survivors have the same hopes, fears, and tribulations. Though our perspectives and experiences differ, there is something deep in the core of each of us that connects us. We must all be mindful of how we differ and what we share while we make certain all voices are heard.

I have also learned that wherever you travel and whatever you see, there are good people out there who can serve as a reminder that anything can be accomplished if we listen to one another and hold true to our vision. While it is easy to accept defeat, movements never happen overnight. Progress is occurring. We are nothing without collaboration: we are stronger together.

Key Points

- Including the voices of survivors is essential to solving the backlog and changing the criminal justice response to rape victims.
- A diverse array of survivor's voices needs to be heard, supported, and empowered.
- Testing all kits, and collecting DNA from criminals convicted for other crimes, will populate CODIS in ways that can help solve rape cases. One person's stranger rapist is another person's known perpetrator.
- There are many dedicated people working to solve the SAK backlog, improve the system, provide trauma-informed care, and ensure justice. Change happens when we all work together.

Discussion Questions

1 How can we empower survivors to join the SAK effort without risking re-traumatization?
2 How does Natasha's experience provide a firsthand experience of how the brain processes trauma?

Further Reading

Alexenko, N. S. (2018). *A survivor's journey: From victim to advocate*. Amazon Publishing.

Section II

Where are we now?

Present reform efforts

6 SAKI training and technical assistance

Partnering with SAKI sites for success

Patricia A. Melton and Amanda R. Young

Author Note and Funding Acknowledgment

This project was supported by Grant No. 2019-MU-BX-K011 awarded by the Bureau of Justice Assistance. The Bureau of Justice Assistance is a component of the U.S. Department of Justice's Office of Justice Programs, which also includes the Bureau of Justice Statistics, the National Institute of Justice, the Office of Juvenile Justice and Delinquency Prevention, the Office for Victims of Crime, and the SMART Office. Points of view or opinions in this document are those of the authors and do not necessarily represent the official position or policies of the U.S. Department of Justice.

The Value of Training and Technical Assistance in Supporting a National Initiative

Undoubtedly, not testing sexual assault kits results in failure to support survivors of sexual assault and missed opportunities to hold offenders accountable, including serial sexual perpetrators who are a threat within and across communities. Sexual assault kits accumulate due to a multitude of challenges that are not limited to only resource or capacity issues but also include limited understanding of the value of forensic evidence, lack of policies for sexual assault kit submission and testing, and a lack of cross-disciplinary collaborations for victim-centered services (Campbell et al., 2018; see Chapter 1 for more details). Therefore, solutions intended to resolve unsubmitted sexual assault kits must also address agency communication and cultural dynamics, improve cross-agency coordination, and foster strategies that improve the response to sexual assault by aligning policies with national recommendations and best practices. Legislation that mandates the timely submission and testing of sexual assault kits removes the physical accumulation of sexual assault kits in law enforcement evidence property rooms but does not address gaps in cross-agency collaboration nor the lack of trauma-informed, victim-centered approaches needed to support survivors of sexual assault and improve investigative and prosecutorial outcomes.

Therefore, more is needed to support the alignment of policy to national recommendations and best practices, remove agency silos to improve cross-agency collaboration and promote the formation of a successful multidisciplinary team (MDT), and educate practitioners on the effects of trauma on sexual assault victims to create practices that are trauma-informed and victim-centered. These needs can be effectively addressed through training and technical assistance (TTA).

DOI: 10.4324/9781003186816-9

This chapter will highlight how the SAKI TTA project, referred to as SAKI TTA, supports the SAKI sites in order to generate a more impactful and sustainable SAKI site program. Training refers to in-person or virtual training, which is led by a subject matter expert who is demonstrated to have the experience, knowledge, and skill set required of the topic. Technical assistance refers to resources, including briefs and webinars, teleconferences and web-based video conferences, and other multimedia presentations created by subject matter experts, to assist in the understanding of a topic. We begin by first describing the SAKI program and SAKI TTA model—what it is, how it came to be, how it is structured, and how it supports the goals of SAKI. Next, we describe the key components of the SAKI program for a sustained reformed response to sexual assault. Then, we detail the challenges and lessons learned by SAKI TTA in guiding policy change that is aligned with national recommendations. More specifically, in terms of lessons learned, we expand upon what SAKI TTA recommends and/or provides to address the challenges faced by jurisdictions as they reform their response to sexual assault.

TTA is a critical component of advancing sexual assault response reform. Jurisdictions dedicated to improving their response to sexual assault must look beyond discipline-centric changes and consider multidisciplinary approaches. These need to be grounded in evidence-based solutions that align with national recommendations. Embracing an effective and comprehensive TTA program and implementing key resources from such a program into agency-specific policy is an essential pathway to create a sustainable approach to effectively apply nationally recognized best practices and improve jurisdictional response to sexual assault. The SAKI model, which encourages the use of evidence-based resources (provided under SAKI TTA) in order to create best practice and policy, facilitates jurisdictions with creating an improved community response to sexual assault. This model is the cornerstone of sexual assault response reform and can be adopted by any jurisdiction. This chapter describes many challenges associated with supporting an improved response to sexual assault. SAKI TTA has created plausible evidence-based solutions, presented as resources and key considerations, to address these challenges. The resources created under SAKI TTA are openly available to any agency, not just SAKI grantees, and the SAKI TTA helpdesk can direct requests to specific team members for consultation under the national reach aspect of SAKI TTA. We encourage agencies to incorporate SAKI resources into their own internal training programs and take advantage of the wealth of freely available information on the SAKI TTA website to support changes to policy and practice.

SAKI sites and visitors to the SAKI TTA website are also encouraged to follow the SAKI program on social media. SAKI TTA recognizes social media as a vital method to share information, including success across the SAKI program, in real-time. The SAKI social media network has grown extensively to include SAKI sites, criminal justice and crime laboratory practitioners, researchers, advocates, and survivors. SAKI social media followers are encouraged to see the impact the SAKI program is having across the nation and are inspired by the stories of support to the victims of sexual assault and successful outcomes of these cases.

As a subject matter expert in sexual assault response reform and DNA forensic processing of sexual assault kits, Dr. Melton has dedicated her career to the just resolution of sexual assault cases. She has facilitated policy change and promoted multidisciplinary reform to violent crime. She has served as a project director for SAKI

TTA since its inception in 2015. In that capacity, she has overseen the creation of resources and strategies presented under SAKI TTA and authored a holistic resource for sexual assault response practitioners entitled *Enacting an Improved Response to Sexual Assault: A Practitioner's Guide to Successful Sexual Assault Response Reform*. She also serves as a task force consultant supporting statewide legislative sexual assault response reform for the North Carolina Department of Justice. Dr. Melton's work addresses fundamental issues in the criminal justice system's response to sexual assault at multiple levels of analysis. Her work focuses on guidance for organizational-, community-, and statewide sexual assault response reform to move the field of improved sexual assault response beyond individual agency success toward statewide and national reform. Dr. Melton strives to ensure the impact of her work on society is transformative.

Ms. Young is the SAKI TTA training director and is responsible for the development and execution of in-person and virtual training events hosted under SAKI TTA, including national meetings, regional events, and webinars. She has extensive experience with and knowledge of agency needs associated with sexual assault response reform including policy change, data collection, and multidisciplinary strategies to address unsubmitted sexual assault kits. Ms. Young understands the challenges agencies encounter while improving their response to sexual assault and in collaboration with subject matter experts, coordinates the appropriate TTA support to address such challenges.

As a point of clarification, under SAKI, *unsubmitted sexual assault kits* are kits that have not been submitted to a forensic laboratory for testing and analysis using current methodologies eligible for submission to the Combined DNA Index System (CODIS). They are, by definition, not tested, as they had never been submitted to a crime laboratory for testing with CODIS eligible methodologies. Moreover, an *unsubmitted sexual assault kit backlog* differs from a backlog of submitted sexual assault kits waiting to be tested in the crime laboratory. The SAKI program addresses unsubmitted (therefore untested sexual assault kits) but does not address sexual assault kits that have already been submitted to a crime laboratory and are waiting to be tested, as other federal funding opportunities exist to address that issue.

SAKI: A Model for Enhancing Sexual Assault Response

The Bureau of Justice Assistance (BJA) National Sexual Assault Kit Initiative (SAKI) model incorporates three primary objectives.

1 Inventory all previously unsubmitted sexual assault kits;
2 Form a MDT that convenes regularly to address the issues that lead to an accumulation of unsubmitted sexual assault kits in the jurisdiction; and
3 Designate a SAKI site coordinator who not only serves as the primary point of contact but also has full support from the lead agency to effectively lead the SAKI site team and be responsible for fostering and coordinating across the SAKI site team to ensure the SAKI goals and objectives are met.

As seen in Figure 6.1, there are four purpose areas in the SAKI program designed to meet the progression of the SAKI sites as they advance through the program.

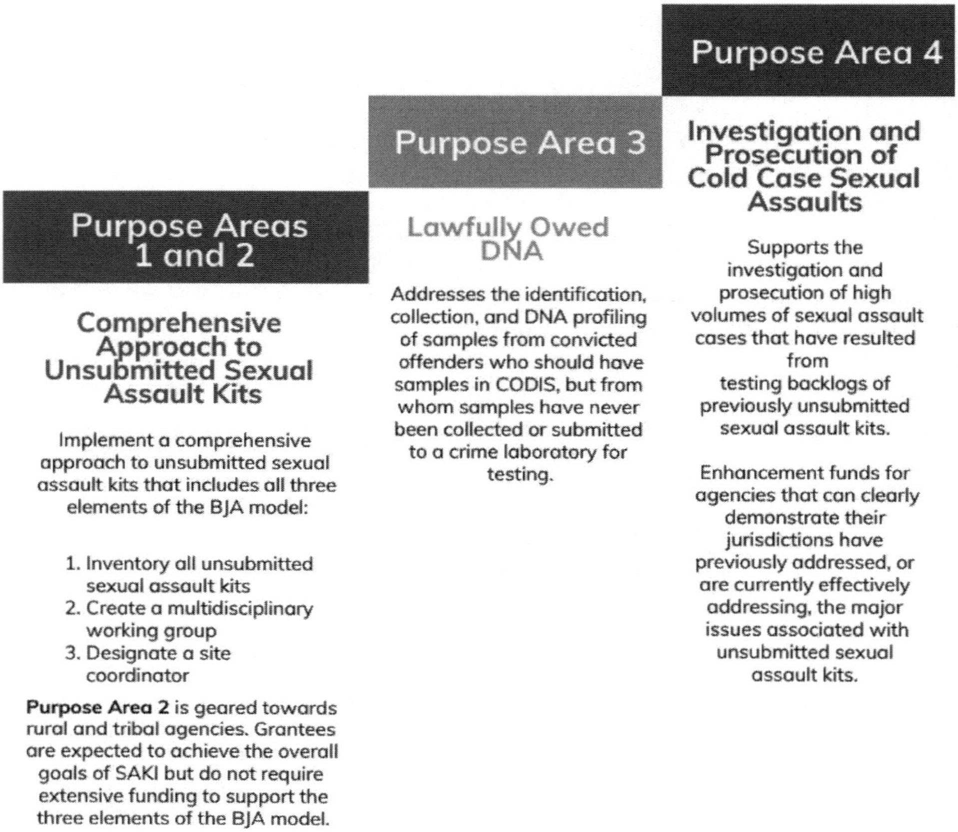

Purpose Area 4

Investigation and Prosecution of Cold Case Sexual Assaults

Supports the investigation and prosecution of high volumes of sexual assault cases that have resulted from testing backlogs of previously unsubmitted sexual assault kits.

Enhancement funds for agencies that can clearly demonstrate their jurisdictions have previously addressed, or are currently effectively addressing, the major issues associated with unsubmitted sexual assault kits.

Purpose Area 3

Lawfully Owed DNA

Addresses the identification, collection, and DNA profiling of samples from convicted offenders who should have samples in CODIS, but from whom samples have never been collected or submitted to a crime laboratory for testing.

Purpose Areas 1 and 2

Comprehensive Approach to Unsubmitted Sexual Assault Kits

Implement a comprehensive approach to unsubmitted sexual assault kits that includes all three elements of the BJA model:

1. Inventory all unsubmitted sexual assault kits
2. Create a multidisciplinary working group
3. Designate a site coordinator

Purpose Area 2 is geared towards rural and tribal agencies. Grantees are expected to achieve the overall goals of SAKI but do not require extensive funding to support the three elements of the BJA model.

Figure 6.1 BJA SAKI Four Purpose Areas

1 Purpose Area 1 is a comprehensive approach to address unsubmitted sexual assault kits. This is the purpose area where most SAKI sites enter the program.
2 Purpose Area 2 is also a comprehensive approach to sexual assault, however, it is tailored for small agencies such as rural or tribal agencies.
3 Purpose Area 3 is the expansion of DNA databases to assist with sexual assault investigations and prosecutions, specifically through the collection of lawfully owed DNA from convicted offenders and, as state laws permit, arrestees.
4 Purpose Area 4 supports the investigation and prosecution of cold case sexual assaults and is intended for jurisdictions that have already addressed the major issues associated with the accumulation of unsubmitted sexual assault kits. Purpose Area 3 and Purpose Area 4 are considered more advanced stages of the SAKI program. The majority of sites enter at Purpose Area 1, requiring foundational training, whereas others enter at Purpose Area 4, requiring more advanced training. The rate at which an individual site progresses through the program also differs among the sites.

As of August 2021, there are 71 SAKI sites, consisting of 25 statewide sites, 29 citywide sites, 13 countywide sites, 3 multicounty sites, and 1 district site. Many sites have received more than one SAKI award across multiple purpose areas. SAKI sites, both currently and previously funded, represent approximately 57% of the US population, or 328.2 million people. The SAKI TTA team typically provides resources to over 4,600 practitioners per month and has a distribution list of over 5,000 individuals. As of November 2020, SAKI TTA has conducted more than 90 in-person events, authored over 35 technical briefs, and hosted over 80 webinars.

SAKI Training and Technical Assistance: A Collaborative Partner to SAKI Sites

In 2015, BJA implemented the SAKI program to create a coordinated, community-based response to the issues of unsubmitted sexual assault kits and foster an improved response to sexual assault. BJA understood that jurisdictions entering the SAKI program were going to need dedicated assistance to achieve the goals of the program and that just providing funding would not address the root causes as to why unsubmitted sexual assault kits accumulated in the first place nor effectively prevent future accumulations of unsubmitted sexual assault kits. While federal funding supports the capacity and enhancement needs of the SAKI sites, TTA provides the needed resources, education, and guidance to build the foundation for trauma-informed approaches that change how agencies investigate and prosecute these cases while also supporting the healing process needed by victims of sexual assault.

For these reasons, TTA for jurisdictions is vital to the success of SAKI and for the larger goal of reforming the response to rape. A comprehensive TTA plan facilitates the creation of a strategic process with milestones, goals, and actions to ensure a successful and sustainable approach for addressing sexual assault cases (Melton, 2020). Under SAKI, addressing previously unsubmitted sexual assault kits allows for an internal review of agencies' methods for investigating and prosecuting sexual assault cases. SAKI TTA partners with the SAKI sites to assist with strategies for policy review and provides insight for modification of policies to align with national recommendations, hence improving a SAKI site's ability to support sexual assault cases.

The SAKI TTA Team: Multidisciplinary, Evidence-Based, and Practitioner-Based

The SAKI TTA program is funded by BJA and led by RTI International. The SAKI TTA team is a multidisciplinary group of experts with combined decades of experience in sexual assault response reform. The SAKI TTA team includes sexual assault and criminal justice researchers, former crime laboratory practitioners, former law enforcement officers, prosecutors, sexual assault nurse examiners, victim and family advocates, and members from national law enforcement organizations (see Box 6.1). One of the key factors for creating an improved response to sexual assault is the formation of a MDT, therefore, one of the elements that has made the SAKI TTA project so successful is that the project team functions as a model MDT (see Figure 6.2).

Box 6.1

The SAKI TTA team

SAKI TTA Team

The SAKI TTA Team is composed of the following agencies:
- RTI International
- International Association of Chiefs of Police
- AEquitas
- Michigan State University
- Joyful Heart Foundation
- Rape, Abuse, and Incest National Network
- SANE-SART Resource Service
- Project: Cold Case

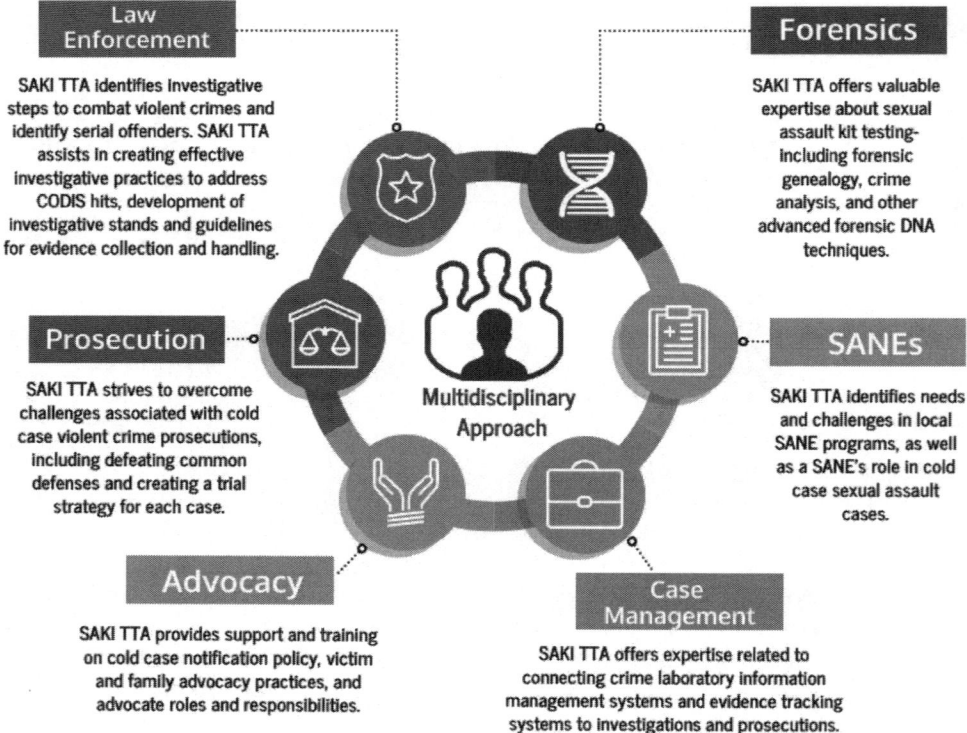

Law Enforcement

SAKI TTA identifies investigative steps to combat violent crimes and identify serial offenders. SAKI TTA assists in creating effective investigative practices to address CODIS hits, development of investigative stands and guidelines for evidence collection and handling.

Forensics

SAKI TTA offers valuable expertise about sexual assault kit testing- including forensic genealogy, crime analysis, and other advanced forensic DNA techniques.

Prosecution

SAKI TTA strives to overcome challenges associated with cold case violent crime prosecutions, including defeating common defenses and creating a trial strategy for each case.

Multidisciplinary Approach

SANEs

SAKI TTA identifies needs and challenges in local SANE programs, as well as a SANE's role in cold case sexual assault cases.

Advocacy

SAKI TTA provides support and training on cold case notification policy, victim and family advocacy practices, and advocate roles and responsibilities.

Case Management

SAKI TTA offers expertise related to connecting crime laboratory information management systems and evidence tracking systems to investigations and prosecutions.

Figure 6.2 A Multidisciplinary Approach to Sexual Assault Response Reform

In addition to having a team that represents an MDT highly similar in structure to the MDT a SAKI site would implement, the SAKI TTA team creates resources from both a researcher and practitioner perspective. The researcher's perspective ensures that SAKI TTA resources are aligned with national recommendations and best practices and are grounded in peer-reviewed research. The research element is critical as its conclusions result from the robust scientific process as opposed to generalized assumptions and anecdotal information. The practitioner perspective brings in the practical experience viewpoint and ensures that SAKI TTA resources take into consideration the challenges associated with a SAKI site implementing the information from a resource into actual policy and practice. Therefore, SAKI TTA resources go beyond providing general solutions to a challenge by providing key steps to implement a sustainable solution. This combination is essential to effectively support SAKI sites in reaching their program goals and fostering a sustainable improved approach to sexual assault.

SAKI TTA: An Innovative Training and Technical Assistance Model

The resources provided under SAKI TTA are generated through an innovative process which includes: (a) tailoring resources to meet the needs of SAKI sites, (b) obtaining feedback on the impact of the resources and modifying as necessary, and (c) assessment of impact through metrics associated with an improved response to sexual assault. This process is conducted through a series of phases that results in the sustainability of the TTA, as indicated by the SAKI site's ability to improve their response to sexual assault (see Figure 6.3). To successfully provide TTA, the SAKI TTA team must understand the overarching vision, mission, and goals of the SAKI program and work with each SAKI site to align their own individual needs and goals to the overarching milestones of the SAKI program. This partnership between the SAKI TTA team and the SAKI sites ensures a holistic community response to sexual assault is created within each site.

SAKI TTA: Comprehensive and Customized Support for SAKI Sites

Despite the planning and thoughtfulness that goes into applying for a SAKI award, it can be challenging for a site to begin addressing the goals and objectives. In fact, progression is not a linear process but rather requires that multiple objectives be addressed simultaneously. This complexity can feel overwhelming; hence SAKI TTA works closely with SAKI sites to tailor an action plan that breaks down the complexity into smaller components. Action planning allows sites to track progress and highlight incremental successes. By working collaboratively with the SAKI sites through a model grounded in frequent communication and transparent collaboration, the SAKI TTA team customizes resources to address SAKI site nuances. The SAKI TTA team begins building a relationship with each SAKI site as part of the onboarding process via a welcome packet including a plan for immediate next steps, an overview of program requirements, and guidance on milestones and goals defined by each purpose area.

Key Components for Successful Sexual Assault Response Reform

SAKI sites must address several objectives that are considered the building blocks for an improved response to sexual assault (see Figure 6.4). SAKI TTA supports

Figure 6.3 Supporting Sustainability through TTA

these objectives through multimedia resources. The section below describes how SAKI sites must address these objectives and details the support that the SAKI TTA provides.

The SAKI Unsubmitted Sexual Assault Kit Inventory: Accounting for Unsubmitted Sexual Assault Kits across the Nation

A key objective of the SAKI program is to conduct an inventory of previously unsubmitted sexual assault kits. This task is complicated by the lack of electronic records systems that effectively track the location, existence, and testing status of sexual assault kits. Often, these are papers or microfiche records that must be reviewed manually. Once these records have been reviewed and a list of unsubmitted sexual

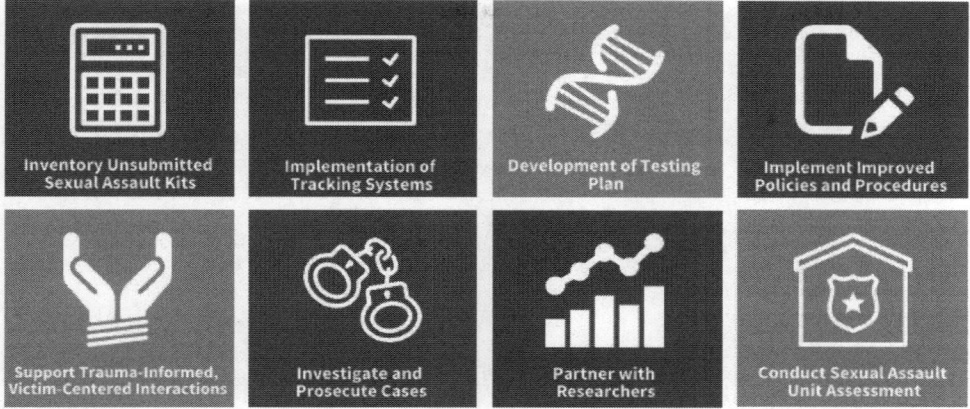

Figure 6.4 Key Objectives for Success in SAKI

assault kits is obtained, the existence of these sexual assault kits must be verified oftentimes by manually locating the sexual assault kits in evidence property rooms. The inventory process requires coordination and collaboration across multiple agencies including the crime laboratory, law enforcement, hospitals, rape crisis centers, and other community agencies, where it is possible that sexual assault kits may have been collected and stored. The inventory also requires dedicated personnel to conduct the records review, verify the existence and location of the sexual assault kits, and track the data. This process becomes increasingly more complex when deployed across a large geographical area such as a state or a cluster of multiple jurisdictions. In both cases, the number of agencies involved in the inventory process may reach well into the hundreds.

The SAKI program provides a clear metric on the magnitude of unsubmitted sexual assault kits through the requirement that SAKI grantees conduct an inventory and submit the inventory data. As of March 2021, SAKI grantees have inventoried 127,388 unsubmitted sexual assault kits. This number will continue to increase as more SAKI grantees complete their inventories. SAKI TTA recommends that the inventory approach be discussed within the SAKI site MDT to ensure awareness of the policies associated with the collection and storage of unsubmitted sexual assault kits. SAKI TTA provides customized inventory support to each SAKI Site by assisting with developing a tailored inventory plan that includes milestones and checkpoints, providing review and insight to inventory processes, and assisting with the required BJA inventory certification process.

Implementation of Tracking Systems for Sexual Assault Kits to Prevent the Future Accumulation of Sexual Assault Kits

The ability to properly track sexual assault kits from collection through testing and case adjudication is a key factor in preventing the accumulation of unsubmitted sexual assault kits. SAKI TTA assists SAKI sites with considerations for what functionalities may be important in a sexual assault kit evidence tracking system. Considerations may include multiagency access, case information, tracking requirements, status reports, and a public facing interface where victims of sexual assault can obtain information about the testing status of their sexual assault kit. Conversations may also include suggestions regarding the implementation of a new system or modifications to a current system. As implementing an evidence tracking system may be costly, SAKI TTA also provides insight on funding opportunities and options that may be acquired in discrete phases but that build on each other to create a sustainable solution over time.

Creating an Effective Testing Plan for Sexual Assault Kits

The SAKI program emphasizes the testing of sexual assault kits to ensure forensic DNA profiles obtained from sexual assault evidence are entered into the CODIS database. CODIS has proven to be a powerful tool for the generation of investigative leads and for linking multiple cases together, thereby identifying serial perpetrators (see Chapter 7 for more details). SAKI TTA provides each SAKI site with guidance in developing a testing plan to effectively test all the sexual assault kits identified in the inventory. The testing plan must take into consideration crime laboratory capacity concerns; therefore, SAKI TTA assists SAKI sites with improving communication and collaboration with the testing laboratory to ensure adequate resources are available and information sharing is maximized. SAKI TTA also supports SAKI sites with advanced DNA testing methodologies including forensic genetic genealogy (see Box 6.2 for the DOJ definition of forensic genetic genealogy).

SAKI TTA Guides Policy Change Aligned with National Recommendations: Challenges and Lessons Learned

SAKI sites must create policies that improve cold case sexual assault investigations and prosecutions, thereby ensuring just resolutions to these cases whenever possible while also supporting the healing process for victims of sexual assault by ensuring that sites have access to the most recent research and national recommendations supporting resolving cold case sexual assaults. Detailed below is suggested guidance and support for several key policy changes integral to sexual assault response reform.

Providing Resources for Improved Sexual Assault Investigation Policies

Challenges. Cold case sexual assaults are difficult and demanding cases for law enforcement to investigate. Additionally, addressing a backlog of unsubmitted sexual assault kits creates another set of demands for law enforcement—reestablishing a relationship and trust with the victim and community, addressing questions regarding testing delays, and concerns about community safety through offender accountability. SAKI TTA assists sites with the review and creation of policies that support cold case sexual assault investigations, including staffing for case reviews, CODIS hit prioritization, and non-DNA investigative approaches. Recommendations include conducting case reviews to determine if additional forensic testing is warranted or if additional investigative leads are possible (e.g., witness and victim interviews).

As mentioned previously, SAKI sites must also create a testing plan to address the submission of the cold case sexual assault kits in their SAKI inventory. As testing

Box 6.2

DOJ definition of forensic genetic genealogy

Forensic Genetic Genealogy

The **DOJ Interim Policy Forensic Genealogical DNA Analysis and Searching** provides these definitions: The term 'forensic genetic genealogical DNA analysis and searching,' or 'FGGS,' means the forensic genetic genealogical DNA analysis of a forensic or reference sample of biological material by a vendor laboratory to develop an FGG (forensic genetic genealogical DNA analysis) profile and the subsequent search of that profile in a publicly-available open- data personal genomics database or a direct-to-consumer genetic genealogy service.

progresses, the influx of SAKI sexual assault kits submitted to the crime laboratory will result in investigators receiving an influx of CODIS hits. Investigators are typically not prepared to address a significant amount of CODIS hits received at one time.

Lessons learned. SAKI TTA advises that sites create a CODIS hit prioritization system and follow-up policies to be prepared to effectively address the inflow of CODIS hits they will receive from the testing of sexual assault kits in their inventory.

Supporting Trauma-Informed, Victim-Centered Engagement with Victims of Sexual Assault

Challenges. As mentioned earlier, jurisdictions addressing unsubmitted sexual assault kits have the additional challenge of addressing the investigative and testing failures—to the sexual assault victims and the community. Victim advocates (community- and system-based) are essential to supporting the healing process of survivors of sexual assault. But these are not the only entities charged with supporting survivors. Community- and system-based advocates, law enforcement system advocates, and prosecutor-based system advocates all play a vital role in providing support to victims at various steps of the judicial process.

Lessons learned. SAKI TTA recommends that for more effective law enforcement and victim advocate partnership, each entity should seek to better understand and value each other's role and work as a united team to support the victim. SAKI sites should also review their victim notification, engagement, and interviewing policies to ensure that all interactions with victims are conducted in a trauma-informed, victim-centered manner. For law enforcement, conducting a victim interview in a trauma-informed, victim-centered manner is very different from the training they have received on interrogating suspects. SAKI TTA provides extensive resources to conduct trauma-informed, victim-centered interviewing and provides clarification on why the law enforcement/victim advocate partnership is crucial to successful victim interviews.

Challenge. SAKI grantees must also create a victim notification policy with the intent of providing key case information in a trauma-informed manner and building a rapport to maintain victim engagement through the criminal justice system while the victim chooses to participate. Policies associated with contacting victims of sexual assault cold cases require consideration of the risk of re-traumatization as these sexual assault cases may have occurred many years ago. Acknowledgment of the failure to test the sexual assault kit with a sincere apology is often beneficial to the healing process for victims of cold case sexual assaults (Joyful Heart Foundation, 2016).

Lessons learned. SAKI TTA assists sites with strategies on providing a sincere apology to victims and being transparent with the status of their case. A victim notification policy is a living document that includes roles for both victim advocacy and law enforcement and should be reviewed periodically within a SAKI site's MDT to ensure incorporation of the SAKI site's observations and experiences with victims in their community.

Providing Trauma-Informed Training for Improved Policy and Practice

Challenges. Foundational to these policy changes is ensuring criminal justice practitioners are educated in the effects of trauma on a sexual assault victim, thereby shifting the previous criminal justice culture away from rape myths and false stereotypes to one that recognizes the impact of trauma on a victim of sexual assault and works collaboratively with victim advocacy to ensure victim safety and healing.

Lessons learned. SAKI TTA emphasizes not only understanding trauma and how it may affect a victim of sexual assault but also a law enforcement/victim advocacy partnership and a prosecutor/victim advocate partnership to support sexual assault victims through the entire process. The SAKI TTA team has created resources and on-demand virtual trainings covering the effects of trauma and how to create trauma-informed, victim-centered policy and practice.

Providing Resources and Assistance for Resolution to Cold Case Sexual Assaults

Challenges. Sexual assault cases are some of the most challenging cases to prosecute as these cases are often complicated by factors that may not affect other types of violent crimes, such as lack of eyewitnesses and failure to understand that trauma may result in delayed reporting or other responses that a jury may misinterpret. Sexual assault cases are complicated further by the fact that oftentimes the assailant is known to the victim—an intimate partner; a family member, relative, or close family friend of the victim; or someone respected in the community. All these factors are true for cold case sexual assaults. However, cold cases are further complicated by the passage of time, which impacts available evidence and witness memories, and by the prior investigation (especially when not conducted in a trauma-informed manner). On the other hand, prosecuting cold case sexual assaults demonstrates to the community and victims of sexual assault that the criminal justice system will not tolerate this violent crime and will support victims of sexual assault by seeking just resolution to these cases whenever possible.

Lessons learned. SAKI TTA provides resources and training on successful courtroom strategies to address these challenges ensuring jurors connect with and understand the victim's experience. SAKI TTA also emphasizes victim safety and support through advocacy during the entire judicial process and has created resources, conducted trainings and interactive workshops covering the many challenges associated with prosecuting cold case sexual assaults. In the trainings, SAKI sites are encouraged to discuss the challenges of their cases to receive insight from SAKI TTA subject matter experts and their peers so that they may learn about new approaches that could be implemented in their jurisdiction.

Recognizing the Benefits of Partnering with Researchers and Crime Analysts

Challenges. The reasons associated with the accumulation of unsubmitted sexual assault kits are complex, vary across agencies, and often involve intra-agency cultures that have evolved over time and are difficult to resolve. Identifying the root causes associated with unsubmitted sexual assault kits requires careful review of policies and practices from all disciplines involved and effective collaboration across the MDT to evaluate resources, data, and limitations—all without creating an atmosphere of blame. Collecting and assessing key metrics associated with previously unsubmitted sexual assault kits provides insight into preventing future accumulations and victimization, improves investigation and prosecution, and thereby increases public safety.

Lessons learned. SAKI TTA provides resources to sites on the role of a crime analyst and partnering with researchers. Site-specific data may include trends in investigation and prosecution, outcomes of the testing (number of sexual assault kits yielding DNA eligible for CODIS entry, the number of CODIS hits obtained, etc.), number of victims willing to engage with the criminal justice system, feedback from victims on the agency's notification approach, and victimology trends.

Lessons learned. SAKI TTA assists with information sharing across all of the sites, fosters researchers and crime analyst discussions through a quarterly working group, and provides subject matter expertise to understand what outcomes data analysis can provide as well as how these outcomes can inform policy. Furthermore, SAKI TTA collates the resulting information and observations of the evidence base to draft and disseminate recommendations at a national level.

SAKI TTA Conducts Sexual Assault Unit Assessments as an Indicator of Sustainable Change

In partnership with BJA, SAKI TTA created the SAKI Sexual Assault Unit (SAU) assessment as a specialized form of technical assistance for law enforcement agencies of SAKI sites to improve their overall response to sexual assault. A variety of sources are used to conduct the assessment with the SAKI site including a policy review, a case file review of sexual assault cases over a multiyear period, and interviews with key practitioners including investigators, patrol officers, unit supervisors, command staff, representatives from the crime laboratory and forensic medical personnel including sexual assault nurse examiners. At the conclusion of the SAU, an in-person briefing with agency leadership is conducted to review the findings and recommendations. The SAU identifies areas of success as well as areas of improvement to which SAKI TTA provides customized resources.

Discussion: Advancing Reform through the SAKI Program

The SAKI program is not just about inventorying and testing previously unsubmitted sexual assault kits. SAKI grantees must create policies that improve practices associated with the investigation and prosecution of cold case sexual assaults while also supporting the victims—many of whom will learn for the first time that their sexual assault kit languished on the shelf untested for many years. SAKI grantees must determine the causes for the untested kits, acknowledge this failure, commit to making changes, and rebuild trust with their communities and victims of sexual assault. In other words—comprehensively reform their response to rape. Through these actions, SAKI sites build a sustainable, improved response to sexual assault that includes supporting victims of sexual assault, preventing the future accumulation of unsubmitted sexual assault kits, and ensuring sexual assault cases are investigated in a trauma-informed manner and prosecuted to the fullest extent possible.

The SAKI program has grown from an initial cohort of 20 sites in 2015 to currently 71 sites—25 of which are statewide sites. SAKI TTA has maintained pace with the growth of the SAKI program by continuously working to identify and address the challenges faced by these jurisdictions, improving the resources generated, and creating innovative approaches to meet the increased scope of the project. The SAKI TTA team supports the SAKI grantees by levering the cumulative experience of several years as the SAKI program TTA provider, the SAKI TTA team's collective experience in sexual assault response reform, and through the knowledge of the issues the SAKI sites encounter in their SAKI program. SAKI TTA recognizes that as the SAKI sites progress through their goals and the SAKI program, there will always be a need for foundational training and resources in addition to advanced topics. SAKI sites enter the program at different stages of progression in sexual assault response reform. Additionally, SAKI TTA encourages SAKI sites to incorporate SAKI resources into their own internal training programs or training academies for their own internal sustainability. SAKI TTA values peer-to-peer learning and fosters a network of relationships across the different SAKI sites so that the grantees can support each other and share their experiences, lessons learned, and improved practices with each other.

As mentioned earlier, agencies addressing sexual assault response reform that are not part of the SAKI program can access and benefit from leveraging the materials, knowledge, and expertise freely available through SAKI TTA. In many cases, foundational work on sexual assault response reform, such as the formation of a MDT, securing support and buy-in from key stakeholders, and conducting a preliminary review of practices, policies and outcomes associated with sexual assault cases to identify gaps, barriers, challenges, and areas of improvement can all be done, and perhaps should be done, prior to submitting an application for SAKI funding. Through these actions, an agency may also create a better understanding of not only how the different purpose areas funded under the SAKI program may apply to them, but also if other funding streams may be more applicable and, ideally, how to use multiple funding streams for comprehensive support to resolve violent cases. For example, oftentimes, agencies believe that SAKI funding isn't applicable to their goals as they have addressed an inventory of unsubmitted sexual assault kits, have legislation in place mandating submission of sexual assault kits, or do not have a backlog of untested sexual assault kits. Under the SAKI program, Purpose Area 4 is designed for agencies that have already addressed the root causes of unsubmitted sexual assault kits but do need support specifically for the investigation and prosecution of cold case sexual assaults. Looking even deeper into issues associated with addressing sexual assault and rape, research clearly indicates that our system of collecting, processing, and entering convicted offender profiles into the CODIS database is faulty. Sexual assault cases may not be resolved because of the lack of convicted offender samples in CODIS. SAKI TTA has resources available to support jurisdictions addressing gaps in the collection, tracking, and processing of lawfully owed DNA samples. Additionally, SAKI TTA resources provide support to jurisdictions beyond addressing sexual assault kit processing to include supporting victims of sexual assault and improving investigative and prosecutorial approaches for sexual assault cases. In short, to effectively create sustainable, trauma-informed sexual assault response reform, jurisdictions will likely need to address the challenges and issues previously described in this chapter. SAKI TTA has provided freely available resources to address these challenges in order to support a national improved response to rape.

SAKI sites and visitors to the SAKI TTA website are encouraged to follow the SAKI program on social media (see Box 6.3 for social media handles associated with SAKI). SAKI TTA recognizes social media as a method to share information, including success across the SAKI program, in essentially real-time. The SAKI social media network has grown extensively to include SAKI sites, criminal justice and crime laboratory practitioners, researchers, advocates, and survivors. SAKI social media followers are encouraged to see the impact the SAKI program is having across the nation and are inspired by the stories of support to the victims of sexual assault and successful outcomes of these cases.

Box 6.3

Images associated with the sexual assault kit initiative

 @SAKInitative

 @sakinitative

In conclusion, SAKI TTA has been a trusted partner of the BJA SAKI program, supporting SAKI sites and jurisdictions across the nation since the inception of the program in 2015. The resources provided by SAKI TTA positively impact jurisdictions tackling unsubmitted sexual assault kits and an improved response to sexual assault by addressing challenges and providing assistance to meet their sexual assault response reform goals. SAKI TTA supports the creation of sustainable approaches for addressing sexual assault cases through evidence-based policies and practices aligned with national recommendations. By creating a web-based platform with a multimedia design, SAKI TTA has ensured freely available, sustainable resources for any jurisdiction addressing unsubmitted sexual assault kits and an improved response to sexual assault now and in the future.

Key Points

- Funded by the Bureau of Justice Assistance, the National Sexual Assault Kit Initiative leads the nation in supporting jurisdictions in an improved response to sexual assault.
- The SAKI program aims to create a coordinated community response to sexual assault that promotes survivor healing and ensures just resolution to sexual assault cases through a comprehensive, trauma-informed, and victim-centered approach.
- SAKI supports the SAKI sites by building jurisdictional capacity to prevent future accumulations of unsubmitted sexual assault kits and supporting the investigation and prosecution of cases associated with unsubmitted sexual assault kits.
- The SAKI TTA team assists in the development, implementation, and dissemination of best practices, as well as in the creation of policies and protocols for addressing systemic issues that lead to large numbers of unsubmitted sexual assault kits and preventing those issues from reoccurring in the future.

- The SAKI TTA program, led by RTI International and in partnership with a team of subject matter experts from various organizations, offers expertise, resources, training, and assistance to jurisdictions as they establish trauma-informed, victim-centered, evidence-based sustainable practices for:

  - Inventorying, tracking, and testing sexual assault forensic evidence from unsubmitted sexual assault kits;
  - Supporting survivors of sexual assault through victim-centered practices that promote healing;
  - Conducting trauma-informed investigations and prosecutions of cold case sexual assaults; and
  - Encouraging a partnership with researchers and crime analysts to better understand the factors that lead to a jurisdiction's accumulation of unsubmitted sexual assault kits.

Discussion Questions

1 What stakeholders should be included in a MDT?
2 What cold case sexual assault investigation policies and practices should be reviewed?
3 How does the victim advocate's role support law enforcement?
4 What are the key considerations for engaging with victims of cold case sexual assaults?
5 What are some of the issues resulting in sexual assault cases not be prosecuted?
6 What are some of the communication strategies for informing the community about sexual assault response reform?
7 How does lawfully owed DNA impact sexual assault cases?

Further Reading

SAKI Website: A clearing House of Valuable Resources

The SAKI website, https://sakitta.org, is a sustainable one-stop shop for criminal justice practitioners looking to find solutions, recommendations, and promising practices for addressing cold case sexual assaults and violent crime. The website hosts all the virtual resources, including the SAKI Virtual Academy, the SAKI Toolkit, SAKI webinars, SAKI recommendations for effective practices, and SAKI news and events. The resources on the website are not restricted to SAKI sites but are openly available to any agency seeking to improve their response to sexual assault.

Practitioner Guidance for Enacting an Improved Response to Sexual Assault

Addressing unsubmitted sexual assaults is a complex process for jurisdictions to undertake. However, criminal justice agencies have the power to create a strategic, sustainable plan for an improved response to sexual assault that aligns with current best practices and national recommendations. *Enacting an Improved Response to Sexual Assault: A Criminal Justice Practitioner's Guide* (https://www.rti.org/rti-press-publication/improved-response-sexual-assault) will help prosecutors and law enforcement agencies create a process with milestones, goals, and suggested actions, all designed to support a successful and sustainable approach for addressing sexual assault cases.

Lawfully Owed DNA, the Other Side of CODIS

Recent research, practitioner experiences, and media reports have confirmed that the CODIS database is not consistently populated with DNA profiles from convicted offenders and arrestees. Not effectively tracking, collecting, and processing lawfully owed DNA samples results in delinquencies in the ability of CODIS to make connections across cases and may therefore delay the identification of individuals and investigative leads for sexual assault cases. For further discussions on the issue of lawfully owed DNA, see Perspectives on Addressing the Collection, Tracking, and Processing of Lawfully Owed DNA Samples (https://forensiccoe.org/collecting-tracking-processing-lawfully-owed-dna-report/).

References

Campbell, R., Feeney, H., Pierce, S. J., Sharma, D. B., & Fehler-Cabral, G. (2018). Tested at last: How DNA evidence in untested rape kits can identify offenders and serial sexual assaults. *Journal of Interpersonal Violence*, *33*(24), 3792–3814. https://doi.org/10.1177/0886260516639585

Joyful Heart Foundation. (2016, March). *Navigating notification: A guide to re-engaging sexual assault survivors affected by the untested rape kit backlog.* Retrieved from https://issuu.com/thejhf/docs/navigatingnotification

Melton, P. A. (2020). *Enacting an improved response to sexual assault: A criminal justice practitioner's guide.* RTI Press. RTI Press Occasional Paper No. OP-0066-2007 https://doi.org/10.3768/rtipress.2020.op.0066.2007

United States Department of Justice Bureau of Justice Assistance. (2021, May 28). *BJA FY 21 National Sexual Assault Kit Initiative (SAKI).* Bureau of Justice Assistance. https://bja.ojp.gov/sites/g/files/xyckuh186/files/media/document/O-BJA-2021-94003.pdf

7 Advancing our understanding of sexual assault offenders

Rachel E. Lovell, Angela Williamson, Timothy G. Keel, Thomas Dover, and Mary Weston

Author Note and Funding Acknowledgment

This project was supported in part by Grant Nos. 2015-AK-BX-K009, 2016-AK-K016, and 2018 AK-BX-0001 awarded by the Bureau of Justice Assistance. The Bureau of Justice Assistance is a component of the U.S. Department of Justice's Office of Justice Programs, which also includes the Bureau of Justice Statistics, the National Institute of Justice, the Office of Juvenile Justice and Delinquency Prevention, the Office for Victims of Crime, and the SMART Office. Points of view or opinions in this document are those of the author and do not necessarily represent the official position or policies of the U.S. Department of Justice. A pilot research project was supported by a research grant from the Cuyahoga County Prosecutor's Office.

For decades, forensic evidence from hundreds of thousands of sexual assault kits (SAKs) remained untested in evidence storage facilities across the United States. As a result of the U.S. Department of Justice (DOJ) SAK initiative, 76 jurisdictions (to date) have received funding from this initiative primarily to inventory untested kits, submit them to a forensic lab for DNA testing, and investigate and prosecute the cases resulting from the testing (where applicable) (sakitta.org, 2022, Chapter 1).

Social and behavioral science research from the initiative is emerging rapidly as a result of the SAK initiative. This research, coupled with recent advancements in forensic technologies, demonstrates that some of what we thought we knew about sexual assault offenders was incomplete and inaccurate. This chapter explores how these two components—research and forensics—intersect in informative ways. First, we summarize how recent research and forensic advancements are shedding new light on sexual assault offenders and their behaviors. Second, we provide case study examples and implications for practice as guidance to law enforcement professionals on how these advancements can be used to inform the investigation and prosecution of sexual assault offenders.

Background of Authors

The authors of this chapter have divergent but overlapping areas of expertise. We bring our distinct perspectives to the topic and provide key lessons learned and recommendations. Rachel Lovell, PhD (co-editor of this book) is an applied criminologist and methodologist whose research focuses on gender-based violence, particularly sexual violence, and SAKs.

DOI: 10.4324/9781003186816-10

Angela Williamson has a PhD in Molecular Biology and over 16 years of experience as a forensic specialist working on complex criminal cases and missing/unidentified persons' investigations. Williamson has worked in state and private forensic labs and performed serological screening and DNA analysis on thousands of major crime cases. Currently, she is the Supervisor, Forensics Unit/FBI Violent Crime Apprehension Program (ViCAP) Liaison at the U.S. Department of Justice, Bureau of Justice Assistance (BJA). She developed and oversees the entire National Sexual Assault Kit Initiative (SAKI) in addition to other forensic-based programs at BJA.

Timothy Keel has an MS in Management and Leadership with over 40 years of law enforcement experience. He is a former Detective Lieutenant in the Baltimore Police Department, Homicide Unit. He is now a certified behavioral analyst "Profiler" in the FBI's Behavioral Analysis Unit (BAU).

Thomas Dover has a PhD in Computational Criminology and is a crime analyst in the FBI's BAU. He has over 25 years of experience providing analytical assistance to local, state, and federal agencies in investigating and prosecuting violent crimes. Dover's research focuses on modeling criminal behavior and offender decision-making, case-linkage analysis, identifying and reducing analytical and investigative bias, and developing methods to structure and automate case analysis techniques.

Mary Weston has a JD and has been an Assistant Prosecuting Attorney in the Cuyahoga County Prosecutor's Office since 2006. She joined the Cuyahoga County SAK Task Force when it was formed in 2013 and currently functions as its supervisor, overseeing all aspects of cold case sexual assault and homicide investigations and prosecutions.

Case Studies

The case studies provided in this chapter are primarily drawn from Cuyahoga County (Cleveland, Ohio) for three main reasons. First, Lovell has directed an action research project in collaboration with the Cuyahoga County SAK Task Force, led by the Cuyahoga County Prosecutor's Office, since early 2015. Second, the Task Force is an early adopter of the SAK initiative and has recently completed testing and investigating over 7,000 previously untested SAKs[1] resulting in over 800 indicted defendants (to date). Therefore, the Task Force has numerous illustrative examples and is far enough along in the process for the case studies to be discussed publicly. Finally, as a prosecutor and SAK Task Force supervisor, Weston has extensive knowledge of these cases.

Implications for Practice

The implications for practice sections have been written primarily by those with firsthand knowledge of law enforcement operational practices (Williamson, Dover, Keel, and Weston). The goal for these is to speak directly to those tasked with investigating, prosecuting, and working with sexual assault offenders to increase case solvability, improve public safety, and prevent further victimization.

Advancing What We Know About Sexual Assault Offenders

Prevalence of sexual recidivism and sexual reoffending

Sexual assault offending

Serial sexual assault offending is more common than we thought. Why? Because our ability to identify serial sexual assault offending and serial sexual assault offenders has been limited by incomplete information.

First, most sexual assaults go unreported to law enforcement (National Research Council, 2014). Sexual assault is the most underreported violent crime in the United States (Rennison, 2001). Rates of sexual assault (vs. reported sexual assaults) indicate that sexual assault impacts a significant portion of the population—one in five women and one in 38 men in the United States have experienced a completed or attempted forced penetration in their lifetime (Smith et al., 2017), with women and girls of color and LGBTQ populations experiencing sexual assault at higher rates than white, heterosexual, and cisgender women (Smith et al. 2017; Walters et al., 2013).

Second, even when sexual assaults are reported to law enforcement, arrests and convictions are rare. Out of every 100 sexual assaults, approximately a third are reported to law enforcement (Morgan & Thompson, 2022), 19 lead to arrest (Morabito et al., 2019b), and 5 lead to a conviction (plea or guilty verdict) (Morabito et al., 2019a). Case attrition is discussed in greater detail in Chapter 2 of this book. Therefore, what we know about sexual assault offenders is primarily based on those *convicted* of a sexual assault offense—the 5%. Unfortunately, studies based solely on convicted offenders vastly underrepresents sexual assault offending in general and serial sexual assault offending specifically.

Sexual recidivism and sexual reoffending

How common is serial sexual assault offending? The answer to this question depends on what and how we define serial and how we know about the multiple offenses. Criminal recidivism most often implies repeated adjudication in the criminal justice system (Deslauriers-Varin & Beauregard, 2013), meaning that the offender is connected to two or more crimes separated via arrest and/or conviction (Lovell et al., 2017), i.e., being "caught" (also referred to as "detected" or, more specifically, adjudicated) once and then being "caught" at least one more time. Yet, the level and nature of the recidivism matter—namely, *sexual recidivism* (for a sexually based crime) is different from *general recidivism* (for a non-sexually based crime). This operational definition stands in contrast to *repeat offending*, which means committing a crime and a subsequent crime (in a separate incident) regardless of whether the person was "caught" for one or more of the crimes. *Repeat sexual assault offending (serial sexual assault offending)* is committing a sexually based crime and then a subsequent sexually based crime, regardless of being caught for the offense.

The most recent *sexual recidivism* rates of sexual assault offenders in the United States come from a large representative sample of prisoners released from 30 states in 2005 and followed for nine years post-release. Approximately 8% of the released prisoners who had been convicted of a sexual offense were arrested for a subsequent sexually based offense within those nine years (Alper & Durose, 2019). Of note, this 8% sexual recidivism relies solely on official criminal justice system records—a *completed* prison sentence for a sexual offense followed by a *subsequent arrest* for another sexual offense within a limited time frame (nine years)—which, as discussed above, is a substantial undercount of sexual reoffending.

Self-reported sexual reoffending rates are much higher than recidivism rates. Since an estimated 95% of all offenders who commit sexual assault are male (Sandler & Freeman, 2009), one study chose to focus on the behavior of male college students. They found that 35% of these males reported some likelihood of committing a sexual assault if given the opportunity without being caught (Malamuth, 1981)—indicating a sizable number of potentially motivated sexual assault offenders given certain circumstances. In studies of commuter college students and military recruits, between 62% and 71% of men who self-reported ever sexually assaulting, attempting to sexually assault, or using coercion to sexually assault, did so more than once (Lisak & Miller, 2002; McWhorter et al., 2009). However, self-reported offending estimates also have significant limitations in that offenders must be able to recall, admit, and self-define these offenses as nonconsensual (LeBeau, 1985).

In summary, much of what we know about serial sexual assault offenders is based on those caught more than once by the criminal justice system or those who self-report serial sexual criminality. Both methodologies are likely to depict an unrepresentative picture of all serial sexual assault offending. *This is where data from the sexual assault kits come into play.*

Following up on testing DNA in previously untested kits enables a second look at past investigative practices. The DNA evidence collected from these kits can be used to connect previously unlinked sexual assaults by more objective means and without relying on adjudication or self-report. Additionally, SAKs include evidence gathered at the time of collection. This provides a more representative picture of reported sexual assaults because the availability of DNA for testing is not dependent on a successful adjudication. *In other words, data from kits provide a more accurate discernment of the extent and nature of serial (or repeat) sexual assault offending.*

Serial sexual assault offending from the SAK initiative

So how much serial sexual assault offending is being identified from SAK initiatives? Wayne County (Detroit, Michigan) and Cuyahoga County (Cleveland, Ohio)—two early adopter SAK initiative jurisdictions addressing a large number of untested kits—found that between a fourth and a third of the suspects connected to the now-tested kits can be identified as serial sexual assault offenders (Campbell et al., 2019; Lovell et al., 2018). While these numbers are much higher than the sexual recidivism estimates of 8%, they are likely still undercounts the rate of serial sexual assault offending for several reasons. First, they only pertain to sexual assaults committed in the respective SAK initiative jurisdictions, not those in surrounding counties or other states. Second, using DNA from previously untested SAKs to establish serial sexual assault offending is predicated on circumstances in which,

- A victim reported the sexual assault,
- A kit was collected,

- Law enforcement retained the kit, and
- Law enforcement personnel submitted the kit for testing.

Furthermore, the suspects had to be connected to these now tested kits in at least one of two ways—as a named suspect and/or through DNA. If connected by DNA, two additional criteria were necessary for the kits to be linked to each other.

- The kit included enough DNA from the suspect to meet eligibility for testing and
- The kit had enough DNA information to meet federal DNA database eligibility.

A breakdown with any of these criteria means the DNA did not make it into the system, and the sexual assaults would not be linked. In other words, *the rates of serial sexual assault offending are likely even higher than these a-fourth-to-a-third estimates.*

Case study from the Cuyahoga County SAK initiative

The most prolific serial sexual assault offender identified as part of the Cuyahoga County SAK initiative is connected by DNA to 22 rape kits in northeast Ohio. The sexual assaults started in 1995 when Ford was 28 years old and ended almost a decade later when he was finally caught at 37. Given that all of these sexual assaults were stranger sexual assaults and that it was only DNA that connected him to these sexual assaults, *the extent of his serial sexual assault offending would not have been known had it not been for the now-tested sexual assault kits* (Lovell et al. 2022).

Implications for practice

Based upon the preponderance of evidence from these now tested kits, *we recommend that law enforcement start a sexual assault investigation by strongly considering that a sexual assault offender has done this before, will continue to do this in the future, or both.* We encourage law enforcement to adjust how they consider the actions of sexual assault offenders. Based on the findings across SAK initiative jurisdictions, it is clear that many sexual assault offenders do not just commit one offense and stop. It is important to recognize that a significant proportion of these offenders will continue to sexually reoffend until they are apprehended and/or after they are released.

Consistency of sexual assault offenders' modus operandi and/or victim preference

Common perceptions of serial sexual assault offenders have been that they:

- Maintain a victim "type"—consistently sexually assault victims with certain characteristics, often demographic characteristics, such as victims of a particular age range, race/ethnicity, hair color, height, body structure, etc.
- Maintain a consistent relationship "type" with regard to whom they sexually assault—only strangers, only intimate partners, only acquaintances, and
- Maintain a consistent method of offending or *modus operandi (MO).*

Why do these assumptions remain? Because without testing all of the kits and revisiting past practices, *much of the repeat sexual assault offending that did not fit the offender's pattern remained unknown to law enforcement.* Investigative practices in many law enforcement agencies tend to address a sexual assault allegation as an isolated event or use the offender's MO and presumed victim preferences to potentially link other sexual assaults to that offender. Data from the SAKI indicate that these practices should be reevaluated.

Case study from the Cuyahoga County SAK initiative

The research partner for the Cuyahoga County SAK Task Force recalls when she first began collaborating, she would sit in on Task Force meetings as prosecutors summarized the cases soon going to trial (Lovell & Dissell, 2021). The cases often involved serial sexual assault offenders whose crimes had been linked together through DNA because these types of cases were prioritized for prosecution (Lovell et al., 2018). In those cases, prosecutors would often say things like, "he (the defendant) has these two (sometimes three, four, or more) rapes, and then there's the other one." They would then describe the facts of the linked cases. Inevitability, the "two" were similar, and the "other one" did not fit the pattern. The researcher frequently wondered *what about the other one? How many of these offenders have an other one? What can be learned from the other one?*

These early participant observations guided the direction of the ongoing research. The research team examined the characteristics of the sexual assaults committed by suspects connected to more than one sexual assault in the sample. They considered the victim's relationship to the perpetrator, the characteristics of the victims, the perpetrator's means of access to the victim, MO, etc. Armed with these unique data from the SAK initiative, the research team found that sexual assault offenders often "crossed over"—meaning they sexually assaulted victims who varied by relationship status, age, race/ethnicity, and even gender (Lovell et al., 2017).

For example, one offender was connected to three sexual assaults via DNA—two females in separate incidents and another incident where the suspect was linked to the sexual assault of a 29-year-old sleeping male in a group home. Another offender was one of four suspects involved in the sexual assault of a 13-year-old girl at a party (a stranger) and 2 months later sexually assaulted his 3-year-old son. In yet another series, the offender was linked to the sexual assaults of two women in separate offenses. One victim was his 13-year-old "girlfriend" (he was 20 years old). His MO involved manipulation of the victim in that sexual assault. In the other sexual assault, he vaginally, orally, and anally penetrated a stranger, keeping a gun to her head during the entire assault—a much more gratuitously violent sexual assault (Lovell et al., 2017).

Implications for practice

Previous to the success of DNA in identifying suspects across cases, the "traditional" method for linking serial sexual assault offenses was to concentrate on the offender's MO. The investigator's experience plays a significant role in interpreting a suspect's MO (including a deviation from it). Profilers in the FBI's BAU have experience interpreting offenders' behaviors on serial sexual assaults. BAU members consider several key factors in explaining offenders' deviations from an MO and their preferred victim selection process:

- *Desirability*—Who/what the sexual predator wants in a perfect situation is their preferred target. This is what drives them to commit crimes and engage in illegal activity.
- *Availability*—Who is available for the offender to target at that particular time. Many offenders choose to commit a sexual assault on a "less ideal" target rather than wait for the "perfect victim."
- *Vulnerability*—After looking at who is available to target, the sexual predator may assess if there is someone else more vulnerable to target. Offenders typically choose the easier target with a greater chance of a successful outcome—i.e., the sexual assault and getting away with it.

Another factor that has to be considered when assessing an offender's MO is that an MO is not "fixed" and may necessarily change for the offender to successfully offend. MO involves the practical behaviors employed by the offender. However, the offender's behavior is also an expression of his[2] fantasy, which may change due to the offender's internal affect, interests, and intentions. Therefore, an offender's behavior—including MO—is complex and exists at the intersection between the offender's internal drivers, external opportunities, and the environment that he must navigate.

To successfully sexually assault the victim, an offender must be minimally capable of adapting to a range of inhibitors and opportunities. For instance, he may intend to commit a sexual assault along a bike path. To do so, he may reason that he can wait for a victim, sexually assault her, and then run away with little risk. In reality, when he attempts to do so, he may find that a passerby interrupts the sexual assault, and he is nearly caught. Given these circumstances, different offenders may react differently.

- One offender may try again with little consideration of changing his MO.
- Another offender may learn from nearly being caught that he must isolate the victim and either abducts the next victim and attempts to move her away from the path into the woods or completely changes and opts to break into a house with a lone victim that he can isolate.
- Yet another offender may be driven by opportunity. His next victim may be someone that he is apt to be situationally isolated like a family member or intimate partner.

Each of these adaptations can look very different in terms of MO, even though they are all the result of the offender's internal drivers and their behavioral manifestation given the environmental opportunity.

Even considering these very complex factors, the BAU acknowledges and touts that behavior is trumped by DNA. Behavior is generally interpretive and, as such, is always "interpreted" with incomplete information. On the other hand, DNA can provide definitive evidence by positively identifying a specific suspect and connecting him to the victim and/or scene. This can provide investigators with conclusive evidence for linking the offender (known or otherwise) to other cases. These cases, which may or may not look similar and may or may not have similar victims, have become the best evidence for identifying, linking, and convicting suspects.

Data from the SAK initiative and the examination of previously untested SAKs demonstrate that offenders do not always choose the same type of victim, even if that is the offender's original preference. Therefore, when attempting to link cases together, investigators must factor potential divergence from an MO and victim type preference into their investigations when trying to link cases. The SAK initiative has taught us to cast a broader net.

Criminal versatility of sexual assault offenders

Sexual assault offenders are often viewed as a certain type of offender—one that solely or primarily commits sexually based crimes; however, recent research contradicts this assumption. Sexual assault offenders frequently commit other types of crimes (general offending) in addition to sexual assault offenses (sexual assault offending). In a study of prisoners released in 1994, in 15 US states, 3 years after their release, 5% of sexual offenders were arrested for another sexually based crime and 43% for any crime (Langan et al., 2003). However, general recidivism rates for those convicted of sexually related crimes are lower than for those convicted of non-sexually related crimes (Alper & Durose, 2019). In an analysis of defendants from the 75 largest counties in the United States who were referred to prosecutors on rape charges, 37% had at least one prior felony conviction, and 10% had five or more felony convictions (Reaves, 2013).

Our current understanding of the general and sexual assault offending behavior of sexual assault offenders has been limited because of the available methods by which criminal offending is assessed, tracked, and identified. *This is where data from the sexual assault kits come into play.* These data allow researchers to overcome some of these limitations by examining the general and sexual assault offending behaviors of large numbers of undetected sexual assault offenders (those not previously arrested and/or convicted of the sexual offenses associated with the kits), thereby allowing for a more expansive view of general and sexual assault offending. Some of these other offenses may have been precursors of, or related to, sexual assaults; however, many of them simply may show that these offenders are criminally versatile.

Case study from the Cuyahoga County SAK initiative

A prolific serial rapist and murderer identified in Cuyahoga County were linked to the rapes of seven women and the killing of one of them during a 15-year span. He is currently serving a 25-years-to-life sentence. Between rapes, he was in and out of prison for vehicle theft, felonious assault, arson, burglary, theft, and robbery. But until thousands of previously untested kits in Cuyahoga County were tested, including those connected to this offender, he had never been arrested for nor convicted of rape.

This offender is an extreme but not unique example of many of the undetected serial sexual assault offenders identified as part of the SAK initiative in Cuyahoga County. Many of these undetected sexual assault offenders have high rates of serial criminality—being arrested for multiple serious (often violent) felonies—not just rape. In one study from Cuyahoga County, these undetected sexual assault offenders had an average of almost seven and a half arrests for serious crimes, with the top decile having almost 19 arrests. However, because of underreporting and significant amounts of attrition for rape charges within the criminal justice system, two-thirds did not have an arrest for rape in their criminal history (Lovell et al., 2020a).

Implications for practice

While many sexual assault investigators understand that offenders may have other crimes directly or indirectly connected to sexual assaults, having previously untested kits tested and DNA profiles uploaded to the federal DNA database (called the Combined DNA Index System or "CODIS") has been an eye-opening lesson that indicates that most, if not all, sexual assault offenders commit other offenses, such as peeping, stalking, burglaries, and other crimes related to their search for a victim; robberies and thefts (possibly to support their crimes); drugs (possibly to use as a ruse); and trespassing (intelligence-related)—but also other types of crimes not related to sexual assault offending.

This information can and should be used for a variety of reasons. First, by conducting an analysis of minor crimes in the area, combined with a suspect's description, investigators are more likely to be able to obtain suspect information, including name and habits. Investigators may be able to collect evidence that links the now identified suspect to the rape when there had previously been no identifiable suspect. Second, by having a better understanding of the offender's likely prior acts, investigators have additional avenues to explore that may lead to additional criminal charges aside from the sexual assault(s). Additional charges may increase the probability of successful prosecution and may also result in a longer sentence.

Ensuring eligible individuals have their DNA in the federal DNA database

CODIS is the program and software that centralizes DNA profiles collected from individuals arrested and/or convicted of qualifying offenses across federal, state, and local forensic laboratories (Federal Bureau of Investigation, 2002). CODIS began in 1990 as a pilot project across 12 US states to help identify suspects and link crimes. It has taken decades to populate. As of October 2021, CODIS contained almost 20 million DNA profiles connected to individuals and 1.1 million profiles connected to crimes—profiles that remain in the database to help solve cold, current, and future crimes (Federal Bureau of Investigation, 2021).

Until recently, because so many SAKs had remained untested, potentially hundreds of thousands of profiles connected to suspected sexual assault offenders had not been entered into CODIS. Traditionally, even when kits were tested, they were primarily only connected to cases where victims were sexually assaulted by strangers *and* interested in participating in the prosecution, which resulted in a limited and unrepresentative number of sexual assault offenders being entered into CODIS (Luminais et al., 2017). *This is where data from the sexual assault kits come into play.*

The SAK initiative demonstrates why the practice of only testing kits collected from victims of stranger rape who were interested in prosecuting their offender was shortsighted. By testing all the kits—those associated with sexual assaults committed by non-strangers, from incidents that occurred outside the statute of limitations, and from victims who did not want to prosecute—law enforcement has continued to populate CODIS, identify previously unknown suspects, and connect previously unconnected crimes. Moreover, sexual assault is a type of crime that frequently results in a suspect leaving their DNA, making the collection of a kit particularly probative. Why? Because these DNA profiles extend beyond the crime in question.

In 2016, the US DOJ SAK initiative began providing funding to current SAK initiative sites to address issues of "owed" DNA. Lawfully owed DNA swabs are swabs that legally should have been collected and entered into CODIS based upon a qualifying offense but were not. This was done with the recognition that the more (lawful) profiles uploaded in the CODIS, the more robust the database becomes, thereby increasing the probative value in testing the kits via the increased probability of DNA matches in CODIS.

Case study from the Cuyahoga County

While many sexual assault offenders have prior arrests or convictions, this does not necessarily mean that their DNA has been collected and uploaded into CODIS. The identification of one high-profile Cleveland-area convicted serial rapist and murderer highlighted a systemic problem of not collecting and/or not entering lawfully owed DNA profiles from suspects into CODIS. In 2009, after discovering the bodies of 11 decomposing women in his home, officials also discovered that his DNA should have been in CODIS (but was not) after previously receiving a 15-year prison sentence for rape. Later, it was determined that his DNA had been collected, but his DNA was never entered into CODIS (Dissell, 2011).

While Cuyahoga County had documented failures with collecting lawfully owed DNA from offenders (Dissell, 2011), it remained unknown *how many individuals lawfully owed their DNA*. The Cuyahoga County Prosecutor's Office and its research partner (led by Lovell) are collaborating on a project to identify individuals who owe DNA, swab them, and follow up on what happens after their DNA profiles are entered into CODIS. This undertaking was funded through the BJA's SAK initiative. Through these efforts, almost 15,000 people were confirmed to owe DNA based on qualifying offenses committed in the county. Efforts remain underway to swab as many of these "missed" individuals as possible and address collection issues in the county.

Implications for practice

Investigators cannot assume that an offender's DNA is already in CODIS. Typically, eligible convicted offenders from whom DNA lawfully can be collected include those arrested, facing charges, or convicted of any felony. Felonies can include murder, sexual abuse, kidnapping, or other qualifying state offenses (DNA Analysis Backlog Elimination Act, 2000). Investigators also need to remain aware of local and state laws impacting their ability to upload convicted offender DNA to CODIS. These include state DNA laws, most of which only allow entry of a suspect's DNA into CODIS for convictions associated with crimes after 1994 or 1995 when these laws were enacted. As such, many offenders (incarcerated, paroled, or deceased) associated with older cases may not have had their DNA entered into CODIS. For example, in Ohio, state law prohibits law enforcement from compelling an individual to provide DNA if they were previously "missed" (e.g., should have been swabbed but were not) unless they are currently under the supervision of the criminal justice system (Lovell et al., 2020b).

As standard practice at the start of an investigation, law enforcement should first verify with their local or state CODIS administrator or statewide law enforcement databases (where applicable) that specific individuals of interest are in CODIS. Data should be collected and analyzed regarding where the "misses" are occurring, e.g., certain agencies or units within agencies, certain critical contact points in the criminal justice system, etc. This type of analysis will help determine if training would improve collection rates within the criminal justice system.

Exhausting all options for obtaining a DNA profile from collected evidence

The SAK initiative has primarily focused on SAKs that were never subjected to forensic analysis. However, given the rapid advancements in forensics technology, SAKs previously subjected to forensic testing that did not produce a DNA profile suitable for CODIS upload (or did not produce a CODIS hit) are an untapped source for gathering leads in unsolved crimes. In other words, some previously tested SAKs contain certain items of evidence that remain untested or were tested using older forensic technologies. This evidence may benefit from the application of newer and more advanced DNA methodologies. *This is where data from the sexual assault kits come into play.*

Early forensic testing of kits typically included only blood typing. Once DNA testing was more widely available, kits were often first serologically screened for the presence of bodily fluids (namely semen) before undergoing DNA testing and may have been tested using antiquated DNA methodologies (e.g., RFLP or DQAlpha) that are not eligible for CODIS entry. If the screened samples did not include the presence of foreign DNA (presumably belonging to the male suspect), they did not progress to DNA analysis.

These are defined as *partially tested SAKs* within BJA's SAK initiative. It is standard practice in many forensic labs to test the most probative samples—usually the vaginal, anal, and oral swabs—as determined by the lab's testing protocol or by the forensic specialist and based upon information provided in the SAK's medical documentation (see Chapter 16 for more details about what happens at the lab after the kit has been submitted). Thus, it is common for older kits to have items that were either not tested at all or were not tested using CODIS-eligible methodologies (for instance, they were only screened for serology). Additional items contained in the kits (victims' clothing, sheets, pubic hair combs, etc.) are typically tested only when specifically requested by law enforcement and approved by the lab. This usually occurs in instances when the tested samples from the kit did not produce a CODIS-eligible profile.

So, why is this important? It means that often there is forensic evidence contained in the kit that has not been fully leveraged and might help identify offenders in unsolved crimes. Below we detail a case study where this additional review and testing resulted in the conviction of a serial sexual assault offender.

Case study from the Cuyahoga County SAK initiative

In 2000, a 33-year-old woman was waiting at a bus stop when an unknown male in a vehicle approached, parked, exited his vehicle, and put a gun to her head. He forced her into his vehicle, drove to a parking lot behind an apartment building, and forced vaginal intercourse, ejaculating on the victim's stomach. As the perpetrator was cleaning himself up with a t-shirt, the victim unlocked the passenger door and fled, flagging down a city bus. She was later transported to the hospital, where a SAK was collected.

The victim's SAK was first tested—for serology—in 2012 by the state lab. This was the standard operating procedure at the time. The vaginal samples, oral samples, pubic hair combings, abdomen swabs, and genital swabbing from the kit were all negative—meaning "no semen identified." The only evidence not tested at the lab were the fingernail scrapings, head hair standard, and nasal mucous sample (Raible, 2021).

In 2017, at the request of the Cuyahoga County SAK Task Force, the state lab agreed to test the untested items in the kit. This time these same items were tested using the current standard operating procedures of the lab—the "straight-to-DNA" method, meaning no screening for serology first. They also retested the skin stain swabs from the victim's abdomen but with the "straight-to-DNA" method. This retest of the skin swabs from the victim's abdomen resulted in a CODIS hit to a named offender. The same male DNA profile was on the swab of the pubic hair comb that had never been tested. To rule out the possibility that the male DNA profile belonged to the victim's consensual partner, Task Force investigators showed a photo array containing the offender's photo to the victim in 2017. She could not identify the suspect as her assailant, but she confirmed that nobody in the photo array was a consensual partner.

The suspect in this 2000 rape was indicted and pleaded guilty to rape and kidnapping with firearm specifications and is now serving a 19-year prison sentence. This outcome is a direct result of the Task Force taking a second look at kits subjected to older forensic technologies to identify (potentially) never-tested items and/or retesting items in the kits using more advanced DNA technologies. This example is also illustrative of how forensic evidence contained in the kits could be fully leveraged to help identify sexual assault offenders in unsolved sexual assaults.

Implication for practice

What we are learning from the SAK initiative is that just because the kits have been previously subjected to some type of forensic testing, it should not be assumed that the forensic evidence has been fully leveraged. The work being done in Cuyahoga County is evidence of the value in consistently reviewing forensic evidence in cases where more current technologies may advance the investigation and produce leads. As detailed in Chapter 16, not all laboratories use the same techniques, and not all techniques are as sensitive or successful in terms of generating probative DNA profiles, especially in cold cases where the DNA might be degraded or present at low levels. DNA methodologies are also rapidly evolving. An item that failed to yield a DNA profile three to five years ago may hold valuable DNA evidence that could be obtained with a newer methodology. The SAK initiative has demonstrated the value of examining cold case sexual assaults in order to solve past cases and prevent future ones by getting violent offenders off the streets (Lovell et al., 2021).

The SAK initiative also demonstrates the need to view case files as "living" documents to be examined regularly. To fully leverage forensic evidence to solve crimes, law enforcement must have the tools in place to keep up with investigative advancements. One tool that helps keep case files accessible is searchable case file software. Although most law enforcement agencies now have electronic case management systems, digitized files are not always easily searchable. Often, electronic case files contain PDF documents in electronic file folders. The details of the crime and descriptions or lists of available evidence are buried in the reports' narratives—text that is not easily searchable and requires a person to examine the documents one at a time for each potential inquiry. This lack of searchability presents significant barriers to linking cases, identifying patterns, and leveraging forensic evidence. Future technological advances in law enforcement should include advancements in the accessibility and degree of interaction with criminal justice information.

Using forensic evidence as corroborating evidence

The SAK initiative has demonstrated that kits provide much more to law enforcement than identifying unknown suspects in cases where victims are willing and able to participate in the investigations and prosecutions (Luminais et al., 2017). SAKs can also be used to provide strong corroborating evidence of a victim's account of the crime and can even rule out suspects as perpetrators. *This is where data from the sexual assault kits come into play.*

Case study from the Cuyahoga County SAK initiative

In 2006, a woman and her 21-year-old son attended a work party in downtown Cleveland. After they left, they were entering their vehicle when an unknown male with a gun got in the back seat and ordered the woman to drive. The attacker forced her to drive to an industrial area with which he seemed familiar (and later it would be noted as being near his residence) and ordered both victims out of the car. The attacker forced the woman's son into the car's trunk and slammed down the trunk's lid. He demanded the female victim's wallet, then pulled down her pants and raped her. The sexual assault was disrupted by the woman's son, who broke free from the trunk through the car's back seat. The son tried to fight off the attacker, but the attacker shot the son in the chest (he survived) and then fled on foot.

The woman went to the hospital and a SAK was collected. The SAK was tested in 2006. Items in the SAK only contained the DNA of the victim's husband and did not contain any other DNA that could be attributed to the attacker, likely because the rape was interrupted. Crime scene investigators lifted a palm print from the car's trunk, but it did not produce a print that could be added to AFIS (the fingerprint identification database). In 2016, as part of the SAK initiative, the Task Force reviewed the file and noticed the female victim's pants were still being held in the police property room but had never been tested. The state lab agreed to take samples from the waistband of the pants, where the attacker had placed his hands to pull them down. Analysts obtained a male DNA profile from the waistband that was suitable for CODIS upload. It was uploaded and produced a hit to a known offender. The Task Force then requested that the palm print from the car's trunk be directly compared to the known offender's palm prints, and they were a match. He was indicted and later convicted of rape, kidnapping, and attempted murder and sentenced to 36 years in prison.

Implications for practice

With the absence of DNA from semen in the original testing of the kit, the above case study demonstrates the value in fully leveraging the forensic DNA through more recent technological advancements and the value in using the existing forensic evidence as corroborating evidence. The evidence strongly supports the victim's account of this crime by finding forensic evidence that matched what the victims' said happened—the palm print from the trunk and the DNA on the waistband.

There are many reasons why DNA would not be present in kits (e.g., no ejaculation, condom use, no penile penetration, delayed reporting). On the SAK Task Force, the testing produced a CODIS-eligible profile in 61% of the never-tested kits, meaning 39% did not have a CODIS-eligible profile (Lovell et al., 2021). The Task Force was able to get a result for this horrendous crime by taking a second look. It was one of 271 indictments in cases that previously had no offender DNA in the SAK uploaded to CODIS as of December 2020 (Lovell et al., 2021).

Expanding beyond CODIS and into forensic genetic genealogy (or forensic genealogy) to identify sexual assault offenders

The increased access to forensic genetic genealogy (FGG) by law enforcement is a very recent development in the forensic field. BJA's SAK initiative defines this as the combined use of traditional genetic profile information contained in publicly available DNA databases with publicly available genealogical research on family histories to help narrow down the list of suspects. *This is where data from the sexual assault kits (plus recent forensic advancements) come into play.*

FGG can be used in instances where there is sufficient DNA evidence from the crime to produce a profile eligible for upload into CODIS, but the upload fails to produce a match to a known offender. The genetic information is uploaded "into one or more publicly-available open-data personal genomics DNA databases or direct-to-consumer genetic genealogy services. The FGG profile is then compared by automation against the genetic profiles of individuals who have voluntarily submitted their biological samples or entered their genetic profiles into these [genetic genealogy services]" (U.S. Department of Justice, 2019, p. 3) This process produces a potentially short(er) list of (often distantly) related suspects.

This is where the genealogists take over. They take the shortlist and extensively research suspects, construct family trees, and search genealogy archives to narrow down the list of potential suspects even further to provide an investigative lead (or leads) on the suspect's identity. Below we detail a recent example of how this has been used to identify an offender.

Case study from the Cuyahoga County SAK initiative

As part of the SAK initiative in Cuyahoga County, there are nearly 200 indicted John Does—DNA profiles obtained from a now-tested SAK that are uploaded to CODIS but do not produce hits to known offenders. This means the DNA profile is from an individual whose DNA is not in CODIS (because otherwise, a "hit" would have resulted). The Task Force indicted these unique DNA profiles to stop the statute of limitations clock (20 years for most of these cases) in the hope that they will be identified at some later point. With FGG, the Task Force does not have to passively wait until the offender commits a qualifying crime that would put them into CODIS.

FGG has now been able to identify some of these sexual assault offenders. For example, one case that was solved by FGG involved a woman sexually assaulted by a stranger who broke into her Cleveland home in 1999. Her kit was tested as part of the SAK initiative. The results produced a CODIS-eligible DNA profile, but that profile did not match any known offender in CODIS. The DNA profile obtained from the SAK was indicted in 2018 as Cuyahoga County's 133rd John Doe indictment. In 2020, this kit was one of 20 kits identified by the state crime lab as a good candidate for FGG. In 2021, the Task Force sent the DNA profile to a private genealogy lab. Later that year, the lab provided the Task Force with the name of a suspect. Investigators on the Task Force surveilled the suspect and obtained a beverage bottle that he discarded. The state crime lab obtained DNA from the bottle, which matched the DNA in the victim's SAK. Task Force investigators then obtained the suspect's DNA standard for confirmation analysis and his DNA was confirmed to be the source of the DNA in the SAK. Cuyahoga County prosecutors then amended the name of the defendant on the indictment from "John Doe #133" to the suspect's true name.

Implications for practice

The use of FGG, in accordance with the DOJ Interim Policy (U.S. Department of Justice, 2019), should be considered in cases where sufficient DNA is available and prior uploads to CODIS failed to provide an investigative lead. FGG provides another avenue to leverage DNA evidence to mine ever-expanding public databases to identify offenders. FGG is particularly useful where the offender has a minimal or negligible criminal record or is deceased. These offenders are less likely to have an offender DNA sample in CODIS and, as such, would most likely never be identified without the application of FGG. Investigators should consider FGG as another valuable tool to identify violent offenders and provide answers to victims and families.

Using forensic evidence in interviews with suspected sexual assault offenders

As previously explained, the use of SAK initiative funds to analyze previously untested kits has led to an unparalleled opportunity for investigators to obtain corroborative evidence and identify previously unknown offenders. In the past, when DNA testing first became available, labs' "turnaround" times—the amount of time it takes to test a SAK—were long, often taking a year or more. This meant that investigations were delayed and that results were often not available before the suspect interview (National Institute of Justice, n.d.). Now, with shorter turnaround times, forensic evidence plays a more immediate role in investigations.

This final "lesson learned" is a bit different from the others. It is not so much about using data from SAKs to examine *past* practices to inform current investigative practice. Instead, this lesson pertains to how *current SAK initiative* practices can inform *current and future* investigative practices. This is due to the cold case nature of these cases. Interviews in the SAK initiative cases can now begin with forensic information in hand.

Implication for practice

Should an investigator be fortunate enough to obtain identifiable DNA evidence and locate the subject, the next step is "the interview." *Other than obtaining basic information, we would recommend not conducting a formal interview of a key subject until forensic examinations are completed. We recognize that may not always be possible in a new case but should be the standard in an unresolved cold case.* Before the actual interview, the investigator will typically conduct an extensive background on who the subject is (e.g., where they have lived, worked, marital status, etc.) and their criminal record to understand better what types of crimes they have committed. A timeline should also be developed with as much information as possible.

As tempting as it may be to do otherwise, investigators should consider not telling a suspect during the interview that his DNA was found on the evidence. Instead, interviewers should seek to obtain the suspect's full account of what happened. Often, suspects will strategically seek to distance themselves from the crime by lying about it; for instance, they may deny that they ever had sex with the victim or claim to be unfamiliar with the crime location. It is critical to obtain statements that will undermine a later manufactured defense of consent (often concocted after the benefit of legal counsel).

The interview should start friendly and create an atmosphere of cooperation. The interview is about getting accurate and pertinent information from the interviewee. Investigators should remember that a "negative statement" is as good or better than a denial statement. Examples of negative statements include: "I never met her," "I've never been there," or "I was out of state during that time, so it couldn't have been me." These types of statements (which should be video recorded) are ideal for use by a prosecutor and make it difficult for the defendant to claim later the sexual act was consensual, which is a typical tactic once DNA evidence is presented.

Should the interviewee state that he knew the victim intimately and that it had always been consensual, the interviewer should concentrate on getting accurate details specific to the sexual assault offense and concentrating on possible inconsistencies that may signify deception.

As previously stated, the data from the SAK initiative have more clearly indicated that many offenders (a) do not go after just one type of victim, (b) offend more often than is reported, and (c) typically engage in other crimes (both in terms of personal financial gain and in their search for a victim). Having this knowledge, the investigator/interviewer should take extra effort to review previous crimes that may be connected to the suspect. Knowledge is power and may lead the interviewee to believe that law enforcement knows more about him than he anticipated, putting the interviewer in a better position to obtain more accurate and relevant information.

Discussion

The SAK initiative has engendered a fantastic opportunity to explore sexual assaults and sexual assault offending behavior spanning decades and large geographical areas. Never before has there been the ability to assess sexual assault and sexual assault offenders at this scale and with this scope. This chapter explores eight lessons learned from this initiative that expands our knowledge of sexual assault offending by coupling recent research and forensic advancements. The chapter also presents the illustrative case studies from Cuyahoga County's SAK initiative and provides implications for incorporating these lessons for current and future investigations and prosecutions. The information provided here increased our collective understanding of sexual assault offending behavior and forensic advancements.

Key Points

The SAK initiative has advanced our understanding of sexual assault offending behavior in eight key ways.

- The prevalence of sexual reoffending is much higher than prior research suggests.
- There is less consistency in sexual assault offenders' *modus operandi* and greater diversity in their victim preference than prior research suggests.
- Sexual assault offenders are more criminogenic and criminally versatile than prior research suggests.
- Just because someone should have their DNA in CODIS does not mean they do. This has major implications for the robustness of CODIS.
- Just because a kit was subjected to some forensic testing does not mean all the options for forensically testing the evidence have been exhausted. This has significant implications for fully leveraging forensic evidence to identify offenders in unsolved crimes.
- In addition to DNA testing, evidence collected from kits can be used to corroborate victims' (and witnesses' and suspects') accounts of the crime.
- Recent advancements in FGG allow for the solving of crimes beyond the limits of the CODIS database.
- The SAK initiative provides helpful lessons to investigators on how to use forensic evidence in interviews with suspected sexual assault offenders in current crimes.

Discussion Questions

1 Before reading this chapter, what were some of your ideas about "typical" sexual assault offending behavior?
2 The SAK initiative research presented derives from victims of sexual assault who had kits collected, which is not likely to be representative of all victims of sexual assault. In what ways do you think this affects the lessons presented here?
3 FGG is controversial due to privacy concerns related to DNA. What are your thoughts on when and how this technique should and should not be used by law enforcement to solve crimes?

Notes

1 These ~7,000 kits are primarily from sexual assaults that occurred from 1993 through 2011. Almost all of them are from the Cleveland Police Department. Approximately 5,000 were kits prior to the formation of the SAK initiative had never been submitted for forensic testing and 2,000 had some prior forensic testing but not in alignment with current forensic technologies or practices.

2 We use the male pronoun for an offender because the vast majority of sexual assault offenders are male (U.S. Department of Justice, Federal Bureau of Investigation, 2019). This is with the acknowledgment that not all sexual assault offenders are male.

Further Reading

Beauregard, E., Rossmo, D. K., & Proulx, J. (2007). A descriptive model of the hunting process of serial sex offenders: A rational choice perspective. *Journal of Family Violence*, 22(6), 449–463. https://doi.org/10.1007/S10896-007-9101-3

Guerrini, C. J., Wickenheiser, R. A., Bettinger, B., McGuire, A. L., & Fullerton, S. (2021). Four misconceptions about investigative genetic genealogy, *Journal of Law and the Biosciences*, 8(1), lsab001, https://doi.org/10.1093/jlb/lsab001

Woodhams, J., Tonkin, M., Burrell, A., Imre, H., Winter, J. M., Lam, E. K. M., ten Brinke, G. J., Webb, M., Labuschagne, G., Bennell, C., Ashmore-Hills, L., van der Kemp, J., Lipponen, S., Pakkanen, T., Rainbow, L., Salfati, C. G., & Santtila, P. (2018). Linking serial sexual offences: Moving towards an ecologically valid test of the principles of crime linkage. *Legal and Criminological Psychology*, lcrp.12144. https://doi.org/10.1111/lcrp.12144

References

Alper, M., & Durose, M. (2019). *Recidivism of sex offenders released from state prison: A 9-year follow-up (2005–14)* (NCJ 251773). U.S. Department of Justice, Bureau of Justice Statistics. https://www.bjs.gov/content/pub/pdf/rsorsp9yfu0514.pdf

Campbell, R., Pierce, S., Ma, W., Feeney, H., Goddman-Williams, R., & Sharma, D. (2019). Will history repeat itself? Growth mixture modeling of suspected serial sexual assault offending using forensic DNA evidence. *Journal of Criminal Justice*, 61, 1–12. https://doi.org/10.1111/CICO.12108

Deslauriers-Varin, N., & Beauregard, E. (2013). Investigating offending consistency of geographic and environmental factors among serial sex offenders: A comparison of multiple analytical strategies. *Criminal Justice and Behavior*, 40(2), 156–179.

Dissell, R. (2011, May 17). "Anthony Sowell's DNA collected in prison is missing; 200 other untested samples discovered" *The Plain Dealer*. http://blog.cleveland.com/metro/2011/05/anthony_sowells_dna_collected.html

DNA Analysis Backlog Elimination Act of 2000, Pub. L. No. 106-546. (2000). https://www.congress.gov/106/plaws/publ546/PLAW-106publ546.pdf

Federal Bureau of Investigation. (2002, May 14). Testimony, Dwight E. Adams, Assistant Director, Laboratory Division, FBI, Before the Senate Judiciary Committee Subcommittee on Crime and Drugs, Washington, D.C. https://archives.fbi.gov/archives/news/testimony/the-fbis-codis-program

Federal Bureau of Investigation. (2021, October). CODIS-NDIS Statistics. https://www.fbi.gov/services/laboratory/biometric-analysis/codis/ndis-statistics

Langan, P. A., Schmitt, E., & DuRose, M. (2003). *Recidivism of sex offenders released from prison in 1994* (B. of J. S. US Department of Justice, Trans.; NCJ 198281). U.S. Department of Justice, Bureau of Justice Statistics. https://www.bjs.gov/content/pub/pdf/rsorp94.pdf

LeBeau, J. L. (1985). Some problems with measuring and describing rape presented by the serial offender. *Justice Quarterly, 2*(3), 385–398. https://doi.org/10.1080/07418828500088621

Lisak, D., & Miller, P. (2002). Repeat rape and multiple offending among undetected rapists. *Violence and Victims, 17*(1), 73–84.

Lovell, R. E., & Dissell, R. (2021). Dissemination and impact amplified: How a researcher–reporter collaboration helped improve the criminal justice response to victims with untested sexual assault kits. *Journal of Contemporary Criminal Justice, 37*(2), 257–275.

Lovell, R., Luminais, M., Flannery, D. J., Overman, L., Huang, D., Walker, T., & Clark, D. R. (2017). Offending patterns for serial sex offenders identified via the DNA testing of previously unsubmitted sexual assault kits. *Journal of Criminal Justice, 52*, 68–78.

Lovell, R., Luminais, M., Flannery, D. J., Bell, R., & Kyker, B. (2018). Describing the process and quantifying the outcomes of the Cuyahoga County sexual assault kit initiative. *Journal of Criminal Justice, 57*, 106–115. https://doi.org/10.1016/j.jcrimjus.2018.05.012

Lovell, R., Huang, W., Overman, L., Flannery, D., & Klingenstein, J. (2020a). Offending histories and typologies of suspected sexual assault offenders identified via untested sexual assault kits. *Criminal Justice and Behavior, 47*(4), 470–486. https://doi.org/10.1177/0093854819896385

Lovell, R., Klingenstein, J., Huang, D. & Weston, M. (2020b). *Final report: Outcomes from efforts to swab offenders who lawfully "Owe" DNA in Cuyahoga County.* The Begun Center for Violence Prevention Education and Research at Case Western Reserve University. http://hdl.handle.net/2186/ksl:2006068202

Lovell, R.E., Sabo, D. & Dissell, R. (2022). Understanding the geography of rape through the integration of data: Case study of a prolific, mega-mobile serial stranger rapist identified through rape kits. *International Journal of Environmental Research and Public Health, 19*, 6810, https://doi.org/10.3390/ ijerph19116810

Lovell, R. E., Singer, M., Flannery, D. J., & McGuire, M. J. (2021). The case for "investigate all": Assessing the cost-effectiveness of investigating no CODIS hit cases in a sexual assault kit initiative. *Journal of Forensic Sciences, 66*(4), 1316–1328. https://doi.org/10.1111/1556-4029.14686

Luminais, M., Lovell, R., & Flannery, D. (2017). *Perceptions of Why the Sexual Assault Kit Backlog Exists in Cuyahoga County, Ohio and Recommendations for Improving Practice.* Begun Center for Violence Prevention Research and Education at the Jack, Joseph and Morton Mandel School of Applied Social Sciences at Case Western Reserve University. http://hdl.handle.net/2186/ksl:2006061457

Malamuth, N. (1981). Rape proclivity among males. *Journal of Social Issues, 37*(4), 138–157.

McWhorter, S. K., Stander, V. A., Merrill, L. L., Thomsen, C., J., & Milner, J. S. (2009). Reports of rape perpetration by newly enlisted male Navy Personnel. *Sexual Abuse: A Journal of Research and Treatment, 24*, 204–218.

Morabito, M. S., Pattavina, A., & Williams, L. M. (2019a). It all just piles up: Challenges to victim credibility accumulate to influence sexual assault case processing. *Journal of Interpersonal Violence, 34*(15), 3151–3170. doi:10.1177/0886260516669164

Morabito, M. S., Williams, L. M., & Pattavina, A. (2019b). *Decision making in sexual assault cases: Replication research on sexual violence case attrition in the United States, 2006–2012.* Inter-university Consortium for Political and Social Research. https://www.ncjrs.gov/pdffiles1/nij/grants/252689.pdf. Accessed June 22, 2020.

Morgan, R. E., & Thompson, A. (2022 February). *The nation's two crime measures, 2011–2020.* (B. of J. S. US Department of Justice, Trans.; NCJ 03385). U.S. Department of Justice, Bureau of Justice Statistics. https://bjs.ojp.gov/content/pub/pdf/ntcm1120.pdf

National Institute of Justice. (n.d.). *Sexual assault kits: Using science to find solutions.* U.S. Department of Justice. https://nij.ojp.gov/sites/g/files/xyckuh171/files/media/document/unsubmitted-kits.pdf

National Research Council. (2014). *Estimating the incidence of rape and sexual assault.* National Academies Press.

Raible, T. (Host). (2021, August 27). Just partially tested sexual assault kits. (No. 173). In Just Science. RTI. https://forensicrti.org/episode-173-just-partially-tested-sexual-assault-kits/

Reaves, B. (2013). *Felony defendants in large urban counties, 2009-statistical tables.* U.S. Department of Justice, Bureau of Justice Statistics. https://www.bjs.gov/content/pub/pdf/fdluc09.pdf

Rennison, C. M. (2001). *Criminal victimization 2000, changes 1993–2000 with trends 1993–2000.* https://bjs.ojp.gov/content/pub/pdf/cv00.pdf

sakitta.org. (2022). SAKI grantee sites. https://www.sakitta.org/sakisites/

Sandler, J. C., & Freeman, N. J. (2009). Female sex offender recidivism: A large-scale empirical analysis. *Sexual Abuse: A Journal of Research and Treatment, 21,* 455–473. https://doi.org/10.1177/1079063209347898

Smith, S. G., Basile, K. C., Gilbert, L. K., Merrick, M. T., Patel, N., Walling, M., & Jain, A. (2017). *National Intimate Partner and Sexual Violence Survey (NISVS): 2010–2012 state report.* National Center for Injury Prevention and Control, Centers for Disease Control and Prevention (Atlanta, GA).

Smith, S. G., Zhang, X., Basile, K. C., Merrick, M. T., Wang, J., Kresnow, M. J., & Chen, J. (2018). *The national intimate partner and sexual violence survey: 2015 data brief–updated release.* National Center for Injury Prevention and Control, Centers for Disease Control.

U.S. Department of Justice. (2019). *Interim policy: Forensic genetic genealogical DNA analysis and searching.* https://www.justice.gov/olp/page/file/1204386/download

U.S. Department of Justice, Federal Bureau of Investigation. (2019). *National incident-based reporting system: Victims Sex by Offense Category.* ttps://ucr.fbi.gov/nibrs/2019/tables/pdfs/victims_sex_by_offense_category_2019.pdf

Walters, M. L., Chen, J., & Breiding, M. J. (2013). *The National Intimate Partner and Sexual Violence Survey (NISVS): 2010 findings on victimization by sexual orientation.* National Center for Injury Prevention and Control Centers for Disease Control and Prevention. https://www.cdc.gov/ViolencePrevention/pdf/NISVS_SOfindings.pdf

8 Current issues in understanding sexual victimization

Veronique N. Valliere

Author Note

The opinions or points of view expressed in this document are solely those of the author and do not reflect the official positions of any participating organization or the U.S. Department of Justice.

The woman was confused—he had never done this before, and it felt wrong. She said she "froze" and got "stiff." The victim was "in shock," thinking to herself, "This can't be right. What is he doing?" She tried to scoot away from his hands, but she had "nowhere to go." The victim purposefully kept her eyes closed tightly. She was thinking, "If I make eye contact, he will think I like it." Throughout the time he was assaulting her, the victim did not want to create a confrontation. "I was naked—he is huge," she said. She lay there "weighing options." Should she scream? Run out, go naked into the lobby? She began sliding down, trying to get off the table in the "least confrontational way." She began feeling nauseous, lying there with her eyes clenched shut, her heart racing, sweating, with a dry mouth. She said she was sweating so profusely, the sweat "started rolling down [her] ass." In the months following the assault by her massage therapist, the victim has developed enduring symptoms. She has panic attacks, intrusive memories, and disruptions to her sexual experiences. She suffers shame, guilt, and negative cognitions about herself, men in general, and intimacy. This victim did not report her assault until several other victims came forward.

This is the description from a victim of sexual assault with whom I worked. She was assaulted in a professional setting while getting a massage. As a clinical and forensic psychologist with over 25 years of experience treating offenders and victims of violence, I have had the opportunity to be involved with hundreds of victims through providing treatment, conducting evaluations, or consulting on their civil or criminal cases. I am frequently retained to provide expert witness testimony related to victim reactions and perpetrator characteristics. I have also worked with thousands of sexual offenders who know and can describe the behavior of their victims, which they use to their advantage. I have learned a great deal which I have made available for others through my book *Understanding Victims of Interpersonal Violence: A Guide for Investigators and Prosecutors* (Valliere, 2019).

Sexual assault continues to be a significant public health issue, complicated by persistent misinformation and misunderstanding of victims and the impact of trauma, both during and after an assault. The brief vignette that opens this

DOI: 10.4324/9781003186816-11

chapter captures the array of issues many victims of sexual assault face both during and after a sexual assault. The above victim's responses superficially appear to be counterintuitive and counterproductive. As the reader or observer, one might wonder: *why she did not run, why she did not report the assault, and how she could possibly be ashamed and guilty for something she did not deserve and did not give consent to?* Despite the #MeToo movement, despite the media and educational efforts of advocates, victims of sexual assault continue to encounter substantial stigma and misinformation regarding their response to sexual assault, even from educated professionals and helpers. Beyond the fact that persistent myths and misinformation continue to be a societal hurdle to disclosure and reporting (see Chapter 3) and interfere with a just and trauma-informed response to survivors, these myths and biases can also profoundly impact the investigation and prosecution of sexual assault cases, cases in which sexual assault rape examination kits (SAKs) can play a critical role.

This chapter has several purposes. The overall aim of the chapter is to provide education to combat misinformation and faulty expectations about victim behavior. It will provide a better understanding of what we now know about the impact of trauma both during and after an assault in order to more accurately understand the experience of victims. An accurate understanding of these issues is needed to better inform crucial decision-making, including decision-making that impacts the attainment and testing of rape kits.

In the sections that follow, trauma will be defined. This is followed by a section on the impact of fear on the victim and development and expression of trauma. The third section will explore how trauma impacts the victim's response during and following an assault. Finally, the last section will describe the enduring impact of trauma on the victim. Please see Chapter 5 for a first-hand account of a survivor's journey post-rape and in response to the long-delayed testing of her sexual assault kit (SAK).

What Is Trauma and What Causes It?

Trauma, as a term, has been used interchangeably to describe an event itself or the response to an event. The DSM defines trauma as the personal experience of a highly disturbing or damaging event (American Psychiatric Association, 2013). The event must be terrible, causing serious injury or a severe threat to one's life or physical or psychological integrity. Sexual assault commonly produces trauma in victims. Sexual maltreatment can produce trauma even if the sexual abuse does not include physical contact. Finding out someone has secretly videotaped a private sexual or intimate act, being exposed to someone's penis in a nonconsensual situation, and being sexually harassed are all acts of sexual maltreatment that can produce trauma.

What causes trauma?

In general, there are a number of elements of an event that are thought to contribute to the traumatic nature of it. The American Psychiatric Association (2013), in the diagnostic requirements for a trauma-related disorder, characterizes a traumatic event as one that poses actual or threatened death, serious injury, or sexual violence. Factors such as the degree of terror and helplessness experienced by the victim, the presence or lack of social supports, the frequency and duration of the event(s), the level of betrayal, the unpredictability of the event, and the preexisting factors of the victim are all contributors to defining if an event is traumatic (American Psychiatric Association, 2013; National Institute of Mental Health, n.d.). Not all terrible events cause trauma.

Additionally, there is no way to ascribe rankings to the presupposed severity of the event and its impact. Trauma is highly personal. The development of or protection from trauma is affected by a host of (or a multitude of) factors, including the victim's personality, experience, culture, prior history, and experience during the assault. A victim who is regularly raped by her drunk husband might suffer less profound trauma than a patient whose doctor rubs his erect penis against her during an office visit. Abrahams et al. (2013) provide one example of a study that contradicts the belief that violent sexual assault causes more psychological harm than less violent assaults. In fact, victim self-blame, a contributor to trauma and depression, is greater in assaults that are less violent and more confusing to the victim (Kahn et al., 2003). Violent assaults are more easily identified as wrong, resulting in less victim-blaming. What is important in working with victims of assault is to **never assume** the level of impact that a victim experiences from an assault of any type.

When does trauma start?

The appearance and development of trauma are complicated. It does not necessarily have a predictable appearance or course. Generally, trauma is thought of acute or chronic—acute trauma appearing close in time to the traumatic event while chronic trauma endures over time. Trauma may have an impact on a victim of assault during that assault. Or a victim might not develop trauma until well after the sexual assault or abuse. Trauma might not be a consequence of one event but a result of accumulated experiences. Trauma can be confounded by elements of love, betrayal, dependency, and an accumulation of events. There are a limited number of diagnoses in the 5th edition of the Diagnostic and Statistical Manual (DSM5, American Psychiatric Association, 2013) used by American clinicians to identify mental disorders. Most victims of assault will not develop a diagnosable chronic trauma disorder, though they will suffer with traumatic impacts of the assault on a subclinical level, like anxiety, depressive symptoms, intrusive memories, or intimacy disruptions. The development of trauma can come later when the victim is able to label the behavior of the perpetrator. For instance, a child who cannot cognitively or emotionally appreciate the intention and gratification of someone who sexually abuses them and the meaning of the sexual acts might develop trauma as they mature, becoming better able to fully understand the abuse on a different level. There is research indicating that a victim's negative experiences with the criminal justice system and law enforcement or other types of "disastrous disclosures" can be the cause of the victim's trauma, not the assault itself (Valliere, 2019).

Are all victim reactions and responses to assault related to trauma?

While appreciating the impact of trauma is imperative in understanding victim behavior, trauma is not the only thing that drives victim responses and reactions to sexual assault. Trauma is one influence; it is important to be aware of the myriad of factors that victims negotiate in their decision-making and reactions. Each and every victim brings with them internal factors, previous experiences, and external factors that help them navigate a sexual assault. There are social influences, including power and status. A victim might be from a culture that dictates behavior, whether it is sexual behavior, gender-normed behavior, or reporting behavior. There might be a preexisting relationship with the offender that highly influences the victim's perception, reactions, and strategy during the assault. The victim might have prior experiences with abuse that have taught them how to react. The offender might have engaged in behavior that dictates the victim's reactions. There are far too many influences on victim response to address in this chapter; however, the victim can likely inform an investigator or clinician about these influences if properly and empathically interviewed. There is a movement in the field to train investigators in trauma-informed interviewing of victims of assault, something proving to be beneficial to victims and law enforcement officers (Lathan et al., 2019, 2021).

Also, it is crucial to remember two other things when attempting to understand a victim's behavior and response to assault. First, there are normal human processes at play even during sexual assault. As depicted in Box 8.1, cognitive biases play a huge role, both for the victim and for the community who is attempting to understand and evaluate the victim's behavior. A key example of this is *hindsight bias*. Hindsight bias is the bias that allows us to rewrite history. It is our tendency to revisit the past with new information without the recognition that we are using this new information (Kahneman, 2011). It is the bias that compels victims to ask, "Why did I go out with him? Why didn't I scream? Why didn't I see the red flags?" Society judges victims this very same way, especially in the legal process, scrutinizing each and every decision to determine the "dumb" choices the victim made and how they were to blame for the outcome. Somehow, it is forgotten that the victim could not predict the outcome at the time they were making these decisions. "People asked me 'what did you expect' when you picked a male massage therapist," a victim recently stated to me, "I answered them that I expected a massage!" This is only one example of a bias that impacts a victim. Another example is the belief that in a "just world" or karma, bad things do not happen to good people or things happened for a reason. Many of

---

Box 8.1

How do biases impact victims?

Biases are cognitive schemas that organize the world for humans, unconsciously causing an inclination to hold on to a particular perspective. They provide speedy and efficient ways to organize information, especially in regard to threat or risk. But they are inaccurate. For victims, biases contribute to disbelief, failure to recognize an assault when it does not fit the typical definition of rape or assault, and denial of the attacker's intention, motivation, and character. Through attribution bias, victims can give inaccurate reasons or causes for behavior, like thinking, "If he wasn't drunk, he wouldn't have raped me," or "I provoked the assault by flirting." Loss aversion can drive a victim to stay with an abuser. Others rely on biases to judge the victim, form expectations for behavior, and identify perpetrators. For example, the halo effect, a bias that makes us think of people as "good" when they perform good acts, contributes to the disbelief of allegations—"he's not like that."

us maintain the belief that we can control things and protect ourselves by making "good" decisions. Women are regularly schooled and advised on avoiding "dumb" choices to make regarding sexual assault.

Second, research continues to demonstrate that society persistently believes rape myths (Lonsway et al., 2001). In the common internalized narrative the public carries, sexual assault is a clearly identifiable, chaotic, often violent event that occurs between strangers and includes some type of penetration. Many of our faulty expectations of victims come from those persistent myths about rape and sexual assault. Not only does the public maintain those beliefs, but victims do as well. This leads to a victim's confusion about an assault that does not fit the narrative of "real rape," resulting in an array of behaviors reflecting this confusion. A victim who does not label a sexual assault accurately might not act in ways that would presumably protect them, like escaping, stopping contact with the offender, resisting physically, or doing other behaviors that are expected by victims. The bottom line is that individuals respond to assault individually and unpredictably. There is no set of responses that are to be expected, that "prove" someone was assaulted, or that can be reliably predicted based on knowing only a few details of the traumatic event.

Despite the fact that there is no "typical" response to violence, professionals in the clinical and criminal justice arena often rely on using victim responses to judge victim credibility or offender culpability. Long et al. (2013) wrote, "These fallacies have been reinforced for centuries by public discourse, inadequate laws created by misguided and uneducated legislators, and the various defense strategies designed to discredit victims by the exploitation of common rape myths." Faulty

---

Box 8.2

What are issues that are commonly faced by male victims?

In general, most victims are female or identify as female. When a victim identifies and is seen as male, there are additional internal and external barriers to help-seeking (Valliere, 2019). These include:

- Demands of traditional masculinity in regards to vulnerability, weakness, and help-seeking;
- Stereotypes of male sexuality, promiscuity, and receptiveness;
- Male sexual response;
- Failure to identify women as perpetrators or attackers;
- Shame and stigma;
- Victim-blaming and poor experience with law enforcement; and
- Minimization of the assault and impact.

Males are not the only victims who face additional barriers to help or reporting. LGBTQ+ victims, rural victims, victims of color, incarcerated victims, and disabled victims all have added challenges when victimized by sexual assault (Valliere, 2019). Assess and acknowledge each victim's potential barriers to reporting and help-seeking to properly support and address a victim.

expectations not only contribute to victim-blaming and failure to appreciate and understand victim response, but they also contribute to the failure of the criminal justice system to hold offenders accountable. When laypeople rely on myths and misinformation, they may inaccurately label a victim as a liar, minimize the offenses the victim has endured, and dismiss the victim's allegations and testimony about violence.

Victims face the impact of misinformation throughout the experience of sexual assault. We have a relatively limited understanding of sexual offenders' behaviors (Lovell et al., 2020) and continued problematic expectations of victim response (Valliere, 2019). People tend to believe that danger is foreseeable and preventable, relying on stereotypes about people who assault and situations that "invite" sexual assault. The barriers that victims face in reporting, help-seeking, and participating in prosecution are immense. As highlighted in Box 8.2, these decisions are complicated. They are complicated by other reasons as well: sexual identity, cultural affiliations, race, gender, access to services, poverty, experiences with law enforcement, and more. Understanding trauma and its impact on victim behavior is one way to decrease these barriers and facilitate appropriate and supportive responses to victims from law enforcement and other helpers.

Fear, Threat, and Trauma

First and foremost, it is our body's job to survive and defend. When we are attacked, physically or psychologically, we react first in a primal way. During an attack, the brain's primary and immediate response is to defend itself, whether this is a physical, emotional, or sexual assault. When a threat is identified, when the victim understands that the attack is inevitable, regardless of how the process of that attack occurred, fear or self-defense is the natural response (Kozlowska et al., 2015). This sense of threat activates several physiological responses in victims of attack and also among those who experience repeated lesser sexual traumas, like sexual harassment.

Is it fear or something else?

The word fear, however, is used interchangeably in the literature to describe both subjective, affective experience and physiological responses. Some advocate a differentiation between the use of the word fear—a conscious cognitive experience—and defense—the physiological response to a threat (LeDoux & Pine, 2016). Fear is a word typically used to describe an emotional experience, not a physical one. Physiologically, the body can respond to threats in order to defend itself, even without the conscious feeling of fear. It is useful to understand these differentiations, especially as victims may not experience or identify fear as a primary response to an assault. In fact, many victims use words that do not reflect fear to describe their emotions during the assault. Instead, they use words like confused, shocked, or uncomfortable.

Likewise, fear or terror is often not a response to coercive events or assaults that occur when the victim is intoxicated, asleep, or unconscious. By understanding the body's response to threat through a defense circuitry that is automatic and unconscious, we can better accept that trauma can have an impact on a victim even when the victim is not consciously experiencing terror or fear.

Additionally, it is important to recognize fear can result from other sources rather than the assault itself. Victims might fear the violation, the humiliation, or the perpetrator. They might fear being seen in a vulnerable position or as violated or they might fear the consequences that might ensue from the attack. A victim can fear that the attack might be worse if the abuser is provoked. Victims can fear getting pregnant or a disease. A myriad of fear-based thoughts can go through a victim's mind during an attack—or no thoughts at all as terror and fear make the victim freeze. Freeze is a reaction that is discussed in greater detail below.

Emotional impact of fear

Fear, as an emotion, magnifies our prediction of harm and decreases our likelihood of engaging in risky options like fighting back (Baron, 2007). Fear may cause someone to overestimate the danger of resistance, perceive another as capable of being more violent than they might be, or feel peril when considering enacting an unfamiliar behavior. The cognitive impact of fear leads victims to make choices to submit to attacks, placate the offender, or just "wait until it is over." While the expectation is that a victim will fight earnestly to protect themselves from being assaulted, overcome fear, and act in their own defense requires the development of habits for self-defense (Hopper, 2018), which most victims are unlikely to have. Moreover, if the victim has a prior history of abuse, they might rely on old habits, like submission, dissociation, or pacification of the offender that have worked in the past.

Fear may not only influence the victim's decisions during an assault but after as well, pervading decision-making throughout the victim's experience. The victim might fear retaliation from the perpetrator or others. They might fear that no one will believe them. The consequences of disclosure are a source of profound anxiety and fear for victims (see Chapter 3). There can be many sources of fear or anxiety for the victim, all of which should be explored and acknowledged as affecting the victim's behavior. The fear of consequences and not being believed might arise immediately, overshadowing the assault itself. These are not unwarranted fears; studies show that not being believed, negative experiences with law enforcement, social supports, or the prosecutor can be more traumatic than the assault itself (Valliere, 2019).

Physiological impact of fear

Fear and/or the activation of the defense circuitry has a profound physiological impact. We have evolved to defend ourselves; we are hardwired to respond in ways that will promote the probability of survival. Physiological responses to threats are complex, unconscious, and often out of our control. When faced with a serious threat, a series of neurobiological responses occur. This is referred to as the "defense cascade" (Kozlowska et al., 2015). This defense cascade produces a number of unmanageable and misunderstood effects on the victim that can affect the victim later in terms of self-blame, trauma, memory, disclosure, and decision-making.

Freezing

Most have heard of the flight or fight response, the response that activates the body for a call to action. However, the first physiological response to a threat is to freeze. The freeze response is effective because it allows a threatened being to avoid being detected (like a prey animal in the brush) and gives time to process and assess danger. Freezing helps the body prepare for action (Roelofs, 2017). Freezing is generally an immediate but transient response. When the person experiences shock or disbelief about what is happening, freezing can be more prolonged with the body and brain unable to process the experience event. Many victims will say they were "shocked," that their mind "went blank," or that they "shut down" during the assault. These experiences are common with the freeze response.

Prior trauma or adverse experiences can "prime" someone to experience freezing (Kozlowska et al., 2015). A victim who freezes might experience more terror or a profound sense of helplessness during the assault. "I was literally frozen," the victim explained when she awoke to find the perpetrator penetrating her from behind, "I tried to open my mouth to scream and nothing came out. I have never felt anything like that before. Then it was too late anyway." This feeling of helplessness can lead many victims to a diminished sense of competency, greater self-recrimination and confusion, and an amplified feeling of vulnerability. "I always thought I knew what I would do in that situation," a victim reported, "Now I don't trust myself. I will never say I know myself again." This victim now carries pepper spray and a weapon all the time. She feels vulnerable and exposed after her assault, a dramatic change from the athletic, independent woman who would backpack in the woods alone.

Tonic immobility

A victim who freezes during an attack can get trapped in a response known as "tonic immobility." Tonic immobility is a primal defense mechanism, often known as "playing dead" when faced by a threat in order to confuse or discourage the attacker. In humans, it is elicited in situations when escape or fighting is impossible (Kozlowska et al., 2015). In the sexual assault literature, it is sometimes referred to as "rape paralysis." While freezing is brief, tonic immobility can last substantially longer and occurs later in the defense cascade (Roelofs, 2017). There is evidence that humans experience tonic immobility (Volchan et al., 2011), and sexual assault is the most likely event to trigger it. Victims who experience tonic immobility, both men and women, are more likely to have post-traumatic symptoms (Coxwell & King, 2010).

Call to action: The sympathetic nervous system

After the body freezes, a response activated by the parasympathetic nervous system, whose job is to slow things down, the sympathetic nervous system kicks in, producing the fight or flight response. This takes some time, as physiologically, the body must shift from passive to active defending (Roelofs, 2017). In the meantime, the assault might be finished and the immediate threat is over. A sexual assault can be over in seconds or minutes - before the victim can fully appreciate or even identify the event. The physiological response to fight or flee can be mitigated by the victim's conscious decision-making, like to submit. It can also take a different than expected form, like a victim who seeks flight mentally by dissociating, the defense mechanism that allows a victim to "check out" or separate from the event psychologically. Despite the conscious decision-making or behavioral outcome, the victim will still experience the physiological response to the fear. The victim of a sexual assault during a massage cited at the start of this chapter described this, saying, "I just laid there. My heart was pounding so hard. I was sweating so badly that sweat was rolling down my ass." The attacker kept telling her to "relax" during the assault, commenting on how taut her muscles were. This victim had the physiological response to the assault while controlling her outward behavior—inside, she was panicking.

Actual physical flight from a situation sounds simple but is very complicated. It requires the victim to assess not only the situation in its entirety but also to determine the practicality and consequences of flight. "I could only imagine having to run out of the room naked, wrapped in a sheet, without my keys," a victim thought. An attempt to escape during an assault, or even after, might result in more serious consequences than the assault itself. It might trigger physical assault or backlash from the perpetrator. It might bring attention from outsiders who may pose a danger to the victim, like friends of the attacker, or someone else might be endangered by the victim's behavior, like a child. One victim was shot at by her husband in their home and was able to escape. However, the children were left in the home. Her husband took the children hostage, requiring a SWAT team to come to rescue them.

The fight response is even more unlikely during an attack. In a study focused solely on convicted rapes of victims by strangers, only 17% engaged in active physical violence, mainly kicking during the rape (Woodhams et al., 2011). While the sympathetic nervous system floods the body with adrenaline and other chemicals, preparing the body for action, these chemicals impair thinking and decision-making. When the victim has no strategy for fighting, what ensues is a panicked response that is often ineffective for self-defense (Roelofs, 2017).

Cognitive Impact of Trauma

Neurobiology is complex. The brain is full of structures with different functions that impact heart rate, respiration, memory, thinking, and behavior during an assault. Their interactions are multifaceted, involved, unconscious, and reflexive. *What is simple is to understand that a traumatic event or threat floods the brain with numerous chemicals that affect how a victim perceives, decides, and remembers.* These hormones or chemicals include adrenaline, cortisol, oxytocin, and others. This flood of chemicals significantly impacts how the brain processes information, affecting structures of the brain, including the hippocampus, amygdala, and prefrontal cortex. The structures of the brain compete with one another and get disorganized, inhibiting the proper functioning in terms of memory formation and consolidation and thinking and reasoning (Campbell, 2012; LeDoux & Pine, 2016; Schwabe, 2017).

Memory and trauma

The issue of trauma and memory has been long debated and studied in the literature (see Crespo & Fernandez-Lansac, 2016 for a review). Issues of false memory, suggestibility, and recall have been studied and written about extensively (e.g., Brainerd & Reyna, 2005; Williams & Banyard, 1999). Traumatic events are associated with periods of forgetting or failure to recall the event at all, called traumatic amnesia, in a significant percentage of victims (American Psychiatric Association, 2013). Psychological defenses of denial, dissociation, depersonalization, and repression/suppression impact memory as well. These defenses disrupt the normal integration of cognitive function, including memory, perception, consciousness, and behavior, often following a traumatic event (American Psychiatric Association, 2013).

Memory is complex and involves several different components: encoding, storage, and recall. The structures of the brain that get disorganized during a traumatic event can disrupt the encoding and accuracy of the memory (Cozolino, 2017). The hippocampus, the structure of the brain responsible for organizing and encoding memory, is sensitive to stress chemicals. Trauma can cause this structure to be less effective, resulting in fragmented or temporally disorganized memories. A victim might have missing pieces of events or remember them in a somewhat disorganized order (Schwabe, 2017). Characteristics of the event, the offender, and even the forensic interview, can also impact memory and disclosure processes, as summarized in Box 8.3.

This is not to say that a victim's memory is fraught with relevant inaccuracies. In fact, stress and arousal may facilitate specific and long-lasting memories for salient and important elements of a traumatic or stressful event (Hoscheidt et al., 2014; Mather & Sutherland, 2011). A victim may remember the subjectively most important details or more details closer to the event while forgetting or never encoding more peripheral or less proximal details. Traumatic memory for salient details can be "burned in" someone's mind, sometimes referred to as a flashbulb memory. For example, a victim may vividly remember the smell of the perpetrator's breath and the feel of his erection against her while forgetting the order of events or what she was wearing. This does not correspond well with the need for chronology, detail, and "facts" that are the focus of a criminal investigation. Often the assumption can be that the victim would or should have access to information as if the memory was a recording. When it is not, the victim can be judged as lying by interviewers.

In the experience of a traumatic event, what is central or important to a victim might not be important to a third party who did not experience that event. The same is true for peripheral details. Multiple events, especially those that more or less follow a routine, can get confused regarding peripheral details, as opposed to the unique or central elements to a victim that might characterize the assault. A simple Internet search of Dr Blasey-Ford's issues with recall regarding her allegations of being assaulted by Brett Kavanaugh illustrates the substantial ongoing discussion regarding this issue, along with other issues of victim recall. For another example of this, see Chapter 5, Alexenko's first-hand account of her sexual assault, where she remembers the gun held by the perpetrator but was not able to describe the perpetrator.

Thinking, deciding, and trauma

Thinking under stress is difficult. The brain relies on "fast" thinking—emotional, reflexive, and automatic (Kahneman, 2011). Again, neurobiological responses to stress and threat decrease the activity of the executive functioning of the brain, occurring in the prefrontal cortex. We begin to rely on engrained reflexes and habits (Kozlowska et al., 2015). Victims talk about going on "automatic pilot." Victims who

---

Box 8.3

Considerations that impact memory and disclosure

There are many issues that need to be considered in understanding a victim's memory or disclosure. These include:

- **Multiple interviews**—multiple interviews are necessarily going to produce "inconsistencies" as recall and tell of any single event repeatedly is going to change in subtle or incidental details.
- **Impact of interviewer**—the interviewer will have a significant impact on what is disclosed and how it is disclosed, as well as how it is documented. What is asked, how it is asked, and the interviewer's interest and judgment all impact the interview and disclosure.
- **Purpose of the interview**—Different types of interviews elicit different information.
- **Repeated assaults or trauma**—events can become confused or commingled for peripheral details when assaults occur repeatedly by the same offender.
- **Passage of time**—the passage of time necessarily includes some erosion of peripheral details, forgetting, or inaccuracy of memories that were not revisited or reinforced.
- **Influence of the offender**—The offender can have an influence on how the victim remembers or interprets events, especially when the sexual assault is not clear and overt.
- **Intoxication**—intoxicants can impact memory formation and recall. Shame of the victim for using intoxicants can impact disclosure.

---

were previously assaulted rely on previously learned strategies for survival. Many victims report not being able to think at all, experience confusion, or have thoughts they believe are unrelated or "crazy" in the context of the assault. "All I could think about was if the kids were going to come home or if dinner would be ready," one victim said to describe her confusion. She reflexively thought about things involved in her daily schedule. Planning for escape or resistance was not possible for her. This disorganization can compromise decision-making, strategizing, or judgment.

Finally, the experience of intense fear or terror can leave victims exhausted. There is an adrenal dump in self-protection and recuperation. Exhaustion can set in and cause severe lethargy. Other short-term physical and cognitive effects include, among others, difficulty concentrating, distortions of perception, depersonalization, helplessness, or disorientation (SAMHSA, 2014). The victim might be literally unable to consider escape or leaving. Referred to as quiescent immobility, it is the state of complete exhaustion that occurs after a trauma when the victim has returned to a state of relative safety, like when an attack is over (Kozlowska et al., 2015). While adaptive for healing, it is maladaptive for the expectations we place on victims. Victims who fall asleep in bed with the attacker are confronted with disbelief about the allegations. After all, if they had just been raped, wouldn't they want to get help? "He came," the victim explained, "He always fell asleep after he came. It was over. I knew it was over." This victim provides an example of both her exhaustion as well as the subjective assessment of threats that victims make in order to guide their decisions.

Enduring Impact of Trauma and Sexual Assault

Sexual assault almost always has enduring effects on the victim. These effects can be physical, behavioral, or psychological. Sexual assault is the traumatic event most likely to cause post-traumatic stress disorder (PTSD) when compared with other types of trauma, though the minority of sexual assault victims develop PTSD (Domino et al., 2020). While the impact of sexual assault might not produce symptoms that rise to a diagnosable level, sexual assault almost always changes the victim.

Trauma-related disorders and symptoms

The most commonly known disorder related to trauma is PTSD (American Psychiatric Association, 2013). PTSD is described diagnostically as a disorder that occurs following a traumatic event. The symptoms of the trauma persist for more than a month after the stressor. Symptoms that occur right after the assault up to a month are diagnosed as acute stress disorder. The symptoms are clustered in four general categories: intrusive symptoms, avoidance symptoms, negative alterations in cognitions and mood related to the trauma, and increases in arousal and reactivity. The victim with PTSD can experience intrusive thoughts or memories of the assault, flashbacks, dreams, or nightmares. The victim will actively avoid thoughts, feelings, or triggers reminding them of the assault. Negative thoughts involving self-blame, negative expectations or beliefs about others or themselves ("I am damaged"), or distorted thoughts about causes or consequences can be present. The victim may experience feelings of isolation, estrangement, or detachment from others. They may lack interest in activities or fail to experience pleasure in things they used to enjoy. Irritability, a heightened startle response, sleeping, and concentrating difficulties are all hallmarks of hyperarousal. Self-destructive or reckless activities reflect the victim's difficulties with impulsivity and reactivity. The development of PTSD can be mitigated or facilitated by the victim's social support system, relationship with the offender, or perception of the event (Domino et al., 2020).

Victims of sexual assault may receive diagnoses that reflect increased anxiety or depression. Some adults and children who have been traumatized and abused might be misdiagnosed or incompletely diagnosed. A victim who is diagnosed with attention deficit hyperactivity disorder (ADHD) might actually be displaying symptoms of trauma. Another who has "anger issues" or chronic depressive symptoms may instead have irritability or dysphoria related to trauma-related cognitions and feelings; for these individuals, treatment with a focus on the trauma may help.

Other effects of sexual assault

Most victims of sexual assault suffer from changes in a number of other psychological or emotional spheres that are subclinical or not captured by diagnostic descriptions or symptoms. Victims can suffer from a change in their worldview. "She now has her eyes wide open to the possibility that people are not what you think," the victim's aunt said, describing how the world had become more dangerous for her niece. Some victims lose their faith. For some, their lives change because they can no longer engage in their usual routines, including self-care. Many lose friends, become more socially restricted, or stop doing certain activities. This might be a result of distrust, feelings of betrayal, or a reaction to the judgment they experienced from others. Retaliation by third parties or on social media for reporting is a real thing. Many victims lose a sense of competency, worth, or lovability because of their feelings of shame, humiliation, or self-blame. Some victims may be rejected from their family or culture, especially if that victim is perceived to be at fault for the sexual assault. It is important to recognize the myriad of effects sexual assault can have, not just the symptoms it produces in victims.

What Does This Have to Do with Rape Kits?

Rape kits are more easily obtained when the victim has knowledge about, support from, and positive expectations for the investigative process. From the very start of an investigation of sexual assault, the victim is subject to numerous players in the process—law enforcement, SANEs, advocates, and others. If a victim is faced with judgment, ignorance, or even hostility from law enforcement, investigators, advocates, or other first responders, the likelihood that the victim will cooperate with an investigation and participate in an intrusive sexual assault examination is vastly diminished. If an investigator or prosecutor decides, based on ignorance of victim dynamics, that a victim is not credible or has acted in an "unbelievable" way and that they are not going to pursue prosecution, they have determined that testing the rape kit is useless. Untested raped kits are, at least in part, due to a negative assessment of the victim—the victim's behavior, cooperation, likability, and perceived credibility. If these assessments are based on bias, if the victim has already had a negative experience in the process, or if the victim does not cooperate because of the bias and judgment, justice will likely be denied.

Discussion

As society learns more about sexual assault and victimization, we are better able to understand the psychology of victims and recognize the short and long-term effects of victimization. We are making strides in no longer labeling the behaviors of victims as noncredible, nonsensical, or counterintuitive. Research on victim experiences and trauma processes has enlightened our responses to victims as law enforcement, advocates, helpers, friends, and members of juries. However, there is a long way to go.

It is important to remember that sexual assault is disorienting, disorganizing, and damaging. When a victim reports the assault, they are subject to a level of scrutiny and demands that are incredible. The process of investigation can be as or more traumatizing than the assault itself, including the intrusive experience of a sexual assault examination. The expectations and judgments about victim behavior and memory are immense and often unrealistic. Through education about and confrontation of myths and misinformation, a more reasonable set of demands for victims can be established. While we have made progress, there is more to go in order to properly understand, support, and safeguard victims of sexual assault. As we improve, victims will be more likely to come forward and cooperate, resulting in a greater value for and use of rape kits.

Key Points

- Victims face continued misinformation and problematic expectations regarding their response to victimization.
- Trauma is a physiological event as well as a psychological event.
  - Freeze is part of the response set, not just flight or fight.
  - A victim's physiological response affects behavior both during and after an assault.
  - Memory, recall, and the development of traumatic symptomatology can all be affected by the physiological response to trauma.
- The impact of trauma is highly personal and individualized. There are many factors that impact victim response to trauma. A victim's experience of and response to a traumatic event is influenced by an array of factors—internal, external, and social.
- Fear has a powerful bearing on the victim's experience and response to assault.
- Victims face numerous barriers to reporting and help-seeking, barriers that are heightened by having a minority status.
- Sexual assault has an enduring impact, not only producing diagnosable symptoms of the trauma but creating alterations in the perceptions and experience of the world for the victim.
- The attainment, testing, and use of sexual assault examination kits are significantly impacted by addressing the lack of or inaccuracy of knowledge about victim behavior.

Discussion Questions

1 What beliefs and biases do you maintain about victimization, victims, or perpetrators?
2 What are some of the common assumptions about victimization, victim response, and perpetrators?
3 Have you ever experienced a traumatic event in which your response surprised you?
4 How does the criminal justice system potentially cause more trauma to a traumatized victim?
5 How can this information be used to improve healthcare and criminal justice responses to sexual assault survivors?

Further Readings

Hopper, J. (July 24, 2015). Sexual Assault: Brain, behavior, and memory. https://www.youtube.com/watch?v=dwTQ_U3p5Wc
Valliere, V. (2019). *Understanding victims of interpersonal violence: A guide for investigators and prosecutors*. London: Routledge Press.

References

Abrahams, N., Jewkes, R., & Mathews, S. (2013). Depressive symptoms after a sexual assault among women: Understanding victim-perpetrator relationships and the role of social perceptions. *African Journal of Psychiatry, 16*, 288–293. https://www.ajol.info/index.php/ajpsy/article/view/91159

American Psychiatric Association. (2013). *Diagnostic and statistical manual of mental disorders—5th edition.* American Psychiatric Association.

Baron, J. (2007). *Thinking and deciding* (4th ed.). Cambridge University Press.

Brainerd, C., & Reyna, V. (2005). *The science of false memory.* London: Oxford University Press.

Campbell, R. (2012, December 3). "The neurobiology of sexual assault." *An NIJ Research for the Real World Seminar.* National Institute of Justice: US Department of Justice. https://www.nij.gov/multimedia/presenter/presenter-campbell/Pages/welcome.aspx

Coxwell, A., & King, M. (2010). Adult male rape and sexual assault: Prevalence, revictimization, and the tonic immobility response. *Sexual and Relationship Therapy, 25*(4), 372–379. doi: 10.1080/14681991003747430

Cozolino, L. (2017). *The neuroscience of psychotherapy: Healing the social brain.* W.W. Norton & Company.

Crespo, M., & Fernandez-Lansac, V. (2016). Memory and narrative of traumatic events: A literature review. *Psychological Trauma, 8*(2), 149–156. doi: 10.1037/tra0000041

Domino, J., Whiteman, S., Weathers, F., Blevins, C., & Davis, M. (2020). Predicting PTSD and depression following sexual assault: The role of perceived life threat, post-traumatic cognitions, victim-perpetrator relationship, and social support. *Journal of Aggression, Maltreatment, & Trauma*, 1–19. https://doi.org/10.1080/10926771.2019.1710634

Hopper, J. (2018, September 5). "Why it's time for sexual assault self-defense training." *Psychology Today.* http://www.psychologytoday.com

Hoscheidt, S., LaBar, K., Ryan, L., Jacobs, W. J., & Nadel, L. (2014). Encoding negative events under stress: High subjective arousal is related to accurate emotional memory despite misinformation exposure. *Neurobiology of Learning and Memory, 112*, 237–247. https://doi.org/10.1016/j.nlm.2013.09.008

Kahn, A., Jackson, J., Kully, C., Badger, K., & Halvorsen, J. (2003). Calling it rape: Differences in experiences of women who do or do not label their sexual assault as rape. *Psychology of Women Quarterly, 27*, 233–242. https://doi.org/10.1111/1471-6402.00103

Kahneman, D. (2011). *Thinking fast and slow.* Farrar, Straus and Giroux.

Kozlowska, K., Walker, P., McLean, L., & Carrive, P. (2015). Fear and the defense cascade: Clinical implications and management. *Harvard Review of Psychiatry, 23*(4), 263–287. 10.1097/HRP.0000000000000065

Lathan, E., Langhinrichsen-Rohling, J., Duncan, J., & Stefurak, J. (2019). The promise initiative: Promoting a trauma-informed police response to sexual assault in a mid-size Southern community. *Journal of Community Psychology, 47*(7), 1733–1749. https://doi.org/10.1002/jcop.22223

Lathan, E., Langhinrichsen-Rohling, J., Stefurak, J., Duncan, J., & Selwyn, C. (2021). Trauma informed sexual assault investigations training: Lessons learned attempting to enhance sexual assault-related understanding and reduce rape myth beliefs and burnout among police officers. *Policing: A Journal of Policy and Practice*, 1–21. https://doi.org/10.1093/police/paab076

LeDoux, J. & Pine, D. (2016). Using neuroscience to help understand fear and anxiety: A two-system framework. *American Journal of Psychiatry, 173*(11), 1083–1093. https://ajp.psychiatryonline.org/doi/pdf/10.1176/appi.ajp.2016.16030353

Long, J., Kristiansson, V., & Mallios, C. (2013). When and how: Admitting expert testimony on victim behavior in sexual assault cases in Pennsylvania. *Strategies in Brief, 18*, 1–7. http://www.ncdsv.org/images/AEquitas_When-and-How-Admitting-Expert-Testimony-on-Victim-Behavior-in-PA-Issue-18_5-2013.pdf

Lonsway, K. A., Welch, S., & Fitzgerald, L. F. (2001). Police training in sexual assault response: Process, outcomes, and elements of change. *Criminal Justice and Behavior, 28*(6), 695–730. doi: 10.1177/009385480102800602.

Lovell, R. E., Williamson, A., Dover, T., Keel, T., & Flannery, D. J. (2020). Identifying serial sexual offenders through cold cases. *Law Enforcement Bulletin* (official publication of the U.S. Federal Bureau of Investigation), May. https://leb.fbi.gov/articles/featured-articles/identifying-serial-sexual-offenders-through-cold-cases

Mathers, M., & Sutherland, M. (2011). Arousal-biased competition in perception and memory. *Perspectives in Psychological Science*, 6(2), 114–133. 10.1177/1745691611400234

National Institute of Mental Health. (n.d.). *Post-traumatic stress disorder*. National Institute for Mental Health. Retrieved January 21, 2022 from https://www.nimh.nih.gov/health/topics/post-traumatic-stress-disorder-ptsd

Roelofs, K. (2017). Freeze for action: Neurobiological mechanisms in animal and human freezing. *Philosophical Transactions of the Royal Society B*, 372, 20160206. http://dx.doi.org/10.1098/rstb.2016.0206

SAMHSA (2014). *TIP 57: Trauma-informed care in behavioral health services*. Retrieved January 21, 2022 from https://store.samhsa.gov/product/TIP-57-Trauma-Informed-Care-in-Behavioral-Health-Services/SMA14-4816

Schwabe, L. (2017). Memory under stress: From single systems to network changes. *European Journal of Neuroscience*, 45(4), 478–489. https://doi.org/10.1111/ejn.13478

Valliere, V. (2019). *Understanding victims of interpersonal violence: A guide for investigators and prosecutors*. Routledge Press.

Volchan, E., Souza, G., Franklin, C., Norte, C., Rocha-Rego, V., Oliveira, J., David, I., Mendlowicz, M., Coutinho, E., Fiszman, A., Berger, W., Marques-Portella, C., & Figueira, I. (2011). Is there tonic immobility in humans? Biological evidence from victims of traumatic stress. *Biological Psychology*, 88, 13–19. 10.1016/j.biopsycho.2011.06.002

Williams, L., & Banyard, V. (Eds.). (1999). *Trauma and memory*. Sage.

Woodhams, J., Hollin, C., Bull, R., & Cooke, C. (2011). Behavior displayed by female victims during rapes committed by lone and multiple perpetrators. *Psychology, Public Policy, and Law*, 18(3), 415–452.

9 Current victim notification procedures

Victim and process impacts across two SAKI sites

Heather C. Melton, Emma C. Lathan, and Jennifer Langhinrichsen-Rohling

Author Note and Funding Acknowledgement

This work was supported in part by the Bureau of Justice Assistance, Grant/Award Number: 2015-AK-BX-K003 to the Mobile, Alabama Police Department with a sub-award to the University of South Alabama (PI: Langhinrichsen-Rohling). However, the views in this chapter are solely those of the authors and do not represent the official positions of the DOJ, the BJA, or the Mobile Police Department.

It has become clear that many sexual assault kits (SAKs) are never submitted to a crime laboratory for testing for a variety of reasons (Campbell et al., 2017a). In fact, in the early 2010s, it was estimated that there were over 200,000 unsubmitted SAKs in the United States (Strom & Hickman, 2016). More recent evidence suggests that the number of unsubmitted SAKs was previously underestimated; between 300,000 and 400,000 unsubmitted SAKs exist across the United States (Strom et al., 2021). As jurisdictions began to rectify the backlog by testing these previously unsubmitted SAKs, several important questions have emerged: *If, when, and how should victims be notified of this testing effort, particularly if it requires telling victims that their SAK was unsubmitted previously? Given that prosecutorial decisions often hinge on victim engagement with the criminal justice system, how might victim notification (VN) be conducted to facilitate the choice to re-engage while promoting healing and resisting re-traumatization?* Many SAKI sites have wrestled with these questions in the absence of data related to different VN decisions.

This chapter is written by authors located at two different SAKI-funded sites: the state of Utah (HM) and Mobile, AL (JLR, EL). Heather Melton (HM) served as the researcher for the Utah SAKI site. She is an Associate Professor of Sociology and the Director of Criminology at the University of Utah. Her research is centered around gender-based violence and the criminal justice response to it. Jennifer Langhinrichsen-Rohling (JLR) served as the PI for the Mobile, AL action-oriented research-community SAKI partnership for many years prior to relocating to the University of North Carolina—Charlotte, where she is currently a Professor in the Clinical concentration of the Health Psychology doctoral program. She is well known for her research on intimate partner violence, stalking, and sexual assault. She has recently been named as a researcher on the Charlotte, NC SAKI team. Emma Lathan (EL) conducted her dissertation with data from the Mobile, AL SAKI site and is now completing her post-doctoral fellowship at Emory University School

DOI: 10.4324/9781003186816-12

of Medicine with the Grady Trauma Project. Both JLR and EL were actively involved in the development, adaptation, and evaluation of the Mobile VN protocol.

Both sites chose to delineate and then enact a VN process. The authors of this chapter tracked outcomes related to each chosen policy. Thus, this chapter offers findings related to two "real-world" VN policies as well as lessons learned, modifications made, and recommendations for best practices moving forward. We highlight the specifics of VN related to previously unsubmitted SAKs with long-time delays, as well as how recent findings apply to future VN practices

Victim Notification

At the broadest level, victim notification (VN) is an ongoing and important part of the criminal justice process; thus, there are precedents to consider when embarking on a previously unsubmitted SAK-oriented VN process (National Center for Crime Victims, 2014) Given the existence of VN processes and that the term "victim" has traditionally been used within the criminal justice system to refer to someone who directly experiences a crime, we use the terms "victim" and "victim notification" as opposed to "survivor" and "survivor notification" throughout this chapter. Within the criminal justice system, a VN refers to any situation in which a victim is provided information about their case, their offender, or any part of their interaction with the criminal justice system (i.e., efforts related to the investigation and prosecution of their case). It can also refer to victims being notified when their offender is released from incarceration. For example, the Victim Notification System (VNS) is a free computer-controlled system of the U.S. Department of Justice which informs victims of federal crimes about the release or escape of the offender(s) who perpetrated that crime. It is also known as Crime Victim Notification (CVN) or State-wide Automated Victim Notification Service (SAVNS) (U.S. Legal, n.d.). Forty-seven states, plus the District of Columbia and Puerto Rico, use some version of an automated system for this purpose (Irazola et al., 2015).

This chapter specifically refers to "cold" case SAK VNs, or the process of telling a victim about the forensic results that emerged from testing their previously unsubmitted SAK that only recently has completed DNA analyses. Please see Chapter 20 for a discussion of the development of a national SAK VN policy that could include informing victims that their SAK was part of the backlog, regardless of whether DNA results are obtained.

An added complication to the VN process is the fact that the cases attached to the previously unsubmitted SAKs are often considered "cold" given the time that has elapsed since the crime was committed and evidence collection. Victims may have a range of reactions when learning that their SAK has only recently been tested, despite evidence collection occurring months to years prior. Emotions could include being angry, confused, upset, or relieved, among many other possibilities. According to the National Institute of Justice (NIJ), being reminded of the previous assault may also cause re-traumatization, which could include flashbacks and other symptoms of post-traumatic stress disorder. An upsetting reminder of the previous assault may also impact current substance use or abuse and/or affect sobriety (National Institute of Justice [NIJ], 2016). These reactions may not be confined to the victim but instead, create a ripple effect across the victim's intimate and social network. Current and past family members, partners, and friends may also have strong reactions to SAKI-related VNs. These reactions can also affect the victim's decision to re-engage with the criminal justice system.

Thus, it is critical that those conducting the VN (i.e., the "notifiers") are aware of the possibility of varied responses to VN and seek to decrease the likelihood of a negative reaction. Best practice suggests that agencies and/or groups engaging in VN consider potential victim reactions ahead of time (Campbell et al., 2017b, see Chapter 20). Another best practice is to develop a SAKI site-specific VN protocol to ensure a victim-centered, trauma-informed process is routinely used by notifiers. This needs to be done to ensure a victim-centered, trauma-informed notification process is being implemented at each SAK site. *Victim-centered* means that the needs of the victim are at the center of all decisions. *Trauma-informed* means that the response must support the victim's emotional and physical safety, foster recovery by providing resources and services, and educate all involved in the response (Campbell et al., 2018). The goal of the trauma-informed VN procedures is to prevent re-traumatization by recognizing and responding to trauma reactions in ways that are healing and restorative.

Specific to a SAKI VN protocol, several things must be considered: safety and privacy, risk of re-traumatization, current needs, secondary victimization, and risk of lifetime poly-victimization (Sexual Assault Kit Initiative, n.d.). When thinking about safety and privacy, the notifier must:

- Consider the victim's current situation—Sexual assault disclosure is relatively rare, and the victim might not have disclosed to those closest to them, in the past or at the current time. Thus, the notifiers should be mindful not to jeopardize the individual's privacy. For example, the notifiers may need to speak to the victim in a private location and/or ask, "Is now a good time?" before divulging information.
- Consider whether the VN itself could re-traumatize the victim. Notifiers should consider the date and time that the assault occurred in order to avoid a repeat trauma on the anniversary of the assault; notifiers may also want to avoid named holidays.
- Be prepared to offer support for difficult emotions and physical reactions aroused by the VN. Notifiers also need to be prepared to offer resources for other forms of support, such as physical and mental health care or housing and food assistance. Victims may have experienced secondary victimization or institutional betrayal in prior encounters with the justice system. Past negative experiences may impact the victim's response to the current notification and the notifiers.
- Consider and respond to negative reactions by addressing the role of the system in the victim's personal experience of trauma. Whether notifiers should offer an apology for previous institutional betrayals is a topic of ongoing debate (see Chapter 20).
- Be aware that the original victimization or experience of crime can increase the risk of future victimization (Barnes et al., 2009), and the victim might have experienced many types of victimizations over their lifetime (e.g., poly-victimization). It is possible that chronic victimization experiences will impact how a victim responds to the current VN.

VN, particularly "cold" case VN, presents complexities that must be addressed to ensure a victim-centered, trauma-informed notification. Thus, best practice suggests that protocols considering these issues be developed prior to conducting VNs. More specifically, VN protocols should be tailored to fit each site's individual needs and developed with input from the notifiers to increase the likelihood that it is practical and relevant and will be used consistently (Campbell et al., 2017b).

Aims of Victim Notification

VN serves several important purposes. First, many assert that it is the victims' right to know about their case, including any potential results from DNA testing. Indeed, this is written into the Crime Victims' Right Act of 2004. Specifically, it states that "Victims have the right to be informed of the services they are entitled to receive; any public court proceedings related to the crime; and the status of the accused, including any release or escape from custody." While states vary in their statutes on victims' rights, many do include this type of language in their laws. For example, this language is written directly into the Utah Victims Bill of Rights (Utah Code Section 77-37 & 77-38).

Second, if there is a chance of future legal action, victims need to be notified to determine if they want to engage in legal proceedings. Notifying the victims in an attempt to re-engage them with the legal process is a practical matter. Law enforcement and prosecutors need to know the status of victim participation if the case is reopened or to move forward with prosecution based on the testing of the SAKs. Victim participation is often deemed necessary by the legal system for successful prosecution (NIJ, 2016). In fact, prosecutors often cite a lack of victim participation as a reason not to move forward with a case (O'Neal et al., 2015; Spohn & Holleran, 2001).

Regardless of potential legal procedures, many victims are eligible for additional services related to their reported sexual assault. This is particularly true in many of the SAKI sites where victim therapeutic funds were written into the SAKI program. *Thus, part of the objective of a SAKI, VN goes beyond justice system outcomes and centers on supporting the victim.* This support is particularly important in shaping a victim's potential future engagements with the criminal justice system. Feeling supported and having their well-being cared for will potentially increase their willingness to interact with the criminal justice system (Aherns et al., 2016).

Specific to these previously untested SAKs, some have argued that another purpose of notification is to "right the wrong" of not testing the kits in the first place (Campbell et al., 2017b). To many, the fact that these SAKs were never tested demands the justice of testing, an acknowledgment of the wrong, and an apology to those victims impacted, regardless of any other purpose or potential future outcome. However, knowing the purpose of a notification is important because it has implications for VN notification protocols and decisions.

Types of Notification and Best-Practices

How to Notify

Several advocacy and victim service agencies, including the Joyful Heart Foundation and the Office for Victims of Crime, have outlined best practices for victim-centered, trauma-informed VN (see Chapter 18). Suggestions for beginning the process include bringing a multidisciplinary team (MDT) together to develop a site specific VN protocol, being flexible, providing VN training, and knowing your community (Office of Victims of Crime, n.d.). However, there is an ongoing debate among stakeholders, including law enforcement, prosecutors, victim advocates, and survivors, as to the "best" way to notify victims (Aherns et al., 2016).

Most jurisdictions conduct VNs related to offender release either by mail or phone, although other methods may include in-person or email VN. Similar to VN in "cold" sexual assault cases, each VN method has advantages and disadvantages.

Specifically, *notification by mail* might be preferred by some victims as they may be more likely to read and attend to an official letter. Mail VN also facilitates contact with those who are not easily accessible by phone or email, due lack of access to reliable phone or internet. On the other hand, safety and privacy issues may arise from mail VNs (i.e., the letter could be opened and read by someone other than the intended recipient), and this strategy may not be optimal for reaching those who frequently relocate.

Another option for VN is a *phone notification*. Phone calls can be more confidential than open-access mail. In line with the empowerment and control aspects of trauma-informed VNs, a phone message allows the victim to decide when or if it is best for them to return the notifiers' call. After the phone call, the victim can then choose the details of when and where to meet in person to receive more details. They can also decide, based on the phone call, not to have a second conversation. Setting up a future meeting via telephone may provide the victim with more time to make decisions about how to proceed and gather a support network. However, for some victims, a phone call about their SAK might seem too impersonal. Like mail, a phone message is also subject to confidentiality concerns; many do not answer unknown or unexpected calls on their cell phone, and obtaining an up-to-date phone number can be challenging.

In recent years, *email notifications* have increased in frequency. Email may be many people's primary contact preference and/or main mode of official communication. Email also offers a pathway for immediate and ongoing contact with a victim. Similar to mail and phone VNs, an email may be considered too impersonal for the initial contact, and it can be difficult to determine if the intended recipient viewed the email. Additionally, an email could be lost through a spam filter or deleted due to questioned credibility.

Finally, *in-person notification* is an option. Many argue that in-person notification shows that criminal justice personnel are taking sexual assault, testing, and any potential future cases seriously. In-person VN lays the groundwork for a victim-centered, trauma-informed response and allows the notifiers to address any immediate victim needs (e.g., crisis intervention, mental health, resources). However, just like all VN methods, there are some potential concerns associated with in-person VN. First, an in-person notification that takes place when family or friends are present might violate the victim's privacy, especially considering the victim may not have revealed their sexual assault history to others. Second, given the criminal justice system previously failed to do their due diligence related to the victim's case, the victim might understandably mistrust law enforcement. Police presence at an in-person VN could trigger a negative reaction that might impact a victim's willingness to re-engage with the system. Third, in-person VN is the most time-consuming and logistically difficult method of notification. An additional issue is determining whether it would be better for the VN to be scheduled (i.e., the victim is contacted beforehand, the VN has a set meeting time and can be prepared for emotionally and physically) or unscheduled (i.e., the notifiers locate the victim in-person without prior contact).

Who Notifies

An additional VN question pertains to the choice of which victims to notify: *Is it best to only notify certain victims (i.e., only those with cases that hit to an identified offender in the Combined DNA Index System [CODIS], only if law enforcement plans to further investigate the case based on the testing results, only if the district attorney's office agrees to prosecute the case) or to notify all whose SAKs are now being tested?* In a study exploring the perceptions of both professionals and victims, Busch-Armendariz et al. (2015) found that while professional standards state that all victims have the right to be notified, both professionals and victims expressed mixed reactions to the institution of a broad, "notify all" policy. Other research, however, suggests some victims support widespread notification. Perhaps, VN should not be viewed as a "one-size-fits-all" process, particularly when it pertains to victims with cases that were in the backlog of untested SAKs (Aherns et al., 2016; Sulley et al., 2018).

Assessing Victim Notification in Cold Case SAKs

Research on the SAK VN process is nascent but expanding. Campbell et al. (2018) evaluated VNs implemented in Detroit as part of an NIJ-funded project on previously unsubmitted SAKs. In this project, there was a preference for in-person VN. Campbell et al. (2018) found that most victims did <u>not</u> have a strong negative emotional reaction to the in-person VN, and more than half of those notified decided to re-engage with the system. However, the amount of time between kit collection and testing was related to the victim's emotional reaction, such that the more time between SAK collection and VN, the more negative reaction at VN. Finally, victims who were assaulted by known others (i.e., non-stranger assault) were less likely to re-engage than victims who were assaulted by a stranger (Campbell et al., 2018).

Moreover, The Joyful Heart Foundation examined 98 practitioners' and survivors' preferences for SAK VN. They concluded that survivor choice, information in the process, confidentiality and safety, and an empathic response were the most preferred strategies (Ahrens et al., 2016). In another study of previously unsubmitted SAKs (Sulley et al., 2018), a standardized VN letter that was being considered for use was evaluated by participants. They regarded this method of delivery as potentially re-traumatizing for victims (Sulley et al., 2018). Conversely, trust, personal agency, decision-making, and practical issues (e.g., respect for privacy and safety, need for specific information, and need for victim-centered research) were listed as key ingredients for a positive VN experience (Sully et al., 2018).

Given the scant research on VN, we present case studies of two SAKI sites' VN processes in the section below. These case studies are drawn from two separate jurisdictions—one statewide site (Utah, HM) and one city-based site (Mobile, Alabama, JLR, EL). The sites' VN policies are described and compared via preliminary data to expand our cross-jurisdictional understanding of the VN and gain a better understanding of both current VN processes and the best directions for future practice.

Case Study #1: Utah

This case study includes results obtained via four different strategies assessing the VN processes used across the state of Utah:

a   A survey was voluntarily completed by victim advocates and/or law enforcement after they concluded each VN.
b   After VN completion, an anonymous survey was administered to victims.
c   In-depth interviews were conducted with the main SAKI victim advocates for the statewide site.
d   Additional findings were generated through focus groups that were comprised of law enforcement officers or victim advocates who participated in VNs.

To start the process in Utah, a 14-page VN protocol was created by a MDT comprised of victim advocates, law enforcement, SANE nurses, prosecutors, and others (see Chapter 21 for more information on MDTs in SAKI) with the aim to serve as a victim-centered/trauma-informed resource for agencies to use as they began the VN process in these cold cases. This protocol covered the "who, what, why, when, and how" of conducting a VN and was disseminated at various meetings and trainings as well as to individual agencies located across Utah. *It emphasized flexibility while encouraging in-person notifications. The inclusion of a victim advocate in the VN was strongly recommended.* However, in the end, jurisdictions across Utah independently decided how to conduct VNs at their site. Thus, a variety of VN methods were attempted and subject to evaluation.

As of the project's end (September 2019), 76 victims were recommended to be notified based on a multiple stakeholder case review process. During this process, a team of law enforcement, SANE nurses, victim advocates, prosecutors, and a crime lab representative determined whether VN was warranted. This team made a recommendation after reviewing all the information from a case attached to one of the previously unsubmitted SAKs, including the new testing results (Melton, 2021). Data reported below were obtained from 34 victim advocates/notifiers from seven agencies who undertook one of the recommended VNs. In addition, six victim surveys were returned from 76 victims recommended for notification (7.8%). Results are presented in the following tables and charts.

Quantitative Survey Findings

As shown in Table 9.1, among the 34 victim advocate/notifier surveys completed after a VN, seven agencies were represented,

- In 7 cases, a police officer conducted the notification alone (20.6%),
- In 11 cases, a victim advocate conducted the notification alone (32.4%), and
- In 16 cases (as recommended by the VN state protocol), a victim advocate and a police officer conducted the VN together (47.0%).

Table 9.1 Describing the Utah Victim Notification Processes

Characteristics of VN Process	N = 34 responses, 7 agencies
Notification	
Just advocate	11 (32.4%)
Just law enforcement	7 (20.6%)
Advocate & law enforcement officer	16 (47.0%)
Scheduled	14 (41.2%)
Unscheduled	20 (58.8%)
Location	
In person	19 (55.8%)
Over the phone	15 (44.2%)
Perception of physical reaction	
Positive	14 (41.2%)
Neutral	8 (23.5%)
Negative	12 (35.3%)
Perception of emotional reaction	
Positive	17 (50.0%)
Neutral	5 (14.7%)
Negative	12 (35.3%)
Change in reaction	
More positive	17 (50.0%)
Stayed the same	12 (35.3%)
More negative	2 (5.8%)
Don't know/missing	3 (8.8%)
Questions	
Yes	26 (76.5%)
Questions answered	
Yes	24 (92.3%)
Notifiers feel about the notification	
Positive	25 (73.5%)
Neutral	4 (11.8%)
Negative	4 (11.8%)
Don't know/missing	1 (2.9%)

Moreover, in terms of completing the VNs,

- 14 were scheduled (41.2%),
- 20 were unscheduled (58.8%),
- 19 were conducted in person (55.9%), and
- 15 occurred over the phone (44.1%).

Regarding notifiers' perceptions of the victim's body language in response to the information being presented (i.e., physical reaction),

- 12 notifiers perceived a negative physical reaction from the victim (35.3%),
- 14 perceived a positive physical reaction (41.2%), and
- 8 perceived a neutral physical reaction (23.5%).

In terms of notifiers' perceptions of the victim's emotional reactions,

- 12 notifiers perceived a negative emotional reaction (35.3%),
- 17 perceived a positive emotional reaction (50.0%), and
- 5 perceived a neutral emotional reaction (14.7%).

In terms of the change in the reaction over the course of the VN,

- 17 notifiers (50.0%) perceived that the victim became more positive over the course of the VN,
- 2 notifiers (5.9%) perceived that the victim became more negative over time,
- 12 (35.3%) perceived the victim to have no change in reaction, and
- 3 notifiers (8.8%) indicated that they did not know or the data were missing.

Finally, in terms of the VN process overall,

- 26 victims had questions (76.5%),
- 24 notifiers felt the victim got their questions answered (70.5%), and
- 25 of the victims (74%) felt positive about the VN overall, according to the notifiers.

Notably, as shown in Figures 9.1, 9.2, and 9.3, statistical analyses indicated that *notifiers were significantly more likely to perceive VNs that were scheduled (p < 0.05), were conducted in-person (13 vs. 4, p < 0.01), and had a law enforcement officer present (p < 0.01) as eliciting a positive emotional response from the victim than VNs that were unscheduled, were conducted by phone and did not have a*

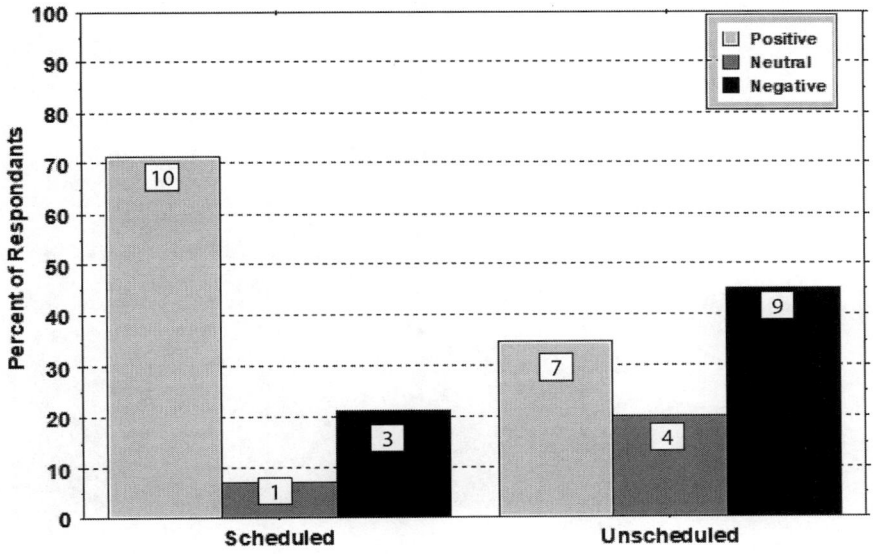

Figure 9.1 Significant Differences in Victims' Perceived Emotional Reaction by Whether the Visit Was Scheduled vs. Unscheduled

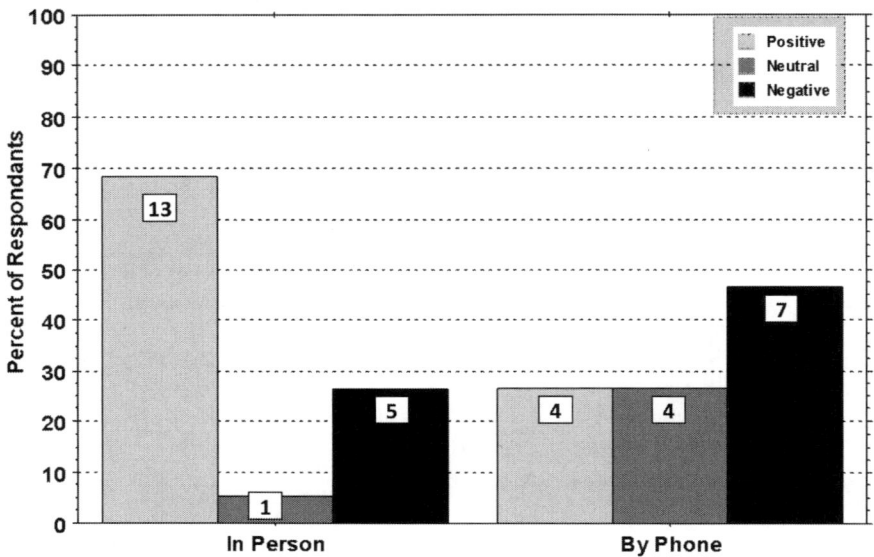

Figure 9.2 Significant Differences in Victims' Perceived Emotional Reaction by Whether the Visit Was in Person vs. by Phone

law enforcement officer present. The notifiers also rated the VNs as getting more positive over time; at least six of the victims originally perceived to have a negative emotional reaction were rated as having a more positive reaction over time. In two cases, the notifiers indicated that the emotional reaction became more negative over the course of the VN process. This indicates that from the notifiers' perspective,

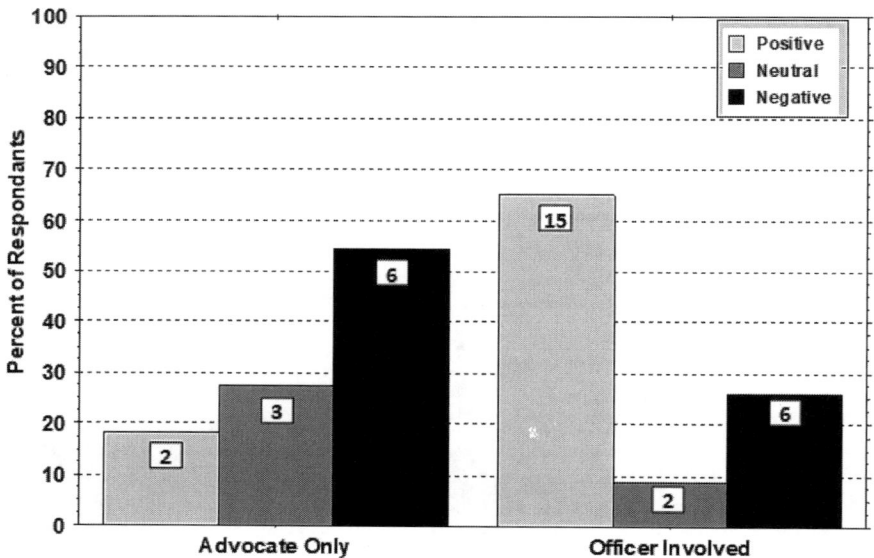

Figure 9.3 Victim Notifications Conducted by an Advocate Only vs. Law Enforcement Officer and/or an Advocate

victims tended to respond more positively across the course of the VN, regardless of their initial emotional response.

Qualitative Findings

Notifiers also had the opportunity to provide comments about the VN. Themes centered on their perceptions of what worked, what did not work, and what could be improved. In terms of what worked, *in-person VN was viewed as preferable compared to over the phone*. One advocate wrote,

> I think in-person made the difference. Although the victim did not have much of a reaction, I felt because we were there in person, the victim wanted to move forward. It made her feel that the police department was serious about working her case. Another said, "Being in person at the victim's home worked well. The in-person interaction was crucial. Having both a victim advocate and police presence was also important".

And another,

> In person was so important for this victim. She said that she definitely needed to feel cared about and supported and a phone call would <u>not</u> have provided that. She was honored that we cared enough to wait and tell her in person.

When addressing what did not work, advocates expressed frustration regarding the amount of time it took to test kits. Comments included:

- "She had to wait so many years, now she does not want to go forward with the case," and
- "That we are doing this 8 years later than when she filed the report and put herself out there."

Notifiers were also frustrated by their lack of information. For example, one victim advocate wrote, "It was hard not being able to tell the victim who the identified suspect was or what his name was, or even let her know that he is incarcerated."

Finally, advocates commented on their need for more training to be fully prepared to conduct a VN. They also reiterated the need to respect a victim's decision about re-engagement. For example, an advocate wrote, "[Advocates] need more training in CODIS, rape kit testing and DNA. Victims want to understand that portion of their case, even more than understanding the investigation or whether or not their case will move forward."

While relatively fewer responses were obtained from victims, those who responded expressed an array of reactions to their VN. For example, several victims mentioned liking that the VN was conducted in person. One victim said, "Liked the in-person notification. Felt supported and was not alone." Others expressed frustration, particularly related to their unanswered questions. One victim wrote,

> I had lots of questions surrounding who the suspect was that was identified through a DNA match. The investigator said he could not tell me who was

identified at this time due to the investigation. It is hard to wait. I have been wait-ing for so many years. I know that they are trying to help and complete a solid investigation but maybe contact me once you are at the point in the investigation that I can know who the suspect is.

Interestingly, no victim spontaneously indicated that they wanted an apology. However, caution should be used when considering this finding, as only six victim surveys were returned. Further, although not a part of the formal policy, regret and/ or an apology may have been expressed by some notifiers or perceived by victims, and therefore, it was not lacking.

Interviews/Focus Groups with Key Stakeholders

Each SAKI Victim Advocate was interviewed prior to being involved in a focus group with other victim advocates. A second focus group occurred with law enforcement representatives. One component of these interviews was to gather VN perspectives. Data indicate that all participants knew there was an existing VN protocol; most were using it but to varying degrees. Several strengths of the existing protocol were highlighted: it was developed with involvement from different agencies and disci-plines; it was research-based; and agencies received individualized training. However, some concerns with the protocol were raised. Law enforcement expressed concerns that the existing protocol is too restrictive, while victim advocates noted that the cur-rent protocol is too lengthy and potentially traumatizing. Of note, victim advocates also raised concerns about not being fully utilized by law enforcement.

Case Study Summary

This research sheds light on victim, advocate, and law enforcement perceptions of the VN process and protocol. Findings suggest that there is no universal agreement or standardized administration of VNs in cases involving previously unsubmitted SAKs. Yet, it is clear that VNs should continue.

Findings also highlight steps that should occur post-VN. Victims identified the amount of time that they have already waited as problematic. If appropriate, the system should avoid letting more lag time accumulate once victims have been re-engaged. Victim advocates need continued training on the VN protocol and aspects of the forensic evidence process.

The VN protocol should be consistently followed, but flexibility should be afforded. This includes encouraging law enforcement to incorporate and utilize their victim advocates. Preliminary analysis indicates that in-person, scheduled notifica-tions involving a victim advocate and a law enforcement officer may be the most victim-centered/trauma-informed approach.

Case Study #2: Mobile, Alabama

Mobile, AL recently faced a backlog of untested SAKs, with 1,412 kits certified by the National Sexual Assault Initiative (SAKI). As of December 2018, all kits selected for submission to the forensic lab by the MDT were sent for testing ($n = 757$). A priori, the City of Mobile Police Department (MPD) and the multidisciplinary SAKI team (MDT) chose to evaluate each case to determine the need for submission rather than using a forklift approach. Thus, the site continues to be in the process of receiving forensic CODIS hits.

The MDT decided only to notify victims if their SAK testing resulted in a CODIS hit. Because the mean amount of time from sexual assault report to VN was roughly 15 years, most survivors were unaware of their cases' standing. Several had even forgotten about making a report. Prior to developing a site-specific VN protocol, the team was aware that the process must be handled with care. As noted by Campbell et al. (2015), VN may constitute an emotional and physical risk to rape survivors, "which may or may not be mitigated by the information provided (e.g., testing results, CODIS hits, suspect identification) and opportunities for action and/or closure (e.g., investigation and prosecution)" (p. 232).

As described below, the Mobile SAKI site initially held an MDT workshop to construct their evidence-based, trauma-informed protocol. The hope was to provide relevant case-related information, offer and connect the victim to additional services, and determine the victim's willingness to re-engage with and participate in the criminal justice process. Next, a Victim Notification Team (VNT), comprised of lead sex crimes detectives, psychologists/researchers, the assigned sex crimes prosecutor, victim advocates, and a sexual assault nurse examiner (SANE), was formed and tasked with policy implementation as well as locating and notifying rape survivors. Following a Plan, Do, Study, Act protocol, the VNT modified the policy multiple times due to practical limitations and low rates of victims choosing to re-engage with the justice system. For example, one policy change that occurred promoted the greater inclusion of the designated sex crimes prosecutor in the VN experience. This was done to help prepare victims for court delays and grand jury experiences, as these were noted sources of victim frustration.

To create the site's VN policy, MDT members first collected materials from other SAKI sites with VN policies. Specifically, materials were collected from the national SAKI website; Rebecca Campbell, a psychologist and principal investigator on the Detroit SAKI grant (see Chapter 1); and Lonsway and Archambault's (2017) summative report on multiple SAKI sites' development of a VN protocol. Second, following the lead of the Detroit SAKI site, VNT team members participated in an all-day retreat to develop a VN protocol. Third, Campbell et al.'s (2015) Nine VN Discussion Questions, which outline key decision points in the development of a VN protocol, were used as a guidepost for policy development. See Table 9.2 for a list of Campbell et al.'s questions and Mobile MDT's accompanying implementation plan.

Importantly, the VN protocol underwent three phases of revision (discussed in detail below) for two distinct reasons. First, the Mobile SAKI site and VNT were established early in the National SAK initiative. Updated materials and lessons learned from other sites were being disseminated continuously over the course of VN policy development leading to adaptations and adoptions of emerging best practices.

Second, as the process of notifying victims began, some members of the VNT voiced concerns about using VN strategies in use at other sites. Other SAKI sites' VN policies were not built for our unique community and the specific challenges it faces. For example, in Alabama, felony cases must be presented to a grand jury to determine whether they can move forward to district court; however, we do not have a statute of limitations for rape charges. As many other sites have not required a grand jury

Table 9.2 Campbell et al.'s Nine Questions and Mobile SAKI's Responses and Implementation Plans

Campbell et al.'s (2015) nine discussion questions	*Mobile SAKI's implementation—Victim Notification Policy 3.0*
Question 1: How should victim notification be approached?	The Victim Notification Team's (VNT) approach to victim notification would be modified on a case-by-case basis.
	The VNT consists of the assigned case investigator, specialized sex crimes prosecutor, and victim advocate.
Question 2: When and why are victims notified and how does this vary by DNA results?	On a case-by-case basis, victims who had a SAK submitted to ADFS for testing as a result of the grant initiative will be contacted and informed of testing results when a CODIS hit is received from their SAK.
	Special circumstances (i.e., CODIS hit is to the originally named suspect(s), victims with physical and/or intellectual disabilities, young or advanced age, offender linked to other cases, and/or contextual or cultural factors) may warrant adaptations agreed upon by the VNT.
	The victim can be contacted before the SAK is submitted for forensic testing or while pending results if a need for early notification is established by the VNT.
Question 3: Who makes the decision that a victim will be notified?	The VNT (i.e., victim advocate, specialized sex crimes prosecutor, assigned case investigator).
Question 4: What should be achieved during the first contact?	The primary goal of the initial phone contact is to schedule a more in-depth meeting in person to discuss the status of the SAK.
	If the victim declines a second, in-person meeting, they will be informed of the status of the SAK by phone, given an opportunity to ask questions and be asked for permission for future contact.
Question 5: Who should make the first contact with the victim?	The assigned case investigator and victim advocate will make the first contact. The specialized sex crimes prosecutor may be present if deemed necessary.
Question 6: How should the first contact be made?	Initial contact should be attempted by phone. If all attempts to contact by phone are exhausted (e.g., disconnected or changed numbers, multiple messages left), the VNT will attempt to notify in person.
	A case review meeting will be held prior to each victim notification to establish a notification approach that takes into account the suspect's criminal history, the victim's past experiences with law enforcement, and the need for additional resources. The case review meeting will be attended by the research team, VNT, supervisor, and additional community advocates, as necessary.

(Continued)

Table 9.2 Campbell et al.'s Nine Questions and Mobile SAKI's Responses and Implementation Plans   *(Continued)*

Campbell et al.'s (2015) nine discussion questions	*Mobile SAKI's implementation—Victim Notification Policy 3.0*
Question 7: What information should be given to victims at the first contact?	Information will not be withheld if the victim asks for additional information in the initial notification (by phone or in person). The victim will be given the advocate's contact information and a list of community resources.
Question 8: What should happen after the initial contact?	If the victim agrees to a second in-person visit, they will be informed in person of the status of the SAK and given an opportunity to ask questions. More detailed follow-up interviews will be conducted at another time and place unless the victim requests to move forward during the second in-person meeting. The VNT team will assess the victim's willingness to re-engage with the criminal justice system and ask permission to follow up.
Question 9: How should victim notification staff be trained?	All members of the VNT should receive trauma-informed, victim-centered sexual assault investigations training.

presentation and may need to prioritize certain cases due to time in the system, our VN policy was tailored. Victims who chose to re-engage in AL had to face two potential processes: preparation and presentation to a grand jury and then a subsequent trial. Ongoing consideration of the victim experience in the criminal justice process resulted in three iterations of the VN policy.

Victim Notification Policy 1.0.

In September 2016, the existing VN policy stated that a victim advocate and the assigned case investigator will notify the victim of testing results, either by phone or in person, with the goal of scheduling a second, in-depth and in-person meeting. The VN policy also outlined that information would not be withheld if the victim asks for it during the initial notification and attempts to avoid scheduling the VN on important dates to the victim (birthday, date of assault, court dates, etc.) would be made. During VN, the victim was to be given the advocate's contact information as well as a list of community resources. This phone contact was expected to be brief and lead to a second in-person visit. A priori, it was expected that the victim would be informed of the status of their SAK and the resultant DNA findings at this meeting. To reduce distress and enhance cognitive recall, more detailed follow-up interviews were supposed to be conducted at another time and place (a third meeting) unless the victim requested to move forward with an interview during the second in-person meeting. Follow-up interviews were to be conducted at the local Rape Crisis Center or at another location requested by the victim, with an advocate present.

   The initial policy did recognize that the team's approach to VN would likely need to be modified on a case-by-case basis. The following three scenarios are examples of special circumstances that the VNT recognized as potentially warranting adaptations. First, if the CODIS hit is to a known suspect who was originally named by the victim, victim contact may not be necessary if the case is still not going to proceed. Second, additional representatives will be involved in the VN as needed for victims with physical and/or intellectual disabilities, young or advanced age, and/or if there are known contextual or cultural factors. Third, if the victim currently resides out of jurisdiction, due consideration will be given to participation of the victim's local advocate and law enforcement agencies in the VN process.

Victim Notification Policy 2.0

In August 2018, the VN protocol was updated to incorporate lessons learned from initial VNs and additional recommendations from other sites. The updated policy stipulated that the victim can be contacted before the SAK is submitted for forensic testing or while results are pending if, for example, facts of the case need to be established or redetermined prior to SAK submission. In order to avoid retraumatizing the victim, however, early notification will only occur if it is in the best interest of the investigation as determined by the lead investigator, the designated supervisor, and VNT. At this time, an addendum was added to the original VN policy to give the victim the opportunity to prohibit the police department, district attorney's office, and rape crisis advocates from communicating with the media about details of the case.

Victim Notification Policy 3.0

In January 2019, the VN policy underwent another revision. The revised VN policy recommended that all initial notifications be first attempted with a phone contact. Discomfort with in-person initial notifications had continued to be expressed by law enforcement and advocates. The update also stipulated that a case review meeting will be held prior to each VN to establish a notification approach that considers the suspect's criminal history, victim's past experiences with law enforcement, and the need for additional resources; the case review meeting will be attended by the lead investigator, supervisor, victim advocate, research team member, and prosecutor. Prosecutors will now be required to attend VNs for cases that are high priority or involve a known serial offender. Moreover, in addition to the investigator, supervisor, and VNT determining the benefits and risks of notification before a CODIS hit is returned, the specialized sex crimes prosecutor will also help establish the need for early notification. Phase 3 specified that efforts will be made to obtain a buccal (i.e., confirmation) swab from the alleged perpetrator prior to VN to reduce the victim's wait time for confirmation and potential prosecution.

Outcomes on VNs To-Date

Victim re-engagement is key for successful investigation and prosecution of cold case sexual assaults (NIJ, 2016). As of March 2020, 66 VNs have been conducted at the Mobile, AL SAKI site; all cases were associated with a kit that came back with a CODIS hit to a suspect. However, 18 of 66 cases (27.3%) could not move forward to prosecution due to:

- the suspect being deceased ($n = 11$, 16.7%),
- the victim offering new information that closed the case ($n = 3$, 4.5%),
- lack of jurisdiction ($n = 1$, 1.9%), or
- a lack of new leads, sufficient evidence, or needed information ($n = 3$, 4.5%).

Of the 48 cases that could move forward with further investigation and/or prosecution,

- 58.3% of the victims indicated that they were not willing to re-engage with the criminal justice system after VN ($n = 28$),
- 22.9% could not be reached after the original VN ($n = 11$),
- 16.7% were willing to re-engage ($n = 8$), and
- 1.9% were unsure of whether to proceed ($n = 1$).

Stakeholders initially expressed concern that locating and notifying victims of the status of their long-neglected SAKI case (i.e., VN) after a CODIS hit would be poorly received or even re-traumatizing. After debate, the decision to notify first via telephone was agreed upon. To determine response to VNs, police, and advocates rated each victim's contact for emotional reactions and perceived willingness to re-engage with the criminal justice system. Of the 66 VNs to date, emotional response data were provided by notifiers for between 49 and 54 VNs. Contrary to expectation, many victims were rated as having positive or neutral emotional responses to notification. Specifically,

- 27.8% of victims were rated as happy or excited the case was reopened ($n = 15$) and
- 38.7% of victims responded "matter-of-factly" to contact ($n = 19$).

However, there were also negative responses,

- 36.5% of victims had negative emotional responses ($n = 19$), e.g., tension, anxiety, suspicion of investigators, trembling, or crying.
- 3.8% of victims indicated the VN process was re-traumatizing ($n = 2$).

Overall, our findings suggest, when using trauma-informed, victim-centered VN protocols, positive or "matter-of-fact" victim responses occur the majority of the time, but more may be needed to foster re-engagement.

Of note, of the cases that could move forward ($n = 48$), only 16.7% ($n = 8$) indicated a willingness to proceed after VN. Given that some other SAKI sites report substantially higher rates of victim re-engagement (e.g., 57% using in-person notification; Campbell, 2018), the team considered whether other factors might be associated with re-engagement including the original case charge (i.e., rape 1 or 2, suspicious circumstances, rape, and sodomy, or other), noted cooperation in original investigation, and emotional reaction during VN.

Although small sample size prohibited use of robust statistical tests, chi-square analyses were conducted to determine differences among three groups: victims willing to re-engage, victims unwilling to re-engage, and disengaged victims (i.e., could not be reached after initial VN). Chi square analyses revealed that the groups did not significantly differ in terms of original case charge, X^2 (6, $N = 47$) = 11.64, $p = 0.07$ (e.g., 57% of those whose case was originally marked as having a concurrent rape and sodomy charge were willing to re-engage vs. 13% of those with a rape 1 or 2 case charge, 10% with suspicious circumstance case charges vs. 0% with other case charges [e.g., "investigation," domestic violence]), cooperation in original investigation, X^2 (2, $N = 46$) = 1.80, $p = 0.41$, or emotional response to notification (e.g., positive, X^2 (2, $N = 41$) = 4.13, $p = 0.13$; matter-of-fact reaction, X^2 (2, $N = 37$) = 0.54, $p = 0.76$; negative, X^2 (2, $N = 39$) = 1.02, $p = 0.60$).

Case Study Summary

Despite low rates of re-engagement with the criminal justice system, the MDT recognized that VNs provide a crucial opportunity for trauma-informed practice. Namely, VNs provide victims with a choice they were not previously afforded—whether and how to proceed with investigation and prosecution. It is important to note, however, that VNs require trauma-informed protocols and interdisciplinary teams to resist re-traumatization and reestablish trust. Overall, MPD's SAKI team found victim re-engagement is difficult to predict—many victims indicated they moved on and were in a different place, while others remained hurt by how the original investigation was handled. This site's VNT is continuing to conduct VNs as CODIS hits arise.

Cross-Site Comparisons: Similarities and Differences

Taken together, these case studies highlight the importance of developing a VN protocol that is victim-centered and trauma-informed, practical and consistently used, and viewed by stakeholders of varying disciplines as a key component of the criminal justice process. These case studies also outline potential variations in the VN process, as each SAKI site has unique considerations (e.g., state laws, community culture, average level of trust in law enforcement). Findings across the two case study sites were highly consistent in relation to emotional response. Namely, at both sites, the minority of victims responded to VN negatively, suggesting our previous concern about re-traumatization by conducting well-planned VNs is largely unwarranted. Despite the lack of universal agreement or VN standardization in cases attached to previously unsubmitted SAKs, both sites indicate it is crucial that SAKI sites consistently yet flexibly adhere to their VN protocol and allow victim well-being and community safety to guide their decision-making.

Discussion

VN is an important part of the criminal justice response to sexual assault cases, particularly those in which SAKs were not previously tested. Victims have the right to know the overall status of their case and evidence. The VN process is not only crucial for victims to determine the next steps in their potential cases but also for the criminal justice system to have the opportunity to make amends for the wrong that was committed against them via its initial failure to test their kits. While sparse, research is addressing the best ways to accomplish VNs in cold cases. It appears that in-person notifications in which both a law enforcement officer and a victim advocate are involved elicit the most positive response, perhaps because in-person VN indicates to victims that the system is taking their case seriously. However, VN protocols need to be flexible to consider how the victim might experience the notification based on their previous and current circumstances. More research is needed to continue to solidify best practices. In particular, it is important to explore the long-term impacts of the VN as well as how specific types of VNs impact victims' re-engagement with the criminal justice process. While these VNs will continue to be relevant to "cold" cases, our focus shifts to the implications of this research for our general response to sexual assault and SAKs.

Clearly, the wait time between the incident and SAK submission, CODIS hits, grand jury presentations, and trial is a larger, systemic issue (see Chapter 1). Therefore, this research has multiple implications for the broader system level. First, unnecessary lag-time should be avoided. Second, in current cases, victims should be notified of the status of their case immediately after a CODIS hit is received. Third, a universal tracking system needs to be implemented, so victims have a reliable way of checking the status of their kit and investigation throughout the process. Finally, those doing the notifying need to be armed with the most up-to-date information about the case. If notifiers cannot share information with the victim at the time of the notification, they must be prepared to be transparent and explain why. Only when VNs are consistently conducted in a victim-centered, trauma-informed way will we begin to make amends for the past and position sexual assault victims to achieve the justice they deserve.

Key Points

The following are some key points from this chapter:

- VN is an important part of the criminal justice process.
- Good VN protocols can help the justice system be more victim-centered and trauma-informed.

- VN should occur after involvement from multiple disciplines, training, and protocols are developed.
- VN protocols need to be flexible and fluid as additional research is disseminated and issues arise in the specific jurisdictions where VNs are occurring.
- VNs can be in-person, over the phone, via email, or via US mail. There are pros and cons to each method.
- VN in cases that involve previously untested SAKs is a victims' right. It needs to occur to determine if the victim wants to re-engage with the system. Ideally, it should also occur to make amends for the past wrong of not testing the SAK.
- Research at the Utah site suggests that in-person notifications may afford the best opportunities to be victim-centered and trauma-informed.
- The Mobile, AL site reveals that most victims had a positive or matter-of-fact emotional reaction to the VN. However, relatively few victims made a choice to re-engage with the criminal justice system at this site.
- VN in these "cold" cases can and should inform current VN practices in newer cases of sexual assault.

Discussion Questions

1. Discuss each method of VN that can be used. What implications does the method used in a VN potentially have? Based on this chapter and the research presented, what do you think is the best VN policy and why?
2. How can notifiers anticipate how a particular victim may respond to a VN? If they cannot, what might they do to mitigate a negative response?
3. How do you rectify the many different objectives that might go into a particular VN (i.e., the victim who needs/wants/has a right to information, law enforcement/prosecutors who need to know if a victim will participate so they can move forward with a case, victim advocates who want to support/protect the victim, and so on)? Can all these needs be served while employing a victim-centered, trauma-informed notification process?
4. Discuss why having representatives from multiple disciplines (particularly law enforcement and victim advocacy) is preferable. What do the representatives from these different disciplines bring to the VN process?

Further Reading

Ahrens, C. E., Swavola, L., & Dahlgren, S. (2016). *Comprehensive technical report of the joyful heart foundation victim notification project*. Joyful Heart Foundation. https://web.csulb.edu/~cahrens/JHF_Technical_Report_FINAL.pdf

Busch-Armendariz N., Donde, S., Vohra-Gupta, S., Heffron, L. C., Kalergis, K., & Lee, A. (2015). *How to notify victims about sexual assault kit evidence: Insight and recommendations from victims and professionals* (NIJ 2011-DN-BX-0002). University of Texas at Austin.

Campbell, R., Shaw, J., & Fehler-Cabral, G. (2018). Evaluation of a victim-centered, trauma-informed victim notification protocol for untested sexual assault kits. *Violence Against Women*, 24(4), 379–400.

Melton, H. C. (2021). A multidisciplinary response to sexual assault: The case review process for previously unsubmitted sexual assault kits. *Journal of Criminological Research, Policy, and Practice* (online ahead of print). https://doi.org/10.1108/JCRPP-11-2020-0068

Pinchevsky, G. M. (2018). Criminal justice considerations for un-submitted and untested sexual assault kits: A review of the literature and suggestions for moving forward. *Criminal Justice Policy Review, 29*(9), 925–945.

Sexual Assault Kit Initiative. (n.d.). *Re-engaging cold case victims.* https://www.sakitta.org/toolkit/docs/Re-engaging-Cold-Case-Victims-Factors-to-Consider.pdf

References

Ahrens, C. E., Swavola, L., & Dahlgren, S. (2016). *Comprehensive technical report of the joyful heart foundation victim notification project.* Joyful Heart Foundation. https://web.csulb.edu/~cahrens/JHF_Technical_Report_FINAL.pdf

Barnes, J. E., Noll, J. G., Putnam, F. W., & Trickett, P. K. (2009). Sexual and physical revictimization among victims of severe childhood sexual abuse. *Child Abuse and Neglect, 33*(7), 412–420.

Busch-Armendariz N., Donde, S., Vohra-Gupta, S., Heffron, L. C., Kalergis, K., & Lee, A. (2015). *How to notify victims about sexual assault kit evidence: Insight and recommendations from victims and professionals* (NIJ 2011-DN-BX-0002). University of Texas at Austin.

Campbell, R. (2018). Why police "couldn't or wouldn't" submit sexual assault kits for forensic DNA testing: A focal concerns theory analysis of untested rape kits. *Law & Society Review, 52*(1), 73–105.

Campbell, R., Fehler-Cabral, G., Bybee, D., & Shaw, J. (2017a). Forgotten evidence: A mixed methods study of why sexual assault kits (SAKs) are not submitted for DNA forensic testing. *Law & Human Behavior, 41*(5), 454–467.

Campbell, R., Fehler-Cabral, G., & Horsford, S. (2017b). Creating a victim notification protocol for untested sexual assault kits: An empirically supported planning framework. *Journal of Forensic Nursing, 13*(1), 3–13. doi: 10.1097/JFN.000000000000000139

Campbell, R., Fehler-Cabral, G., Pierce, S., Sharma, D.B., Bybee, D., Shaw, J., Horsford, S., & Feeney, H. (2015). The Detroit sexual assault kit (SAK) action research project (ARP). U.S. Department of Justice.

Campbell, R., Shaw, J., & Fehler-Cabral, G. (2018). Evaluation of a victim-centered, trauma-informed victim notification protocol for untested sexual assault kits. *Violence Against Women, 24*(4), 379–400.

Irazola, S. P., Williamson, E. J., Niedzweiecki, E., Debus-Sherrill, S., & Sun, J. (2015). Keeping victims informed: Service providers' and victims' experiences using automated notification systems. *Violence and Victims, 30*(3), 533–544.

Lonsway, K.A., & Archambault, J. (2017). *Victim impact: How victims are affected by sexual assault and how law enforcement can respond.* End Violence Against Women International.

Melton, H. C. (2021). A multidisciplinary response to sexual assault: The case review process for previously unsubmitted sexual assault kits. *Journal of Criminological Research, Policy, and Practice, 7*(3), 270–281. https://doi.org/10.1108/JCRPP-11-2020-0068

National Center for Crime Victims. (2014). *Cold case victim notification: Sample policy,* http://www.ncdsv.org/images/NCVC_Cold-case-victim-notification-sample-policy_2014.pdf

National Institute of Justice. (2016). *Notifying sexual assault victims after testing evidence,* https://www.ojp.gov/pdffiles1/nij/249153.pdf

O'Neal, E.N., Tellis, K., & Spohn, C. (2015). Prosecuting intimate partner sexual assault: Legal and extra-legal factors that influence charging decisions. *Violence Against Women, 21*(10), 1–22.

Office of Victims of Crime. (n.d.). *Victim Notification.* Retrieved from https://ovc.ojp.gov/topics/victim-notification

Sexual Assault Kit Initiative. (n.d.). *Re-engaging cold case victims,* https://www.sakitta.org/toolkit/docs/Re-engaging-Cold-Case-Victims-Factors-to-Consider.pdf

Spohn, C. & Holleran, N. (2001). Prosecuting sexual assault: A comparison of charging decisions in sexual assault involving strangers, acquaintances, and intimate partners. *Justice Quarterly, 18*, 651–688.

Strom, K. J. & Hickman, M.J. (2016). Untested sexual assault kits: Searching for an empirical foundation to guide forensic case processing decisions. *Criminology and Public Policy, 15*(2), 593–601.

Strom, K. J., Scott, T., Feeney, H., Young, A., Couzens, L., & Berzofsky, M. (2021). How much justice is denied? An estimate of unsubmitted sexual assault kits in the United States. *Journal of Criminal Justice, 73*, 101746. doi.org/10.1016/j.jcrimjus.2020.101746

Sulley, C., Wood, L., Heffron, L. C., Westbrook, L., Levy, N., Donde, S. D., & Busch-Armendariz, N. (2018). "At least they're workin' on my case?" Victim notification in sexual assault "cold" cases. *Journal of Interpersonal Violence, 36*(9–10), 4360–4380. doi:10.1177/0886260518789905

U.S. Legal. (n.d.). *Victim notification,* https://definitions.uslegal.com/v/victim-notification-system/

Utah Code Section 77-37 & 77-38. (2022). Victim's rights, 1-9. Accessed on July 11th, 2022 at Le.utah.gov/xcode/Title77/Chapter37/77-37.html

10 Transforming police response to sexual assault from the inside out

A case study of the Mobile, Alabama, sexual assault kit promise initiative

Jennifer Langhinrichsen-Rohling, Emma C. Lathan, Tres Stefurak, and Jessica Duncan

Author Note and Funding acknowledgement

This work was supported in part by the Bureau of Justice Assistance, Grant/Award Number: 2015-AK-BX-K003 to the Mobile, Alabama Police Department with a sub-award to the University of South Alabama (PI: Langhinrichsen-Rohling). However, the views in this chapter are solely those of the authors and do not represent the official positions of the DOJ, the BJA, or the Mobile Police Department.

Sexual assault is one of the most challenging crime categories for which to obtain justice. As the most likely cause of post-traumatic stress disorder (Liu et al., 2017), sexual assault is also one of the most difficult personal experiences from which to recover emotionally. From a justice perspective, difficulties associated with responding to, adequately investigating, and subsequently prosecuting rape, as compared to other types of crime, are evident. Sexual assault has a particularly low rate of being cleared by arrest and a high rate of being cleared by exceptional means (Walfield, 2015). Throughout the criminal justice process, many victims experience unwarranted challenges to their credibility and uninformed responses to their traumatic reactions, resulting in distrust of the system, secondary trauma, and experiences of institutional betrayal (Smith & Freyd, 2014). There is considerable case attrition through the process, as well as victim disengagement and discouragement (Chapter 2). Even among the small number of sexual assault cases making it fully through the criminal justice system, there are low conviction rates upon trial (Nitschke et al., 2019).

Adding to these bleak realities is the still-evolving discovery of many police departments' systematic failure to submit sexual assault kits (SAKs), which often contain crucial DNA evidence, for forensic testing—often referred to as the "rape kit backlog." Estimates suggest that as many as 300,000–400,000 unsubmitted or backlogged SAKs reside in law enforcement custody across the United States (Strom et al., 2021). Strom and Hickman (2010) refer to this state of affairs as "justice denied."

It is within this problematic, systemic context that one dedicated police officer uncovered the existence of numerous unsubmitted SAKs within the custody of the City of Mobile Police Department (MPD) in Mobile, Alabama. These SAKs were discovered in a variety of places, including a too-small evidence room, agency lockers, and an off-site storage facility. Some belonged to other police jurisdictions but had yet to be returned (e.g., nearby New Orleans, the neighboring city of Prichard).

DOI: 10.4324/9781003186816-13

Strangely, some SAKs were found intact but were labeled as "destroyed." These SAKs came from women who had experienced a stranger rape as well as from women raped by a known offender. They included cases investigated by current fellow officers as well as SAKs obtained many years prior. Many were accompanied by minimal investigative paperwork.

Choosing to stay late and work weekends, this solo officer began the tedious process of rounding up and inventorying the SAKs, while hunting down each SAK's necessary documentation to enable submission to the state forensic lab. Given the voluntary nature of this work and the limited amount of time this officer could allocate, this officer concentrated on SAKs connected to cases he deemed as the most concerning and also as having the highest probability of being successfully prosecutable. Thus, began the Mobile, Alabama National Sexual Assault Kit Initiative (SAKI) Promise Initiative.

SAKI Funding: The Start of the Promise Initiative

As noted elsewhere in this book (see Chapters 1 and 6), as this effort was voluntarily occurring in Mobile, the Bureau of Justice Assistance (BJA) began issuing calls to fund the cataloging and submission of unsubmitted SAKs in US jurisdictions with documented SAK backlogs. These potential grants requested a new level of police-prosecutor-forensic lab-advocate collaboration through the establishment of a multidisciplinary team (MDT). They also required the adoption of particular strategies to inventory SAKs, resolve the current backlog, and, if possible, prevent its recurrence. Specifically, the funding was designed to (1) confirm the extent of the backlog; (2) identify underlying causes that led to the backlog; (3) develop, implement, and evaluate a plan for testing the untested SAKs, and (4) develop, implement, and evaluate a procedure for notifying victims if and when a SAK produces a DNA hit in the Combined DNA Index System (CODIS).

In 2016, MPD applied for and was awarded its first official BJA SAKI grant. This galvanized the local effort. As with many urban police departments located across the United States, MPD was already coping with the challenges of (1) limited resources and personnel shortages that included an underfunded and overworked state forensic lab and the absence of a Special Victims Unit (SVU) or a Family Justice Center (FJC); (2) infrastructure gaps (e.g., an outdated and overcrowded evidence room, lack of private interview rooms for traumatized victims, difficult-to-access off-site storage facilities); and (3) lack of standardized communication channels (with other jurisdictions, among officers changing roles in the department, and to provide information to victims in a transparent up-to-date fashion). MPD was also grappling with historic and ongoing racial, political, and cultural tensions. Obtaining resources that were dedicated to addressing the police department's response to sexual assault provided a needed foundation for this transformational process.

Of course, with these resources came structure and stipulations to promote accountability. The first requirement was that each site develops an MDT to address the backlog. The importance of fully utilizing an MDT to address and redress the criminal justice response to sexual assault cannot be overstated (see Chapter 21). However, for police departments, this also raises several immediate and important decisions: *Who belongs on the MDT as partners with the police department, and what decision-making power do they have? How will these new processes and part-ners impact long-standing, although potentially less formal, relationships with the state crime lab and prosecution?* Because these relationships are needed with crimes other than sexual assault, there was risk in the change process. These initial MDT-related issues are described more throughout this chapter.

Once the MDT was constituted, other essential decisions needed to be faced; decisions that would have both short- and long-term implications for the police department, rape victims, perpetrators, the state forensic lab, local prosecution and the District Attorney's (DA) office, the local rape crisis center, and across time, the community. In the current chapter, we articulate seven more key decision points faced by the MDT and MPD as a whole (see Table 10.1). We provide these decision points as a way to inform other police departments who are seeking to transform their institution-specific and criminal justice-as-a-whole response to sexual assault from the "inside out."

The perspectives offered here were generated by the authors of this chapter, who constitute the original University of South Alabama SAKI research team. As part of a research-action team nested in a community-academic partnership, we functioned as collaborators, co-participants, investigators, consultants, and scientists across three different multiple-year SAKI grants awarded to MPD. Dr. Langhinrichsen-Rohling, now a Clinical Health Psychology Professor at the University of North Carolina, Charlotte, served as the Principal Investigator of two of these grants. She has amassed over 30 years of research focused on intimate partner violence, trauma, stalking, and sexual assault. Dr. Tres Stefurak, a Professor in the Clinical-Counseling Doctoral Program at the University of South Alabama, is the Principal Investigator of Mobile's third SAKI grant. His research focuses on trauma and other mental health needs among system-involved youth, mixed methods research and program evalua-tion, as well as law enforcement responses to victims of violence. Emma Lathan and Jessica Duncan served as paid graduate assistants on the project. Emma focused on enhancing victims' interactions with representatives of the criminal justice system, namely by evaluating the MDT's newly developed protocol used to notify victims of the current status of their case (i.e., victim notification, see Chapter 9) as well as a mandatory, police department-wide trauma-informed sexual assault investiga-tions training. Jessica's research focused on evaluating sources of bias that may lead law enforcement and other officials to view rape victims as less credible, which may potentially explain why SAKs were unsubmitted historically.

It is important to note that the decision points we are highlighting in this chapter are being described as sequential; however, most were revisited and re-envisioned at multiple points in the project. Many continue to generate discussion; some remain unsettled among MDT members. Thus, our initial recommendation is that any police department planning to embark on "inside out" transformation with regard to their sexual assault response should prepare for a multiyear, multi-partner journey with many iterative processes. *It is a marathon, not a sprint.* Moreover, fully embracing the cyclic public health change model of Plan, Do, Study, Act (PDSA) and applying it to all key decisions and policy changes, and in the process acknowledging that changes will be ongoing, is likely to reduce frustrations among various stakeholders who may expect one new decision to fix the issue (PDSA; Moen & Norman, 2009). We also suggest that all stakeholders formally acknowledge and, if possible, agree to assess their organizational readiness for change, as overall

Table 10.1 Eight Key Decision Points, Questions, and Challenges with Site Transformation

Eight key decision points	Emerging questions	Potential challenges
1. DEFINING THE BACKLOG	Where are all the SAKs? Who should be collecting and counting all the kits in the possession of the police department? Which ones have been submitted already? Which one should be officially counted in the backlog? How can the evidence storage and tracking system be improved?	If the effort is originating in the police department, it will likely be difficult to reconsider the submission of cases that fellow officers have deemed "suspicious" or unfounded. In some departments, being taken off the street to work in the evidence room is considered a temporary assignment (often due to a field-related concern). This may increase the possibility that the evidence room/storage areas are not well-organized and documented. These areas may have also been managed by a number of different people with an array of skill sets.
2. THE MULTIDISCIPLINARY TEAM	Who should be invited to the team? How can the MDT be integrated into police business? What happens when old team members leave and new team members join the MDT? Should there be confidentiality paperwork signed? How often and with what stipulations? How often should the team meet? Who is in charge? How is the lack of agreement handled?	Use of an MDT is a different way of conducting police business. The degree to which other voices can be considered and utilized relates to how much transformation can occur. Bringing new partners into the MDT is particularly challenging. Specifically, the inclusion of researchers, the media, and/or survivors as stakeholders in the MDT is likely to generate concerns from criminal justice stakeholders. Other MDT members may struggle with feeling less empowered (advocates, SANEs) in the process. Sustaining the MDT beyond the lifecycle of a grant requires intentional effort and a shared mission that stretches beyond the backlog.
3. ALLOCATION OF ENERGY	How should the energy, resources, and attention be distributed in order to sufficiently and simultaneously address SAKS from the past, the present, and the future? How will current cases be handled while the backlog is being addressed? Who is in charge of the organizational change needed to prevent a future backlog?	Depending on the size of the department, some personnel may need to be fully dedicated to addressing the backlog. These cases have unique challenges. Dedicating personnel to sexual assault cases allows staff to gain particular competencies and skills. Not all staff will be interested, skilled, or well-suited to this work. Staff selection processes may need to be updated. Key personnel will need to be a part of policy decisions and organizational change; however, they may not attend the weekly MDT meetings.

(Continued)

Table 10.1 Eight Key Decision Points, Questions, and Challenges with Site Transformation (Continued)

Eight key decision points	Emerging questions	Potential challenges
4. SUBMITTING THE BACKLOG	What SAKs should be submitted to the forensic lab, and in what order? What is the current and ongoing capacity of the associated forensic lab?	Prioritizing SAKs for submission is likely to generate controversy and expose underlying biases related to sexual assault, victims, and perpetrators. However, the forklift approach may just move the backlog from the police department to the forensic lab. If this lab is also responsible for processing evidence from other crimes (e.g., homicides, robberies) and other jurisdictions (state labs), this can be problematic for the overall health of the police department.
5. VICTIM NOTIFICATION	Who, what, when, where, and how should this process be undertaken?	This work may be traumatizing for staff. Criminal justice personnel may be particularly challenged by victims who choose not to re-engage with the system
6. TRACKING OUTCOMES	What do we need to measure to see the impact of our efforts? Should our team include a research partner? Will they understand our context and maintain confidentiality as needed? Will the data reflect the hard work we are doing or will we be further criticized?	Tracking implementation and outcomes requires effort and additional buy-in. Research partners bring much to the effort. However, use of a community-based participatory strategy to identify useful indicators and to interpret obtained findings is essential. If the research team members are viewed as evaluators rather than partners, team members, and potential consultants, collaboration may be more difficult. Relationships are essential.
7. CHANGING POLICE POLICY AND PRACTICE (INTERNAL)	What would need to be put into place to prevent another backlog?	Key changes points include training and use of trauma-informed interviewing at the outset; a policy of thoroughly investigating all reports, regardless of the likelihood of prosecution; a submit all kits for forensic testing policy; consideration of who has what role in the department (evidence room, SVU) with an eye to matching competencies to specialized training to positions.
8. CHANGING POLICE POLICY AND PRACTICE (EXTERNAL PARTNERSHIPS)	How do we maintain, change, and expand our partnerships to promote our ability to achieve justice and support victims? How do we encourage another partner to transform their organization from the inside out?	Academic-agency partnerships are valuable. Tracking all the points where communication can be dropped or priorities are misaligned can highlight potential growth points. Adoption of shared communication or software tracking systems (that face all external partners as well as the victim) might reduce the frequency of justice denied.

readiness is a joint function of motivation, general capacity, and innovative-specific capacity within and across agencies (Scott et al., 2017). With these caveats, and as depicted in **Table 10.1**, we offer a description of the challenges experienced, lessons learned, and decisions adopted.

First Key Decision Point: The Multidisciplinary Team

Who should be on the team? How can a multidisciplinary team be integrated into police business? What are the relationships among "new" partners and how will these change relationships with existing partners?

In response to the funding, the first official step was to form an MDT. The first iteration of the MDT consisted of the following stakeholders: the original police officer who voluntarily dedicated himself to this project; the police captain for the sex crimes unit; several detectives who were assigned to the project once funding materialized; a rape crisis advocate and a key administrator from the local rape crisis agency (both had a long-standing and positive history of collaboration with the police department); an assistant DA who was assigned to the project through the DA's office; and representatives from the state forensic lab.

Several months after creating the MDT, members of the partnered research team (i.e., the current authors) were invited to and included in these meetings. Including psychological (rather than criminal justice) researchers from the local university, with both professors and graduate students, raised concerns among some MDT stakeholders. These seemed to center on vulnerability related to "airing dirty laundry," getting input from people who did not understand police processes and distrust of those who were perceived to be "book" but not "street" smart. To allay some of these concerns, all MDT participants formally agreed to confidentiality with regard to some specific team processes as well as with regard to all private, confidential, and case-related information; documents to this effect were generated and signed by all team members.

Gendered dynamics emerged early on, with the advocates, graduate students (EL, JD), and the clinical and the counseling psychologist Principal Investigators (JLR, TS) often representing stereotypical female-focused concerns related to victim rights (e.g., test all kits, start by believing, advocating for trauma-informed care); while the police, prosecutor, and forensic lab representatives disproportionately represented stereotypical male-focused concerns related to the rights of the perpetrator (e.g., fears of entering someone into CODIS who did not belong there, worries that a consensual partner might be wrongly accused of a horrendous crime, victim credibility suspicions and case examples of false reports of rape). These tensions waxed and waned. One result was a change in the gender make-up of the MDT with the deliberate inclusion of two female prosecutors and a female police officer in year two.

Other ongoing controversies related to MDT included the following:

1 Should the MDT include a survivor? If yes, how would this person be identified, and what would their role be?
2 Should the MDT include a representative from the media? If yes, how could this person help increase the public's knowledge of the Promise Initiative and support for change? Conversely, would this inclusion increase or decrease the likelihood of SAKI-related lawsuits?

3 How should differences in opinions and approaches be handled? Who should get the final say?

4 Where and when should the MDT meet? Is it problematic to hold all the MDT meetings in the Chief of Police's conference room within MPD or reasonable given their role?

5 What is the purpose and format of the MDT? Who should set the meeting agenda?

These latter questions were key at the group's onset but also re-emerged once all SAKs were submitted for testing. Answers to other questions changed over time. For example, a media representative was added to the team in year two, with no appreciable change in lawsuits, and although multiple conversations occurred regarding the importance of including survivors' voices in the process, this did not occur.

Second Key Decision Point: Defining the Backlog

Who should be collecting and counting all the kits in the possession of the Mobile Police Department? Which SAKs should be officially "counted" as part of the backlog?

Once the MDT was constituted, efforts quickly shifted toward making decisions about which SAKs to submit and in what order. The process of identifying which kits could be accurately described as "unsubmitted" and thus counted in the backlog was immediately found to be more complicated than anticipated. MPD started with an initial estimate of unsubmitted SAKs; this number was generated by the original solo officer. However, once the SAK effort became grant-funded, confusion quickly arose as to which SAKs preceded the grant (e.g., those that had already been tagged for submission and in some cases, had already been submitted were considered pre-SAKI by the solo officer) vs. SAKs not worked by the original investigating officer. It was argued that these could properly be considered "in the grant" as unsubmitted SAKs. Some argued that all of the SAKs should count in the national total of backlogged SAKs; others were adamant that pre-grant police work should be separated from grant-funded work. Eventually, it was decided that the original box of hand-selected cases—most but not all—were attached to unsubmitted SAKs, should not count in the official SAKI total.

Next, once the paperwork was obtained and collated back with the SAK, we determined that a significant number of the SAKs included in the initial grant tally as unsubmitted actually had been previously submitted. Some were found to have been both previously submitted and tested with current technology (e.g., not meeting criteria of this grant). Others were found to have been previously submitted and tested, however, they were tested using now obsolete DNA technology. This second group was included in the SAK backlog total. Further still, many SAKs were originally labeled as unsubmitted, however, once the corresponding paperwork was obtained, we realized the SAK had been previously submitted and contained no biological material. These remained in our backlog total; however, many acknowledged that there would likely be little additional forensic value in submitting these SAKs for testing. Overall, the key result of these discoveries was that the total number of truly unsubmitted SAKs, with potentially testable DNA was substantially lower than MPD's initial estimate. This messy determination was frustrating, confusing, and time-consuming for stakeholders.

However, this process led to two important insights for the police department. First, the current systems used to catalog and track SAK processes, paperwork, and kits were inadequate. It was too difficult to determine the status of any particular SAK. This led the MDT to pursue the adoption of a computerized tracking system for old and current sexual assault cases. Second, a future-oriented approach materialized. Specifically, MDT members wondered aloud if future advances to forensic testing would occur, such that kits would need to be retested in the future. If so, a good-sized, permanent, temperature-controlled, and well-organized storage system for SAKs was essential, as Alabama does not have a statute of limitations for felony sexual assaults (2014 Code of Alabama 15-3-5). Preventing future backlogs would require infrastructure and organizational investment. These needs were addressed in subsequent funding proposals. Ultimately, out of the original 1,412 inventoried SAKs,

- 655 were determined to not require further testing. This final number reflects multiple decision points. First, it was determined that 295 kits had actually already been submitted to state forensic labs at an earlier point, but no biological evidence was contained within them ("no DNA" cases). These SAKs were not re-submitted, as there was no DNA profile suitable for uploading to CODIS.
- Next, 64 of the kits were determined to have already been tested with the most recent technology available. These kits were reconnected with their paperwork and not re-submitted.
- In 165 of the cases, the victim had named their offender, and forensic scientists confirmed that the named offender's DNA was already in CODIS. Thus, MDT police investigators and prosecutors argued that re-submission of these SAK was not necessary. The research team found themselves at odds with this decision, as submission of such kits would seemingly have the potential to offer corroboration if the DNA in the kit matched, as expected, to the named offender and that offender had not yet been tried for this crime.
- In another 11 cases, the SAKs had previously been submitted, and the offenders' DNA was already uploaded to CODIS; these cases were not re-investigated nor re-opened as the case had been previously adjudicated.
- In another 11 cases, the assistant DA recommended not submitting the SAK, as their opinion was that evidence contained in the kit would not impact any potential or forthcoming investigations or prosecution. Many of these cases had already been brought to the grand jury unsuccessfully, perhaps due to insufficient evidence.
- In 8 cases, the MPD did not have jurisdiction over the case. Decisions were made about how to return these kits to their rightful jurisdiction.
- Finally, after a review by current MPD detectives, the designated SAKI prosecutor, and a third-party investigator from the prosecutor's office, in 101 of the cases, it was determined a sexual crime did not occur, and the federal criteria for submission to CODIS were not met. These cases were also not submitted.

Third Key Decision Point: Allocation of Energy

How should we distribute our energy, resources, and attention in order to sufficiently and simultaneously address SAKs from the past, present, and future?

A question that will almost immediately face any sexual assault MDT is how to best prioritize multiple stakeholders' time, energy, and resources. The MDT will also need to determine allocations among three competing directions:

- Ferreting out underlying causes for the local backlog to understand and address the context in a tailored fashion (the past);
- Addressing the testing of backlogged kits and cold case efforts while maintaining focus on sexual assault cases that are occurring in real-time (the present); and/or
- Implementing training initiatives, issuing new standard operating procedures, and updating old or adopting new policies that will serve to prevent the reoccurrence of a backlog (the future).

With guidance from the national SAKI Training and Technical Assistance team, our site primarily chose to use existing research evidence (i.e., materials gathered from other sites) to address the past rather than a local self-probe. This reduced reactivity and defensiveness while simultaneously allowing the lion's share of resources to be directed to the present and the future.

Specifically, accumulated evidence, including that obtained from two national surveys of police departments' reasons for not using all types of DNA evidence (i.e., 1,700 law enforcement agencies, Lovrich et al., 2003; 2,250 police departments, Strom & Hickman, 2010), indicated that the inability to react to technological advances, ongoing rape-related biases and beliefs, and resource scarcity are prime factors in police department decisions to not to submit a SAK for testing. For example, both studies found that the most commonly cited reason for not submitting DNA evidence was the absence of an identified suspect for the crime (e.g., a stranger sexual assault). This is potentially unsurprising since the submission of DNA evidence of an unknown perpetrator was considered relatively futile prior to the onset of CODIS in 1990. Prior to CODIS, a reference sample from a suspect was required to consider DNA from an unknown perpetrator as probative evidence in a prosecution. Technological advances, in conjunction with greater utilization of CODIS, have increased the utility of entering both known and unknown perpetrators into the database (see Chapters 7 and 16).

Second, both surveys found that police were less likely to submit evidence for DNA testing if a perpetrator was in the process of being or had already been indicted or if there was no specific request from the prosecutor (Tasca et al., 2013). This finding is consistent with police tendency to utilize a "downstream" orientation in their decision-making. Use of the downstream orientation, with police attempting to determine if the case will be able to be successfully prosecuted prior to a full investigation, is useful for an overworked and underpaid officer and an under-resourced criminal justice system. However, it is a pathway by which rape myths and victim credibility judgments can strongly influence kit submission.

Finally, there was a consistent pattern of citing under-resourced forensic labs as the reason for not submitting and potentially utilizing DNA evidence. For example, part of Detroit's explanation for their lack of SAK submission was the real-world limitations imposed by the police department's chronically depleted resources (i.e., resource scarcity; Campbell, R et al., 2017). Qualitative interviews related to Mobile's SAKI also highlighted resource scarcity as a factor in the lack of kit submission, not only within the police department but across all stakeholders intersecting with SAKs including investigators, forensic lab staff, prosecutors, victim advocates, and medical providers conducting the initial exam of the victim.

Fourth Key Decision Point: Submitting the Backlog

Which SAKs should be submitted to the forensic lab and in what order?

Given the ongoing resource scarcity issues facing MPD and the Alabama state forensic lab, many MDT meetings focused on selecting the procedure by which unsubmitted SAKs would be chosen for submission, and in what order. Generally, in these debates, the "forklift" approach (i.e., send all kits) was pitted against the practice of prioritizing SAK submission based on MDT-selected factors. The "forklift" approach generated concern among stakeholders for two primary reasons. First, this approach fails to account for important contexts surrounding a given victim, perpetrator, or even the actual SAK. For example, some victims were deemed as less credible, and consequently, the crime less prosecutable. If prosecution is not likely, it was argued that submission and testing of that kit should not be prioritized. Second, these same stakeholders worried about regulating kit submission to a randomized process, particularly if a re-review suggested that the rape was violent, the victim was likely credible, and there was the potential that the perpetrator could be a serial predator. It was argued that the safety of the community should be a priority when considering the order of SAK submission to the crime lab. Conversely, an opposing group argued that it is this type of decision-making (i.e., making decisions based on what cases they deem to be prosecutable, what victims they deem to be credible, what rapes they deem to be serious) that has led rape victims to feel betrayed by the system and has given police the power to influence the process based on rape myths, which has ultimately resulted in a lack of SAK submission. This latter group argued for the use of a randomized SAK submission process.

Both groups perceived their motive to be ethical: prioritize submission of cases perceived to be more prosecutable or against perpetrators perceived to be more dangerous to protect the community vs. prioritize an equal-access-to-testing decision process to reduce the influence of bias, promote equity, and pursue justice for all victims. In these discussions, numerous victim credibility biases were articulated. Specifically, victim participation in substance abuse (B. Campbell et al., 2015; Schuller & Stewart, 2000), prostitution (B. Campbell et al., 2015; Page, 2007), voluntarily associating with their alleged perpetrator (Campbell & Fehler-Cabral, 2018), and having difficulty remembering details of the crime (Alderden & Ullman, 2012; B. Campbell et al., 2015; Venema, 2014) were all cited as confounding factors that would reduce the likelihood of indictment and successful prosecution.

Given these upcoming barriers, submitting these SAKs last fit with some stakeholders' anticipated low odds of eventual success. In contrast, victims whose rapists were unknown to them, who had not been involved in substance abuse or prostitution, and whose verbal accounts were clearer and more consistent were highlighted as cases needing to be prioritized for early kit submission. The nature of this debate was not about whether all unsubmitted SAKs should be eventually submitted (this was confirmed after some kits were removed from the backlog count as noted above), but rather which should be sent to the crime lab first. The stakes were heightened when the state crime lab indicated that they would not be able to test a substantial influx of old cases at once, at least not in combination with their regular caseload.

Instead, they requested a small number of additional backlogged kits be submitted each month. Thus, the adoption of a submission process was necessary.

Ultimately, the MDT chose to pursue a "both/and" approach; this entailed both using the MDT to review and select some SAKs for priority testing and submission, as well as randomly selecting an equal number of kits from the pool of SAKs that police and prosecutor stakeholders had judged as a lower priority. This compromise was brokered by two pieces of information. First, emerging evidence from other SAKI sites was demonstrating that CODIS hits were coming back to cases that were initially judged as non-credible, suspicious, or non-prosecutable in relatively equal rates to cases that were prioritized initially. Second, several other SAKI sites, including some that were similar to Mobile, were fielding lawsuits from survivors whose cases had been dropped due to police bias. The MDT felt that the inclusion of a random process of SAK selection for submission would provide greater equity for survivors while generating a defensible police process. Other police departments may face different factors affecting which kits to submit first, including prioritizing cases whose statute of limitations is expiring or prioritizing cases that have a potential serial rapist, as this is substantially more common than was originally anticipated (see Chapter 7).

Fifth Key Decision Point: Victim Notification

When, and if, should victims be notified that this process is occurring, and, specifically, that their kit is involved in the Promise Initiative? How should the victim notification process be conducted?

In addition to testing unsubmitted SAKs, SAK initiatives have also been tasked with notifying sexual assault victims of the current status of their case (victim notification or VN; national best practices for VN are offered in Chapter 20, and Mobile's experience with VN is compared to Utah's VN process in Chapter 9). While each SAKI site has crafted its own VN policy, one main aim of VN is to inform victims of the CODIS results while increasing their willingness to re-engage with the criminal justice system (i.e., "victim cooperation"). Victim participation is particularly important for both investigative and/or prosecutorial success in sexual assault cases (NIJ, 2016). Developing, implementing, and evaluating a VN policy requires numerous factors to be considered (see Chapters 9 and 20).

Many of the VN decisions made by the Mobile MDT came from a consideration of victim's rights balanced with concerns about unnecessarily re-traumatizing a victim who may have "forgotten about," "gotten over," or "moved on from" a long-ago sexual assault. From a victim's rights perspective, everyone connected with an unsubmitted SAK should be notified that they are part of the Promise Initiative. The Mobile MDT decided to handle this perspective through the airing of a public service announcement (PSA). This PSA described the Promise Initiative and included cameos by the DA, the lead sexual assault advocate, and the Police Chief. An open-access webpage was also created; this webpage outlined the procedure and purpose of the initiative and encouraged individuals to contact MPD if they were a victim of sexual assault and if they believed their case or SAK was among those that were unsubmitted. However, few survivor-initiated contacts were received and no direct, broad-scale VN efforts were conducted.

The trauma-informed perspective was reflected in multiple ways in the adopted Mobile VN policy. First, VN was to occur only if a CODIS hit was returned and there was new information to relay. Second, VN was designed to include a police officer and an advocate. The appointment was to be made via phone in order to give the survivor the choice of when, where, and how to meet for the in-person VN. Later, it was determined that all survivors should have the option of having their follow-up VN take place at the newly established FJC, which was located off-site from the police department.

The MDT wanted the VN policy to accomplish two distinct aims: facilitate healing and promote justice. However, different stakeholders had different degrees of investment in these two aims. SAKI prosecutors rely on getting victims re-engaged with the criminal justice system. While other SAKI sites have reported victim re-engagement rates ranging from 57% (R. Campbell et al., 2015a) and higher (Lovell et al., 2016), the re-engagement rate obtained in Mobile was considerably lower. This led to a re-examination of the literature to identify factors associated with victim re-engagement. Campbell et al. (2018) reported that time since assault, age at the time of the assault, and relationship to perpetrator significantly influenced willingness to re-engage with the criminal justice system. Specifically, individuals notified more than nine years after the assault, aged 16–24 at the time of the assault, and those assaulted by a known vs. stranger perpetrator were less willing to re-engage. Among adolescent victims, characteristics of the assault, victim-blaming experiences, and social support were associated with re-engagement (Feeney et al., 2018). Furthermore, sexual assault victims who did not feel comfortable during their initial interview or during VN were less likely to disclose information (Greeson et al., 2016; Patterson & Campbell, 2012), and those who perceived investigator empathy as low were less likely to willingly move forward with the case (Maddox et al., 2011).

Once the existing literature was consulted, MDT discussions focused on what local factors might be influencing reduced rates of victim willingness to re-engage. MDT stakeholder disagreement was common; however, consensus built around (1) the added difficulties of needing victims to testify at a grand jury before a trial could be guaranteed and (2) notifier tension surrounding giving a victim voice and choice as consistent with trauma-informed care vs. needing or even requiring victim participation, particularly in the case of a serial predator. There was little agreement about the frequency and duration of contact that would be perceived as supportive vs. pressured or even borderline abusive. The timeline for discussing or determining the choice to re-engage was also controversial; some stakeholders wanted very early indications of this decision for case planning or case closing purposes. In keeping with these tensions, the VN policy was revised multiple times (see Chapter 9).

Sixth Key Decision Point: Tracking Outcomes

What do we need to measure to see the impact of our efforts?

Typical Outcomes from Previous SAK Initiatives

Jurisdictions that have adopted SAK initiatives have varied in multiple ways, including organizational structures (i.e., which agency is leading the initiative; composition of the MDT); submission policies (i.e., "forklift"/test all vs. prioritization/ selective testing); and victim notification policies (i.e., rape crisis advocate present vs. just law enforcement; in-person vs. telephone notification). Further, previous SAK initiatives have targeted a variety of outcomes, including CODIS hit rates (Lovell et al., 2018), successful grand jury indictment and prosecutions (Davis & Wells, 2019), or frequency of victim willingness to re-engage with the criminal justice system, as discussed previously. Decisions about which outcomes to track faced the MDT all along the journey. We learned that one of the benefits of having an academic-community partnership is having the capacity to track outcomes. However, like other decisions highlighted in this chapter, we were reminded that buy-in from all stakeholders continues to be essential as outcomes can be used in helpful and unhelpful ways.

Other lessons emerged. For example, in terms of benefits, greater buy-in (from team members and from administrators) occurred when successes were made tangible. Inside-out change is a long process; achieving and celebrating benchmarks along the way fueled continued motivation. Operationally defining site specific outcomes (i.e., what is a realistic rate of victim re-engagement?, what is the expected rate of success at grand jury?) also generated important conversations about needed training or process changes across the system. Adding metrics at the beginning of the process made it easier to obtain grant funding for later efforts and allowed for direct comparisons across sites, providing fuel for the national learning process. Outcome measures also provided a clear pathway toward greater accountability to the public.

Some potential downfalls associated with decisions related to outcome tracking include heightened defensiveness and reactivity in an already politically charged environment. This was noticed most when researchers highlighted data collected from other SAKI sites; many other sites were perceived to be substantially different in ways that would preclude generalizability. Researchers also faced repeated stakeholder concerns that outcome data or process metrics could be used inappropriately, resulting in poor job reviews, lawsuits, and/or misunderstandings of police or prosecutor realities and contexts. At the larger level, moving toward an evidence-based, outcome focused approach, challenges the reliance on clinical- or experienced-based decision-making, and requires multiple systems to engage in a paradigm shift toward standardized procedures. It can also slow the process at the beginning, which runs contrary to a fix-it-quickly mindset. Building in evaluation shifts the process to include both short-term and long-term thinking.

CODIS Hits

One common outcome goal is to track CODIS hits related to submitting the SAKs. Base rate data is available from existing SAKI sites. For example, in Houston, 21% of all tested SAKs received DNA hits; Los Angeles' rate was 18%; Detroit's rate was 29%; and New Orleans' rate was 14% (Waltke et al., 2018). One of the highest CODIS hit rates found in SAKI work was in Cuyahoga County, Ohio (39%) (Lovell et al., 2018). Cuyahoga County (Cleveland) submitted nearly 5,000 SAKs and indicted 524 defendants (Lovell et al., 2018). Conversely, 6,660 SAKs were tested in Houston, yet there were 29 indictments (Driessen, 2015). As of January 2020, the Mobile Promise Initiative submitted 757 SAKs for forensic testing—139 received hits in CODIS (18.4%), with 129 cases having offender hits and 54 cases having forensic hits. Thirty-two of the hits obtained were to serial sexual offenders, defined by BJA as having another officially documented perpetration of rape or sexual assault.

Nine cases are at the point where they are preparing to be, or have already been, presented to a grand jury. Of these, only four cases have resulted in indictments and moved to the trial phase. Of these four, one was dismissed. The presiding judge ruled the prosecution could not move forward because the offender was a minor at the time of the alleged crime. Two other cases are currently pending trial. To date, one offender has been found guilty as a direct result of a Promise Initiative CODIS hit.

Seventh Key Decision Point: Changing Internal Policy and Practice

What needs to be addressed within the police department, so there is never another backlog?

With one of the largest backlogs in the country—and arguably one of the more daunting undertakings of the SAK initiatives—Detroit has been highly successful in implementing institutional practices to provide justice and prevent future injustice. For instance, the police department and its leadership have supported new evidence-based training on trauma-informed, offender-focused investigational methods (Campbell et al., 2015b). Following Detroit's lead, Mobile implemented victim-centered and trauma-informed approaches and trainings; developed a specialized sexual assault unit comprised of specialized investigators and prosecutors; renovated the SAK evidence rooms; and adopted an innovative evidence-tracking system.

Changes in Police Policies

Mobile also chose to develop new standard operating procedures for officers investigating sex crimes, focusing specifically on trauma-informed investigation procedures. The commanding officer for sex crimes, working in collaboration with the MDT and after attending multiple trainings sponsored by the Department of Justice, developed the policies and organizational changes described hereafter.

Submit All Kits

As documented previously in Detroit, Campbell and Fehler-Cabral (2018) found that, in addition to funding and staffing limitations, concerns over victim credibility and cooperation influenced why SAKs were not submitted by police. Further, Goodman-Williams et al. (2019) found no support for the practice of prioritizing kits for submission based on specific features associated with the offender, the victim, or the nature of the assault. This research suggests that submitting all kits is both an ethically and an empirically supported practice. In Mobile, the adoption of a submit all kits policy was controversial for several reasons. First, police stakeholders argued that there are not all reports of rape are "real." They had concerns about submitting a kit to CODIS that came from a rape that they did not believe occurred. This concern was supported by professionals from the state crime lab who reminded MDT participants that evidence of a crime having occurred (as determined by the presiding law enforcement agency) is a requirement for CODIS submission. The final decision was to have the policy assert that all kits were to be submitted unless there was irrefutable evidence that the alleged rape did not happen (i.e., material evidence that this could not have happened as reported by the victim). The policy change was eventually supported by the sex crimes detectives, who reported greater clarity in their work. One stated, "When detectives let personal feelings get involved, things go wrong, you are better to follow procedures that time has been put into developing and sleep well at night …"

Special Victims Unit and Family Justice Center

A second important internal change was to create a stand-alone, off-site, SVU within the police department and, eventually, an off-site FJC. Prior to receiving the SAKI funding, investigators were assigned rape and sexual assault cases alongside other cases such as property crime. Through the efforts of the MDT and with support from SAKI funding, an SVU was created within the MPD, staffed with dedicated investigators whose sole focus was sexual assault investigation. These investigators joined and participated in the SAKI MDT. They were also supported to attend multiple professional development workshops on trauma-informed investigation procedures.

In addition to mounting a fully devoted SVU, the police department decided to move forward in their relationship with the local rape crisis center and the DA's office to create an FJC. The FJC allowed investigators, rape crisis advocates, and assistant DAs to be housed in a single location, a building on-site of the rape crisis center's parent organization. This meant victims now had a "one-stop shop" and would not have to go to multiple destinations after their initial rape exam. The FJC also promotes more effective communication by housing team members and stakeholders in the same place. Proximity facilitates the timely sharing of information and strategy and can result in closer relationships among partners. It also equalizes the power dynamics among stakeholders by providing meetings away from any particular stakeholder's primary space (e.g., not at the police department's central office or at the DA's office). This important advancement was likely aided by key stakeholders working more closely together as part of the SAKI grant.

Police Academy & Ongoing Professional Development

Another internal change was to extend the push toward trauma-informed care and changed responses to sexual assault beyond the SVU investigators, rape crisis advocates and prosecutors, and onto all sworn officers as well as incoming cadets. Specifically, members of the MDT crafted a series of professional development workshops (Lathan et al., 2019). The workshops focus on various aspects of trauma-informed policing, including ways to reduce officer bias toward rape victims, trauma-informed interviewing strategies, and the importance of applying due diligence to all evidence, SAK and otherwise, that emerge in the aftermath of a rape. This latter emphasis is to help officers avoid the corrosive effects associated with "downstream orientation" or the overt focus on what officers believe will be prosecutable, rather than performing a thorough investigation that includes gathering evidence and interviewing potential witnesses. This training also emphasized the importance of following new sexual assault standard operating procedures, chief among them to submit all SAKs.

Foregoing the use of the "Suspicious Circumstances" Label

During the inventory phase of the Mobile site's project, a significant subset of sexual assault cases (n = 351, or 25%) was discovered; these cases were labeled "Suspicious Circumstances." Investigators on the MDT stated that Mobile's police department has historically used this label to indicate that one or more of the officers involved in the case did not believe the victim's report of a sexual crime. On behalf of the goal of reforming practices, protocols, and policies that generated a backlog, the MPD has now implemented a Standard Operating Procedure that disallows officers use of the "Suspicious Circumstances" label as code for concerns about victim credibility. Now, this designation is only allowed to be used in cases where the victim is unable to confirm an assault occurred. For example, this label is allowed if the victim states they lost consciousness and suspects they may have been assaulted. In other words, a designation of suspicious circumstances is now only used if the *victim* is suspicious that they were assaulted or unsure of what precisely happened. The label is no longer meant to convey that police are suspicious of the victim or doubt their credibility. Furthermore, if a victim says they were assaulted, the officers will now label the crime that the victim reported (e.g., Rape First Degree, Sodomy, etc.) rather than indicating what the officer thinks "might" have happened. On the other hand, if officers can confirm that a victim's report of sexual assault was a false or baseless allegation (i.e., they have enough evidence to theoretically charge the reportee with false reporting), they have now been directed to use the official crime label accepted by the Uniform Crime Reporting program, "Unfounded."

Eighth Key Decision Point: Maintaining, Changing, and Expanding External Partnerships

How do we maintain, change, and expand our partnerships to promote our ability to achieve justice and support victims? How do we encourage other partners to transform their organizational response to sexual assault from the inside out?

The criminal justice system is complex. With regard to sexual assault, a substantial amount of coordination of information and exchanging of evidence has to occur for the process to be effective. In Mobile, the official response often flows from the responding police officer to the hospital (SANEs conducting a sexual assault forensic examination to obtain a SAK, potentially with the inclusion of an advocate), to assigned investigators (potentially from an SVU) who re-engage with the victim at an FJC (housed off-site from the police department, with the inclusion of an advocate) to the forensic lab to prosecution. The collected SAK has to move from the hospital to the police evidence room and onto the forensic lab. It has to be accompanied by the required paperwork, which provides the forensic analyst with cues about what to test. Information about the testing eventually returns to the police department. At various points in the process, the sex crimes prosecutor is likely to be consulted, and at some point, the case transfers from the police to the prosecution as the primary lead of the criminal justice process. Given current wait times in the criminal justice system, the time from crime to trial (if a trial happens) can be considerable; multiple updates and communications to the victim are required to facilitate continued engagement, voice, and choice in the process.

Recognition of this complexity has led jurisdictions like Mobile to create a FJC. Closer relationships among those working to transform the response to sexual assault from the inside out are also a catalyst for greater organizational change. Divergent perspectives on the same mission not only led to police officers reflecting on their policies and procedures but also led police officers to question the policies and practices of other stakeholders. These exchanges focused on sexual assault responses but were extended to consider how the SAKI efforts might be directly and indirectly impacting responses to other types of crime (homicides, assault). The collective impact from SAKI has yet to be determined but may be considerably broader than ever anticipated.

Conclusions

This chapter considered key decision points faced by MPD, an urban police department attempting to change their response to sexual assault from the "inside out" via SAKI. SAKI sites differ substantially in who leads the change effort (e.g., prosecution, police, advocates) and at what level (e.g., city, county, state). We argue that any urban police department that chooses to address its stockpile of unsubmitted SAKs is simultaneously afforded an opportunity for organizational growth. These opportunities are maximized through the active use and empowerment of an MDT, committed stakeholders, and transparent debate at critical decision points, as well as through the enactment of policy, procedure, and partnership changes. As members of the Mobile, AL MDT and as on-site researchers embedded in an academic-community partnership, we highlight eight controversial decisions our site faced, diverse viewpoints offered, decisions rendered and revisited, and outcomes obtained in order to provide a potential guide for other institutions hoping to transform their response to sexual assault from the "inside out." Tackling and then sustaining this type of change requires institutional courage and is aided by buy-in from all levels. It can also be supported or slowed by the behaviors of key external partners. Attention to and regular communication among all stakeholders through an engaged MDT that persists through challenges is a roadmap for success.

Key Points

- Engagement in a multidisciplinary SAKI team is a multiyear, multi-partner journey with many iterative processes. Success requires organizational readiness and commitment.
- The simultaneous remediation and future-oriented prevention of backlogged SAKs require infrastructure and organizational investment in both time and resources.
- Change from the inside out, through institutional policy and practice initiatives like victim-centered and trauma-informed approaches, accountable standardized operational procedures, and submit all kits initiatives, serves to create sustainable reform.

Discussion Questions

1 How do you think the SAKI project might go differently if it is primarily led by a city police department, state government, or the local prosecutor's office? What are the advantages and disadvantages of having the police department be responsible for changing its old (and potentially ongoing) response to sexual assault?

2 What do you think are the advantages and disadvantages of a "both/and" approach to submitting previously untested SAKs? Would this be the method you would choose? Why or why not?

3 What are some communication strategies that you think are beneficial on an MDT? Why would these be necessary in the context of SAKI?

Further Reading

Campbell, B. A., Fehler-Cabral, G., Pierce, S. J., Sharma, D. B., Bybee, D., Shaw, J., Horsford, S., & Feeney, H. (2015). *The Detroit sexual assault kit (SAK) action research project (ARP) final report.* Award #2011-DN-BX-0001. Accessed on February 27 at https://ovc.ojp.gov/library/publications/detroit-sexual-assault-kit-sak-action-research-project-arp-final-report

Home | Sexual Assault Kit Initiative (SAKI). (n.d.). Retrieved March 22, 2022, from https://www.sakitta.org/

Lathan, E., Langhinrichsen-Rohling, J., Duncan, J., & Stefurak, J. T. (2019). The promise initiative: Promoting a trauma-informed police response to sexual assault in a mid-size southern community. *Journal of Community Psychology, 47*(7), 1733–1749. https://doi.org/10.1002/jcop.22223

Lovell, R., Luminais, M., Flannery, D. J., Bell, R., & Kyker, B. (2018). Describing the process and quantifying the outcomes of the Cuyahoga County sexual assault kit initiative. *Journal of Criminal Justice, 57*, 106–115. https://doi.org/10.1016/j.jcrimjus.2018.05.012

References

Alderden, M. A., & Ullman, S. E. (2012). Creating a more complete and current picture: Examining police and prosecutor decision-making when processing sexual assault cases. *Violence Against Women, 19*(5), 671–673. https://doi.org/10.1177/1077801212453867

Campbell, B. A., Menaker, T. A., & King, W. R. (2015). The determination of victim credibility by adult and juvenile sexual assault investigators. *Journal of Criminal Justice, 43*(1), 29–39. https://doi.org/10.1016/j.jcrimjus.2014.12.001

Campbell, R., & Fehler-Cabral, G. (2018). Why police "couldn't or wouldn't" submit sexual assault kits for forensic DNA testing: A focal concerns theory analysis of untested rape kits. *Law & Society Review, 52*(1), 73–105. https://doi.org/10.1111/lasr.12310

Campbell, R., Fehler-Cabral, G., Bybee, D., & Shaw, J. (2017). Forgotten evidence: A mixed methods study of why sexual assault kits (SAKs) are not submitted for DNA forensic testing. *Law and Human Behavior, 41*(5), 454–467. https://doi.org/10.1037/lhb0000252

Campbell, R., Fehler-Cabral, G., Pierce, S. J., Sharma, D. B., Bybee, D., Shaw, J., Horsford, S., & Feeney, H. (2015a). *The Detroit sexual assault kit (SAK) action research project (ARP) final report.* Award #2011-DN-BX-0001. Accessed on February 27 at https://ovc.ojp.gov/library/publications/detroit-sexual-assault-kit-sak-action-research-project-arp-final-report

Campbell, R., Shaw, J., & Fehler-Cabral, G. (2015b). Shelving justice: The discovery of thousands of untested rape kits in Detroit. *City & Community, 14*(2), 151–166. https://doi.org/10.1111/cico.12108

Campbell, R., Shaw, J., & Fehler-Cabral, G. (2018). Evaluation of a victim-centered, trauma-informed, victim notification protocol for untested sexual assault kits. Violence Against Women, 24(4), 379–400. https://doi.org/10.1177/1077801217699090

Code of Alabama. (2014). *Title 15—CRIMINAL PROCEDURE. Chapter 3—LIMITATIONS ON PROSECUTION. Section 15-3-5—Offenses having no limitation.* (n.d.). Justia Law. Retrieved February 24, 2022, from https://law.justia.com/codes/alabama/2014/title-15/chapter-3/section-15-3-5/

Davis, R. C., & Wells, W. (2019). DNA testing in sexual assault cases: When do the benefits outweigh the costs? *Forensic Science International*, 299, 44–48. https://doi.org/10.1016/j.forsciint.2019.03.031

Driessen, K. (2015, February 23). City done with lab testing of rape kit backlog. *Chronicle*. Retrieved from http://www.chron.com/news/politics/houston/article/City-donewith-Lab-testing-of-rape-kit-backlog-6096424.php

Feeney, H., Campbell, R., & Cain, D. (2018). Do you wish to prosecute the person who assaulted you?: Untested sexual assault kits and victim notification of rape survivors assaulted as adolescents. *Victims & Offenders*, 13(5), 651–674. https://doi.org/10.1080/15564886.2018.1426668

Goodman-Williams, R., Campbell, R., Sharma, D. B., Pierce, S. J., Feeney, H., & Fehler-Cabral, G. (2019). How to right a wrong: Empirically evaluating whether victim, offender, and assault characteristics can inform rape kit testing policies. *Journal of Trauma & Dissociation*, 20(3), 288–303. https://doi.org/10.1080/15299732.2019.1592645

Greeson, M. R., Campbell, R., Bybee, D., & Kennedy, A. C. (2016). Improving the community response to sexual assault: An empirical examination of the effectiveness of sexual assault response teams (SARTs). *Psychology of Violence*, 6(2), 280–303.

Lathan, E., Langhinrichsen-Rohling, J., Duncan, J., & Stefurak, J. T. (2019). The promise initiative: Promoting a trauma-informed police response to sexual assault in a mid-size southern community. *Journal of Community Psychology*, 47(7), 1733–1749. https://doi.org/10.1002/jcop.22223

Liu, H., Petukhova, M. V., Sampson, N. A., Aguilar-Gaxiola, S., Alonso, J., Andrade, L. H., Bromet, E. J., de Girolamo, G., Haro, J. M., Hinkov, H., Kawakami, N., Koenen, K. C., Kovess-Masfety, V., Lee, S., Medina-Mora, M. E., Navarro-Mateu, F., O'Neill, S., Piazza, M., Posada-Villa, J., ... World Health Organization World Mental Health Survey Collaborators. (2017). Association of DSM-IV posttraumatic stress disorder with traumatic experience type and history in the World Health Organization World Mental Health Surveys. *JAMA Psychiatry*, 74(3), 270–281. https://doi.org/10.1001/jamapsychiatry.2016.3783

Lovell, R., Flannery, D., Overman, L., & Walker, T. (2016). *What happened with the sexual assault reports? Then vs. now*. Begun Center for Violence Prevention Research and Education.

Lovell, R., Luminais, M., Flannery, D. J., Bell, R., & Kyker, B. (2018). Describing the process and quantifying the outcomes of the Cuyahoga County sexual assault kit initiative. *Journal of Criminal Justice*, 57, 106–115. https://doi.org/10.1016/j.jcrimjus.2018.05.012

Lovrich, N. P., Pratt, T. C., Gaffney, M. J., Johnson, C. L., Aspien, C. H., Hurst, L. H. & Schellberg, T. M. (2003). *National forensic DNA study report: Final report*. Washington D.C. National Institute of Justice.

Maddox, L., Lee, D., & Barker, C. (2011). Police empathy and victim PTSD as potential factors in rape case attrition. *Journal of Police and Criminal Psychology*, 26(2), 112–117. https://doi.org/10.1007/s11896-010-9075-6

Moen, R., & Norman, C. (2009). *Evolution of the PDCA cycle*. Accessed on February 22, 2022 at https://rauterberg.employee.id.tue.nl/lecturenotes/DG000%20DRP-R/references/Moen-Norman-2009.pdf

National Institute of Justice. (2016). Notifying sexual assault victims after testing evidence. Accessed on July 11, 2022 at https://www.ojp.gov/pdffiles1/nij/249153.pdf

Nitschke, F. T., McKimmie, B. M., & Vanman, E. J. (2019). A meta-analysis of the emotional effect for female adult rape complainants: Does complainant distress influence credibility. *Psychological Bulletin*, 145(10), 953–979. https://doi.org/10.1037/bul0000206

Page, A. D. (2007). Behind the blue line: Investigating police officers' attitudes towards rape. *Journal of Police and Criminal Psychology*, 22(1), 22–32. http://dx.doi.org/10.1007/s11896-007-9002-7

Patterson, D., & Campbell, R. (2012). The problem of untested sexual assault kits: Why are some kits never submitted to a crime laboratory? *Journal of Interpersonal Violence*, 27(11), 2259–2275. http://dx.doi.org/10.1177/0886260511432155

Schuller, R. A., & Stewart, A. (2000). Police responses to sexual assault complaints: The role of perpetrator/complainant intoxication. *Law and Human Behavior*, 24(5), 535–551. http://dx.doi.org/10.1023/A:1005519028528

Scott, V. C., Kenworthy, T., Godly-Reynolds, E., Bastien, G., Scaccia, J., McMickens, C., Rachel, S., Cooper, S., Wrenn, G., & Wandersman, A. (2017). The Readiness for Integrated Care Questionnaire (RICQ): An instrument to assess readiness to integrated behavioral health and primary care. *American Journal of Orthopsychiatry*, 87(5), 520–530. https://doi.org/10.1037/ort0000270

Sexual Assault Kit Initiative Training and Technical Assistance. (2020). *Sexual Assault Kit Initiative*. Department of Justice. Washington, D.C.: Office of Justice Programs.

Smith, C. P., & Freyd, J. J. (2014). Institutional betrayal. *American Psychologist*, 69(6), 575–587. https://doi.org/10.1037/a0037564

Strom, K. J., & Hickman, M. J. (2010). Unanalyzed evidence in law-enforcement agencies: A national examination of forensic processing in police departments. *Criminology & Public Policy*, 9(2), 381–404. https://doi.org/10.1111/j.1745-9133.2010.00635.x

Strom, K., Scott, T., Feeney, H., Young, A., Couzens, L., & Berzofsky, M. (2021). How much justice is denied? An estimate of unsubmitted sexual assault kits in the United States. *Journal of Criminal Justice*, 73, 101746. https://doi.org/10.1016/j.crimjus.2020.101746

Tasca, M., Rodriguez, N., Spohn, C., & Koss, M. P. (2013). Police decision making in sexual assault cases: Predictors of suspect identification and arrest. *Journal of Interpersonal Violence*, 28, 1157–1177.

Venema, R. M. (2014). Police officer schema of sexual assault reports: Real rape, ambiguous cases, and false reports. *Journal of Interpersonal Violence*, 31(5), 1–28. https://doi.org/10.1177/0886260514556765

Walfield, S. M. (2015). When a cleared rape is not cleared: A multilevel study of arrest and exceptional clearance. *Journal of Interpersonal Violence*, 31(9), 1767–1792.

Waltke, H., LaPorte, G., Weiss, D., Schwarting, D., Nguyen, M., & Scott, F. (2018). Sexual assault cases: Exploring the importance of non-DNA forensic evidence. *National Institute of Justice Journal*, 279, 1–14. https://nij.gov/journals/279/Pages/non-dna-evidence-in-sexual-assault-cases.aspx.

11 Seeking justice through sexual violence prosecutions

Jennifer Gentile Long, Patricia D. Powers,
Holly Fuhrman, and Jennifer Newman

The prosecution of sexual violence is unlike the prosecution of other crimes. Sexual violence poses distinctive challenges for prosecutors and other professionals in the criminal justice system and often involves uniquely vulnerable victims. The crimes themselves—how they are committed, who commits them, who is victimized—are widely misunderstood by those who have not been educated about perpetrator-victim dynamics (see Chapters 3, 4, 7, and 8). And the behavior of victims in response to the trauma of these devastating crimes is often misconstrued. While many criminal justice professionals have educated themselves about these dynamics and behaviors, the general public (including jurors) continues to be influenced by myths and misconceptions. Too often, law enforcement and prosecutors "weed out" the more difficult cases based on a perception that the cases will prove to be "unwinnable"—that the legal and factual challenges are insurmountable (see Chapter 2). In some cases, victims are deemed "uncooperative" or "unreliable" when, in reality, their behaviors are symptoms of significant trauma (see Chapter 8). Disappointingly few cases make it to trial and even fewer result in conviction. Moreover, the problem is self-perpetuating: to the extent that police and prosecutors are not vigorously pursuing more challenging cases, they are not developing and honing the skills necessary to build sexual assault cases that will result in convictions.

However, conviction rates tell only part of the story about whether a prosecutor's office—or a prosecutor—is successful in handling cases involving sexual violence. If difficult or challenging cases fall by the wayside early in the process, they are generally not factored into the rate of conviction. While there may be a thin veneer of success in terms of conviction rate, the reality is that serial perpetrators, or those who are clever in their choice of victim, escape justice, while victims who have been violated in the most personal and devastating way are left to their own remedies, without the support of the criminal justice system. Studies examining the testing of previously backlogged sexual assault kits in just three cities—Cleveland, Memphis, and Detroit—have revealed over 1,250 suspected serial rapists linked to assaults occurring all over the United States (End the Backlog, 2017).

If conviction rates are not a reliable measure of success, what is? The answer lies in the quality of the prosecution's response. In prosecuting sexual violence, more so than with other crimes, the process is as important as—or more important than—the legal outcome in achieving a just result. The entire process of thorough investigation

DOI: 10.4324/9781003186816-14

and meticulous prosecution yields many benefits, regardless of whether any individual case results in conviction:

- Prosecutors and investigators hone skills and refine strategies that increase the likelihood of conviction in future cases.
- Better prepared cases shine a light on the full range of an accused's conduct, exposing predatory behavior, exploitation, manipulation, and intimidation.
- Serial offenders are identified so that future victimizations can be prevented.
- Law enforcement and prosecutors come to recognize the prevalence of cross-over offenders—individuals who victimize both persons they know (intimate partners, acquaintances) and those they don't know.
- Evidence is developed that may be admissible in other cases involving the same perpetrator.
- Trauma-informed responses reduce re-traumatization in victims.
- Victims see their cases are taken seriously and obtain a measure of validation and closure.
- Victim safety, privacy, and confidentiality are respected and protected.
- Victims are encouraged to report crimes.
- Community relations are strengthened by consistent messaging from prosecutors in a position of leadership.
- Communities are made safer.
- Jurors and judges are educated in dynamics of sexual assault and how trauma may affect victim behavior.
- Improved coordination and cooperation between criminal justice professionals allows all involved to share information, knowledge, and expertise—streamlining the process for victims and allowing agencies to make the best use of available resources.

This chapter explains in detail the problems that have arisen as a result of over-reliance on conviction rates in cases of sexual violence. It identifies the core principles that should inform a model response to these crimes to further the goals of justice—i.e., offender accountability, victim well-being, and community safety. Finally, it discusses how prosecutors can broaden definitions of "success" in the prosecution of sexual violence and how they can measure their current response as well as efforts toward improvement.

This chapter was developed by AEquitas, a nonprofit organization focused on developing, evaluating, and refining strategies related to the prosecution of gender-based violence and human trafficking. This work is done by a team of experts, many of whom are experienced former prosecutors who specialized in prosecuting sexual violence and related offenses in jurisdictions across the United States. This chapter was adapted from the Model Response to Sexual Violence for Prosecutors (RSVP Model), a three-volume resource developed by AEquitas and its partners at the Urban Institute (Urban) and the Justice Management Institute (JMI).[1] The RSVP Model is available at theRSVP.org.

A brief note about terminology—across the United States, sex crimes are named and defined differently. The criminal acts range from sexual penetration to sexual contact or exposure, with additional elements ranging from physical force to lack of consent. This chapter will use the terms rape, sexual assault, and sexual violence interchangeably when referring to any of these crimes. We also chose to use the term victim rather than survivor as this term parallels their status within the justice system.

The Accountability Gap: Incidence of Sexual Violence vs. Prosecution and Conviction Rates

"Sexual violence is a deeply traumatic crime that can cause severe damage to survivors' emotional, spiritual, and psychological well-being" (Hanson, 2014, para. 1). Studies estimate that 1 in 5 women and 1 in 71 men have been raped at some point in their lives (Black et al., 2011). Sexual assault victimization is both physically and psychologically harmful. In addition to the physical harm, which studies show one in three female victims and one in six male victims experience, victims suffer from an invasion of personal autonomy and dignity (Tjaden & Thoennes, 2006). In fact, the largest proportion of crime victims suffering from post-traumatic stress disorder is sexual assault survivors (Campbell & Wasco, 2005).

Yet despite the prevalence of sexual violence—and the harms that it causes—disappointingly few offenders are ever held accountable through the criminal justice system. More than two-thirds of sexual assault victims do not report the assaults committed against them to police for reasons that include fear, embarrassment, trauma, loyalty toward or fear of the perpetrator, distrust in the criminal justice system, and a belief that the criminal justice system is an inappropriate vehicle for resolving their experiences of violence (Cohn et al., 2013; Herman, 2011; Tjaden & Thoennes, 2006).

Even when victims do report sexual assault, it is not always a given that their cases will be investigated and prosecuted. Regardless of the intentions of system professionals to achieve justice, and despite their beliefs in the strength of their offices' responses to these crimes, research reveals that arrest rates, prosecution rates, and conviction rates for sexual violence are staggeringly low (Beichner & Spohn, 2005; Kingsnorth et al., 1998; Rockey et al., 2012; Spohn et al., 2001). In one six-site study, for instance, researchers found that between 80% and 89% of cases reported to the police were either never referred to the prosecutor's office or were declined for prosecution (Campbell et al., 2014). The backlog of sexual assault kits has been the most tangible sign of the gap between reported sexual assaults and arrest, prosecution, and conviction. Historically, thousands of victims of sexual assault have not only reported cases to law enforcement but presented for medical care and forensic evidence collection (Strom et al., 2009); many of these cases remained dormant until the DOJ's Sexual Assault Kit Initiative (SAKI) provided funding for testing backlogged sexual assault kits and training for system professionals. And while SAKI has made an enormous dent in the testing of kits, the challenge persists—while there is limited data on the remaining backlog across the United States, recent reports from individual jurisdictions reveal worrying numbers of still-untested kits (Hanson, 2021). This enduring problem is reflective of the larger crisis of staggering case attrition in the criminal justice system—what researchers have dubbed "[o]ne of the most enduring realities of sexual assault" (Spohn & Tellis, 2014, p. 101).

What causes the gap between reports of sexual assault and actual prosecutions? Is law enforcement failing to investigate or refer cases for prosecution? Are officers "exceptionally clearing" these cases (Spohn & Tellis, 2012) based on perceptions about downstream decision-making? (Morabito et al., 2019; Pattavina et al., 2015)[2]

Are cases being referred for prosecution but then declined based on inadequate or inaccurately analyzed investigations? Are triable cases being declined for some other reason?

Answers to these questions can be gleaned from attrition studies (AEquitas, 2017), reports from untested sexual assault kits (AEquitas, 2017), investigative reports (Knezevich & Rentz, 2016; Miller & Armstrong, 2015), victim feedback (AEquitas, 2017; Wood et al., 2015), and anecdotal evidence, including multidisciplinary participant feedback at trainings. Among the likely explanations are:

- credibility assessments grounded in sexual violence myths (e.g., regarding assaults committed against acquaintances and intimate partners, persons in the commercial sex industry, or intoxicated victims, see Chapter 3);
- unconscious biases related to age, race, and socioeconomic status of the victim or offender (Beichner & Spohn, 2005; Kingsnorth et al., 1998; Rockey et al., 2012; Spohn et al., 2001)[3];
- lack of information and training about sexual violence perpetration, victimization, and trauma;
- agency resource shortages (Campbell et al., 2015); and
- concerns over conviction rates (Campbell et al., 2015; Long & Nugent-Borakove, 2014).

When it comes to investigation and prosecution of cold case sexual assaults, additional factors are likely at play. These may include the perceived effect of the impact of time on victims, witnesses, and evidence, as well as concerns related to pre-accusatorial delay, reflecting a dire need for specialized cold case training.

Collectively, these factors paint an unacceptable picture of the criminal justice response to sexual assault—a picture that is distressing for the countless prosecutors seeking justice and devastating for the countless victims who deserve it. The crisis also has significant implications for victim and community safety. Testing of backlogged sexual assault kits has revealed that serial sex offending is more common than previously estimated: roughly a third to a quarter of offenders identified through SAKI are serial sexual offenders connected to at least two sexual assault kits associated with a criminal report (see Chapter 7). Research examining the testing of kits has also shown that serial sexual offenders do not always have the same *modus operandi* or specialized marks of their offense; such offenders may assault strangers, as well as persons known to them (see Chapter 7).

Improving the response to sexual violence will not only increase the number of cases investigated and prosecuted but will encourage more survivors to report their assaults and reduce the occurrence of these crimes as communities identify more perpetrators.

The Core Principles Guiding Best Practices in Sexual Assault Prosecution

Prosecutors' dedication to seeking justice can make it difficult to see and accept failures. When we, as prosecutors, hear survivors say that they feel ignored or abandoned by the system, our defenses kick in. We stubbornly insist that survivor perceptions are not accurate—not in our jurisdictions. *However, a better response is to truly listen* to survivors' feedback, acknowledge that our approach may not be fully achieving our goals, and examine how our practices can be improved. This involves reviewing our disposed cases to determine trends in outcomes; assessing our policies and practices against best practices; reviewing the most current scientific, social scientific, and forensic research; and enhancing our awareness of advanced DNA technologies, among numerous other strategies.

Below, we describe the core principles of a model response to sexual violence, as well as strategies for bringing these principles to life through office-level and case-level practices. By employing the strategies described below, prosecutors will be better equipped to seek justice for victims, hold offenders accountable, collaborate with other criminal justice stakeholders to end the current backlog of sexual assault kits, and ultimately prevent future backlogs.

Trauma-Informed Prosecutorial Approaches

A trauma-informed approach requires prosecutors to understand how trauma affects victims of sexual violence and to interact with victims in a manner that minimizes re-traumatization and maximizes their engagement with the criminal justice system. Victims are unique individuals—as are all people—and their responses to trauma can be just as diverse. When recounting the details of sexual violence, victims may cry, laugh, talk loudly and aggressively, exhibit a flat affect, or shut down entirely. Victims may "cope" by attempting to ignore or normalize what happened to them (Kristiansson & Whitman-Barr, 2015; see also Chapter 8), prompting them to be angry or confrontational when pressed for information. Trauma may also impact a victim's ability to recount the details or the chronology of the assault and surrounding events. They may have triggers, such as sounds or smells, which cause them to relive some aspect of their assault. Victims experiencing these effects may also attempt to self-medicate using drugs or alcohol. The effects of trauma can be exacerbated for victims of intimate partner sexual assault, who repeatedly endure both physical and sexual violence at the hands of a trusted partner, as well as for Black, Indigenous, and People of Color (BIPOC) victims, who may have experienced generational trauma caused by racial violence, systemic discrimination, and/or familial patterns of abuse (Thomas, 2021).

Prosecutors should also be mindful of the trauma of reopening cold cases, where DNA evidence is matched years—or even decades—after a victim is assaulted. In such cases, victims face unique challenges when engaging with the criminal justice system, particularly when it comes to testifying at trial. Whether a victim has been able to place their trauma behind or has carried it with them, facing their offender at trial may reopen old wounds and lead to re-traumatization.

Prosecutors can employ numerous strategies to mitigate the effects of trauma on the victim and on the criminal case. These may include—but are not limited to—collaborating with allied professionals, including system-based and community-based advocates, to ensure victims receive any needed services, including counseling, medical care, civil legal assistance, and safety planning; tailoring victim interviews to elicit sensory and experiential details; and requesting accommodations for victim testimony, such as the presence of victim advocates or support animals near the witness stand.

190 Jennifer Gentile Long, Patricia D. Powers, Holly Fuhrman et al.

Cold cases require consideration of additional strategies to mitigate victim trauma. For example, prosecutors may consider working closely with advocates, law enforcement, and other allied professionals to determine a protocol for notifying victims of CODIS (the federal DNA database, see also Chapters 7 and 16) hits or reopened cases. These and other strategies are discussed in detail in AEquitas and SAKI resources (Sexual Assault Kit Initiative, n.d.b).

Victim-Centered Prosecutorial Approaches

A victim-centered approach to sexual assault appreciates the central role victims play in the judicial process and considers their needs throughout. The best possible case outcomes not only hold the offender responsible for their actions, but account for the victim's history, experience, and perspective, as well as the impact of the criminal justice process on their lives and their family, school, or workplace, and community.

Prosecutors should understand that, although they have a duty to seek accountability for offenders, pursuit of this duty cannot come at the expense of the victim's well-being. This means that practices that are recognized as being harmful to victim safety, such as the use of material witness warrants (U.S. Department of Justice, 2022) should be reserved for the most serious of cases and utilized only under the most extreme circumstances, if at all. It also means that victims should have access to civil attorneys and community-based professionals who can maintain victim confidentiality and zealously advocate for the victim's interests, which may sometimes run counter to the prosecutor's interests (Sexual Assault Kit Initiative, n.d.a).

A victim-centered approach also requires that victims are kept informed at all stages of the criminal justice process. During pre-trial, for example, prosecutors can let victims know when they intend to file motions to admit or keep out certain evidence or when court dates get delayed. Prosecutors should also meet and thoroughly prepare victims for trial by practicing direct and cross-examination, as well as discussing anticipated defense strategies and how the prosecutor plans to address them.

Offender-Focused Prosecutorial Approach

By recognizing that offenders purposefully, knowingly, and intentionally target victims whom they believe they can assault with impunity (see Chapter 7), prosecutors can persistently focus on the offender's actions and intent and oppose defense tactics to deflect the focus onto the victim. An offender-focused approach is driven by an accurate and unbiased analysis of a case and applicable law, as well as a thorough understanding of offender conduct and offender-victim dynamics. The rights of crime victims are always protected to the best of the prosecutor's ability.

Prosecutors can narrow the focus on serial sexual offenders, in particular, by litigating motions to introduce evidence of the offender's prior acts under Rule 404(b) of the Federal Rules of Evidence or its local equivalent. Defendants in sexual violence cases commonly assert that the victim had consented to sexual activity. Evidence of prior acts can help overcome the consent defense by establishing the perpetrator's intent, preparation, or common scheme or plan for the assault. In some cases, the defendant's identity will be at issue—but if the defendant used distinctive methods of carrying out the assault, evidence of previous assaults can be used to identify or support the identification of the defendant. Prior acts evidence can also be utilized to rebut a claim of mistake of fact—for instance, in a case where the defendant claims that he did not know a victim was too intoxicated to consent but has a history of similar assaults. In these cases, the prosecutor may have evidence of prior victims who had reported sexual assault by the defendant under the same or similar circumstances. Such evidence may show a common scheme or plan to isolate and assault intoxicated victims. When the prosecutor's office has multiple cases involving similar assaults on multiple victims, they can seek to join these cases where the evidence meets this standard; if joinder is not allowed, the prosecutor may still bring in evidence regarding other victims by way of 404(b).

It should be noted that admission of 404(b) evidence is one of the most litigated areas on appeal (Long et al., 2017). A sound 404(b) strategy requires a specialized prosecutor who can lay a clear record as to the admissibility of the evidence under as many theories as applicable and prepare a sample cautionary instruction for the jury's consideration of such evidence. Prosecutors should ensure that the judge in their cases articulates the legal reasoning and analysis supporting a decision to permit admission of 404(b) evidence. They can request that the court address each of the proffered theories individually and in the alternative. This should be done on the record and, if possible, by written decision.

Multidisciplinary

Research has shown that a system working collaboratively to provide a coordinated response will encourage more victims to access services and participate in the criminal justice process, more effectively hold offenders accountable, and help improve victim and community safety. Collaboration enables prosecutors and allied professionals to share resources, educate one another, evaluate and refine their practices on a continual basis, adapt in response to emerging issues, and ensure the sustainability of their practices.

Sexual Assault Response Teams (SARTs) are multidisciplinary teams that coordinate the community's response to sexual assault. They are an invaluable resource for prosecuting sexual violence crimes. SARTs "[e]nsure justice and create a more compassionate and streamlined response, [allowing] service providers [to] intervene in a way that speaks to the context of each victim's circumstance and respects the unique roles of the different professionals involved in responding to sexual assault" (Office of Victims of Crime, 2011, para. 1). SART team members typically include several "core" members including prosecutors, advocates, law enforcement, forensic examiners, and medical personnel, but may also include professionals from other disciplines, such as crime lab analysts, dispatchers, civil and victim's rights attorneys, faith-based providers, federal grant administrators, policymakers, culturally specific organizations, corrections, probation, parole, and sex offender management professionals, to name a few.

SARTs or multidisciplinary teams often pursue two primary goals. The first is to promote regular contact and coordination among disciplines as they respond to individual cases. This allows allied professionals to ensure a holistic response to victim needs while enhancing relevant aspects of the criminal justice response (AEquitas, 2017). SART members can also provide expertise on physical, behavioral, and forensic evidence. In the context of a cold case, for instance, a crime lab analyst may be able to provide invaluable insight into advanced DNA technologies that could help establish investigative leads for identifying unknown offenders. SARTs can also review cases after the fact to assess how they were handled and to determine steps for improvement moving forward.

The second goal of a SART is to improve the broader community response by identifying gaps in victim services, mapping existing networks of support and expertise, raising concerns and offering solutions to better integrate and improve existing practices, developing new sustainable practices (adapting best practices from other jurisdictions where appropriate), and developing a plan for receiving and responding to feedback. For instance, as mentioned earlier, individual SART members can offer their unique perspectives to help develop a victim notification protocol (Sakitta.org 2022) and provide support for victims when a cold case is reopened or results in a CODIS hit (Powers & Knecht, 2019).

Specialized Prosecution

Prosecutors must understand offender-victim dynamics in various types of sexual assault cases, as well as assumptions and misconceptions widely held by both laypeople and professionals. Specialized investigative practices provide enhanced knowledge and require greater skill to uncover relevant and probative evidence while keeping victims engaged throughout the process. Specialized trial expertise provides enhanced knowledge and requires greater skill to explain common gaps in evidence and counter deeply entrenched myths and assumptions about victim credibility—including how victims respond to trauma and what victimization looks like. Specialized prosecution units promote the development of such expertise, provide access to focused training, and present opportunities for collaboration with law enforcement and community partners.

Because victims of sexual violence—like victims of intimate partner violence—are uniquely vulnerable to intimidation by the offender and the offender's friends, family, and allies, *prosecutors who specialize in these crimes are well-versed in the dynamics of intimidation and thus well-positioned to respond when intimidation occurs.* They are able to identify subtle indicators of intimidation, collaborate with victims and advocates to establish an appropriate safety plan, and introduce evidence of the defendant's intimidation of the victim at trial to ensure accountability. Intimidation evidence can be used to bring additional charges or establish consciousness of guilt. Specialized sexual violence and intimate partner violence prosecutors also have the experience and training to introduce testimony of a victim who has been intimidated out of coming to court under Rule 804(b)(6) of the Federal Rules of Evidence and its local equivalents (AEquitas 2012).[4]

Specialized prosecutors are also better able to build rapport and trust with victims, which may enable them to develop new evidentiary leads. Their experience in sexual violence cases also enables them to appreciate the relevance of certain evidence, which may be overlooked by a less experienced or non-specialized prosecutor. For instance, prosecutors can ask victims questions about the circumstances under which they disclosed and to whom, leading to corroboration of the victim's testimony; elicit sensory, emotional, and physiological details of the assault, which provides powerful evidence for juries; and work with the victim to uncover any information pertaining to anticipated defenses.

Prosecutors who have identified possible defense strategies are better prepared to counter these defenses in their case-in-chief and to file motions precluding the defense from introducing irrelevant or prejudicial evidence. Evidence that does not tend to make a fact at issue more or less likely, which is designed only to shame a victim or turn the opinion of the jury against them, should not be presented at trial. These defense strategies can include:

- Discrediting the victim's memory or perception of events (typically where alcohol is involved) or directly challenging their credibility, or portraying the victim as having "buyer's remorse"—someone who later regrets a voluntary act.
- Trying to prove a motive to fabricate, attempting to pierce the rape shield by questioning the victim about prior sexual activity, or presenting other evidence to impugn the victim's character for the purpose of making the jury dislike the victim.
- Minimizing evidence of force by focusing on the victim's prior consensual acts with the perpetrator, characterizing any injury as trivial or an accidental byproduct of "rough sex."

To the extent that defense strategies rely on improper evidence, they can be opposed with motions to exclude the evidence. Victim-blaming strategies not involving improper evidence can be effectively countered at trial through carefully planned testimony and argument. For example, where defendants allege that the victim had a motive to fabricate, prosecutors can ask victims to describe how they felt during medical-forensic examinations or interviews with the responding officer and then ask the jury why the victim would endure that humiliating process if the assault did not occur. While it is never proper for the prosecutor to express a personal belief in the victim's truthfulness, it is important to always project confidence in the victim's veracity and reality of the harm suffered.

Research-Informed Prosecutorial Approaches

Prosecutorial decisions must be driven by the most current and accurate scientific, sociological, and legal research. Innovative practices to improve responses to sexual violence must be research-informed and implemented to determine their true value. Where effective, these practices should be sustained, re-evaluated, and refined for improvement and ongoing relevance to changing conditions.

For example, research, as well as the experiences of Sexual Assault Medical Forensic Examiners (SAMFEs), has shown that a lack of physical injury is not inconsistent with a crime of sexual violence (Commonwealth v. Minerd, 2000; State v. McMillian, 1996; State v. Presley, 2003). Even a minor child disclosing past sexual abuse with no genitourinary injuries will not always present with injury (Brochmann & Dahl, 2017). Armed with this knowledge, prosecutors can utilize experts to explain to juries the significance of injuries—or lack thereof—in sexual assault cases.

Research, as well as the expertise of allied professionals, can also aid prosecutors' understanding of victim behaviors. As discussed earlier, many aspects of victim behavior that make a sexual assault case challenging for jurors (and possibly for prosecutors and police)—delayed reporting, piecemeal disclosure, gaps in recall, inconsistencies in the victim's account—may be attributable to trauma. Studies by neuroscientists indicate that memories of traumatic events may be fragmented, inaccessible, or less readily retrieved than other memories (see Chapter 8). Chemical changes in the brain during traumatic events affect the ability of victims to recall and recount details of the event. It is important for first responders, investigators/ detectives, and prosecutors to have at least a rudimentary understanding of this phenomenon, so they do not draw erroneous conclusions about victim credibility and can interview the victim using trauma-informed techniques that will elicit as much detail as possible (Powers & Campbell, n.d.).

While knowledge of the available research is useful, prosecutors should avoid employing experts to testify about the neurobiology of trauma at trial. Persons with true expertise on the topic are extremely limited in number and likely costly to retain; much information on the neurobiology of trauma remains unknown; introduction of such evidence may prompt defense requests to view victims' counseling records; and there's a likelihood that such testimony could lead to impermissible diagnoses or conclusions that evade the province of the jury. Prosecutors who have a basic understanding of the available research can instead utilize other experts—law enforcement, advocates, clinical psychologists, and others who commonly work with persons who have experienced traumatic events—who can educate juries about victim responses to trauma without discussing the science (Thomas, 2021).

Criminal justice professionals can also benefit tremendously from knowledge of advanced DNA technologies, which can identify donor profiles from mixed samples and generate leads that result in the apprehension and prosecution of unknown suspects. The expanded use of publicly searchable databases, familial searching through CODIS in permitting jurisdictions, phenotype testing to generate genetic-based descriptions of unknown suspects, and forensic genetic genealogy has opened the door to cutting-edge investigations in both cold and current cases of sexual assault (see Chapter 7). Prosecutors who recognize the potential of these techniques can work collaboratively with investigators to identify suspects and hold offenders accountable (Powers & Marra, n.d.). Effectively presenting DNA expert testimony at trial requires intensive planning and collaboration with analysts. Prosecutors should work with experts to understand the science of DNA, as well as its potential and limitations. Close collaboration enables prosecutors to develop strategies for explaining complex concepts to a jury, as well as to anticipate and prepare for challenges and issues that arise during litigation.

Finally, research into serial offending and cross-offending can provide criminal justice professionals with critical context in evaluating, investigating, and prosecuting cases. Research into backlogged sexual assault kits tested through SAKI has shown that of individuals linked with more than one kit, only 56.6% exclusively assaulted strangers, while only 15.1% assaulted only known victims (Lovell et al., 2017). This means that almost one-third of the serial offenders assaulted both a stranger *and* a non-stranger, challenging what we commonly believe about serial sexual assault. Prosecutors should treat every sexual assault as one involving a possible serial perpetrator. They should advocate for expeditious testing of DNA, even in cases where the defendant admits to intercourse but claims consent, and work with law enforcement to pursue additional avenues for identifying other victims.

Performance-Driven Prosecutorial Approaches

Improving the overall response to sexual violence requires the assessment of key elements of our practice through performance management. How do we determine if a best practice is truly effective? How can we measure our own progress in improving our practice? Historically, conviction rates have been used as the primary measure of "success" for prosecutors because they represented the only readily accessible data (Long & Nugent-Borakove, 2014). Conviction rates alone, however, are weak indicators of a jurisdiction's response to sexual assault. They can also be misleading—when difficult or complex cases are "weeded out" before trial, charging, or arrest, the result is a deceptively high conviction rate (Rasmusen & Ramseyer, 2009).

A wide variety of meaningful outcomes can occur that are not directly related to the binary result of conviction or acquittal but which nevertheless help ensure accountability for perpetrators and safety for victims and communities. Such outcomes include victim satisfaction with the criminal justice process itself (as opposed to the disposition), as well as with the prosecutor's use *of every legitimate means* to bring about a just outcome. Conviction rates fail to take these measures into account, and thus a more comprehensive performance management system is needed. A critical aspect of any performance management process involves measuring the rates and reasons for case attrition—i.e., cases in which victims did not report their assault to law enforcement, cases closed by law enforcement without being referred to prosecutors, and cases in which prosecutors declined to bring charges (see Chapter 2). This pre-emptive "weeding out" process is rarely the result of conscious or callous disregard for victim and community safety but rather of office policies and practices that direct the declination or dismissal of sexual violence cases characterized by so-called "difficult" issues. These may include, but are not limited to, alcohol use by the victim and/or perpetrator, a current or former relationship between the victim and the offender, lack of physical force, lack of physical injury, "non-intuitive" victim behaviors, issues related to passage of time, and complicated DNA evidence.

By documenting the rates of case attrition at various stages in the criminal justice process, as well as the reasons why cases are unreported, closed, and declined, prosecutors will have better insight into the scale of sexual violence in their communities and may uncover common issues that reveal areas for improvement. For instance, learning why victims do not report sexual violence can provide insight into how the criminal justice system can enhance victims' ability to report while uncovering patterns associated with reported cases that were closed or rejected can reveal unconscious biases, resource issues, and a need for particularized training and technical assistance.

Outcomes for all cases—both those that proceed through the system and those that do not—can be disaggregated by relevant victim characteristics or demographics (e.g., race, gender identity or sexual orientation, income group, disability status). This information can provide staff valuable insights for identifying training needs as well as a factual understanding of the community they are serving. This data may provide insight relevant to interactions with victims, particular victim vulnerabilities, and case outcomes specific to particular subgroups. Information pertaining to different groups also can help indicate the extent to which equal access to justice issues are present.

Efforts to measure performance in sexual violence prosecutions should also consider case complexity. Understanding the impact of complexity on case processing and outcomes in one's own jurisdiction is an important part of assessing prosecutors' capacity (i.e., their level of knowledge and experience) to properly evaluate the relevance of particular factors present in their cases and to achieve the best possible outcomes. It effectively exposes areas where additional prosecution training or technical assistance is needed, as well as areas where community, law enforcement, or judicial education is necessary. Accounting for case complexity will also provide the necessary context for case outcomes.

For example, jurisdictions with high conviction rates may be rejecting cases perceived to be too difficult or complex, whereas jurisdictions with lower conviction rates may be taking such cases to trial—perhaps losing some of them but affording victims a forum for justice and prosecutors an opportunity to refine and improve their trial skills. Prosecutors and their offices should never be penalized for advancing complex cases that might lower their conviction rate, nor should they be encouraged to decline complex cases to ensure high conviction rates. Encouraging prosecutors to take on difficult cases requires their offices to develop a system that consistently captures the complexity of their cases, examines how those cases are being handled, and permits identification of those areas where improvements can be made.

In addition to contextualizing case outcomes by measuring case attrition and complexity, prosecutors have the opportunity to incorporate an array of success metrics that are not focused on case dispositions. Even if a case results in a resolution that falls short of the charges or sentence pursued by the prosecutor, the implementation of best practices throughout the life of the case, from initial evaluation and charging through resolution, can generate a high quality of procedural justice for the victim and the public. A comprehensive definition of case success should thus account for the prosecution's efforts to bring about justice.

A "best practices" checklist can help measure the level of procedural justice in our cases. It can also be used as the basis for regular meetings between unit chiefs and line-level prosecutors to examine the actions taken throughout the case and identify areas for improvement. Did we file a 404(b) motion? If not, should we have? Do we have the necessary training and skills, and access to experts, to work on cases involving complex DNA technologies? If not, how will we build our capacity and identify experts?

Finally, any definition of success in sexual violence cases should account for victims' experiences in the criminal justice system. Whatever the final disposition of an individual case, a victim's experience is impacted by the level of respect, dedication, expertise, and temperament of the professionals handling their cases. Although prosecutors' offices rarely survey victims, it can be helpful to systematically obtain feedback over time from victims regarding their perceptions of the quality of their experiences with various components of the criminal justice process. Victim survey findings can provide all partners (victim advocacy, law enforcement, medical providers, and prosecutors' offices) with: (a) a comprehensive picture of progress; (b) an understanding of which problem areas need to be addressed (e.g., through training and technical assistance); (c) feedback on the extent to which identified problems are improving or getting worse; and (d) knowledge regarding which aspects of the criminal justice response enhance victim safety and/or victim perceptions of justice.

Conclusion

Sexual violence is far more prevalent than an examination of convictions would indicate. And recent efforts to test backlogged sexual assault kits have revealed that serial sexual offenders are more numerous than we thought. While prosecutors work consistently and tirelessly to achieve justice in these cases, the data revealed through SAKI, the high rates of case attrition, and the experiences of survivors have shown us that current efforts are simply not enough.

There are many ways in which prosecutors can improve their practices—not only to hold more offenders accountable and make communities safer but enable more victims to report their assaults and to ensure that they feel heard and respected by the system. This involves working with, rather than against, victims' trauma; centering victims' needs throughout the criminal process; anticipating defense strategies and zealously countering attempts to introduce irrelevant evidence; applying relevant research; working with other system stakeholders and community partners; and consistently evaluating and refining practices. Prosecutors in the field do not have to do this alone; national training and technical assistance providers, like AEquitas, are available to help implement the strategies discussed throughout this chapter (TA2TA, n.d.).

Ultimately, there is never a guarantee of a successful case disposition, no matter how aggressively a prosecutor seeks justice on a victim's behalf. Yet, when prosecutors use every legitimate means to bring about justice, positive outcomes will be achieved. Prosecutors hone their skills and refine strategies to increase the likelihood of convictions in future cases, serial offenders are identified and exposed, myths and biases are eradicated, and victims obtain a measure of validation and closure.

Key Points

- Sexual assault prosecutors need a specialized skill set that is honed by trying cases with varying levels of complexity.
- Conviction rates only tell part of the story about whether a prosecutor's office or a prosecutor is successful. Multiple performance metrics are needed and these should be routinely monitored.
- The goals of justice include offender accountability, victim well-being, and community safety. The prosecutorial process can yield benefits not captured by conviction rates.
- Best-practice prosecutorial approaches are trauma-informed, victim-centered, offender-focused, specialized, and research-informed.
- Strategies associated with best-practice prosecution include mitigating the effects of victim trauma, coordinating with a multidisciplinary team, preparing victims for all stages and aspects of the criminal justice process, anticipating defense strategies, and keeping abreast of emerging forensic technologies.

Discussion Questions

1 How do sexual assault prosecutorial strategies differ from strategies for trying other types of crime?

2 These authors argue that more sexual assault cases should be brought to trial, even if they don't result in conviction. What are their reasons for this?
3 This chapter highlights key principles underlying best practices for prosecuting sexual assault. What are they? Which ones would you prioritize and why?

Funding Acknowledgment

The writing of this chapter was supported by Grant No.15JOVW-21-GK-02220-MUMU awarded by the Office on Violence Against Women, U.S. Department of Justice. The opinions, findings, conclusions, and recommendations expressed in this publication are those of the authors and do not necessarily reflect the views of the Department of Justice, Office on Violence Against Women.

Notes

1 This chapter is adapted from the *Model Response to Sexual Violence for Prosecutors (RSVP Model).* Many present and former AEquitas staff contributed to the RSVP Model: Jennifer Long, CEO; Jane Anderson, Jonathan Kurland, Patricia Powers, and John Wilkinson, Attorney Advisors; Teresa Garvey, Viktoria Kristiansson, and Dalia Racine, former Attorney Advisors; Charlie Whitman-Barr, former Senior Associate Attorney Advisor; Holly Fuhrman, Senior Associate Attorney Advisor; Mary MacLeod and Jennifer Newman, Associate Attorney Advisors; and Mary Katherine Burke, former Associate Attorney Advisor. Harry Hatry, Distinguished Fellow at the Urban Institute; Janine Zweig, Associate Vice President for Justice Policy at Urban; Elaine Borakove, President of JMI; and Rey Cheatham Banks, Senior Program Manager at JMI also contributed to the RSVP Model.
2 Downstream decision-making occurs where criminal justice professionals decide not to investigate or refer a case for prosecution based upon their perception that a particular type of case will be declined by prosecutors or by their prejudgment of the merits of the case—that a jury will not convict.
3 Sexually exploited persons may not self-identify as victims of sexual violence (Farrell et al., 2012).
4 Although it is rare for sexual violence cases to proceed absent victim testimony, there are distinct cases in which it may be possible to proceed utilizing Rule 804(b)(6) and its local equivalents. For more information on motions under forfeiture by wrongdoing, see AEquitas (2012).

References

AEquitas. (2012, October). *The prosecutors' resource: Forfeiture by wrongdoing.* https://aequitasresource.org/wp-content/uploads/2018/09/The_Prosecutors_Resource_Forfeiture_by_Wrongdoing.pdf
AEquitas. (2017). Sexual Assault Justice Initiative: annotated bibliography. https://aequitasresource.org/wp-content/uploads/2018/09/SAJI-Annotated-Bibliography-June-2017.pdf
Beichner, D., & Spohn, C. (2005). Prosecutorial charging decisions in sexual assault cases: Examining the impact of a specialized prosecution unit. *Criminal Justice Policy Review, 16*(4), 461–498. https://doi.org/10.1177/0887403405277195
Black, M. C., Basile, K. C., Breiding, M. J., Smith, S. G., Walters, M. L., Merrick, M. T., Chen, J., & Stevens, M. R. (2011). *The national intimate partner and sexual violence survey: 2010 summary report.* National Center for Injury Prevention and Control, Centers for Disease Control and Prevention. https://www.cdc.gov/violenceprevention/pdf/nisvs_report2010-a.pdf

Brochmann, N. D., & Dahl, E. S. (2017, May). The virginity fraud. [Video] TED. https://www.ted.com/talks/nina_dolvik_brochmann_and_ellen_stokken_dahl_the_virginity_fraud?language=en

Campbell, R., Bybee, D., Townsend, S. M., Shaw, J., Karim, N., & Markowitz, J. (2014). The impact of sexual assault nurse examiner programs on criminal justice case outcomes: A multisite replication study. *Violence Against Women, 20*(5), 601–625. https://doi.org/10.1177/1077801214536286

Campbell, R., Fehler-Cabral, G., Pierce, J., Sharma, D. B., Bybee, D., Shaw, J., Horsford, S., & Feeney, H. (2015). *The Detroit Sexual Assault Kit (SAK) Action Research Project (ARP), Final Report (No. 248680)*. National Criminal Justice Reference Center. https://www.ojp.gov/pdffiles1/nij/grants/248680.pdf

Campbell, R., & Wasco, S. (2005). Understanding rape and sexual assault: 20 years of progress and future directions. *Journal of Interpersonal Violence, 20*(1), 127–131.

Cohn, A., Zinzow, H. M., Resnick, H. S., & Kilpatrick, D. G. (2013). Correlates of reasons for not reporting rape to police: Results from a national telephone household probability sample of women with forcible or drug-or-alcohol facilitated/incapacitated cape. *Journal of Interpersonal Violence, 28*(3), 455–473.

Commonwealth v. Minerd, 562 Pa. 46, 753 A.2d 225 (2000).

End the Backlog. (2017). *Test rape kits. Stop serial rapists.* https://www.endthebacklog.org/backlog-why-rape-kit-testing-important/test-rape-kits-stop-serial-rapists

Farrell, A., McDevitt, J., Pfeffer, R., Fahy, S., Owens, S., Dank, M., & Adams, W. (2012). *Identifying challenges to improve the investigation and prosecution of state and local human trafficking cases.* Urban Institute. http://www.urban.org/publications/412592.html

Hanson, B., (2014, July 30). *The importance of understanding trauma-informed care and self-care for victim service providers.* Office of Violence Against Women: Blog. https://www.justice.gov/ovw/blog/importance-understanding-trauma-informed-care-and-self-care-victim-service-providers

Hanson, M. (2021, July 3). Untested rape kits on Massachusetts: Advocates worry budget proposal will leave 6,300 kits untested, but state senator says aim is to test all. *MassLive.* https://www.masslive.com/boston/2021/07/untested-rape-kits-in-massachusetts-advocates-worry-budget-proposal-will-leave-6300-kits-untested-but-state-senator-says-aim-is-to-test-all.html

Herman, S. (2011). *Parallel justice for victims of crime.* National Center for Victims of Crime.

Kingsnorth, R., Lopez, J., Wentworth, J., & Cummings, D. J. (1998). Adult sexual assault: The role of racial/ethnic composition in prosecution and sentencing. *Journal of Criminal Justice, 26*(5), 359–371.

Knezevich, A., & Rentz, C. (2016, December 9). Maryland lawmakers call for uniform police standards on rape kits. *Baltimore Sun.* http://www.baltimoresun.com/news/maryland/politics/bs-md-rape-kits-reaction-20161209-story.html

Kristiansson, V., & Whitman-Barr, C. (2015). Integrating a trauma-informed response in violence against women and human trafficking prosecution. *Strategies, 13.* https://aequitasresource.org/wp-content/uploads/2018/09/Integrating-A-Trauma-Informed-Response-In-VAW-and-HT-Strategies.pdf

Long, J. G., Garvey, T. M., Anderson, J., & Kristiansson, V. (2017). Evidence of other "bad acts" in intimate partner violence, sexual violence, stalking, and human trafficking prosecutions. *Strategies, 31.* https://evawintl.org/wp-content/uploads/Aequitas-Evidence-of-Other-Bad-Acts-IPV.pdf

Long, J. G., & Nugent-Borakove, E. (2014). Beyond Conviction Rates: Measuring Success in Sexual Assault Prosecutions. *Strategies, 12.* https://evawintl.org/wp-content/uploads/beyond-conviction-rates.pdf

Lovell, R., Luminais, M., Flannery, D. J., Overman, L., Huang, D., Walker, T., & Clark, D. R. (2017). Offending patterns for serial sex offenders identified via the DNA testing of previously unsubmitted sexual assault kits. *Journal of Criminal Justice, 52*, 68–78. https://doi.org/10.1016/J.JCRIMJUS.2017.08.002

Miller, T. C., & Armstrong, K. (2015, December 16). An unbelievable story of rape. *The Marshall Project and Pro Publica.* https://www.propublica.org/article/false-rape-accusations-an-unbelievable-story

Morabito, M., Williams, L., & Pattavina, A. (2019). *Decision-making in sexual assault cases: Replication research on sexual violence case attrition in the U.S.* National Institute of Justice. https://www.ncjrs.gov/pdffiles1/nij/grants/252689.pdf

Office of Victims of Crime. (2011). *What is a SART?* SART toolkit. https://ovc.ncjrs.gov/sartkit/about/about-sart.html

Pattavina, A., Morabito, M., & Williams, L. (2015). Examining connections between the police and prosecution in sexual assault case processing: Does the use of exceptional clearance facilitate a downstream orientation. *Victims and Offenders, 11*(2).

Powers, P., & Campbell, R. (n.d.). *Achieving justice at trial: Direct examination of victims of violent crimes.* Sexual Assault Kit Initiative. https://www.sakitta.org/conviction-integrity/view.cfm?id=35

Powers, P., & Knecht, I. (2019). *The prosecutor's role in survivor notification.* Sexual Assault Kit Initiative. https://www.sakitta.org/toolkit/index.cfm?fuseaction=tool&tool=6

Powers, P., & Marra, M. (n.d.). *Advancing justice with DNA technologies.* Sexual Assault Kit Initiative. https://www.sakitta.org/conviction-integrity/view.cfm?id=21

Rasmusen, E. B., & Ramseyer, M. (2009). Convictions versus conviction rates: The prosecutor's choice. *American Law and Economics Review, 11*(1), 47–78. http://dx.doi.org/ahp007

Rockey, J., Matheson, S., Farr, H., Mayhew, M. R., Murphy, S., & Edwards, K. M. (2012). *Pathways to justice: The movement of adult female sexual assault cases across the New Hampshire criminal justice system.* White Papers and Other PIRC reports, 8. https://scholars.unh.edu/pirc_reports/8

Sakitta.org (2022). Victim notification toolkit. https://www.sakitta.org/toolkit/index.cfm?fuseaction=topic&topic=1

Sexual Assault Kit Initiative. (n.d.a). *Community- and systems-based advocates.* RTI International. https://media.dojmt.gov/wp-content/uploads/Community-and-Systems-Based-Advocacy.pdf

Sexual Assault Kit Initiative. (n.d.b). *Unique aspects of prosecuting cold case sexual assault.* RTI International. https://www.sakitta.org/toolkit/docs/SAKI_Brief_UniqueAspects-ProsecutingColdCaseSA.pdf

Spohn, C., Beichner, D., & Davis-Frenzel, E. (2001). Prosecutorial justifications for sexual assault case rejection: Guarding the "gateway to justice." *Social Problems, 48*(2), 206–235.

Spohn, C., & Tellis, K. (2012). The criminal justice system's response to sexual violence. *Violence Against Women, 18*(2), 160–192.

Spohn, C., & Tellis, K. (2014). *Policing and prosecuting sexual assault: Inside the criminal justice system.* Lynne Rienner Publishers. ISBN: 978-1-62637-024-1.

State v. McMillian, No. C-950523, 1996 WL 233866 (Ohio Ct. App. 1996, May 8).

State v. Presley, No. 02AP–1354, 2003 WL 22681425 (Ohio Ct. App. 2003, November 13).

Strom, K. J., Roper-Miller, J., Jones, S., Sikes, N., Pope, M., & Horstmann, N. (2009, October). *Survey of law enforcement forensic evidence processing 2007.* Final Report. Washington, D.C.: U.S. Department of Justice, National Institute of Justice.

TA2TA. (n.d.). Grantees. https://www.ta2ta.org/grantees.html

Thomas, D. (2021, October 12). First, do no harm: The neurobiology of trauma, and trauma informed investigations. *AEquitas.* https://www.youtube.com/watch?v=0AX9KN_1Nac

Tjaden, P. G., & Thoennes, N., (2006). *Extent, nature, and consequences of rape victimization: Findings from the national violence against women surgery.* U.S. Dept. of Justice, Office of Justice Programs, National Institute of Justice. https://www.ncjrs.gov/pdffiles1/nij/210346.pdf

U.S. Department of Justice, (2022). *FY 2022 Solicitation Companion Guide: OVW grant programs & post-award information.* https://www.justice.gov/ovw/page/file/1463936/download

Wood, M., Lepanjuuri, K., Paskell, C., Thompson, J., Adams, L., & Coburn, S. (2015). *Victim and witness satisfaction survey.* Crown Prosecution Service. https://www.cps.gov.uk/sites/default/files/documents/victims_witnesses/cps_victim_and_witness_survey_sept_2015.pdf

12 Current trends in sexual assault medical forensic exams and examiners

Julie L. Valentine and Nancy R. Downing

Author Note

These authors have no funding to disclose. The opinions or points of view expressed in this document are solely those of the authors and do not reflect the official positions of any participating organization or the U.S. Department of Justice.

Introduction

The Violence Against Women Act (VAWA), passed in 1994 and reauthorized in 2000, 2005, and 2013, guaranteed the rights of sexual assault survivors to receive Sexual Assault Medical Forensic Examinations (SAMFEs, or *exams*) at no cost to survivors. While SAMFEs may be conducted by health-care practitioners without expertise in forensics or competence in trauma-informed care, current recommendations are for examinations to be conducted by Sexual Assault Nurse Examiners (SANEs or *nurses*) or other health-care providers with specialized forensic examiner training (National Institute of Justice, 2017). National standards have been established for both adult/adolescent and pediatric SAMFEs (Office on Violence Against Women, 2016; Office on Violence Against Women (OVW), U.S. Department of Justice, 2013). Due to the inherent connection between SAMFEs and SANEs, issues related to SANE practice and programs also impact SAMFEs. Additional best practice recommendations for SAMFEs were published in the *National Best Practices for Sexual Assault Kits: A Multidisciplinary Approach* (National Institute of Justice [NIJ], 2017). The International Association of Forensic Nurses is the professional organization that sets standards for forensic nursing practice and developed the SANE education guidelines for both adult/adolescent and pediatric SANEs (International Association of Forensic Nurses, 2018).

As other chapters in this book extensively detail, the collection of forensic evidence from a survivor of sexual assault using a victim-centered and trauma-informed approach is vital for holding offenders accountable and aiding in survivors' healing process. The focus of this chapter is on the sexual assault kit (SAK) collection process, highlighting current guidelines, recent advancements, and future directions for SAMFEs and SANEs. This chapter's authors are experienced SANEs and forensic nursing researchers who have been actively engaged with developing policy to improve survivor outcomes at state and national levels. Dr. Valentine is the Associate Dean of Undergraduate Studies and Research at Brigham Young University

DOI: 10.4324/9781003186816-15

College of Nursing and a certified SANE. Her research focus areas are sexual violence, intimate partner violence, and criminal justice system response to sexual violence. Dr. Valentine conducts multidisciplinary, collaborative research studies to promote sexual assault case reform and benefit victims and case processing. Dr. Valentine served on the National Institute of Justice to the Sexual Assault Forensic Evidence Reporting (SAFER) Act Working Group in the development of national best practice policies in sexual assault cases, *National Best Practices in Sexual Assault Kits: A Multidisciplinary Approach* (2017). Dr. Downing has been a forensic nurse since 2004 and is an Associate Professor in the Center of Excellence for Forensic Nursing at Texas A&M University. She teaches in the Master's level forensic nursing program and conducts research related to intersections of violence, substance use, and health outcomes, including development of a statewide telehealth SANE program in Texas. She addresses policy and legislation surrounding forensic nursing through her roles on the Texas Forensic Science Commission, International Association of Forensic Nurses Board of Directors, and Vice Chair of the National Institute of Standards Organization of Scientific Area Committees for Forensic Science Forensic Nursing Subcommittee.

Current Guidelines for Sexual Assault Medical Forensic Examinations

The national protocols for adult/adolescent and pediatric SAMFEs provide general guidelines related to the care of sexual assault victims and specific recommendations on exam procedures (U.S. Department of Justice, 2013, 2016). Both national protocols emphasize:

- using a multidisciplinary team approach;
- ensuring confidentiality;
- collecting informed consent;
- providing options for reporting and mandates;
- providing victim-centered care; and
- staying current with the justice system infrastructure related to examinations.

The protocols also describe specific recommendations for sexual assault forensic examiners (SAFEs), sexual assault evidence collection kits (SAKs), and exam facilities and equipment. Information on SAMFEs includes guidelines for health care and injury evaluation, drug-facilitated sexual assaults, evidence collection and packaging, written documentation, photographic documentation, discharge planning, and follow-up health care. Post-sexual assault medications generally include prophylactic medications to prevent pregnancy and sexually transmitted infections depending on the nature of the sexual assault and age of the victim. Medication guidelines vary based on current Centers for Disease Control and Prevention guidelines which adapt as needed to incorporate new research and evidence-based practice information (Centers for Disease Control and Prevention, 2021).

The most recent recommendations for SAMFEs emerged from a multidisciplinary working group that was established through the SAFER Act of 2013 (National Institute of Justice, 2017). Focus areas of the 2017 guidelines include adopting trauma-informed care and greater emphasis on utilizing a multidisciplinary, patient-centered approach. The new guidelines also include

- expanded time recommendations between assaults and SAMFEs;
- reduced the number of collected swabs to help concentrate potential DNA material, and
- including the collection of touch DNA evidence.

Additionally, with the emergence of more sensitive DNA analysis testing methods, specific guidelines to reduce DNA cross-contamination were provided, including SANEs wearing gloves and masks during evidence collection and packaging. Guidance on evidence collection in sexual assault cases in which victims were unconscious or lacked memory of the events is also presented in the *National Best Practices* document.

In addition to SAMFE guidelines from the national protocol documents and *National Best Practices for Sexual Assault Kits*, the federal VAWA and state-level legislation and policies also inform SAMFEs. The VAWA reauthorization of 2013 clarified that sexual assault victims were entitled to SAMFEs regardless of law enforcement investigative involvement. Sexual assault cases in which victims opt to receive SAMFEs with evidence collection but not participate in criminal justice system involvement are referred to as *non-investigative cases* at the time of evidence collection (Office on Violence Against Women, 2017). In some areas of the United States, these cases are referred to as non-report, anonymous, or Jane Doe SAKs. However, in other areas of the country, law enforcement agencies are notified of the sexual assault, but investigations are not pursued unless victims choose to engage with the criminal justice system. Non-investigative SAKs are not an option for pediatric cases or vulnerable adults due to mandatory reporting guidelines. The current Office on Violence Against Women recommendation is to not submit non-investigative SAKs to crime laboratories for analysis. Non-investigative SAKs are kept for varying amounts of time based on individual state statutes, giving victims extra time to decide whether to formally report the sexual assault. See Chapter 13 for an expanded discussion of these non-investigative SAKs.

State legislation impacts guidelines for SAMFEs, specifically regarding chain of evidence, storage, crime laboratory submission, and evidence tracking (End the Backlog, n. d.). The majority of state legislation on SAKs has been enacted to address testing unsubmitted SAKs (those never submitted for forensic testing) and to prevent future "backlogs" of untested SAKs. Although these legislative guidelines do not affect the actual examination, they do impact SAMFE multidisciplinary policies and discharge information and must be incorporated into examiner policies. Current national recommendations are that SAKs should not be stored in health-care facilities but within criminal justice locations (National Institute of Justice, 2017). Multiple challenges exist in exploring the extent of SAK storage in health-care facilities, as these kits are not under criminal justice jurisdiction. In jurisdictions with SAK Initiative funding, health-care facilities have been encouraged to submit any stored kits to respective law enforcement agencies and/or state crime laboratories. Moving forward, health-care facilities are strongly advised to submit SAKs to law enforcement within seven days (National Institute of Justice, 2017).

Current Guidelines for Sexual Assault Nurse Examiners and Programs

SANEs are registered and advanced practice nurses with specialized education in caring for patients reporting sexual assault and collecting evidence for SAKs. The educational degrees of SANEs range from diploma programs to associate through doctoral degrees. The International Association of Forensic Nurses developed the approved 40-hour SANE training program guidelines based upon the U.S. Department of Justice national training standards (U.S. Department of Justice, 2018) and offers online SANE courses. The International Association of Forensic Nurses has an approval process to evaluate and recommend SANE educational programs in the United States and Canada that meet the U.S. Department of Justice and International Association of Forensic Nurses requirements (International Association of Forensic Nurses, 2021b). In addition to completion of the approved SANE educational program, SANEs must complete clinical practicum requirements.

Some SANE programs elect to meet requirements to take the American Nurses Credentialing Center board-certified credentialing examination to become SANE-A®, board-certified SANE for adult/adolescent patients, and/or SANE-P®, board certified SANE for pediatric patients. According to the American Nurses Credentialing Center (2010), certification in a nursing specialty ensures professionals have met specialty practice standards, demonstrates a commitment to the specialty, provides a sense of pride and accomplishment, promotes consumer confidence, and protects the public. In the case of forensic nursing, certification can also support a nurse's qualification as an expert witness and promote juror confidence. National certification for SANE-A and SANE-P is available through the International Association of Forensic Nurses Commission for Forensic Nursing Certification. As of April 2021, 1,292 nurses had achieved SANE-A certification, and 548 nurses had achieved SANE-P certification across the United States (Downing, 2021).

Board-certified SANEs are required to complete continuing education requirements to maintain their credentialing. The International Association of Forensic Nurses is the leading organization providing SANE education through annual conferences, online programs, webinars, and *Journal of Forensic Nursing* articles with continuing education examinations (International Association of Forensic Nurses, 2021a). Educational offerings are strongly encouraged for all SANEs to maintain professional expertise.

Eight states currently offer state SANE certification or credentialing (Office for Victims of Crime, n.d.). Often, state credentialing programs are practice-oriented and intended to demonstrate competency based on educational and skills-based criteria, with requirements for continuing education and clinical practice to maintain credentials. State credentialing programs are typically managed by offices of attorney generals, state departments of health, or state boards of nursing. State credentialing is a means to demonstrate forensic nurses have received appropriate SANE education, are knowledgeable in their specialty, and aware of state laws. Since it is not necessary in most states to be SANE credentialed or certified to provide SAMFEs, state credentialing is a way for states to set a standard level of practice. A downside of state credentialing is that it may act as a deterrent to achieving national certification (Downing, 2021). National certification is offered by the Commission for Forensic Nursing Certification at the International Association of Forensic Nurses. Nurses can be certified as adult/adolescent SANEs (SANE-A) or pediatric SANEs (SANE-P). National certification differs from state credentialing as it represents achievement of the highest standards of SANE practice. Nurses must meet eligibility requirements, including approved SANE education and 300 practice hours, prior to taking a proctored SANE certification examination. The examination was developed and is updated following a rigorous process including a job analysis study, a standard setting study to determine a passing score, item writing workshop, and psychometric item analysis (International Association of Forensic Nurses, n. d.). As with other nursing specialties, specialty certification beyond holding a registered nursing license is not required to practice. Requiring state credentialing or SANE certification to practice would severely restrict access to SANEs, which is especially critical in rural areas where there are nursing shortages and existing nurses may lack the resources needed to obtain and retain certification.

SANEs generally practice in community-based or hospital-based settings. Community-based programs operate independently of specified hospital systems. In community-based SANE programs, nurses may care for patients presenting to free-standing clinics or they may travel to different hospital emergency departments or clinics. In hospital-based SANE programs, one or more hospitals in a jurisdiction may be designated as the care facility for conducting SAMFEs. Community-based programs are more likely to face financial challenges in maintaining the private space, equipment, and personnel to run the program. However, hospital-based programs may require patients to transfer from the facility where they first presented for care to designated SAMFE facilities for their examination; this may be less than ideal for patients. SANEs in rural communities often practice independently as the only health-care provider with expertise in conducting SAMFE. Technology to connect rural SANEs with established SANE programs in more urban areas is a growing trend (Walsh et al., 2019).

As SANE programs continue to expand, the International Association of Forensic Nurses is working toward the development of a voluntary SANE program accreditation program as a way to verify that high-quality, evidence-based care is being provided. Accreditation can demonstrate SANE programs meet pre-established practice standards. Benefits of accreditation include having expert program review and guidance on improving practices, increased community and patient confidence in the quality and safety of care, enhanced ability to recruit staff, improved risk management, and support for the framework development needed to achieve and maintain high-quality programs (Joint Commission, 2021).

Recent Advancements in Sexual Assault Medical Forensic Examinations

Advancements in SAMFEs include technological and practice advancements which impact examinations, evidence collection, and SAK contents and instructions.

Advancements in examinations and evidence collection

Principles of informed consent, trauma-informed interactions, and utilizing a patient-centered approach continue to frame SAMFEs, while improvements in DNA technology have resulted in changes to examination and evidence collection guidelines. Research has shown that probative or meaningful DNA evidence can be obtained 120 hours or more after sexual intercourse (Speck & Ballantyne, 2015). *Probative DNA* evidence refers to DNA results from forensic analysis that provide value to the investigation or prosecution of a crime, such as the development of a partial or full DNA profile of the suspect. Thus, the timeframe for evidence collection following sexual assault has expanded from 72 hours to 120 hours or more based upon jurisdiction policies (National Institute of Justice, 2017). This gives survivors considerably more time to determine how they want to interact with the health care and criminal justice systems after the sexual assault.

Forensic advancements

The ability to develop probative DNA analysis findings is also dependent upon the type of DNA analysis methods employed by publicly funded crime laboratories. Crime laboratories conduct *short-tandem repeat* (STR) DNA tests, as this is the current standard DNA testing method that develops DNA profiles that could be admissible into the Federal Bureau of Investigations (FBI) Combined DNA Index System (CODIS) (Federal Bureau of Investigation, n.d.). Some crime laboratories also use STR testing methods specific to the Y-chromosome or male chromosome, referred to as Y-STR tests. Y-STR analysis can potentially develop helpful DNA information when less biologic material is available than is needed for traditional STR analysis in sexual assault cases (Purps et al., 2015). Y-STR profiles are not as discriminating as traditional STR testing methods but can aid in identifying families through the male lineage. For more information on forensic testing of SAKs when they get to the lab, see Chapter 16.

WHY DOES THIS MATTER?

SANEs and other forensic examiners should be familiar with the testing methods of their jurisdiction's crime laboratory, as this information can influence evidence collection decisions and information provided in SAMFE paperwork. Generally, best practice recommendations are to collect any potential evidence because the ability to develop probative DNA profiles is unknown until tested.

As the sensitivity of DNA analysis has evolved, smaller amounts of biologic material are required to develop DNA profiles, indicating that evidence can now be collected for potential trace biologic material, such as in *touch DNA* (Valentine et al., 2021). Recent guidelines for collecting touch DNA samples in groping and sexual assault cases include using sterile, moistened swabs on touched areas of skin and collecting touched clothing (Valentine et al., 2021). National guidelines for obtaining touch DNA in sexual assault cases were not provided until the *National Best Practices* recommendations, as previous guidelines only addressed the collection of biological fluids (National Institute of Justice, 2017). Inclusion of touch and trace DNA in sexual assault cases will only be achieved through education of law enforcement, forensic examiners, forensic scientists, victim advocates, criminal justice professionals, and the public to ensure that victims of groping and/or sexual assault cases not involving bodily fluids also receive SAMFEs with evidence collection.

Given that recent advancements in DNA testing have increased sensitivity, there is more concern regarding cross-contamination of collected biological evidence.

SAMFE guidelines have always included wearing gloves during evidence collection, but current recommendations are also for forensic examiners to wear masks and avoid talking while collecting and packaging evidence (National Institute of Justice, 2017). Evidence related to the impact of these recommendations is currently lacking.

Advancements in injury identification

In addition to DNA advancements, improvements in injury identification and documentation have substantially influenced SAMFE practices. Assessment of injuries following sexual assault has important implications for the investigation and prosecution of sex crimes. Studies indicate that the presence of injuries is associated with greater law enforcement reporting by victims (Downing et al., 2020; Fisher et al., 2013) and greater likelihood cases will progress through the legal system (Campbell et al., 2009; Holleran et al., 2010; Johnson et al., 2012). Victims, law enforcement, prosecutors, and jurors should be educated on the many reasons injuries may not be present following sexual assault and that injuries should not be necessary to prove a sexual assault occurred. Furthermore, multidisciplinary partners and the public should be educated that psychological injuries such as posttraumatic stress disorder, anxiety, depression, suicidal ideation, and substance use, although less visible, can be more persistent and debilitating than physical injuries following sexual assault (Kilpatrick et al., 2013).

Studies examining the presence of injuries identified on victims' bodies or anal/genital areas during SAMFEs vary widely in the proportion of victims who have visible injuries (Kennedy, 2013). Most studies indicate a significant portion of patients do not have either bodily or anal/genital injuries (Sommers et al., 2012). Injuries may not be prevalent because victims frequently report they did not fight back during the sexual assault. Victims may have also been incapacitated by alcohol or other substances (Anderson et al., 2017). Though SANE programs do not typically document why patients did not fight back, retrospectively, victims have stated they were too scared, "just wanted it to be over," or were afraid of being physically injured (Möller et al., 2017).

Other potential reasons injury prevalence has varied considerably between studies include study design (e.g., lack of blinding), examiner experience, visualization techniques (e.g., naked eye, magnification, toluidine blue dye), and whether non-specific injury findings (e.g., redness, tenderness) were documented as injuries (Kennedy, 2013). A recent study comparing anogenital injury in consensual versus non-consensual sexual intercourse found anogenital injury was over two times more likely to be present in patients reporting non-consensual intercourse, though the prevalence of each injury type was low in both groups (Sommers & Fargo, 2021).

Due to the importance of injury documentation in investigation and prosecution, enhanced techniques to identify and/or better visualize bodily and anogenital injuries are often used by forensic nurses. For example, colposcopes and enhanced camera systems may be used to visually magnify anogenital areas during an examination or to magnify anogenital images after examination to better identify and/or visualize small anogenital injuries. *A National Protocol for Sexual Assault Medical Forensic Examinations: Adults/Adolescents* ("*National Protocol*") states, "the colposcope is an important asset in the identification of microscopic trauma" (Office on Violence Against Women, 2013, p. 68). However, some forensic medical practitioners have called into question the value of colposcopes to visualize anogenital injuries, arguing the significance of minor injuries in the prosecution of sexual assault is questionable and cannot distinguish between consensual and non-consensual intercourse (Rogers et al., 2019; Walker, 2015).

Similar arguments could be made about the use of toluidine blue dye to visualize and document anogenital injuries. Toluidine blue dye is a nuclear stain that attaches to nucleated cells. Therefore, when it is placed on skin that is normally non-nucleated (i.e., epidermis), and toluidine blue dye uptake is positive, this indicates injury to the surface layer, which could corroborate a patient's history of sexual assault, though again, it cannot determine whether sexual contact was consensual. The *National Protocol* (Office on Violence Against Women, 2013) states the purpose of toluidine blue dye is to "highlight" external anogenital trauma (p. 98) and not to identify injuries that are not visible without it, presumably to mitigate the issue of identifying injuries so minor as to not be of evidentiary value. However, others have found toluidine blue dye is useful for identifying injuries that were missed using only visual inspection (Hirachan, 2019; Zink et al., 2010). The SANE profession would benefit from greater guidance, supported by evidence, on consistent use of toluidine blue dye and whether to use it only for highlighting detected injuries or for identifying injuries not otherwise observed.

While some have expressed concerns regarding the significance of enhanced anogenital injury visualization methods, others have argued the forensic nurse's role is to collect all possible evidence, reserving evidentiary value for the courts (Zink et al., 2010). These conflicting opinions have yet to be resolved among SANEs. Some jurisdictions include policies calling for the use of colposcopes, enhanced imaging, and/ or toluidine blue dye (Office on Violence Against Women, 2013). However, there are surprisingly few evidence-based publications examining how documentation of anogenital injuries using enhanced visualization techniques have impacted sexual assault investigation and prosecution. Multidisciplinary discussions between forensic nurses, law enforcement, prosecutors, and defense attorneys regarding best SANE evidence collection and documentation practices would provide further insight into the issues discussed here. The advent of the National Institute of Standards and Technology's Organization of Scientific Area Committees for Forensic Science national multidisciplinary subcommittee on standards for sexual assault examinations is a promising step toward developing standards. The impact of these techniques on patients should also be systematically examined as they could potentially be traumatic (Caswell et al., 2019).

Advancements in documenting blunt force trauma

An emerging technology to improve visualization and documentation of blunt force trauma is the use of alternate light sources for examining bruises (Scafide et al., 2020). Alternate light sources refer to lights of isolated ultraviolet, visible, or infrared wavelengths that are utilized while wearing colored goggles to block reflected light to better visualize substances or injury (Marin & Buszka, 2013). The *National Protocol* (Office on Violence Against Women (OVW), U.S. Department of Justice, 2013) states that alternate light sources can be used to identify subtle injury, but it does not provide guidance on how to use it for this purpose. More familiar is the use of alternate light sources for detecting semen on clothing or skin that fluoresces

(Pollitt et al., 2016). However, when used to visualize blunt force trauma such as bruises, alternate light sources can be used to detect absorption, not fluorescence. When blood escapes from blood vessels under the epidermal layer, the escaped blood can be visualized as absorption using alternate light sources.

A recent randomized controlled crossover study found 415 and 450 nanometer alternate light sources using a yellow filter were better at detecting evidence of bruising at sites of known blunt force trauma than white light (Scafide et al., 2020). This technology may be especially helpful in identifying blunt force trauma in patients with dark skin colors, for whom visualizing bruises through highly pigmented dermal layers can be difficult (Scafide et al., in press). This may result in injuries not being properly visualized or appreciated by law enforcement, potentially contributing to cases not progressing in the legal system (Deutsch et al., 2017). Scafide and colleagues developed a Bruise Visibility Scale and Alternate Light Sources Visibility Scale for clinical use (Scafide et al., 2021); its use in clinical settings is currently being evaluated.

While the use of alternate light sources to improve bruise visibility is a promising new area of forensic nursing, it comes with important caveats. False positives can occur when other conditions (Scafide et al., 2020) and even topical products produce absorption under alternate light sources (Pollitt et al., 2016). For these reasons, alternate light sources should only be used when there is a reported history of blunt force trauma at the site to better visualize, not detect, known areas of injury (Scafide et al., 2020).

Additional studies may identify how alternate light sources can be used to detect injuries in the absence of history, similar to more recent evidence in support of using toluidine blue dye to detect and not just highlight already visible injuries. Even if validated for detecting injuries, use of toluidine blue dye and alternate light sources, like use of colposcopes, are advanced forensic nursing skills. They should not be used without proper training regarding how to distinguish between false positives and normal findings. Failure to do so can have potentially harmful consequences, including contributing to misidentified suspects, wrongful convictions, or protracted legal procedures through poorly collected evidence (Johnson, 2021).

Additionally, contrast filters on colposcopes and enhanced camera systems can be applied to photographs to improve the visualization of identified injuries. Contrast filters work by stretching the intensity range of images to improve contrast (Sudhakar, 2017). This technique preserves the original photographs and does not require specialized skills. However, no studies validating its use in medical forensic exams or how it is used in investigation and prosecution were found. Advances in the identification and visualization of injuries related to sexual assault have the potential to improve evidence documentation, which can be beneficial to the investigation and prosecution of these crimes.

Advancements in sexual assault kit contents and instructions

Standardized recommendations for SAK contents and instructions are published in national guidelines (Office on Violence Against Women, 2013, 2016; National Institute of Justice, 2017). Oversight and established reviews of SAKs and SAFME paperwork should be conducted by designated agencies in each jurisdiction. Current guidelines do not recommend the inclusion of slides in SAKs to create smears for the evaluation of spermatozoa. Forensic laboratories have improved analysis methods to detect spermatozoa. With the increased concern of DNA cross-contamination, as mentioned previously, masks and gloves should be included in SAKs for use by forensic examiners.

SAKs should contain easily understandable evidence collection and packaging instructions in case SAFMEs are completed by health-care providers without specialized training. SANEs and forensic examiners should consider the SAFME paperwork as the primary means to communicate information about collected swabs or other evidence to forensic scientists to guide laboratory analysis. With the ability to develop probative DNA profiles from epithelial cells, saliva, blood, or semen, it is helpful for forensic examiners to note the type of contact connected to body swabs to inform DNA analysis decisions.

Some jurisdictions have incorporated forensic electronic medical records rather than paper forms, although hard-copy instructions and forms should still be in SAKs. Forensic electronic medical records are beneficial to improve the dissemination of the SAFME paperwork to forensic science and criminal justice system partners. Additionally, forensic electronic medical records may be more time-efficient than paper charting.

As with all electronic health records, very secure standards and procedures must be employed to ensure privacy and confidentiality. In jurisdictions with electronic SAK tracking systems with victim portals, information on accessing the portal and tracking the SAK should be included within the SAK to guarantee this information is shared with victims. A legislatively mandated electronic SAK program in Texas has tracked over 14,000 SAKs since September 1, 2019, with 23.6% of victims logging into the system (Texas Department of Public Safety, 2021).

Influences and Future Trends

SAFMEs will continue to evolve based upon technological advancements and SANE practice changes. Evidence collection, documentation, and packaging need to be responsive to continued DNA and scientific advancements. This responsiveness is dependent upon strong collaborative relationships between SANEs or forensic examiners and multidisciplinary partners. Relationships can be strengthened through involvement in sexual assault response teams through scheduled in-person and virtual meetings. Texas passed a law in 2021 requiring all counties to participate in sexual assault response teams; it will be helpful to examine the impact of this law on increasing access to trauma-informed responses to sexual assault.

Content, paperwork, and instructions in SAKs need to adapt to incorporate research advances and current evidence-based practice recommendations. Continued updates to SAKs are challenging in the current landscape of differing SAKs based upon jurisdiction preferences. A proposal for a standardized, national SAK has been made to ensure evidence-based practice recommendations are established nationally. A standardized, national SAK would support health-care equity and quality in SAFMEs throughout the United States.

A future direction for forensic nursing includes the forensic nurse hospitalist (Berishaj et al., 2020). Forensic nurse hospitalists would be available to provide specialized care whenever staff have concerns about a patient's health and safety related to abuse, neglect, or questionable death. Increasingly, forensic nurses are expanding care beyond sexual assault to provide care for patients impacted by intimate partner violence, strangulation, assault, child or elder abuse/neglect, human trafficking, and other forms of non-accidental trauma. Beyond serving as fact and expert witnesses in cases for which they provided direct patient care, SANEs contribute valuable skills as legal consultants and expert witnesses in sexual assault legislation, practice changes, and civil and criminal cases (Valentine, 2018).

Advancements to increase access to SANEs

The issue of access to SANEs continues to be the greatest challenge. The Government Accounting Office reported a shortage of SANEs in the United States, especially in rural areas (Clowers, 2018). This is important due to findings that SAMFEs conducted by SANEs, compared with non-SANE health-care providers, resulting in more effective evidence collection (Sievers et al., 2003), greater admissibility of evidence in court, and up to 83% greater likelihood the case will proceed through the justice system (Campbell et al., 2012, 2014; Fehler-Cabral et al., 2011; Toon & Gurusamy, 2014). Attorneys, law enforcement, and survivor advocates in rural areas have reported issues with evidence collection and unrealistic juror expectations related to DNA and solving cases that can be mitigated by SANE involvement in SAMFEs (Annan, 2014).

Transferring patients

Several strategies to address access to SAMFEs have been employed. For example, a 2013 law in Texas mandated all hospitals with emergency rooms provide SAMFEs to patients who do not want to transfer to hospitals with SANEs. Despite this, a 2017 Police Foundation report found most rural hospitals still preferred to transfer patients (Davis et al., 2017). They also found the basic evidence collection course required to perform SAMFEs was not sufficient to prepare nurses to provide this specialized care.

Thus, increasing access to SANEs, and not merely SAMFEs, is optimal. To increase the SANE workforce, the U.S. Health Resources & Services Administration (HRSA) awarded over $8.1 million to 20 academic institutions to provide SANE education in 2018 and renewed the program in 2020. The HRSA-SANE program provides total funding to support nurses in achieving SANE education and certification, removing the financial constraint.

Even with increased SANE education for rural nurses, practical constraints limit the ability of rural hospitals to provide 24-hour SANE services. The low volume of patients seeking SAMFEs means rural nurses have difficulty attaining and maintaining proficiency. Furthermore, SANEs practicing with limited experience, and in isolation, risk protocol fidelity drift when they lack access to expert continuing education and peer review. For these reasons, it is understandable that some rural hospitals prefer to transfer patients to hospitals with SANEs so patients can receive the highest standard of care.

Unfortunately, transferring patients to hospitals where SANEs are available can have several negative impacts. Most people who are sexually assaulted do not seek medical treatment (Sabina & Ho, 2014; Zinzow et al., 2012). Survivors of sexual assault may feel stigmatized by health-care providers and perceive being treated as though they were "not normal" (Kennedy & Prock, 2018). This stigma can be exacerbated when patients are informed by the hospital where they seek care that "we don't do that here" and have to be transferred to a hospital with a SANE program. Transportation issues, fatigue, and intoxication can prohibit patients from self-transporting to referred facilities, and patients may decide not to go (Fehler-Cabral et al., 2011). Fragmented care creates risk of added trauma from having to repeat the sexual assault history and patients may be faced with additional emergency room charges. Transfers also cause delays in time-sensitive medical treatments such as pregnancy and HIV prophylaxis, and time-sensitive evidence may be lost or become contaminated with multiple health-care provider contacts.

TeleSANEs

A more recent strategy to increase access to expert SANEs is through telehealth (teleSANE). TeleSANE is an innovation that prevents transfers from hospitals without full-time expert SANEs while still providing access to expert SANEs. In 2013, the Office for Victims of Crime (OVC) funded the first teleSANE program in Massachusetts, the National Telenursing Center, which aimed for a national scope including serving military and tribal communities (Walsh et al., 2019). In 2016, the OVC released a notice of funding opportunity (NOFO) for the development of a statewide teleSANE program, which was awarded to Pennsylvania State University, and the SAFE-T Center was created (Miyamoto et al., 2021). In 2019, the NOFO was released again to fund statewide teleSANE programs and four sites were selected (Avera Health in South Dakota, Texas A&M University, Tundra Women's Coalition in Alaska, and the University of Arkansas for Medical Sciences). In addition to the six OVC-funded sites, states and hospital systems have also developed their own teleSANE programs, representing a rapid expansion of this innovation to increase access to SANE expertise. The goals of the OVC project are to improve access to experienced SANEs through telehealth and ensure more patients receive patient-centered and trauma-informed care using Duffy's (2010) quality-caring model.

TeleSANE differs from most traditional telehealth programs (AAACN, 2018) in that it provides real-time consultation with a remote health-care provider who is providing direct care to a patient. The teleSANE engages with both the health-care provider and the patient using a model that has been referred to as real-time tripartite consultation (Deldar et al., 2016). In provider-to-provider telehealth models, the locus of responsibility for the encounter is at the patient location (AAACN, 2018). Thus, the teleSANE is not the direct care provider, does not make nursing diagnoses, does not document the patient history or exam findings, and does not maintain evidence custody.

Despite the rapid growth of teleSANE care, no data have been reported regarding whether it improves health or legal outcomes. The OVC technical assistance provider, the International Association of Forensic Nurses (IAFN), is collecting standardized data from each of the 2019 OVC teleSANE grantees to better understand impacts on patients, bedside clinicians, teleSANEs, and advocates. To our knowledge, no cases using teleSANE have been prosecuted, so currently, there are no data on how having a teleSANE might impact prosecution. Data from the NTC show the most common types of assistance requested of teleSANEs during encounters included monitoring/reviewing, evidence collection, exam procedures, and documentation (Walsh et al., 2019), suggesting teleSANEs are positioned to impact evidence collection and documentation quality. While teleSANEs are not providing direct patient care, the remote provider documents a teleSANE was present during the exam and provided guidance where needed. To this end, it is expected teleSANE providers will be subpoenaed to testify, also providing increased access to expert SANE testimony in rural areas. For more information about SAMFEs in rural areas, see Chapter 14.

Attrition is another critical issue that inhibits access to SANEs (Clowers, 2018). Rural SANEs often practice in isolation and are less likely to be certified (Thiede & Miyamoto, 2021). In addition, risk of vicarious traumatization may contribute to attrition (Raunick et al., 2015; Wies & Coy, 2013). Burnout and moral distress related to the COVID-19 pandemic (Sagherian et al., 2020) may contribute to even greater SANE attrition as SANE is typically a secondary professional role taken in addition to another nursing role (Mitchell et al., 2022).

Many SANE programs struggle to maintain adequate funding to keep their program operational. Maier (2012) surveyed a sample of 40 SANE programs and found that 72% reported funding challenges to provide SAMFEs. Poor funding results in the inability to purchase new equipment, provide forensic continuing education, and adequately compensate SANEs. Funding challenges contribute to SANE attrition and can decrease SAMFE availability and quality.

Discussion

The quality of SAFMEs is highly dependent upon access and availability to SANEs or other specialty educated health-care professionals. While the International Association of Forensic Nurses has grown from a few dozen nurses when founded in 1992 to over 6,000 members today, many areas in the United States lack SANEs to provide specialized care. Steps must be taken to increase the number of SANEs in the United States.

The reliability and validity of forensic disciplines have become increasingly scrutinized. For example, a National Academy of Sciences report found forensic science disciplines, in general, lacked rigorous certification programs for forensic scientists. Forensic science disciplines also lacked strong standards and protocols for forensic analysis and reporting of results; some forensic techniques were not supported by sufficient evidence nor peer-reviewed studies of their reliability (National Academy of Sciences, 2009). Forensic nursing will likely undergo scrutiny similar to other forensic professionals as SANEs become more visible. Judges, attorneys, and jurors will increasingly expect forensic nursing to meet specified standards of education, knowledge, and experience.

Currently, there are no minimum education requirements for registered nurses to practice as SANEs; SANEs can be nurses with diploma-based education or have associate's, bachelor's, master's, or doctorate degrees. SANE training programs also vary. The International Association of Forensic Nurses developed SANE Education Guidelines (International Association of Forensic Nurses, 2018) via an expert consensus panel and has an approver unit to review SANE education curricula. At this time, International Association of Forensic Nurses SANE education approval is voluntary and obtaining approval verifies programs meet the criteria and ensures nurses who complete them are eligible to sit for SANE certification exams. Certification is also voluntary. Peer review of SANE practice is also recommended (Office on Violence

Against Women, 2013) but is not required. Thus, it is possible to perform SAMFEs with no standardized educational background, training, certification, or peer review.

With the advent of an Organization of Scientific Area Committees for Forensic Science Forensic Nursing Subcommittee (Organization of Scientific Area Committees for Forensic Science, 2021), standards for SANE practice should increase, which will benefit patient care. It is expected that improving SAMFE processes and availability will lead to healthier and safer communities.

Additional research on the impact of care provided by SANEs on patients, forensic science, and criminal justice system outcomes is necessary to develop evidence-based practice guidelines. *The Constructed Theory of Forensic Nursing Care* (Valentine et al., 2020) suggests that forensic nurses with specialized education improve multidisciplinary outcomes for patients affected by violence and trauma and provides a framework for conducting forensic nursing research. Research trials to test this assertion are necessary.

Addressing health inequities and establishing commitments to social justice are priority areas for all nursing specialties, as described in the Futures of Nursing Report 2020–2030 (National Academies of Sciences, Engineering, and Medicine, 2021). The International Association of Forensic Nurses Strategic Plan notes the first strategic plan pillar of Social Justice as a core value informing and directing forensic nursing practice (IAFN, 2018). For forensic nursing, health equity is achieved when all patients affected by violence receive equal, compassionate, and skilled forensic nursing care. Regarding SAMFEs, this goal is only achievable in the United States with a substantial increase in SANE services.

Key Points

- SAMFE, SAKs, and SANE practice must continually adapt to technology, such as touch DNA evidence analysis, and practice advancements, such as program accreditation.
- Evidence supports better health care and legal outcomes when SANEs are involved in sexual assault examinations and testimony, though the quality of SAMFEs is highly dependent upon the expertise of the forensic examiner.
- SANE certification and program accreditation are voluntary but recommended as both indicate high-quality and evidence-based forensic nursing care.
- Access to specialized SANE care, especially in rural and underserved areas, must be improved throughout the U.S to ensure equity and quality in SA responsiveness and SAK evidence collection. State and federal funding for SANE education and telehealth SANE practice are strategies to increase access to SANE expertise.
- New and advanced technologies in SANE practice to identify and collect evidence in sexual assault cases can improve the ability to successfully investigate and prosecute sexual assault cases. Forensic nursing and forensic science research are necessary to establish and support SAMFE evidence-based practices.

Discussion Questions

1 What are the foremost research gaps related to SAMFEs and SANE practice?
2 What are the best strategies to increase SANE access and services across the United States?
3 How do we increase sustainability and funding of SANE programs?

4 What is the role of SANEs within the criminal justice system? What are the pros and cons of having state and national certification processes be mandatory?
5 What are the next steps in establishing a national, standardized SAK?

Further Reading

National Institute of Justice. (2017). *National best practices for sexual assault kits: A multi-disciplinary approach.* https://www.ncjrs.gov/pdffiles1/nij/250384.pdf

U.S. Department of Justice. (2013). *A national protocol for sexual assault medical forensic examination: Adults and adolescents* (2nd ed.). https://www.ncjrs.gov/pdffiles1/ovw/241903.pdf

U.S. Department of Justice. (2016). *A national protocol for sexual abuse medical forensic examinations: Pediatrics.* https://www.justice.gov/ovw/file/846856/download

U.S. Department of Justice. (2017). *Sexual assault kit testing initiatives and non-investigative kits: White Paper.* https://www.justice.gov/ovw/page/file/928236/download

U.S. Department of Justice, Office on Violence Against Women. (2018). *National training standards for sexual assault medical forensic examiners* (2nd ed.). https://cdn.ymaws.com/www.safeta.org/resource/resmgr/docs/Training_SexualAssaultForens.pdf

Valentine, J. L., Sekula, L. K., & Lynch, V. A., (2020). Evolution of forensic nursing theory—Introduction of the constructed theory of forensic nursing care: A middle-range theory. *Journal of Forensic Nursing, 16*(4), 188–198.

References

American Academy of Ambulatory Care Nursing (AAACN). (2018). (6th ed.). AACN.

American Nurses Credentialing Center (ANCC). (2010). *Why certify? The benefits of nursing certification.* https://www.medscape.com/viewarticle/717805

Anderson, L. J., Flynn, A., & Pilgrim, J. L. (2017). A global epidemiological perspective on the toxicology of drug-facilitated sexual assault: A systematic review. *Journal of Forensic and Legal Medicine, 47,* 46–54.

Annan, S. L. (2014). We desperately need some help here. The experience of legal experts with sexual assault and evidence collection in rural communities. *Rural & Remote Health, 14*(4), 2659.

Berishaj, K., Boland, C. M., Reinink, K., & Lynch, V. (2020). Forensic nurse hospitalist: The comprehensive role of the forensic nurse in a hospital setting. *Journal of Emergency Nursing, 46*(3), 286–293.

Campbell, R., Bybee, D., Townsend, S. M., Shaw, J., Karim, N., & Markowitz, J. (2014). The impact of sexual assault nurse examiner programs on criminal justice case outcomes a multisite replication study. *Violence Against Women, 20*(5), 607–625.

Campbell, R., Patterson, D., & Bybee, D. (2012). Prosecution of adult sexual assault cases a longitudinal analysis of the impact of a sexual assault nurse examiner program. *Violence Against Women, 18*(2), 223–244.

Campbell, R., Patterson, D., Bybee, D., & Dworkin, E. R. (2009). Predicting sexual assault prosecution outcomes: The role of medical forensic evidence collected by sexual assault nurse examiners. *Criminal Justice and Behavior, 36*(7), 712–727.

Caswell, R. J., Ross, J. D., & Lorimer, K. (2019). Measuring experience and outcomes in patients reporting sexual violence who attend a healthcare setting: A systematic review. *Sexually Transmitted Infections, 95*(6), 419–427.

Centers for Disease Control and Prevention. (2021). Sexual assault and abuse and STIs. https://www.cdc.gov/std/treatment-guidelines/sexual-assault.htm

Clowers, A. N. (2018). *Sexual assault: Information on the availability of forensic examiners.* U.S. Government Accountability Office. https://www.gao.gov/assets/gao-19-259t.pdf

Davis, R. C., Camp, T., Howley, S., Wells, W., & Knecht, I. (2017). *Impact of SB1191 on accessibility of sexual assault exams in TX.* Police Foundation.

Deldar, K., Bahaadinbeigy, K., & Tara, S. M. (2016). Teleconsultation and clinical decision making: A systematic review. *Acta Informatica Medica, 24*(4), 286–292.

Deutsch, L. S., Resch, K., Barber, T., Zuckerman, Y., Stone, J. T., & Cerulli, C. (2017). Bruise documentation, race and barriers to seeking legal relief for intimate partner violence survivors: A retrospective qualitative study. *Journal of Family Violence, 32*(8), 767–773.

Downing, N. R. (2021). International Association of Forensic Nurses President's message. *Journal of Forensic Nursing, 17*(2), E18–E22.

Downing, N. R., Adams, M., & Bogue, R. J. (2020). Factors associated with law enforcement reporting in patients presenting for medical forensic examinations. *Journal of Interpersonal Violence, 37*(5–6), 3269–3292. https://doi.org/10.1177/0886260520948518

Duffy, J. R. (2010). Joanne Duffy's quality caring model. *Nursing Theories and Nursing Practice, 3,* 402–416.

End the Backlog. (n. d.). Backlog map. https://www.endthebacklog.org/#explore_backlog_map

Federal Bureau of Investigation. (n. d.). Frequently asked questions on CODIS and NDIS. https://www.fbi.gov/services/laboratory/biometric-analysis/codis/codis-and-ndis-fact-sheet

Fehler-Cabral, G., Campbell, R., & Patterson, D. (2011). Adult sexual assault survivors' experiences with sexual assault nurse examiners (SANEs). *Journal of Interpersonal Violence, 26*(18), 3618–3639.

Fisher, B. S., Kaplan, A., Budescu, M., Fargo, J., Tiller, D., Everett, J., & Sommers, M. (2013). The influence of anogenital injury on women's willingness to engage with the criminal justice process after rape. *Violence and Victims, 28*(6), 968–983.

Hirachan, N. (2019). Use of toluidine blue dye in detection of anogenital injuries in consensual sexual intercourse. *Journal of Forensic and Legal Medicine, 64,* 14–19.

Holleran, D., Beichner, D., & Spohn, C. (2010). Examining charging agreement between police and prosecutors in rape cases. *Crime & Delinquency, 56*(3), 385–413.

International Association of Forensic Nurses. (2018). *Sexual Assault Nurse Examiner (SANE) education guidelines.* https://www.forensicnurses.org/page/EducationGuidelinesAccess

International Association of Forensic Nurses. (2021a). *Board-certified SANE-A nurses.* https://www.forensicnurses.org/search/custom.asp?id=2093

International Association of Forensic Nurses. (2021b). *Education Offerings.* https://www.forensicnurses.org/page/EducationMainPage

International Association of Forensic Nurses. (n. d.). *Certification 101.* https://www.forensicnurses.org/wp-content/uploads/2021/05/Certification_101.pdf

Johnson, M. B. (2021). *Wrongful conviction in sexual assault: Stranger rape, acquaintance rape, and intra-familial child sexual assaults.* Oxford University Press.

Johnson, D., Peterson, J., Sommers, I., & Baskin, D. (2012). Use of forensic science in investigating crimes of sexual violence: Contrasting its theoretical potential with empirical realities. *Violence Against Women, 18*(2), 193–222.

Kennedy, K. M. (2013). Heterogeneity of existing research relating to sexual violence, sexual assault and rape precludes meta-analysis of injury data. *Journal of Forensic and Legal Medicine, 20*(5), 447–459.

Kennedy, A. C., & Prock, K. A. (2018). "I still feel like I am not normal": A review of the role of stigma and stigmatization among female survivors of child sexual abuse, sexual assault, and intimate partner violence. *Trauma, Violence, & Abuse, 19*(5), 512–527.

Kilpatrick, D. G., Resnick, H. S., Milanak, M. E., Miller, M. W., Keyes, K. M., & Friedman, M. J. (2013). National estimates of exposure to traumatic events and PTSD prevalence using DSM-IV and DSM-5 criteria. *Journal of Traumatic Stress, 26*(5), 537–547.

Maier, S.L. (2012). Sexual assault nurse examiners' perceptions of funding challenges faced by SANE programs: "It stinks." *Journal of Forensic Nursing, 8*, 81–93.

Marin, N., & Buszka, J. M. (2013). *Alternate light source imaging: Forensic photography techniques.* Anderson Publishing.

Mitchell, S. A., Charles, L. A., & Downing, N. (2022). Increasing access to forensic nursing services in rural and underserved areas of Texas. *Journal of Forensic Nursing, 18*(1), 21–29.

Miyamoto, S., Thiede, E., Dorn, L., Perkins, D. F., Bittner, C., & Scanlon, D. (2021). The Sexual Assault Forensic Examination Telehealth (SAFE-T) Center: A comprehensive, nurse-led telehealth model to address disparities in sexual assault care. *The Journal of Rural Health, 37*(1), 92–102.

Möller, A., Söndergaard, H. P., & Helström, L. (2017). Tonic immobility during sexual assault: A common reaction predicting posttraumatic stress disorder and severe depression. *Acta Obstetricia et Gynecologica Scandinavica, 96(8)*, 932–938.

National Academy of Sciences. (2009). *Strengthening forensic science in the United States: A path forward.* National Academies Press.

National Academies of Sciences, Engineering, and Medicine. (2021). *The future of nursing 2020-2030: Charting a path to achieve health equity.* The National Academies Press. https://doi.org/10.17226/25982.

National Institute of Justice (NIJ). (2017). National best practices for sexual assault kits: A multidisciplinary approach. NIJ. https://www.ojp.gov/pdffiles1/nij/250384.pdf

Office for Victims of Crime. (n. d.). *Sexual assault nurse examiners.* https://www.ovcttac.gov/saneguide/management-of-sane-programs/sexual-assault-nurse-examiners/

Office on Violence Against Women (OVW), U.S. Department of Justice. (2013). *A national protocol for sexual assault medical forensic examination: Adults and adolescents* (2nd ed.). https://www.ncjrs.gov/pdffiles1/ovw/241903.pdf

Office on Violence Against Women (OVW), U.S. Department of Justice. (2017). *Sexual assault kit testing initiatives and non-investigative kits: White paper.* https://www.justice.gov/ovw/page/file/928236/download

Office on Violence Against Women (OVW), U.S. Department of Justice. (2016). *A national protocol for sexual assault medical forensic examination: Pediatric.* https://www.ncjrs.gov/pdffiles1/ovw/241903.pdf

Organization of Scientific Area Committees for Forensic Science. (2021). *Forensic nursing sub-committee.* https://www.nist.gov/organization-scientific-area-committees-forensic-science/forensic-nursing-subcommittee

Pollitt, E. N., Anderson, J. C., Scafide, K. N., Holbrook, D., D'Silva, G., & Sheridan, D. J. (2016). Alternate light source findings of common topical products. *Journal of Forensic Nursing, 11*(3), 97–103.

Purps, J., Geppert, M., Nagy, M., & Roewer, M. (2015). Validation of a combined autosomal/Y-chromosomal STR approach for analyzing typical biological stains in sexual assault cases. *Forensic Science International: Genetics, 19*, 248–252. http://dx.doi.org/10.1016/j.fsigen.2015.08.002

Raunick, C. B., Lindell, D. F., Morris, D. L., & Backman, T. (2015). Vicarious trauma among sexual assault nurse examiners. *Journal of Forensic Nursing, 11*(3), 123–128.

Rogers, A., McIntyre, S. L., Rossman, L., Solis, S., Bacon-Baguley, T. A., & Jones, J. (2019). The forensic rape examination: Is colposcopy really necessary? *The American Journal of Emergency Medicine, 37*(5), 999–1000.

Sabina, C., & Ho, L. Y. (2014). Campus and college victim responses to sexual assault and dating violence: Disclosure, service utilization, and service provision. *Trauma, Violence, & Abuse, 15*(3), 201–226.

Sagherian, K., Steege, L. M., Cobb, S. J., & Cho, H. (2020). Insomnia, fatigue and psycho-social well-being during COVID-19 pandemic: A cross-sectional survey of hospital nursing staff in the United States. *Journal of Clinical Nursing.* https://doi.org/10.1111/jocn.15566

Scafide, K. N., Downing, N. R., Kutahyalioglu, N. S., Sebeh, Y., Sheridan, D. J., & Hayat, M. J. (2021). Quantifying the degree of bruise visibility observed under white light and an alternate light source. *Journal of Forensic Nursing, 17*(1), 24–33.

Scafide, K. N., Downing, N. R., Kutahyalioglu, N. S., Sheridan, D., Langlois, N. E., & Hayat, M. J. (in press). Predicting alternate light absorption in areas of trauma based on degree of skin pigmentation: Not all wavelengths are equal. *Forensic Science International*.

Scafide, K. N., Sheridan, D. J., Downing, N. R., & Hayat, M. J. (2020). Detection of inflicted bruises by alternate light: Results of a randomized controlled trial. *Journal of Forensic Sciences, 65*(4), 1191–1198.

Sievers, V., Murphy, S., & Miller, J. J. (2003, December). Sexual assault evidence collection more accurate when completed by sexual assault nurse examiners: Colorado's experience. *Journal of Emergency Nursing, 29*, 511–514.

Sommers, M. S., Brown, K. M., Buschur, C., Everett, J. S., Fargo, J. D., Fisher, B. S., & Zink, T. M. (2012). Injuries from intimate partner and sexual violence: Significance and classification systems. *Journal of Forensic and Legal Medicine, 19*(5), 250–263.

Sommers, M. S., & Fargo, J. D. (2021). Discriminating between consensual intercourse and sexual assault: genital-anal injury pattern in females. *Journal of Forensic and Legal Medicine, 79*, 102138.

Speck, P., & Ballantyne, J. (2015). *Post-coital DNA recovery study. Final report submitted to National Institute of Justice*. US Department of Justice. https://www.ncjrs.gov/pdffiles1/nij/grants/248682.pdf

Sudhakar, S. (2017, July 9). *Histogram equalization: Image contrast enhancement*. https://towardsdatascience.com/histogram-equalization-5d1013626e64

The Joint Commission. (2021). *Benefits of Joint Commission accreditation*. https://www.jointcommission.org/resources/news-and-multimedia/fact-sheets/facts-about-benefits-of-joint-commission-accreditation/

Texas Department of Public Safety. (2021). *Sexual assault evidence tracking program*. https://www.dps.texas.gov/section/crime-laboratory/sexual-assault-evidence-tracking-program

Thiede, E., & Miyamoto, S. (2021). Rural availability of sexual assault nurse examiners (SANEs). *The Journal of Rural Health, 37*(1), 81–91.

Toon, C., & Gurusamy, K. (2014). Forensic nurse examiners versus doctors for the forensic examination of rape and sexual assault complainants: A systematic review. *Campbell Systematic Reviews, 10*(5), 1–56. https://doi.org/10.4073/CSR.2014.5

U.S. Department of Justice. (2017). *Sexual assault kit testing initiatives and non-investigative kits: White Paper*. https://www.justice.gov/ovw/page/file/928236/download

U.S. Department of Justice, Office on Violence Against Women. (2018). *National Training Standards for Sexual Assault Medical Forensic Examiners* (2nd ed.). https://cdn.ymaws.com/www.safeta.org/resource/resmgr/docs/Training_SexualAssaultForens.pdf

Valentine, J. L. (2018). Forensic nursing: Overview of a growing profession. *American Nurse Today, 13*(12), 42–44.

Valentine, J. L., Presler-Jur, P., Mills, H., & Miles, S. (2021). Evidence collection and analysis for touch deoxyribonucleic acid in groping and sexual assault cases. *Journal of Forensic Nursing, 17*(2), 67–75. https://doi.org/10.1097/jfn.0000000000000324

Valentine, J. L., Sekula, L. K., & Lynch, V. A. (2020). Evolution of forensic nursing theory—Introduction of the constructed theory of forensic nursing care: A middle-range theory. *Journal of Forensic Nursing, 16*(4), 188–198.

Walker, G. (2015). The (in)significance of genital injury in rape and sexual assault. *Journal of Forensic and Legal Medicine, 34*, 173–178.

Walsh, W. A., Meunier-Sham, J., & Re, C. (2019). Using telehealth for sexual assault forensic examinations: A process evaluation of a national pilot project. *Journal of Forensic Nursing, 15*(3), 152–162.

Wies, J., & Coy, K. (2013). Measuring violence: Vicarious trauma among sexual assault nurse examiners. *Human Organization*, 72(1), 23–30.

Zink, T., Fargo, J. D., Baker, R. B., Buschur, C., Fisher, B. S., & Sommers, M. S. (2010). Comparison of methods for identifying ano-genital injury after consensual intercourse. *The Journal of Emergency Medicine*, 39(1), 113–118.

Zinzow, H. M., Resnick, H. S., Barr, S. C., Danielson, C. K., & Kilpatrick, D. G. (2012). Receipt of post-rape medical care in a national sample of female victims. *American Journal of Preventive Medicine*, 43(2), 183–187.

13 Current trends with anonymous reporting

Lessons learned from Duluth, Minnesota

Mary Faulkner

In 2015, the City of Duluth Police Department (DPD) found itself in the unenviable position of having the most unsubmitted sexual assault kits (SAKs) in the state of Minnesota. This inventory included SAKs with accompanying police reports ("standard" or "unrestricted" SAKs) and those that were without a named victim and had no accompanying report. They were only identified by a unique number ("anonymous" or "restricted" SAKs). DPD was also awarded federal Sexual Assault Kit Initiative (SAKI) funding in 2015 to collaborate with Saint Louis County Attorney's Office, the Program for Aid to Victims of Sexual Assault (PAVSA), and the state crime laboratory, the Minnesota Bureau of Criminal Apprehension (MN BCA), to address previously unsubmitted SAKs. DPD formed a SAKI working group to test SAKs and to identify and tackle underlying issues that left SAKs untested. These efforts focused on addressing both the standard and anonymous SAKs and providing victim-survivors with opportunities to re-engage with law enforcement and advocacy services.

The City of Duluth and the Sexual Assault Kit Initiative

Duluth is a port city in northeastern Minnesota on the shores of Lake Superior. Duluth has a population just shy of 90,000. It is known for its cold temperatures and Ellen Pence's visionary work on domestic violence intervention, known as the Duluth Model. This model uses Power and Control Wheels to demonstrate that violence is not limited to isolated acts of abuse but rather patterns of behavior where one partner seeks to intimidate, isolate, manipulate, and threaten the other. The Duluth Model promotes the use of a coordinated community response (CCR) or regular collaboration of stakeholders in law enforcement, prosecution, advocacy, and other allied fields to establish protocols to support victim-survivors and hold offenders accountable. While developed for domestic violence, CCRs have also been a promising development for sexual assault reform.

DPD has participated for over 20 years with the Southern Saint Louis County Sexual Assault Multidisciplinary Action Response Team (SMART), whose mission is to ensure a victim-centered community response to sexual assault by utilizing a culturally competent and multidisciplinary approach. The SMART has implemented and sustained a number of promising programs including the creation of a community-based Sexual Assault Nurse Examiner (SANE) program housed at PAVSA, an Anonymous Reporting Protocol, and a Trafficking Awareness Task Force. Importantly, a solid foundation of criminal justice system collaboration was in place as sexual assault reform efforts began in our region and across the state.

DOI: 10.4324/9781003186816-16

In partnership with the Saint Louis County Attorney's Office and PAVSA, DPD implemented the Bureau of Justice Assistance (BJA) SAKI model's three essential elements: the completion of a certified inventory of unsubmitted SAKs, the designation of a Site Coordinator, and the formation of a multidisciplinary working group. By 2016, DPD had instituted a "test-all" policy directing Sex Crimes Abuse and Neglect (SCAN) Unit investigators to submit all incoming unrestricted SAKs for testing to the MN BCA within 30 days. The working group identified factors that led to the inventory of unsubmitted SAKs (including but not limited to): (1) lack of policies and protocols on SAK testing; (2) understaffing and instability within the SCAN Unit; (3) lack of an understanding of the value of forensic evidence, particularly in cases that may hinge on issues of consent; (4) inability to establish and maintain communication with and participation from victim-survivors; and (5) lack of understanding of victim-survivor's trauma responses. To date, 444 previously unsubmitted, unrestricted SAKs from 1993 to 2015 have been tested resulting in:

- 203 CODIS uploads and 116 CODIS hits.
- 187 victim-survivors have been notified that their SAKs are now tested, and 126 victim-survivors have opted to either re-engage with law enforcement or advocacy services.
- 36 cases have been referred for charges, 20 suspects have been charged, 4 defendants have accepted plea deals, 2 were convicted at jury trials, and 8 suspects are pending trial.

I serve as the Site Coordinator for the DPD SAKI project. The BJA requires each site to identify a Site Coordinator. I am housed at the police department but am an advocate with the community-based rape crisis center PAVSA. Site Coordinators have three important roles. Firstly, I am the facilitator for our multidisciplinary working group which includes representatives from law enforcement, prosecution, advocacy, forensic medicine, forensic science, mental health care, and academia. Our full working group meets quarterly, and we have two subcommittees, a Protocol and Policy Development subcommittee and a Case Review subcommittee which meet biweekly and as needed, respectively. At these meetings, I work to gather input from team members and build consensus for the project's trajectory.

Secondly, I track our progress through the stages of reform including conducting a BJA-certified inventory, submitting and testing the unrestricted SAKs, notifying victim-survivors, and investigating and prosecuting cold cases. This includes tracking the creation of deliverables, such as protocols and outreach materials and submitting quarterly performance reports to document our progress and identify our challenges and successes.

Finally, and most importantly, this role requires cultivating a "Janus-faced" perspective. I need to be able to reflect on past practices and identify historical factors that had impeded the sexual assault response and then apply that analysis to improve current practices. Our working group views the mission of addressing anonymous SAKs as an important aspect of our comprehensive sexual assault reform, as detailed below.

Anonymous Reporting Protocol Implementation (2008)

The Southern Saint Louis County SMART developed and implemented its Anonymous Reporting Protocol in 2008. Locally, the term Anonymous was adopted while other communities adopted similar practices but used terms such as Jane Doe, blind, third-party, non-investigative, and restricted reporting kits, among others (Lonsway & Archambault, 2020; Office on Violence Against Women [OVW], 2017). The PAVSA SANE Program dispatches on-call SANEs to conduct forensic exams at three local emergency departments and maintains confidential records for those victim-survivors who were unsure about or declined to report their assault to law enforcement. All patient-identifying information is sealed within the SAK. The SANE calls Saint Louis County 911 Dispatch as the third-party reporter of a sexual assault and provides them with an approximate location. 911 Dispatch then generates a unique Incident Complaint Report (ICR) number for the SAK that includes the appropriate jurisdiction. In turn, participating law enforcement agencies agree to retrieve, inventory, and store anonymous SAKs that are labeled with only the unique ICR number.

At the time of implementation, there were five participating law enforcement jurisdictions in Minnesota—DPD, Saint Louis County Sheriff's Office, Hermantown Police Department, University of Minnesota-DPD, Proctor Police Department, Superior Police Department, and Douglas County Sheriff's Office (the latter two jurisdictions are in neighboring Wisconsin). All have agreed to store anonymous SAKs in perpetuity. This agreement to store anonymous SAKs in law enforcement property and evidence units has kept them from being left in hospital refrigerators where the chain of custody could not be assured. Anonymous SAKs are ineligible for testing by the MN BCA because they lack a corresponding police report. PAVSA advocates assist victim-survivors if they later choose to convert their SAKs from anonymous to standard and then need to make an accompanying report to law enforcement. Once converted, an investigation can commence and the SAK is eligible for testing.

While a significant improvement in trauma-informed practice, there are limitations to this Anonymous Reporting Protocol. Victim-survivors under age 18 and vulnerable adults are screened for mandatory reporting and may not be able to choose anonymity. If an incident warrants a mandated report, the SANE would make the patient's identity and circumstances of abuse known to Saint Louis County Initial Intervention Unit or Adult Services and facilitate a report to the appropriate law enforcement jurisdiction. If an incident occurred outside of the seven participating jurisdictions, the SAK would not be collected and stored by an appropriate law enforcement agency. It would remain locked in the emergency department refrigerator and only be retained as long as space permitted. Similarly, if emergency department medical professionals rather than a SANE conducted the forensic exam and the patient declined to report to law enforcement, the SAK would remain at the hospital. Without accompanying police reports, these SAKs were not considered to be evidence. Locally, these SAKs became known as "Non-Reports." They exist outside of both the standard process of reporting to law enforcement and the Anonymous Reporting Protocol with no guidelines for storage or retention. See Chapter 12 for more information on SAFMEs, Chapter 15 for SAFMEs within a university setting, and Chapter 3 for a review of the literature on disclosure.

Key Aims of the Anonymous Reporting Protocol

The Anonymous Reporting Protocol primarily aimed to meet the needs of victim-survivors in our community, in particular, those who may be reluctant to file a police report and, if required to report, might forgo medical care in the aftermath of a sexual assault. Secondarily, medical personnel and SANEs are part of a collaborative process with law enforcement that worked to outline the storage, retention, or conversion of these SAKs. Ledray and Kraft (2001) indicated that most SANE programs already had in place a "widely followed policy" to conduct "a complete evidentiary examination for sexual assault survivors, even if no police report has been made" (Ledray & Kraft, 2001, p. 396). In their estimation, the advantages include the preservation of evidence and the additional decision time for victim-survivors who are uncertain about whether or not to report. The disadvantages identified were the costs incurred by victim-survivors and/or SANE programs, the possible loss of other evidence (such as clothing and bedding), and concerns over the victim-survivor's credibility. In a six-month period in 2000 and 2001, the Minneapolis (MN)-based SANE program, Sexual Assault Resource Services (SARS) reported that 78 out of 206 or 38% of women who sought a forensic exam arrived at the hospital uncertain about reporting (Ledray & Kraft, 2001). They also identified factors that may influence whether or not a victim-survivor would be uncertain about reporting including the relationship between victim-survivor and perpetrator, the presence of any weapons during the assault, and whether or not the victim-survivor had used alcohol prior to the assault (Ledray & Kraft, 2001, p. 399).

Thirdly, the protocol was developed to be in compliance with the 2005 Violence Against Women Act (VAWA) provision regarding the availability of forensic medical exams but in the absence of statewide guidance. This provision, which has become known as Forensic Medical Compliance states:

> Nothing in this section shall be construed to permit a State, Indian tribal government, or territorial government to require a victim of sexual assault to participate in the criminal justice system or cooperate with law enforcement in order to be provided with a medical forensic exam, reimbursement for charges incurred on account of such an exam or both (42 USC.A § 3796gg-4(d)(1), 2005).

While the "letter of the law" did not dictate that communities needed to create an anonymous reporting protocol, anonymous reporting was seen as a means to meet the "spirit of the law." In 2013, Training and Technical Providers for End Violence Against Women International (EVAWI) argued that the provision was a broad attempt to improve the response to sexual assault. While there may be accompanying benefits for the criminal justice system, the primary goal is to improve the victim's experience. They write:

> ... victims benefit when they have prompt and unobstructed access to a medical forensic exam—which provides both medical care and social services at the moment when they are most needed and when they are most likely to facilitate physical and psychological healing. By eliminating barriers such as payment considerations and the immediate pressure to decide whether or not to talk with law enforcement, victims are more likely to feel they have real and meaningful access.
> (Lonsway et al., 2013, p. 12)

While VAWA provides the impetus to develop an anonymous reporting protocol, it did not offer a framework or template. In 2011, the Minnesota Coalition Against Sexual Assault (MNCASA) published the "Minnesota Model Policies for Forensic Compliance: How to Ensure Victims of Sexual Assault in Your Community Receive the Care that Federal and State Law Require," which details the gaps in Minnesota statute (referred to as "restricted SAKs"):

1 There is no Minnesota or federal law that dictates where restricted evidentiary SAKs or other evidence collected in a restricted case must be stored.
2 There is no federal or Minnesota law that dictates how long restricted SAKs or additional evidence collected in restricted cases must be kept.

There are no provisions in either VAWA 2005 or Minnesota law requiring the submission or DNA or toxicology analysis of restricted SAKs (Gonsalves, 2011, p. 55, p. 66, p. 81, respectively).

Southern Saint Louis County (MN), like many other communities, relied on its existing criminal justice collaborative relationships to implement and maintain its own anonymous reporting option for victim-survivors and, in doing so, contributed to a patchwork of practices across the state.

The Statewide Inventory of Unsubmitted SAKs (2015)

In 2015, all MN law enforcement jurisdictions were also required to participate in a one-time statewide accounting of unsubmitted SAKs. For this audit, "untested rape kit" was defined as a SAK that has been used to collect evidence and (1) had not been submitted to the Bureau for DNA analysis but had been cleared for testing through *the written consent of the victim*; or (2) had been submitted to the Bureau for DNA analysis but the analysis has not been completed. The MN BCA provided each law enforcement jurisdiction with a spreadsheet to enter the following information on each untested SAK: ICR number, date of the incident, date of collection, and the reason why the kit was not submitted. The reasons were chosen from a drop-down list of seven possibilities. One of the drop-down options for why the kit was not submitted was "Anonymous/Blind Report." Because of this, DPD included its anonymous SAKs on the spreadsheet even though these SAKs had not been cleared for testing through the victims' written consent.

The Minnesota audit found 3,482 untested SAKs stored by law enforcement across the state (Feshir, 2015; News Tribune Staff, 2015). Minnesota BCA spokesperson Oliveira offered the following preliminary reasons why SAKs were not submitted for testing, "The kit adds no value to a case, the case was closed, a suspect confessed, a criminal complaint was never filed, prosecutors declined the case, investigation revealed the sex was consensual and the victim either refused to participate or filed a false report" (Bjorhus & Webster, 2015). Once the numbers were released, advocates questioned whether the inventory of untested SAKs was larger than expected because of the inclusion of anonymous SAKs and/or other SAKs that may not be cleared for testing with victims' consent (Bjorhus & Webster, 2015). DPD topped the list with 578 untested SAKs, which constituted about 17% of the total in MN (*n* = 3,482). In line with the concerns of advocates, nearly 30% of DPD's inventoried SAKs were categorized as Anonymous/Blind Report. Moreover, DPD's 130 anonymous SAKs accounted for 75% of the anonymous SAKs reported

Table 13.1 Duluth Police Department Responses to the "Reason for Not Submitting for Testing" from MN Statewide Accounting of Untested Rape Kits—2015

Victim elected not to participate further in the criminal justice process	213
Other	189
Anonymous/blind report (no victim info)	130
Prosecution declined	19
Kit not relevant for prosecution (kit results not needed—CONSENT)	14
Current investigation	9
Kit not relevant for prosecution (kit results not needed—CONFESSION)	4
TOTAL	**578**

Sources: Minnesota Department of Public Safety Bureau of Criminal Apprehension [MN BCA], 2015; Bjorhus, 2015; Sinner & Webster, 2015.

statewide (*n* = 175). In other words, anonymous SAKs comprised a sizable portion of all the untested SAKs and the majority of anonymous SAKs in MN were inventoried at DPD (Table 13.1).

DPD attributed the "wide swings in the numbers" among the different law enforcement agencies to confusion as to which SAKs should be counted as unsubmitted and whether anonymous should be included. Some saw the large numbers of untested anonymous SAKs at DPD as an indicator of "progressive" and "victim-centered" practices that allow victims more voice and choice (Prather & Zamora, 2015).

A year after the inventory, "victim choice" and "victim consent" became key criteria shaping the discussion of unsubmitted SAKs in the media. Advocates voiced that their primary concern was ensuring that victim-survivors requesting forensic exams were not turned away at their local hospitals or experiencing lengthy wait times, particularly in rural areas, and not necessarily whether or not SAKs were tested, particularly those without victims' consent (Bjorhus, 2016). For more information on important medical care provided to victim-survivors during a forensic exam, see Chapter 12. Advocates also advised that there could be more SAKs at hospitals and clinics that were not counted in the "official" inventory numbers since the official inventory only covered SAKs found within law enforcement sites (Bjorhus, 2016).

Issue of Storing the SAKs

In an article detailing the storage of untested SAKs in hospital's emergency departments, SANE Ellen Johnson of Regents Hospital in Saint Paul is quoted as saying that she was willing to keep SAKs not released to law enforcement by victim-survivors for up to three years if she has the fridge space, even though the official policy is ninety days. Describing this reporting option Johnson says, "They didn't have a lot of choice about what happened, so they have a lot of choices now" (Vezner, 2017). Johnson also notes that she attempts to notify victim-survivors before disposing of the SAKs (which are referred to as "orphans" in the article and would be "non-reports" in our region) but is hampered by the inability to leave a message because it may not be safe or secure. MNCASA Medical Forensic Policy Program Coordinator Jude Foster further explained the confusion around SAKs stored at hospitals. Using the term "restricted" for these SAKs, she stated that it was a matter of perspective. "Hospitals see restricted kits as being evidence that doesn't belong in their facilities.

Law enforcement, on the other hand, doesn't consider them evidence because they haven't received a report. This discrepancy creates a rift in some communities" (Feshir, 2020).

Next, there's the issue of charges being brought from a stored, restricted SAK. For example, a 2018 Ramsey County case involved a victim-survivor who decided to report to police seven months after the SAK was collected and stored at Hennepin County Medical Center (HCMC). The investigator on the case learned that the SAK was about to be destroyed and asked the facility to hold it for her, offering a short-term solution of purchasing HCMC a refrigerator so they could keep it in storage (Feshir, 2020). The media coverage of the SAKs captures the confusion among practitioners about the nature of anonymous SAKs, terminology, storage, retention, and the need for statewide standardization rather than a patchwork of regional practices.

The attention placed on SAKs as a result of the audit led to a series of statewide reforms. In 2018, the MN legislature set a 60-day time frame for unrestricted SAKs to be submitted to the crime lab. Unrestricted and restricted were codified as the two main descriptors for SAKs—unrestricted being those with victims' consent for testing and restricted being those without consent. In Southern Saint Louis County and throughout the state, restricted replaced anonymous as the designated term for SAKs collected without an accompanying police report. In 2021, the MN BCA mandated centralized storage of restricted SAKs at their facility for a period of 30 months and instituted a uniform consent form that delineates the difference between an unrestricted and a restricted SAK (Table 13.2).

MN has now become home to three SAKI sites with the addition of the MN Department of Public Safety in 2018 and the City of Minneapolis Police Department in 2020. The state legislature has also passed a "test-all" policy for standard (or unrestricted) SAKs, procured a statewide tracking system with a web-based portal for victim-survivors and overhauled the criminal sexual conduct (CSC) statutes including the elimination of the statute of limitations for 1st through 4th degree CSC. These statewide changes have increased standardization of the sexual assault response and provided increased equity of access to victim-survivors.

Table 13.2 Timeline of Minnesota Statewide Sexual Assault Reform

2015	One-time statewide accounting of untested sexual assault kits (SAKs) held by law enforcement
2015	City of Duluth Police Department (DPD) awarded Sexual Assault Kit Initiative (SAKI) funds
2018	MN Office of Public Safety awarded SAKI funds
2019	Statewide timelines for handling unrestricted SAKs from hospital to law enforcement to the MN Bureau of Criminal Apprehension (MN BCA) laboratory
2020	City of Minneapolis Police Department (MPD) awarded SAKI funds
2021	Mandatory testing of all unrestricted SAKs
2021	Statewide restricted SAK storage by MN BCA
2021	Overhaul of Criminal Sexual Conduct (CSC) statutes including the elimination of the statute of limitations for 1st to 4th degree CSC
2022	Launch of statewide kit tracking web-based database accessible to victim-survivors

Sources: Bjorhus (2018), Cox (2022), Montemayor (2021)

Assessment of the Anonymous Reporting Protocol (2016–Present)

DPD's inclusion of anonymous SAKs in its inventory and the promotion of its victim-centered, progressive Anonymous Reporting Protocol suggest that, in order to achieve comprehensive sexual assault reform, its efforts must be evaluated, with the guiding principle that anonymous SAKs deserve the same level of attention given to previously unsubmitted standard SAKs. With those SAKs, the working group asked: what factors left them untested? And with anonymous SAKs, the complementary question is: why have so few anonymous SAKs been converted to criminal investigations?

In line with the research on outcomes from anonymous SAKs (Gonsalves, 2011), we have identified the need to track the conversion rate of anonymous SAKs and their related investigative and prosecution outcomes. Gonsalves (2011) cites several preliminary studies with conversion rates: Department of Defense in 2005 (25%) then in 2008 (14%); one county in Florida between 2007 and 2009 saw a 25% conversion rate; and a Twin Cities, Minnesota program saw a 25% conversion rate in 2010. These rates are in line with Ledray and Kraft (2001). On average between 2008 and 2015, the PAVSA SANE program conducted 100 sexual assault exams per year with 20 patients choosing the anonymous option. Generally speaking, 20% of SAKs collected have been anonymous. Few reports are converted to investigations and even fewer have been prosecuted ($n = 3$). While these figures are averages, they place our local conversion rates much lower than those of other jurisdictions.

The high number of anonymous SAKs inventoried between 2009 and 2015 ($n = 130$) indicates that victim-survivors find this option appealing, but the low conversion rate raises a number of concerns about victim-survivors' informed consent, their understanding of the conversion procession, and the effectiveness of advocacy follow-up. To address these concerns, we took a back-to-basics approach toward enhancing the Anonymous Reporting Protocol in four ways: (1) explicitly informing victim-survivors that anonymous SAKs would not be tested, (2) providing them with information sheets that indicate which option they chose and how to get additional information, (3) instituting a more robust schedule of outreach to these victim-survivors, and (4) creating a standing agenda item on anonymous reporting at monthly SMART meetings. These monthly discussions of the Anonymous Reporting Protocol help the team to stay familiar with the process and have the potential to address any issues or concerns in a timely manner.

The lack of conversions from anonymous to standard reports may indicate that victim-survivors did not fully understand their chosen reporting option at the time of the exam and the next steps once they left the hospital. SANEs and advocates have the responsibility to provide victim-survivors with clear information about the criminal justice system during their forensic medical exams. They provide the reporting options available while also seeing to their medical needs and providing emotional support. Our first change to the anonymous reporting process: SANEs explicitly asked patients if they want their SAK to be tested. Generally speaking, SANEs ask victim-survivors if they had thought about whether or not to make a report to law enforcement. SANEs would review two documents (specific to our regional protocol) with the victim-survivors: (1) an Authorization for Use and Disclosure of Specific Health Information which included a Release to Law Enforcement Based on Reporting Options and (2) Anonymous/Third-Party Reporting Option Information

Sheet. Victim-survivors would select their reporting option on the Authorization form and sign it, and they would be provided copies of both documents if they chose the anonymous reporting option.

In reviewing these forms, neither mention SAK testing for either the standard or anonymous SAKs. Neither SANEs nor advocates had been trained to proactively inform patients that if they chose the anonymous option, their SAK would not be tested. Under the new guidance beginning in 2016, SANEs now notify victim-survivors who chose anonymity that their SAKs will not be tested unless and until they follow up and "convert" them. This additional information allows victim-survivors to weigh their options in light of what will happen to their SAKs.

Emerging trauma-informed practices, however, advise that victim-survivors of sexual assault may not retain all of the information shared with them when they are in the emergency room undergoing a sexual assault forensic exam (Campbell, 2016; Campbell et al., 2015). So, upon discharge, patients are now provided with an information sheet specific to either standard report or the anonymous reporting option. These information sheets are written in accessible language and refer victim-survivors back to PAVSA's 24/7 Helpline for confidential support, safety planning, accompaniment to interviews and/or hearings, and other advocacy services. PAVSA is also working to develop and maintain more robust follow-up to victim-survivors with anonymous SAKs including outreach at six months and a year after their exam.

Future Efforts

Our working group also plans to approach the 130 inventoried anonymous SAKs with a modified version of the process used to address the nearly 450 unrestricted SAKs. The first step is the creation of an inventory of anonymous SAKs including the elements comparable to the BJA-certified inventory of standard SAKs including ICR, date of collection, victim-survivor's name, victim-survivor's age, identified perpetrator (if available), and relationship between victim-survivor and perpetrator (if available). Victim-identifying information will be held confidential by the Site Coordinator, SANE Coordinator, and Victim Advocate.

Once the inventory is complete, the second phase is Victim Notification. With standard SAKs, our site notified victim-survivors once their SAKs were tested to completion. DPD submits SAKs only to the MN BCA and does not contract with private laboratories for SAK testing. As previously mentioned, the MN BCA does not test SAKs without an accompanying police report or the victim's signed consent.

Subject matter experts at the Department of Justice Office's OVW and EVAWI agree that SAKs without consent for testing should not be tested (Lonsway & Archambault, 2011; OVW, 2017; Price, 2010). On the issue of testing, a 2017 OVW white paper uses the term "non-investigative" SAKs to describe SAKs from those who have chosen not to report a sexual assault to law enforcement and have not otherwise consented to test the kit (OVW, 2017).

Testing without victim consent may have the following unintended consequences:

1 undermining victims' rights;
2 eroding community trust in law enforcement; and
3 drawing down already-limited resources.

In a training bulletin published in 2013 and revised in 2021, Lonsway and Archambault posed the question—*Should we test anonymous kits?* They defined anonymous SAKs as referring to the evidence collected and documented during a forensic medical exam that was obtained from a victim who has not yet personally reported the sexual assault to law enforcement. However, they also point out that the victim is actually not anonymous to the nurse or to other medical professionals suggesting that the term "anonymous" is a misnomer. They acknowledge a shift in their own thinking on terminology when their bulletin was revised in 2021:

> In our early writing on the topic, we advocated for agencies to implement a protocol for anonymous reporting. However, as innovation and reform have continued, it has become clear to us that the emphasis on anonymity has masked the more important questions of *what will happen to a report once it is made* (emphasis theirs). We have therefore shifted toward a more general language of "alternative reporting options," which may include anonymity for victims, non-investigative responses from law enforcement, and/or other components designed to increase victims' access and participation. (p. 6)

Lonsway and Archambault (2020) agree with OVW's position that evidence associated with these "non-investigative reports" should not be tested. They provide three reasons—lack of documented victim consent, lack of documentation of a crime, and inability to exclude consensual partners. Thus, the terminology associated with these SAKs, as well as the processes post obtaining these SAKs, continues to evolve.

Submittal for testing, therefore, will only occur if victim-survivor consent is acquired. The Victim Advocate will adapt the existing Victim Notification Protocols with attention to the particular sensitivity of re-engaging those victim-survivors who had opted for anonymity (see Chapter 20 on VN policies). The Victim Advocate is an employee of PAVSA, the community-based sexual assault crisis center, rather than a system-based advocate and has confidentiality to discuss the victim's options without being required to share information with law enforcement. The Victim Advocate will conduct the notification to re-engage with victim-survivors to see if they would like to convert their SAKs to allow for testing. They will also offer other advocacy services such as counseling and support groups. Some victim-survivors may use this outreach as an opportunity to engage in supportive services and may once again decline contact with law enforcement. If victim-survivors opt for conversion, then they can sign a release of information to allow their identifying information to be shared with the designated DPD investigators and meet to give their statement. The resulting data from these efforts—number of victim-survivors located, number notified, and number who chose conversion and re-engagement with law enforcement—will complement the performance measures for previously unsubmitted standard SAKs. We will also track the number of converted SAKs submitted for testing and any CODIS uploads and hits resulting from testing, as well as any investigative and prosecutorial outcomes.

As previously mentioned, data related to the Anonymous Reporting Protocol has been incomplete and reliant on averages. Our goal is to build a complete set of data on Anonymous Reporting from 2008 to the present. This set will include the total number of Anonymous SAKs completed by the SANE program, number of Anonymous SAKs for each of the seven participating jurisdictions, number of conversions to standard reports, length of time between exam and conversion, number of CODIS uploads and hits, and related investigative and prosecution outcomes. For 2021, we report a total of 151 SANE exams conducted with 24 victim-survivors opting for anonymous reporting, with anonymous reporting accounting for about 16% of the total exams. Of these 24, six victim-survivors later converted their SAKs to standard reports, placing the conversion rate at 25%. Tracking these metrics will help to determine if there are any discernible trends following our assessment of the protocol. For example, are victim-survivors less likely to choose anonymous reporting if they are informed explicitly that those SAKs are not tested? And are victim-survivors more likely to convert their anonymous kits with the additional information and follow-up provided?

The Southern Saint Louis County Anonymous Reporting Protocol was developed to meet local needs and to comply with federal law in the absence of statewide guidance. Now, there are a number of statewide sexual assault mandates in MN, and our local practices are changing to reflect this progress. First, we are transitioning our language from the categories of standard, anonymous, and non-report to unrestricted and restricted reports, respectively. SANEs and medical professionals are incorporating the use of the statewide uniform consent form for SAK testing rather than locally developed documents. Finally, restricted (formerly known as anonymous) SAKs are being shipped from hospitals directly to the MN BCA. We eagerly await the launch of the statewide SAK tracking system which will allow victim-survivors to securely access information about the location and status of their SAK.

Conclusion

Addressing anonymous SAKs fits well into the goals of comprehensive reform projects like the SAKI. With the appropriate partners collaborating and great care paid to the maintenance of necessary confidentiality, a parallel process of inventorying, notification, and cold case investigation and prosecution of these SAKs can be developed. Victim-survivors rely on alternative reporting options to navigate uncertainty around participating in the criminal justice system, and reform efforts should evaluate and enhance these options. The same guiding principles can be applied to approach alternative reporting methods in a process that is multidisciplinary, victim-centered, trauma-informed, and holistic in nature. Reforms' effects should also put federal, state, and local initiatives in conversation with one another. SAKI has provided the opportunity for the City of DPD to have the necessary financial resources as well as access to nationally renowned subject matter experts to implement emerging best practices and, in turn, become a resource and a partner for other jurisdictions, large and small, who are committed to sexual assault reform.

Key Points

- There are a variety of terms used nationally to describe alternative reporting options, including, but not limited to, Anonymous, Blind, Jane Doe, Non-Investigative, and Restricted. Effective terminology centers the victim-survivor and informs them about the status of their SAK.
- Anonymous Reporting Options are not merely about VAWA Medical Forensic Compliance. They are an integral part of sexual assault response and meet a need for victim-survivors in our community. Close to 40% of victim-survivors arrive at the hospital undecided about reporting to law enforcement.

- Victim-survivors make a number of important decisions during a forensic medical exam. It is important to explicitly discuss SAK testing so that they can make an informed decision about whether or not to make a report to law enforcement.
- Due to the effects of trauma on memory, SANEs and advocates should provide victim-survivors with information sheets about their chosen reporting option upon discharge and offer robust follow-up contacts to answer questions and explain the next steps.
- As with other "cold cases" of sexual assault, a case review of Anonymous Reporting SANE reports may provide qualitative and quantitative data that would inform comprehensive sexual assault reform.

Discussion Questions

1 What strategies can SANEs and advocates put in place to provide clarity around criminal justice procedures that can follow a forensic exam?
2 What promising practices can be developed to provide robust post-exam follow-up? How might technology and alternative means of communication assist victim-survivors in engaging with law enforcement and advocacy on their terms at their preferred intervals?
3 What messaging should be included in any public service announcements to increase both the community and victim-survivors' understanding of the available reporting options and how to re-engage with advocacy or law enforcement when they are ready?
4 What qualitative and/or quantitative data should be collected from anonymous/restricted reporting case files to better understand why victim-survivors chose that option?
5 What metrics beyond conversion rates and successful prosecution would indicate that an anonymous or restricted reporting option is meeting victim-survivors' needs?

Funding Acknowledgment and Author Note

This project was supported by Grant No. 2018-AX-BK-0002 awarded by the Bureau of Justice Assistance. The Bureau of Justice Assistance is a component of the Department of Justice's Office of Justice Programs, which also includes the Bureau of Justice Statistics, the National Institute of Justice, the Office of Juvenile Justice and Delinquency Prevention, the Office for Victims of Crime, and the SMART Office. Points of view or opinions in this chapter are those of the author and do not necessarily represent the official position or policies of the U.S. Department of Justice.

Further Reading

Heffron, L. C., Busch-Armendariz, N. B., Vohra, S. S., Johnson, R. J., & Camp, V. (2014). Sexual assault survivors time to decide: An exploration of the use and effects of the nonreport option. *The American Journal of Nursing*, 114(3), 26–36. http://www.jstor.org/stable/24466461

Henniger, A. L., Iwasaki, M., Carlucci, M. E., & Lating, J. M. (2019). Reporting sexual assault: Survivors' satisfaction with sexual assault response personnel. *Violence Against Women*, 1–21. https://doi.org/10.1177/1077801219857831

Stahl, B., Bjorhus, J., Webster, M., & Covington, H. (2018, January 25). Justice denied: When rape is reported and nothing happens. How Minnesota's criminal justice system has failed victims of sexual assault. *Star Tribune*. https://www.startribune.com/denied-justice-series-when-rape-is-reported-and-nothing-happens-minnesota-police-sexual-assault-investigations/487400761/

Sully, C., Wood, L., Cook Heffron, L, Westbrook, L., Levy, N., Donde, S. D., & Busch-Armendariz, N. (2018). "At least they're workin' on my case?" Victim notification in sexual assault "cold" cases. *Journal of Interpersonal Violence*, 36(9–10), 1–21. https://doi.org/10.1177/0886260518789905

References

Bjorhus, J. (2015, November 12). State officials detail backlog of rape kits. *Star Tribune*. https://www.startribune.com/police-agencies-in-minnesota-disclose-tally-of-untested-rape-kits/346861582/

Bjorhus, J. (2016, August 28). Citing victims' wishes, costs, agencies aren't rushing to test old rape kits. *Star Tribune*. https://www.startribune.com/old-rape-kits-no-statewide-rush-to-test/391208701/?refresh=true

Bjorhus, J. (2018, February 27). Minnesota drafts new rape kit protocols with timetables to test. *Star Tribune*. https://www.startribune.com/minnesota-drafts-new-rape-kit-protocols/475339213/

Bjorhus, J., & Webster, M. (2015, September 2). Thousands of unprocessed rape kits sit on shelves in Minnesota. *Star Tribune*. https://www.startribune.com/thousands-of-unprocessed-rape-kits-sit-on-shelves-in-minnesota/324018681/

Campbell, R. (2016, September 26). *The Neurobiology of Trauma: What You Need to Know about the Brain and Trauma* [Webinar]. Sexual Assault Kit Initiative. https://www.sakitta.org/toolkit/index.cfm?fuseaction=tool&tool=48

Campbell, R., Feeney, H., Fehler-Cabral, G., Shaw, J., & Horsford, S. (2015). The national problem of untested sexual assault kits (SAKs): Scope, causes, and future directions for research, policy, and practice. *Trauma, Violence, & Abuse*, 18(4), 1–14. https://doi.org/10.1177/1524838015622436

Cox, P. (2022, July 13). New Minnesota Rape Kit Tracking System Promises More Accountability. *Minnesota Public Radio*. https://www.mprnews.org/story/2022/07/13/new-minnesota-rape-kit-tracking-system-promises-more-accountability

Feshir, R. (2015, November 13). BCA finds nearly 3,500 rape kits across MN. *Minnesota Public Radio*. https://www.mprnews.org/story/2015/11/12/minnesota-untested-rape-kits

Feshir, R. (2020, April 13). Bill would set standard for preserving rape kits in Minnesota. *Minnesota Public Radio*. https://www.mprnews.org/story/2020/04/13/bill-would-set-standard-for-preserving-rape-kits-in-mn

Gonsalves, S. G. (2011). Minnesota model policies for forensic compliance. Published by the Sexual Violence Justice Institute (SVJI), Minnesota Coalition Against Sexual Assault.

Ledray, L., & Kraft, J. (2001). Evidentiary examination without a police report: Should it be done? Are delayed reporters and nonreports unique? *Journal of Emergency Nursing*, 27(4), 396–400. https://doi.org/10.1067/men.2001.117421

Lonsway, K. A., & Archambault, J. (2011). Reply to article "Receiving a forensic medical exam without participating in the criminal justice process: What will it mean?," *Journal of Forensic Nursing*, 7, 78–87. https://doi.org/10.1111/j.1939-3938.2011.01102.x

Lonsway, K. A., & Archambault, J. (2020). *Should we "test anonymous kits?"* End Violence against Women International. https://evawintl.org/wp-content/uploads/2013-10_TB-Should-We-Test-Anonymous-Kits.pdf

Lonsway, K. A., Huhtanen, H., & Archambault, J. (2013, Revised 2021). *The earthquake in sexual assault response: Implementing VAWA Forensic Compliance*. End Violence against Women International. https://evawintl.org/wp-content/uploads/Module-14_Forensic-Compliance.pdf

Ledray, L., & Kraft, J. (2001). Evidentiary examination without a police report: Should it be done? Are delayed reporters and nonreports unique? *Journal of Emergency Nursing, 27*(4), 396–400. https://doi.org/10.1067/men.2001.117421.

Minnesota Department of Public Safety Bureau of Criminal Apprehension. (2015). Statewide Accounting of Untested Rape Kits. https://dps.mn.gov/divisions/ojp/forms-documents/Documents/2015%20Inventory%20Appendices.pdf

Montemayor, S. (2021, June 30). Lawmakers close gaps in Minnesota's sex assault laws with public safety bill. *Star Tribune*. https://www.startribune.com/lawmakers-close-gaps-in-minnesota-s-sex-assault-laws-with-public-safety-bill/600073316/

News Tribune Staff. (2015, November 12). Police agencies in Minnesota disclose tally of untested rape kits. *Duluth News Tribune*.https://www.duluthnewstribune.com/news/3881721-police-agencies-minnesota-disclose-tally-untested-rape-kits

Office on Violence Against Women, United States Department of Justice. (2017, January). *Sexual Assault Kit Testing Initiatives and non-investigative kits*. White Paper. https://www.justice.gov/ovw/page/file/928236/download

Prather S., & Zamora, K. (2015, December 8). Agencies say they are following the law with untested rape kits. *Star Tribune*. https://www.startribune.com/agencies-say-they-re-following-the-law-with-untested-rape-kits/360876411/

Price, B. (2010). Receiving a forensic medical exam without participating in the criminal justice process: What will it mean? *Journal of Forensic Nursing, 6*, 74–87. https://doi.org/10.1111/j.1939-3938.2009.01063.x

Sinner, C., & Webster, M. (2015, November 12). Look up how many untested rape kits your city has. *Star Tribune*. https://www.startribune.com/look-up-how-many-untested-rape-kits-your-city-has/346924692/?refresh=true

Vezner, T. (2017, February 17). This nurse's refrigerator is full of untested rape kits. Here's why. *Twin Cities Pioneer Press*. https://www.twincities.com/2017/02/17/rape-kits-accumulate-untested-amid-struggle-over-how-to-handle-backlog/

14 Current issues in providing sexual assault medical forensic exams in rural areas

Bridget Diamond-Welch, Mattie Jones, and Brianna Zimmer

Author Note

The opinions or points of view expressed in this chapter are solely those of the authors and do not reflect the official positions of any participating organization or the US Department of Justice.

Providing Sexual Assault Medical Forensic Exams in Rural Areas

The National Sexual Assault Kit Initiative (SAKI) is dedicated to reforming the criminal justice response to sexual assault and facilitating equity, justice, and healing for survivors. Central to this mission is the discovery of thousands of untested sexual assault kits (SAKs) located in numerous jurisdictions across the United States. Given the centrality of the SAK to recent efforts, general questions are raised including *How are SAKs completed initially? What factors make a quality SAK? Can all SAKs provide the type of data relied upon for analyzing patterns of perpetration and use in criminal justice proceedings? And, of primary importance, how are sexual assault survivors treated when they have their SAMFE done and SAK collected?*

This chapter, in conjunction with Chapter 12 in this book, provides an overview of the exams that lead to the completion of a SAK and how the quality and accessibility of these examinations can impact survivors. The particular focus of this chapter rests on the evidence that there is differential access to quality exams across the United States. The implications of geography-based differences in access to high quality SAK collection are described. The authors will then discuss four different strategies for dealing with rural SANE/SAFE shortages, which include (1) a focus on training over certification, (2) mobile units, (3) traveling nurses, and (4) telehealth.

The lead author of this chapter, Bridget Diamond-Welch, PhD, is an Associate Professor of research and the Director for research and evaluation of the School of Health Sciences at the University of South Dakota (SD). She is the named researcher with SD's 2019 SAKI grant from the Bureau of Justice Assistance and an evaluator on a current telehealth sexual assault medical forensic exam (SAMFE) grant. The chapter's co-authors are both undergraduate researchers on the SD SAKI grant. This chapter concludes with a discussion of what research is needed to evaluate the effectiveness of each of these four methods.

DOI: 10.4324/9781003186816-17

The Sexual Assault Medical Forensic Exam and the Health-Care Professionals That Provide Them

A SAMFE straddles both the health care and the criminal justice systems as an examination that treats injuries (and other health concerns) and gathers evidence of a crime. The exam is completed by a health-care professional. According to the Department of Justice (2013), a SAMFE includes:

> Gathering information from the patient for the medical forensic history; an examination; coordinating treatment of injuries, documentation of biological and physical findings, and collection of evidence from the patient; documentation of findings; information, treatment, and referrals for STIs, pregnancy, suicidal ideation, alcohol and substance abuse, and other nonacute medical concerns; and follow-up as needed to provide additional healing, treatment, or collection of evidence.

Given the technical skills required for accurate evidence collection and the unique nature of sexual assault, best practices outlined by the National Institute of Justice (2017) include specialized training for the health-care professionals who provide these exams. Nurses who receive this training are frequently referred to as sexual assault nurse examiners (SANEs) or sexual assault forensic examiners (SAFEs). It is important to point out that there are two kinds of SANE training—SANE-A (adult certified) and SANE-P (pediatric certified). Given that the needs of adults and children are different and that the limited research on SANEs has largely focused on SANE-A, this review will focus solely on adult SAMFEs or SANE-As.

Individuals who come to the emergency room for post-sexual assault care may be requesting a SAMFE for immediate reporting, may be requesting it for potential reporting at a later time or may be coming primarily to receive medical attention. It is essential for the well-being of these individuals that they are treated in a trauma-informed and patient-centered manner, regardless of their reason for coming to the emergency room. The short-term and long-term impacts of sexual assault victimization are well-documented across victimization groups (Campbell et al., 2009; Elliott et al., 2004; Peterson et al., 2011, see also Chapter 8). There are consequences to physical and sexual health (e.g., risk of sexually transmitted infections, eating disorders, somatic problems), adverse psychological effects (e.g., fear, anxiety, post-traumatic stress disorder), and social affects (e.g., isolation, loss of trust, fear of intimacy). The consequences experienced can vary due to personal characteristics of the victim (e.g., gender or age), the assailant (e.g., relationship to victim), the assault itself (e.g., type of coercion or forced used), and the response of others (e.g., level of victim blame or social support; Ullman, 2010, see also Chapters 3 and 8).

When a health professional who interacts with a survivor of sexual assault is inexperienced, espouses rape myths, or is disrespectful to the patient, the result can be secondary victimization of these survivors (Ranjbar & Speer, 2013). Secondary victimization is a re-traumatization experienced by the survivor of assault based on their treatment by responders such as health-care providers. This has been documented to occur when the survivor receives inadequate care, experiences long wait times (with Littel, 2001 providing an upward bound of waiting for ten hours without being allowed to use the bathroom), being refused HIV prophylaxis when indicated or emergency contraception (such as Plan B) because of the beliefs of providers or the hospital system (Campbell & Raja, 1999). Littel (2001) argues that addressing the trauma caused by ill-prepared health professionals was an impetus for the development of SANE programs through which health-care professionals are trained on how to properly conduct exams in a non-victim blaming manner.

Research into the effect of SANE programs has found that the use of a trauma-informed approach by these clinicians has a positive impact on the psychological well-being of sexual assault patients (see Campbell et al., 2005 for a review). Important elements to a trauma-informed and patient-centered SAMFE include making the patient feel cared for, providing them with support, compassion, and information, while listening and believing them (Campbell et al., 2008). Patients should also feel that they have choice and control about what happens during a SAMFE (Department of Justice, 2013). Implementing trauma-informed and patient-centered care not only improves psychological outcomes, but also improves judicial process outcomes (e.g., Campbell, 2008; Campbell et al., 2012; Sievers et al., 2003).

While more research is needed on the impact of SANEs on the long-term well-being of patients, it is clear that they can, at the least, ensure that patients are not retraumatized and, at the most, have a positive long-term effect on recovery. *The problem becomes that sexual assault survivors do not have equal access to this care.* Whether a particular emergency room has SANEs on staff, on call, or available through different arrangements varies widely across the United States. In the next section, we will discuss how rurality impacts the availability of SANE services, with a focus on examples from SD. The data reported come from over three years of qualitative interviews with SANEs, county and hospital administration, judicial system actors and others, and meeting observations (e.g., at SANE trainings and legislative discussions) undertaken by the first author of this chapter, who lives in SD and is the researcher associated with the state's SAKI grant from the Bureau of Justice Administration.

The Challenge of Geography

Rural areas may lack in people, but those people experience interpersonal violence (IPV) at similar rates as those in urban areas—and frequently this violence is more chronic and severe (Edwards, 2015). Further, given lack of access to resources, rural victims may have worse psychological, social, and health outcomes (Peek-Asa et al., 2011). With services being so remote, and the extensive demand for existing services, rural victims may not be able to access services at all (Dawson, 2017).

Individuals in rural areas also face different barriers to services compared to their urban counterparts. For example, the low population may result in the health-care provider knowing both the patient and the perpetrator. These complex pre-existing dual relationships can often result in people feeling like they cannot receive confidential services and potentially fearing they may not be believed over their abuser. Limited access to public transport is another issue (Thomas et al., 2020 for review). These issues can be further exacerbated on tribal lands as a design of colonized processes (Deer, 2015). As Box 14.1 indicates, SD provides an excellent example of a rural area with high rates of sexual violence.

Overall, research is limited on access to SANE services in rural areas. A report commissioned by the US Government Accountability Office (GAO) reviewed

---

Box 14.1
_____

South Dakota: A rural state example

With only 11.7 people per square mile (US Census, 2021), SD meets the federal designation of a "rural" state. According to Health Resources and Services Administration, 60 of the state's 66 counties are completely designated (59 counties) or partially designated (1 county) as a primary care health professional shortage area. This means that the federal government has designated these areas as suffering a shortage of primary care, mental health, and dentists. Given this overall lack, it is unsurprising that in 2021 there are only nine fully certified SANE nurses. This count includes both SANE-A and SANE-P. More than 50% of these nurses are employed in the two cities in the state—though some of them deliver services to rural areas through telemedicine (as discussed in this chapter).

At the same time, SD had the third highest rate of rape in the United States in 2019, with 72.6 per 100,000 in the state compared to 42.6 in the United States at large (McMahon et al., 2021). While this data relies on only rapes reported to law enforcement, recent unpublished data obtained by the first author indicates that these rates skyrocketed during COVID. This data includes reports from all community victim services organizations who obtain state funding and what types of victims they are seeing. In 2019, there were 590 individuals who received services for sexual assault. In 2020, that number increased by 369% to 2,768.

---

information on six states and found that, especially in rural areas, hospitals were unable to meet the demand for SAMFEs. As indicated above, rural hospitals reported that they often had to send survivors to other hospitals (often very long distances away) in order to receive exams. For those that did have a SANE on staff, the hospitals were frequently unable to provide 24-7 access—again resulting in travel or long wait times.

In SD, health-care practitioners and advocates frequently reported this very concern—patients having to wait hours (one report of over eight hours) for the hospital to even begin the SAMFE, which can result in survivors feeling retraumatized by a system that is seemingly ignoring them. Long waits can also complicate access to other resources that are not available 24-7 in rural areas. One SANE nurse provided an example of a particular patient who was left waiting in this hospital for hours before her kit was completed:

> They're left waiting in the emergency room in [omitted] County for hours to do the kit and then they're still given prescriptions to go fill somewhere else. The pharmacy's not open on Sundays, it's not open after hours. And that's how it is in a lot of rural communities. So, they don't have the ability to even get the, the Plan B or the, you know, medications that they need to prevent STDs in a timely fashion.

Transportation often is the responsibility of the patient. With the lack of public transportation, this can make it nearly impossible for survivors to get to SAMFE services.

The GAO argued that this lack of SANE supply occurs because of three challenges: (1) low levels of training opportunities, (2) weak support for SANE programs from important stakeholders (such as hospital administration), and (3) low retention rates for SANEs. While the next section will address limited training opportunities specifically, the GAO found that hospital administration reported low support because of the "low number of sexual assault cases treated each year" (Clowers, 2016, p. 8). This concern was repeated by stakeholders in SD, with one SANE reporting:

> Since critical access facilities have a low volume of these cases, it's difficult to remain competent. So, I would say there are pockets of critical access and rural hospitals that have not had any of this training and there are gaps.

There also seems to be issues, in some areas, with law enforcement support of SANEs. Speaking to one nurse about her experience during COVID, she indicated that she saw almost no sexual assault patients. Yet, we know, given the reported numbers (see Box 14.1), that sexual assaults were still occurring. She commented:

> We never closed the ER. We always would take sexual assault patients. But our numbers dropped to almost nothing. Come to find out, police were telling victims the ER was closed and they couldn't get a kit done. I don't know if they just didn't want the hassle or if they really just didn't know we were open.

Although not covered in the GAO report, findings in SD also indicate that there may be a lack of buy-in for important elements of a quality SAMFE. For example, in one county in SD, a county administrator reported that they would not pay for any SAMFE that included the "morning after pills on them" because "we don't think our voters would want us to." Of note, state law requires that the county where the assault occurs pays for the SAMFE and all associated medications. Meanwhile, a few 100 miles away in a Sovereign nation (discussed further below), the nurse practitioner reported that the "pharmacy just makes up a box of medications" (Plan B or Ella, HIV drugs, nausea medication), and the nurse just will "take that box back with us to the sexual assault room."

It is not surprising that, given these conditions, there is a high turnover for SANEs. Lack of administrative report results in SANE nurses frequently not being paid to be on-call, for working overtime, or (as found by the GAO) being paid "significantly less than other on-call medical professionals" (Clowers, 2016, p. 8). In SD, the treatment of patients frequently rests on the efforts of a few dedicated nurses. In one town, the nurses have negotiated for HIV medication at a reduced cost to supply to all patients who have an indicated need, but they will not be paid overtime to provide care. SANE programs vary greatly. A few are high functioning and fully staffed 24 hours a day, 7 days a week. Most others are struggling, understaffed, or non-existent—with the majority of care resting in the hands of one or two nurses.

SAMFE and Sovereign Nations

The problem of geography is not just one of urban/rural divide. There are 574 recognized Sovereign Nations across the United States. SD shares geography with nine. Each Nation has its own land, economy, laws, culture, and practices. Each has its own access to resources—including health-care systems. There are federally funded health services provided by Indian Health Services (IHS). IHS has facilities across 37 states and is located on and off tribal lands. While IHS health care is theoretically available to all Native peoples, IHS is underfunded, understaffed, access can be remote, and waits long (Sequist, 2021; Zuckerman et al., 2004).

To expand services, different tribes have supplemented care in various ways. The result is that it is impossible to summarize sexual assault services across Tribes. Some tribes have no real local access to SANEs, while others have dedicated sexual assault exam teams (even if they are not certified SANEs, they are SANE knowledgeable). To provide an overview, we will discuss one Nation and its access to SANEs—Pine Ridge.

Pine Ridge is home to the Oglala Lakota Sioux Tribe. The reservation lands cover over 3,400 square miles, making it one of the largest to share geography with the United States and the largest for SD. While the Pine Ridge IHS facility has (at least until recently) had a strong sexual assault examination team, this one facility can be hundreds of miles away when a survivor needs it. Further, Pine Ridge is deemed as a place with persistent poverty (40% in 2019). According to the USDA, about 27% of Oglala Lakota County (the primary county covering Pine Ridge) is food insecure. It is also marked as an area that is a food desert (lacks access to healthy food) and many people are without individual transport. There is a reservation bus, but its schedule is not always reliable. For example, we were informed it stopped running during COVID—further isolating people from services.

In communities with lack of access to basic resources and difficulty getting transport to services, there are inherent challenges in provisioning trauma-informed sexual assault care. The challenges faced by many survivors were summarized in one person's story provided by her SANE:

> And so she didn't have a ride to come in and it was way out in the districts about, you know, 45 miles away and she doesn't have running water. She hasn't had electricity. So she, you know, went from home to home, kinda trying to figure out what she should do. And finally came to the hospital at 10:30 at night last night, you know, 72 hours later because she had finally hitchhiked and made it into town.

This has many important implications—here we will name two. The first and most important is that this woman did not have the ability to receive any type of support after being traumatized. Her struggle to receive the basic health care that we conceive of as a human right is not setting her on the path toward healing. The second is that after three days, the evidence of her assault will have degraded. This could make it even more difficult for her to pursue a criminal justice outcome to her case—if she desired to do so. In our conversations, her case exemplified the struggles of many.

We do not want to paint the Oglala Lakota Sioux Tribe as victims of poverty. There is great resilience, community, art, and communal care that is inspiring. There is no better example of this than the work being done by a few dedicated nurses in the IHS facility. Not only does the single-payer style health care allow the nurses to just bring in a box of all the medicine needed during the exam (as discussed above), the nurses bring cultural healing practices to the SAMFE to provide complete patient care:

> You know, after they've had that exam done and they've cleaned up and they've smudged or sometimes we'll use essential oil. Well, you know, to help them calm down. And the interviewers are like, what did you do to her? She's so calm. She's so like put together and she can just tell us her story. And that's, that's a huge win for us because then ... the patients walk away with a better feeling that they have done everything in their power to work in the process and the process works better because they're more cooperative.

Yet, this case study provides one further example of some of the difficulties this chapter discusses. Recently, the head nurse that ran the program moved away from Pine Ridge. Currently, the sexual assault program is suffering, though some nurses are signed up for training to learn more even if they do not get certified.

We would argue that the goal of every state should be to provide the same high-quality level of trauma-informed and patient-centered care to survivors of sexual assault—no matter where they present for services—urban, rural, or Sovereign Nation. Yet, as the above discussion has made clear, the reality is: The geography of where you seek a sexual assault care will vastly impact the quality of care that you may receive and your chance for revictimization. States across the country are implementing attempted solutions to this problem. The rest of this chapter will address four: (1) focusing on training rather than certification, (2) employing mobile units, (3) hiring traveling nurses, and (4) utilizing telehealth.

Implementing Solutions

Training vs. Certification

The International Association of Forensic Nursing (IAFN) has created certification practices for SANEs. For SANE-A, certified nurses with two years on the floor must complete 40 hours of classroom training (e.g., medical forensic history-taking, specimen collection, photography, and courtroom testimony) and 40 hours of clinical labs that go over the in-person skills needed (e.g., how to swab different areas for DNA, toxicology, and how to document an injury). The cost of this training can be up to several 100 dollars, rivaling the cost of the exam itself. Beyond actual fiduciary costs, the amount of time and the travel required for rural nurses to attend a hands-on lab can be significant barriers to rural nurses receiving this training.

As reviewed by Thiede and Miyamoto (2021), different states have different laws regulating who can perform a SAMFE. Like their state of analysis, which was Pennsylvania, SD has no statewide requirements. In this situation, "facilities (i.e., hospitals or health-care systems) determine who will provide sexual assault care and make independent determinations of training and certification requirements, if any" (p. 82). Nursing schools across SD do not require training in this area, meaning many nurses have no knowledge of how to perform the SAMFE. According to interviews, many are hesitant to perform an exam due to that lack of knowledge and trepidation over having to testify. This trepidation and lack of training push survivors to go elsewhere for their care or potentially decide not to have an exam at all, highlighting the aforementioned negative psychological and health effects on survivors.

Given the lack of SANE-certified nurses in many rural areas, one response is to move away from stressing certification and instead focus on providing training in different skills areas. IAFN has recognized that when a SANE is not available, the next best thing is to train the medical personnel who will provide the exam with some basic knowledge. In reaction to this, they have developed a free webinar: "No SANE in Sight" (International Association of Forensic Nurses, n.d.). SD has followed this lead by offering free skills labs across the state to any nurse who would like to participate. These efforts are supported by grant funds.

The logic of this is sound. Provide training when certification is not possible. The obvious drawbacks are that the nurses who have training rather than certification will not be exposed to all of the information IAFN has determined as necessary for a quality SANE examiner. As it stands, we are unaware of any systematic evaluation of whether these efforts have improved outcomes for sexual assault survivors or not in states with this approach.

Nurses with SANE training may also seek IAFN certification after meeting rigorous education and clinical practicum hours and passing a written certification exam. IAFN certification is the only certification recognized by the American Nurses Credentialing Center—a subsidiary of the American Nurses Association—that administers certification exams for both registered and advanced practice nurses (see Chapter 12).

Mobile Units

Mobile health clinics are an alternative means of care for rural and underserved populations. Units consist of vehicles equipped with equipment and tools needed for clinicians to provide comprehensive care directly to patients. Due to the current lack of implementation of mobile care units for medical forensic exams, little research exists on what these types of mobile care units look like. Theoretically, mobile units would be staffed with SANEs and equipped with SAKs and all other equipment necessary to complete a full medical-forensic examination. Local SANEs would be able to travel to communities and events with high rates of sexual assaults. This practice would allow SANEs to travel directly to the victim, provide care, complete a SAK, and provide victims with local resources. These units would prevent victims from experiencing the undue burden of seeking comprehensive care after a sexual assault.

Mobile health clinics offer an innovative way to address problems with serving sexual assault victims in rural communities, but they do have limitations. One such limitation is the fragmentation of care. While patients can receive comprehensive care within the mobile care unit, existing units have recognized the complications with ensuring patients attend follow-ups with local institutions (Yu et al., 2017). This issue is exacerbated when units do not have established relationships with local hospitals and clinics. Another issue that arises is financial limitations. Obtaining and maintaining vehicles creates a financial burden, especially as the vehicles age. A study on mobile health care found that 58% of surveyed units identified financial limitations as their most significant burden (Post, 2007).

Because of the mobile nature of these units, they must be small and compact. The size of units can lead to concerns of confidentiality between patients within the unit (Yu et al., 2017). However, this concern can be negated through limiting the number of patients allowed within the unit at one time. Spatial constraints can also limit the capacity for medical equipment which may result in a lower quality of care (Yu et al., 2017). Finally, a major limitation to mobile care units is logistical. The mobile nature of units requires a reliance upon generator power (Yu et al., 2017). A loss of power can result in problems with maintaining refrigerated samples and may cause issues with internet access, in turn resulting in problems with record management (Yu et al., 2017).

While mobile units may experience limitations, they also provide communities with great benefits. Rural areas often lack a large number of SANEs which increases the importance of providing access to sexual assault examinations to rural and underserved populations. Mobile clinics can drive directly into communities that lack proper sexual assault care in order to mitigate common problems that may prevent sexual assault victims from seeking treatment. These problems may include lack of time and resources, transportation issues, difficulties in making appointments, long wait times for care, and administrative processes (Hill et al., 2016). The goal of mobile care units is to provide health care to rural and underserved populations. It is especially important to serve female and minority patients in these settings, as they have been demonstrated to be the most highly victimized and under supported (Bach et al., 2021). In a mobile health clinic study, out of 811 mobile health clinics, over half of the patients seeking care were women and ethnic minorities (Malone et al., 2020).

Another positive for mobile units is the reduction of cost of treatment. These mobile units can reduce charges incurred in traditional hospital settings. Increased access reduces the likelihood of long-term hospitalization (Hill et al., 2016). According to this research, mobile units provide a sense of trust between patients, providers, and the overall community. Qualitative research on mobile health units demonstrates that patients value the informal nature of the mobile units and these units instill more trust because of the effort made to drive to victims and into communities. They provide an intermediary connection between patients and the larger health institutions. By entering the community and allowing patients to come to them, units offer the benefit of providing patients a sense of control over their health-care decisions. As discussed above, this sense of control is especially important when dealing with victims of sexual assault. Evidence indicates that patients utilizing mobile units have increased self-confidence in their participation in the health-care system (Hill et al., 2016).

While much of the research on mobile care units focus on their overall effectiveness and their implementation, most articles only focus on units that provide basic health care such as screenings and preventative check-ups. The one article focusing on victims of sexual assault only addresses the possible utilization of mobile health units to address acute care needs post assault (Gilmore et al., 2019). Evidence presented indicates that both participants and providers found use of the unit to be a positive experience; they recognized that it fills a specific need. Future research should focus on the benefits and limitations of creating a mobile health unit that specifically provides sexual assault examinations and is staffed with SANEs.

Traveling Nurses

Travel nurses are hospital staff who can choose a temporary placement at hospitals that are experiencing staffing shortages. Recently, travel nursing has become a popular career choice for many medical professionals because it can offer an increase in pay, flexibility within their schedule, and the opportunity to travel. Travel nursing jobs often offer competitive financial opportunities in the form of free housing, increased pay rates, and other benefits (Spader, 2011). Additionally, the supply of travel nurses became a necessity for many hospitals during the COVID-19 pandemic (Gottlieb & Zenilman, 2020). As the profession of travel nursing grows within the medical field, it offers a possible solution toward expanding sexual assault care within rural areas. To address the lack of SANE nurses within rural areas, hospitals could employ travel nurses to fill employment gaps and provide more comprehensive care. This could reduce the distance sexual assault survivors have to travel to receive a SAK examination.

Hospitals are often facing staffing shortages in vital departments, so they fill their gaps using travel nurses. As reviewed by Poikus et al. (2020), managers and hospital officials often use travel nurses to reduce the effects of employment shortages that would otherwise negatively impact patient care. The Community Tracking Study found that 75% of the hospital respondents relied on supplemental nurses; this number reflects the projected 10% increase in the growth of the career (Aiken et al., 2007; Poikus et al., 2020).

There is mixed information about the effectiveness of traveling nurses. On the concerning side, one study found that an overall increase in temporary nurses led to a decrease in the safety and care of patients and an increased strain on traditional nursing staff (Aiken et al., 2007; Bae et al., 2010). However, another study by Clarke and Sloane (2007) found that the traveling nurses were not to blame for nurse strain and patient care. Rather, high numbers of travel nurses were indicative of an institution that already had these safety and care issues; these hospitals had decided to use traveling nurses as a potential solution to their pre-existing liabilities. They concluded that hospitals should focus on inadequate resources as their primary issue (Clarke & Sloane, 2007).

It may not be surprising that traveling nurses themselves can face challenges when they are put into a new location. These challenges may include being put in an environment in which they are unfamiliar with the culture, have to cope with moving, uncertainty, new relationships and procedures, and travel logistics while working in chronically under-staffed hospitals. These nurses frequently report feelings of loneliness and isolation (Poikus et al., 2020). Undoubtedly part of the reason for this is that the traditional nurses worry about how travel nurses will work in their unit and may have negative perceptions related to higher salaries of travel nurses.

Nonetheless, the implementation of traveling SANEs could fundamentally impact the response to sexual assault victims in rural areas. Providing traveling SANEs would relieve pressures on traditional nurses who might otherwise be untrained to handle the heightened care and trauma-informed, medical, and forensic considerations needed for sexual assault victims. These traveling nurses would be able to offer a victim-centered, trauma-informed response which is crucial to victims in rural areas.

Overall, limited research exists on the existence of traveling SANEs. More research must be conducted to better understand the benefits and limitations of traveling SANEs on victims of sexual assault, hospital institutions, and the justice process.

Telehealth SANEs

Telehealth, or telemedicine, has become an increasingly common mode of health-care provision across health-care domains. Spurred by social distancing concerns associated with the COVID-19 pandemic, patients and providers both have a better attitude toward telehealth use resulting in rates of use that are 38 times higher than use prior to COVID-19 (Bestsennyy et al., 2021). In recent years, several projects have developed to provide SAMFEs through telehealth technology (e.g., Miyamoto et al., 2021; Walsh et al., 2019).

While models may vary from location to location, generally telehealth SAMFEs follow the same general spoke-and-hub model. A hub site employs SANE-qualified nurses (can be both adult and pediatric) 24-7 to staff telehealth calls for spoke sites (the locations—here largely rural—that do not employ their own SANE). The spoke sites receive training, technical assistance, and guidance from the hub site. When a sexual assault victim presents at a local hospital, that hospital connects to the telemedicine hub. Once connected, the hub SANE nurse runs the SAMFE, directing the spoke nurse on what to do in the room. The trained SANE ensures that questioning, documentation, imaging, and all other interactions are done in a trauma-informed and patient-centered manner, which includes particular attention to the confidentiality of the patient.

There is some initial evidence that supports the use of telemedicine as a solution to issues faced in rural areas. A review by Walsh and Meunier-Sham (2020), found that both child and adult patients were not resistant to the technological aspects of the examinations. They further found that there were few technological issues and that nurses came to accept the use of it over time. However, there is still much we do not know about telemedicine—particularly in terms of its ability to provide trauma-informed and patient-centered care. Fortunately, greater research on this is being conducted in the context of the COVID-19 pandemic that should demonstrate results related to these outcomes. Of concern, however, many of the current rural telemedicine programs are operating via grants (e.g., OVC & OVW). If and when this money runs out, it is unclear whether rural critical access hospitals will continue to fund these efforts.

Discussion

The primary goal of any state should be that a survivor of sexual assault occurring within that state should receive the same level of quality trauma-informed and patient-centered care, regardless of the geography where that assault occurs. As this chapter has clearly indicated, this is not what is currently taking place across the US States that have rural areas and those that share their geography with Sovereign Nations may have many additional challenges to provisioning quality care—specifically in terms of providing the experts needed to guide that care.

Existing at the juncture between health care and the criminal justice system, the SAMFE is an exam that requires special knowledge and preparation. The best current indication of that knowledge is SANE certification. However, hospitals in rural areas may not be able to support this training for their nurses, may not find them necessary due to the low level of cases that present to the hospital, and therefore have difficulty maintaining SANEs due to their high turnover. This chapter provides some information from experiences of those within SD, with a specific look into the Oglala Sioux Tribe and the Pine Ridge Reservation, as examples of some of the issues rural areas face (see Box 14.1).

There have been several solutions floated for dealing with SANE shortage in rural areas. This chapter discussed four: stressing training over certification, provisioning mobile units, traveling nurses, and telehealth. Overall, there is a lack of empirical evidence that any of these methods will successfully provide quality SAMFE across different geographies. It is likely that one area may need one solution, and another area may benefit from a different approach. For example, telehealth does not seem like a solution when a person would still need to travel a 100 miles to reach the closest telehealth provider. At the same time, mobile units may not be a feasible solution to provision SAMFEs in a location that already has a critical access hospital—even if that hospital does not have a SANE. Likely, a combination of solutions should be deployed to reach the goal of providing equitable and accessible, high quality care to sexual assault survivors within rural areas. Stressing training—making all nurses SANE-knowledgeable if not certified, could pay dividends for patients who then may not face being turned away or being victim-blamed by untrained staff.

As such, this chapter should serve as a call to the sexual assault field to study access to quality SAMFEs in their states, to include particularly remote areas and health-care-disenfranchised communities. Through first mapping the terrain, the needed solution(s) may become apparent. Moreover, when solutions are attempted, evaluation of that effort should be undertaken to understand how to best provision care for sexual assault survivors. Through this process we can help rural health-care providers ensure their patients get the best care possible.

Key Points

- SAMFEs are complicated exams that merge health-care needs with collecting forensic evidence. They are best done by trained professionals (called SANEs).
- A quality SAMFE that is trauma-informed can have positive impacts on survivors of sexual assault as well as on their criminal justice cases. A bad experience can result in retraumatization of the sexual assault survivor.
- Rural areas have high rates of sexual victimization and experience strain providing specialized sexual assault response services. This extends to providing SAMFEs.
- Rural areas frequently do not have SANEs on staff. If they do have them, they frequently aren't available 24-7. This can be due to low access to training, lack of support from the administration, and high turnover of SANE nurses in rural areas.
- One potential solution is not to require SANE certification but instead to expand training. While this has sound logic, there is no current research that we are aware of that evaluates the effectiveness of this approach.

- Another potential solution is to provide mobile clinics. In this solution, the SANEs travel to the geographic location where the assault occurred. There is a lack of information on the effectiveness of these solutions in terms of sexual assault, but there is evidence that this solution is very costly.
- Traveling nurses are another potential solution. However, there is mixed evidence that traveling nurses can shore up under resourced hospitals. There is no research, of which we are aware, on the use of traveling nurses to provide SANE services.
- Telehealth or telemedicine is the final solution we presented to address the rural SANE shortage. These programs are currently underway and being examined for the ability to provide trauma-informed care. However, most seem to be grant funded and the continued ability to support the cost of these programs is unclear.

Discussion Questions

1 The COVID-19 Pandemic has increased general comfort with online procedures, including but not limited to meetings, social events, and even doctor's appointments. How do you think you would feel about having your SANE nurse be connected to you through a computer rather than having this nurse present in the room?

2 Read "The Case of Pine Ridge." Given the information you learned about this sovereign nation, which solution to rural SANE access do you believe would work best? Worst? Explain.

3 We have discussed four potential solutions to the SANE shortage in rural areas. Can you think of different solutions?

4 This review focused on SANE-A. Do you think any of these solutions would work better or worse for pediatric (usually under 18, but defined based on biological development) cases of sexual assault? Explain.

Further Reading

Campbell, R., Patterson, D., & Bybee, D. (2012). Prosecution of adult sexual assault cases: A longitudinal analysis of the impact of a sexual assault nurse examiner program. *Violence against Women, 18*(2), 223–244. https://doi.org/10.1177/1077801212440158

Campbell, R., Patterson, D., & Lichty, L. F. (2005). The effectiveness of sexual assault nurse examiner (SANE) programs: A review of psychological, medical, legal, and community outcomes. *Trauma, Violence, & Abuse, 6*(4), 313–329.

Clowers, A. N. (2016). *Sexual assault: Information on the availability of forensic examiners*. United States Government Accountability Office. https://www.gao.gov/assets/gao-19-259t.pdf

Deer, S. (2015). *The beginning and end of rape: Confronting sexual violence in Native America*. University of Minnesota Press.

Walsh, W. A., & Meunier-Sham, J. (2020). Using telehealth for pediatric, adolescent, and adult sexual assault forensic medical examinations: An integrative review. *Journal of Forensic Nursing, 16*(4), 232–239. https://doi.org/10.1097/JFN.0000000000000303

References

Aiken, L. H., Xue, Y., Clarke, S. P., & Sloane, D. M. (2007). Supplemental nurse staffing in hospitals and quality of care. *The Journal of Nursing Administration*, 37(7–8), 335–342. https://doi.org/10.1097/01.nna.0000285119.53066.ae

Bach, M. H., Beck Hansen, N., Ahrens, C., Nielsen, C. R., Walshe, C., & Hansen, M. (2021). Underserved survivors of sexual assault: A systematic scoping review. *European Journal of Psychotraumatology*, 12(1). https://doi.org/10.1080/20008198.2021.1895516

Bae, S., Mark, B., & Fried, B. (2010). Use of temporary nurses and nurse and patient safety outcomes in acute care hospital units. *Health Care Management Review*, 35(4), 333–344. https://doi.org/10.1097/HMR.0b013e3181dac01c

Bestsennyy, O., Gilbert, G., Harris, A., & Rost, J. (2021, July 9). *Telehealth: A quarter-trillion-dollar post-COVID-19 reality?* McKinsey & Company. https://www.mckinsey.com/industries/healthcare-systems-and-services/our-insights/telehealth-a-quarter-trillion-dollar-post-covid-19-reality

Campbell, R. (2008). The psychological impact of rape victims' experiences with the legal, medical, and mental health systems. *American Psychologist*, 63(8), 702–717. https://doi.org/10.1037/0003-066X.63.8.702

Campbell, R., Adams, A. E., & Patterson, D. (2008). Methodological challenges of collecting evaluations data from traumatized clients/consumers: A comparison of three methods. *American Journal of Evaluation*, 29(3), 369–381.

Campbell, R., Dworkin, E., & Cabral, G. (2009). An ecological model of the impact of sexual assault on women's mental health. *Trauma, Violence, & Abuse*, 10(3), 225–246.

Campbell, R., Patterson, D., & Bybee, D. (2012). Prosecution of adult sexual assault cases: A longitudinal analysis of the impact of a sexual assault nurse examiner program. *Violence against Women*, 18(2), 223–244. https://doi.org/10.1177/1077801212440158

Campbell, R., Patterson, D., & Lichty, L. F. (2005). The effectiveness of sexual assault nurse examiner (SANE) programs: A review of psychological, medical, legal, and community outcomes. *Trauma, Violence, & Abuse*, 6(4), 313–329.

Campbell, R., & Raja, S. (1999). Secondary victimization of rape victims: Insights from mental health professionals who treat survivors of violence. *Violence and Victims*, 14(3), 261–275. https://doi.org/10.1981/0886-6708.14.3.261

Clowers, A. N. (2016). Sexual assault: Information on the availability of forensic examiners. *United States Government Accountability Office*. https://www.gao.gov/assets/gao-19-259t.pdf

Dawson, B. (2017). *Rural community violence: An untold public health epidemic*. National Rural Health Association.

Deer, S. (2015). *The beginning and end of rape: Confronting sexual violence in Native America*. University of Minnesota Press.

Department of Justice. (2013). A national protocol for sexual assault medical forensic examinations – adults/adolescents. 2nd Edition. https://www.ojp.gov/pdffiles1/ovw/241903.pdf

Edwards, K. (2015). Intimate partner violence and the rural–urban–suburban divide: Myth or reality? A critical review of the literature. *Trauma, Violence, & Abuse*, 16(3), 359–373.

Elliott, D. M., Mok, D. S., & Briere, J. (2004). Adult sexual assault: Prevalence, symptomatology, and sex differences in the general population. *Journal of Traumatic Stress*, 17(3), 203–211.

Gilmore, A. K., Davidson, T. M., Leone, R. M., Wray, L. B., Oesterle, D. W., Hahn, C. K., Flanagan, J. C., Gill-Hopple, K., & Acierno, R. (2019). Usability testing of a mobile health intervention to address acute care needs after sexual assault. *International Journal of Environmental Research and Public Health*, 16(17), 3088. https://doi.org/10.3390/ijerph16173088.

Gottlieb, J. D., & Zenilman, A. (2020). When nurses travel: Labor supply elasticity during COVID-19 surges. *Becker Friedman Institute*. https://bfi.uchicago.edu/wp-content/uploads/2020/11/When-Nurses-Travel.pdf

Hill, C., Ricks, M., & Yu, S. (2016). A literature review of the scope & impact of mobile health clinics. *Mobile Health Map*. https://static1.squarespace.com/static/509ab226e4b058edb8efe5a9/t/592ed75bc534a537fbb91943/1496242030963/A±Literature±Review±of±the±Scope±and±Impact±of±Mobile±Health±Clinics±2016.pdf

International Association of Forensic Nurses. n.d. Caring for the sexually assaulted patient when there is no SANE in sight. https://www.forensicnurses.org/page/NoSANEInSight

Littel, K. (2001). Sexual assault nurse examiner (SANE) programs: Improving the community response to sexual assault victims. *U.S. Department of Justice*. http://www.vawnet.org/sites/default/files/assets/files/2016-09/OVC_SANE0401-186366.pdf

Malone, N. C., Williams, M. M., Smith Fawzi, M. C., Bennet, J., Hill, C., Katz, J. N., & Oriol, N. E. (2020). Mobile health clinics in the United States. *International Journal for Equity in Health*, *19*(1). https://doi.org/10.1186/s12939-020-1135-7

McMahon, T., Walstrom, B., & Kerkvliet, J. (2021, March). Sexual violence in South Dakota: 2019 data report. *South Dakota Department of Health*. https://doh.sd.gov/documents/Prevention/2019_SD_SexualViolenceReport.pdf

Miyamoto, S. et al. (2021). The implementation of the sexual assault forensic examination telehealth center: A program evaluation. *Journal of Forensic Nursing*, *17*(3), E24–E33. https://doi.org/10.1097/JFN.0000000000000337

Miyamoto, S., & Thiede, E. (2021, April 4). *Rural availability of sexual assault nurse examiners*. Penn State Social Science Research Institute. https://ssri.psu.edu/news/rural-availability-sexual-assault-nurse-examiners

National Institute of Justice. (2017). National best practices for sexual assault kits: A multidisciplinary approach. https://www.ojp.gov/pdffiles1/nij/250384.pdf

Peek-Asa, C., Wallis, A., Harland, K., Beyer, K., Dickey, P., & Saftlas, A. (2011). Rural disparity in domestic violence prevalence and access to resources. *Journal of Women's Health*, *20*(11), 113–118.

Peterson, Z. D., Voller, E. K., Polusny, M. A., & Murdoch, M. (2011). Prevalence and consequences of adult sexual assault of men: Review of empirical findings and state of the literature. *Clinical Psychology Review*, *31*, 1–24.

Poikus, K. N., Abraham, S. P., & Gillum, D. R. (2020). The lived experiences and the factors affecting assimilation of travel nurses into the culture of assigned nursing unit. *International Journal of Science and Research Methodology*, *16*(4), 189–223.

Post, P. (2007). Mobile health care for homeless people: Using vehicles to extend care. *National Health Care for the Homeless Council*. https://nhchc.org/wp-content/uploads/2019/08/mobilehealth.pdf

Ranjbar, V., & Speer, S. A. (2013). Revictimization and recovery from sexual assault: Implications for health professionals. *Violence and Victims*, *28*(2), 274–287. https://doi.org/10.1891/0886-6708.11-00144

Sequist, T. D. (2021). Improving the health of the American Indian and Alaska native population. *Journal of the American Medical Association*, *325*(11), 1035–1036. https://doi.org/10.1001/jama.2021.0521

Sievers, V., Murphy, S., & Miller, J. J. (2003). Sexual assault evidence collection more accurate when completed by sexual assault nurse examiners: Colorado's experience. *Journal of Emergency Nursing*, *29*(6), 511–514.

Spader, C. (2011). Opportunity knocks for travel nurses. *Nursing*, *111*(1), 36. https://doi.org/10.1097/01.NAJ.0000392860.82683.e0

Thiede, E., & Miyamoto, S. (2021). Rural availability of sexual assault nurse examiners (SANEs). Journal of Rural Health, *37*(1), 81–91.

Thomas, T. L., Nobrega, J. C., & Britton-Susino, S. (2020). Rural health, forensic science and justice: A perspective of planning and implementation of a sexual assault nurse examiner training program to support victims of sexual assault in rural underserved areas. *Forensic Science International: Reports*, 2. https://doi.org/10.1016/j.fsir.2019.100053

Walsh, W. A., Meunier-Sham, J., & Re, C. (2019). Using telehealth for sexual assault forensic examinations: A process evaluation of a national pilot project. *Journal of Forensic Nursing*, *15*(3), 152–162. https://doi.org/10.1097/JFN.0000000000000254

Ullman, S. E. (2010). *Talking about sexual assault: Society's response to survivors*. American Psychological Association.

US Census. (2021). QuickFacts South Dakota: Population estimates, July 1, 2021. https://www.census.gov/quickfacts/SD

Yu, S. W. Y., Hill, C., Ricks, M. L., Bennet, J., & Oriol, N.E. (2017). The scope and impact of mobile health clinics in the United States: A literature review. International Journal for Equity in Health, 16(1), 178–189. https://doi.org/10.1186/s12939-017-0671-2

Zuckerman, S., Haley, J., Roubideaux, Y., & Lillie-Blanton, M. (2004). Health service access, use, and insurance coverage among American Indians/Alaska Natives and Whites: What role does the Indian Health Service play? *American Journal of Public Health*, 94(1), 53–59. https://doi.org/10.2105/ajph.94.1.53

15 Caring for sexual assault victim-survivors on college campuses

Candice N. Selwyn, Carolyn Dolan, Sarah Koon-Magnin, Tres Stefurak, and Alison Rudd

As a consequence of both increased public discourse about sexual assault in general and with a focus on several high-profile cases in particular, the need for systemically addressing sexual assault on college and university campuses is receiving greater attention from the public, higher education administration, and government bodies. This chapter seeks to provide an overview of the landscape of sexual assault on college and university campuses and share lessons learned from both the greater campus-based sexual assault literature as well as efforts to implement a campus-based sexual assault nurse examiner (SANE) program offering completion of sexual assault evidence collection kits (SAEK) also known as sexual assault kits (SAKs) on-site at a mid-sized university in the Southeast.

Through funding awarded by the Office for Victims of Crime (OVC; 2020-V3-GX-0164), our team joined together to develop and launch a sustainable, campus-based SANE program at the University of South Alabama (USA), referred to throughout the chapter as HEART: promoting Health, Empowerment, and Recovery from Trauma. We look forward to sharing the many lessons we have learned in our work thus far.

The contributors of this chapter have diverse backgrounds, which is reflected in the interdisciplinary nature of the work described here. Candice Selwyn is the Project Director of HEART and a Research Assistant Professor in the College of Nursing at USA with a PhD in clinical-counseling psychology with an expertise in the provision of trauma-informed healthcare. Professor Carolyn Dolan, Clinical Director of HEART, is a nurse practitioner and the Project Director for a HRSA continuation grant at USA. Her SANE experience spans over 20 years and includes SANE-Pediatric (2021) and SANE-Adult certification (2019). She is also an attorney and a past president (2018) of The American Association of Nurse Attorneys (TAANA). Sarah Koon-Magnin is an Associate Professor in the USA Department of Political Science and Criminal Justice and has PhD in crime, law, and justice. She has published extensively in the area of sexual assault and is particularly interested in the disclosure experience for victims and those receiving the disclosures and promoting trauma-informed responses. Tres Stefurak is the Associate Dean and Professor of Counseling Psychology in the College of Education & Professional Studies at USA and has a PhD in counseling psychology. Most recently, he has been one of the research partners for the City of Mobile, AL's SAKI grants funded by the Department of Justice. Alison Rudd serves as Training Coordinator for HEART and is an Associate Professor of Simulation and a Certified Healthcare Simulation Educator (CHSE) at USA. She also has an active clinical practice with the USA Department of Emergency Medicine as a

DOI: 10.4324/9781003186816-18

board-certified family nurse practitioner and certified SANE. For the past 12 years, she has coordinated multiple SANE clinical skills labs at the USA state-of-the-art simulation center, now an approved training site by the International Association of Forensic Nurses (IAFN).

The Problem of Sexual Assault in Higher Education

In a sample of over 180,000 undergraduate and graduate students across 33 universities, an average of 13% reported experiencing some form of sexual assault while in college (Cantor et al., 2020). Even more alarming, an average of 26% of undergraduate women and 23% of undergraduate transgender, non-binary, and/or gender-questioning students report being sexually assaulted during college (Cantor et al., 2020).

Students who report experiencing sexual assault during college often describe going out of their way to avoid the perpetrator of the assault, being afraid for their safety, losing interest in their daily activities, withdrawing from friends and family members, struggling with nightmares and sleep difficulty, and feeling detached. Furthermore, students who have been sexually assaulted report decreased class attendance, difficulty concentrating in class and on studies, difficulty completing assignments and taking exams, and difficulty going to work (Cantor et al., 2020). As such, colleges and universities must make sexual assault prevention and trauma-informed response to sexual assault disclosure a top priority if they are to succeed in educating and enriching students.

In line with the improved cultural understanding of the many forms of sexual assault following the #MeToo movement, the most recent data available from the Association of American Universities (AAU) Campus Climate Survey on Sexual Assault and Misconduct (2020) indicate a substantial increase in college students' knowledge of the definition of sexual assault and sexual misconduct between 2015 and 2019 (Cantor et al., 2020). Congruently, the rate of sexual assault reported by undergraduate and graduate women, as well as undergraduate men, increased within this same time period (Cantor et al., 2020); this change should not necessarily be interpreted as an increase in sexual assault incidents (although that possibility cannot be discounted), as the change may also be the result of student's increased understanding of the varying types of sexual assault. Students also reported an increase in knowledge of where to get help when an assault has occurred, where to report on campus, and what will happen when a report is made on campus; yet, the rate of students who report feeling "very" to "extremely" knowledgeable about reporting sexual assault and receiving help on campus remains below 40%, indicating a majority of students are not adequately prepared to report an assault or receive services when needed (Cantor et al., 2020).

Unfortunately, gains in knowledge of definitions of sexual assault and processes for reporting an assault have not uniformly translated to gains in perceptions of support by college and university officials. Undergraduate women's belief that administration officials would take their report seriously decreased between 2015 and 2019, whereas men and transgender, non-binary, and/or gender-questioning students' beliefs increased (Cantor et al., 2020). Overall, both women and transgender, non-binary, and/or gender-questioning students are significantly less likely to believe their report will be taken seriously or that officials would conduct a fair investigation. This pattern is even more pronounced among students who have personally experienced a sexual assault (Cantor et al., 2020). These data suggest the students most vulnerable to experiencing assault are also those least likely to view making a report as worthwhile.

Barriers to Reporting Sexual Assault

It is widely acknowledged that sexual assault is the most under-reported violent crime (Rennison, 2002). College students are even less likely to report sexual assault to police than non-enrolled college-aged peers (Sinozich & Langton, 2014). The AAU Campus Climate Survey on Sexual Assault and Misconduct (2020) determined that 15% of students surveyed contacted at least one campus-based program or resource following their experience of sexual assault. Of the students who contacted at least one resource:

- 47% contacted campus counseling services,
- 24% contacted student health services,
- 21% contacted their Title IX office,
- 18% contacted campus-based victims' services, and
- 11% contacted campus law enforcement (Cantor et al., 2020).

Common reasons cited by students for not seeking a resource on campus included:

- the belief that the incident could be handled alone,
- the assault was "not serious enough,"
- it would be too emotionally difficult to make a report,
- the resource could not help,
- feelings of embarrassment and shame, and
- desire to not get the perpetrator in trouble.

Congruent with the findings discussed above, women and transgender, non-binary, and/or gender-questioning students were especially likely to endorse these concerns. Transgender, non-binary, and/or gender-questioning students were also much more likely to report concern their gender would result in their report being minimized or misunderstood (Cantor et al., 2020). Regarding the belief the assault was "not serious enough," students noted factors such as:

- not experiencing a physical injury as a result of the assault,
- involvement of alcohol,
- initial consent during the sexual encounter,
- the belief "events like this seem common," and
- experiences of involuntary arousal during sexual assault (Cantor et al., 2020).

Awareness of such barriers is crucial for developing effective campus-based programming to improve systemic response to sexual assault.

Unique Barriers to Reporting Sexual Assault on College and University Campuses

In addition to the barriers cited above, students are likely to also face unique challenges in reporting a campus-based sexual assault that victim-survivors in community settings may be less likely to encounter. As previously noted, most students remain unaware of how to report, to whom to report, and the processes that will take place following a report of sexual assault on campus. Therefore, even those who may desire to make a report will likely encounter systemic challenges for making such a report.

While victim-survivors within the community have one primary legal option for formally reporting sexual assault (i.e., municipal law enforcement), college students have two processes—Title IX and/or campus police. Without a sufficient understanding of the processes involved in reporting to Title IX and/or campus police, students already in vulnerable post-traumatic states may encounter unexpected hindrances, become discouraged, and disengage from the process and/or needed supportive care.

In theory, students who elect the route of reporting to Title IX may be even less likely to receive a sexual assault medical forensic examination (SAMFE) than those who elect to report to campus police due to differing procedures for responding to sexual assault reports, although additional research is needed. This dynamic is even more complicated by ever-changing rules and regulations to which colleges and universities adhere, particularly surrounding Title IX processes (Kidder, 2020), and varying perceptions of the role of campus police compared to local and state law enforcement (Youstin & Kopp, 2021).

One such factor students are often not aware of that impacts both Title IX and the campus police response to sexual assault is that of jurisdiction. Sexual assaults are investigated and prosecuted within the jurisdiction in which the sexual assault occurred. Therefore, if a student is sexually assaulted off-campus in a jurisdiction outside of their college or university, neither Title IX nor campus police is responsible for investigating (though the Title IX office may still be able to assist the student by connecting them to support services). Students are often unaware of this fact until they attempt to report an experience of sexual assault or seek medical services on account of sexual assault that occurred off-campus and are met with a reality that conflicts with their expectations. SAEKs are also often processed by the department of forensic sciences within the region of the case's jurisdiction. In communities in which campus police have little collaboration with municipal police departments, students may find the process of reporting and submitting a SAEK for processing even more challenging to navigate.

Most states do not require mandatory reporting of adult sexual assault cases, leaving the decision to report to the victim-survivor themselves; however, colleges and universities who receive federal funding are required to compel faculty, staff, and administrators to forward disclosures of sexual assault or misconduct to the Title IX office. Institutions often interpret this requirement broadly and classify nearly all employees as mandatory reporters (Holland et al., 2018). If a victim-survivor discloses an assault to a trusted professor, resident advisor, or other college or university employee, they may not be aware that the disclosure is now required to be forwarded on to the Title IX office. As a result, the disclosure may be shared without the student's consent, triggering an investigation the student may not have wanted in the first place.

Though the empirical research at this point is limited, scholars have voiced significant concerns about compelled disclosure (Weiss & Lasky, 2017). A key concern is that victim-survivors may feel that their autonomy is being undermined, as their experience is shared with individuals to whom they did not choose to disclose. In addition to the potential harm caused by taking this important decision out of the victim-survivors' hands, mandatory reporting may also enhance the likelihood of experiencing secondary victimization (i.e., retraumatization), which is more common when a sexual assault is disclosed to a formal source of support (Campbell et al., 2001). Although this policy may be intended to increase reporting and accountability for sexual assault on campuses, the opposite could also be true (Holland et al., 2018). Surveys of undergraduate students' perceptions of mandatory reporting policies generally suggest that they support compelled disclosure and view it as useful (Mancini et al., 2016; Newins & White, 2018). However, approximately one-fifth of students report that they would be less likely to disclose an assault to a college or university employee because of the existence of compelled disclosure policies (Mancini et al., 2016; Newins & White, 2018). This is a substantial portion of the undergraduate population and suggests that for some students, mandatory reporting policies are having the opposite of their intended effect.

Lastly, it is critical to acknowledge the historical mishandling of sexual assault reports on campuses as another potential barrier to reporting. Similar to the ways in which mishandling of sexual assault reports led to a backlog of untested SAKs within municipalities (Bureau of Justice Assistance, 2021, see Chapter 1), there are unfortunately many examples of institutions of higher education minimizing or denying the presence of sexual assault on their campuses despite evidence to the contrary. Colleges and universities are often highly motivated to protect their reputations, and acknowledgment of sexual assault on campus runs the risk of tarnishing institutions' prestige and deterring future students (Smith & Freyd, 2014). This may partially explain why while 32% of college presidents agreed sexual assault was prevalent on campuses, only 6% saw this as an issue for their campus (Dolamore & Richards, 2020). When trusted institutions on which students depend fail to prevent sexual assault, normalize contexts in which assault occurs, complicate reporting procedures, and/or respond to reports in dismissive ways that deny the experience of the victim-survivor, they are engaging in behaviors consistent with the concept of institutional betrayal (Smith & Freyd, 2014). At the individual victim-survivor level, those who experience intuitional betrayal suffer worse physical and mental health outcomes and are more likely to disengage from care (Smith & Freyd, 2014). At the organizational level, increased awareness of cases of institutional betrayal perpetrated by reputable, respected institutions of higher education may lead student victim-survivors to forego reporting due to expectations for a poor response from the administration.

Campus-Based Resources for Victim-Survivors of Sexual Assault

Consistent with the governmental response to unsubmitted SAKs through the creation and support of the Sexual Assault Kit Initiative (SAKI), demand for campus-based resources for students affected by sexual assault has increased as awareness of the prevalence and impact of sexual assault on college and university campuses has risen. Many colleges and universities have developed and launched both prevention and response activities that seek to reduce the overall prevalence of sexual assault and assist those who have been assaulted. Yet, there remains room for improvement. Namely, although colleges often offer advocacy and counseling services to students who report sexual assault, most colleges and universities lack healthcare services focused on caring for students who have been sexually assaulted (i.e., SAMFEs). The value of access to care from a SANE following sexual assault is widely cited. Because they emphasize a trauma-informed response, SANE's are less likely than other medical professionals to cause secondary victimization (i.e., retraumatization) and are more likely to help empower the patient by emphasizing their ability to withhold consent throughout the exam (Campbell et al., 2005). Research also indicates that cases progress further in the criminal justice system when a SANE exam with evidence collection is conducted (Campbell et al., 2012). Mock juror studies suggest that participants are more likely to believe testimony provided by a SANE than a non-SANE registered nurse (Golding et al., 2015), and prosecutors view SANE testimony as a valuable part of their case (Schmitt et al., 2017).

The recognition of the important role of forensic nursing in caring for those affected by sexual assault has led various federal agencies to fund both training and education grants focused on increasing the supply of SANEs within local communities and programmatic grants focused on establishing and sustaining SANE programs on college and university campuses. The remainder of this chapter will focus on lessons learned from one such programmatic initiative to establish a campus-based SANE program offering SAEKs at a mid-sized university in the Southeast United States. Lessons learned focus on three domains: administrative lessons, multidisciplinary team (MDT) lessons, and clinical service delivery lessons.

The HEART Project: Promoting Health, Empowerment, and Recovery from Trauma

Administrative Lessons

Begin with sustainability in mind

Establishing and sustaining SANE programming on a college or university campus requires specially trained personnel across key departments (student health, counseling, advocacy, and law enforcement), examination space, equipment and supplies, and an infrastructure for both medical record keeping and storage of potential forensic evidence. HEART elected to work toward sustainability at the outset of the initiative by working within the university's existing infrastructure as much as possible (i.e., performing SAMFEs out of the existing student health facility on campus; training existing staff; recruiting additional staff who are dedicated to the project) and seeking examination reimbursement from the state crime victim's compensation commission.

Obtain and sustain buy-in

As with any systemic intervention, obtaining buy-in from administration and departmental leaders is critical to the success of the overall program. A successful campus-based sexual assault prevention and response program involves partnerships across the college and/or university system to include departments most likely to encounter students who have experienced sexual assault. Examples include but are not limited to academic affairs, Title IX, fraternity and sorority life, athletics, housing, multicultural student affairs, and disability services, in addition to key direct service departments such as student health, counseling, advocacy, and law enforcement.

Form an advisory board

One method of obtaining and sustaining buy-in from administration and departmental leadership is to form a campus-based advisory board that serves to unite administration around the topic of sexual assault on campus and remove barriers to effective service provision for students affected by sexual assault. In developing an advisory board, consider the inclusion of not only administration and departmental leadership but also student and community leaders. Including students on the program's advisory board ensures the board stays up to date on the current pulse of the student body and that programmatic decisions are informed by students' perspectives. Incorporating community leaders into the campus-based advisory board facilitates transparency and accountability to individuals outside the college or university structure, an important component for the institution of higher education, which has a reputation for inappropriately addressing sexual assault.

Develop a vision, mission, and set of shared values

Implementing a systemic sexual assault prevention and response program is best guided by a vision, mission, and set of values shared among the multidisciplinary advisory board and direct service team. In developing a shared set of values focused on a common vision and mission, the group is setting a roadmap for decision-making at later stages of program implementation.

Through several group discussions among core MDT members, HEART identified its vision and mission, as well as a set of six core values: trauma-informed, victim-survivor-centered, confidentiality, inclusivity and cultural humility, collaboration, and commitment to excellence. In facing a choice point throughout program development and implementation, HEART revisited its vision and mission and opted for the route that was most aligned with our guiding values.

Work closely with Title IX and legal counsel

Although SANE programs are first and foremost medical care, data and specimens gathered throughout the SAMFE are also forensic in nature and subject to subpoena should a case go to trial. As such, all programmatic policies, procedures, and practices should undergo scrutiny prior to launching the SANE program to ensure they are in line with state and federal requirements. Working closely with the college or university's Title IX office and legal counsel is invaluable in developing a clear, compliant process that can be explained to students as they seek services and make an informed decision about their care.

Give extra thought to confidentiality and privacy

One such policy that requires extra thought and consultation with Title IX and legal counsel is that of students' confidentiality and privacy when seeking care for sexual assault on campus. As mentioned earlier in this chapter, many colleges and universities classify most of their faculty, staff, and administrators as mandatory reporters of sexual assault under Title IX. This can create barriers to ensuring students' confidentiality when they seek services for experiences of sexual assault on campus. Developing a close working relationship with your Title IX office can assist in determining which university employees are exempt from the mandatory reporting requirement. HEART direct service staff (healthcare providers, advocates, and counselors) are all considered to be confidential resources, meaning they cannot be compelled to disclose a student's report of sexual assault to either Title IX or campus law enforcement.

Further, while SANE programs typically fall under the Health Insurance Portability and Accountability Act (HIPAA), SANE programs housed on campuses that offer care solely to students are most likely to fall under the Family Educational Rights and Privacy Act (FERPA). According to FERPA, as soon as a student's medical record is used for any purpose other than medical care, even in the instance a student obtains their own personal copy of their medical record, the medical record becomes part of the student's educational record, which is subject to different disclosure regulations. In essence, FERPA allows the disclosure of a student's educational record without the student's explicit consent in numerous circumstances.

As results of a SAMFE are arguably even more sensitive in nature than typical medical records, protection of their privacy is imperative. Moreover, students are entitled to be provided with relevant information regarding the privacy of their medical records to make an informed decision about seeking a SAMFE. Importantly, although FERPA *allows* disclosure of a student's educational record without their consent under various circumstances, the disclosure is not required, and colleges and universities may develop their own policy to provide an additional layer of protection for a student's SAMFE records. HEART worked closely with the university's legal counsel to ensure a student's SAMFE record would not be released without their written permission barring a subpoena, in line with HEART's guiding principle of being trauma-informed and providing students with as much control over the process as possible.

Lastly, colleges and universities may consider results of the SAMFE as evidence to be included in Title IX proceedings (Veidlinger, 2016). In these instances, a SANE may be called as either a fact or expert witness in sexual misconduct proceedings on campus. It is important to discuss this possibility with the Title IX office, legal counsel, and SANEs performing SAMFEs on campus prior to launching services so that students can be properly informed of the role of the SAMFE and SANE in the Title IX process. If results of the SAMFE are to be used in Title IX proceedings, SANEs should be included to interpret and provide context for findings (Veidlinger, 2016).

Multidisciplinary Team Lessons

As is recommended practice among community-based sexual assault response programs (e.g., SARTs, MDTs), HEART included multiple departments from across campus to provide the most streamlined and consistent response to sexual assault possible. In a higher education setting, typical partners include SANEs and other health professionals, as applicable, advocates, counselors, law enforcement officers, Title IX staff, and research partners. These specific departments were recruited for the HEART MDT as they were those identified to be most likely to encounter students in the acute aftermath of sexual assault (i.e., first responders) and as having a distinct role to play in sexual assault response on campus.

Orient and train the MDT

Building an MDT should begin by ensuring all MDT members are on the same page about the central mission of the group and have the knowledge necessary to perform their role on the MDT in a manner that is consistent with the team's guiding values. Achieving this will likely require multiple, regularly scheduled training sessions and MDT meetings.

The ramp-up to launching HEART included four biweekly trainings on topics including the overall goals and objectives of the project, neurobiology of trauma, victim-survivor-centered communication, and facilitating victim-survivor engagement in care through collaboration. In addition to presenting up-to-date information on these relevant topics, members of the MDT engaged in breakout room discussions about how these concepts would be relevant to their own specific roles on the MDT. Breakout rooms were organized to include a representative from each MDT department (healthcare, advocacy, counseling, law enforcement), as each member plays a distinct role in responding to victim-survivors of sexual assault. During breakout room discussions, each member of the MDT not only clarified their own role in finer detail but also better understood the roles and responsibilities of their other teammates that respond to victim-survivors.

The two-month training series culminated in a simulated *in-situ* training exercise conducted in collaboration with the university's simulation department. During the in-situ training exercise, the MDT responded to a simulated report of sexual assault by a standardized patient on-site at the student health center and engaged with the standardized patient in a trauma-informed manner according to each team member's role (e.g., SANE obtained consent and explained process of exam, advocate offered support and additional follow-up services, law enforcement introduced self, took a preliminary report, and explained the process of filing a police report, etc.). This training served two purposes—to practice the skills just learned in the four-part training series and to identify remaining gaps in the response process.

Focus on building and maintaining collegial relationships

In addition to guaranteeing a basic knowledge of trauma-informed principles, these early training sessions served the secondary purpose of team building. An MDT's strength is in bringing various points of contact from responding agencies together to promote a consistent response to sexual assault victim-survivors. Yet, the performance of the MDT is also dependent on the willingness of its members to be open and honest in communication with members from departments across campus. Building trust and collegial relationships among team members is a necessary initial step to forming an effective MDT. HEART sought to facilitate the development of trust among team members through regularly scheduled MDT meetings and trainings that varied in formality. Informal meetings that allowed time for members to get to know each other on a more personal level appeared to be particularly helpful.

Praise varying perspectives and normalize disagreement

Bringing members together from various disciplines and departments across campus is not only beneficial for determining if continuity of care is being provided to victim-survivors but also for evoking varying perspectives capable of ultimately improving the entire response process. MDT members need to both know and value the roles of their teammates to work together most effectively. Understanding where one team member's role ends and another team member's role begins allows each MDT member to provide the best care possible within their role without taking on too much responsibility for tasks outside their role.

As MDT members' roles differ, so do their goals. Given discipline-distinct goals and roles on the MDT, disagreement among team members is both normal and expected. In fact, a lack of disagreement among members of the MDT from differing disciplines could indicate a lack of trust and open communication. Thus, it is important that the MDT is a safe space to share a variety of perspectives and opinions and that members treat each other with respect as the team works toward the shared mission of serving victim-survivors of sexual assault. Creating such a space may be difficult to implement and involve some growing pains as members get to know each other and share new cases. After the MDT is established, it may be useful to bring in an external partner for feedback and to help center the group around its mission. Because this person is an outsider (i.e., not a member of the MDT or campus community) and thus not privy to the specific conversations or disagreements that may have taken place within the group, they are able to view the big picture and draw attention back to the organizing mission and values of the group.

SANE Clinical Service Delivery Lessons

Prioritize medical care and patient autonomy

SAMFEs, while forensic in nature, are first and foremost medical care. When presenting for a SAMFE, victim-survivors (referred to as patients within the medical context of the SAMFE) should initially be evaluated for acute injuries warranting immediate medical attention (e.g., excessive bleeding, signs of non-fatal strangulation, head injuries, etc.). As campus-based student health centers are most often not capable of treating acute, emergent injuries, a transfer to an emergency department (ED) may be necessary to ensure the victim-survivor is medically stable. For this reason, it is important that the team establish a robust relationship with a local ED. Whether the ED be inside the academic institution or not, it is important that ED providers understand the sexual assault screening and care process at the student health center, operate inside a trauma-informed framework with patients, and practice closed-loop communication with the SANE or other student health clinical representative so that effective follow-up can be maintained.

Further, while a SAEK should be offered to all victim-survivors who present for care within 120 hours of the assault, the entire MDT must respect the victim-survivor's decisions about the type of services in which they wish to engage. Through HEART, victim-survivors have complete discretion over which services they decide to utilize and which they decline. Victim-survivors may choose to receive a SAMFE with or without the inclusion of the SAEK. If they choose to have a SAEK performed during their SAMFE, they are also in complete control of which aspects of the SAEK are completed and may decline any aspect of the exam. Victim-survivors may also choose to receive a SAMFE with a SAEK but decline to report the assault to law enforcement (i.e., anonymous SAEK). Alternatively, they may decide to contact an advocate, see a counselor, and/or report to law enforcement but decline a SAMFE.

Victim-survivors are informed of all the support services available to them (both verbally and in writing), as well as the potential consequences of choosing or declining each service and are supported to make decisions about which, if any, services they decide to utilize.

Collaborate closely with support advocates

Advocates are essential to the work of not just the MDT broadly but specifically to the work of the SANE. To minimize opportunities for the SAMFE to be challenged on the grounds of provider bias should the victim-survivor's case go to trial, SANEs must remain both patient-centered, as they would with any patient under their care, and neutral toward the results of the SAMFE. Advocates, however, have no duty to remain neutral toward the outcomes of the SAMFE. To the contrary, the advocate's role is to be exclusively focused on supporting the psychosocial needs of the victim-survivor throughout the lengthy process of recovering from an experience of sexual assault. In this manner, advocates benefit not just the victim-survivor but also the SANE by allowing the SANE to focus solely on the provision of high-quality forensic healthcare.

HEART focused both on increasing the capacity of the university's existing support advocate program by offering additional education and training, including simulation-based training opportunities with standardized patients, and by partnering with the local community-based advocacy program for additional support as needed. Specifically, given the campus-based advocacy program was new to providing support to victim-survivors during SAMFEs, HEART partnered with a community-based advocacy program to offer campus advocates opportunities to shadow advocates during SAMFEs performed at the local hospital-based SANE program. The community-based advocacy program has also been invaluable in providing psychosocial support to campus-based advocates, as many of the campus-based advocates are new to their role. Finally, campus advocates participated in a simulation-based training with standardized patients, which allowed them to practice their role and receive immediate, timely feedback from the seasoned community-based advocacy supervisor. SANEs also participated to enhance the realism of the encounter and facilitate an ongoing, healthy relationship between the SANEs, campus advocates, and community-based advocates.

Ensure SAMFEs adhere to best practices

SANEs should ensure they adhere to the National Protocol for SAMFEs (US Department of Justice Office on Violence against Women, 2013), as well as standards of practice for forensic nursing, professional ethics, and applicable laws. Professional nursing ethics principles include beneficence, non-maleficence, autonomy, veracity, fidelity, fairness (justice), and accountability for nursing acts (American Nurses Association, 2015). Having policies and procedures in place that adhere to the national protocol and standards of practice for forensic nursing is critical for supporting SANEs in their work on campuses. With clear, concrete guidance, the SANE, MDT, and victim-survivor are all aware of what to expect under typical circumstances.

Regularly scheduled peer review for quality assurance purposes can assist in ensuring best practices are being utilized. SANE peer review consists of a de-identified group review of patient documentation, evidence collection techniques (if a SAEK was performed), and photographs taken during the SAMFE. This process allows SANEs to share feedback and expertise, as well as build additional skills for future patient encounters. Results of the peer review process may also be shared with other members of the MDT, as applicable, to identify remaining training needs and gaps in service provision processes. HEART elected to adopt a process of de-identified peer review for every patient encounter overseen by HEART's Clinical Director and in collaboration with the SANE call team.

Resources were also specifically allocated to ensure professional development and practice currency of HEART SANEs. Continuing education opportunities were offered to local SANEs and covered topics such as trauma-informed care, evidence collection, hymenal assessment, and male anogenital exams. HEART SANEs were also supported in joining the state chapter of the IAFN and attending the annual conference to partner with forensic nurses across the nation and stay up-to-date on SANE practices (for more information, see Chapter 12).

Develop a positive working relationship with local law enforcement

Although SANEs must remain mindful of their role as healthcare providers and distinguish themselves from functions of law enforcement and criminal justice, a positive working relationship with local law enforcement is beneficial for supporting an effective SANE program.

Campus police are an especially important resource for addressing sexual assault on university and college campuses. While campus police officers are typically employed directly by the university, they often have privileges comparable to those of a municipal or state police officer, capable of conducting a complete investigation and making arrests as needed. In relation to campus-based sexual assault, campus police are critical to launching an investigation, ensuring proper chain of custody and timely processing of SAEKs, and referring cases to the District Attorney's Office for possible prosecution, as appropriate.

HEART worked closely with campus law enforcement to develop trauma-informed policies and procedures specifically related to SAEKs. For instance, once a SAEK has been performed by a HEART SANE, our campus law enforcement agency assumes custody of the SAEK within 72 hours of the kit's completion. All SAEKs are submitted immediately for processing with the patient's permission. For patients who wish to delay processing, HEART negotiated with campus law enforcement to store anonymous kits indefinitely to allow patients sufficient time to consider submitting their kits.

Focus on SANEs' self-care and prevent vicarious trauma

Assisting victim-survivors who have experienced sexual assault can be emotionally demanding, leading to symptoms of vicarious trauma (VT), compassion fatigue, and burnout among SANEs (Raunick et al., 2015). However, it's important to note VT and burnout can be prevented through conscious effort and systemic support (Flarity et al., 2016). HEART prioritized the prevention of VT and burnout from its inception through two primary mechanisms: (1) professional development via continuing education offerings to increase SANEs' perceptions of self-efficacy in providing care to sexual assault victim-survivors and (2) psychosocial support via group debriefing sessions to be facilitated by the university's employee assistance program (EAP) to remind SANEs they are not alone in their work and provide a safe space to validate and normalize their reactions to caring for patients affected by violence. HEART members were encouraged to utilize the university-provided EAP, if needed, to minimize VT and sustain role satisfaction. Most importantly, at every HEART-related meeting, VT was openly discussed, and team members were encouraged to share. Making VT part of the "everyday" conversation, normalized the process, and instead of feeling ashamed, team members felt validated.

Discussion

Trauma-informed response to students who have experienced sexual assault requires special considerations, as campuses present not only unique barriers but also unique opportunities. Students may be hesitant to report sexual assault due to the numerous factors discussed throughout this chapter and campuses often lack key resources, specifically SAMFEs and SAEKs performed by trained SANEs. Yet, campuses are also often a tighter-knit community ripe with possibilities for multidisciplinary collaboration and maintenance of evidence-based, timely knowledge due to their academic nature. This chapter has highlighted key considerations for the formation of a campus-based SANE program that includes the offering of SAEKs through lessons learned from an initiative in the Southeastern United States.

As the nation moves forward in its attempt to reconcile past mishandlings of sexual assault through initiatives such as SAKI, higher education must remain a prime target given both the level of risk present during college and the inherent strengths campuses possess for the possibility of a cohesive, trauma-informed response. Compared to municipalities that must attempt to coordinate across potentially dozens of facilities and agencies to address community-based sexual assaults, relevant departments on campuses are most often housed under a single university system, easing the logistics of coordinated communication and response. Further, many colleges and universities have several of the key services needed to provide comprehensive care to sexual assault student victim-survivors already at their disposal (i.e., general healthcare, Title IX advocacy, and counseling). With relatively minor adjustments to existing infrastructures, a comprehensive SANE program offering SAEKs can be implemented on campuses, potentially increasing the number of student victim-survivors who receive trauma-informed healthcare following experiences of sexual assault. In bolstering the support offered to students following sexual assault, colleges and universities are not only better caring for the students under their supervision but also more likely to meet the overall mission of higher education—to enrich the lives of students as they work toward a quality education and meaningful career.

Key Points

- The campus environment differs from a general community setting in important ways. Service providers should consider their unique context when designing programs.
- Providing campus-based resources may help overcome barriers to service provision, particularly those relating to cost, transportation, and availability.

- A successful campus-based program requires input from many departments on campus. Each of these groups brings its own goals and perspectives that may lead to conflict within the MDT. Ground rules for communication and collaboration should explicitly allow this possibility and recognize the need for respectful consideration of each individual on the team.
- Though not available on every campus or in every community, SANEs offer valuable services in their ability to respond in a trauma-informed manner, collect and document usable evidence, and link victim-survivors to additional services in the community.

Discussion Questions

1 In what ways does responding to sexual assault in the campus environment setting differ from assaults in the community?
2 Should mandatory reporting requirements apply to disclosures by college students? In what ways might this policy be problematic?
3 Why is buy-in from key administrators and stakeholders so important to the development of a new program?
4 Discuss the key stakeholders who should be included in multidisciplinary responses to sexual assault within your own community. Why are they important and what should their roles and responsibilities entail?
5 How does the presence of a SANE program improve sexual assault response?

Author Note and Funding Acknowledgment

This publication was produced by the University of South Alabama under 2020-V3-GX-0164, awarded by the Office for Victims of Crime, Office of Justice Programs, US Department of Justice. The opinions, findings, and conclusions or recommendations expressed in this chapter are those of the contributors and do not necessarily represent the official position or policies of the US Department of Justice.

Conflict of Interest to Disclose

The authors have no conflicts of interest to disclose.

Further Reading

Donde, S. D., Ragsdale, S. K., Koss, M. P., & Zucker, A. N. (2018). If it wasn't rape, was it sexual assault? Comparing rape and sexual assault acknowledgment in college women who have experienced rape. *Violence against Women*, 24(14), 1718–1738.
Kafonek, K., & Richards, T. N. (2017). An examination of strategies for the prevention of gender-based violence at four-year institutions of higher education. *Journal of School Violence*, 16(3), 271–285. https://doi.org/10.1080/15388220.2017.1318576
Moylan, C. A., & Javorka, M. (2020). Widening the lens: An ecological review of campus sexual assault. *Trauma, Violence, & Abuse*, 21(1), 179–192. https://doi.org/10.1177/1524838018756121
Sinozich, S., & Langton, L. (2014). Rape and sexual assault among college-age females, 1995–2013. *BJS Special Report*.

References

American Nurses Association. (2015). Code of ethics with interpretative statements. Silver Spring, MD: Author. Retrieved from http://www.nursingworld.org/MainMenuCategories/ EthicsStandards/CodeofEthicsforNurses/Code-ofEthics-For-Nurses.html

Bureau of Justice Assistance. (2021, August 19). *Sexual assault kit initiative (SAKI): Overview: BJA*. Bureau of Justice Assistance. Retrieved October 25, 2021, from https://bja.ojp.gov/ program/sexual-assault-kit-initiative-saki/overview

Campbell, R., Bybee, D., Kelley, K.D., Dworkin, E. R., & Patterson, D. (2012). The impact of sexual assault nurse examiner (SANE) program services on law enforcement investigational practices: A mediational analysis. *Criminal Justice and Behavior, 39*, 169–184.

Campbell, R., Patterson, D., & Lichty, L. F. (2005). The effectiveness of sexual assault nurse examiner (SANE) programs: A review of psychological, medical, legal, and community outcomes. *Trauma, Violence, & Abuse, 6*(4), 313–329.

Campbell, R., Wasco, S. M., Ahrens, C. E., Sefl, T., & Barnes, H. E. (2001). Preventing the "second rape": Rape survivors' experiences with community service providers. *Journal of Interpersonal Violence, 16*, 1239–1259.

Cantor, D., Fisher, B., Chibnall, S., Harps, S., Townsend, R., Thomas, G., Lee, H., Kranz, V., Herbison, R., & Madden, K. (2020). *Report on the AAU Campus Climate Survey on Sexual Assault and Misconduct*. i–433.

Dolamore, S., & Richards, T. N. (2020). Assessing the organizational culture of higher education institutions in an era of #MeToo. *Public Administration Review, 80*(6), 1133–1137. https://doi.org/10.1111/puar.13179

Flarity, K., Nash, K., Jones, W., & Steinbruner, D. (2016). Intervening to improve compassion fatigue resiliency in forensic nurses. *Advanced Emergency Nursing Journal, 38*(2), 147–156. https://doi.org/10.1097/TME.0000000000000101

Golding, J. M., Nesa, E., Wasarhaley, K. R., Lynch, A. L., & Magyarics, C. L. (2015). Improving the credibility of child sexual assault victims in court: The impact of a sexual assault nurse examiner. *Behavioral Sciences & the Law, 33*, 493–507. https://doi.org/10.1002/ bsl.2188

Holland, K. J., Cortina, L. M., & Freyd, J. J. (2018). Compelled disclosure of college sexual assault. *American Psychologist, 73*(3), 256–268. https://doi.org/10.1037/amp0000186

Kidder, W. C. (2020). (En)forcing a foolish consistency?: A critique and comparative analysis of the Trump administration's proposed standard of evidence regulation for campus Title IX proceedings. *Journal of College and University Law, 45*(1), 1–49.

Mancini, C., Pickett, J. T., Call, C., & Roche, S. P. (2016). Mandatory reporting (MR) in higher education: College students' perceptions of laws designed to reduce campus sexual assault. *Criminal Justice Review, 41*, 219–235.

Newins, A. R., & White, S. W. (2018). Title IX sexual violence reporting requirements: Knowledge and opinions of responsible employees and students. *Journal of Aggression, Conflict, and Peace Research, 8*, 74–82.

Raunick, C. B., Lindell, D. F., Morris, D. L., & Backman, T. (2015). Vicarious trauma among sexual assault nurse examiners. *Journal of Forensic Nursing, 11*(3), 123–128. https://doi. org/10.1097/JFN.0000000000000085

Rennison, C. M. (2002). *Rape and sexual assault: Reporting to police and medical attention, 1992-2000*. US Department of Justice, Office of Justice Programs.

Schmitt, T., Cross, T. P., & Alderden, M. (2017). Qualitative analysis of prosecutors' perspectives on sexual assault nurse examiners and the criminal justice response to sexual assault. *Journal of Forensic Nursing, 13*, 62–68.

Smith, C. P., & Freyd, J. J. (2014). Institutional betrayal. *American Psychologist, 69*(6), 575–587. https://doi.org/10.1037/a0037564

US Department of Justice Office on Violence against Women. (2013). A national protocol for sexual assault medical forensic examinations: Adults/adolescents. Available at https://www.ojp.gov/pdffiles1/ovw/241903.pdf

Veidlinger, R. L. (2016). IX: Role of sexual assault nurse examiners in campus sexual assault proceedings. *The Journal for Nurse Practitioners*, *12*(2), 113–119. https://doi.org/10.1016/j.nurpra.2015.09.002

Weiss, K. G., & Lasky, N. V. (2017). Mandatory reporting of sexual misconduct at college: A critical perspective. *Journal of School Violence*, *16*(3), 259–270. https://doi.org/10.1080/15388220.2017.1318575

Youstin, T. J., & Kopp, P. M. (2021). Role variations and perceptions of campus police versus local and state law enforcement. *Policing: A Journal of Policy and Practice*, *15*(2), 1491–1506. https://doi.org/10.1093/police/paaa054

16 Behind the scenes of the forensic lab

Forensic decision-making for sexual assault kit testing

Charlotte Lopez-Jauffret

Author Note

The opinions or points of view expressed in this chapter are solely those of the author and do not reflect the official positions of any participating organization or the US Department of Justice.

The length of time from submission of SAKs to the lab and then to completion—also referred to as processing time—varies widely across jurisdictions. This can affect the quality of information obtained by the investigating agencies and can later affect the likelihood of arrest or convictions based on said information. The lack of consistent government regulation within the realm of sexual assault testing results in inconsistencies in criminal case outcomes and demonstrates a government failure in sexual assault responses. These kits are taken to labs where forensic scientists are making decisions as to what are the most probative items to test within them but are limited to the number of items they can test within a kit depending on where it is processed, such as a state or private laboratory. In addition, laboratory procedures and monetary costs play a large role in what can be processed for DNA within a SAK. Each of these factors is taken into account by the forensic scientist, and these decisions may have vast effects.

The impacts of these decisions are understudied. Even more so, the factors that influence scientists' decision-making processes require more attention. Each sample selected for testing in the kit has a financial cost to the laboratory and individuals, but who determines these costs and how many samples are allowed per SAK? In the sections that follow, this chapter breaks down how kits are currently tested and provides case examples to illustrate testing plans and decision-making.

As a previous forensic scientist testing hundreds of kits in a private laboratory and as a previous forensic intelligence analyst researching the aftermath of testing, it is apparent that the outcome of how many samples tested, and what gets tested, is grossly understudied. Furthermore, the consequences of the testing are, unfortunately, an afterthought for forensic scientists. Forensic scientists are trained not to put weight on the outcomes of testing but instead to focus on processing the sample for the presence of DNA. The nature of the job is to remain neutral.

However, as a researcher with a goal to reform the response to sexual assault, it is imperative to further explore the decision-making processes of forensic scientists in the lab. Specifically, why are there limits to the number of samples tested in a kit? Are people aware the limits exist? What are the variations in protocols to help determine

DOI: 10.4324/9781003186816-19

what types of samples? This chapter aims to highlight the relationship between SAKs and forensic scientist decision-making on testing and begin to present preliminary research needed to answer some of these questions.

Background of Laboratories and Forensic Scientists

Once a kit is collected and submitted for testing, where does it go and who conducts the testing? Forensic labs can either be private or publicly funded. Within the United States, there are approximately 400 crime labs, with the majority of the labs being privately funded (Siegel, 2019). Publicly funded labs include government labs, such as the FBI crime lab and state crime labs. In addition to publicly funded state crime labs, jurisdictions might also have publicly funded county labs or city labs, which can exist within police departments (although many have started to separate themselves to become independent labs) (see Box 16.1).

Within these laboratories are forensic scientists who process cases and make decisions as to what gets tested and when. In order to become a forensic scientist in a lab, one must obtain the necessary background for a particular forensic discipline. Historically, forensic scientists were members of police departments dedicated to the testing of evidentiary items without explicit education requirements (Houck & Siegel, 2009). However, this is no longer the case, as the field of forensic science has advanced and specialized. Current forensic disciplines include forensic biology, latent fingerprints, firearms, and digital evidence. For the purposes of this chapter, we will focus on forensic biology as it is the most common testing type used in SAK testing. Forensic biology testing includes testing for the presence of biological fluid such as blood, semen, and saliva (Li et al., 2015). In order to become a DNA analyst, a forensic scientist must have a minimum of a BA/BS in biology, chemistry, or forensic science, and have taken coursework in statistics, population genetics, molecular biology, and biochemistry (Li et al., 2015).

Once educational requirements are met, there is additional training required by the quality assurance standards (QAS) of the laboratories. The QAS are determined by the FBI to ensure that any and all DNA profiles obtained from evidentiary items are acquired through standard operating procedures (SOPs) and accredited laboratories (FBI, 2020). The SOPs detail how to proceed with the testing of biological evidence. They are used to ensure consistency across testing (specifically for the types of materials used) and detail what steps need to be completed at the various stages of testing.

However, most SOPs do not detail explicitly what samples need to be taken forward for DNA testing. In fact, many only include guidelines as each case has differing levels of probative information (DC Department of Forensic Sciences, 2018; Houston

---

Box 16.1

Lab independence?

Do you think forensic labs should be independent of law enforcement agencies? How would we implement this separation and what would it look like?

Forensic Science Center, 2016; Indiana State Police, 2018). Probative information refers to explicit information included in the SAK paperwork, previously provided to the health-care professional by the victim. The level of information provided helps guide the scientists to determine which samples will more likely have DNA presumed to belong to the perpetrator (oftentimes called *foreign* DNA). So, it is up to the forensic scientist with their knowledge and experience (both educational and professional), who is randomly assigned, to determine which samples and how many (if not dictated by the SOP) will proceed with DNA testing.

Contents of a SAK

What is included (and not included) in a SAK? Forensic scientists examine the contents of a SAK to determine which items should be tested. Unfortunately, what is included in a SAK can vary substantially among jurisdictions (RAINN, n.d.). (See Figure 16.1 for the contents of a typical SAK.) According to the national protocol for sexual assault medical forensic examinations for adults/adolescents (Office of Violence Against Women, 2013), SAKs are required at minimum to contain:

- A kit container. Specifically, a container that has identifying information and evidence initiation forms to commence a chain of custody.
- Paperwork that includes a checklist of which items have been collected and from where on the body. This paperwork is what differs most between jurisdictions and in part drives the decisions of forensic scientists.
- Diagrams and synopsis information pertaining to details of the crime and where the victim was touched on their body.
- Specific evidentiary items (where applicable). Perianal/anal swabs, vaginal/penile swabs, oral swabs, body swabs, hair samples (jurisdiction specific), and patient's clothing (jurisdiction specific).

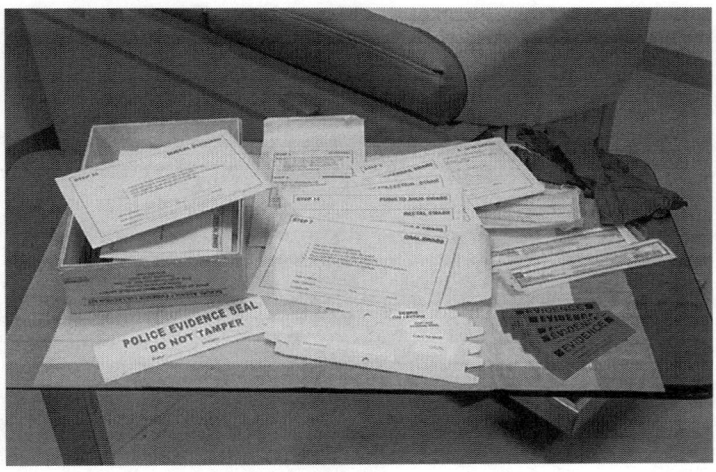

Figure 16.1 Example of Contents in a SAK

Source: Zak Gowans, Brigham Young University (2022).

Box 16.2

What is a DNA extract?

A *DNA extract* is the DNA portion of an evidentiary sample after testing is completed.

Box 16.3

What is a perianal swab?

Perianal swabs refer to the area between the rectum and the vagina. These swabs are often more comfortable to obtain as they are not inserted. They are also beneficial for testing purposes as there can be leakage between the vagina and the rectum.

- Evidence collection materials (to effectively store and maintain evidence). Some of these items include swab boxes/tubes and collection envelopes.
- A DNA sample from the victim (known or reference swab). This is used to be able to determine the portion of the profile that belongs to the victim compared to the "foreign DNA." DNA samples from victims are not entered into CODIS.

Testing Sexual Assault Kits

Once the kit is obtained, what types of evidence can DNA be obtained from it? DNA is most commonly presumed to be found in biological samples such as blood, semen, or saliva (Butler, 2009). However, DNA can also be found in "touch" samples. *Touch DNA* refers to cells left behind through contact when an individual touches something, e.g., ropes, knives, etc. (Butler, 2009). Touch DNA may also be on an individual who was touched by another person, even without any biological secretions. Touch DNA can occur with strangulation, grabbing onto clothing, or even holding hands. Unfortunately, touch samples are not an ideal source of DNA compared to blood, semen, or saliva (Butler, 2009; Williamson, 2012). Additionally, not all touch samples are equivalent. Touch DNA samples can differ depending on the type of contact the individual has with an object, better samples can be obtained with increased pressure or if the person has touched the item for a longer period of time (Valentine et al., 2021). So, if and when other potential sources of DNA are available, other than touch, those tend to be prioritized when proceeding to identify an individual. This is especially true if the total number of samples is limited during testing. This is largely because there is a higher chance of obtaining a profile from a sample that was obtained via a bodily fluid rather than through touch.

Now, what happens next? Prior to examining any evidentiary items, forensic scientists first read the case synopsis typically included in the paperwork within the kit. This synopsis contains very pertinent information as to what happened during the assault. Unfortunately, not all case synopses are the same. They can differ based on the level of information provided by the victim, what is actually recorded by the sexual assault nurse examiner (SANE), and even the jurisdiction (RAINN, n.d.). There is also no consistent methodology as to what is required of the SANE to include in the case synopsis (Campbell et al., 2005, see also Chapter 12). Among this variation, each scientist must make decisions based upon the synopsis of the rape documented in the kit's paperwork and what evidence is present in the SAK in front of them in order to determine the most effective testing plans. Many scholars highlight this inconsistency as a case efficiency issue for testing, as not every scientist may select the same items for testing, especially if they are limited in their selection (Strom et al., 2017).

But, what determines the number of samples that are permitted to be tested from one SAK? The answer is far more complex than just a given number. First, testing of SAK cases can occur in multiple rounds and at varying labs. Each lab has its own SOP for processing cases. For state laboratories, most SOP are public. However, this is not always the case with private labs, as it is considered proprietary information. Consequently, the number of samples selected for testing from the kits may be different depending on the lab that is processing the kit.

For example, according to the National Institute of Justice (NIJ), testing of kits ideally should occur in a multi-tiered testing approach (National Institute of Justice, 2017; see Figure 16.2). In this model, kits are preliminarily evaluated to determine which items are likely to be most probative, meaning that the item is most likely to result in obtaining a DNA profile. What this NIJ model does not indicate is *how many* samples this can include or *how* to determine which items are likely to be the most probative. *This determination is made by the forensic scientist and is subjective, based upon what the scientist reads and what information is provided.* Moreover, there is even variation in what is included in the kit, not solely the information provided in the kit paperwork. So, in testing a kit whether in the recommended model from NIJ or not, there is a high degree of variability, regardless of how many rounds of testing are performed.

There is also a monetary cost to testing more samples—including for multiple rounds of testing (Speaker, 2019; see also Chapter 17 for more information). Forensic scientists have a finite number of samples in the hopes of obtaining probative results. If no foreign DNA (presumed to belong to the perpetrator) is found, the case would have to be assessed again using a second set of finite samples. Each round of testing incurs a monetary cost to the lab and/or the funding agency. There is also a cost of time to both the victim, who may be patiently awaiting results, or an alleged perpetrator awaiting trial.

The NIJ model fails to specify who approves multiple rounds of testing and neglects to recognize that multiple rounds of testing are limited at private laboratories. The number of rounds of testing allowed is contingent on which lab it is sent to, as their SOPs vary, as do their contractual agreements with government labs. At state labs or other government-funded labs, it is at the discretion of the scientist or the agency funding the testing, dictated through the SOP, to determine if multiple rounds of testing would be useful. However, some kits are outsourced to private labs. At the private labs, contracts are negotiated between the vendor lab and the funding agency/state lab. These contracts entail how much the funding agency will pay for the testing of samples, and, because a monetary amount is provided, outsourcing labs are limited to certain numbers of samples per case and, thus,

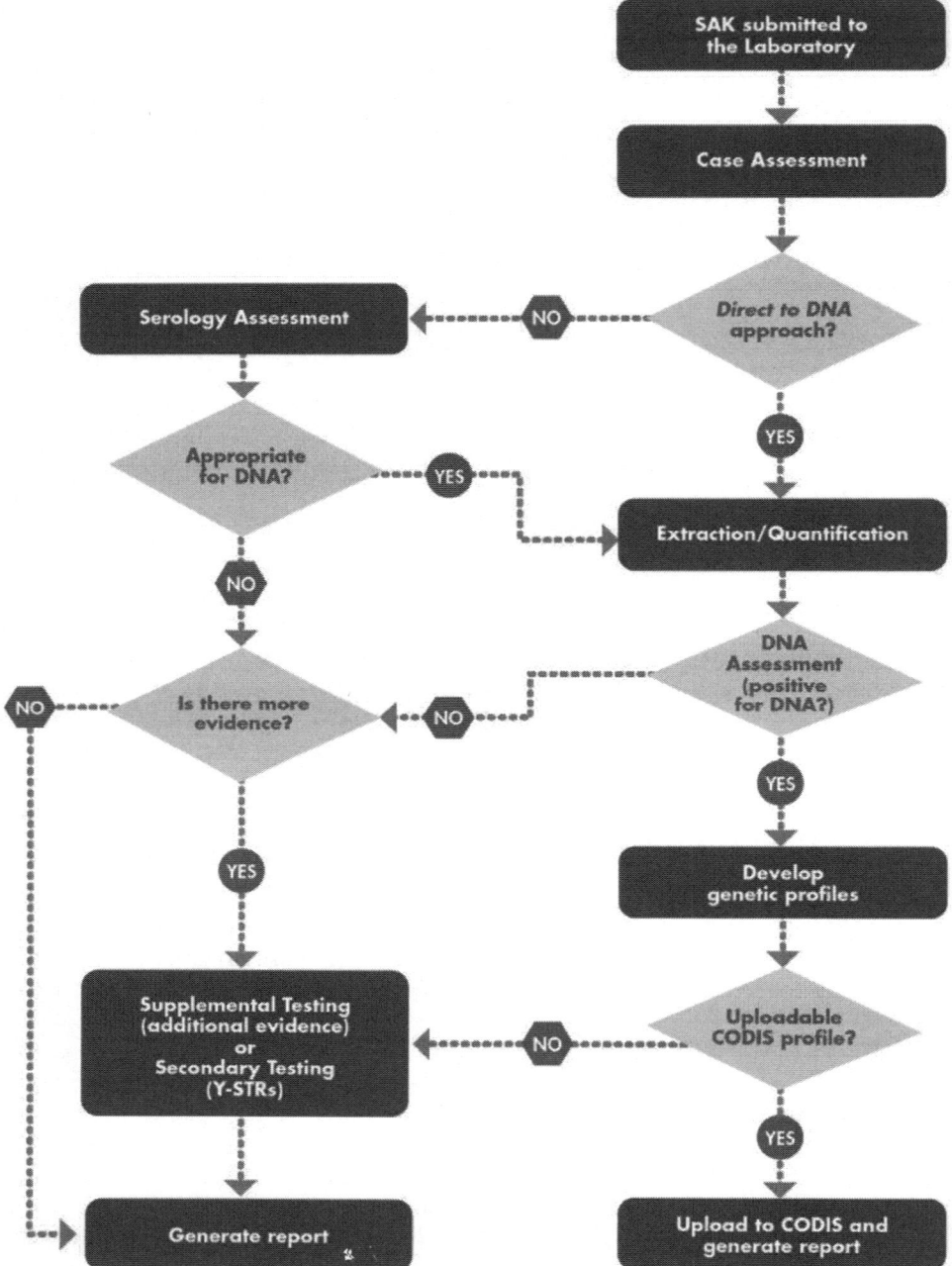

Figure 16.2 Recommended High-Throughput Process Flow for Sexual Assault Kits from the National Institute of Justice

Source: National Institute of Justice (2017).

Figure 16.3 High-Throughput Process for Private Laboratories

Source: Amended Figure from the National Institute of Justice (National Institute of Justice, 2017).

rounds of testing. Figure 16.3 demonstrates what traditionally occurs at private labs with only one round of testing.

Private laboratories are often limited to one round of testing and confined to what is dictated in their contractual agreements. One study determined the cost efficiency differences for evidence collected from property crimes between testing in state labs ("in house") compared to private ("outsourcing") and found that in some jurisdictions outsourcing *per sample* was $400 due to the contractual agreements, but the same samples cost between $108 and $280 in house (Roman et al., 2009). For sexual assault cases, the cost is much higher—costing between $236 and $2,300 per kit (Department of Justice (DOJ), 2006; Hobbs, 2011). The costs in these studies were purely for testing alone regardless of the case outcomes. Oftentimes the prices differ drastically, as outside laboratories are for-profit businesses compared to state laboratories. However, despite the price, it is often more beneficial to send the cases to outside laboratories to eliminate a backlog and abide by testing parameters (Sexual Assault Victims' Rights Act, 2019). The price increase does not stop at the testing level. Another study determined that the average cost of a SAK to reach conviction was $16,000 (Davis & Wells, 2019). This includes the cost of testing as well as the legal costs to reach a conviction. Notably, these studies do not show *how many* samples are tested in each of the cases to reach conviction or not.

An added complexity when looking at the cost and number of samples to test is that one sample does not necessarily yield one DNA extract. SAK samples are first presumed to have sperm present and go through what is called a differential extraction process.[1] In this process, the DNA is separated into two fractions: the sperm fraction and the epithelial fraction. The epithelial fraction contains skin cells that are non-specific to male or female DNA, but the sperm fraction specifically targets DNA from spermatozoa (Butler, 2009). This means that if one sample is selected for testing in a SAK, and is presumed to have sperm present, it will yield two DNA extracts. The number of samples dictated at the beginning of testing oftentimes does not take this into account, which can have downstream effects for the cost determination. Due to the costs, one study recommends tiered testing with the first rounds of testing to only include the three most probative samples (Wang et al., 2020). This study also found that there are no significant effects in applying this methodology to SAK testing (Wang et al., 2020).

So how many samples does one test? And for how many rounds? There is a balancing act in determining the number of samples to be tested in the first round of testing and this affects the possibility of outcomes and future testing. Overall, the likelihood of a sample having DNA and the tiered testing approach have the largest impact on which items will proceed with DNA testing. If the most probative items are presumed to have DNA, and are thus likely to be tested first, this may affect the chances of additional rounds of testing, and if anything can and should be tested next.

Box 16.4

Test all?

Should there be a requirement related to testing all evidence sample types per jurisdiction? Why or why not?

Forensic scientists serve as the gatekeepers in determining which samples get tested and when (Strom et al., 2017). Coming full circle to our earlier question: so, who and what determines the limit (if there is one) for how many samples are tested per SAK? Additional research is needed to decipher how forensic scientists determine which samples may proceed with DNA testing. What one scientist may deem as more probative another scientist may not, especially under the confines of a limited number of samples, less specific paperwork, and with cost considerations in mind.

Terms to remember

Table 16.1 provides a list of common forensic terms and definitions.

After the testing

What happens after the testing is complete? Forensic scientists often do not know what happens after the testing—the investigation and eventual prosecution of the case. The job of the forensic scientist is to solely test, write the lab report and speak to those findings (when needed or asked to do so). However, the goal in obtaining DNA within a sample is to *identify* an individual, but identification is not typically the end result.

Primarily, the identification process first starts by testing the evidence for potential biological data and then using the Combined DNA Index System (CODIS) for (ideally) final identification of an individual. CODIS is a DNA national database used by criminal justice entities that retain DNA profiles from convicted offenders, as well as unknown profiles that are attributed to the putative perpetrator(s)

Table 16.1 Common Forensic Terms and Definitions

Term	Definition
Differential extraction	Extraction process used when there is a presumed presence of sperm.
Sperm fraction	Sperm fraction resulting from differential extraction.
Epithelial fraction	Non-sex specific fraction resulting from differential extraction.
SOP	Standard operating procedures used by laboratories mandated by accrediting bodies to ensure the effective processing of evidence.
CODIS	Combined DNA Index System—DNA system that contains all profiles attributed to a putative perpetrator or those convicted of a crime.
Outsourcing	The process labs take to send excess casework to private laboratories for testing.

of a crime. This system is often used as an investigative tool to aid agencies in associating profiles with the putative perpetrator(s) (CODIS and NDIS Fact Sheet, 2016). However, not all evidentiary samples associated with the putative perpetrator are eligible for CODIS upload or search. Additionally, not every type of CODIS hit is associated with a named suspect. This is a common misconception about CODIS.

In order for a DNA profile to be deemed CODIS eligible, it must: be generated by an accredited laboratory that follows the Federal Bureau of Investigation's (FBI) QAS, meet the minimum locations of the DNA needed for upload, and the profile acquired from the evidentiary sample must be attributed to the putative perpetrator (CODIS and NDIS Fact Sheet, 2016). These regulations are in place to ensure that no victim profiles are uploaded. Only after passing the threshold of eligibility, the evidentiary profile may be uploaded into CODIS. Once uploaded, the CODIS database continuously searches for potential hits as additional crimes occur and more profiles are uploaded to the database.

However, if a hit does occur, it does not necessarily provide a name. A hit can link multiple cases together, provide a name (to which the profile is attributed), or both. A CODIS hit where a name is provided is known as an offender hit (a hit to an offender). A CODIS hit where a name is not attributed to a profile but is attributed to other cases is called a case-to-case hit. Sometimes a profile from one case can hit more than one case, including a named offender (offender hit). In other words, one profile can provide several different types of leads.

Based on the type of hit, varying investigative information can be provided to the investigative or prosecutorial agency and lead to differing outcomes. These can be arrests and/or convictions. Unfortunately, however, the linear association between the three is frequently presumed (that a CODIS hit will result in an arrest and an arrest will lead to a conviction). But not all arrests lead to convictions, just like not all CODIS hits lead to arrest. Each hit is considered a lead and does not automatically imply an arrest or conviction. In the case of sexual assault, sometimes the hit links to a consensual partner of the victim and not a suspect. In those instances, once a further investigation occurs to confirm it is the consensual partner, this DNA is (supposed to be) removed from CODIS. This is done to remove the possibility of being falsely associated with the sexual assault offense. Again, it all comes down to *if* DNA is obtained and if not, *what* samples were tested.

After the testing: Case outcomes

A backlog, defined by the NIJ, is "One that has not been tested 30 days after it was submitted to the laboratory" (Nelson, 2010). Due to this, there has been an ongoing conversation within the criminal justice community as to why the backlogs specifically at the lab exist and if testing the kits, years after the alleged offense, are worth testing in terms of cost (Wang & Wein, 2018). However, there are essential aspects of testing the kits that are not purely financial. They can also be useful as evidentiary samples for investigative purposes; identification to an alleged perpetrator is one of them. Identification of suspects, though, is only a possibility if the evidence is tested. The same is true for arrests. It all starts with the testing of the SAKs.

It is unknown to the full extent how large of a backlog there is of SAKs (Ritter, 2013). Recently though, it is estimated that there are currently up to 400,000 untested SAKs in the United States based on known counts from 2014 to 2018 in 15 states (Strom et al., 2021). Unfortunately, the identification of the backlog stems from a variety of issues within the criminal justice system. Specifically, police department submission of the kits is a known issue that prevents testing as well as prosecution (Campbell et al., 2017). However, addressing the backlog of the kits still does not ensure their prosecution.

Current policies attempt to address the backlog testing of SAKs in an effort to prevent future assaults from happening and attempt to give case closures to victims. Unfortunately, these policies are ineffective because the increased testing of kits does not ensure the prosecution of the cases. Additionally, the evidence obtained within a kit is oftentimes insufficient to proceed with prosecution because no contextual information is included. For example, there is an existing policy in Washington, DC called The Sexual Assault Victims' Rights Act of 2019 (SAVRAA), which mandates the testing of a SAK to be completed within 90 days (Sexual Assault Victims' Rights Act, 2019). This increased speed of testing, though, does not ensure arrests or prosecution, especially if the burden to provide the kits to the lab relies on police departments. The submission process of SAK often lies on the investigative agency and not the prosecutorial one (Patterson & Campbell, 2012). The constant shift in processes and movement in submission responsibility causes some SAK to sit for extended periods of time prior to being processed. But, despite their shelf life, their likelihood of prosecution is still the same (Campbell et al., 2017). Studies show that less than half of sexual assault cases, regardless of forensic evidence, are even prosecuted (Campbell et al., 2012; Peterson et al., 2012).

So, a logical response to the demonstrated inefficiencies in the prosecution and testing of SAK is to look at outside case-specific information that may aid in the prosecution of these offenses *in conjunction* with what is being tested and shift pressure from testing kits alone to looking at kits with contextual information gathered outside of the kit.

If there were increased government intervention in the investigation process, an overall understanding of the external factors, and which samples are more probative, this could aid in the prosecution of the cases. In doing this, there could be targeted strategies implemented to acquire evidence and contextual data outside of the SAK. These items may play a role in the perpetuation of an offense and may also play a role in the likelihood of prosecution. More importantly, kits, in conjunction with the investigative information obtained outside of the kit, can lead to increased case closures through either arrests or convictions.

Decision-Making and Case Examples

What guidance is provided to forensic scientists making these testing decisions? The overall testing goal is to use the samples that are presumed to not only be DNA rich but also have a reasonable expectation that the alleged perpetrator's DNA is present in the sample and simultaneously be the most probative. However, in order to determine this, forensic scientists must evaluate all of the information provided within the kit to determine which samples can proceed with testing. This is referred to as a "hierarchy of propositions" (Cook et al., 1998). Essentially, forensic scientists determine what additional information can be provided in testing a particular sample. The scientists decipher the information provided and determine which samples and how many, if not dictated by protocols, can aid the requesting agency in filling in gaps.

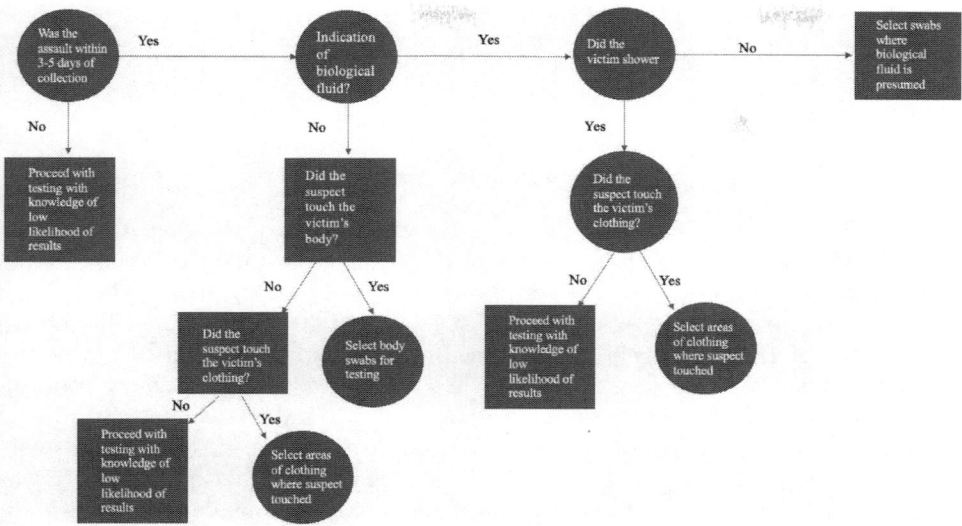

Figure 16.4 Decision-Making Tree for Forensic Scientists

In order to have effective decision-making, forensic scientists look at the varying details provided to determine which samples to proceed with (see Figure 16.4). These details can vary per kit as no two cases are the same. For illustrative purposes, below, I provide different case scenarios to highlight how the decision-making process occurs for the forensic scientist and how it may differ per case. Circling back to the various sources of DNA (touch or biological secretion), there are also other factors that can affect which samples are more likely to yield probative results. These will be highlighted in the case scenarios.

Case 1

Synopsis provided in the paperwork

Female victim states that she was walking home from the bar. Male suspect was following behind her and tapped her on the left shoulder. Victim turned around and was hit in the face by the suspect. The suspect began to pin the victim down with his hands and assault her. Victim indicates she was vaginally assaulted and does not remember if the assailant wore a condom. Victim states that the assailant also licked her face and various parts of her chest. After the assault, the victim quickly went home and discarded her clothing prior to getting examined for a SAK. The victim obtained the kit the same night of the assault.

Evidence collected

The following items of evidence were collected in Case 1's SAK:

- Vaginal swab
- Anal/perianal swab

- Buccal swab (known DNA swab)
- Face swab of cheek
- Swab of breasts
- Swab of mouth

Going through the flow chart

Based on the case synopsis and evidentiary swabs collected, the first observation is that the kit was collected the same day of the assault. This increases the chances of DNA being present within a sample as it degrades over time. The second observation from this case synopsis indicates that there is presumed biological fluid (saliva) on the victim's chest as well as potential semen (vaginally). Although there is an indication that the suspect touched the victim's clothing, none was collected within the kit. If testing were to proceed, as Wang et al. (2020) recommend with three samples, we would only proceed with the testing of the vaginal swab, breast swab, and perianal swab. Even though there is no indication that there was anal penetration, proceeding with the anal swab is recommended as oftentimes, there is leakage and movement of fluids from the vaginal area to the perianal/anal area.

If no probative DNA samples were obtained from the first three swabs selected, the forensic scientist would then proceed with the mouth swab and the face swab of cheek. Despite the fact that these samples are likely to yield probative results because they are from biological fluids, and they were taken the night of the offense, the testing would have been limited because of the number of samples. In this case, more efficient testing could be accomplished if all items proceeded with testing in the hypothetical first round.

Case 2

Synopsis provided in the paperwork

Male victim states that they were at a party when the assault occurred. The victim was alone in the room with another male suspect. The suspect pinned the victim to the bed tearing the victim's shorts and anally penetrated him. The victim says that he was able to fight back and scratch the suspect's face. The victim also states that he recalls the suspect putting on a condom during the assault. After the assault, the victim went home and showered. Two days later, the victim obtained a SAK and brought the shorts that he wore the night of the offense.

Evidence collected

The following items of evidence were collected in Case 2's SAK:

- Anal swab
- Fingernail clippings
- Victim's shorts
- Buccal swab (known DNA swab from the victim)

Going through the flow chart

Based on the case synopsis, the testing plan is not as clear as the first case scenario. First, the victim showered after the assault which affects the likelihood of DNA being obtained (RAINN, n.d.). This would cause the forensic scientist to look at other potential items other than any swabs collected directly from the body of the assailant. Additionally, the kit was collected two days after the assault and there was showering. This lowers the likelihood of DNA being present in the sample even more. So, if this case were to follow a tiered testing approach, the only most probative item to proceed with testing would be the torn shorts. However, if testing were to proceed with the three samples, all of the evidentiary items obtained in this kit could proceed with testing. Even though the case information is the same, the SOPs and the forensic scientist deciphering the case may have different interpretations as to what is considered most probative.

Future Directions for SAK Testing

Highlighted throughout this chapter was the use and decision-making of forensic scientists as a mechanism toward case closures and prosecutions. Collected evidence is only a portion of the necessary information in order to proceed with case closures. Testing kits alone is not a solution for a reformed response to rape. Rather, further evaluation is needed to determine where the kit is being tested and what is in the kit. Specifically, we need to consider how many items there are within the kit and which ones will increase case closures.

Moving forward, future studies of SAK testing should seek to address the following:

1 What is the financial cost to the lab to test all items of evidence included in a SAK? In doing this, are similar prosecution levels achieved?
2 What other characteristics (outside of the kit) affect the chances of prosecution?
3 What are the outcomes of multiple rounds of testing for sexual assault cases?

Much more research needs to be done to answer these questions. By furthering research like this, forensic labs will be able to triage case information and prosecutorial entities will be able to evaluate what information is more effective in closing cases. Testing of sexual assault cases should not be restricted depending on where the kit goes. Additionally, kits should not be limited to certain rounds of testing. Criteria should be determined to test the efficacy of samples, and if a sample contained within the kit meets those requirements, a full case should be tested. In creating multiple rounds of testing, many kits may fall through the cracks, as it is still unclear who determines if a kit can go through more than one round of testing. The victims of the assault should not bear the weight of extended time for multiple rounds of testing.

Key Points

- There are different types of DNA samples: (1) touch and (2) those presumed to come from biological fluid (e.g., blood, semen, saliva)

- State and private labs can have varying strategies for SAK testing

  - Can be determined monetarily or through tiered testing approaches

- Just because a sample is tested doesn't mean: (1) DNA is present and (2) an individual is identified
- Results for forensic scientists are different than for attorneys or victims
- Based on what evidence is in the kit, and what information is present not every item will be tested
- The decision-making process of which samples are tested is in part subjective

Discussion Questions

1 Should there be a limit to the number of samples tested per SAK?
2 What is the monetary cost of a SAK? How should it be determined?
3 Who should pay the expense for the kit testing (i.e., victims, labs, lawyers, the public)?
4 Who should pay for the collection and storage of the SAKs?

a How would this be funded?

5 Who should decide which and how many samples are tested?
6 Should there be a defined set of samples to test? If so, only in certain instances (e.g., the victim does not recall what occurred during the assault)?

Note

1 Most reported sexual assault cases have a male suspect. However, kits where there is a female suspect go through a separate extraction process as there is no sperm or Y chromosome in female DNA. Evidence where there is presumed to have same-sex DNA does not go through the differential extraction process.

Further Reading

Mourtgos, S. M., Adams, I. T., Nix, J., & Richards, T. (2021). Mandatory sexual assault kit testing policies and arrest trends: A natural experiment. *Justice Evaluation Journal*, 4(1), 145–162.

National Institute of Justice. (n.d.). *Sexual assault kits using science to find solutions.* https://nij.ojp.gov/sites/g/files/xyckuh171/files/media/document/unsubmitted-kits.pdf

National Research Council. (2009). *Strengthening forensic science in the United States: A path forward.* National Academies Press.

Pinchevsky, G. M. (2018). Criminal justice considerations for unsubmitted and untested sexual assault kits: A review of the literature and suggestions for moving forward. *Criminal Justice Policy Review*, 29(9), 925–945.

Wells, W., Fansher, A. K., & Campbell, B. A. (2019). The results of CODIS-hit investigations in a sample of cases with unsubmitted sexual assault kits. *Crime & Delinquency*, 65(1), 122–148.

References

Butler, J. M. (2009). *Fundamentals of forensic DNA typing.* Academic Press.

Campbell, R., Feeney, H., Fehler-Cabral, G., Shaw, J., & Horsford, S. (2017). The national problem of untested sexual assault kits (SAKs): Scope, causes, and future directions for research, policy, and practice. *Trauma, Violence, & Abuse, 18*(4), 363–376. https://doi.org/10.1177/1524838015622436

Campbell, R., Patterson, D., & Bybee, D. (2012). Prosecution of adult sexual assault cases: A longitudinal analysis of the impact of a sexual assault nurse examiner program. *Violence against Women, 18*(2), 223–244.

Campbell, R., Patterson, D., & Lichty, L. F. (2005). The effectiveness of sexual assault nurse examiner (SANE) programs: A review of psychological, medical, legal, and community outcomes. *Trauma, Violence, & Abuse, 6*(4), 313–329.

CODIS and NDIS Fact Sheet. (2016, June 8). Retrieved July 23, 2021, from https://www.fbi.gov/services/laboratory/biometric-analysis/codis/codis-and-ndis-fact-sheet

Cook, R., Evett, I. W., Jackson, G., Jones, P. J., & Lambert, J. A. (1998). A hierarchy of propositions: Deciding which level to address in casework. *Science & Justice, 38*(4), 231–239.

Davis, R. C., & Wells, W. (2019). DNA testing in sexual assault cases: When do the benefits outweigh the costs? *Forensic Science International, 299*, 44–48.

DC Department of Forensic Sciences (2018). *FBS01 – General procedures for forensic biological evidence examination.* https://dfs.dc.gov/sites/default/files/dc/sites/dfs/publication/attachments/FBS01%20-%20Guidelines%20for%20Forensic%20Biological%20Evidence%20Examination.pdf

Department of Justice (DOJ), Office of State Budget and Management. (2006). *Cost study of DNA testing and analysis.* Retrieved from https://files.nc.gov/ncosbm/documents/files/3-1-2006FinalDNAReport.pdf

Federal Bureau of Investigations (FBI). (2020). *Quality assurance standards for forensic DNA testing laboratories.* https://www.fbi.gov/file-repository/qas-guidance-document-070120.pdf

Hobbs, J. M. (2011). *Testing failure: Prompt analysis of sexual assault evidence. 10 ideas for equal justice.* Retrieved from https://www.scribd.com/document/61681245/10-Ideas-for-Equal-Justice-2011

Houck, M. M., & Siegel, J. A. (2009). *Fundamentals of forensic science.* Academic Press.

Houston Forensic Science Center (2016). *Forensic biology DNA SOP manual.* https://houstonforensicscience.org/sop/1jRJOAZcZ3qTWQGgyXLXmSfnywFsy.pdf

Indiana State Police. (2018). *Standard operating procedure: Victim sexual assault kit evidence submission requirements.* https://www.in.gov/isp/files/Sexual%20Assault%20Kit%20Evidence%20Submission.pdf

Li, R., Norman, S., & Schober, J. (2015). *Forensic biology.* CRC Press.

National Institute of Justice. (2017). *National best practices for sexual assault kits: A multidisciplinary approach.* https://www.ojp.gov/pdffiles1/nij/250384.pdf

Nelson, M. (2010). *Making sense of DNA backlogs: Myths vs. reality.* National Institute of Justice, Office of Justice Programs, US Department of Justice.

Office on Violence against Women, US Department of Justice. (2013). *A national protocol for sexual assault medical forensic examinations: Adult/adolescents* (2nd ed.). (Report #NCJ 228119). https://www.ncjrs.gov/pdffiles1/ovw/241903.pdf

Patterson, D., & Campbell, R. (2012). The problem of untested sexual assault kits: Why are some kits never submitted to a crime laboratory? *Journal of Interpersonal Violence, 27*(11), 2259–2275. https://doi.org/10.1177/0886260511432155

Peterson, J., Johnson, D., Herz, D., Graziano, L., & Oehler, T. (2012). *Sexual assault kit backlog study.* The National Institute of Justice.

RAINN. (n.d.). *What is a sexual assault forensic exam?* Retrieved July 28, 2021, from https://www.rainn.org/articles/rape-kit

Ritter, N. (2013). Untested evidence in sexual assault cases. *Sexual Assault Report, 16*(3), 33–34.

Roman, J. K., Reid, S. E., Chalfin, A. J., & Knight, C. R. (2009). The DNA field experiment: A randomized trial of the cost-effectiveness of using DNA to solve property crimes. *Journal of Experimental Criminology, 5*(4), 345–369.

Sexual Assault Victims' Rights Act § 201 (2019). https://ovsjg.dc.gov/sites/default/files/dc/sites/ovsjg/service_content/attachments/Sexual%20Assault%20Victims%27%20Rights%20Amendment%20Act%20of%202019.pdf

Siegel, J. A. (2019, February 7). *Crime laboratory. Encyclopedia Britannica.* https://www.britannica.com/science/crime-laboratory

Speaker, P. J. (2019). The jurisdictional return on investment from processing the backlog of untested sexual assault kits. *Forensic Science International: Synergy, 1*, 18–23.

Strom, K., Hendrix, J., Parish, W., & Melton, P. (2017). *Efficiency in processing sexual assault kits in crime laboratories and law enforcement agencies.* RTI International. https://www.ojp.gov/pdffiles1/nij/grants/250682.pdf

Valentine, J. L., Presler-Jur, P., Mills, H., & Miles, S. (2021). Evidence collection and analysis for touch deoxyribonucleic acid in groping and sexual assault cases. *Journal of Forensic Nursing, 17*(2), 67–75.

Wang, Z., MacMillan, K., Powell, M., & Wein, L. M. (2020). A cost-effectiveness analysis of the number of samples to collect and test from a sexual assault. *Proceedings of the National Academy of Sciences, 117*(24), 13421–13427.

Wang, C., & Wein, L. M. (2018). Analyzing approaches to the backlog of untested sexual assault kits in the USA. *Journal of Forensic Sciences, 63*(4), 1110–1121.

Williamson, A. L. (2012). Touch DNA: Forensic collection and application to investigations. *Journal of the Association of Crime Scene Reconstruction, 18*(1), 1–5.

17 Current understanding of the cost-effectiveness of testing sexual assault kits

Paul J. Speaker

Author Note

The opinions or points of view expressed in this chapter are solely those of the author and do not reflect the official positions of any participating organization or the US Department of Justice.

Advancements in Understanding the Cost-Effectiveness of Testing Sexual Assault Kits

The previous chapters highlight the recent history and developments with sexual assault kit (SAK) testing, including the more recent attempts to catalog and test the previously unsubmitted SAKs (see Chapters 1, 6, and 10). The arguments supporting the testing of all cataloged and untested SAKs are convincing on ethical grounds but have run into the age-old economic problem of unlimited wants but limited resources. Faced with such a dilemma, economists conduct cost-benefit analyses to weigh the potential gains from an activity and compare the gains achieved by the commitment of the same funds toward alternative uses. The objective is to take the limited funds and apply them toward the highest valued uses with the eventual result in the greatest degree of satisfaction or value. Detailing the costs and benefits of an activity permits the calculation of a metric, return on investment (ROI), which measures the net benefit (i.e., benefits net of costs) relative to the total costs of the action. Since we express ROI as a percent return, decision-makers may compare the ROI of one activity directly with alternative uses of funds. For example, a policy maker could assess the ROI of testing SAKs and compare it with the ROI from spending those funds on an additional police car or the ROI from infrastructure investment.

The discussion of testing the unsubmitted SAKs has dominated much of the recent focus on responses to sexual assault, but as we learn more, the discussion extends to policies toward the testing of all newly submitted SAKs (see Chapter 18). The current chapter introduces the economic argument for the degree of testing SAKs, including unsubmitted SAKs, backlogs of submitted SAKs, and *de novo* SAKs moving forward. Economic theory and statistical analysis provide the foundation for the development of objective evidence for policy makers to rely on as a supplement to moral and ethical arguments for action.

Economic Measures

Economists evaluate opportunities for action by comparing the benefits from a particular action with the corresponding costs from taking that action (Houck &

DOI: 10.4324/9781003186816-20

Speaker, 2020; Hunt et al., 2019; Kurimski et al., 2017). The benefits may involve easily identified gains such as monetary returns. For example, a share of common stock purchased for $1.00 today that is sold for $1.25 a year from today yields a gain or net benefit of $0.25. However, in many circumstances, those benefits represent expected costs avoided. For example, the purchase of a home alarm system reduces the likelihood of a home robbery; in this case, the economic benefit we measure is the expected loss avoided. Rather than measuring some received benefit, the metric estimates what would have happened if that specific action had not been taken.

The ultimate decision regarding taking a course of action follows from maximizing the gains from the benefits over the costs, subject to available resources. For public sector decisions (i.e., government), society must receive benefits that exceed the costs expended. The measure of the additional benefits compared to the additional costs is then expressed as either the dollar benefit per dollar expended or as an ROI, where ROI = (benefits – cost)/costs. Both the percentage metric ROI and the dollar benefit per dollar extended permit easier comparison to alternative uses of public funds. Since every government entity will have a budget limitation, each must choose among many alternative investments that offer positive ROI. A ranking of projects based upon ROI offers some objective support for conducting that project in comparison to conducting other projects to reach other societal goals.

The ROI from Testing the Backlog and Unsubmitted SAKs

Crime scene investigation (CSI), popularized with various television programming, suggests a somewhat romantic occupation populated by dazzling scientists with unparalleled access to technology. *Law & Order: Special Victims Unit* is one such program that has highlighted the capability of the testing of SAKs in support of the investigation of sexual assaults. While the CSI-type programs provide a sense of the capability of the science, the reality faced by forensic crime laboratories is a lack of funding and associated resources for the quick turnaround time (TAT) analysis that is typically depicted in these television programs. For example, a sample of crime laboratories in 2020 indicated that TAT for DNA testing ranged from 16 to 816 days, with a median TAT of 143 days (Speaker, 2021). More than half of the crime laboratories in this sample demonstrated a backlog of more than 70% of submitted cases.[1] That backlog only references the cases that were submitted to crime laboratories. Recent estimates of the unsubmitted cases suggest that roughly 350,000 SAKs have yet to be sent to the forensic laboratory for testing (Campbell & Fehler-Cabral, 2020; Lovell et al., 2021; Strom et al., 2021).

Various studies have broached the ethical, moral, and justice arguments for the testing of SAKs and sought to examine why such a high volume of SAKs never reached the forensic laboratory (see Chapters 1 and 2). These studies have been joined by economic examination of the testing of the unsubmitted and untested SAKs (Speaker, 2019b; Wang, et al., 2020; Wang & Wein, 2018). The economic analyses ask the simple question as to whether the economic benefits from testing SAKs outweigh the economic costs from doing so. These economic studies provide additional support to the ethical, moral, and justice arguments for the testing of SAKs as they conclude that there is a high ROI to society for testing all SAKs (Briody, 2000; Campbell & Fehler-Cabral, 2020; Doleac, 2017; Doleac, 2021; Speaker, 2019a).

Consider what constitutes a measurable benefit from the testing of SAKs. A successful program of investigation (including testing and perpetrator identification) leading to conviction could prevent a further assault by the perpetrator. Additionally, the testing may add value via the avoidance of misidentification should the test exonerate a suspect. By preventing additional assaults by that perpetrator, potential future victims do not have to endure the pain, suffering, and treatment from a subsequent assault. There are many types of savings in the form of avoided expenses to treat the physical and mental trauma, lost productivity, and post-assault security expenditures.

To measure these savings, several questions must be resolved. Among those questions:

- What happens if a SAK is not examined?
- How frequently does a rapist continue to assault if left unchecked?
- How frequently is a DNA profile of the assailant obtained from a SAK?
- If a DNA profile is obtained, how likely is it to result in a CODIS hit?
- If there is a CODIS hit, what is the likelihood of a conviction?
- What are the costs borne by the survivors of sexual assault?
- What are the costs to the rest of society when a sexual assault occurs?
- What are the costs that we expect to avoid if SAKs are tested?

Several studies address these questions and when the answers are combined, we obtain measures of the benefits from testing SAKs. The role of the economist is to take the research by sociologists, psychologists, statisticians, mathematicians, and economists to provide a profile of the "typical" costs avoided.

Cost-Benefit analysis (or marginal cost vs. marginal benefit analysis) estimates the additional benefits from a particular action against the additional costs associated with that action. Wang and Wein (2018) utilized the marginal cost-marginal benefit technique when they evaluated the efficacy of testing the approximately 350,000 untested SAKs that are part of the US backlog. They used the outcomes from several efforts by jurisdictions to identify and test the previously unsubmitted SAKs (Bashford, 2013; Campbell et al., 2017; DeLisi et al., 2010; Lussier et al., 2011). Taking a conservative approach that adopts outcomes from several studies, they developed a mathematical model to provide a lower estimate of the societal benefits from testing these SAKs.

Consider the Questions Posed Above

What happens if a SAK is not examined?

Evidence suggests that if left unchecked, the perpetrator often continues to assault (see Chapter 7). The survivor of the assault must deal with the physical and emotional toll of the assault. That toll includes immediate medical costs to deal with the physical pain and injury as well as long-term costs to treat the mental and psychological trauma (see Chapter 8). Additional costs include increased expenditures for security, diminished productivity and the resultant lost income, and the costs to others, such as friends, family, and the community.

How frequently does a rapist continue to assault if left unchecked?

Answering this question requires some sense of the typical length of the active career of a rapist who has never been caught. Lussier et al. (2011) investigated the behavior of rapists who avoided conviction and yet acknowledged their criminal behavior after the statutes of limitation had expired for their assaults. The results were widely distributed, however, the average number of assaults per perpetrator was 7.1 times per year. Additionally, the period of activity during which the rapist was active varied considerably but followed well-known statistical distributions with an average active period before the first conviction of 3.69 years. Taken together, the 7.1 sexual assaults per year multiplied by the average of 3.69 years of activity equals an average of 26.22 sexual assaults after the first assault and prior to conviction. *Thus, the benefit from testing a SAK from the first assault is the avoidance of an additional 26.22 sexual assaults.*

The next two questions seek to determine: **How frequently will a DNA profile of the assailant be obtained from a SAK? How frequently will an obtained profile provide a match to a profile in the DNA database?** Wells et al. (2016) provide comparative CODIS hit rates from samples of untested SAKs in Detroit, Los Angeles, and New Orleans to consider results from the SAK testing program in Houston. They found similar CODIS hit rates across jurisdictions. Since Wang and Wein (2018) concentrated on the testing of previously unsubmitted SAKs, they limited their analysis to prior studies that tested all uncovered and previously unsubmitted SAKs from various projects. Following the Detroit testing of all previously untested SAKs, they used the relative frequency of "hits" of 0.316 in place of the probability of finding a DNA profile. A "hit" refers to a SAK that yields a CODIS-eligible DNA profile. *This probability indicates that for every 100 kits tested, between 31 and 32 SAKs can be expected to yield a DNA hit.*

If there is a CODIS hit, what is the likelihood of a conviction?

To illustrate how this estimate was generated, consider the New York City effort to uncover and test all of the unsubmitted SAKs in Manhattan (Bashford, 2013). Table 17.1 highlights the outcomes, where 35% of the unsubmitted SAKs yielded DNA beyond the DNA of the survivor. Unfortunately, nearly 60% of those profiles were associated with a crime for which the statute of limitations had expired. Some

Table 17.1 Testing Manhattan SAKs

Tested	3,777
No DNA	2,448
Hits	1,329
Statute run out	792
Missing victim or police file	32
Victim won't press charges	30
Victim recanted or compromised	76
DNA not conclusive	29
Already arrested	279
Open cases	44
Convictions	49

Box 17.1

News headlines are teasers that may mislead

Headline: "After 3 Years and $1.5 Million Testing Rape Kits, Alaska Made One New Arrest."

By Kyle Hopkins, Anchorage Daily News, Dec. 30, 2020

Upon seeing such a headline, you might have the pre-conceived notion that testing the backlog of untested SAKs is an expensive and fruitless venture. What value should be attached to the testing of previously shelved SAKs?

10% of those profiles involved cases where either the police file was missing or the person victimized could not be contacted, recanted, or would not press charges. Another 21% of those profiles connected with individuals already under arrest for other criminal charges. Ultimately, at the time of the Bashford presentation, 3.7% of the profiles resulted in a conviction for the sexual assault (see Box 17.1).

The next question to consider is **"What are the costs borne by the survivor of sexual assault?"** Placing a dollar value on horrific events can seem a bit cold, but that is the task asked of economists in any situation of loss ranging from vehicle or workplace accidents to medical malpractice to terrorist attacks. The economics of crime is no exception. DeLisi et al. (2010) collected an extensive sample that included victims across five categories of criminal activity (homicide, rape, armed robbery, aggravated assault, and burglary) to ascertain the cost to victims and society from various crimes. Their sample accounted for a variety of costs borne by the victims of crime, including the costs for medical care (physical and psychological), lost income from expected future earnings, public sector expenditures in support of crime victims, the value of any property damage or losses, and a monetization of losses from deterioration in the quality of life. For the survivors of rape, the sample yielded a wide range of victim costs with a high of $2.24 million. *However, the average victim cost from a sexual assault was determined to be $172,348.*[2]

What are the costs to the rest of society when a sexual assault occurs?

DeLisi et al. (2010) included an assessment of the additional costs beyond those of the crime victim. These costs include costs to the justice system (policing, courts, jails, and prisons), productivity losses from the offense, and willingness-to-pay (WTP) expenditures. WTP represents those expenditures that arise as a means to avoid crime, such as personal security expenditures (e.g., home alarm system) and behavior modifications to avoid being victimized (e.g., ride share in place of walking), insurance costs, and social expenditures to enhance safety and avoid crimes (e.g., enhanced street lights). *As with the victim costs of sexual assault, the sample from rape cases saw a wide range of WTP expenditures going as high as $4.81 million, with an average WTP expenditure of $370,228 (2021 dollars).* Thus, by combining the direct survivor costs with the other societal costs, a single sexual assault has an average monetized expense of $558,916. This represents the benefit to society (i.e., cost savings) for each sexual assault that is avoided.

Wang and Wein (2018) then estimated the net benefits from testing SAKs using results from prior studies on the relative frequency of convictions (Bashford, 2013), the relative frequency of DNA hits from SAKS (Campbell et al., 2016), the relative frequency of sexual assaults (Lussier et al., 2011), the years of activity of rapists (Lussier, 2014) combined with the costs of SAK testing (DeLisi et al., 2010) and the direct and indirect costs from sexual assault (DeLisi et al., 2010). To obtain the estimated returns from testing, Wang and Wein multiplied the estimated probability of a conviction by the probability of a DNA hit from testing by the expected number of sexual assaults avoided by the direct and indirect costs from a sexual assault. They did this to address this question. **Given this testing of all of the previously unsubmitted SAKs, was it worth it?** Wang and Wein demonstrate that yes, the monetary benefits to society far exceed the costs of testing. *In their conservative estimation, they show the returns to be $81 for every $1 spent or a societal ROI exceeding 8,000%.* However, when more detail on the cost of testing is considered, the societal gains are even more substantial (Speaker, 2019b). Table 17.1 includes some 44 cases that were unresolved at the time of the Bashford presentation. When the open cases are subjected to the same probability conditions, the expected benefit from testing increases dramatically—more than double the conservative estimates from Wang and Wein. *"Now that there is an economic argument to buttress the moral argument, there are no excuses: The backlog must be tested" (Wein, 2018).*

Wang and Wein emphasize that this estimate represents the lower bound of the benefits from testing and only indicates benefits derived from a conviction after the first assault. Many benefits are not included in the measures highlighted above. The DNA analysis conducted by forensic scientists is an objective process intended to lead the justice system toward truth. Conviction is the only outcome measured above. Exoneration also has benefits, as does the testing of SAKs that did not yield a DNA profile. These benefits have not yet been considered in economic analyses conducted to date.

The Cost of Testing

Detailed information on the cost of testing is available from Project FORESIGHT (Houck et al., 2009) with updated information available annually on the cost of DNA testing (e.g., Speaker, 2021). The economic interpretation of the net benefits from examining the unsubmitted SAKs found in Wang and Wein (2018) relies on a single estimate for the cost of testing. The analysis used a cost of DNA testing of $1,641, based on a conservative cost figure from a few jurisdictions. The economics underlying the cost of testing is a little more complicated than presented in the conservative demonstration undertaken by Wang and Wein.

One law in economics is the Law of Diminishing Marginal Returns (LDMR), which indicates that as we add more resources to the provision of goods and services, eventually, the rate of increase in output falls. This leads to the economic concept of economy of scale; namely, there is a best size for all enterprises. To illustrate, consider two different businesses: a coffee shop, such as Starbucks, and a big box retailer, such as Walmart. It would be unprofitable for a Starbucks to occupy the same space as the big box retail store. It would have wasted space and been too expensive to generate a profit. On the other hand, a Walmart would not fit within the coffee shop space. In each case, it would be too costly for the businesses to survive as their competitors will operate at lower costs and push them out of business.

Now, consider an operation that does not have to generate profits to remain in business. Most forensic DNA laboratories operate in the public sector to serve a political jurisdiction. As a government entity, these laboratories do not face the market factors that would force an operation to perfect economies of scale (i.e., the lowest average cost possible for that activity). Figure 17.1 illustrates the average cost of DNA casework analysis from the 146 DNA laboratories Project FORESIGHT submissions for the fiscal year 2020 (Speaker, 2021). Figure 17.1 illustrates a point for each laboratory's average cost relative to its corresponding caseload. The overlaying curve represents the econometric estimate of the relationship between caseload and average cost for this data. The downward-sloped portion of the U-shaped curve shows the economies of scale that are achieved as caseload is increased, while the upward-sloped portion of the curve illustrates the diseconomies of scale as caseload increases beyond perfect economies of scale. Notice that the vast majority of public sector DNA laboratories operate along the downward-sloped portion, which suggests that the lab's average costs will continue to fall for some time as the laboratory increases its analysis of DNA cases. The jurisdiction's crime rate will influence the ability to achieve greater economies of scale, as will local restrictions on the activity of the laboratory. A higher crime rate will result in more evidence sent to the laboratory and lower average costs, but greater crime is not desired. An expansion of "for fee" services, such as genealogical DNA analysis, could also help to lower average costs, provided the jurisdiction permits such practices by the laboratory. The vast majority of the laboratories illustrated by the data points in Figure 17.1 have unrealized gains from economies of scale. DNA analysis of previously unsubmitted SAKs will result in lower average costs and greater returns on investment.

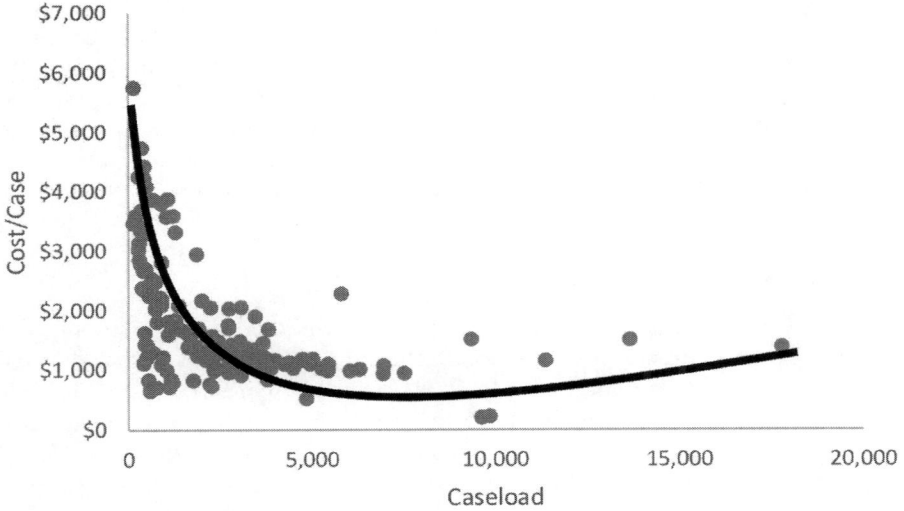

Figure 17.1 DNA Casework Cost/Case vs. Caseload

The Return from Testing de novo SAKs

While a great deal of attention has been placed on the unsubmitted SAKs, there is also a nationwide movement to consider "test all" policies for SAKs. Similar economic procedures may be used to estimate the net benefits from such policies (Speaker, 2019b; Wang et al., 2020). Reconsider the details in Table 17.1 when viewed as SAK laboratory submissions immediately following an assault. *Even if the same DNA hit rate is experienced, the ability to include cases where the statute of limitations has not run out or where the perpetrator is not already under arrest would lead to a much higher expected benefit in testing.*

Table 17.1 illustrates this situation. In this example, the statute of limitations had run its course for 792 of the cases. Another 279 cases found the DNA match, but it was with someone already imprisoned. Imagine instead that the SAKs for these cases had not been warehoused and instead had been immediately tested. **Doing this, the expected CODIS hit rate rises from 3.7% of the unsubmitted cases to an estimated 28.76% of the *de novo* cases (Speaker, 2019b).**

The relationship between a greater level of testing and the average cost of that testing is a dynamic relationship. For the laboratories illustrated in Figure 17.1, nearly 98% of them operate on the downward-sloped portion of the average cost curve. If they were to increase the DNA testing of SAKs, they could expect their average costs to decline. If a laboratory's jurisdiction allocates additional funding for testing the previously unsubmitted SAKs or adopts a "test all" policy, average costs will decline and the corresponding ROI will increase.

For example, the typical jurisdiction that analyzes 1,000 DNA cases per year would receive the benefits of $558,916 for each sexual assault case and incur an average cost of $1,806. This yields an ROI of 30,848%, which is even more dramatic than the conservative estimate by Wang and Wein (2018). The dynamic situation illustrated above from economies of scale suggests that a doubling of cases to 2,000 cases per year would raise the ROI to 38,903% as average costs fall to $1,433. A laboratory would continue to realize huge gains until it reaches perfect economies of scale.

These dramatic gains raise questions as to why such funds have not been allocated to date. The forensic laboratory competes with other worthwhile endeavors for the allocation of public funding. Perhaps the answer rests simply with the telling of the economic story in support of the ethical and moral arguments to test all SAKs. ROI offers a convenient and compelling metric to assist in the direction of public funds among competing uses from infrastructure to justice.

The Value from Additions to the DNA Database

SAK research using economics, statistics, and mathematical modeling continues to evaluate the value of forensic investigation in the administration of justice. The use of DNA databases has coordinated attempts to connect the perpetrators of crime with the DNA profiles collected to date. To determine value, studies often begin with a look at the relative frequency of matches between a DNA sample and the DNA database as a proxy for the probability of matches for other offenses.

While the technique of assigning probabilities from the relative frequency proxy is an accepted practice, Campbell et al. (2016) point out that care must be taken to not misuse this technique when it comes to sexual assault cases. In their examination of the previously untested SAKs, they note that decisions to prioritize stranger over non-stranger assault cases suffer from an erroneous use of the relative frequency of DNA database hits. Cases of non-stranger assaults often never made it to testing in the forensic laboratory since the identification of the alleged assault was known. However, should the accused individual commit a sexual assault in the future (stranger or non-stranger case), there would be no possibility of a match.

The lack of testing was a self-perpetuating problem. A CODIS hit cannot be realized if a profile has not been entered into the DNA database. Non-stranger sexual assault cases are more likely to have lower hit rates as long as a practice of not testing non-stranger assaults persists. Each non-stranger assault could be a repeat sexual assault by either a serial non-stranger rapist or a stranger rapist. This lower relative frequency of hits to the database is not an indication that stranger cases should be prioritized; rather, it suggests that a lower hit rate is a product of poor historical decision-making.

What happens when there is an addition to the DNA database? Doleac (2017) demonstrates that each addition (not merely DNA hits) offers a gain to society that may reach as high as $20,000. Recent data from Project FORESIGHT (Speaker, 2021) finds that a sample of over 150 forensic laboratories maintains a median DNA sample cost of $301 to the laboratory for DNA analysis and $55 to upload to the DNA database. *Looking at the societal benefits relative to the costs of analysis and inclusion in the DNA database yields an ROI that exceeds 5,500%.*

The societal benefits from including additional entries into the DNA database extend beyond catching and convicting criminals. Benefits include the potential deterrence effect through a reduction in the willingness to commit additional crimes. This has a particularly pronounced impact on the prevention of sexual assaults. As the DNA database expands to include more profiles, the greatest deterrence comes with reductions in sexual assaults (Anker et al., 2021). For each one percent increase in profiles in the DNA database, there is a 2.7% reduction in the occurrence of sexual assaults.

Innovations in SAK Testing

One benefit that comes out of the embarrassment of having an estimated 350,000 untested SAKs in the United States, has been efforts to enact "test all" laws and/or the extension or elimination of the statute of limitations regarding conviction for sexual assaults (see Chapter 18). Test all laws speed up the societal returns highlighted in the studies summarized above (e.g., Anker et al., 2021; Campbell et al., 2016; Doleac, 2017; Speaker, 2019b; Wang & Wein, 2018), among others. In addition to efforts to enact test all policies, Wang et al. (2020) address the question of the efficiency of testing within the samples contained in a SAK. Should all samples (e.g., vaginal, oral, anal, neck, breasts, and underwear) within a SAK be tested? If prioritization among samples determines testing, is it best to rely upon the expert opinion of a medical professional (e.g., the sexual assault nurse examiner, or SANE) or a machine learning algorithm?

Each sample tested comes at a cost, and the budgets of the forensic laboratory are limited, so the testing of all samples within a SAK may prevent or delay the testing of a sample from another SAK. Suppose that a SAK contains five swabs from different locations on the body of the victim. Wang et al. (2020) consider these expert opinions vs. machine learning algorithms to determine the most likely samples to yield a usable DNA profile. *Although they find that machine learning outperforms the medical experts, they conclude that the ROI comes from a test all swabs policy over a selective testing procedure* (see Chapter 16 for more information).

Advancements with the use of familial DNA (i.e., searching the DNA database for siblings, parents, children, cousins, and any other blood relatives) to identify potential perpetrators of assault have also gained attention, particularly via the voluntary expansion of databases through interest in genealogy.[3] The number of individuals interested in their family's origins has grown in recent years. The private services that provide these ancestral backgrounds have cooperated with law enforcement in some situations for access to the private databases, which have served to identify through familial DNA the connections to perpetrators of various crimes. The ethical, moral, and legal arguments with respect to the use of these extra-criminal databases are ongoing, but these databases have the potential impact to influence the identification of the perpetrators of crimes.

Recent advances in rapid DNA technology hold great promise to identify perpetrators more quickly and avoid the repeat offenses of the serial criminal. A recent test program by the Kentucky State Police Forensic Laboratory (KSPFL) demonstrated the effectiveness of rapid DNA technology (ANDE, 2019; Schreiner, 2019; Speaker & Wells, 2021). The KSPFL, like many forensic laboratories, has been faced with increased demand for DNA services that have far outpaced the growth in funding for DNA casework. However, the result for KSPFL, as with DNA laboratories nationwide, has been a continual lengthening of the TAT for the processing of the DNA analysis. For KSPFL, that TAT grew to nearly ten months. Prioritization might reduce that TAT for a particular case, but the dilemma for the laboratory in such prioritization is the horrific nature of case submissions from sexual assaults to homicides and how to determine any criteria to place one case ahead of others.

On the other hand, rapid DNA technology permits the determination of a DNA profile in under two hours (see Box 17.2). The KSPFL test program sought to determine the reliability of the technology and whether the time savings from reduced TAT were worth the expense of the technology. To assess the rapid DNA technology vs. the traditional technology, the SAKs prepared by the SANEs included the preparation of two additional swabs. One of the two additional swabs was randomly selected for testing using the rapid DNA technology, while the standard SAK swabs were submitted to the laboratory for traditional testing, and the results were compared.[4] The results of the test program were encouraging. The comparison of the rapid DNA

Box 17.2

Rapid DNA—Kentucky first in nation to adopt Rapid DNA for sexual assault investigations: Rapid DNA testing of sexual assault evidence kits leads to identification of suspects within hours (Kentucky State Police, 2019)

If the TAT for processing the DNA from a sexual assault drops from over ten months, down to within two hours, how much would you be willing to pay for the adoption of this technology?

technology with traditional testing yielded consistent identification when sufficient foreign biological material was found in the SAK. Likewise, the cost-effectiveness of the rapid DNA technology supported the adoption of this technology. *As noted above from Lussier et al. (2011), the frequency of the sexual assaults from the untested rapist implies that the KSPFL adoption of rapid DNA for the immediate testing of swabs recovered from the sexual assault examination avoids an estimated six additional sexual assaults.* The monetized value of these avoided sexual assaults approaches $3.5 million[5]

Economic Expectations

If policy makers determine that the additional investment in testing will be implemented, then what will it cost to do so?

For nearly all forensic laboratories, increased funding for the testing of SAKs will result in greater returns on investment than currently realized. The justification for funding will be strengthened, and survivors in particular and society in general will benefit from that funding. Test all policies have significant benefits that derive from the immediacy of the testing to help curtail further assaults from the same assailant and from the high value of additions to the DNA database as a deterrent. Investing in the expansion of entries to the DNA database offers the least expensive alternative to the reduction in sexual assaults and the corresponding highest ROI.

Beyond the efforts to measure the impact of growth in the DNA database, early examination of case submissions suggests that efforts to reduce the TAT for DNA analysis have even greater dynamic benefits. Since most forensic laboratories do not bill the policing agencies for submission of evidence, price is replaced by queuing time to receive results. When TAT is reduced, there tends to be an increase in the submissions of casework to the forensic laboratory. FORESIGHT data suggests that a one percent reduction in TAT will increase DNA submissions by 1.2%. That increase may come from all sources of DNA analysis, including increased reporting of sexual assaults as faster action is taken in support of the survivors of sexual assault. Regardless of the source cases, the ROI will continue to climb, providing even greater economic justification for increased resource allocation for testing.

Conclusion

The economic problem of unlimited wants and limited resources forces policy makers to make choices on the expenditures of public funds. Although there are strong ethical and moral arguments to allocate funds to the testing of SAKs, funding must come from somewhere else in the public budget. The use of business metrics, such as ROI, permits the comparison with alternative uses of funds. Wang and Wein's (2018) statistical modeling provided a conservative estimate of the ROI from testing previously unsubmitted SAKs with roughly $81 in benefits for every dollar spent. Extending that analysis to the testing of *de novo* SAKs, Speaker (2019b) estimates the ROI for different sized laboratories and shows that jurisdictions with larger laboratories can take advantage of economies of scale and realize ROI levels exceeding $389 in benefits for every dollar spent.

The societal benefits from the testing increase as the time between the sexual assault and the resulting testing is reduced. Future developments with rapid DNA testing should continue to increase the societal ROI for testing all SAKs as the societal benefits increase with the reduced wait time. The ROI may improve even further as economies of scale permit the rapid DNA manufacturers to operate at lower costs and pass some cost savings to the testing laboratories and booking stations.

Key Points

- Allocation of funding for SAK testing competes with limited available funding for other public goods like arts, infrastructure, and social welfare programs. Public good funding choices require complex cost-benefit analyses and decision-making based not only on moral and ethical grounds but on the grounds of economic ROI.
- The use of business metrics like ROI allows for a direct comparison across alternative uses of funding; this type of analysis further strengthens the argument for testing all kits.
- Significant measurable benefits of testing a SAK include the prevention of further assaults, prevention of spent public resources (e.g., law enforcement, policy makers) time, and money, and the prevention of monetary costs to survivors and society (upwards of $560,000 per assault).
- Monetary benefits to society far outweigh the cost of testing, with a conservative estimate of $81 saved for every $1 spent on testing. More comprehensive analyses suggest a ROI exceeding $389 in benefits for every dollar spent.
- An important benefit from testing a SAK from the first assault is the avoidance of an additional 26.22 sexual assaults.
- With regard to the lab, the best ROI comes from a test all swabs policy over a selective testing procedure.
- Recent research indicates that adoption of rapid DNA for the immediate testing of swabs recovered from the sexual assault examination avoids an estimated six additional sexual assaults. These have a monetized cost of 3.5 million dollars (Speaker & Wells, 2021).
- Increased submission of DNA and population of CODIS, in conjunction with continuous technological advancements in DNA testing will increase ROI.

Discussion Questions

1 The "economic problem" highlights the limitations of budgets to satisfy all wants. To do one thing means giving up something else. If there were a cap on public funding, what would you give up in order to allocate more funds toward the testing of SAKs (at the local, state, or national levels)? Can you support your choices with economic data?

2 The Denmark experience (Anker et al., 2021) with the expansion of DNA databases to include non-violent crime, resulted in dramatic reductions in sexual assaults as the database grew. Should similar policies be adopted in the United States and other countries as a means to reduce sexual assaults?

3 Currently, only a small portion of sexual assaults are reported. What impact will a "test all SAKs" policy have on the reporting of sexual assaults?

Notes

1 "Although no official definition exists for the DNA backlog, the National Institute of Justice (NIJ) defines a backlogged case as one that remains untested for 30 days after it has been submitted to a laboratory" (US Department of Justice Office of Justice Programs, 2011).

2 The original costs of crime presented by DeLisi et al. (2010) used monetary costs in 2008 dollars. The values presented here have been adjusted by the Consumer Price Index (CPI) to reflect 2021 dollars.

3 The prominence of self-testing kits via companies such as 23andMe, AncestryDNA, and Family Tree DNA have permitted people to inexpensively discover details of their roots. DNA testing expands the traditional genealogy search of historical records to uncover biological details embedded in the family tree. The voluntary self-testing expands the non-criminal databases that might be searched to identify individuals with DNA profiles that contain family traits that match those of a suspected perpetrator of an assault or other crime.

4 The KSPFL tested the rapid DNA technology of the ANDE 6C Rapid DNA system.

5 This follows the societal benefits highlighted by DeLisi (2010), updated for inflation using 2021 price indices. The TAT for DNA casework for KSPFL was 320 days. Combined with the DeLisi updated societal cost of a sexual assault of $558,916 and the 7.1 sexual assaults per year from the untested perpetrator, estimates that (320/7.1 assaults avoided) times $558,916 savings per assault avoided yields savings of $3.479 million.

Further Reading

Aldy, J. E., & Viscusi, W. K. (2008). Adjusting the value of a statistical life for age and cohort effects. *The Review of Economics and Statistics*, 90(3), 573–581.

Levitt, S. D., & Dubner, S. J. (2010). *Freakonomics: A rogue economist explores the hidden side of everything*. William Morrow.

Talib, N. (2007). *Fooled by randomness: The hidden role of chance in life and in the markets*. Penguin.

References

ANDE. (2019). *Kentucky case study*. Retrieved from ANDE: https://www.ande.com/kentucky-case-study/

Anker, A. S., Doleac, J. L., & Landersø, R. (2021). The effects of DNA databases on the deterrence and detection of offenders. *American Economic Journal: Applied Economics*. https://www.aeaweb.org/content/file?id=12854

Bashford, M. (2013). *How New York City tackled its backlog*, Webinar presented for the National Center for Victims of Crime, March 2013. Retrieved June 2, 2021. https://www.nationalpublicsafetypartnership.org/clearinghouse/Content/Resource Documents/New%20York%20City%E2%80%99s%20Sexual%20Assault%20Kit%20 Backlog.pdf

Briody, M. (2000). The effects of DNA evidence on sexual offence cases in court. *Current Issues in Criminal Justice*, 14(2), 159–181. https://doi.org/10.1080/10345329.2002.1203 6257

Campbell, R., Feeney, H., Fehler-Cabral, G., Shaw, J., & Horsford, S. (2017). The national problem of untested sexual assault kits (SAKs): Scope, causes, and future directions for research, policy, and practice. *Trauma, Violence, & Abuse*, 18(4), 363–376. https://doi.org/10.1177/1524838015622436

Campbell, R., & Fehler-Cabral, G. (2020). "Just bring us the real ones": The role of forensic crime laboratories in guarding the gateway to justice for sexual assault victims. *Journal of Interpersonal Violence*, 1–28. https://doi.org/10.1177/0886260520951303

Campbell, R., Javorka, M., Sharma, D. B., Gregory, K., Opsommer, M., Schelling, K., & Lu, L. (2020). A state census of unsubmitted sexual assault kits: Comparing forensic DNA testing outcomes by geographic and population density characteristics. *Journal of Forensic Sciences, 65*(6), 1820–1827. https://doi.org/10.1111/1556-4029.14554

Campbell, R., Pierce, S., Sharma, D., Feeney, H., & Fehler-Cabral, G. (2016). Should rape kit testing be prioritized by victim–offender relationship? *Criminology & Public Policy, 15*(2), 555–583. https://doi.org/10.1111/1745-9133.12205

DeLisi, M., Kosloski, A., Sween, M., Hachmeister, E., Moore, M., & Drury, A. (2010). Murder by numbers: Monetary costs imposed by a sample of homicide offenders. *Journal of Forensic Psychiatry and Psychology, 11*(4), 501–513. https://doi.org/10.1080/14789940903564388

Doleac, J. (2017). The effects of DNA databases on crime. *American Economic Journal: Applied Economics, 9*(1), 165–201. https://doi.org/10.1257/app.20150043

Doleac, J. (2021, February 1). *How DNA databases deter crime*. Retrieved from Bloomberg: https://www.bloomberg.com/opinion/articles/2021-02-01/dna-databases-are-better-crime-deterrent-than-long-prison-time

Hopkins, Kyle. (2020, December 30). After 3 years and $1.5 million testing rape kits, Alaska made one new arrest. *Anchorage Daily News*. https://www.propublica.org/article/after-3-years-and-1-5-million-testing-rape-kits-alaska-made-one-new-arrest

Houck, M. M., Riley, R. A., Speaker, P. J., & Witt, T. S. (2009). FORESIGHT: A business approach to improving forensic science services. *Forensic Science Policy & Management: An International Journal, 1*(2), 85–95. https://doi.org/10.1080/19409040902810723

Houck, M. M., & Speaker, P. J. (2020). Project FORESIGHT: A ten-year retrospective. *Forensic Science International: Synergy, 2*, 275–281. https://doi.org/10.1016/j.fsisyn.2020.08.005

Hunt, P. E., Saunders, J., & Kilmer, B. (2019). Estimates of law enforcement costs by crime type for benefit-cost analyses. *Journal of Benefit Cost Analysis, 10*(1), 95–123. https://www.cambridge.org/core/journals/journal-of-benefit-cost-analysis/article/estimates-of-law-enforcement-costs-by-crime-type-for-benefitcost-analyses/0A1A55F70324FDBAA947FF1F18AA1B74

Kentucky State Police. (2019). *Kentucky first in nation to adopt rapid DNA for sexual assault investigations*. https://kentuckystatepolice.org/hq-4-10-19/

Kurimski, L. M., Speaker, P. J., & Bassler, J. R. (2017). Project FORESIGHT and return on investment: Forensic science laboratories and public health laboratories. *Forensic Science Policy & Management: An International Journal, 8*(1), 1–12. https://doi.org/10.1080/19409044.2017.1280099

Lovell, R. E., Singer, M., Flannery, D. J., & McGuire, M. J. (2021). The case for "investigate all": Assessing the cost-effectiveness of investigating no CODIS hit cases in a sexual assault kit initiative. *Journal of Forensic Sciences*. https://doi.org/10.1111/1556-4029.14686

Lussier, P. (2014). Criminal career of sex offenders. In Weisburd, D. & Bruinsma, G. (Eds.), *Encyclopedia of criminology and criminal justice* (pp. 787–800). Springer-Verlag.

Lussier, P., Bouchard, M., & Beauregard, E. (2011). Patterns of criminal achievement in sexual offending: Unravelling the "successful" sex offender. *Journal of Criminal Justice, 39*, 433–444.

Schreiner, B. (2019). *Kentucky to use rapid DNA tests for sex assault cases*. Retrieved from Associated Press: https://www.apnews.com/689a03bd0433413cacf36753ae757ae3

Speaker, P. J. (2019a). The jurisdictional return on investment for DNA database. *Forensic Science International: Synergy, 1*(1), S13–S14. https://doi.org/10.1016/j.fsisyn.2019.02.038

Speaker, P. J. (2019b). The jurisdictional return on investment from processing the backlog of untested sexual assault kits. *Forensic Science International: Synergy, 1*(1), 18–23. https://doi.org/10.1016/j.fsisyn.2019.02.055

Speaker, P. J. (2021). *Project FORESIGHT Annual Report, 2019–2020*. West Virginia University Research Repository. https://researchrepository.wvu.edu/faculty_publications/3008

Speaker, P. J. & Wells, R. (2021). The return on investment from rapid DNA testing of sexual assault kits: The Kentucky State Police forensic laboratory experience. *Medical Research Archives*, 9(11). https://doi.org/10.18103/mra.v9i11.2600

Strom, K. J., Scott, T., Feeney, H., Young, A., Couzens, L., & Berzofsky, M. (2021). How much justice is denied? An estimate of unsubmitted sexual assault kits in the United States. *Journal of Criminal Justice*, 73, 101746. https://doi.org/10.1016/j.jcrimjus.2020.101746

U.S. Department of Justice Office of Justice Programs. (November 2011). *The DNA backlog*. OJP Fact Sheet. https://www.ojp.gov/sites/g/files/xyckuh241/files/archives/factsheets/ojpfs_dnabacklog.html.

Wang, Z., MacMillan, K., Powell, M., & Wein, L. M. (2020). A cost-effectiveness analysis of the number of samples to collect and test from a sexual assault. *Proceedings of the National Academy of Sciences*, 117(24), 13421–13427. https://doi.org/10.1073/pnas.2001103117

Wang, C., & Wein, L. M. (2018). Analyzing approaches to the backlog of untested sexual assault kits in the U.S.A. *Journal of Forensic Sciences*, 63(4), 1–12. https://doi.org/10.1111/1556-4029.13739

Wein, L. M. (2018). *The sexual assault problem we can't afford to ignore*. Accessed June 2, 2021. https://www.cnn.com/2018/03/22/opinions/rape-kits-should-be-tested-says-research-wein/index.html

Wells, W., Campbell, B., & Franklin, C. (2016). *Unsubmitted sexual assault kits in Houston, TX: case characteristics, forensic testing results, and the investigation of CODIS hits*. US Department of Justice. https://www.ojp.gov/pdffiles1/nij/grants/249812.pdf

18 Eliminating the rape kit backlog
Federal and state legislative responses

Ilse Knecht, Mateo Cello, and Burcu Sagiroglu

Author Note

The opinions or points of view expressed in this chapter are solely those of the authors and do not reflect the official positions of any participating organization or the US Department of Justice.

The First Rape Kit Reform Efforts, and the Origins of the Six Pillars of Reform

The Joyful Heart Foundation was founded in 2004 by Law and Order Special Victims Unit (SVU) actress, director, and advocate, Mariska Hargitay. Through playing Detective Olivia Benson on Law and Order SVU, Hargitay learned a tremendous amount about the crime of rape. She also experienced the long-lasting impact of rape on survivors. Letters from fans of the show poured in across the years; many were testimonies from survivors sharing their stories of abuse. As Hargitay became informed about the topic, she was shocked and saddened by the prevalence and variety of sexually based crimes (e.g., sexual assault, domestic violence, human trafficking, rape) and how trauma impacts survivors, many for their entire lives. She felt she had to answer these survivor letters in a meaningful manner. With this desire in mind, she created the Joyful Heart Foundation with the mission to transform society's response to sexual assault, domestic violence, and child abuse, support survivors' healing, and end sexual violence.

In 2009, Hargitay met Wayne County Prosecutor, Kym Worthy, at a congressional hearing about the backlog of unsubmitted SAKs and learned of the more than 10,000 untested rape SAKs in Detroit alone. Soon after this meeting, Joyful Heart started working closely with local stakeholders in Detroit to address the problem. Joyful Heart's involvement in the national SAK issue then expanded to Cleveland, Los Angeles, Memphis, and many other jurisdictions. The organization has helped these jurisdictions by raising awareness of the existence of the backlog, providing guidance and technical assistance to jurisdictions working to address their backlog, and helping with fundraising efforts. In 2010, Joyful Heart Foundation named "ending the rape kit backlog" its top advocacy priority.

To increase visibility and create a hub for information about the SAK backlog, Joyful Heart Foundation launched www.endthebacklog.org, which was the first online repository dedicated to tracking rape kit reform (RKR) at the city, state, and national levels. This resource also sought to increase awareness about the sheer

DOI: 10.4324/9781003186816-21

number of untested SAKs. While working city by city was having an impact, it soon became clear that the problem was widespread, and statewide and national legislative reforms were needed. In 2015, Joyful Heart began to identify, analyze, and catalog each state law being enacted to address or end the backlog. At the same time, Joyful Heart was collecting and disseminating legislative options among state jurisdictions, and both legislators and stakeholders were requesting the development of a model comprehensive reform bill. The Joyful Heart Foundation has responded to this request.

In 2016, the Joyful Heart Foundation, in partnership with Civitas Public Affairs Group, developed a grassroot, survivor-focused, and actionable nationwide campaign to end the rape kit backlog. The campaign plan was developed following a thorough review of the work in this area, which included interviews with nearly 75 trusted experts including advocates, survivors, prosecutors, investigators, crime lab personnel, and local, state, and national leaders. This was followed by a 50-state analysis of the policy opportunity landscape. The 50-state assessment formalized the following six essential pillars for states to achieve comprehensive RKR:

1 *Annual statewide inventory:* Counts of all untested rape SAKs on a reoccurring basis to understand the scope of the problem, where the system is breaking down, and to monitor progress. This aids in creating greater accountability and transparency for all stakeholders.
2 *Mandatory testing of backlogged SAKs:* Eliminate the existing backlog by requiring law enforcement agencies to submit all previously untested SAKs to the lab and requiring these kits to be tested.
3 *Mandatory testing of new SAKs:* Prevent future backlogs by requiring law enforcement agencies to promptly submit all newly collected SAKs to the lab and requiring the lab to test these kits within a specific time frame.
4 *Tracking system:* Create a statewide system that allows designated individuals (mainly victims, law enforcement agents, hospital staff, and lab staff) to follow the path of a rape kit throughout the chain of command: hospital, local law enforcement agency, analysis process at the lab, and final disposition.
5 *Victims' right to notice:* Grant victims the right to receive information about the status and location of their SAKs.
6 *Funding for reform:* Allocate the appropriate amounts of state funding to implement these reforms.

Before the creation of the six-pillar approach in 2016, there was no standardized way to understand and analyze the severity of the backlog problem in the United States. This made the goal of eliminating the backlog even more challenging. At this time, there was no consensus on how many untested SAKs were sitting on shelves, their locations, next steps, or how to prevent the future backlog of untested SAKs. Joyful Heart's national research initiative and the creation of this agenda allowed us to determine what each state had achieved with regard to RKR, and what work still needed to be carried out. This set the groundwork for our legislative campaign. Now that we knew what needed to be done in each state, we could begin providing information to local legislators to enact reforms addressing the six pillars.

Of note, our campaign is ongoing, and it will not end until every state has cleared its state SAK backlog and passed legislation that speaks to all six pillars. This work is essential because creating systemic changes via legislation and policy will withstand stakeholder changes and shifting priorities (e.g., a lab director's retirement or a new police chief who doesn't elevate rape as an important crime). Enacting and implementing legislation are the best way to ensure that there will never be another backlog of unsubmitted sexual assault kits (SAKs) in the United States.

First attempts at reform

Below, we review some of the first RKR laws ever passed, as they will provide more insight on how Joyful Heart's mission got started, where we are today, and where we are headed.

In 2002, Illinois passed HB3172, creating the Sexual Assault Evidence Collection Program that coordinates the distribution, collection, analysis, and maintenance of SAKs under the leadership of Illinois State Police (ISP). Following this law, in 2003, the Illinois state budget allocated annual funding for the program. In 2010, Illinois lawmakers passed the first comprehensive RKR law, SB3296. This included the requirement of an inventory of untested SAKs in law enforcement departments, mandated time-sensitive testing of the SAKs that were discovered, and timelines for the testing of newly collected SAKs. Over time, the Illinois legislature has built upon the Sexual Assault Survivors Emergency Treatment Act, passing legislation requiring tracking of SAKs, trauma-informed training for law enforcement personnel, and survivors' rights to know the status of their SAKs.

California followed Illinois. In 2003, the state enacted AB898, granting victims the right to be informed whether a DNA profile was obtained from testing their rape kit, if the profile was uploaded into the DNA database, and if the DNA profile matched another profile in the database. This law was novel for its time. Through this law, the California legislature demonstrated an understanding of the importance of this type of information for survivors. Their understanding has been backed by research demonstrating that access to the status of their cases can promote healing for survivors of sexual assault. Conversely, a lack of knowledge can be harmful to their well-being (Joyful Heart Foundation, 2016).

Eight years later, Texas was the third state to enact RKR legislation. In 2011, the state legislature enacted SB1636, requiring law enforcement agencies to send all newly collected SAKs to a crime lab for testing within 30 days. The law directed the lab to test the SAKs "as soon as is feasible." The statute also required law enforcement agencies to count the untested rape SAKs in their storage facilities and to have them analyzed by September 2014. In 2013, Texas added to this law by granting victims the right to access information about the location and status of their kit. Texas continued improving its rape kit handling laws and enacted HB8 in 2019; this law tightened the time frame for the submission and analysis of newly collected SAKs and prohibited the destruction of kits, which has been a problem in some states in the past.

Another early adopter of RKR legislation was Colorado. In 2013, state lawmakers passed HB1020 requiring all law enforcement agencies to report the number of untested SAKs in their possession to the Colorado Bureau of Investigation (CBI). The law also required the testing of all previously untested SAKs within 120 days of enactment and mandated law enforcement to send new SAKs for testing within 21 days.

While most reform across states is legislated, some jurisdictions have addressed backlog elimination and rape kit handling procedures through non-legislative measures. Three of the pillars proposed by the Joyful Heart Foundation—inventory, backlog testing, and tracking—can be achieved through alternative means, such as a governor's executive order, an attorney general's initiative, or grant funding. Furthermore, a state lab can create and implement a tracking system without law behind it. An attorney general can use their position to strongly pressure law enforcement to send all their backlogged SAKs in for testing and they can pay for it from the state's budget, which removes a large barrier to submission. In numerous states, inventories have been carried out without laws being enacted because of the efforts of the state lab, state auditor, attorney general, or governor.

However, Joyful Heart strongly asserts that progress made toward the pillars of inventory, backlog testing, and tracking is more effective, and sustainable, when legislated. For example, having a law that requires the creation of a rape kit tracking system typically results in a legal mandate that all parties that handle a rape kit must participate in the system, which is central to its success; this cannot be effectively *required* without law. Mandating the testing of newly collected SAKs and creating rape kit handling timelines must be in law or kit submission and testing will vary among precincts, resulting in unequal access to the law for survivors, and often a continuation of practices that contributed to the formation of the initial backlog. A victim's right to know the status of their kit must be in statute in order for it to be a "right." The funding pillar is accomplished through the budget and appropriations process, which is considered legislation. Receiving federal grant funding is not enough for a state to be considered invested in reform; the state must commit to reforming through its own budget. While three pillars can be adopted without law, permanence is key to real RKR, and state law is the best way to ensure that the pillars stand throughout time.

RKR legislation has transformed the way SAKs are handled across the country from collection to final disposition. Today, 45 states have passed legislation improving rape kit processing; just five have not. Enacting laws to improve the handling and processing of SAKs is vital to a safe and just society. These laws not only ensure that every rape kit connected to a reported crime is tested in a timely manner but also demonstrate to survivors and communities as a whole that elected officials and other leaders consider sexual violence a top priority. RKR laws not only ensure that SAKs are tested expeditiously but also shine a bright light on how the criminal justice system has traditionally ignored and deprioritized sexual assault (with the backlog as a symptom of this larger dysfunction). Legislation to improve the management of untested SAKs also improves the system's overall response to sexual violence survivors.

Trends in Rape Kit Legislation

Since the first law in 2002, 45 states and Washington, DC have passed 164 bills related to Joyful Heart's six pillars of legislative reform. These laws expanded access to justice for more than 134,000 survivors every year and have impacted more than 315 million Americans. To date, 11 states and Washington, DC have reached full legislative RKR by enacting all six of Joyful Heart's pillars: Connecticut, Hawaii, Illinois, Kentucky, Massachusetts, Michigan, Nevada, Oregon, Texas, Utah, and Washington.

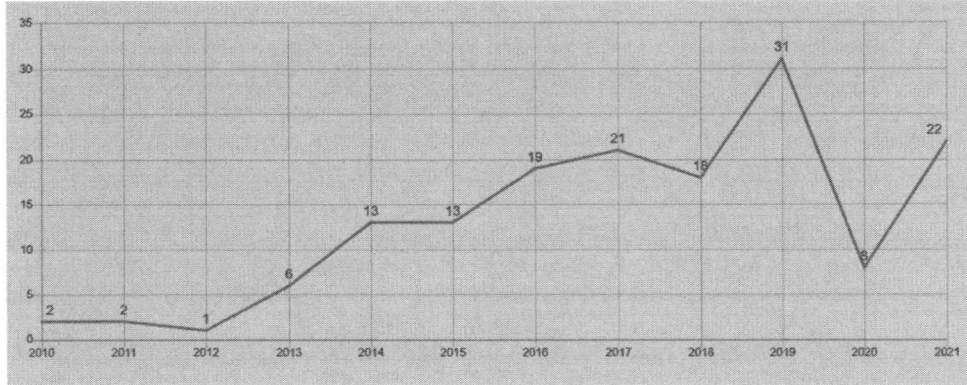

Figure 18.1 Passed Bills by Year 2010–2021

As a result of Joyful Heart's efforts:

- 32 states and Washington, DC have inventory laws in place, with 14 states requiring a one-time inventory and 18 states mandating a recurring inventory
- 30 states and DC grant survivors the right to notification about their SAKs
- 33 states and DC mandate the testing of newly collected SAKs; 9 states require testing of backlogged kits by law[1]
- 34 states and DC have established a kit tracking system
- 29 states and DC have allocated state funding to implement these reforms

Over the last decade, legislative trends show great progress in the implementation of rape kit legislation reform. Not only are more states passing rape kit-related legislation, but there has also been an upward trend in terms of total RKR bills passed per year. Figure 18.1 shows the increasing number of RKR bills passed per year. We see a peak in 2019, and a valley in 2020. The valley is likely explained by the COVID-19 pandemic when state funds were allocated toward handling this health crisis. We also suspect that the amount of bills passed in 2021 has been affected by the pandemic, as it was still very much of public concern during this time period. Even so, the amount of bills passed in 2021 is similar to the levels of 2018 and 2017.

Figure 18.1 demonstrates that state legislatures have recognized the magnitude of this issue and have begun to pass legislation that seeks to improve how SAKs are handled and processed. The 2021 results are promising, especially considering that states are still financially recovering from the pandemic. Current results indicate that the positive trend that existed before 2020 could very well continue in 2022 and beyond.

In addition, inspection of the data indicates that there may be a positive relationship among these three pillars: funding, inventory, and forward testing (see Figure 18.2). We see that when the number of funding bills increases, so does the amount of forward testing and inventory bills. Future research is needed to determine the nature of these relationships and what drives them.

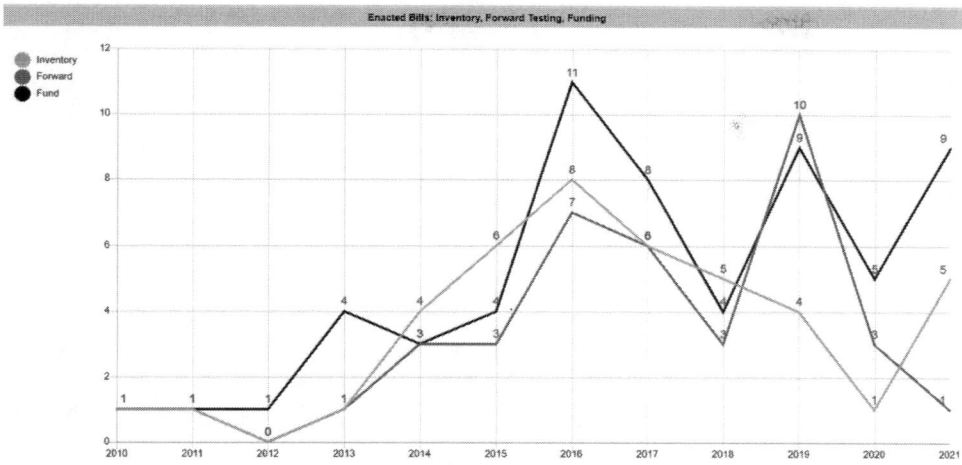

Figure 18.2 Number of Enacted Bills by Pillar: Inventory, Forward Testing, Funding 2010–2021

Sufficient funding allocated from a state's budget ensures that crime labs, law enforcement, prosecutors, and victim advocates have the resources necessary to test SAKs, investigate cases, support survivors, and prosecute offenders. Twenty-seven states that passed bills to grant state funds toward ending the backlog have allocated more than $173 million to end the backlog and test more than 147,000 SAKs (Joyful Heart Foundation). These bills aimed to end the backlog, fund crime labs, implement relevant reforms, and test future kits. These states granted $6 million on average to end the backlog, ranging from $157,000 in Montana to $69 million in Texas.

Another point of interest is that RKR bills tend to come out of bipartisanship. Since the earlier bills passed in 2010, the majority of the bills were co-introduced by Democratic and Republican sponsors. In total, out of 156 bills that passed, 80 bills had bipartisan sponsorship, 26 bills had only Democratic sponsorship, 19 bills had only Republican sponsorship, and the remaining bills were either introduced by legislative committees or were budget bills without a legislator's sponsorship. This seems to demonstrate the beneficial nature of bipartisan support in pushing RKR legislation into law (see Figure 18.3).

After a legislative session under the shadow of the pandemic in 2020, 33 states introduced 57 bills related to Joyful Heart's six pillars of legislative reform in 2021. As of October 2021, 18 of these states have passed 22 bills. See Table 18.1 for an exhaustive list as of the Fall of 2021. Among the states that passed bills related to the six pillars,

- Five states required an inventory of untested SAKs
- One state mandated the testing of backlogged SAKs
- One state improved its kit handling timelines
- Five states required the establishment of a tracking system by law
- Eight states granted survivors the right to know the status of their SAKs or improved such laws
- Nine states granted first-time or additional funding for RKR[2]

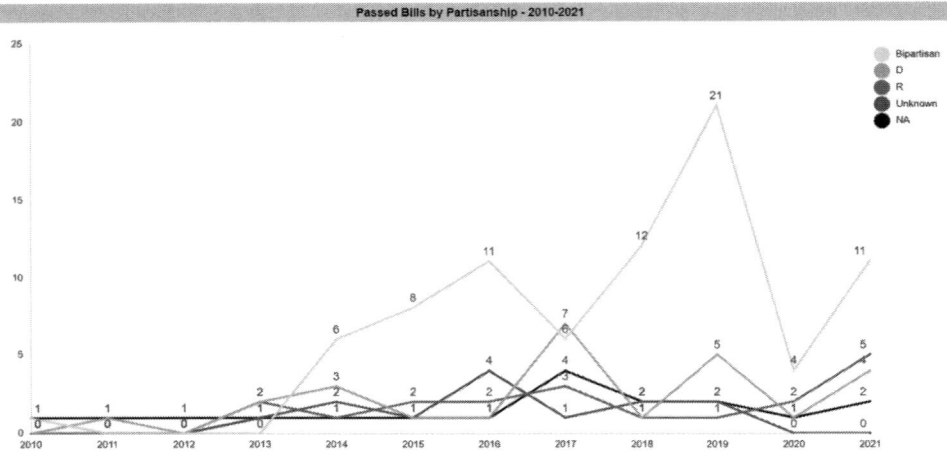

Figure 18.3 Number of Enacted Bills by Partisanship

Barriers to the Advancement of the Field

Over the last decade, there has been steady growth in the adoption of RKR laws, and the number of states adopting this legislation. Despite the difficulties brought by the COVID-19 pandemic, we anticipate similar levels of pre-pandemic legislative growth

Table 18.1 2021 Enacted Legislation as Indicated by Joyful Heart Foundation Data Collection

State	Bill number	Pillar
Alabama	HB137	Victims' rights
California	SB129	Funding (additional)
California	SB215	Tracking (additional)
Colorado	HB1143	Victims' rights
Connecticut	HB6689	Funding (additional)
Florida	HB673/SB1002	Tracking
Georgia	HB255/HB193	Inventory (additional), tracking
Illinois	Illinois State Budget FY2021	Funding (additional)
Illinois	HB1739	Tracking (additional), victims' rights (additional)
Iowa	HF426	Tracking, victims' rights
Maryland	HB0588/SB0491	Funding (additional)
Massachusetts	HB4013	Inventory, backlog, funding (additional)
Missouri	HB12	Funding
Montana	HB310	Victims' rights
Montana	HB693	Inventory
North Dakota	SB2281	Inventory, tracking
Ohio	HB110	Funding
Oklahoma	HB2546	Victims' rights
Tennessee	HB39/SB1035	Forward testing (additional), tracking, victims' rights
Texas	HB1/SB1	Funding (additional)
Washington	HB1109	Victims' rights (additional)
Washington	HB1094/SB5092	Inventory, funding (additional)

in the years to come. Future research will be needed to document the accuracy of this prediction.

Certainly, existing data indicate that the pace of reform has been extraordinary, and in just the past few years has ticked up notably. However, two barriers stand in the way of nationwide reform. In this next section, we first highlight two ongoing challenges: lack of compliance and lack of funding. It should be noted that there are potential solutions to these problems and the next section will also discuss some ways to successfully address and diminish these barriers.

Compliance issues

Over the last two years, Joyful Heart Foundation has focused on recording issues of non-compliance with RKR-related legislation. We have already uncovered several instances in which certain state agencies are not following the laws their government has enacted. For example, in April 2020, the state's Attorney General released the one-time statewide audit mandated by AB3118 in California. The law states that "each law enforcement agency, medical, forensic laboratory, and any other facility that receives, maintains, stores, or preserves sexual assault evidence kits shall conduct an audit of all untested sexual assault kits in their possession" and *shall participate in the statewide audit*. However, the report shows that only 149 law enforcement agencies and crime labs actually participated in the audit, while there are over 500 police agencies in the state. The report also notes that no medical facilities provided information for this report, a clear instance of non-compliance. Thus, while the audit yielded a total of 13,929 backlogged SAKs in California, we know that this number is likely to represent only a fraction of the true total number of untested SAKs in the state.

Similarly, in New York, the state comptroller released a report in May 2020 that documented non-compliance by the state's crime labs. The report indicated that labs were not testing either newly collected SAKs or backlogged SAKs within the 90-day time period established by the law (A10760, 2016). Also in New York, many police agencies did not comply with state statute established through SB980 (2018), which requires said agencies to report, on a quarterly basis, the number of untested SAKs in their possession. Failure to comply with inventories keeps the public in the dark about the state of the backlog and makes it difficult to create a plan of action. Instances like these in New York and California illustrate the lack of transparency and accountability that has existed far too long around rape kit testing. These findings also highlight difficulties with implementation and compliance with legislation.

Similar instances of non-compliance have occurred in Texas. In 2019, the state passed The Lavinia Masters Act (HB8), which mandated law enforcement to carry out a one-time inventory of untested SAKs in their possession. Again, participation in this audit was incomplete: Dallas Sheriff's Department, Fort Worth Police Department, Houston Police Department, San Antonio Police Department, and Tarrant County Sheriff's Department were among the many law enforcement agencies that did not participate in the mandated inventory. Due to this non-compliance and the resulting incomplete inventory, Texas does not know the true extent of its backlog and cannot fully allocate the necessary resources to combat it.

California, New York, and Texas are not the only states that have had issues of non-compliance. We have also found similar problems in other states such as Pennsylvania and Massachusetts. More work needs to be done to ensure that when a RKR law is passed, improvement in the handling and processing of SAKs follows. Residents of the state, and most importantly survivors, deserve full compliance with RKR laws.

Lack of resources

A second problem is a lack of resources dedicated to processing and handling SAKs. In September of 2019, Joyful Heart conducted a nationwide survey regarding RKR policies in each of the fifty states. The goal of the survey was to receive insight from individuals from diverse professional backgrounds about how SAKs are being handled and processed in their respective states. The survey, conducted online (with some interviews conducted via phone) had more than 50 questions. We received 112 individual responses, with an overall response rate of 32% from all 50 states. Participants included: Sexual Assault Nurse Examiners (SANEs), law enforcement officials, forensic lab staff, advocates, prosecutors, state and city agency officials, and SAKI site coordinators.

While survey comments indicated that most participants believed that the state labs and hospitals were doing their best in terms of collecting and testing SAKs, participants routinely mentioned that lack of funding and heavy caseloads prevented the labs from testing SAKs in a timely manner. About one in three respondents said that their labs lack sufficient resources to carry out the testing of newly collected SAKs. If labs cannot test SAKs in a timely manner, then it is almost certain that a new backlog of untested SAKs will form at the crime lab.

A 2016 study demonstrated a substantial return on investment in processing SAKs: carrying out comprehensive RKR is cheaper for communities in the long run. Lovell et al. (2021) explain that rape is costly to victims and includes psychological and tangible logistical costs including medical expenses, lost workdays, and out-of-pocket expenses, making prevention of future rapes crucial. The researchers then compared the costs to the victim, to the costs of testing a rape kit, and found that the cost to the victims is more than 92 times higher than the cost of testing and investigating the rape kit. Savings come from following up the testing with thorough investigations and prosecutions; in other words, by getting offenders off the street and thereby preventing future rapes (Singer et al., 2016). For a current economic analysis, see Chapter 17.

Addressing These Barriers

Solving non-compliance

Legislative language

Joyful Heart has closely monitored states' attempts to create compliance mechanisms. We suggest that the best way to assure reform statutes are being followed is by inserting compliance clauses directly into RKR bills. An example is Kentucky's SB63 (2016). This law includes a clause:

> Local law enforcement agencies who wish to obtain funds from the Law Enforcement Foundation Program fund must have a written policy and procedures manual related to sexual assault examinations that has been approved by the Justice and Public Safety Cabinet no later than January 17th 2017.

Tying funding to compliance could also be effective. In Kentucky's case, a clear procedure related to sexual assault examinations approved by the Justice and Public Safety Cabinet could lead, in theory, to a more comprehensive way to interact with victims and process SAKs. However, it should be noted that while the manual may be comprehensive, there are no clauses here to ensure that law enforcement agencies are following the manual they created.

Likewise, Texas' HB8 (2019) threatens the loss of funds for not following what is stated in the bill: *Failure to comply with the requirements of this subchapter may be used to determine eligibility for receiving grant funds from the department, the office of the governor, or another state agency.* The spirit of this clause is good, but the word *may* still implies this is only a mere possibility instead of certainty. In light of the fact that it has already been determined that some police agencies in Texas are not complying with the inventory mandate in HB8, it will be interesting to see whether the state of Texas deems these agencies ineligible for grants.

From Joyful Heart's research, binding adherence to the statute to funding is the only way we have seen states try to combat non-compliance in RKR. Enforcing these mechanisms lies with the state and to date, we have no examples of that occurring.

Watchdog figures

Another way to address non-compliance is through the establishment of a watchdog figure who is supported by the state. Some states have created a position whose responsibility is to assure that statutes are being followed and that citizens' rights are being protected. An example of how these watchdog figures have played an important role in the field of RKR can be found in Pennsylvania. The state's Auditor General is the chief fiscal watchdog of the commonwealth. He or she is responsible for using audits to ensure that all state money is spent legally and properly. In 2015, Pennsylvania Auditor General Eugene DePasquale played an impactful role in ensuring compliance with the rape kit inventory. In that year, Act 27 was passed, which mandated an inventory of rape kits across the state. DePasquale released a report signaling low law enforcement participation and lack of funding to the Department of Health, which is the entity required to collect such information. DePasquale also found that the state labs, the entities responsible for testing SAKs, were underfunded. The Auditor General played a key role in making non-compliance visible. It should be noted that the Auditor General's role is generally reactive in that they highlight existing non-compliance rather than prevent it. However, watchdog figures could prove to be an effective way to solve issues of non-compliance and are an additional avenue to consider.

A similar position we have seen is that of the ombudsperson. These are state officials who work to address citizens' complaints against the state itself. As an example, South Carolina has a Crime Victims Ombudsman, whose job is to ensure that "victims of crime are served equitably and treated fairly by the South Carolina criminal justice system and its victim service organization" (South Carolina Attorney General's Office). Figures like this have the potential to help survivors locate their kit, and learn whether it has been tested or not, though we have no evidence of this occurring in South Carolina.

Compliance with enacted legislation by the corresponding criminal justice agencies is a topic that needs to be researched and addressed. There is limited evidence as to which are the most effective ways to assure stakeholders are following state statutes. The field needs more information on how to achieve compliance and respond to non-compliance, which mechanisms work, which do not, and how to implement effective mechanisms.

Addressing the lack of resources

Using state funds

Lack of resources is another significant problem perpetuating the problem of untested SAKs. The most obvious way to address this issue is to allocate public funds to the handling and processing of SAKs. Research suggests that testing every kit saves communities money (Lovell et al., 2021). They analyzed the cost of testing never tested SAKs in Cuyahoga County, Ohio. Factoring in the cost of testing SAKs and other related expenses, the study calculated the overall cost-effectiveness of testing approximately 5,000 unsubmitted SAKs, engaging survivors, investigating, and (where applicable) prosecuting cases. The study found that each kit tested produced an estimated net savings of $5,127 to the community. Cuyahoga County saved $26.5 million by testing and following up on the testing via investigations and prosecutions—thereby preventing future rapes. Legislators should not be hestant to advocate for the allocation of public funds to testing rape SAKs. From a purely fiscal point of view, it will save the state money in the long run.

Applying for federal grants

If states are unwilling to invest more of their money to carry out RKR, there are other ways to address the issue of lack of resources. One mechanism is through applying for federal grants. Today, the nation has three federally run programs designed to improve the way sexual assault SAKs are managed: The Sexual Assault Kit Initiative (SAKI), Sexual Assault Forensic Evidence–Inventory, Tracking, and Reporting (SAFE-ITR) Program, and The Debbie Smith Act.

SAKI is a Department of Justice program created to provide local communities with funding and technical assistance to test previously unsubmitted SAKs in police and hospital storage facilities, create multi-disciplinary teams to investigate and prosecute cases connected to the backlog, and address the need for victim notification and reengagement with the criminal justice system. The US Congress has approved between $41 and $45 million each year for this unique program since 2015. Grants have been awarded to 70+ sites, including law enforcement agencies, prosecutors' offices, victim-serving agencies, Attorneys General, and Governor's offices all throughout the nation.

SAFE-ITR is a Bureau of Justice Assistance Program, which is located within the U.S. Department of Justice. The program looks to obtain a true scope of the number of SAKs in possession of police agencies and to understand how these SAKs move throughout the criminal justice system. From 2016 to 2020, the program allocated over $11 million, through 18 awards. The program is currently responsible for the creation of six tracking systems, with more in progress in the coming years (Bureau of Justice Assistance, 2022).

The third major federal funding program is The Debbie Smith Act, which addresses DNA backlogs at crime labs and does not fund any downstream needs as SAKI does. This piece of legislation was first passed in 2004, as part of the Justice for All Act (P.L. 108-405). The current law authorizes up to $151 million in grants for states and localities for testing DNA evidence, training for lab personnel, and providing up-to-date and efficient lab equipment. This law was reauthorized in 2008 and 2014, when it was extended through the fiscal year of 2019 (P.L. 113-182). In 2013 the Sexual Assault Forensic Evidence Reporting Act (SAFER Act, H.R. 354 in the 113th Congress) was enacted to require 75% of Debbie Smith Act funds to be used to process the backlog of untested SAKs. This law also provides grants to conduct audits of unprocessed SAKs to help track the backlog of hundreds of thousands of untested DNA SAKs sitting in labs across the country. SAFER also mandated the Department of Justice to create a report with national rape kit handling guidelines.

These three funding opportunities allow states to receive federal dollars to improve the way they handle and process SAKs. Applications for and maintenance of federal money received through these grants are beneficial avenues through which states can address concerns related to the lack of resources needed to improve the criminal justice's response to sexual assault.

Conclusion

This chapter explored the development of Joyful Heart's six-pillar legislative framework to end the rape kit backlog. The six-pillar framework is important because it provides a way to track progress, see which states are moving toward comprehensive reform, and determine which states need additional support to improve SAK handling and processing. The six-pillar framework is also essential for informing policy efforts and allowing stakeholders to determine where more resources or attention is needed. There is an ongoing need for research to investigate whether or not there are any more elements that should be included in this framework. We also need to focus on how to secure compliance with state laws. That is, once a state has adopted all six pillars, is there anything else that must be done to assure SAKs are dealt with in a comprehensive manner?

There has also been advancement of legislation that covers Joyful Heart's six pillars of comprehensive reform. Five of the six pillars are adopted by around two-thirds of states: forward testing (33 states), inventory (32 states), victim notification (30 states), funding (29 states), and tracking (27 states). The least addressed pillar is the backlog (only 9 states passed laws). By overall reform, inventory is the most common pillar (42 states), followed by tracking (34 states), forward testing (33 states), backlog (31 states), victims' right to notification (30 states), and funding (31 states). Joyful Heart's first priority is the inventory pillar, because we know that a statewide count of backlogged SAKs is critical for displaying the extent of the problem. It also provides a baseline from which states move forward. Consistent with our priority, mandating an inventory is the most achieved pillar.

Looking at pillar trends, beginning in 2010, there has been a steady increase in legislation passed, with a peak in 2019. In 2020, we saw a dip which is believed to be a result of the social and economic hardship brought on by the pandemic. In 2021 we saw a rise in bills to levels similar to pre-pandemic legislative trends. This implies that stakeholders, including state legislators, have not forgotten the importance of passing legislation to achieve comprehensive RKR. In the coming years, there is reason to believe that legislative bills will continue to be passed as advocates at state and local levels remain committed to the fight for justice and to ensuring the rights of survivors of sexual assault.

Two obstacles to the advancement of RKR—non-compliance of RKR legislation and lack of funding—were discussed. Although there has been great legislative progress, there is still a need to achieve full comprehensive reform nationwide. There are various ways to address these obstacles, from inserting compliance measures within RKR bills, to applying for federal grants. There are ample opportunities for further research, including the use of additional effective compliance measures, or ways to maximize kit testing to be more economical and efficient.

The RKR field is complex. More laws are being passed, but we are also seeing obstacles that may limit progress. At Joyful Heart, we believe the field is headed in the right direction, that momentum is on our side, but that there is still considerable work to be done.

Key Points

- The Joyful Heart Foundation created a legislative framework that would provide a path to comprehensive reform around the way SAKs are handled nationwide.
- This framework is comprised of six pillars: (1) annual statewide inventory of untested SAKs, (2) mandatory testing of backlogged SAKs, (3) mandatory testing of newly collected SAKs, (4) establishment of a kit tracking system, (5) granting victims the right to know the status and location of their kit, and finally, and (6) establishing funding to carry out these previous five pillars.
- Since 2010, we have seen a steady increase in the number of bills introduced and passed that seek to improve the way SAKs are handled and processed.
- The COVID-19 pandemic caused a dramatic dip in the number of pillar bills passed.
- In 2021 as states recovered, we saw the amount of enacted pillar bills increase to pre-pandemic levels.
- The majority of RKR bills had bipartisan sponsorship.
- Though we have made great progress, there are still issues to address: non-compliance to existing RKR laws and lack of funding to carry out these reforms.
- There are potential solutions to these problems. As for non-compliance, adding compliance clauses to rape kit-related legislation and having state-level watchdog figures monitor compliance could ameliorate the issues. For lack of funds, states should commit to public safety as a priority and allocate more of their funds to facilitate testing and storage of SAKs, and/or apply for available federal grants.

Discussion Questions

1 Moving forward, is there a need to add more pillars to the six-pillar framework advanced by the Joyful Heart Foundation in order to fully cover "comprehensive reform"? In other words, can a state that has adopted all six pillars improve any further in the way they handle and process SAKs, or in the way victims gain information about their kit as it moves through the justice system?
2 Do you believe there will be an increase in legislation in 2022? 2023? 2024? Why or why not?
3 What other compliance methods can be applied to the RKR field? How can states ensure that reform bills are being enacted?

Further Reading

Bureau of Justice Assistance. (2018). *Unsubmitted sexual assault kits: Navigating the process from inventory to adjudication—A guide for Holistic Cold Case Sexual Assault Reform* (pp. 1–13).
Jeanguenat, A. (2018). *Understanding DNA testing and reporting: Unsubmitted sexual assault kits.* Department of Justice's Bureau of Justice Assistance.
Peterson, J. Johnson, D., Herz, D. Graziano, L. & Oehler, T. (2012). *Sexual assault kit backlog study.*

Notes

1 A total of 31 states are testing their backlogged kits through legislative or non-legislative means. They are Alaska, Arizona, Colorado, Connecticut, Delaware, Florida, Georgia, Hawaii, Illinois, Iowa, Kansas, Kentucky, Maryland, Massachusetts, Michigan, Missouri, Montana, Nevada, New Mexico, New York, North Carolina, Ohio, Oklahoma, Oregon, Pennsylvania, Texas, Utah, Virginia, Washington, West Virginia, and Wisconsin.
2 There is a bill currently being debated in Wisconsin that, if passed, would change these totals.

References

BJA Fact Sheet. (2021). *Sexual assault forensic evidence—inventory, tracking, and reporting (SAFE-ITR),* July 2021.
Bureau of Justice Assistance. (2022, January). *National sexual assault kit initiative infographic.* https://bja.ojp.gov/library/publications/national-sexual-assault-kit-initiative-infographic
Campbell, R., Feeney, H., Pierce, S. J., Sharma, D. B., & Fehler-Cabral, G. (2016). Tested at last: How DNA evidence in untested rape kits can identify offenders and serial sexual assaults. *Journal of Interpersonal Violence, 33*(24), 3792–3814. https://doi.org/10.1177/0886260516639585
Campbell, R., Shaw, J., & Fehler–Cabral, G. (2015). Shelving justice: The discovery of thousands of untested rape kits in Detroit. *City & Community, 14*(2), 151–166. https://doi.org/10.1111/cico.12108
Crime Victim Ombudsman. (n.d.). *South Carolina Attorney General.* https://www.scag.gov/inside-the-office/crime-victim-services-division/crime-victim-ombudsman/
Joyful Heart Foundation. (2016). *Navigating notification: A guide to re-engaging sexual assault survivors affected by the untested rape kit backlog.*

Lovell, R., Singer, M., Flannery, D., & McGuire, M. (2021) The case for "investigate all": Assessing the cost-effectiveness of investigating no CODIS hit cases in a sexual assault kit initiative, *Journal of Forensic Sciences*, 66(4).

Office of the Attorney General Xavier Becerra, Division of Law Enforcement Bureau of Forensic Services. (2020). *Statewide audit of untested sexual assault forensic evidence kits 2020 report to the legislature.* https://oag.ca.gov/sites/all/files/agweb/pdfs/publications/ag-rpt-audit-usasfe-kits-2020.pdf

Office of the New York State Comptroller, Thomas P. DiNapoli, State Comptroller Division of State Government Accountability. (2020). *Processing of sexual offense evidence collection kits.* https://www.osc.state.ny.us/files/state-agencies/audits/pdf/sga-2020-19s44_0.pdf

Sexual Assault Forensic Evidence – Inventory, Tracking, and Reporting (SAFE-ITR) Program, Funding (2022) https://bja.ojp.gov/program/safe-itr/funding

Singer, M., Lovell, R., & Flannery, D. (2016). *Cost Savings and Cost Effectiveness of the Cuyahoga County Sexual Assault Kit Task Force.* The Begun Center for Violence Prevention Education and Research at the Jack, Joseph and Morton Mandel School of Applied Social Sciences at Case Western Reserve University. http://hdl.handle.net/2186/ksl:2006061446

Section III

Where do we want to be?

Envisioning a future reformed response

19 Advancements in trauma-informed training and interviewing for law enforcement and prosecutors

Bradley A. Campbell

History of Trauma-Informed Training for Sexual Assault Responders

Research on sexual assault case processing has revealed that police decisions to arrest, and prosecutors' decisions to accept charges, often rely on misconceptions about sexual assault and survivors (Lapsey et al., 2021; Spohn et al., 2001). Specifically, police and prosecutors often make faulty judgments about survivor credibility and case convictability (Bostaph et al., 2021; Campbell et al., 2015). These judgments are often based on common rape myths and perceptions held by practitioners about "good" cases that are likely to move forward in the criminal justice process (Bollingmo et al., 2007; Estrich, 1987). For example, studies have found that police and prosecutors have often adhered to the myth that "true" sexual assault cases involve an unknown offender who uses force and/or weapons, and a survivor who resisted the attack and sustained visible injuries (Estrich, 1987). Other studies have shown that some practitioners also have followed misconceptions about the behavior of sexual assault survivors. In sum, these studies have demonstrated that often practitioners believe "true" survivors will report victimization immediately (Alderden & Ullman, 2012; Frazier & Haney, 1996; LaFree, 1981), will be emotionally expressive—or visibly upset (Bollingmo et al., 2007), and will be able to recall all details of an assault directly after victimization (Campbell et al., 2015). For cases that do not fit these myths, practitioners may question survivor credibility, perceptions about case convictability are reduced, and case attrition is common (Frohmann, 1991, 1997; Kerstetter, 1990). In relation to the decision to test sexual assault kits (SAKs), these myths can also affect practitioner decisions to submit and request SAKs for testing (Campbell & Lapsey, 2021; Campbell & Fehler-Cabral, 2018).

Following these misperceptions when making decisions in sexual assault cases is problematic, as most cases do not reflect these common myths (Lonsway, 2010). Indeed, most survivors know their perpetrator (Smith et al., 2018), few offenders use force or a weapon (Sinozich & Langton, 2014), and many survivors do not report to the police at all, let alone immediately after the assault (Lorenz et al., 2021, see Chapter 3). Additionally, due to the neurobiological effects of trauma on the brain (Van der Kolk, 2015), many survivors are inconsistent when recalling the details of an assault (Franklin et al., 2020; Lonsway, 2010), display a range of emotions when reporting, and can be unable to recount all details of an assault immediately after victimization (Campbell, 2012; see also Chapter 8). Finally, research has also documented that between 37% and 70% of survivors experienced tonic immobility—a natural "freeze" response to extreme fear or trauma—inhibiting their ability to resist

DOI: 10.4324/9781003186816-23

an attacker because they are physically unable to move (Marx et al., 2008; Moller et al., 2017).

In light of these well-documented contradictions to myths about sexual assault cases and survivors, advocates have pushed for reforms to change sexual assault response training for police and prosecutors since the 1970s and 1980s (Field, 1978; Vito et al., 1983). This call for more training focuses on educating practitioners about the realities of sexual assault cases, how to improve the treatment of sexual assault survivors by the criminal justice system, and, more recently, trauma-informed responses to survivors. Trauma-informed training aims to educate officers about the neurobiological effects of trauma and encourages methods of interviewing and interacting with survivors that can improve survivor well-being, increase survivor engagement with the justice system, and can ultimately help practitioners conduct strong investigations to hold offenders accountable (Ahrens, 2006; Campbell et al., 2021; Lathan et al., 2021). These approaches to sexual assault investigations incorporate the four "R's" of trauma-informed care that highlight the importance of (1) realizing the extent of trauma, (2) recognizing the signs of trauma, (3) responding with trauma-informed care and policies, and (4) resisting retraumatization (SAMHSA, 2014). For example, interviews conducted with survivors of sexual assault revealed the importance of acknowledging trauma, treating survivors with empathy and respect, allowing survivors a voice in the investigative process, and reducing the retraumatizing effects of the criminal justice system and processes (Lorenz et al., 2021; Maier, 2008). Indeed, recent research has demonstrated that when criminal justice actors engage with survivors in a trauma-informed manner, survivors are less likely to report self-blame (Murphy-Oikonen et al., 2020) and are more likely to continue engaging with the criminal justice process (Bostaph et al., 2021; Lorenz et al., 2021).

Though advocates have pushed for reforms to change sexual assault response training for police and prosecutors over the last five decades (Field, 1978), few jurisdictions have implemented trauma-informed training programs, and even fewer empirical evaluations of such programs exist in the published literature (Sleath & Bull, 2017). A cursory search of the published literature dating back to 1975 revealed just over 20 studies that explicitly evaluated police sexual assault training programs, while no evaluations of such training for prosecutors were identified (see Chapter 11). Existing training evaluations generally support the efficacy of sexual assault training for police officers and investigators (see Campbell & Lapsey, 2021). For example, several studies revealed that trauma-informed training can improve officers' short- and long-term perceptions of survivors (Campbell et al., 2021; Franklin et al., 2020), knowledge of trauma-informed investigative practices (Campbell et al., 2020; Darwinkel et al., 2013; Lathan et al., 2021; Tidmarsh et al., 2020), behavior in mock interviews with survivors (Tidmarsh et al., 2021), and survivor engagement with investigators in real cases (Mourtgos et al., 2021).

Untested SAKs and the Adoption of Trauma-Informed Training in the United States

While in graduate school, I (B. Campbell) worked with Dr. William Wells of Sam Houston State University (SHSU) on the Houston, TX Sexual Assault Kit Backlog Action Research Project from 2011 to 2015. Some of my earliest research on police responses to sexual assault indicated that sexual assault investigators yearned for specialized training to improve responses to survivors of sexual assault. During the summer of 2011, during interviews we conducted with 44 members of the adult and juvenile sex crimes unit in the Houston Police Department (HPD), we found that though most investigators did not have formal training in sex crimes, several investigators believed sexual assault investigations training would be helpful to improve police response to survivors (Campbell & Wells, 2014). Based on this finding, my research assignment was to identify training options to meet the needs of these investigators. Though some training resources were identified (see Campbell & Wells, 2014), as noted above, few jurisdictions had adopted training programs for sexual assault response and not much was known about the effectiveness of these programs. Over the past 12 years, it has been rewarding to see the advances in the understanding of the backlog of untested SAKs in several other jurisdictions, especially the creation and evaluation of training programs focused on improving sexual assault investigations.

Indeed, the discovery of backlogs of untested SAKs across the United States has pushed several agencies and organizations to develop and adopt new training programs in the last ten years. Beginning with Rebecca Campbell's (2012) discussion of the neurobiology of trauma and sexual assault survivors, trauma-informed training for sexual assault response has become more mainstream. Information on trauma-informed response to sexual assault survivors is widely available online via training briefs from End Violence Against Women International, the International Association of Chiefs of Police, and the National Sexual Assault Kit Initiative (SAKI). For example, SAKI has compiled several training resources for police and prosecutors to effectively respond to survivors of sexual assault in a trauma-informed manner. SAKI offers both a virtual academy (https://academy.sakitta.org/) and a toolkit (https://www.sakitta.org/toolkit/index.cfm) that provide detailed information for the investigation and prosecution of sexual assault cases. In the SAKI virtual academy, police and prosecutors can complete self-paced online training programs that cover topics such as trauma-informed approaches to survivor interactions, planning for investigations and prosecutions, how to minimize retraumatization of survivors, and how to overcome challenges in both new and cold case investigations. Similarly, the SAKI toolkit provides several training resources and checklists for each stage of an investigation or prosecution (see Chapter 6).

In terms of in-person trauma-informed trainings, which were sparked by the discovery of untested SAKs across the United States, at least three cities (Houston, TX; Salt Lake City, UT; Mobile, AL) and one state (Commonwealth of Kentucky) that addressed their backlog have implemented and evaluated trauma-informed training curricula in the last ten years. As shown in Table 19.1, each of these jurisdictions has implemented different training curricula. At the city level, individual police departments developed training programs aimed at a broad audience of both patrol officers and investigators. First, after addressing a backlog of more than 6,500 untested SAKs (Wells et al., 2016), the Houston, Texas Police Department (HPD) implemented four hours of department-wide in-service trainings that covered the neurobiology of trauma, best practices for responding to sexual assault and domestic violence, as well as several community resources available to survivors (Franklin et al., 2020). In their evaluation of the HPD program, Franklin et al. (2020) used a pre- and post-test survey design to assess officers' misperceptions of survivors' responses to trauma both

Table 19.1 Training Programs and Evaluations from Jurisdictions that Addressed Backlogged SAKs

Authors	Study site (audience)	Design	Training program	Outcome measures and effects
Franklin et al. (2020)	Houston, TX (all sworn officers)	Pre- and post-test • 514 pre-training surveys • 468 post-training surveys	Four hours of instruction • Best practices for responding to sexual and family violence • Neurobiology of trauma • Resources available for survivors	Officer misperceptions of trauma • Reduced officers' misperceptions of trauma
Mourtgos et al. (2021)	Salt Lake City, UT (all sworn officers)	Pre- and post-test • 77 pre-training cases • 55 post-training cases	Four hours of instruction • Understanding offenders • Neurobiology of trauma • Rape myth acceptance • Research on false allegations • Victim interviews • Departmental policy	Officer behavior and victim engagement • Increased victim engagement with investigators
Lathan et al. (2021)	Mobile, AL (all sworn officers)	Pre- and post-test • 331 pre-training surveys • 229 post-training surveys	Two hours of instruction • Neurobiology of trauma • Officers' role in sex crimes investigations • Benefits of testing SAKs	Officer knowledge of trauma and perceptions of victims • Increased knowledge of trauma • No effect on perceptions of victims
Campbell et al. (2020)	Kentucky (officers sent by agency to mandatory state training)	Randomized experiment • 250 training group surveys • 114 control group surveys	Forty hours of instruction • Sexual assault laws • Victim-centered response • Neurobiology of trauma • Victim interviewing • Role of SAKs in investigations • Misconceptions about survivors	Officer knowledge and perceptions of victims • Reduced misconceptions about survivors • Increased knowledge of laws • Increased knowledge of trauma-informed practice

before and after completion of the training. A comparison of pre- and post-training results indicated that the training was effective and significantly reduced misperceptions of trauma.

Like the HPD training, the Salt Lake City, Utah Police Department (SLCPD) also created a four-hour block of in-service training; however, the SLCPD program focused directly on the relationship between trauma-informed responses to sexual assault investigations and survivor engagement with sex crimes detectives (Mourtgos et al., 2021). Specifically, the SLCPD curriculum covered research regarding sexual assault offenders, survivor vulnerabilities exploited by offenders, the neurobiology of trauma, rape myth acceptance, research on the small percentage of false allegations, as well as survivor interview techniques and new department policies for responding to sexual assault. Mourtgos and colleagues assessed changes in survivor engagement by comparing six months of pre-training reports with six months of post-training reports. Findings indicated that survivor engagement—defined as survivors' continued participation with an investigator after making a report—significantly increased in the post-training period. Finally, Lathan et al. (2021) evaluated the effectiveness of a two-hour trauma-informed training that educated officers in the Mobile, Alabama Police Department (MPD) about the neurobiology of trauma, officers' role in sex crimes investigations, and the benefits of testing SAKs. The study assessed officers' perceptions of survivors and knowledge of trauma using pre- and post-training surveys. While results indicated that officers' perceptions of survivors—measured using a rape myth acceptance scale—were unchanged by the training, officers' knowledge of the neurobiology of trauma faced by survivors of sexual assault significantly increased.

Taken together, these studies provide evidence that short training programs offered by individual jurisdictions can have a positive impact on officer knowledge of trauma-informed responses and survivor engagement with investigations. To provide an example of a (much longer) statewide training and an evaluation design that could be used in other jurisdictions, the section below describes an evaluation I led that assessed the effectiveness of Kentucky's statewide mandated trauma-informed sexual assault investigation training program.

Untested SAKs and Kentucky's Trauma-Informed Sexual Assault Investigations Training

After working on the Houston SAK Backlog Action Research Project and graduating from Sam Houston State University, I was hired by the University of Louisville's Department of Criminal Justice in 2015. Through a serendipitous encounter, Dr. William Wells connected me with the Kentucky State Police Crime Lab Director and the Director of the Kentucky Association of Sexual Assault Programs, who were embarking on an effort to address the backlog of untested SAKs in Kentucky. Based on this encounter, I was fortunate to be connected with the Kentucky Sexual Assault Kit Backlog efforts in 2016. Upon joining the statewide task force as the lead research partner, I was elated to learn that Kentucky was in the early stages of implementing several reforms, *including a new state-mandated sexual assault investigations training program*. Specifically, after a 2015 audit identified more than 4,500 untested SAKs, the Kentucky Legislature passed the 2016 Sexual Assault Forensic Exam (SAFE) Act to reform the state's criminal justice response to

---

Box 19.1
___

Sexual assault reform in Kentucky

- SAFE Act (or KRS 15.384)

  - Beginning 01/01/2017, mandatory 40-hour training for all law enforcement agencies

- Number of officers required based on agency size

  - Agencies with 4 or fewer officers = 1 officer must attend
  - Agencies with 5–29 officers = 2 officers must attend
  - Agencies with 30 or more officers = 4 officers must be trained

---

sexual assault survivors (Kentucky SAFE Act of 2016). A portion of the SAFE Act required that beginning January 1, 2017, at least one officer from every Kentucky law enforcement agency must attend a *40-hour* training focused on trauma-informed sexual assault investigations. Box 19.1 illustrates the number of officers required to attend the training based on agency size. The training program was developed by the Kentucky Department of Criminal Justice Training (KY DOCJT). The course is a comprehensive 40-hour training program that covers several topics related to trauma-informed investigations including Kentucky sexual assault laws, survivor-centered responses to sexual assault survivors (e.g., neurobiology of trauma, community coordinated responses, survivor interviewing), the role of SAKs in investigations, and common misconceptions about sexual assault cases and survivors (see Box 19.2 and Campbell & Lapsey, 2021; Campbell et al., 2021 for a complete list of training topics).

Box 19.2
___

KY DOCJT sexual assault investigations training course: Topics covered

1 Kentucky laws
2 Rape myths
3 Victim impact
4 Model law enforcement response
5 SART response
6 Investigative strategy
7 Special communities
8 DNA evidence
9 Forensic examination
10 Offender dynamics
11 Preliminary investigation
12 Victim interview
13 Unfounded cases

Because the training program was new, the KY DOCJT agreed to add an evaluation component to assess the effectiveness of the training on three outcomes: (1) officers' adherence to rape myths, (2) Kentucky sexual assault laws, and (3) knowledge of trauma-informed practices. To accomplish this goal, we used data collected from a randomized survey design to answer the following research questions:

- *RQ1: What are the short- and long-term effects of the KY DOCJT training on police officers' self-reported levels of rape myth acceptance?*
- *RQ2: What are the short- and long-term effects of the KY DOCJT training on police officers' knowledge of Kentucky sexual assault laws?*
- *RQ3: What are the short- and long-term effects of the KY DOCJT training on police officers' knowledge of trauma-informed practices?*

Participants in the evaluation included officers selected by their police department to attend one of 11 KY DOCJT sexual assault training courses delivered between May 2017 and April 2018. Of the 396 officers who attended the course, 364 (92%) completed surveys. To evaluate the impact of the training, we employed a randomized three-group design which allowed us to ensure that changes in the three outcome variables were caused by the KY DOCJT training and not an undetected cause and/or survey questions that primed officers to respond in a certain way. Following this design, each of the eleven KY DOCJT sexual assault courses were randomly assigned to three groups: (1) Group A—pre- and post-training assessment (*n* = 144), (2) Group B—post-training only assessment (*n* = 106), and (3) Group C—pre-training only assessment—no training (*n* = 114). Through this design, we created two treatment groups—Groups A and B—of officers who had completed the KY DOCJT sexual assault training and one control group—Group C—of officers who had not completed the sexual assault training course but completed the pre-training assessments. Table 19.2 displays the study design and the schedule of survey assessments.

Results of the Kentucky Trauma-Informed Training Evaluation

Findings from the descriptive analyses are displayed in Table 19.3 (see also Campbell et al., 2020). The following results are derived from our comparisons of Group A's pre- and post-test scores, and a comparison of Group B's post-test scores with Group C's pre-test scores. In this report, we present only descriptive findings and statistical significance testing to assess whether any changes

Table 19.2 Randomized Three-Group Design and Schedule of Assessments (N = 364)

	Treatment groups		Control group
	Group A (n = 144)	*Group B (n = 106)*	*Group C (n = 114)*
Pre-test assessment	X	–	X
KYDOCJT training	X	X	X
Post-test assessment	X	X	–
Follow-up assessment	X	X	–

Table 19.3 Impact of Training on Outcome Variables

Outcome variable	Group	Test type	Average difference	t-score	Significance (95%)	Effect size d
Rape myth acceptance	A (pre/ post-test)	Paired samples t-test	0.1646 (−10.9%)	5.053	*	0.8422[a]
	C vs. B	Independent samples t-test	0.1864 (−12.1%)	3.370	*	0.4598[b]
Knowledge of KY law	A (pre/ post-test)	Paired samples t-test	0.4321 (−14.1%)	2.459	*	0.4098[a]
	C vs. B	Independent samples t-test	0.9992 (−30.9%)	5.106	*	0.6889[b]
Knowledge of trauma practice	A (pre/ post-test)	Paired samples t-test	0.486 (9.5%)	−7.432	*	1.2387[a]
	C vs. B	Independent samples t-test	0.415 (8.1%)	−3.651	*	0.4926[b]

Notes:

[a] Cohen's *d* standardized mean difference (t-test, equal sample sizes).

[b] Cohen's *d* standardized mean difference (t-test unequal sample sizes).

*$p < 0.05$.

in the dependent variable are statistically significant. (For a full discussion of the multivariable statistical analyses, along with a list of questions used to create outcome measure, see Campbell et al., 2020). We assessed both the short- and long-term effects of the training of officers' knowledge about laws and trauma-informed responses, as well as their perceptions of survivors. The short-term results discussing the impact of the KY DOCJT training are discussed below, followed by a summary of the long-term follow-up assessment and its associated findings.

Short-term results. Rape myth acceptance was measured using an average of officers' responses to 17 questions derived from the Illinois Rape Myth Acceptance— Short Form Scale (IRMA-SF; Lonsway et al., 2001). Based on the IRMA-SF, lower average scores indicate a lower level of rape myth acceptance. A comparison of Group A's pre- and post-training scores indicated a 10.9% reduction in rape myth acceptance. A statistical significance test revealed that this reduction was significant and that training produced a large effect on rape myth acceptance.[1] These results are supported by the comparison of Groups B and C, which produced a statistically significant 12.1% reduction in average rape myth acceptance. Based on this relationship, the data indicated that training had a medium effect on rape myth acceptance when comparing Group C's pre-training scores with Group B's post-training scores.

Knowledge of Kentucky laws was measured using officers' responses to two questions that assessed their understanding of two new laws implemented in 2017 by the SAFE Act, which was combined into a scale with lower average scores representing a higher level of knowledge of Kentucky laws. As shown in Table 19.3, when comparing Group A's pre-training scores and post-training scores, we see a significant increase in officers' knowledge, represented by a 14.1% improvement in knowledge, producing a medium effect size. Similarly, when comparing Group C's knowledge scores with Group B, our analysis detected a significant improvement in knowledge (30.9%), representing a medium effect of training on officers' knowledge of Kentucky law.

Finally, officers' knowledge of trauma-informed practices was measured using four questions. For this outcome, higher scores represent more knowledge. Findings indicated that training significantly improved officers' knowledge of trauma-informed practices in Group A by 9.5%, demonstrating that training had a large effect on officers' knowledge of trauma-informed practice. When comparing Group C with Group B, results also detected a significant increase in knowledge (8.1%), representing a medium effect size.

Long-term results. Because the training was effective at improving officer knowledge and behavior in the short term, the KY DOCJT also sought to assess the long-term effects of the training program. Follow-up surveys were sent to the 250 members of Groups A and B in August and September of 2018. After 3 waves of emails, 71 officers (28%) returned completed surveys. An average of 361 days had passed between the completion of the trauma-informed sexual assault investigations training and the follow-up survey with a minimum of 246 days and a maximum of 466 days.[2]

Using this follow-up survey, we compared officers' average scores for each of our outcome scales (e.g., rape myth acceptance, knowledge of new Kentucky laws, knowledge of trauma-informed practices) with their immediate post-training scores. The results demonstrated that all scores held over time, indicating that the training was effective at improving perceptions of survivors, knowledge of laws, and knowledge of trauma-informed practice in both short and long-term assessments.

Summary of Trauma-Informed Training and Future Directions

Based on findings from the trauma-informed training evaluations discussed here, this type of training shows promising results for improving officer knowledge, perceptions of survivors, and survivor engagement with investigators. However, more training programs should be implemented and evaluated to determine (a) the length and content of training for optimal outcomes, and (b) if trauma-informed training for prosecutors provides similar results. To the first point, the training programs discussed in this chapter evaluated programs of varying length and content, though these programs covered similar topics. To increase our understanding of the most effective training programs, evaluations of similar training programs with varying lengths should be assessed. Second, while training programs for prosecutors exist and are being offered, evaluations of a participant's cognitive, attitudinal, and behavioral outcomes should be conducted. Doing so will begin to build an evidence base to assess the effectiveness of trauma-informed training for prosecutors and determine ideal training modalities to maximize results.

Key Points

- Efforts to address backlogs of untested SAKs have sparked a movement for more trauma-informed training for practitioners
- Jurisdictions that have implemented trauma-informed training programs have demonstrated positive results including improvements in police perceptions of

survivors, knowledge of trauma-informed practice, and improvements in survivor engagement

• More training program implementation and evaluation are needed to determine optimal training length and content evaluations of trauma-informed training for prosecutors are needed to build an evidence base for prosecutor education

Discussion Questions

1 What are the key components of trauma-informed training for professionals (e.g., police officers, prosecutors, advocates)?
2 Should these training programs be mandated? Why or why not?

Funding Acknowledgment and Author Note

This project was supported by Grant No. 2017-AK-BX-009 awarded by the Bureau of Justice Assistance. The Bureau of Justice Assistance is a component of the Department of Justice's Office of Justice Programs, which also includes the Bureau of Justice Statistics, the National Institute of Justice, the Office of Juvenile Justice and Delinquency Prevention, the Office for Victims of Crime, and the SMART Office. Points of view or opinions in this chapter are those of the author and do not necessarily represent the official position or policies of the US Department of Justice.

Notes

1 The magnitude of each relationship is calculated using Cohen's *d* formula for assessing effect size. To calculate Cohen's *d*, or standardized mean difference effect sizes for each of our analyses, we used Wilson's Practical Meta-Analysis Effect Size Calculator (found here https://campbellcollaboration.org/effect-size-calculato.html). Based on Cohen's (1992) recommendations for interpreting the magnitude of *d*, 0.2 is interpreted as a small effect, 0.5 is considered a medium effect, and 0.8 is interpreted as a large effect.
2 To be sure that officers who completed the follow-up assessment did not differ from officers who did not, we conducted balance tests using t-tests for demographic variables. Significant differences were not detected for any of the size demographic variables (gender, age, years in policing, highest level of education, prior sexual assault investigations training, and number of sexual assaults investigated in the last year). These results indicated that our follow-up assessment group was comparable to the full sample.

Further Reading

Campbell, B. A., Lapsey, D. S., Jr., & Wells, W. (2020). An evaluation of Kentucky's sexual assault investigator training: Results from a randomized three-group experiment. *Journal of Experimental Criminology, 16*, 625–647.

Franklin, C. A., Garza, A. D., Goodson, A., & Bouffard, L. A. (2020). Police perceptions of crime victim behaviors: A trend analysis exploring mandatory training and knowledge of sexual and domestic violence survivors' trauma responses. *Crime & Delinquency, 66*, 1055–1086.

Lathan, E. C., Langhinrichsen-Rohling, J. Stefurak, J. T., Duncan, J., & Selwyn, C. N. (2021). Attempting to enhance sexual assault-related understanding and reduce rape myth beliefs and burnout among police officers. *Policing: A Journal of Policy and Practice.* https://doi.org/10.1093/police/paab076

Mourtgos, S. M., Adams, I. T., & Mastracci, S. H. (2021). Improving victim engagement and officer response in rape investigations: A longitudinal assessment of a brief training. *Journal of Criminal Justice*, 74, 1–10.

SAMHSA. (2014). Substance Abuse and Mental Health Services Administration's concept of trauma and guidance for a trauma-informed approach. Retrieved from https://store.samhsa.gov/sites/default/files/d7/priv/sma14-4884.pdf

References

Ahrens, C. E. (2006). Being silenced: The impact of negative social reactions on the disclosure of rape. *American Journal of Community Psychology*, 38, 263–274.

Alderden, M. A., & Ullman, S. E. (2012). Creating a more complete and current picture: Examining police and prosecutor decision-making when processing sexual assault cases. *Violence against Women*, 18, 525–551.

Bollingmo, G. C., Wessel, E. O., Eillertsen, D. E., & Magnussen, S. (2007). Credibility of the emotional witness: Ratings by police investigators. *Psychology, Crime, & Law*, 14, 29–40.

Bostaph, L. G., King, L. L., & Brady, P. Q. (2021). How victim credibility and cooperation influence investigative decision-making: Examining DOJ's gender bias principles for investigating domestic and sexual violence. *Policing: An International Journal*, 44, 612–627.

Campbell, R. (2012). The neurobiology of sexual assault: Implications for first responders in law enforcement, prosecution, and victim advocacy. *NIJ Research for the Real World Seminar*. https://www.ncjrs.gov/App/Publications/abstract.aspx

Campbell, R., & Fehler-Cabral, G. (2018). Why police "couldn't or wouldn't" submit sexual assault kits for forensic testing: A focal concerns theory analysis of untested rape kits. *Law and Society Review*, 52, 73–105.

Campbell, B. A., & Lapsey, D. S. Jr. (2021). Do impulsivity and education moderate the effectiveness of police sexual assault investigations training? Findings from a Solomon four-group quasi-experiment. *Criminal Justice & Behavior*, 48, 1411–1430.

Campbell, B. A., Lapsey, D. S. Jr., & Wells, W. (2020). An evaluation of Kentucky's sexual assault investigator training: Results from a randomized three-group experiment. *Journal of Experimental Criminology*, 16, 625–647.

Campbell, B. A., Menaker, T. A., & King, W. R. (2015). The determination of victim credibility by juvenile and adult sexual assault investigators. *Journal of Criminal Justice*, 43, 29–39.

Campbell, B. A., & Wells, W. (2014). Sexual assault investigator training: perceptions from juvenile and adult sex crimes investigators. A report to the Houston, TX Sexual Assault Kit Action-Research Working Group. Retrieved from: http://houstonsakresearch.org/resources/documents/testing.pdf

Darwinkel, E., Powell, M., & Tidmarsh, P. (2013). Improving police officers' perception of sexual offending through intensive training. *Criminal Justice & Behavior*, 40, 895–908.

Estrich, S. (1987). *Real rape: How the system victimizes women who say no*. Harvard University Press.

Field, H. S. (1978). Attitudes toward rape: A comparative analysis of police, rapists, crisis counselors, and citizens. *Journal of Personality and Social Psychology*, 36, 156–179.

Franklin, C. A., Garza, A. D., Goodson, A., & Bouffard, L. A. (2020). Police perceptions of crime victim behaviors: A trend analysis exploring mandatory training and knowledge of sexual and domestic violence survivors' trauma responses. *Crime & Delinquency*, 66, 1055–1086.

Frazier, P. A., & Haney, B. (1996). Sexual assault cases in the legal system: Police, prosecutor, and victim perspectives. *Law & Human Behavior*, 20, 607–628.

Frohmann, L. (1991). Discrediting victims' allegations of sexual assault: Prosecutorial accounts of case rejections. *Social Problems*, 38, 213–226.

Frohmann, L. (1997). Convictability and discordant locales: Reproducing race, class, and gender ideologies in prosecutorial decision making. *Law & Society Review, 31*, 531–555.

Kerstetter, W. A. (1990). Gateway to justice: Police and prosecutorial response to sexual assaults against women. *Journal of Criminal Law and Criminology, 81*, 267–313.

LaFree, G. D. (1981). Official reactions to social problems: Police decisions in sexual assault cases. *Social Problems, 28*, 582–594.

Lapsey, D. S. Jr., Campbell, B. A., & Plumlee, B. T. (2021). Focal concerns and police decision making in sexual assault cases: A systematic review and meta-analysis. *Trauma, Violence, & Abuse.* https://doi.org/10.1177%2F1524838021991285.

Lonsway, K. A. (2010). Trying to move the elephant in the living room: Responding to the challenge of false rape reports. *Violence Against Women, 16*, 1356–1371.

Lonsway, K. A., Welch, S., & Fitzgerald, L. F. (2001). Police training in sexual assault response: Process, outcomes, and elements of change. *Criminal Justice and Behavior, 28*, 695–730.

Lorenz, K., Dewald, D., & Venema, R. (2021). "I was worried I wouldn't be believed": Sexual assault victims' perceptions of the police in the decision to not report. *Violence and Victims, 36*, 455–476.

Maier, S. L. (2008). "I have heard terrible stories …": Rape victim advocates perceptions of revictimization of rape victims by the police and medical system. *Violence against Women, 14*, 786–808.

Marx, B. P., Forsyth, J. P., Gallup, G. G., Fuse, T., & Lexington, J. M. (2008). Tonic immobility as an evolved predator defense: Implications for sexual assault survivors. *Clinical Psychology: Science & Practice, 15*, 74–90.

Moller, A., Sondergaard, H. P., & Helstrom, L. (2017). Tonic immobility during sexual assault: A common reaction predicting post-traumatic stress disorder and severe depression. *Acta Obstretricia et Gynecologica Scandinavica, 96*, 932–938.

Mourtgos, S. M., Adams, I. T., & Mastracci, S. H. (2021). Improving victim engagement and officer response in rape investigations: A longitudinal assessment of a brief training. *Journal of Criminal Justice, 74*, 1–10.

Murphy-Oikonen, J., McQueen, K., Miller, A., Chambers, L., & Hiebert, A. (2020). Unfounded sexual assault: Women's experiences of not being believed by the police. *Journal of Interpersonal Violence.* https://doi.org/10.1177%2F0886260520978190

Sinozich, S., & Langton, L. (2014). *Rape and sexual assault victimization among college-age females, 1995–2013.* US Department of Justice, Office of Justice Programs, Bureau of Justice Statistics.

Sleath, E., & Bull, R. (2017). Police perceptions of rape victims and the impact on case decision-making: A systematic review. *Aggression and Violent Behavior, 34*, 102–112.

Smith, S. G., Zhang, X., Basile, K. C., Merrick, M. T., Wang, J., Kresnow, M., & Chen, J. (2018). *The National Intimate Partner and Sexual Violence Survey (NISVS): 2015 data brief—Updated release.* National Center for Injury Prevention and Control, Centers for Disease Control and Prevention.

Spohn, C., Beichner, D., & Davis-Frenzel, E. (2001). Prosecutorial justifications for sexual assault case rejection: Guarding the "gateway to justice." *Social Problems, 48*, 206–235.

Tidmarsh, P., Hamilton, G., & Sharman, S. J. (2020). Changing police officers' attitudes in sexual offense cases: A 12-month follow-up study. *Criminal Justice and Behavior, 47*, 1176–1189.

van der Kolk, B. A. (2015). *The body keeps the score: Brain, mind, and body in the healing of trauma.* Viking.

Vito, G. F., Longmire, D. R., & Kenney, J. P. (1983). Can police action deter rape: Two views preventing rape: An evaluation of a multi-faceted program. *Police Studies: International Review of Police Development, 6*, 30.

Wells, W., Campbell, B. A., & Franklin, C. A. (2016). *Unsubmitted sexual assault kits in Houston, TX: Case characteristics, forensic testing results, and the investigation of CODIS hits.* National Institute of Justice, Office of Justice Programs, US Department of Justice.

20 The notification for victims of assault (NoVA)

Innovating future practice through a change process

Caitlin Sulley, Margaret Bassett, Yulanda McCarty-Harris, Melanie Susswein, and Noël Busch-Armendariz

Notification for Victims of Assault (NoVA): A Comprehensive Guide and Its Change Process

We are a group of researchers and educators who have worked in the domain of interpersonal violence, including human trafficking, sexual assault, and intimate partner violence for over two decades. Our vision is for all people to live peaceful and prosperous lives in a world free from violence. We began work on victim notification in cases with untested sexual assault kits (SAKs) in 2011 as members of the Houston SAK Action Research Project funded by the National Institute of Justice (NIJ). We conducted research with survivors on notification experiences, needs, and preferences using an action research approach. Then, we collaboratively developed a victim notification protocol with a multidisciplinary team for the Houston Police Department and evaluated and revised the protocol. We subsequently received funding in 2016 from the Office on Violence Against Women (OVW) to create a national guide on trauma-informed notification practices. Our goal is for our victim notification research and tools to inform and enhance the work of professionals to serve survivors better.

Notification for Victims of Assault (NoVA) is a comprehensive guide about SAK testing and the resulting need for victim notification regarding newly obtained forensic results or to give victims details about the progression of their case after a potentially long and inexplicable delay in the process. NoVA addresses the need for a Coordinated Community Response (CCR) to victim notification to successfully re-engage victims after testing their previously unsubmitted SAKs. NoVA highlights the need to utilize trauma-informed, victim-centered protocols and build effective practices moving forward. The key to lasting change is to create multidisciplinary engagement and collaboration. NoVA is to be used in conjunction with state and federal statutes about confidentiality, and other resources, to seek the most expedient justice in sexual assault cases. NoVA was empirically developed and includes best practices and current science about the necessary steps for victim notification through a CCR.

The NoVA guide was developed from original data, which included interviews and consultations with national experts and practitioners. This chapter's existing literature and contents are reprinted from the original NoVA report with permission from IDVSA, The University of Texas at Austin. Throughout the NoVA guide, we refer to lessons learned in the case studies of Memphis, Tennessee; Detroit, Michigan; and

DOI: 10.4324/9781003186816-24

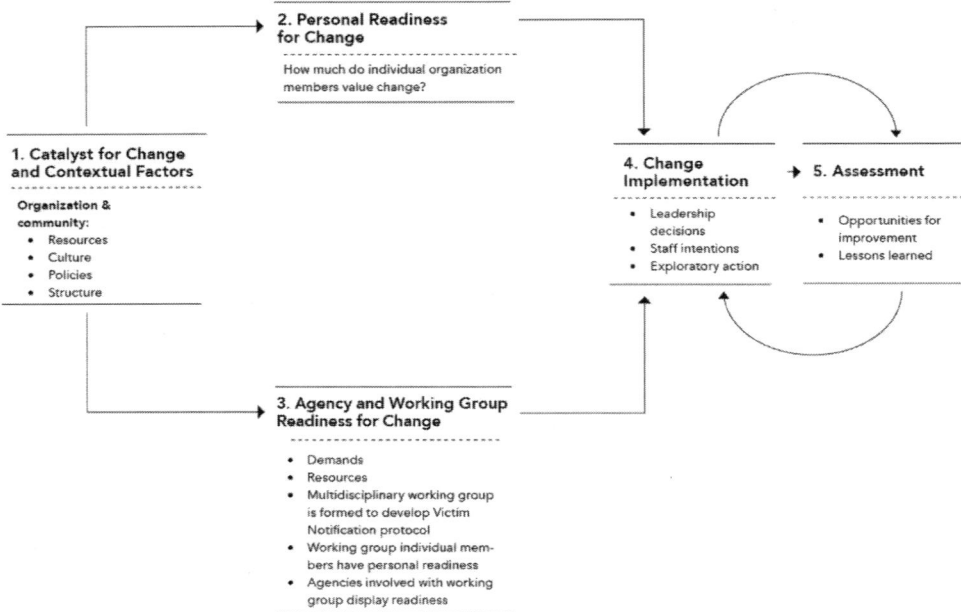

Figure 20.1 NoVA Change Process

Houston, Texas. Memphis has acted to address their untested SAKs and share information about their progress. Detroit and Houston were two projects funded by NIJ beginning in 2011, working to understand and address why kits were left untested.

The NoVA Change Process is based on four overarching principles: (1) victim-centered and trauma-informed, (2) procedural justice, (3) evidence-based and informed practices, and (4) criminal justice. Across these principles, The NoVA guide details a five-step process and provides 13 tools to support the execution of each step. Assessment strategies and tools help determine readiness for change, emphasize lessons learned from communities in Houston, Memphis, and Detroit, and facilitate ways to acknowledge and strategize practical concerns such as budget constraints.

As illustrated in Figure 20.1, NoVA is a *change process* where best practices and current science become standard operating procedures (SOPs). Through this process, the NoVA helps practitioners understand the critical components of victim-centered, trauma-informed notification, and how to apply them in their communities. The NoVA guide includes real-life case studies to assist communities in creating a collaborative, coordinated, and multidisciplinary response to re-engage victims after testing unrequested or untested SAKs.

Section 1. Getting Started Context and Catalyst for Victim Notification

Step 1: Assessing the Context and Catalyst for Change

This step describes how to leverage your community context and current catalyst(s) to better understand and address untested SAKs. Community assessment increases understanding of the climate for testing SAKs and motivations for implementing trauma-informed, victim-centered practices. The state and national context for victim notification, including the background of the national issue and relevant state and national legislation, are vital parts of every community's context.

Before developing a notification protocol, it is essential to assess your community context. Although there are emerging best practices for victim notification, the notification protocols and practices in your community will be unique and will need to be responsive to local needs, resources, histories, alliances, and tensions. Notification protocols should assess for the following issues: macro factors (state and federal laws), scientific evidence and emerging best practices, community factors such as resources and funding, community demographics, and culture, history, and pre-existing and ongoing health and justice inequities.

An important piece of context is identifying the catalyst for change—what is sparking the change to happen now? Changes, including initiating SAK testing or developing a multidisciplinary working group, do not occur independently. There must be an event, incident, person, or shift in thought that facilitates the community to overcome the status quo. Catalysts can be internal (e.g., decisions by leadership) or external (e.g., legal changes or media pressure; receipt of funding)—both scenarios present unique challenges and opportunities. More than one catalyst can exist in a community, and/or multiple catalysts can spur multiple change iterations. Understanding the catalyst(s) in your community helps you to prepare and plan your notification process. For example, an external catalyst like a lawsuit may increase negative pressure or media scrutiny. In this case, your community may need to focus more on protecting the victim's privacy and detailing a strategy to manage the media. On the flip side, external factors may also bring opportunities for increased resources or focused attention from community leadership.

Trauma-informed responses, services, and interviewing

Victims of trauma exhibit a wide range of reactions due to neurobiological processes (see Chapter 8). Reactions can range from lack of emotion to laughing to anxiety and fear, and more. Victims and communities need first responders and service providers to develop the ability to provide trauma-informed care to respond to these varied and potentially unexpected reactions (National Center for Trauma-Informed Care, 2015). We define trauma-informed care as an approach to sexual assault that: recognizes the wide-ranging impact of trauma as well as potential paths to recovery; understands the signs and symptoms of trauma in individuals, families, and community members involved in systems addressing sexual assault; takes steps to integrate evidence-based knowledge on trauma into policies, procedures, and practices; and seeks to prevent re-traumatization. Government and organizational entities that design sexual assault response systems to accommodate the varied consequences of trauma exposure ultimately help to reduce the risk of re-traumatizing those who come to them for help (Elliot et al., 2005). The scientific understanding of trauma continues to evolve. Consequently, responders must stay up to date to have the tools to recognize the impact and effects of trauma on victims.

Building trust with a victim is an especially important component of the interview process, and factors that influence supportive engagement can be communicated to the victim both verbally (e.g., words, tone) and through non-verbal cues (e.g., body language). Law enforcement has an opportunity when they interview victims to demonstrate supportive attitudes and build community trust using trauma-informed interviewing skills (Rich & Seffrin, 2012).

Victims are more likely to be open and provide useful information when they are relatively relaxed, feel that they can trust the investigator, and do not feel threatened or accused by the investigator (Lisak & Markel, 2016). Law enforcement should focus on interactions that build rapport and are validating. Victims also should not be treated or questioned as "witnesses" to their own assaults and put on the defensive (interrogated vs. interviewed); rather, engagement should focus on empathic listening and asking questions to elicit further information about their experience (Lisak & Markel, 2016). The Forensic Experiential Trauma Interviewing (FETI) is considered a best practice for effective, trauma-informed interview techniques (Memon et al., 2010).

The potential consequences and benefits of victim notification

Victim notification practices can have potential consequences and benefits related to trauma reactions and the outcome of a case. Attention to the methods of notification as well as careful consideration of a variety of factors prior to notification are important ways to increase the benefits of victim notification while reducing the likelihood of secondary and tertiary victimization. For example, the psychological consequences of notifying victims in older cases can include bringing up memories or feelings about the assault, triggering additional symptoms such as flashbacks or nightmares, worsening PTSD or other mental health issues, and/or influencing substance use and risky coping behavior (National Institute of Justice, 2016). Notification may also force unwanted disclosure (e.g., having to tell a spouse or child who previously did not know about the assault; Busch-Armendariz et al., 2015a).

While victim notification poses many potential risks, it also provides opportunities for re-engagement and may even generate positive psychological outcomes for victims. Victims interviewed about notification said that the process could lead to a variety of benefits for themselves and others, such as validating their experiences and empowering them, as survivors, with choices (Busch-Armendariz et al., 2015a; see also Chapter 9).

Section 2. Readiness for Change

Step 2: Your Personal Readiness for Change

Before a change can occur, one must be ready and willing to carry out the change. This NoVA step presents the components of personal readiness and describes its critical role. The Tools for Practice section includes personal readiness assessments that you and other members of your organization or team can use to determine your status in the change process.

Practitioners will need "personal readiness" to commit to carrying out change. One major component of personal readiness is a commitment to the sexual assault response field and to victim-centered practice. Readiness also includes an understanding of your own experiences and worldview as well as your willingness to reflect on potential biases or blind spots, particularly regarding members of marginalized communities. While several factors led to large inventories of untested SAKs, victim-blaming attitudes and stereotypes contributed as well (Campbell et al., 2015). Biases in these cases can have a racial or gendered component or be related to a bias against members of sexual minority groups (such as lesbian, gay, bisexual, transgender, queer or questioning, or LGBTQ individuals; US Department of Justice [DOJ], n.d.). These beliefs led to cases not moving forward, SAKs not being submitted for testing, and marginalized victims who felt disbelieved and consequently disengaged from the process.

Before one can be personally ready, understanding one's personal "bandwidth" or capacity to take on new roles and responsibilities is essential. SAK testing and victim notification require a dedicated team of staff members, a great deal of flexibility to handle the extra work that staff members must take on in addition to their often-large workloads, and the emotional stamina to listen to and connect with survivors whose victimization has been forgotten. People at all organizational levels must have personal readiness to receive the support they need from leadership to prioritize SAK testing and victim needs. Step 3 discusses the need for a "change-maker" or "champion"—an individual who has high personal readiness for change and is also willing to lead others toward higher personal readiness. At this intersection of personal commitment, self-reflection, institutional support, and adequate resources, agency and working group readiness for change can occur.

Step 3: Agency and Working Group Readiness for Change

Agency and working group readiness for change must be cultivated alongside personal readiness. These concepts are inextricable, and lasting change toward victim-centered, trauma-informed work cannot be achieved without them. In this step, "agency" refers to an individual organization. "Working group" refers to a multidisciplinary group of professionals, like a Sexual Assault Response Team (SART) or Coordinated Community Response (CCR) group. Research suggests that agencies can best address SAK testing and victim notification by working together in multidisciplinary groups (Campbell et al., 2016). Therefore, this step discusses the change process regarding agency *and* working group readiness for change. In addition, this step addresses common challenges to multidisciplinary work, building effective teams, and making decisions about your team. Some key components in this step include involving all relevant disciplines with the flexibility to incorporate new expertise and resources as they emerge. Teams that are proactive about their dynamics and anticipate opportunities and challenges, like issues of power and group status, internal and external communication, and member engagement, are more likely to succeed (see Chapter 15). This requires ongoing awareness and open collaboration among staff or group members. Therefore, a one-time training addressing bias or how power and privilege are at play is not sufficient. There must be an ongoing commitment that changes the hearts and minds of individuals in order to bring about a victim-centered culture change within an agency or group.

Section 3. Making Change and Assessment

Step 4: Implementing Change, Creating Your Protocol

After you and your community partners assess context, personal and agency readiness, and form your multidisciplinary group, you are ready to begin developing and implementing your notification protocol. Creating and carrying out your protocol

Table 20.1 Procedural Justice in Practice

Procedural justice concept	Definition	Examples in notification
Representation and voice	Victim is heard, has opportunity to speak and represent self.	Victim able to express their frustration with case, SAK not tested until now.
Accuracy	Decisions about case are made based on accurate information.	Professional creates a positive environment for victim and obtains helpful case information.
Neutrality	Decisions are made based on consistent rule application.	Professional contacts victim, despite prior documentation of victim unwilling to cooperate.
Respect and dignity	Victim is treated respectfully and with dignity.	Professional says to victim, "Your case is important," and listens to victim's response.
Fair treatment	Victim's rights are acknowledged, treatment is polite and courteous.	Professional discusses victim's rights and responds patiently to questions.

is the "change" for which you have been preparing. This step is about the practical aspects of victim notification and includes building a protocol for your community, containing notification contact methods, information about the role of advocates in the notification process, and special circumstances like notification with juveniles and non-report (NR) SAKs. NR-SAKs are collected from adult victims who chose not to report the sexual assault to law enforcement and wish to remain anonymous (US DOJ OVW; see Table 20.1).

"Making change" means developing and implementing a victim-centered, trauma-informed victim notification protocol. During development, your working group will make many decisions, including under what circumstances and when victims will be notified, who will conduct notification, what messages will be communicated to victims, and more. Using policies and practices systematically will help your group respond effectively to victims' needs, create lasting change, and aid in investigations of cases with formerly untested SAKs (see Table 20.2).

Victim notification methods

Your group has the option of using several contact methods when attempting to notify victims. Although the needs of individual victims must be considered when deciding which method to attempt, each has general advantages and drawbacks, as summarized in Table 20.3 and described further on the subsequent pages.

NOTIFICATION IN PERSON

In-person notification allows for immediate discussion around victims' questions and crisis intervention, if necessary. It can also provide a more personal approach that can help build trust between practitioners and victims (National Center for Victims of Crime [NCVC], 2011). However, in-person notification can also threaten victims'

Table 20.2 Trauma-Informed Care in Practice

Trauma-informed care elements	*NoVA application*
Safety	Prioritize physical and mental safety: How will notification affect victims' mental health? Is it likely that the victim is currently living with the offender?
Trustworthiness and transparency	Provide accurate, timely information whenever possible, provided the victim has requested this information.
Peer support	Create a peer support group for victims in cold cases to come together and be facilitated by victim advocates.
Collaboration and mutuality	Establish a diverse and equitable multidisciplinary group to develop and implement the victim notification protocol (discussed further in Step 3 of this guide).
Empowerment, voice, and choice	Honor victims' decisions about engagement with the criminal justice system, and allow victims to make choices whenever possible (even if they are choices you don't agree with). Provide the option for victims to "opt-in" to receiving further updates on their case. Meet at the location of the victim's choice.
Cultural, historical, and gender issues	Train all members of the victim notification team on the dynamics of gender-based violence and on historical oppression and disenfranchisement of various groups. Involve community leaders from diverse groups in the system when creating the protocol.

Source: From "Trauma-informed approach and trauma-specific interventions," by the Substance Abuse and Mental Health Services Administration, 2015 (http://www.samhsa.gov/nctic/trauma-interventions).

privacy if family, friends, or others are nearby when the notification team attempts to contact them (NCVC, 2011). Additionally, victims may have had negative experiences with law enforcement at the time of the initial assault and report or among their community.

In a qualitative study in Houston, researchers found that five of seven victim participants reported being treated poorly by law enforcement and experiencing little or no follow-up regarding their original case (Busch-Armendariz et al., 2015b). The unexpected arrival of law enforcement personnel could trigger painful memories, surprise, and shock for these victims. Having a victim advocate present during in-person notifications can help to alleviate some of these concerns (NCVC, 2011).

NOTIFICATION BY PHONE

Phone call notification does not pose the same threat to confidentiality as in-person notification. However, your working group should carefully decide whether to leave voicemail messages and what information to include in any messages (Oregon Attorney General's Sexual Assault Task Force, 2011). Phone notification also gives victims more control over the initial interaction by allowing them the chance to call back at a more convenient time and make their own decisions about if, when, and where to meet in person for further information (NCVC, 2011).

Table 20.3 Strengths and Challenges of Victim Notification Methods

Contact method	Opportunities	Challenges	Best uses
In-person	• Immediate crisis intervention and feedback • More personal approach can help build trust • Confidentiality—can identify who is around at the time of notification	• Can pose a threat to privacy (may not be able to control who is around at the time of notification) • May cause painful memories of negative experiences with law enforcement • Could result in surprise or shock	Initial or follow-up contact
Phone	• Greater confidentiality • Gives victims more control over the initial interaction	• Must be careful regarding voicemail and who answers the phone • Can feel impersonal • Less opportunity for crisis intervention • Phone numbers can frequently change or become disconnected	Initial contact and subsequent follow-up contact based on victim's preferred method of being contacted
Mail	• Some victims may be more likely to receive mail than email • Certified mail can provide greater confidentiality • Victim can open the piece of mail on their own time	• Relocated victims may not receive notification • Victims may not regularly read mail • Very little confidentiality as letters may be intercepted • May come off as impersonal • Provides no opportunity for crisis intervention	Last resort after unsuccessful attempts have been made in-person and by phone
Email	• May be the primary form of communication for some victims • Can reach victims who have relocated • Can include a read receipt to ensure victim has opened it	• Email can be misdirected as spam or overlooked • Can feel highly impersonal • Provides no opportunity for crisis intervention • No way to guarantee that the victim is the one who receives the email	Ongoing notification and information following initial contact
Opt-in notification	• Notify community members about efforts being undertaken • Allow victims to exercise choice and control	• Must be able to reach a large number of victims and provide clear instructions for receiving information	Websites, call centers, and PSAs by local media to alert a wide number of victims that information may be available

Source: Adapted with permission from National Center for Victims of Crime [NCVC] (2011). _Cold case victim notification: Sample policy._ Retrieved from http://victim-sofcrime.org/docs/default-source/dna-resource-center-documents/cold-case-victim-notification-policy.pdf?sfvrsn=2

Unfortunately, phone notifications can feel impersonal, and they do not provide the same opportunities for crisis intervention, support, and information sharing as in-person notifications do. Finding current phone numbers for victims can prove difficult as well (NCVC, 2011).

NOTIFICATION BY MAIL

Some victims may be more likely to notice mail notifications than other forms of communication (NCVC, 2011). Of course, this might not be true for all victims, depending on their usual communication patterns. For example, one victim in Houston stated that had she received a notification letter in the mail, she would have "thrown it away or thought it was a parking ticket" (Busch-Armendariz et al., 2015a). Victims who relocate frequently also might be difficult to contact via mail. Additionally, traditional mail offers very little confidentiality; letters can easily be intercepted or read by new residents or other people with access. Consequently, notification by mail should only be considered in cases where initial in-person and phone attempts to contact victims have been unsuccessful (NCVC, 2011). If your group must conduct notification by mail, certified mail can help alleviate some confidentiality concerns (Busch-Armendariz et al., 2015b).

NOTIFICATION BY EMAIL

Email may be the primary form of communication a victim uses and may more easily reach victims who have relocated than traditional mail. However, spam filters can misdirect emails, and/or victims may overlook an email, so emails used for notification should include a request for read receipt (NCVC, 2011). Emails can also feel highly impersonal and offer no opportunity for support or crisis intervention to the victim. For these reasons, working groups should avoid email for initial contact and use email primarily for ongoing contact, if at all (Busch-Armendariz et al., 2015b; NCVC, 2011).

OPT-IN NOTIFICATION

In addition to the notification techniques described above, your working group may consider "opt-in" options, which allow victims who are interested in receiving updates about their case to reach out to law enforcement or other practitioners. Opt-in techniques include providing information on websites that victims can access, creating call centers, and spreading public service announcements through local media (Busch-Armendariz et al., 2015b). For these campaigns to work, they must reach many community members and provide clear how-to-contact instructions for interested victims.

Victims' preferences for notification in Houston and Detroit

The Houston project found that victims preferred a team approach to notification that included an investigator and a victim advocate. The presence of an advocate often increased victims' willingness to re-engage, even if their original report of the sexual assault had resulted in an initially negative experience with the criminal justice system. Overwhelmingly, survivors indicated that their preferred method of notification was in-person meetings. If in-person notification was not possible, phone contact was preferred over written communication, but victims expressed concerns about privacy, confidentiality, and the impersonal nature of phone and mail contact methods (Busch-Armendariz et al., 2015a). Best practices identified in SAK Action Research Projects in both Detroit and Houston are as follows (Busch-Armendariz et al., 2015a, 2015b; Campbell et al., 2015):

- Develop a protocol using a multidisciplinary team.
- Allow all victims to decide whether to be notified (through opt-in notification options), rather than notification occurring at the discretion of external stakeholders such as law enforcement.
- Empower victims by offering choice and control.
- Provide resources and support during and after notification.
- Communicate with working group partners to have a list of available service options ready when notification begins.
- Have current information about their case and the criminal justice process at the ready as this is crucial to the victim's healing process.

Notification about concrete information is preferred by victims, who reported that news about case status or SAK submission and results provided them with a sense of validation. To maintain victim engagement after initial notification, the personnel conducting notification should not press victims for immediate decisions regarding prosecution or participating in interviews and should instead give survivors time to process the information. Jurisdictions should commit to locating as many survivors as possible, which may involve "hitting the streets," multiple attempts at contact (e.g., 12+ phone calls; 6+ in-person visits), meeting with victims on their own terms (e.g., place and time), in person as possible, and traveling in unmarked vehicles with civilian attire to avoid potential breaches of confidentiality.

Vulnerable and marginalized groups

A notification protocol should thoughtfully consider notification for victims who may be vulnerable and marginalized in the community. Although there are no specific legal parameters for notifying members of marginalized communities, your team should be mindful of physical, intellectual, or developmental disabilities, gender identity and sexual orientation, race and ethnicity, age, socioeconomic factors such as income, and whether the victim has a history of involvement in the sex industry.

Your working group should also consider historical and ongoing oppression and how these oppressions overlap and occur in the criminal justice system and contribute to the mistreatment of victims. Part of assessing your community context is sensitivity to the unique environments that led to untested SAKs, including examining factors that may contribute to unequal treatment and marginalization of certain populations by the criminal justice system. In creating your protocol, aim to avoid further marginalization or alienation of certain groups and individuals from services.

At the individual level, a victim's recovery may be affected by numerous demographic factors such as race/ethnicity, age, and employment or marital status. Many of these factors, like race/ethnicity, can be examined at both individual and macro levels (Campbell et al., 2009). For more discussion, see Step 2 personal readiness considerations and tools.

Your working group should acknowledge societal bias toward victims from under-represented groups and its impact on the agencies, individuals, and systems with which they interact. Your group can combat biases by identifying them and developing targeted strategies to avoid instances where biases could easily affect decision-making. For example, gender biases may cause team members and other professionals to disbelieve victims, misclassify or downplay reports, or inappropriately question the credibility of certain victims. For more information on preventing gender biases in response to sexual assault, see the DOJ's report, "Identifying and Preventing Gender Bias in Law Enforcement Response to Sexual Assault and Domestic Violence" (US DOJ, n.d.).

VICTIMS OF INTIMATE PARTNER SEXUAL ASSAULT

When working with sexual assault victims, it is important to understand the case history, including the relationship between the victim and perpetrator. Sexual violence often co-occurs with intimate partner violence, causing more concern for victim safety (Eby et al., 1995; McFarlane et al., 2005). While the safety of the victim is always an important consideration in victim notification, additional precautions may be necessary for victims of intimate partner sexual assault. Things to consider when planning to engage with a victim whose perpetrator is a current or former intimate partner include determining the location of the perpetrator, preparing to word notifications generically, and engaging in safety planning once victim contact is made (e.g., determining a safe meeting location).

VICTIMS WHO DISCLOSE SUBSEQUENT VICTIMIZATION DURING NOTIFICATION

Women who experience sexual violence are at increased risk for re-victimization, which is the experience of subsequent sexual assault victimizations (Black et al., 2011; Roodman & Clum, 2001). When notifying victims about their SAK being tested, victims may disclose a subsequent assault or incident that was previously unreported. If this happens, the notification team should explain that the victim has the right to report any victimization, including subsequent victimization that occurred after first engaging with the criminal justice system. This is one of many victim rights and building your notification protocol to include your state's code on crime victims' rights, is generally advised. These may include the initial right to receive a sexual assault exam, the right to information about the case as it proceeds, and the right to provide a victim impact statement, among others. These practices are important for both older cases with untested SAKs and current reports of sexual assault. For more information, see the sexual assault Survivors' Bill of Rights Act (2016) in *References*.

SAK TESTING AND NON-REPORT KITS

Recent recommendations from the Office on Violence Against Women (OVW) support honoring victims' wishes about testing non-reported sexual assault kits (NR-SAKs), also known as "non-investigative," anonymous, or even Jane Doe kits (see Chapter 13). NR-SAKs are collected from adult victims who chose not to report the sexual assault to law enforcement and wish to remain anonymous (US DOJ Office on Violence Against Women, 2017; Florida Department of Law Enforcement [FDLE], 2016). Historically, local law enforcement authorities tested SAKs at their discretion (FDLE, 2016). Specifically, OVW cautions that "Testing non-investigative kits without victim consent can undermine victims' rights, weaken community trust of law enforcement, and constitute an imprudent use of finite resources" (US DOJ, 2017). OVW's position is supported by the US military, national victims' advocate organizations, and some state legislatures.

While NIJ has funded research projects on untested SAKs in Houston and Detroit, NR-SAKs were not part of that research. In Detroit, NR-SAKs were precluded from the research. In Houston, NR-SAKs were not a part of the research due to legal mandates that required testing only active investigations where a report had been taken. Although some states have mandated testing of SAKs regardless of the investigation status, most legislation does not specifically address the issue of submitting kits from victims who chose not to report (FDLE, 2016). Only a few states (e.g., Florida and Michigan) currently have policies formally prohibiting testing such kits (US DOJ, 2017).

This guidance recognizes that the criminal justice system may want more information from SAKs for public safety purposes but emphasizes developing alternative reporting options for victims rather than testing unsubmitted SAKs without victims' consent. Alternative options for reporting honor victims' choice and provide options for the report to be converted to a standard/formal report to law enforcement later (US DOJ, 2017). Submitting SAKs without victim consent weakens victims' rights, adds barriers to reporting for victims, damages community trust in the criminal justice system, and wastes limited resources available to respond to other victims' needs. Alternative reporting can include anonymous reporting, third-party reporting (e.g., through a friend or family member), or non-investigative reporting. Often anonymous reporting, third-party reporting, and non-investigative reporting are terms used interchangeably (DOJ, 2017).

Considerations for when to notify victims

Each jurisdiction will be at a different starting point when they come together to develop a notification guide. Some may have yet to inventory untested evidence, while others may have already begun testing sexual assault evidence. Using Figure 20.2, Victim Notification Decision Flowchart, jurisdictions should develop a framework for when notification should occur. Each approach to victim notification has pros and cons to consider, and certain approaches may not be possible for various reasons. Below is a flowchart to consider as notification protocols are developed.

NOTIFYING BEFORE/AFTER TESTING OCCURRED

When clearing inventories of untested SAKs, different jurisdictions will have different testing policies, and not all SAKs will be tested in some states. This may be due to statutes of limitations running out, evidence retention policies, or a lack of resources. Victims have the right to information about their SAK status and testing outcomes. Survivors should ideally be notified before testing occurs and provided clear information about the testing process, or notified if the decision is made that a SAK will not be tested. They should be informed to close the loop on the case and fulfill the

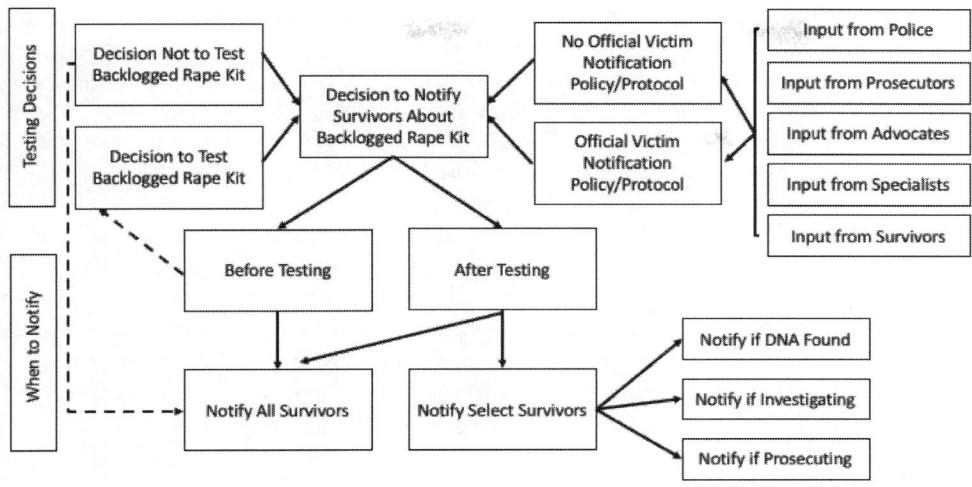

Figure 20.2 Victim Notification Decision Flowchart

victim's right to understand the proceedings related to their kit. This protocol should be reflected in the official notification process.

Notification should include the various outcomes that may occur, such as no DNA evidence or no CODIS hits or a DNA match, and their subsequent options in the criminal justice process. Survivors should be notified at all steps of the process regardless of whether their case will move forward as a result. If possible, survivors should be able to determine the way notification occurs. Regular notification can positively contribute to survivor well-being and process efficacy because it helps survivors know the steps that are about to occur and what will occur afterward. Survivors should also have access to information about their SAK status upon request.

When notifying survivors that their SAKs were tested retroactively, it is important to consider that they may have a strong reaction. Professionals should anticipate the resulting challenges and backlash. Notification protocols should be centered around the provided victim-centered framework to respond to survivors' needs appropriately. Jurisdictions will need to determine whether to notify survivors only if DNA evidence is found or notify them regardless of the testing results. These decisions should be reflected in the official notification protocol and corresponding processes. As much as possible, jurisdictions should notify survivors about the testing status of their SAK in real-time, with regular and consistent updates.

The role of apology

An authentic apology for inadequate sexual assault response conveys genuine compassion, care, and commitment to the public and the victims. Your community partners can come together to make a statement and conduct outreach to rectify issues around SAKs. For example, it is helpful and potentially healing for the public to witness an authentic relationship and connection between law enforcement and advocacy. You may consider bringing in a consultant or expert to assist with developing an apology and/or affirmation of your commitment to addressing sexual violence within your community.

An authentic apology for systemic failures to test SAKs can be an opportunity for reparation in your community. However, an apology may also have legal implications related to admission of wrongdoing (Taft, 2013). You will want to ensure that public apologies or admissions of wrongdoing are vetted and approved, as required, by your agency and jurisdiction.

Any apology conducted in the context of victim notification should be authentic and whole. To be authentic, the apology should acknowledge the harm done by the system to the victim, admit fault on behalf of the system, and express genuine remorse (Taft, 2013). The Joyful Heart Foundation found that survivors valued practitioners who offered an apology early in the process of notification. Victims viewed practitioners' apologizing and taking responsibility for the delay in testing as an important component of establishing trust (Joyful Heart Foundation, 2016).

The role of advocacy

As previously mentioned, victim advocates are practitioners involved in notification who are primarily focused on the victim's needs and who can provide support, information, and resources (Lonsway et al., 2013). Victim advocates can be employed in various ways, affecting the role and confidentiality rules they must uphold (Busch-Armendariz et al., 2015b). Community-based advocates work in a community-based agency, such as a non-profit sexual assault crisis center. Within the criminal justice system, law enforcement agencies, prosecutors' offices, or both usually employ system-based victim advocates (also known as justice advocates). Victim advocates involved in notification are typically system-based victim advocates but may be community-based advocates depending on the resources available in each jurisdiction.

CONFIDENTIALITY AND VICTIM ADVOCATES

It is important that victims and practitioners are aware of the different rules governing confidentiality and privileged communication in the victim-advocate relationship. Although laws vary by state, victims usually have little to no confidentiality with system-based victim advocates but may have higher levels of confidentiality with community-based advocates (Lonsway et al., 2013). Advocates should present information about the limits of their confidentiality to the victim early and repeatedly. While system-based victim advocates can share information provided by the victim to law enforcement on their behalf, victims may also want to simply process the notification experience with the confidentiality that can only be provided by a community-based victim advocate or similar role (e.g., licensed counselor or social worker). In one 2015 study, all victims interviewed reported that they appreciated the support of the system-based victim advocate. One victim stated that the advocate "listened, gave [her] space to cry, let [her] open up, and helped [her] express [her]self" (Busch-Armendariz et al., 2015b). Advocates also provide support to law enforcement by providing care and information to the victim, which helps the officer to fulfill their goals with the victim. Law enforcement also reports that system-based victim advocates also help to explain the neurobiology of trauma observed in victim interactions which helps officers to better understand victim reactions

(Busch-Armendariz & Sulley, 2015). Advocates can provide invaluable support for victims and law enforcement and should be present during notification whenever possible.

Step 5: Assessment and Evaluation

This step introduces evaluation and assessment concepts. There are many different types of evaluation with varying degrees of formality. Evaluations can be useful in measuring aspects of a program or service. Although the idea of an "evaluation" can feel formal or daunting, it is simply a process of reviewing the work that has been done and identifying successes, opportunities for improvement, and lessons learned.

Discussion

The movement to address untested SAKs fundamentally has fairness at its heart and was spurred by grassroots advocacy, national media attention, and state policies and legislation. In 2007, a survey of law enforcement agencies found that almost 20% of unsolved sexual assault cases spanning a five-year period had forensic evidence that had yet to be submitted to crime labs (Ritter, 2011; Strom et al., 2009). Although reasons for not testing sexual assault evidence vary across the country, many communities began auditing, triaging, and testing older and unsubmitted SAKs at that time. The large-scale testing of these SAKs in the United States has led to the re-opening of investigations and subsequent prosecution of cases which necessitates the re-engagement of sexual assault victims.

Major efforts have been established to support the testing, investigation, and prosecution of older SAKs with dedicated resources from federal and state agencies (e.g., District Attorney of New York or DANY, Bureau of Justice Assistance (BJA) Sexual Assault Kit Initiative (SAKI), NIJ DNA Capacity Enhancement and Backlog Reduction Program). Although communities are eager to clear their cache of untested SAKs, much of this is being done without formal protocols for working with victims and ensuring victim-centered practices.

Victim participation is often critical to sexual assault investigations and prosecutions. However, extensive research demonstrates the negative effects of participation in systems that do not understand what victims need and how the trauma impacts them (Peterson et al., 2012; Pinchevsky, 2016; Sacco & James, 2015). To minimize potential trauma, notification protocols should reinforce choice and control for the victims, demonstrate a commitment to survivor well-being, and seek to hold perpetrators accountable.

Driven by research in the field, best practices, and lessons learned, the *Notification for Victims of Assault (NoVA) Change Process* fills a specific need within communities working to clear untested SAKs. The NoVA Guide follows national trends and policies, highlighting the many reasons why SAKs went untested and the dynamics at play that are common across jurisdictions. The solutions also need to be commonly understood, multidisciplinary, and have the best interest of victims and the larger community in mind. The *NoVA Change Process* is guided by the notion that to effectively test the volume of SAKs and notify victims without causing further trauma, individuals, organizations, and teams must engage in thoughtful reflection, informed planning, and ongoing assessment of their protocols and change efforts.

As local and national attention is focused on resolving the problem of untested SAKs in numerous communities, this is an opportune time to make changes that are survivor-centered, collaborative, and can have a long-lasting impact on the criminal justice system.

Key Points

- Change is a process, rather than an event.
- Victim-centered, trauma-informed protocols are essential to achieving procedural justice for victims.
- A victim notification protocol benefits from the engagement of a multidisciplinary team of professionals.
- The *NoVA Change Process* consists of five main components, which are applied to victim notification in Table 20.1. The five components are (1) catalyst for change and contextual factors, (2) personal readiness for change, (3) agency and working group readiness for change, (4) change implementation, and (5) assessment.
- Four overarching principles guide the change process: (1) victim-centered, (2) trauma-informed, (3) procedural justice and evidence-based and informed practices, and (4) criminal justice.

Discussion Questions

1 Describe the catalyst for change in your community. What facilitated the change? Was it related to internal or external decisions or forces? Describe how any historical factors impacted the catalyst for change. What are the hindrances to implementing a victim notification protocol in your community?
2 Describe any events or influences within your community that impact the context of moving forward with victim notification. Describe the cultures present within your community. Describe the related dynamics. How might cultures and their dynamics in the community impact victim notification? What is important to consider about victim notification?
3 What factors in your community are important to consider as you prepare to work on victim notification?
4 What are the state statutes that influence victim notification in your state? Have there been changes in government, resources, or programs for the community that impact victim notification? Describe the relationships and current practices between government services, agencies, and other groups that work collaboratively to respond to sexual assault.
5 What are the biases that may impact your own professional work? What are methods and information you have learned or can learn to counteract them?

Funding Acknowledgment

NoVA was developed based on our research with the Houston Sexual Assault Kit Action Research Project. The Office of Violence Against Women at the United States Department of Justice funded this project with support through Grant No. 2014-TA-AX-K055. The opinions, findings, conclusions, and recommendations expressed in this chapter are those of the authors and do not necessarily reflect the views of the Department of Justice, Office on Violence Against Women.

Conflict of Interest Disclosure

The authors declare that no conflicts of interest exist.

Acknowledgments

This chapter is based on original work made possible as a result of the contributions and support of many people across the nation who are committed to the field of sexual violence, victims, and justice. The authors wish to acknowledge contributors to the original NoVA project, including Sharon Hoefer, Bethany Backes, Mariel Dempster, and Jennifer Thompson. The authors want to recognize the commitment and guidance from professionals who contributed their time and thinking around these issues, including Virginia (Ginger) Baran, Elizabeth Boyce, Emily Burton-Blank, Rebecca Campbell, Michael Crumrine, Kim Farbo, Robin Guidry, Ouita Knowlton, Mary Lentschke, Heather McDonald, Anna Whalley, and Holly Whillock.

Further Reading

Miller, C. (2020). *Know my name: A memoir.* Penguin Books.
Text—H.R.5578—114th Congress (2015–2016): Survivors' Bill of Rights Act of 2016. (2016, October 7). https://www.congress.gov/bill/114th-congress/house-bill/5578/text
US Department of Justice [DOJ]. (2015). Justice Department issues guidance on identifying and preventing gender bias in law enforcement response to sexual assault and domestic violence. https://www.justice.gov/opa/pr/justice-department-issues-guidance-identifying-and-preventing-gender-bias-law-enforcement
Veracities Public Benefit Corporation. (2021). Forensic Experiential Trauma Interviewing (FETI). https://www.certifiedfeti.com/

References

Black, M. C., Basile, K. C., Breiding, M. J., Smith, S. G., Walters, M. L., Merrick, M. T., Chen, J., & Stevens, M. R. (2011). *National intimate partner and sexual violence survey: 2010 summary report.* http://www.nsvrc.org/publications/NISVS-2010-summary-report
Busch-Armendariz, N. B., Donde, S., Sulley, C., & Vohra-Gupta, S. (2015a). *How to notify victims about sexual assault kit evidence: Insight and recommendations from victims and professionals.* Institute on Domestic Violence & Sexual Assault, The University of Texas at Austin.
Busch-Armendariz, N. B., & Sulley, C. (2015). *Does the justice advocate position enhance sex crimes investigations?* https://sites.utexas.edu/idvsa/files/2019/03/IDVSA-Report_Justice-Advocate_Final.pdf
Busch-Armendariz, N. B., Sulley, C., & McPhail, B. (2015b). *Sexual assault victims' experiences of notification after a CODIS hit.* Institute on Domestic Violence and Sexual Assault, The University of Texas at Austin. http://sites.utexas.edu/idvsa/publications/technical-reports/
Campbell, R., Dworkin, E., & Giannina, C. (2009). An ecological model of the impact of sexual assault on women's mental health. *Trauma, Violence and Abuse, 10,* 225–246.

Campbell, R., Fehler-Cabral, G., Pierce, S. J., Sharma, D. B., Bybee, D., Shaw, J., Horsford, S., & Feeney, H. (2015, December). *The Detroit sexual assault kit (SAK) action research project (ARP), final report*. National Institute of Justice, Office of Justice Programs, US Department of Justice. http://www.ncjrs.gov/pdffiles1/nij/grants/248680.pdf

Campbell, R., Greeson, M., Bybee, D., & Kennedy, A. (2016). Improving the community response to sexual assault: An empirical examination of the effectiveness of Sexual Assault Response Teams (SARTs). *Psychology of Violence, 6*(2), 280–291.

Eby, K. K., Campbell, J. C., Sullivan, C. M., & Davidson, W. S. (1995). Health effects of experiences of sexual violence for women with abusive partners. *Health Care for Women International, 16*(6), 563–576.

Elliot, D., Bjelajac, P., Fallot, R., Markoff, L., & Reed, B. (2005). Trauma-informed or trauma denied: Principles of implementation of trauma-informed services for women. *Journal of Community Psychology, 33*(4), 461–477.

Florida Department of Law Enforcement. (2016, October). *Assessment of unsubmitted sexual assault kits: Executive summary*. http://www.fdle.state.fl.us/cms/Forensics/Forensics-Home.aspx

Joyful Heart Foundation. (2016). *Navigating notification: A guide to re-engaging sexual assault survivors affected by the untested rape kit backlog*. Retrieved from http://endthe backlog.org/information-survivors/victim-notification

Lisak, D., & Markel, D. W. (2016). Using science to increase effectiveness of sexual assault investigations, *The Police Chief, 83*, 22–25. Retrieved July 18, 2022 from https://www.policechiefmagazine.org/using-science-to-increase-effectiveness-of-sexual-assault-investigations/

Lonsway, K., Jones-Lockwood, A., & Archambault, S. (2013). *Breaking barriers: The role of community-based and system-based victim advocates*. End Violence Against Women International. https://www.evawintl.org/Library/DocumentLibraryHandler.ashx?id=31

McFarlane, A., Clark, C. R., Bryant, R. A., Williams, L. M., Niaura, R., Paul, R. H., Hitsman, B. L., Stroud, L., Alexander, D. M., & Gordon, E. (2005). The impact of early life stress on psychophysiological, personality and behavioral measures in 740 non-clinical subjects. *Journal of Integrative Neuroscience, 4*(1), 27–40.

Memon, A., Meissner, C. A., & Fraser, J. (2010). The cognitive interview: A meta-analytic review and study space analysis of the past 25 years. *Psychology, Public Policy, and Law, 16*(4), 340–372. doi: 10.1037/a0020518

National Center for Trauma-Informed Care. (2015). About NCTIC. http://www.samhsa.gov/nctic

National Center for Victims of Crime [NCVC]. (2011). *Cold case victim notification sample policy*. https://vrnclearinghousefiles.blob.core.windows.net/documents/Sample%20Policy%20for%20Cold%20Case%20Victim%20Notification.pdf

National Institute of Justice. (2016). Notifying sexual assault victims after testing evidence. Retrieved from https://www.ncjrs.gov/pdffiles1/nij/249153.pdf

Oregon Attorney General's Sexual Assault Task Force. (2011). *Survivor notification: recommendations for Oregon*. Retrieved from http://oregonsatf.org/wp-content/uploads/2011/02/AGSATF-Survivor-Notification-Recommendations-After-Processing-Untested-SAFE-Kits.pdf

Peterson, J., Johnson, D., Herz, D., Graziano, L., & Oehler, T. (2012). *Sexual assault kit backlog study*. https://www.ncjrs.gov/pdffiles1/nij/grants/238500.pdf

Pinchevsky, G. M. (2016). Criminal justice considerations for unsubmitted and untested sexual assault kits. *Criminal Justice Policy Review, 29*(9), 925–945. doi: 10.1177/0887403416662899

Rich, K., & Seffrin, P. (2012). Police interviews of sexual assault reporters: Do attitudes matter? *Violence and Victims, 27*(2), 263–279. doi: 10.1891/0886-6708.27.2.263

Ritter, N. (2011). *The road ahead: Unanalyzed evidence in sexual assault cases.* NIJ Special Report. Washington, DC. https://www.ncjrs.gov/pdffiles1/nij/233279.pdf

Roodman, A. A., & Clum, G. A. (2001). Revictimization rates and method variance: A meta analysis. *Clinical Psychology Review, 21*(2), 183–204.

Sacco, L. N., & James, N. (2015). *Backlog of sexual assault evidence: In brief.* Retrieved from https://fas.org/sgp/crs/misc/index.html

Strom, K., Ropero-Miller, J., Jones, S., Sikes, N., Pope, M., & Horstmann, N. (2009). *The 2007 survey of law enforcement forensic evidence processing.* National Institute of Justice.

Survivors' Bill of Rights Act (2016). 18 U.S.C. § 3772 (2016). https://www.congress.gov/114/plaws/publ236/PLAW-114publ236.pdf

Taft, L. (2013). When more than sorry matters. *Pepperdine Dispute Resolution Law Journal, 13*(181), 181–202.

US Department of Justice [DOJ]. (n.d.). *Identifying and preventing gender bias in law enforcement response to sexual assault and domestic violence.* https://www.justice.gov/opa/file/799366/download

US Department of Justice, Office on Violence Against Women. (2017). *Sexual assault kit testing initiatives and non-investigative kits* [White Paper]. https://www.justice.gov/ovw/page/file/928236/download

21 Envisioning an effective multidisciplinary sexual assault response

The importance of standards, partnerships, and measurable outcomes

Kevin J. Strom, Jim Markey, Hannah Feeney, and Tom Scott

Sexual assault is a serious, deep-rooted problem in our society. In the United States, at least 1 in 5 (19.3%) women and 1 in 71 (1.7%) men are raped during their lifetimes (Breiding et al., 2014). Research on adult survivors has found that nearly 44% of women, 23% of men, and 47% of transgender individuals have experienced a form of sexual violence other than rape (Breiding et al., 2014). For individuals who report their victimization(s) to law enforcement, few cases result in arrest and even fewer result in conviction (Morabito et al., 2019), dispositions due, at least in part, to failures by the criminal justice system to serve these victims adequately (Strom et al., 2021). Effective solutions for combatting sexual assault and establishing a more comprehensive, consistent, and multidisciplinary response that spans the criminal justice system and community-based settings remain a work in progress, as the evidence base for nationally recognized standards still presents major gaps and challenges to those seeking to move the field forward.

Sexual violence presents distinct challenges for law enforcement and co-responding stakeholders, including the broader criminal justice (e.g., prosecution), advocacy (e.g., systems and community-based advocacy), and medical fields (e.g., Sexual Assault Nurse Examiners/Sexual Assault Forensic Examiners [SANEs/SAFEs]). Sexual assault investigations often involve complex and highly personal interactions between a victim, responding officers, and investigators. For example, victims are expected to communicate the details of their traumatic event to law enforcement officers they have never met and often under vulnerable circumstances (e.g., in a hospital). Simultaneously, law enforcement investigators are expected to obtain sensitive and detailed information in ways that allow for a thorough and successful investigation while also providing victim-centered, trauma-informed support. These two responsibilities can produce tension, even under the best of circumstances. Under the worst scenarios, the acceptance of "rape myths" by police affects how they pursue these investigations and the likelihood of making an arrest (Frazier & Haney, 1996; Tasca et al., 2013). Survivors who face cynicism and doubt when reporting crimes to the police report distrust of law enforcement and are more likely to disengage during the investigative process (Campbell, 2008; Campbell & Raja, 1999). However, these negative experiences are not consistent across jurisdictions. Research shows

DOI: 10.4324/9781003186816-25

that the effectiveness of the investigative response differs substantially across US law enforcement agencies (Groeger et al., 2018; Scott et al., 2019).

Individuals' lack of trust in the criminal justice system and in law enforcement's ability to respond effectively to sexual assault, specifically, is keenly demonstrated by sexual assault reporting rates. Despite its high prevalence and significant impact on victims, especially those of marginalized identities, sexual assault is consistently the most underreported violent crime (Morgan & Truman, 2020). To improve victims' reporting experiences, it is imperative that sexual assault survivors receive a consistent and professional response from their law enforcement agency. Rigorous evaluations of sexual assault responses, including investigative practices, would advance our understanding of how best to support victims while also taking effective steps to solve cases. The ultimate goal of these efforts is to develop a robust evidence base for policies and practices that promote comprehensive and consistent actions across the field of sexual assault investigations.

Improving sexual assault response requires a multifaceted approach that has a range of benefits. First, supporting and engaging victims while conducting effective investigations is fundamental to a victim-centered approach. Law enforcement practices should reflect an objective and unbiased response across key activities, including trauma-informed interviewing, evidence collection and processing, the identification and interviewing of suspects and witnesses, and supervisory oversight. Second, protecting public safety and averting patterns of violence is also important, particularly given that sexual assault is widespread, unreported, and too often goes undetected. Research that has documented the serial nature of some sexual offenders, as well as the ways in which offenders can commit a range of sexually motivated crimes, reinforces the importance of a strong and effective law enforcement response within a broader crime reduction strategy (Lisak & Miller, 2002; Lovell et al., 2016, 2017, see also Chapter 7).

The authors of this chapter represent a multidisciplinary team (MDT) that is passionate about supporting sexual assault reform. We have sought to achieve the mutual goals of supporting improvements in jurisdiction-level responses to sexual assault via structured and independent assessments and the longer-term goal of building out the global evidence base and standards for an effective and victim-centered response to sexual assault. The team includes Sgt. Jim Markey (ret.), a nationally recognized expert with more than three decades of experience in the field, the majority of which was spent as a detective or supervisor for the Pheonix Police Department's Sex Crimes Unit. Having investigated thousands of sexual assault cases during his career, he understands the complexity and dynamics of sexual violence and the need for more standardized practices. Dr. Kevin Strom, who has led the SAKI TTA project since its inception in 2015, is a Criminologist who has focused his work on understanding the size and nature of the problem of unsubmitted SAK's and on improving the quality and consistency of victim-focused responses and investigations. He has collaborated with Jim Markey and others on numerous investigative unit assessments that utilized a structured and evidence-based assessment process for supporting agencies in implementing recommended practices. Dr. Hannah Feeney is a Community Psychologist with nearly a decade of experience conducting research on the victimization of marginalized communities. Her areas of expertise include community and systems' response to victimization, help-seeking behavior in survivors, and untested sexual assault kits (SAKs). Mr. Tom Scott,

ABD, is a Social Scientist at RTI who conducts research on policing with a focus on criminal investigations. Much of his work is directed to police practitioners to advance data-driven and evidence-informed policing. He is currently serving as a principal investigator on a Bureau of Justice Assistance-funded project to understand and improve the factors that drive low shooting clearance rates.

This chapter envisions and describes a more integrated, consistent, and victim-centered law enforcement response to sexual violence and discusses recommendations for the field that support sexual assault reform (see Chapters 10 and 19). We describe the necessary role of law enforcement agencies as change agents in developing consistent and evidence-informed practices while improving responses from patrol, investigations, evidence identification and examination, crime and intelligence analysis, and advocacy. Next, we discuss the importance and role of multidisciplinary approaches through the incorporation of MDTs or Sexual Assault Response Teams (SARTs) into a community-level model. In addition to recommended standards for how law enforcement investigative units are organized and operate, we also emphasize the increased integration of allied partners for a multidisciplinary approach, including increased incorporation of victim advocates throughout the police response. Finally, we explain the need for expanding how practitioners in the field identify and evaluate their response to sexual assault by focusing on measures of success that move beyond traditional crime clearance, arrest, and conviction rates. To begin, we discuss the project and focused efforts that serve as the foundation for many of our arguments.

SAKI: Identifying Evidence-Based Standards in Sexual Assault Response

The SAKI program supports state and local jurisdictions in developing effective approaches to sexual assault cases, with an emphasis on inventorying and testing evidence found in SAKs that were previously unsubmitted by law enforcement to a forensic crime laboratory. In 2015, the US Department of Justice, Bureau of Justice Assistance (BJA) developed and implemented the SAKI program. This initiative was in direct response to the discovery of hundreds of thousands of unsubmitted SAKs in possession of law enforcement agencies and other organizations. As a national program to assist law enforcement and their multidisciplinary partners, SAKI is designed to support sexual assault reform, reduce and prevent violent crime, and create a holistic process for engaging and supporting victims. The three primary goals of the initiative were to (1) create a coordinated community response to cold case sexual assault and other violent crimes, (2) build jurisdictional capacity to prevent the reaccumulation of unsubmitted SAKs while also addressing current cases, and (3) support the investigation and prosecution of sexual assault and violent crime cases.

In 2021, SAKI had more than 70 state and local grant sites participating and receiving funding to address their unsubmitted kits while implementing response reform (see www.sakitta.com). SAKI grantees are building community relationships with allied partners that emphasize support for survivors from past and current sexual assault cases. This includes creating or strengthening MDTs or SARTs, which seek to improve law enforcement practices, improve the coordination of resources, and ensure that survivor needs are served. SAKI goals are supported through a comprehensive TTA program (www.sakitta.org) administered by RTI International, a nonprofit research organization. Through this TTA program, SAKI grantees are supported in implementing important response and reform actions. New and enhanced response practices are identified with the goal of establishing a comprehensive response to sexual assault, including clear policies and protocols for all relevant roles, efficient processes for testing and managing evidence, and procedures that ensure all opportunities are taken to fully engage with and support victims.

Sexual Assault Unit Assessments

A key area of technical support provided by SAKI TTA emphasizes law enforcement policy and practice in the form of Sexual Assault Unit (SAU) assessments. These assessments are designed to examine in detail the response processes in place at law enforcement agencies for investigating and prosecuting adult sexual assault cases, including their ability to incorporate victim-centered and trauma-informed practices. The evaluations are carried out for local jurisdictions that have volunteered to learn from the experience. They are designed to provide an independent and structured process for providing key guidance and recommendations and for linking these recommendations with available technical resources for the agencies. The SAU assessments have produced findings and recommendations for both municipal police departments and sheriff's departments (Markey et al., 2021; https://sakitta.rti.org/sau-assessments/index.cfm).

The SAU assessments are designed to thoroughly examine each agency's response to sexual assault by emphasizing their investigative process, including internal and external factors. These assessment methods consisted of (1) a review of agency sexual assault investigative policies, (2) data collection and coding of investigative case files, and (3) internal and external personnel interviews. These methods were used to identify and report key findings and recommendations for the participating agencies. Across the agencies assessed, a number of critical themes were identified. For example, the need for crime scene follow-up in order to collect additional evidence and pursue interviews with key witnesses were areas that law enforcement missed or fell short on when conducting sexual assault investigations.

Objective 1: Establishing Consistent Practices for Law Enforcement Sexual Assault Response

Law enforcement's response to sexual assault benefits from close inspection of current approaches and the push toward a strong evidence base for what works. Critically, agencies should rely on empirical research to guide their decisions and strategies. Research has identified multiple recommendations for law enforcement to assist in developing sound practices, both for criminal investigations broadly and for sexual assault investigations specifically. Some of these improvements can be implemented more efficiently, whereas others have deeper roots in the system and will require a concerted effort to address. Four reviews of the literature—one on homicide investigations (Wellford et al., 2019), one on shooting investigations (Braga, 2021), and two on all criminal investigations (Higginson et al., 2017; Prince et al., 2021)—provide evidence on the topics law enforcement should address and the practices they should implement. Promising practices discussed in these evidence reviews include (1) allocating additional resources to the investigation of serious nonfatal violent crimes like sexual assaults and shootings, (2) enhancing investigator and supervisor oversight and accountability, (3) completing more thorough investigations by locating and processing crime scenes and interviewing all witnesses, and (4) processing all evidence in a timely manner.

Agency-focused evaluations, as were completed as part of the SAKI SAU assessments, can also be a valuable source for findings and recommendations on how to improve the response and investigation of sexual assaults. For example, in a recently published paper examining agency responses to sexual assault, Markey et al. (2021) analyzed pooled data on 491 sexual assault cases that were collected from five of the SAKI SAU assessment sites. Two key overarching findings were that (1) agencies were quick to respond initially and assign detectives to reported sexual assaults in most cases; but (2) detectives often missed investigative opportunities that would support improved case outcomes, which led to victims receiving an incomplete investigation. This is evident from the finding that sexual assault investigators processed rape crime scenes in only one-third of cases, even though most victims promptly reported their assaults. The result was that agencies collected physical and forensic evidence at the crime scene in only one-fifth of cases. The authors also found that, for each additional type of evidence collected, there was an 87% increase in the odds of a suspect's arrest (Markey et al., 2021). These findings align with those of previous studies (Morabito et al., 2019; Wells et al., 2016), suggesting that law enforcement agencies across the nation must dedicate more effort and resources to investigating sexual assaults more thoroughly. *The following fundamental elements should be part of the law enforcement sexual assault response, including investigative follow-up and victim engagement:*

- *Assigning and Having Investigators Respond Promptly*: A critical area that can improve law enforcement response is emphasizing the importance of assigning and having investigators respond promptly. Research has demonstrated a positive correlation between response time and case clearance for homicide investigations (Braga et al., 2019; Wellford & Cronin, 1999), suggesting that faster responses yield more evidence. This likely translates to sexual assault investigations since delayed responses may suggest to victims that law enforcement is uncaring or unhelpful and may result in the loss of witnesses or information.

- *Identifying and Interviewing Victims and Suspects*: Crucial aspects of sexual assault response are the initial identification and contact of the victim, the provision of ongoing support, and overall victim engagement during the investigative process. Delayed or negative interactions can increase negative psychological effects for the victim and may contribute to victims deciding not to participate or withdrawing from the investigative process over time. In contrast, research has shown that positive interactions with the police can improve victims' confidence in their ability to participate in the legal process (Patterson & Campbell, 2010). A victim-centered response should incorporate understanding, empathy, and support for victims when gathering information about the assault and in subsequent interactions.

Across the SAU assessments, in about 75% of reviewed cases, victims were contacted and statements were taken by detectives within 48 hours from when the assault was reported. The level of detail in documented victim statements often varied across cases, sometimes because of the officer's poor documentation practices, and other times because the victim was unable to provide significant details about the incident. Taking steps to obtain all relevant information in an investigation is a core standard practice for any detective involved in an investigation (see https://sakitta.rti.org/toolkit/docs/Core-Standards-for-Sexual-Assault-Investigations.pdf). To accomplish this, the law enforcement officer must conduct thorough and complete interviews with all victims, witnesses, and suspects. Law enforcement agencies should commit to offender-focused investigations, which will support victims making informed decisions about participation that are based on comprehensive investigations.

When conducting victim interviews, a trauma-informed "cognitive style" interview has been shown to yield the most accurate and complete information (Memon et al., 2010). For victims, the interview is an opportunity to provide police with an uninterrupted open-ended narrative of events. To improve accuracy and align with current best practices, officers and detectives should also record statements (via audio or video) made by victims (Archambault & Lonsway, 2008). We have found that in some law enforcement agencies, officers do not consistently record interviews with victims and officers are not provided with clear guidelines for when and how interviews should be recorded. Finally, location is crucial for victim interviewing, with the goal of making victims feel comfortable and supported (Canaff et al., 2020; Sandoval & Adams, 2001). A patrol officer can facilitate a successful preliminary interview by choosing a private location to talk.

One of the most prevalent sources of evidence in a case is a witness. From the SAU assessments, witnesses were found to have been interviewed in only 35% of cases, even though officers documented one or more witnesses were present in 59% of cases. Interviewing a victim, witness, or suspect, and processing the crime scene were all found to increase the odds of a suspect's arrest. However, the presence of a witness in a case was not associated with the likelihood of a suspect arrest. One potential explanation for this finding is that a broad set of persons involved in a case can be defined as witnesses, although some may not have directly witnessed the crime or otherwise have new information that can advance an investigation (Markey et al., 2021).

- *Effectively Collecting, Processing, and Using Evidence*: One clear opportunity for improving the law enforcement response to sexual assault and for increasing arrest rates in sexual assault cases is to implement more consistent practices for the collection and processing of evidence when the initial window of opportunity is available. A pathway for agencies to ensure any potential evidence is collected is to provide a more consistent pattern and protocol of investigative effort across cases. Notably, although all sexual assaults technically involve a crime scene, and although most of the assaults were promptly reported, the crime scene was processed in only a small proportion of cases (Markey et al., 2021). Agencies can also implement policies that define how and when crime scene processing should occur in sexual assault cases and provide training to patrol officers and detectives on how to preserve evidence from the crime scene.

- *Additional Investigative Follow-Up Opportunities*: The SAU assessment findings demonstrated that potentially valuable evidence, such as cell phone communications or social media data, is not routinely collected or utilized by law enforcement during sexual assault cases. For instance, although nearly half of the victims knew their attacker in these cases, detectives investigated or attempted to collect additional evidence associated with victim and suspect cell phone correspondences in only 17% of cases (Markey et al., 2021). This absence of evidence collection appears to contribute to low sexual assault case clearance rates. Case files seldom described detectives asking for or looking more closely into cell phone texts, social media, or dating application communications before or after the assault. Although many cases may have had a justifiable reason for not processing digital evidence or engaging in other investigative actions, including the victim's request to not do so, the case files seldom mentioned the reason that a collected SAK was not submitted or that digital evidence was not collected and analyzed.
- *Leadership and Supervisory Oversight*: Recruiting, training, mentoring, and retaining high-quality detectives are foundational steps toward a sustainable response to sexual assault. Equally important is supervisory oversight within the agency and specific functions that focus on (1) individual personnel performance and growth and (2) overall unit operations and contributions to a collaborative, multidisciplinary response. Appropriate assignment and personnel selection are pivotal to effective specialized unit operations. Experience is key to ensuring effective oversight and review of employee performance and investigations and can also support and provide in-house mentoring opportunities for unit detectives.

Objective 2: The Benefits of Instilling a Multidisciplinary and Holistic Response

Historically, victims seeking to access formal services post-assault (e.g., law enforcement, advocacy, forensic or medical services) encountered fragmented responses that may inhibit their ability to report the crime or participate in the criminal justice process. To mitigate these challenges, some communities have initiated an MDT or SART approach to link together intentionally and proactively all relevant sexual assault stakeholders.[1] MDT/SART structure differs by the community (e.g., meeting about specific cases vs. meeting about policy), but generally, they increase collaboration and communication in ways that streamline a jurisdiction's sexual assault response (Greeson & Campbell, 2013). Importantly, MDT/SARTs bring together diverse perspectives, which can ultimately lead to more sustainable practices. As an example, MDT/SARTs can leverage all available resources for identifying and pursuing suspects in order to obtain justice while also keeping the victim supported, engaged, and safe. One study found that the victims most willing to participate throughout the criminal justice process were also more likely to receive supportive services, including advocacy and forensic nursing or medical services (Davis, 2014). These types of multidisciplinary partners can improve a victim's sense of confidence in the system. Patterson and Campbell (2010) found over 50% of interviewed victims reported that their interactions with SANEs, advocates, or police officers made them confident about the strength of their case and their ability to move forward with the process. Additionally, a quarter of the women stated that being treated with respect by professionals in the system made them want to continue in the process.

Creating a well-functioning MDT can be challenging and requires a concerted effort by a range of partners to be successful. Team members must be knowledgeable in sexual assault response and mechanisms should be in place that ensure open and clear communications. Once the team is formed, it is critical to create roles, responsibilities, and clear objectives as well as a strong, shared logistical and management plan. The setting and maintaining of team rules for engagement and interaction will ensure all the MDT members are able to provide positive input and be productive. Meeting regularly, having set meeting times and agendas, and providing a forum for full participation across the MDT, is important.

A natural step forward that builds from the MDT model is re-envisioning how SAUs are organized. The traditional model is having law enforcement investigators be the primary persons responsible for a wide range of roles. These responsibilities include supporting victims and keeping them engaged, conducting case follow-up, ensuring that all available evidence is maximized (meaning not only collected, processed, and submitted in a timely manner but also ensuring that any forensic results such as hits in the Combined DNA Index System (CODIS) are utilized for the purposes of the case), and for incorporating crime analysis including intelligence linkages. We argue for the expansion of alternative models which would replace this traditional approach with a more holistic SAU that builds on and strengthens relationships with advocates, crime analysts, forensic criminalists, prosecutors, forensic medical examiners, and crime laboratory personnel. The goal for this type of model would be to best utilize the capabilities and roles of these different partners. That would mean ensuring SAU investigators have access to the necessary resources, tools, and capacity to specialize in investigating sexual assault cases, while leveraging advocates for creating a system of stronger support for victims, and forensic and crime analysts for enhanced utilization of forensic evidence and other intelligence.

Objective 3: Rethinking How We Measure and Track Success in Sexual Assault Cases

How law enforcement responds to victims is critical for mitigating the long-term physical, psychological, and financial consequences of victimization (International Association of Chiefs of Police [IACP], 2009; Laxminarayan, 2012). Law enforcement officers are often the first responders on the scene after victims have experienced traumatic events; they also typically interact more with victims than other criminal justice practitioners (Morgan & Oudekerk, 2019). Thus, law enforcement has been a major component in the victim advocacy movement. Many of the early victim service programs of the 1970s were either affiliated with law enforcement agencies or sponsored by the Law Enforcement Assistance Administration (IACP, 2009). These efforts were largely focused on increasing victim participation in criminal investigations and with subsequent stages of prosecution, conviction, and sentencing. The past decade has also witnessed an expansion in initiatives, such as SAKI, that have supported the widespread adoption of victim-centered and trauma-informed practices within law enforcement at the state and local levels. These changes have included a movement to better integrate advocates into the law enforcement response process, with the goal of providing enhanced support for victims of violent crime. As an example, programs such as the Office for Victims of Crime (OVC)-directed Law Enforcement-Based Victim Services Program, which supports the development of agency-based advocacy programs, has grown to more than 70 sites since its inception in 2018 (https://www.theiacp.org/projects/law-enforcement-based-victim-services-lev).

Progress toward implementing more intentional approaches to improve engagement and support of sexual assault victims has brought to the forefront an associated but longstanding need to consider more closely how we are defining and measuring success in sexual assault cases (and in violent crime investigations more broadly). *Research has shown that victims benefit from more holistic approaches that go beyond the justice system response. It is logical that we should be aligning a similar process toward creating a more comprehensive, multidisciplinary approach in terms of measuring outcomes for sexual assault cases.*

Within the field of sexual assault, law enforcement and prosecutors have traditionally measured outcomes that are meant to capture what has been achieved with regard to the criminal justice, practitioner-based role in a sexual assault case. For instance, law enforcement case outcomes are typically measured using arrests and crime clearance outcomes. The Federal Bureau of Investigation's (FBI's) Uniform Crime Reporting (UCR) program provides guidance around how case closure or "clearance" should be documented, including the outcomes for "cleared by arrest" and "cleared by exceptional means" (FBI, 2013). However, these measures do not adequately capture how law enforcement officers and investigators are engaging with or supporting victims. They also fail to capture any broader outcomes for victims or their communities, including measures of victim well-being, closure, or satisfaction with the process. Just because a case was successfully closed does not mean the victim was satisfied, felt safer, or felt that their voice was heard as part of the process.

One opportunity for progress is to develop an expanded framework of outcomes for sexual assault cases that moves beyond the traditional measures of arrests, clearance rates, charges, and convictions. Long and Nugent-Borakove (2014) outline a variety of measurement approaches that can be used to evaluate prosecution-based outcomes that go beyond conviction rates, and a similar model can be used for investigations. These include satisfaction and quality measures (e.g., the extent to which policies were followed, consistent high-quality communication with the victim), efficiency and timeliness measures (e.g., level of effort put forth, time to receive a case disposition), and outcome measures (Long & Nugent-Borakove, 2014). The Office of Violence Against Women is currently funding research to broaden measures of success in the criminal justice system's response to domestic violence, sexual assault, and stalking, which, when published, should provide a grounding framework (https://www.justice.gov/ovw/page/fiie/1159671/download). In our view, a broader framework for evaluating the criminal justice system's response to sexual assaults should address community impacts from sexual assault response efforts. For instance, do community residents feel safer, and are they more likely to report their crimes to the police as the result of specific programs or focused efforts? Are there changes in the known prevalence of sexual assault offending in the community, and are there any changes in recidivism among these offenders? Finally, we argue for the need to collect victim-focused outcomes including victim satisfaction in the services delivered and victim well-being at multiple points in time.

Importantly, when we are considering and prioritizing outcomes, we should not be limited to case disposition. Law enforcement and advocacy services may consider communicating with victims from the onset of their case about their reporting goals and needs. Victims likely have a variety of motivations for reporting their crimes to law enforcement, including seeking justice for themselves, wanting to prevent the crime from happening to someone else, seeking additional resources that are made available through criminal justice reporting (e.g., crime victims' compensation), protecting public safety and preventing subsequent offenders, and wanting to initiate a healing process. As such, in some circumstances, case success may look like connecting victims with advocacy partners who, in turn, can support victims' access to needed resources.

Although the motivations behind victim reporting should not impact law enforcement's approach to conducting high-quality investigations, better understanding victims' goals and needs may help formal helping systems better tailor their response and assess success on a case-by-case basis. For example, some victims may wish to prioritize a decrease in mental health or physical impacts of the assault over prosecution, and thus, perpetrator-focused outcomes would not be a true demonstration of "success." Others may be seeking increased feelings of safety for themselves or their community. Long and Nugent-Borakove (2014) describe measurable accountability indicators around punishment and retribution (e.g., maximum penalty incarceration), deterrence (e.g., timely adjudication to prevent future crimes), rehabilitation (e.g., diversion and treatment programming), and restoration (e.g., restorative justice). Importantly, such indicators may or may not be associated with prosecution of the offender and can instead include outcomes aligned with victim preferences. Given these diverse goals, assessing case outcomes solely on prosecution rates is extremely limited; some victims may be *more satisfied* by outcomes that do not end in arrest or incarceration. Making communities aware of an agency's ability to support diverse outcomes has the potential to improve legitimacy and trust, especially in communities where these improvements are most needed.

It is also important to acknowledge and understand that performance measurement can take place at multiple levels, including at the case level, the investigative unit level, and the law enforcement agency level. Such approaches might include assessments of public safety and whether victims have been effectively served by their communities. Here, the challenge becomes one of measurement; standardized methods of tracking traditional criminal justice case outcomes are flawed, and significant gaps remain in identifying data available across jurisdictions to measure alternative approaches. This limitation also impacts one of the consistent findings from the SAKI SAU assessments: SAU supervisors often do not have the information they need to track investigator and unit-level performance adequately. The lack of effective performance measures also can impact how supervisors manage their investigative staff because they lack the tools and measures to effectively evaluate staff performance or determine what true success looks like for a major case investigative unit.

One opportunity is to expand on work being done through the OVC-funded Victim Outcome and Satisfaction Survey (VOSS), a project developing instrumentation and a survey platform for collecting victim perceptions of the effectiveness and quality of services. The VOSS tool could be broadly used by any criminal justice- or community-based programs that provide support or services to victims of crime. A key focus of the project is on ensuring that the outcome measures used in the tool reflect the diverse intended outcomes of the different forms of help provided by entities that work with victims, including law enforcement agencies. Once the VOSS is finalized, law enforcement agencies could adopt this tool and approach and begin collecting outcome and satisfaction measures from victims. Using the VOSS would enable agencies to track data on whether, after working with officers, victims understand their legal rights and options, have better knowledge of available community resources, know better how to plan for their safety, feel respected, and feel like officers were sensitive to their culture or identity. Additionally, using a standardized tool like the VOSS would allow agencies to benchmark these measures against other agencies and other victim service providers and to be part of broader efforts to measure the impact of federal and state funding for victims nationwide.

The field also needs to focus on how we can improve the most common measures of success currently used across law enforcement for sexual assault outcomes. As an example, a long-term problem with UCR clearance measures is that they are imprecise around what specifically is being measured and how the UCR clearance codes are being used across agencies (Lonsway & Archambault, 2020; Spohn & Tellis, 2014). For instance, in an analysis of sexual assault cases from the Los Angeles Police Department and Los Angeles County Sheriff's Department, researchers determined the two agencies incorrectly used the exceptionally cleared outcome, especially during circumstances where the offender could not be located or when law enforcement submitted the case for prosecution, but prosecutors decided not to move forward with charges because there was insufficient evidence in the case (Spohn & Tellis, 2010, 2014).

Conclusion

The future of law enforcement and greater multisystem response to sexual violence lies in the ability to critique current practices, identify gaps and areas of improvement, create evidence-informed recommendations, and implement and reenforce these practices across the nation. Providing law enforcement with clear direction that is supported by an expanding research portfolio is key to improving response, developing expanded outcomes, and achieving positive change. Having defined direction can also support the creation and adoption of a broader set of standards for all sworn and professional personnel, as well as for key partners (e.g., community-based organizations that seek to better integrate victim-based services).

Evidence-based guidance and training ensure that investigators conduct professional, thorough, and comprehensive investigations via various means, including responding in a victim-centered manner, conducting trauma-informed interviews with victims and witnesses, locating relevant crime scenes and evidence, managing SAKs and other evidence, case review and monitoring, and implementing effective supervisory oversight. Mandatory development of personnel and their skills through training that details the unique aspects of these investigations is complementary to greater multidisciplinary responses that provide a foundation for sustainability and the efficient deployment of finite resources. For example, key partners can work together to ensure that law enforcement response is sustainable across fields (e.g., referrals to community-based advocates are completed effectively) while combating complacency and regression to ineffective or harmful approaches.

Secondly, as goals and expectations around the implementation of best practices expand, particularly as it relates to victim support and evidence management, the field should examine how law enforcement can move beyond the traditional investigative organizational style to incorporate additional partners more effectively. For example, for most SAUs, sworn personnel are responsible for all victim contacts, support, case follow-up, and evidence tracking. Investigative units should consider ways to incorporate and utilize internal and external resources and staffing to support these efforts. This concept should consider the inclusion of systems-based victim advocates, properly staffed professional administrative personnel, property and evidence technicians, crime analysts, and finally, a modern and robust records management system that supports all aspects of a sexual assault investigations.

Next, leadership must also establish clear standards for unit selection, onboarding, and personnel retention. Key to this is identifying agency personnel who are qualified and motivated for these positions. These selections and assignments should follow a clear and standardized agency personnel selection process. For success to be realized, personnel who investigate sexual assault must be able to understand and practice victim-centered, trauma-informed approaches in a consistent manner while simultaneously incorporating all necessary specialized investigative tools and methods. Similarly, SAU supervisors must have the knowledge and experience to oversee an investigative unit, run complex investigations, and develop their personnel.

Finally, the jurisdictional-level response to sexual assault must be holistic and coordinated; it is important to recognize that criminal justice decision-makers (e.g., police, prosecutors) do not operate in vacuums and that their decisions go on to impact other stages of the process. Ultimately, the resources to support improvements in response to sexual assault are a shared responsibility that serves the larger goal of system effectiveness, and, as such, the costs should be borne by all sectors of the system.

Key Points

- The dynamics of sexual assault investigations are unique and can pose challenges, some of which are distinct from other types of criminal investigations. Despite these challenges, it is imperative that victims receive a high-quality level of response regardless of where the crime occurs or what agency responds.
- Law enforcement agencies differ in how they respond to and investigate sexual assault cases. Establishing and reinforcing core standards for law enforcement while continuing to expand the evidence base on what works in terms of policies and practices should be viewed as complementary goals.
- MDTs have been shown to be effective in sexual assault response. We should be thinking about how a multidisciplinary focus could be used to restructure how SAUs are comprised within law enforcement—for example, embedding criminologists or forensic technicians who track, process, and apply forensic evidence to cases including CODIS hits returned from the laboratory; crime analysts who identify linkages across cases; and advocates who ensure that victims are supported and engaged.

- The traditional approach of measuring "case success" based on arrests and convictions is antiquated and does not always align with a victim-centered approach. More comprehensive and victim-focused performance measures are needed for case-level, agency-level, and jurisdictional-level success that account for victim satisfaction, quality, efficiency and timeliness measures, and victim engagement.

Discussion Questions

1   As the field has shifted toward trauma-informed, victim-centered investigative practices, what types of measures do you think should be included to help agencies and communities better understand whether they are having success?
2   What should law enforcement agencies and their partners be doing to engage with communities better to let them know what they are doing to respond to or prevent sexual assault and to get their ideas on what could be improved?
3   What are some steps that can be taken to effectively leverage forensic evidence for sexual assault investigations, such as the utilization of advanced DNA testing and Forensic Genetic Genealogy, while also instituting safeguards to ensure these advances do not violate privacy or ethical protections?
4   What recommendations would you make that could help ensure that victims of sexual assault receive a high-quality and consistent level of response regardless of where the crime is committed or what types of law enforcement agency it is reported to?

Funding Acknowledgment

This project was supported by Grant No. 2019-MU-BX-K011 awarded by the Bureau of Justice Assistance. The Bureau of Justice Assistance is a component of the US Department of Justice's Office of Justice Programs, which also includes the Bureau of Justice Statistics, the National Institute of Justice, the Office of Juvenile Justice and Delinquency Prevention, the Office for Victims of Crime, and the SMART Office. Points of view or opinions in this chapter are those of the authors and do not necessarily represent the official position or policies of the US Department of Justice.

Note

1   While some communities use the terms MDT and SART interchangeably (Office for Victims of Crime [OVC], 2015), they often have distinct purposes. For example, the North Carolina Department of Justice defines SARTs as being responsible for community education and information sharing, while MDTs focus on specific case review (North Carolina Department of Justice, 2020). Because the specific goals of each differ by community, we will refer to them interchangeably in this book chapter.

Further Reading

Markey, J., Scott, T., Daye, C., & Strom, K. J. (2021). Sexual assault investigations and the factors that contribute to a suspect's arrest. *Policing: An International Journal*, 44(4), 591–611.
National Institute of Justice. (2017). *National best practices for sexual assault kits: A multidisciplinary approach.* https://www.ojp.gov/pdffiles1/nij/250384.pdf
Police Executive Research Forum. (2018). *Executive guidebook: Practical approaches for strengthening law Enforcement's response to sexual assault.* Police Executive Research Forum.

Sexual Assault Kit Initiative. (2020). *Core standards for sexual assault investigations.* https://www.sakitta.org/effective-practices/docs/Core-Standards-for-Sexual-Assault-Investigations.pdf

Strom, K., Scott, T., Feeney, H., Young, A., Couzens, L., & Berzofsky, M. (2021). How much justice is denied? An estimate of unsubmitted sexual assault kits in the United States. *Journal of Criminal Justice, 73,* 1–9. https://doi.org/10.1016/j.jcrimjus.2020.101746

References

Archambault, J., & Lonsway, K. (2008). *Incomplete, inconsistent, and untrue statements made by victims: Understanding the causes and overcoming the challenges.* End Violence Against Women International. Retrieved from http://www.ncdsv.org/images/EVAW_IncompleteInconsistentUntrueStatementsMadeByVictims_8-2012.pdf

Braga, A. A. (2021). *Improving police clearance rates of shootings: A review of the evidence.* Manhattan Institute. Retrieved from https://www.manhattan-institute.org/improving-police-clearance-rates-shootings-review-evidence?utm_source=press_release&utm_medium=email

Braga, A. A., Turchan, B., & Barao, L. (2019). The influence of investigative resources on homicide clearances. *Journal of Quantitative Criminology, 35,* 337–364.

Breiding, M. J., Smith, S. G., Basile, K. C., Walters, M. L., Chen, J., & Merrick, M. T. (2014). Prevalence and characteristics of sexual violence, stalking, and intimate partner violence victimization—National Intimate Partner and Sexual Violence Survey, United States, 2011. *MMWR: Surveillance Summaries, 63,* 1–18.

Campbell, R. (2008). The psychological impact of rape victims. *American Psychologist, 63*(8), 702–717.

Campbell, R., & Raja, S. (1999). Secondary victimization of rape victims: Insights from mental health professionals who treat survivors of violence. *Violence and Victims, 14*(3), 261–275.

Canaff, R., Lonsway, K., & Archambault, L. K. (2020). *Trauma-informed interviewing and the criminal sexual assault case: Where investigative technique meets evidentiary value.* End Violence Against Women International.

Davis, M. A. (2014). *Understanding sexual assault survivors' willingness to participate in the judicial system.* Dissertations and Theses. Paper 2094.

Federal Bureau of Investigation. (2013). *Summary Reporting System (SRS) user manual.* US Department of Justice, Federal Bureau of Investigation (FBI).

Frazier, P. A., & Haney, B. (1996). Sexual assault cases in the legal system: Police, prosecutor, and victim perspectives. *Law and Human Behavior, 20*(6), 607–628.

Greeson, M. R., & Campbell, R. (2013). Sexual Assault Response Teams (SARTs) an empirical review of their effectiveness and challenges to successful implementation. *Trauma, Violence, & Abuse, 14,* 83–95.

Groeger, L. V., Fahey, M., & Greenblatt, M. (2018, November 15). Could your police department be inflating rape clearance *rates? ProPublica.* https://projects.propublica.org/graphics/rape_clearance

Higginson, A., Eggins, E., & Mazerolle, L. (2017). Police techniques for investigating serious violent crime: a systematic review. *Trends and Issues in Crime and Criminal Justice [electronic resource], 539,* 1–13.

International Association of Chiefs of Police [IACP]. (2009). *Enhancing law enforcement response to victims: A 21st century strategy.* Retrieved from: https://www.theiacp.org/sites/default/files/all/i-j/IACP_Strategy_REV_09_Layout_1.pdf#page=11

Laxminarayan, M. (2012). Procedural justice and psychological effects of criminal proceedings: The moderating effect of offense type. *Social Justice Research, 25*(4), 390–405.

Lisak, D., & Miller, P. M. (2002). Repeat rape and multiple offending among undetected rapists. *Violence and Victims, 17*(1), 73–84.

Long, J. G., & Nugent-Borakove, E. (2014). Beyond conviction rates: Measuring success in sexual assault prosecutions, *Strategies, 12*, 1–9. https://evawintl.org/wp-content/uploads/beyond-conviction-rates.pdf

Lonsway, K. A., & Archambault, J. (2020). *Clearance methods for sexual assault*. End Violence Against Women International. https://evawintl.org/wp-content/uploads/TBClearnace MethodsforSA1-7Combined.pdf

Lovell, R., Butcher, F., & Flannery, D. (2016). *Cuyahoga County Sexual Assault Kit Pilot Project (SAK) Report on Serial and One-Time Sexual Offenders*. Begun Center for Violence Prevention Research and Education, Case Western Reserve University.

Lovell, R., Luminais, M., Flannery, D. J., Overman, L., Huang, D., Walker, T., & Clark, D. R. (2017). Offending patterns for serial sex offenders identified via the DNA testing of previously unsubmitted sexual assault kits. *Journal of Criminal Justice, 52*, 68–78.

Markey, J., Scott, T., Daye, C., & Strom, K. J. (2021). Sexual assault investigations and the factors that contribute to a suspect's arrest. *Policing: An International Journal, 44*(4), 591–611.

Memon, A., Meissner, C. A., & Fraser, J. (2010). The cognitive interview: A meta-analytic review and study space analysis of the past 25 years. *Psychology, Public Policy, and Law, 16*(4), 340–372.

Morabito, M. S., Williams, L. M., & Pattavina, A. (2019). *Decision-making in sexual assault cases: Replication research on sexual violence case attrition*. Department of Justice.

Morgan, R. E., & Oudekerk, B. A. (2019). *Criminal victimization, 2018*. Bureau of Justice Statistics. NCJ 253043. Retrieved from https://www.bjs.gov/content/pub/pdf/cv18.pdf

Morgan, R. E., & Truman, J. L. (2020). *Criminal victimization, 2019*. US Department of Justice, Bureau of Justice Statistics.

North Carolina Department of Justice. (2020). *What is the difference between a SART and a MDT?* https://ncdoj.gov/hrf_faq/what-is-the-difference-between-a-sart-and-a-mdt/#:~:-text=Most%20NC%20SARTs%20focus%20on,reviews%20of%20sexual%20assault%20cases.&text=How%20can%20I%20learn%20more%20about%20MDTs%20and%20find%20tools%3F%20%C2%BB

Office for Victims of Crime. (2015). *Multidisciplinary Team Models*. Multidisciplinary Team Models. https://www.ovcttac.gov/saneguide/multidisciplinary-response-and-the-community/multidisciplinary-team-models/

Patterson, D., & Campbell, R. (2010). Why rape survivors participate in the criminal justice system. *Journal of Community Psychology, 38*(2), 191–205.

Prince, H., Lum, C., & Koper, C. S. (2021). Effective police investigative practices: An evidence-assessment of the research. *Policing: An International Journal, 44*(4), 683–707.

Sandoval, V. A., & Adams, S. H. (2001). Subtle skills for building rapport: Using neuro-linguistic programming in the interview room. *FBI L. Enforcement Bull, 70*, 1.

Scott, T. L., Wellford, C., Lum, C., & Vovak, H. (2019). Variability of crime clearance among police agencies. *Police Quarterly, 22*(1), 82–111.

Spohn, C., & Tellis, K. (2010). Justice denied?: The exceptional clearance of rape cases in Los Angeles. *Albany Law Review, 74*, 1379–1421.

Spohn, C., & Tellis, K. (2014). *Policing and prosecuting sexual assault: Inside the criminal justice system*. Lynne Rienner.

Tasca, M., Rodriguez, N., Spohn, C., & Koss, M. P. (2013). Police decision making in sexual assault cases. *Journal of Interpersonal Violence, 28*(6), 1157–1177. https://doi.org/10.1177/0886260512468233

Wellford, C. F., & Cronin J. (1999). *An analysis of variables affecting the clearance of homicides: A multistate study*. Justice Research and Statistics Association.

Wellford, C. F., Lum, C., Scott, T., Vovak, H., & Scherer, J. A. (2019). Clearing homicides: Role of organizational, case, and investigative dimensions. *Criminology & Public Policy, 18*(3), 553–600.

Wells, W., Campbell, B., & Franklin, C. (2016). *Unsubmitted sexual assault kits in Houston, TX: Case characteristics, forensic testing results, and the investigation of CODIS hits, final report*. Department of Justice.

22 Washington State's external case review program

Examining the law enforcement and prosecutorial response to sexual assault cases

Antoinette Bonsignore

Author Note

The opinions or points of view expressed in this chapter are solely those of the author and do not reflect the official positions of any participating organization or the US Department of Justice.

The outrageous amount of sexual assault case attrition (RAINN, 2013) represents an imperative for reforming how the criminal justice system responds to sexual assault cases. The Washington State legislature responded to this imperative by enacting legislation to mandate an examination of the law enforcement and prosecutorial response to sexual assault cases to determine how law enforcement training protocols and practices and justice-related protocols can be reformed to reduce case attrition and improve case outcomes. This chapter provides a roadmap for other states' advocates to utilize their state legislature's power to reform the criminal justice system's response to both sexual assault cases and sexual assault survivors.

As an advocate for sexual assault survivors, I used the legislative process to implement tangible reform in how Washington State responds to sexual assault cases while providing accountability and transparency for survivors and the public. Furthermore, my legal background representing domestic violence and sexual assault survivors and my work with the Erie County District Attorney's Office has provided me with the informed experience to tackle the fundamental legal issues that exist in reforming the criminal justice system's response to sexual assault cases. And as a survivor of childhood sexual abuse, I discovered that implementing legislative advocacy into tangible change for survivors provided me with a pathway to address my own past trauma.

The legislative template for advancing justice for survivors began with the idea that I spearheaded as an advocate. That idea was then realized by working with a legislator, Representative Tina Orwall (n.d.), who was pursuing a similar legislative agenda. I recognized that the opportunity to work with and utilize the legislature's power could be harnessed by using my advocacy skills to work with legislators with similar interests. The critical takeaway from the work I am going to present is that legislative action can be used to bring about tangible reform. The first step in realizing that potential is for advocates and advocacy organizations to understand that real change can be accomplished through the traditional avenues epitomized by a state legislative body.

DOI: 10.4324/9781003186816-26

In 2014, I began volunteering with Legal Voice, a Seattle, Washington, non-profit organization that advances the rights of women and girls. Upon joining, I affiliated with Legal Voice's Violence Against Women workgroup and started working to eliminate Washington State's untested sexual assault kits (i.e., SAK, rape kit, or unsubmitted and/or untested kits), which are sometimes referred to as the backlog. Eliminating the backlog was a high priority for the workgroup, as well as for the Washington State legislature. Shortly after I started volunteering, I met Washington State Representative Orwall, who was quickly becoming Washington State's legislative champion for advancing justice for sexual assault survivors. Eliminating the rape kit backlog was her first priority.

In 2015, after a legislative tour of evidence rooms filled with untested sexual assault kits, increased media coverage on the issue, and news coming from other states regarding untested rape kits, a Washington State Attorney General's Office audit revealed a backlog of approximately 10,800 untested rape kits across Washington State (Washington State Attorney General's Sexual Assault Kit Initiative [SAKI], n.d.a; Washington State Attorney General's Sexual Assault Kit Initiative [SAKI], n.d.b). This audit established the imperative for Representative Orwall and the Washington State legislature to find a legislative solution to the state's SAK backlog. This ensuing legislative solution was the first step in the process that eventually established the legislative template for comprehensive reform in how Washington State responds to sexual assault cases. The legislative template detailed here can now serve as a model for advocates pursuing systemic reform in other states and geographic regions.

I begin the chapter by describing how I became involved in the legislative process and implemented the ensuing legislative reform into an operational sexual assault case review program. Next, I briefly describe the issue of attrition and detail the history of sexual assault case review programs and how that history has informed the legislative process in Washington State. Finally, I describe the legislation that created the CSTR program, the findings from a pilot program, and the future directions for the legislation in Washington State and beyond (for a description of other policy initiatives being enacted, see Chapter 18).

Components of Washington State's Legislative Template

The components of the legislative template include: (1) eliminating the state's rape kit backlog and ensuring the backlog could never reoccur, (2) providing accountability and transparency for survivors by securing their rights to information about their cases, (3) establishing statewide victim-centered and trauma-informed training for law enforcement, and (4) beginning to examine that training to understand and potentially address the reasons for the high rate of sexual assault case attrition.

Component 1

The first step in establishing that legislative template involved developing a legislative examination as to why our state had developed such a staggering rape kit backlog and then figuring out how to ensure that the backlog would never occur again. Sounding the alarm for the enormity and urgency of our state's rape kit problem helped us establish widespread bipartisan support for the legislative reforms needed to advance this measure of justice for sexual assault survivors.

Representative Orwall galvanized the Washington State legislature to tackle the state's rape kit backlog by first implementing a statewide, victim-centered, and trauma-informed legislative approach. What does this entail? A *victim-centered legislative program* elevates the survivor's "… priorities, needs, and interests at the center of the work …" (Office for Victims of Crime [OVC, n.d.]). A victim-centered approach to an investigation delivers "non-judgmental assistance" to the survivor and ensures a safe environment wherein survivors will not be re-traumatized (OVC). Moreover, survivors' "… rights, voices, and perspectives are incorporated when developing and implementing …" any system-wide policies that may affect survivors (OVC).

The legislative program devised by Representative Orwall also incorporated a *trauma-informed approach*. A trauma-informed legislative approach is "… delivered with an understanding of the vulnerabilities and experiences of trauma survivors, including the prevalence and physical, social, and emotional impact of trauma … Trauma-informed approaches place priority on restoring the survivor's feelings of safety, choice, and control …" (OVC).

The Joyful Heart Foundation's ENDTHEBACKLOG initiative has championed the imperative need to test all rape kits (Joyful Heart Foundation, n.d.a; Joyful Heart Foundation, n.d.b) (see Chapter 18). Representative Orwall and I collaborated with the Joyful Heart Foundation to figure out how the Washington State legislature could not only end the existing rape kit backlog but also ensure that the legislature would begin to reform how the criminal justice system responds to all sexual assault cases moving forward.

So how was component 1 implemented? Representative Orwall enlisted statewide stakeholders via a collaborative, bipartisan effort involving local advocacy groups, the state crime lab, law enforcement officials, legislators, and victim advocates. In 2015, Representative Orwall began galvanizing support for legislation that would mandate: (a) testing of all current rape kits and (b) logging of the rape kits by law enforcement into the Washington State Patrol evidence collection system within 30 days, which became Washington State House Bill 1068. With the enactment of Washington State House Bill 1068, law enforcement no longer had any discretion to decide whether or not a rape kit would be tested in Washington State (Wash. Legis. H.B. 1068 (2015–16) Washington State House Bill 1068 also established the SAFE (Sexual Assault Forensic Examination) Best Practices Task Force (now known as the SAFE Best Practices Advisory Group) which consists of law enforcement, victim advocates, survivors, hospital representatives, prosecutors, and legislators. This legislation established the critical foundation to guarantee that Washington State's rape kit backlog would never reoccur.

Component 2

Representative Orwall and the Washington State legislature continued their commitment to reforming how the criminal justice system responds to sexual assault cases during the 2016 legislative session by passing House Bill 2530 (Wash. Legis. H.B. 2530 (2015–16) House Bill 2530 implemented a statewide rape kit tracking system that allows victims to go online and check where their rape kit is–hospital, law enforcement agency, crime lab, etc. It also directs the Washington State Patrol to publish a semi-annual tracking system report documenting when rape kits are tested and how long it took for those kits to be tested.

Component 3

During the 2017 legislative session, Representative Orwall again spearheaded the legislative campaign to enact and establish the Washington SAKI Pilot Project, House Bill 1109 (Wash. Legis. H.B. 1109 (2017–18) The legislation created "locally-based multidisciplinary community response teams to conduct cold case investigations tied to previously unsubmitted sexual assault kits." It also required the Washington State Criminal Justice Training Commission (CJTC) to develop victim-centered and trauma-informed law enforcement training protocols (Wash. H.B. Rep., H.B. 1109 (2017–18).

Combined, these three legislative components paved the way for the critical systemic change needed to reform the way Washington State processed rape kits and began reforming the law enforcement response to sexual assault cases. The legislation sought to provide greater accountability for law enforcement while empowering survivors by providing access to information about what is happening with their sexual assault cases. These components have been combined to form a legislative reform template that satisfies the six pillars of legislative rape kit reform developed by the Joyful Heart Foundation (see Chapter 18).

In the section that follows, I briefly detail the extent of sexual assault case attrition in the criminal justice system and the history of external sexual assault case review programs, which provide the framework for the final component of the legislative reform template developed and implemented in Washington.

Background for Component 4—Rape Clearance Rates and Case Attrition: Why Sexual Assault Cases Are Dropping Out of the Criminal Justice System

In a 2018 *ProPublica, Newsy, and Reveal from The Center for Investigative Reporting* (hereinafter *ProPublica*) investigation, *When It Comes to Rape, Just Because a Case Is Cleared Doesn't Mean It's Solved*, it was revealed that police departments often misrepresent rape arrest clearance rates (Yeung et al., 2018). The most striking example of this occurred in Pierce County, Washington, in 2016. In 2016, the Pierce County Sheriff's Office reported 147 sexual assaults. Of these, 87 cases (59%) were labeled as "cleared" when in actuality, they opened investigations for 139 of these cases and made arrests in only 10 cases (7%). The disparity between the reported number of cleared cases and the actual number of arrests was partly based on the misuse of the exceptional clearance designation (Groeger et al., 2018).

How was this done? Law enforcement agencies are permitted to close or clear cases through a coding mechanism known as "exceptional clearance." Federal guidelines (FBI, 2013) authorize the "exceptional clearance" classification for use by police departments to "… clear cases when they have enough evidence to make an arrest and know who and where the suspect is, but can't make an arrest for reasons outside their control" (Groeger et al., 2018). The common perception of "cleared" is that it means solved, when in fact, it is more like "there is nothing else we can do" (Lovell et al., 2020). For those cases that do not lead to an arrest, but there could be more done with the case, they are supposed to be classified as held in abeyance (FBI, 2013).

The reasoning underlying the use of the exceptional clearance case designation most often cited by law enforcement is either that the victim chose to drop the case or the prosecutor declined to file charges (Yeung et al., 2018). Regardless of whether the exceptional clearance designation is being used because of victim non-engagement or prosecutorial decision-making, in both instances, the cases classified under the exceptional clearance designation are misrepresented by law enforcement as cleared ("solved"), even though no actual arrests have occurred. Although the exceptional clearance designation is supposed to be used sparingly, many departments frequently misclassify cases as exceptionally cleared, which can make it appear as if a disproportionate number of them are solved, which they are not (Yeung et al., 2018).

In addition to the frequent misclassifying of the closing reasons for cases of sexual assault, a disturbing investigative report published by the *Star Tribune* in July 2018 found that many basic investigative tasks failed to be completed in a sizable portion of sexual assault cases in Minnesota. *The Star Tribune* reviewed 1,000 rape and sexual assault cases from the 20 law enforcement agencies across Minnesota that reported the highest number of sexual assault reports to the FBI (Stahl et al., 2018). The investigation revealed "... chronic errors and investigative failings by Minnesota's largest law enforcement agencies, including those in Minneapolis and St. Paul" (Stahl et al., 2018, para. 10). In fact, the most basic investigative tasks that would normally be performed in a sexual assault investigation were never completed.

Specifically, records show that in almost a quarter of the cases, police never even assigned an investigator. In about one-third of the cases, the investigator never interviewed the victim. In half the cases, police failed to interview potential witnesses. Most of the cases—about 75%, including violent rapes by strangers—were never forwarded to prosecutors for criminal charges. Overall, fewer than one in 10 reported sexual assaults produced a conviction, records show. Victims see it as a stark betrayal (Stahl et al., 2018, paras. 11–15).

Investigative narratives that highlight the interconnected decision-making between law enforcement and prosecutors have demonstrated this to be a critical determinant of the rate of case attrition. Understanding the parameters of the misuse of the exceptional clearance designation by law enforcement will help evaluate the influence that prosecutorial gatekeeping decisions have on exceptional clearance designations. Accordingly, an assessment of attrition in the investigation process must focus on where and why cases stall in that process. More specifically, three central questions emerge:

1 Why are victims dropping out of investigations?
2 Why is law enforcement failing to make certain arrests? and
3 Why are prosecutors declining to prosecute certain rape cases?

These are the three points of case attrition evaluated in the Washington State external sexual assault case review program.

Some seminal sexual assault case attrition studies have previously examined the interconnected gatekeeping response between law enforcement and prosecutors to better understand where, when, and why sexual assault cases drop out of the criminal justice system (Morabito et al., 2019; Spohn & Tellis, 2012). A review of sexual assault cases at the initial stage of law enforcement investigations should be examined to determine the connection between decisions made by law enforcement that ultimately influence prosecutorial charging decisions.

As stated by Spohn (2021), "The locus of case attrition is the decision to arrest the suspect and the official gatekeepers are the police. But the decision to arrest reflects decision-making between both police and prosecutors. In that the decision to charge is made before the police even make the arrest. Police present the case to prosecutors for a pre-arrest charging evaluation and if the prosecutors accept the case then the police make the arrest and make a formal presentation to prosecutors. If prosecutors reject the case then police have two options, to investigate the case further and try to gather additional evidence, which rarely happens, or close the case and clear it by exceptional means. This generally occurs when the prosecutor has concerns about the credibility of the victim. Accordingly, decisions made by police and prosecutors should not be analyzed in isolation from one another."

Pre-arrest screening results in the overuse and misuse of the exceptional clearance designation. Rape cases reported to law enforcement have very high rates of case attrition (see Chapter 2). As Spohn further noted (2021): "And the cases that are reported rarely result in arrest, prosecution, and conviction. Only so-called "real rapes" with genuine victims are taking seriously by the justice system. The rape reform movement has resulted in mainly symbolic as opposed to instrumental change. Cases involving intimate relationships, on college campuses, and in the military are all on the public and political agendas. Why is it that after almost half a century since the inception of reforms intended to improve the criminal justice response to sexual assault, we are still talking about legitimate rapes and genuine victims?"

The political reality that exists for elected district attorneys needing to demonstrate to the public that they are securing convictions puts pressure on prosecutors to charge only cases that they believe juries will decide to convict. Selecting cases to charge then becomes a matter of which cases juries will accept and which cases they will not accept. Moreover. "[l]ike police, prosecutors also bring to the charging decision their own prejudices and biased perceptions of what a 'real rape' victim looks like, how she behaves, how she should behave, and what her character is" (Leary, 2020). Consequently, the prevalence and acceptance of rape myths by society, and therefore by juries, directly informs prosecutorial charging decisions (Turkheimer, 2019). The rape myths that describe a "real rape" victim include "… views of what a 'real rape' victim looks like (virtuous, injured) and how she behaves afterward (immediately reports), beforehand (reserved), and during the rape (fights back)" (Leary, 2020).

Furthermore, the matter of the true rate of attrition then becomes an issue of transparency and accountability. The attrition rate is generally measured by comparing the number of cases referred to prosecutors vs. the number of cases charged by prosecutors or the number of convictions. However, the true attrition rate should actually be measured by the number of sexual assault cases reported to law enforcement vs. the number of cases charged by prosecutors or the number of convictions. In order to measure the ongoing success of the Washington State sexual assault case review program, there must be an accounting of the number of sexual assault cases reported to law enforcement vs. the number of sexual assault cases charged by prosecutors and the resulting number of convictions. That level of transparency is an issue that Representative Orwall and I are currently working on in order to identify a legislative solution. We believe it is critical to have an accurate accounting of attrition rates starting with the number of reported cases and ending with the number of convictions.

Accordingly, in delineating the steps needed to develop a comprehensive evaluation and comprehend the underlying reasons for the ongoing and substantial attrition of sexual assault cases in Washington State, an external review paradigm must evaluate the interconnected gatekeeping responses to sexual assault cases by both law enforcement and prosecutors (Morabito et al., 2019; Spohn & Tellis, 2012). This comprehensive review provides a foundation to inform the victim-centered and trauma-informed training protocols needed for law enforcement and prosecutors. But, before describing this external case review legislation and process, I first describe the history and framework for case reviews in sexual assault cases.

Background for Component 4—The History of External Sexual Assault Case Reviews

In 1999, in response to a *Philadelphia Inquirer* investigative report, the Women's Law Project began advocating for improving the law enforcement response to sexual assault cases. The *Philadelphia Inquirer* investigative report revealed that the Philadelphia Police Department failed to conduct adequate investigations of thousands of rapes and other sex crimes and *downgraded* those cases into a noncriminal category. The Philadelphia Police Department buried approximately 30% of all sexual assault-related complaints over two decades. It was later established that Philadelphia Police Department officers … "reported using non-crime codes to sideline victims who did not 'fit a certain profile' or were not 'people of substance,' had a history of drug and alcohol abuse, spent time in prison, or had criminal records, were strippers, prostitutes, or had been offered (but not accepted) money for sex, lived in dangerous parts of the city, had mental problems; or were low income" (Women's Law Project, 2013).

In 1999, the then-Philadelphia Police Department Commissioner asked the Women's Law Project to establish an advocacy team to review adult and child sexual assault cases. And in 2000, the Women's Law Project started the annual review of sexual assault cases with the Support Center for Child Advocates, the Philadelphia Children's Alliance, and Women Organized Against Rape. The Women's Law Project team assessed the investigation's completeness and outcome while developing questions and feedback for law enforcement. Furthermore, the case review model identified specific elements of systemic bias in the investigation of sex crimes. Those elements include:

- Victim interrogation instead of an interview,
- Presuming victim not credible,
- Focusing on victim behavior, not accused,
- Threats of and polygraphing victim,
- Threats of and charging victims with crimes,
- More concern for the reputation of the accused than the victim, and
- Discouraging reporting (Women's Law Project, n.d.).

This case review process is now known as the *Philadelphia Model,* and it is recognized as a national best practice (Women's Law Project). This case review model led to significant improvements in the thoroughness and documentation of investigations and the coding of crimes by the Philadelphia Police Department. It also resulted in the reopening of some cases. The Women's Law Project also helped implement the Philadelphia Model around the country. For example, a similar sexual assault case review program currently exists in New York City. However, of particular note, the sexual assault case review programs in Philadelphia and New York City focus solely on reviewing police departments' case files (New York Police Department [NYPD], 2018; Rosenberg, 2018). However, absent an examination of the interconnected decision-making between law enforcement and prosecutors, a sexual assault case review program cannot be comprehensive enough to understand the reasons for the undeniable high rate of sexual assault case attrition. Therefore, the Washington State sexual assault case review program is the only existing case review program that has the tools to examine the underlying reasons for sexual assault case attrition in a fully comprehensive manner. We assert that a comprehensive understanding of attrition cannot be accomplished without examining both the law enforcement and prosecutorial response to sexual assault cases.

Component 4—The Washington State Criminal Justice Training Commission's Case Systems Training Review Program

The beginnings of house bill 1109

After researching ways to uncover the underlying causes for law enforcement and prosecutorial decision-making, I came across research regarding the use of existing case review programs in Philadelphia and New York City. I then decided the best way to advance the need for legislative reform, including a statewide sexual assault case review program, would be using the public forum of an op-ed in the *Seattle Times*. Published in February 2019, my op-ed was titled, *Why are arrest rates for rape in Washington state so underwhelming?* (Bonsignore, 2019). My op-ed and the ensuing case review program legislation were developed partly in response to the *ProPublica* investigation (Yeung et al., 2018).

After publishing the op-ed, I began working with Representative Orwall to develop the necessary legislative language and advance the case review program legislation through the legislature. During the 2021 legislative session, the Washington State legislature approved, and Governor Jay Inslee signed *House Bill 1109* (Wash. Legis. H.B. 1109 (2021–22) This bill created the sexual assault case review program that the CJTC is leading.

Introduction to house bill 1109

Only approximately 16 to 35% of all sexual assaults are reported to law enforcement (Berzofsky et al., 2013; Wolitzky-Taylor et al., 2011) and "… only 9 percent of all rapists get prosecuted. Only 5 percent of cases lead to a felony conviction. Only 3 percent of rapists will spend a day in prison. The other 97 percent walk free" (RAINN, 2013). A more recent study found that "[f]or every 100 rapes and sexual assaults of teenage girls and women reported to police, only 18 lead to an arrest …" (Webster, 2019).

These statistics highlight that far too many sexual assault survivors throughout the United States are denied the most basic semblance of justice within the criminal justice system. This injustice has created an understandable distrust and skepticism of the ability of the criminal justice system to respond to the needs of sexual assault survivors in any meaningful way. The Washington State legislature is attempting to examine this *crisis of confidence* by establishing a pathway toward providing fundamental justice for survivors. As the primary task, the purpose of this enacted legislation is to examine why so many of these cases fail to proceed, thereby creating the Washington State sexual assault case review program.

This sexual assault case review program is different from other programs because it is also trying to determine if the reasons for the high rate of attrition can be addressed and mitigated by improving Washington State's statewide mandated law enforcement training for sexual assault investigators. Essentially, can reforming law enforcement training protocols reduce case attrition and improve case outcomes? This is a central question examined throughout the sexual assault case review program.

Pilot program

The unanimous legislative support for House Bill 1109 and the annual case review program began with a pilot program authorized by the legislature during the 2020 legislative session. The pilot program allowed the CJTC to review closed adult sexual assault case files from law enforcement and prosecutorial agencies. Unfortunately, due to the COVID-19 pandemic, our ability to conduct the pilot program was curtailed, and the case review team could only review law enforcement case files. As a legal and prosecutorial analyst with the Washington State CJTC's sexual assault Case Systems Training Review (CSTR) program, I joined the case review team to complete the pilot program. The case review team includes individuals with backgrounds in law and prosecution, law enforcement, and survivor advocacy.

The pilot program involved the examination of closed law enforcement case files ($n = 31$) from three law enforcement agencies in Whatcom County. The three law enforcement agencies represented a rural, urban, and university community. Each had had some of their law enforcement officers attend the state-mandated law enforcement training for sexual assault investigators.

The pilot program findings demonstrated the need for "immediate training adjustments" and the establishment of additional training protocols. Some of those recommended additions to the law enforcement training protocols included the following (Wallace et al., 2020):

- Provision of sexual assault investigation checklist to patrol officers;
- Question about perceived prosecution barriers in pre-course assessment;
- Provision of a report writing template;
- Involvement of advocates and/or other forms of support in victim interviews;
- Inclusion of Community Resiliency Model facilitators during interview practices;
- Inclusion of report writing examples;
- Inclusion of investigations to update scenarios for interview practices; and
- Added emphasis on co-occurring crimes and lethality assessments.

Another addition to the training protocol that we recommended as a result of our findings from the pilot program included how law enforcement should (1) deal with a victim's recantation, (2) investigate sexual assault cases involving teenagers, and (3) handle interviews with suspects (Wallace et al., 2020).

Furthermore, we found the need for the comprehensive coding of the cases examined in the case review program. We determined that the "...coding should include the identification of cases with arrests made, permanently closed cases, cases referred to prosecution, and exceptionally closed cases. The exceptionally closed cases should include the identification of the point of victim non-engagement, the point of declination [and] the reasons for declination, and the identification of factors leading to attrition and final declination of the case" (Wallace et al., 2020).

We also identified the need for increased coordination and collaboration between law enforcement and prosecutorial agencies investigating sexual assault cases. We argued that the collaboration should include the identification of all collective law enforcement and prosecutorial decision-making, which could lead to or be associated with case attrition. Increased cooperation between law enforcement and prosecutors should consist of an ongoing identification of decision-making factors. The identification of these causality factors will help provide the needed reforms for law enforcement training protocols. The reformed training protocols will facilitate a different type of collaborative working relationship between law enforcement and prosecutorial agencies, one that we hope will create an environment for improved case outcomes.

We also found an increased need to delineate the role that survivors' race and ethnicity have in their experience with the criminal justice system. As we advance, that information will be used to determine the imperative for law enforcement training to be tailored to the specific needs of marginalized survivors. Establishing specific law enforcement training protocols that address the needs of marginalized survivors will hopefully decrease both victim non-engagement and case attrition. Finally, the case files reviewed during the pilot program did not include names of specific advocates or prosecutors, making it challenging to answer follow-up questions. Moreover, when cases were referred for prosecution, the outcomes and reasons for declinations were unknown. Therefore, the case review teams were unable to assess the final disposition of the cases within the totality of the case review.

Nonetheless, the success of the pilot program demonstrated two critical things. First, to improve law enforcement training and eventually develop complementary statewide prosecutorial training, we must review both law enforcement and prosecutorial case files. The legislature did not mandate that we could examine both law enforcement and prosecutorial case files in the pilot program. Accordingly, in response to our findings from the pilot program, which did not include prosecutor case files, the legislature specifically mandated that future case reviews must include case files from both law enforcement and prosecutorial agencies.

Second, we learned that we need the legislature to authorize the CJTC to require law enforcement and prosecutorial agencies to hand over case files for the case review program. Due to the pilot program's success, the legislature specifically established that the CJTC would be authorized to review both law enforcement and prosecutorial case files and that law enforcement and prosecutorial agencies would be required to provide those closed case files to CJTC.

Consequently, the success of the pilot case review program compelled the legislature to enact House Bill 1109, thereby implementing these two critical findings and also expanding the case review program into the current annual program.

The pilot program also served as a vital tool to determine what the case review teams would need in order to establish a successful annual case review program wherein the case reviewing teams could evaluate the response to sexual assault cases from the very beginning to the final disposition of each case. The legislature used those pilot program findings to develop the legislation establishing the current Washington State sexual assault case review program.

The advantage of using a legislative enactment approach to the Washington State sexual assault case review program is that legislative mandates can ensure accountability and objectivity. The fact that the CJTC is now empowered to require law enforcement and prosecutorial agencies to participate in the program is essential to establishing a national best practice for sexual assault case review programs. Moreover, the legislation now requires law enforcement and prosecutorial agencies to identify the race/ethnicity of victims in the closed sexual assault case files that will be reviewed in the next iteration of the case review program. There exists an epidemic of sexual violence affecting Indigenous women in the United States (Futures Without Violence, n.d.; Gilpin, 2016). Washington State, specifically Seattle, has alarmingly high rates of sexual violence affecting Indigenous women (Urban Indian Health Institute, 2018).

One of the keys to addressing this epidemic is understanding the levels of case attrition affecting Indigenous survivors. The purpose for gathering data on race/ethnicity would be to develop specific parameters for victim-centered and trauma-informed training protocols for Indigenous survivors from the information gleaned from the sexual assault case review program. This is imperative since sexual violence in the United States disproportionately impacts marginalized communities, specifically "… women of color, immigrant women, LGBTQIA+ women, and disabled women" (National Organization for Women, 2018) (see Box 22.1). It is critical when we address case attrition affecting marginalized survivors at increased risk of victimization (e.g., women in college [Know Your IX, n.d.]) that we recognize and understand the

---

Box 22.1

Marginalized survivors—Indigenous survivors

- Only 20% of the 104 victims reported their attack to police and only 8% resulted in a conviction of the perpetrator (Urban Indian Health Institute, 2018). Sexual Violence Among Native Women: A Public Health Emergency. Our Bodies, Our Stories: A Report About the Epidemic of Sexual Violence Perpetrated Against Native Women Living in Seattle, Washington: *http://www.uihi.org/wp-content/uploads/2018/08/UIHI_sexual-violence_r601_pagesFINAL.pdf)*
- Many of the women in this study who were raped or coerced did not report the crimes to police, which may indicate a mistrust of law enforcement; however, further research is needed to understand what barriers kept these women from reporting their assaults. This potential mistrust may stem from failure to bring cases to justice. Only 8% of cases of a rape or coercion from a victim's first attack ended in a conviction (Urban Indian Health Institute, 2018). Sexual Violence Among Native Women: A Public Health Emergency. Our Bodies, Our Stories: A Report About the Epidemic of Sexual Violence Perpetrated Against Native Women Living in Seattle, Washington: *http://www.uihi.org/wp-content/uploads/2018/08/UIHI_sexual-violence_r601_pagesFINAL.pdf)*

Box 22.2
___

Marginalized survivors—college survivors

- Only 12% of college student survivors report the assault to the police. Notably, only 7% of survivors of incapacitated sexual assault report their assault to the police. Survivors cite a number of reasons for not reporting: not wanting others to know; lack of proof; fear of retaliation; being unsure of whether what happened constitutes assault; not knowing how to report; and fear of being treated poorly by the criminal justice system (Know Your IX, n.d.).

---

unique political, social, and economic factors that contribute to the case attrition and victim non-engagement affecting these communities (see Boxes 22.2, 22.3, 22.4).

To that end, the sexual assault case review program will enable the CJTC to address the specific victim-centered and trauma-informed needs of marginalized survivors. This can only be accomplished by requiring law enforcement and prosecutorial agencies to identify survivors' race and ethnicity in their individual case files.

Future directions for house bill 1109

We have many questions that need to be addressed as we move forward. Can case attrition be handled solely via the improved law enforcement and prosecutorial victim-centered and trauma-informed training protocols? Are there reasons why case attrition cannot be addressed via reforming law enforcement and prosecutorial training protocols? How can we measure successful training protocols? Which metrics should be used? How can we measure improved case outcomes? Can external case reviews programs address case attrition impacting marginalized survivors? And ultimately, how can we use this case review program to advance accountability for both law enforcement and prosecutorial agencies? In the final analysis, the criminal justice

---

Box 22.3
___

Marginalized survivors—Black survivors

- For African-American women, sexual assault and violence are incredibly pervasive issues that routinely go unreported and under-addressed. Over 18% of African American women will be sexually assaulted in her lifetime. And unfortunately, this percentage only accounts for the number of women who report their abuse. In order to address the issue of sexual violence against Black women, it is imperative that we look at the unique barriers faced by African-American women on a political, economic, and cultural level (National Organization for Women, 2018).
- For every 15 Black women who are raped, only 1 reports her assault. In recent years, there has been an outcry on many Historically Black Colleges and Universities (HBCUs) on the system of silence that has existed around rape for many of their female students (National Organization for Women, 2018).

Box 22.4

Marginalized survivors—people of color survivors

- Approximately 34% of multiracial women, 27% of Alaska Native/American-Indian women, 22% of Black women, and 14.6% of Hispanic women are survivors of sexual violence (2011) (Know Your IX, n.d.).
- Many national studies have failed to measure levels of violence among Asian-American/Pacific Islander communities, citing overly small sample sizes (Know Your IX, n.d.).
- A 2000 Department of Justice report found that 7% of Asian-American women had experienced rape, a number that almost certainly skews low due to the fact that Asian-American women are the least likely to report rape and physical assault of any racial or ethnic group (1998) (Know Your IX. (n.d.).
- A more recent report on domestic violence estimates that 21–55% of Asian women report experiencing intimate physical and/or sexual violence during their lifetime (2015) (Know Your IX, n.d.).

---

system must be accountable to sexual assault survivors and the public in order to promote and ensure public safety.

Discussion and Conclusion

The epidemic of sexual violence and the staggeringly high rate of sexual assault case attrition have established the imperative for the current Washington State external sexual assault case review program to examine the law enforcement and prosecutorial response to sexual assault cases throughout Washington State on an annual basis. External annual sexual assault case review programs examining the law enforcement response to sexual assault cases remain ongoing in Philadelphia and New York City and seven Canadian police agencies (Rosenberg, 2018). The Police Executive Research Forum argues that the external review of sexual assault cases should be routine in law enforcement (Police Executive Research Forum, 2018).

Reforming the law enforcement and prosecutorial response to sexual assault cases in Washington State via an external annual sexual assault case review can provide the necessary tools to begin advancing justice for sexual assault survivors. Closely examining the interconnected decision-making process between law enforcement and prosecutors may not only increase the accountability of that decision-making process for survivors but also provide public accountability. Accountability is how sexual assault cases are investigated cannot be obtained unless we examine that investigatory process from start to finish–from the actions of the responding officers to the law enforcement investigators and through to the final decisions made by the prosecutors.

Washington State's sexual assault case review program has the potential to begin restoring some measure of confidence in the criminal justice system for sexual assault survivors. Restoring that confidence will hopefully increase the level of reporting of sexual assaults to law enforcement.

Challenging the legislative process to advance tangible justice for survivors can provide a pathway for reforming the criminal justice system's response. Consequently, that reform will serve the needs of survivors and promote overall public safety. The foundation for advancing tangible justice and progress through legislative advocacy has only just begun in Washington State. Survivors and advocates have now been handed the keys to deconstruct the factors leading to case attrition and begin the arduous process of improving case outcomes in a victim-centered and trauma-informed manner. Results obtained from that complex process will hopefully reveal the road ahead for reforming the criminal justice system's response to sexual assault cases and thereby advance some semblance of fundamental justice for all survivors.

Key Points

- The staggering prevalence of sexual assault case attrition presents a critical problem regarding how the criminal justice system responds to sexual assault cases and survivors.
- The Washington State legislature has responded to this crisis by creating a groundbreaking sexual assault case review program to identify the critical points of case attrition, including why victims are dropping out of investigations, why law enforcement is not making arrests in certain cases, and why prosecutors are declining to prosecute certain cases.
- Washington State's sexual assault case review program is unique in that it is being empowered by legislation to examine *both* law enforcement and prosecutorial case files. Law enforcement and prosecutorial agencies will be required to provide access to closed adult sexual assault case files.
- The Washington State sexual assault case review program will also develop analyses with an equity focus on reviewing how the criminal justice system responds to marginalized survivors.
- Each annual sexual assault case review will culminate in an analysis designed to improve the victim-centered and trauma-informed law enforcement response to sexual assault cases and help determine how that response should be reformed to serve survivors better.
- Finally, the case review program will try to determine whether sexual assault case attrition can be addressed by reforming both law enforcement and prosecutorial training protocols.

Discussion Questions

1 How can advocates and volunteers contribute to legislative reform?
2 What is unique about this legislative program?
3 How would you improve this program to increase its effectiveness?
4 To what extent is bipartisan support a critical component of the implementation of this program?
5 What types of barriers would prevent this type of program from being implemented nationwide?
6 Can you identify law enforcement and prosecutorial practices that may potentially affect survivor engagement?
7 Can you identify how victim credibility affects prosecutorial charging decisions and the likelihood of an arrest?

8 How do you think that the gatekeeping policies used by both law enforcement and prosecutors facilitate a tendency to close cases via the exceptional clearance designation? What other factors might be at play?

Further Reading

Police Executive Research Forum. (2018). *Executive guidebook—Practical approaches for strengthening Law Enforcement's Response to sexual assault.* https://www.policeforum. org/assets/SexualAssaultResponseExecutiveGuidebook.pdf

Spohn, C., & Tellis, K. (2014). *Policing and prosecuting sexual assault: Inside the criminal justice system.* Lynne Rienner Publishers.

Williams, L. M., Morabito, M., & Pattavina, A. (2018). *Sexual assault case attrition: Key findings from the UML-WCW NIJ-funded research.* American Society of Criminology Annual Meeting, Atlanta, GA. https://www.wcwonline.org/images/pdf/jgbvr/Williams EtAlASC2018.pdf

Women's Law Project. (2016). *Improving police response to sex crimes: The Philadelphia model.* https://www.nsvrc.org/sites/default/files/nsac2016/Tracy_Carol/GenderBiasPolice Accountability.pdf

References

Berzofsky, M., Krebs, C., Langton, L., Planty, M., & Smiley-McDonald, H. (2013). *Female victims of sexual violence, 1994–2010.* https://bjs.ojp.gov/content/pub/pdf/fvsv9410.pdf

Bonsignore, A. (2019, February 8). Why are arrest rates for rape in Washington state so underwhelming? *Seattle Times Opinion.* https://www.seattletimes.com/opinion/why-are-arrest-rates-for-rape-in-washington-state-so-underwhelming/

Federal Bureau of Investigation. (2013). *Uniform Crime Reporting program. Crime in the United States.* US Department of Justice. https://ucr.fbi.gov/crime-in-the-u.s/2013/ crime-in-the-u.s.-2013/offenses-known-to-law-enforcement/clearances/clearancetopic_final

Futures Without Violence. (n.d.). *The facts on violence against American Indian/ Alaskan Native women.* https://www.futureswithoutviolence.org/userfiles/file/Violence% 20Against%20AI%20AN%20Women%20Fact%20Sheet.pdf

Gilpin, L. (2016, June 7). Native American women still have the highest rates of rape and assault. *High Country News.* https://www.hcn.org/articles/tribal-affairs-why-native-american-women-still-have-the-highest-rates-of-rape-and-assault

Groeger, L.V., Fahey, M., & Greenblatt, M. (2018, November 15). Could your police department be inflating rape clearance rates? *ProPublica*: https://projects.propublica.org/graphics/ rape_clearance

Joyful Heart Foundation. (n.d.a). *Campaign to end the backlog.* https://www.endthebacklog. org/ending-backlog-our-approach/campaign-end-backlog

Joyful Heart Foundation. (n.d.b). *Why test all kits?* https://www.endthebacklog.org/backlog-why-rape-kit-testing-important/why-testing-every-kit-matters#:˜:text=Testing%20all%20 kits%20sends%20a,to%20apprehend%20and%20prosecute%20them

Know Your IX. (n.d.). *Statistics.* https://www.knowyourix.org/issues/statistics/

Leary, M. G. (2020). Is the #MeToo Movement for real? The implications for Jurors' Biases in sexual assault cases. *Louisiana Law Review, 81,* 1–38. CUA Columbus School of Law Legal Studies Research Paper No. 2020-3, Available at SSRN: https://ssrn.com/abstract=3721433

Lovell, R., Overman, L., Huang, D., & Flannery, D. (2020). The bureaucratic burden of identifying your rapist and remaining "cooperative": What the sexual assault kit initiative tells us about sexual assault case attrition and outcomes. *American Journal of Criminal Justice.* https://doi.org/10.1007/s12103-020-09573-x

Morabito, M., Williams, L., & Pattavina, A. (2019). *Decision making in sexual assault cases: Replication research on sexual violence case attrition in the U.S.* National Institute of Justice, US Department of Justice: https://www.ncjrs.gov/pdffiles1/nij/grants/252689.pdf

National Organization for Women. (2018). *Black women & sexual violence.* https://now.org/wp-content/uploads/2018/02/Black-Women-and-Sexual-Violence-6.pdf

New York Police Department [NYPD]. (2018). *Response to Office of the Inspector General Report on Special Victims Division.* https://www1.nyc.gov/assets/doi/oignypd/response/OIGReport_on_SVD_Response_62618.pdf

Office for Victims of Crime [OVC]. Office of Justice Programs. (n.d.). *OVC model standards: Glossary.* https://ovc.ojp.gov/sites/g/files/xyckuh226/files/model-standards/6/glossary.html

Orwall, T. (n.d.). Democratic Member of the Washington State House of Representatives. https://housedemocrats.wa.gov/orwall/

Police Executive Research Forum. (2018). *Executive guidebook: Practical approaches for strengthening Law Enforcement's Response to sexual assault.* https://www.policeforum.org/assets/SexualAssaultResponseExecutiveGuidebook.pdf

Rape Abuse and Incest National Network (RAINN). (2013). *Probability statistics: Reporting rates.* https://ocrsm.umd.edu/files/Why-Is-Sexual-Assault-Under-Reported.pdf

Rosenberg, T. (2018, June 27). Rape victim advocates get a role alongside the police. *New York Times Opinion.* https://www.nytimes.com/2018/06/27/opinion/rape-victim-advocates.html

Spohn, C. (2021, May 5). *Policing and prosecuting sexual assault: Lessons from Los Angeles.* Michael J. Hindelang Criminal Justice Center's 19th Annual Lecture. https://m.youtube.com/watch?v=PURRqXijles#

Spohn, C., & Tellis, K. (2012). *Policing and prosecuting sexual assault in Los Angeles City and County: A collaborative study in partnership with the Los Angeles police department, the Los Angeles County sheriff's department, and the Los Angeles County district attorney's office.* US Department of Justice. https://www.ncjrs.gov/pdffiles1/nij/grants/237582.pdf

Stahl, B., Bjorhus, J., & Webster, M. (2018, July 22). Denied justice: When rape is reported in Minnesota and nothing happens. *Star Tribune.* https://www.startribune.com/when-rape-is-reported-in-minnesota-and-nothing-happens-denied-justice-special-report-part-one/487130861/

Turkheimer, D. (2019). *Beyond #MeToo.* 94 N.Y.U. L. REV. 1146, 1159. https://www.nyulawreview.org/issues/volume-94-number-5/beyond-metoo/

Urban Indian Health Institute. (2018, September 14). *Sexual violence among Native women: A public health emergency. Our bodies, our stories: A report about the epidemic of sexual violence perpetrated against Native women living in Seattle, Washington.* https://www.uihi.org/resources/sexual-violence-among-native-women-a-public-health-emergency/

Wallace, J., Stone, E., & Bonsignore, A. (2020). *Case systems training review.* Washington State Criminal Justice Training Commission. https://www.cjtc.wa.gov/docs/default-source/wscjtc/cstr-report-11-30-20.pdf?sfvrsn=f60f13e1_2

Wash. Legis. H.B. 1068 (2015–16). Concerning sexual assault examination kits: https://app.leg.wa.gov/billsummary/?BillNumber=1068&Year=2015&Initiative=false

Wash. Legis. H.B. 1109 (2021–22). Concerning victims of sexual assault: https://app.leg.wa.gov/billsummary?BillNumber=1109&Year=2021&Initiative=false

Wash. Legis. H.B. 1109 (2017–18). Supporting victims of sexual assault: https://app.leg.wa.gov/billsummary?BillNumber=1109&Year=2017

Wash. Legis. H.B. 2530 (2015–16). Protecting victims of sex crimes: https://app.leg.wa.gov/billsummary?BillNumber=2530&Year=2015

Wash. H. B. Rep., H.B. 1109 (2017–18). Supporting victims of sexual assault: http://lawfilesext.leg.wa.gov/biennium/2017-18/Pdf/Bill%20Reports/House/1109%20HBR%20APP%2017.pdf?q=20210722192920

Washington State Attorney General's Sexual Assault Kit Initiative [SAKI]. (n.d.a). *Attorney General's inventory.* https://wasaki.atg.wa.gov/data-and-results/attorney-generals-inventory

Washington State Attorney General's Sexual Assault Kit Initiative [SAKI]. (n.d.b). *Data and results.* https://wasaki.atg.wa.gov/data-and-results

Webster, K. (2019, April 17). *Why do so few rape cases end in arrest?* U Mass Lowell. https://www.uml.edu/news/stories/2019/sexual_assault_research.aspx

Wolitzky-Taylor K. B., Resnick H. S., McCauley J. L., Amstadter A. B., Kilpatrick D. G., & Ruggiero K. J. (2011). Is reporting of rape on the rise? A comparison of women with reported versus unreported rape experiences in the National Women's Study-Replication. *Journal of Interpersonal Violence, 26*(4), 807–832. https://doi.org/10.1177/0886260510365869

Women's Law Project. (2013). *Policy brief: Advocacy to improve police response to sex crimes.* http://www.womenslawproject.org/wp-content/uploads/2017/02/Policy_Brief_Improving_Police_Response_to_Sexual_Assault.pdf

Women's Law Project. (n.d.). *Sexual assault: We work to improve police and institutional response to violence against women.* https://www.womenslawproject.org/domestic-sexual-violence/sexual-violence/

Yeung, B., Greenblatt, M., Fahey, M., & Harris, E. (2018, November 15). When it comes to rape, just because a case is cleared doesn't mean it's solved. *ProPublica*: https://www.propublica.org/article/when-it-comes-to-rape-just-because-a-case-is-cleared-does-not-mean-solved

23 Memphis works to envision a better public health response to sexual assault

Community engagement, prevention, and awareness messaging to change attitudes and behavior

Deborah M. Clubb

Author Note

The opinions or points of view expressed in this chapter are solely those of the author and do not reflect the official positions of any participating organization or the U.S. Department of Justice.

The confirmation of thousands upon thousands of stored and untested sexual assault kits (SAKs) in the late 1990s and early 2000s caused public distress across the nation. Memphis, Tennessee, was one of many communities across the United States with shockingly high numbers of untested kits. The multiagency Memphis Sexual Assault Kit Task Force seized this unique moment in time to foster frank discussions and increase community engagement around preventing and responding to sexual assault. This work centered around the Memphis Says NO MORE campaign. This chapter explores what a public health approach to preventing sexual violence entails and provides examples of how Memphis' public awareness and prevention efforts have been informed by and are consistent with the CDC's public health approach (Centers for Disease Control and Prevention [CDC], 2021, 2022).

Voices of victims/survivors and prevention programming are primary to my work as executive director of the Memphis Area Women's Council where I strive to speak out for women and to identify and combat barriers to full safety, justice, and equity for women and girls in Memphis and Shelby County. My work as a community advocate led to my appointment to the Memphis Sexual Assault Kit Task Force. This task force was created in 2013 to address the city's 40-year inventory of 12,762 stored SAKs—only half of which had been tested at the time of the inventory.

I am the coordinator of the Memphis Says NO MORE campaign, which was created by the Task Force to end domestic violence and sexual assault. The Task Force has now completed DNA testing of all 12,762 kits. We continue to support the investigation and prosecution of cases, notification and support of victims/survivors, and a variety of awareness, education, and messaging efforts to prevent sexual assault. The Memphis Police Department is committed to never allowing another backlog. The Women's Council is committed to providing and supporting the enactment of prevention programming for all ages in all communities and settings with inclusive

DOI: 10.4324/9781003186816-27

messaging and voices, and with a special emphasis on engaging men and boys as allies in ending gender violence.

With wide public awareness of the SAK backlog, rape, a subject that historically bears enormous stigma and fear and was rarely named aloud, became a daily topic of news reports and discussion for law enforcement, elected leaders, advocates, and survivors in Memphis. Along with the laboratory DNA testing, victim advocacy, police investigations, and prosecutions that were generated in response, interest grew in finding ways to galvanize and sustain the community awareness that was initially triggered by the uproar over the stored SAKs. Concern about preventing future assaults and the possibility of repeated future untested SAK backlogs grew. At the national level, some jurisdictions began to educate citizens, striving to change attitudes and behaviors to prevent and end sexual violence. Activism and the eventual enactment of Obama-era policy mandates made sexual assault prevention programming a requirement on many college campuses (Melnick, 2020).

Consent determinations, interventions, trauma recognition, reform of systems, and rebuilding trust all became fodder for prevention messaging in the form of public awareness walks, town hall discussions with police leadership, additional intensive training for law enforcement, and intentional programming on school campuses as mandated by Obama-era Title IX sexual misconduct regulations (see Chapter 15 on SANE reforms on college campuses and Chapters 10, 19, and 21 on reforms within police departments).

Harnessing public health processes to reform our collective response to sexual assault offers multiple avenues for data-based messaging to underpin education, training, awareness, community engagement, and multimedia programming. Advocates, researchers, and preventionists are energized by renewed activism around the rape kit backlog, the #MeToo movement, highly visible celebrity sexual assault cases, and ongoing controversies over the lack of institutional response to gender violence by American military forces. Preventionists are developing and sharing tools and programs that could create a future where sexual assault is averted. These programs have expanded substantially from a focus on helping women prevent their own victimization (via self-defense and safety strategies) to include a greater awareness of the necessity to engage men and boys as informed allies in prevention efforts. Programming has also been adapted to reach beyond school settings and sports teams. In addition, awareness of the dangers to pre-teens has led to a deepening outreach to middle-school-age settings and even to modeling healthy relationship behaviors for children within childcare centers.

Tips and "stranger danger" risk reduction advice aimed at women and girls are still readily available online and on handouts at "rape prevention" events. But most prevention trainers, advocates, and feminists decry putting the burden or responsibility for preventing rape on potential victims. Aiming prevention efforts toward victims seems particularly misguided when as many as eight of ten sexual assaults in the United States are perpetrated by acquaintances, according to the Rape, Abuse, and Incest National Network (RAINN, 2022). What good are self-defense classes, "rape whistles" and admonishments about how to dress and where to go safely if the attacker is a trusted spouse, family member, teacher, friend, clergy, or coach?

Instead of perpetually trying to teach girls how not to get raped while simultaneously increasing the probability of victim blaming, shame, and trauma, our focus should be on teaching boys not to rape. Violence prevention programs that enlighten men and boys about the need for consent and the life-wrecking impact of non-consensual sexual activity can equip them to live in relationships in a more positive and equitable way. With education in place of ignorance and cooperative communication in place of entitlement, the future could see a dramatic change in the tone of first sexual encounters. We would also encourage the promotion of ongoing, healthier relationships among all communities and for all groups.

The Memphis Approach—Change Attitudes, Rebuild Trust

The messages are simple but powerful. Since 2015, the messages have dared people across Memphis and the surrounding metro area to change how they think and act regarding domestic and sexual violence. For example, Memphis Says NO MORE "She was asking for it." NO MORE "Well, she was drunk." NO MORE "What was she wearing?" NO MORE "Not my problem" and NO MORE "Boys will be boys."

Initiated during the city's intensive effort to clear the 40-year stored inventory of SAKs, the Memphis Says NO MORE campaign has peppered storefronts, churches, school hallways, city buses, and airport video screens with well-known local faces and compelling messages in a multimedia campaign. Messages are aimed at ending victim-blaming and encouraging bystanders to step in to prevent violence and offer aid. From the FedEx Forum arena jumbotron to TV spots, the goal has been to change public attitudes while connecting survivors of these traumatic crimes to resources for help and healing. To date, conservative advertising industry estimates say Memphis Says NO MORE has reached about 620,000 individual viewers and has left 1.4 million potential impressions.

Of note, prevention was not the charge initially assigned to the Memphis Sexual Assault Kit Task Force. Instead, the focus was on ensuring the testing of the over 12,000 kits while establishing policies for prompt testing of new kits in order to prevent a future backlog. However, Memphis was unique among the SAKI sites in extending its mandate to the creation of a large-scale awareness campaign to rebuild community trust and change the attitudes, beliefs, and behaviors of its citizens through awareness and prevention efforts.

With the goals of prevention, increased awareness, and rebuilding community trust, localizing the national NO MORE campaign and brand to Memphis made sense. Coordinated by the Memphis Area Women's Council, Memphis Says NO MORE messaging draws on years of interaction with local victims/survivors, advocates, counselors, law enforcement, and attorneys. Outreach tactics included localized printed materials, online tools, training programs, and awareness activities tailored for various audiences and communities. In the section that follows, I detail evidence-based prevention strategies for ending gender-based violence. This is followed by examples of how these strategies have informed Memphis' approach to prevention—much of which was driven by our community's work around addressing our untested SAKs.

Introduction to a Public Health Prevention Approach: Models and Methods

The first question in addressing the complexity of the rape prevention challenge is to discern whether it is a mental health, social, political, medical, or criminal justice problem. Anti-rape activists of the 1970s determined that the prevalence of sexual assault on women was primarily a socio-political challenge as they battled rampant gender-based discrimination, traditional patriarchal power dynamics, and a legal system that revictimized survivors. In 1985, the World Health Organization officially recognized sexual violence as a public health problem. As of 2018, violence against women and girls in the United States and globally continue to be named as a public health epidemic (World Health Organization, 2018).

A public health approach to sexual violence prevention defines the scope of the problem, determines its cause, promotes the development of effective interventions, implements those interventions, and then evaluates interventions with an eye toward disseminating best practices. The World Health Organization (2021) states, "The public health approach is a community-oriented approach that takes the onus from victims and advocates and encourages the entire community (women, men, and youth) to prevent sexual violence."

From the 1960s, American women in many communities, including Memphis, organized themselves to assist and support battered and raped women with emergency shelters and volunteer-staffed rape crisis centers. As a result of demands and lobbying for legislative and policy changes, including federal funding for rape crisis centers in the 1980s and the Violence Against Women Act in the 1990s, services for victims expanded and professionalized. Fruitful collaborations linked criminal justice, mental health, and medical systems. Practitioners in these (at times) disparate systems found the public health approach useful and unifying. Likewise, the WHO and the Centers for Disease Control and Prevention (CDC) embraced and promoted a comprehensive public health model as a useful framework for investigating, understanding, and preventing interpersonal violence in general and sexual violence in particular.

In the nearly 30 years since the initial authorization of the Violence Against Women Act, evaluators have found that brief violence prevention programs presented in isolation are less effective than longer, evidence-based, comprehensive, multilevel strategies. Effective strategies are age-appropriate, offered in sufficient dosage, provided by well-trained staff who utilize socio-culturally relevant material, broad, and based on sound theory (DeGue et al., 2014).

Preventionists often use *a social-ecological model* to understand violence (CDC, 2022). This is a broader framework that offers more sustainable solutions than a "one-size fits all" perpetrators, victims, cultures, and types of rape model (Fielding et al., 2010). The social-ecological model can be used to understand ways of addressing sexual violence at the individual, interpersonal, community, and societal levels. The model helps clarify what might cause or prevent violence and how factors at each level influence each other. At the individual level, age, income, education, substance use, history of abuse, and other personal factors can influence the likelihood of being a victim or perpetrator of violence. Strategies to mitigate these factors include education on safe dating, learning healthy relationship skills and conflict resolution. At the interpersonal level, the influence of close peers and family members is understood to impact one's behavior. Strategies at this level may include educating mentors and parents so they can teach and model positive relationship skills. At the community level, creating safe places for home, school, work, and recreation while reducing conditions that can give rise to violence, such as poverty, neighborhood instability, and residential segregation, may help prevent sexual violence. At the societal level, institutions, community leaders, and policy makers need to recognize and tackle inequities maintained by health, economic, education, and social policies and join this with efforts to bolster household income as well as to provide quality and accessible school and job options (CDC, The Social Ecological Model).

CDC's Rape Prevention Guidance

The CDC's Rape Prevention and Education (RPE) Program was established by the 1994 Violence Against Women Act to develop and strengthen sexual violence prevention efforts at local, state, and national levels. Through the RPE program, the CDC sought to promote efforts to modify or eliminate individual, relationship, community, and societal influences that allow sexual violence perpetration, victimization, and bystander disengagement.

Using this public health model, researchers have explored the risk factors for becoming a perpetrator of sexual violence, thereby giving advocates, campus leaders, and others rich material for developing prevention programs. For example, among common risk factors charted by the CDC were certain sexual behaviors (e.g., multiple sex partners, early initiation of sex, and early and frequent exposure to sexually explicit media); attitudes about sex (e.g., victim-blaming); hostility toward women; perceived peer support of sexual aggression, and close association with hyper-masculine and all-male peer groups. These risk factors give preventionists and advocates clues toward the causes of sexual violence and how to shape messaging, education, and outreach toward preventing violent behavior (see Chapter 7 on offenders).

In 2016, the CDC's National Center for Injury Prevention and Control produced *STOP SV: A Technical Package to Prevent Sexual Violence*, which included strategies for community and policy change toward preventing sexual violence. CDC also published *Sexual Violence on Campus: Strategies for Prevention*, a technical assistance document laying out the best then-available evidence on sexual violence and how to prevent it on college campuses. "The evidence for sexual violence prevention is still emerging, but the problem is too urgent to wait until the field has perfect solutions" (Dills et al., 2016, p. 16).

Sexual Violence Prevention: Using Evidence to Apply What Works

Programs for reducing or preventing sexual violence have flourished in recent decades—from comedy skit-based college tours to bartender training, special hand signals, alongside outreach to athletes and other distinct groups from children to professionals. However, not all are effective. In 2014, DeGue et al. (2014) published a review of 30 years of outcome evaluations ($n = 140$) of primary prevention strategies for sexual violence perpetration. She evaluated their effectiveness in preventing sexual assault perpetration and offered recommendations as to those with promise and those likely not effective. Only two programs passed the rigorous evaluation design review. They were: Safe Dates (Foshee et al., 1996) and Shifting Boundaries (Taylor et al., 2013)—both designed for middle and high school students.

Safe Dates is an educational program that consists of ten 50-minute sessions, one 45-minute play performed by students, and a poster contest. Supported by the CDC, Safe Dates is designed to teach students about the importance of stopping and preventing dating violence perpetration and sexual assault (Foshee et al., 1996). Safe Dates acknowledges that relationship violence can begin as young as sixth grade, with one in four preteens experiencing some kind of abuse (i.e., verbal, physical, emotional, or sexual) from a dating partner. Preventionists recognized the urgent need to incorporate decision-making and healthy relationship skills into family life and education settings for middle schoolers. Safe Dates addresses gender roles, conflict resolution, and includes community resources and materials for parents.

Shifting Boundaries is also school-based and aimed at preventing dating violence among middle schoolers (Taylor et al., 2013). It pairs six classroom sessions with a "building-level intervention" that collects and shares information on "hot spots" in buildings and around the campuses. DeGue and colleagues suggested that a combination of the building-level intervention of Shifting Boundaries and the more extensive curriculum of Safe Dates could be an effective, multilevel community strategy (DeGue et al., 2014).

A third strategy deemed effective by DeGue et al. (2014) was a policy rather than a program. It was the Violence Against Women Act of 1994. This legislation funded criminal justice-related activities associated with a reduction in reported rapes (DeGue et al., 2014). Two other strategies were deemed promising for their potential to impact attitudes and other risk factors—Coaching Boys into Men and Bringing in the Bystander. DeGue and colleagues' research found that single sessions of prevention programs were not effective. However, these authors noted that at the time of their review, 60% of programs offered only one session and most targeted college students. What worked best was a comprehensive program providing skill-enhancing components as well as education and awareness programming aimed at changing beliefs or behavior.

Three prevention concepts that are widely used are detailed below: (1) multimedia messaging, (2) bystander interventions, particularly those with an emphasis on engaging men (see Chapter 25), and (3) social media campaigns. In this chapter, I will describe some of the leading sexual violence prevention efforts that fall into these three categories, their intended audiences, and their content. Each has the potential to equip any or all of us to stop or prevent sexual violence—whether in schools, on college and university campuses, in the workplace or among friends and family.

Strategy One: Multimedia Messaging to End Gender-Based Violence

Across the decades, Americans have been steadily bombarded with pro-health messages about seat belts, drunk driving, first-hand and passive smoking, safe sex, STI transmission, breast self-exams, and much more. Each message is expected to have a noticeable effect on behavior, public policy, and public health as the messages and images became marketing brands.

On March 15, 2013, actress and advocate Mariska Hargitay, founder of the Joyful Heart Foundation, which has a mission to support healing and educate and empower survivors of sexual assault, domestic violence, and child abuse, announced the launch of the NO MORE campaign in a series of events in Washington, DC (see Chapter 18 for more information on the Joyful Heart Foundation). Under the symbol of a blue zero, NO MORE was envisioned as a unified call to action with the tagline "together we can end domestic violence and sexual assault." (NOMORE. Org, 2022).

NO MORE's print and video public service announcements (PSAs) featured athletes, entertainers, and public figures dressed in black and sternly stating "no more" to behaviors such as "boys will be boys" and "she was asking for it." Within several years, with the help of highly visible partners such as the NFL and the donation of millions of dollars in pro bono airtime, NO MORE television PSAs were seen in all 210 major media markets in the United States with 4 billion media impressions in print, broadcast, online and outdoor advertising, in campuses, airports and movie theaters (Joyful Heart Foundation, 2022). Joyful Heart continues to share NO MORE materials and is a leader in policy actions and funding opportunities to eliminate the rape kit backlog through its End the Backlog initiative.

Meanwhile, ongoing development and coordination of the NO MORE campaign became the work of an independent public not-for-profit group, the NO MORE Foundation. It has become the largest coalition of non-profits, corporations, media, schools, and government bodies in partnership to address sexual assault and domestic violence. NO MORE Foundation has 1,400 allied organizations, more than 30 dedicated city, state, or international chapters and an online director of resources in 205 countries and territories. NO MORE Foundation creates and shares award-winning PSAs and open-source customizable tools and resources, including PSAs in Spanish, to help "leverage the power of the media, entertainment, sports, technology, and collective action" (Our Story/NO MORE). In addition to several campaigns tackling domestic violence, NO MORE partnered with Uber to expand the "Stand Up, Don't Stand By" campaign to help prevent sexual assault before it occurs and ensure that a night out stays fun and safe. Publicity material, billboards, posters, a website, social media content and linkage with law enforcement, rape crisis centers, and bars and clubs were developed by Uber and NO MORE for the Uber program that began in Las Vegas and Los Angeles and extended to other United States and Canadian cities.

In September 2021, the 54-nation Commonwealth Secretariat headquartered in London and the NO MORE Foundation announced the #JointheChorus campaign. This is an international initiative designed to recruit men to join the chorus and say no more to gender-based violence against women and girls. Campaign strategies include empowering women economically and socially while assuring quality medical and legal care and support services for those who experience gender violence.

The Memphis Approach: Multimedia Campaign + Public and Professional Training and Awareness

NO MORE is a key component of Memphis' approach. With funding from a local philanthropy, the Memphis Task Force contracted with a professional marketing agency. They designed the logo and branding for a tailored, locally based multimedia campaign. With permission, they adapted the NO MORE blue "zero" logo by adding circles representing the tracks in a vinyl record. This was a nod to Memphis as a historic music center. Memphis Says NO MORE utilizes public events, advertising, printed materials, public events, a website, and public relations to charter its initiative. Metal logo buttons, thousands of palm-sized resource cards, t-shirts, wristbands, stickers, magnets, and posters have been circulated at festivals, civic clubs, campuses, businesses, city, and county facilities. Except for the logo buttons, every "touch" by Memphis Says NO MORE —whether it be in person, on a bus sign, a bracelet, or on a screen—provides a link to survivor services as well as messaging to prevent and end gender violence. Faces, voices, and stories of local media, community and political leaders, and gender violence survivors became the posters and audio tracks for PSAs and video narratives. Since this violence happens in every zip code and to all types of victims, three videos were edited for airing with multiple voices and faces: "Everywhere," "Everyone," and "Silence."

In addition to visual and print media materials, Memphis Says NO MORE hosts trainings for professionals and for the general public to increase awareness, understanding, and action around the community's sexual assault response. Initially, the task force held community updates that outlined the backlog response as mandated by the Memphis mayor's executive order. These conversations and updates were extended. For example, A Community Conversation about Rape for Men featured a rabbi, a minister, a female survivor of rape, and a male survivor of his parent's domestic violence. A Community Conversation on Consent for Youth was hosted in partnership with the University of Memphis; this event brought in specialized trainers from Men as Peacekeepers. Memphis Says NO MORE speakers reach audiences at civic groups, churches, youth programs and workplaces on disclosure, consent, trauma, and support for survivors.

As another example, after Memphis became a SAKI-funded site in 2015, SAKI experts traveled to Memphis for the second summit of "sister" cities—a closed (to the public) conference for jurisdictions working in a multidisciplinary process to test 100% of their SAKs, which at the time was Memphis, Detroit, and Cleveland. As early adopter sites, there was no blueprint for how to best tackle the backlog, so these summits served as an avenue to help the cities learn from each other. The Second Summit was organized by the Memphis Task Force and showcased Memphis Says NO MORE as well as leading researchers in the field of trauma and sexual assault, forensic scientists, law enforcement, practitioners, advocates, survivors, and even the then-mayor of Memphis.

As yet another example, the campaign's target audience and messaging caught the attention of producers of an outdoor music festival who were concerned about rising reports of sexual violence in concert venues nationwide. Memphis Says NO MORE worked with them to create a "Safe Tent" for Mempho Fest concertgoers—a space staffed by victim advocates and counselors who were available throughout the three nights of performances. Other Memphis Says NO MORE volunteers circulated in the crowds with resource cards and bracelets to spread the word about consent and the tent.

Strategy Two: Prevention Through Intervening: Bystander Intervention

Preventionists have increasingly focused on bystander intervention as a primary prevention strategy (CDC). They are working steadily to deepen its impact, especially on campuses, in military settings, and in workplaces. Bystander intervention can increase awareness of a problem and widen the public's perception of whose responsibility it is to solve it, helping reduce the risk of multiple forms of oppressive, abusive, or violent behavior. Students K-3 through college are served by various bystander intervention programs, but many communities focus first and with urgency on college students since the 18–34 age demographic is most at risk for sexual assault (Moracco et al., 2007).

One popular and highly rated program, Bringing in the Bystander, was created by Culture of Respect, a 2013 parent-founded initiative that in 2016 became part of NASPA—Student Affairs Administrators in Higher Education. It aims to help college and secondary institutions end sexual violence and create organizational change (Culture of Respect, 2022). The Culture of Respect stresses campuswide coordination that begins with a detailed evaluation and adherence to six pillars: self-assessment, survivor support, clear policies, multitiered education, public disclosure, and schoolwide mobilization. The Bringing in the Bystander curriculum teaches how to safely intervene in situations in which sexual violence, relationship violence, or stalking are already occurring or might occur. Participants learn how to recognize dangerous behavior, empathize with victims, and accept a role as a bystander equipped with safe methods of intervention (Culture of Respect, 2022). Male and/or female facilitators (professionals or students) are trained in two 3-hour sessions and deliver 4.5 hours of curriculum over several sessions. A booster session also is possible after two months. Content elements include local statistics on sexual and intimate partner violence prevalence and causes; the roles and responsibilities of bystanders in risky situations; role playing to practice intervening and supporting victims; community resources and a pledge committing to being an active bystander.

RAINN, the Rape Abuse & Incest National Network, the leading national advocacy organization for survivors of sexual violence, recommends that prevention campaigns for college campuses employ a three-tiered approach: bystander intervention education to encourage action in response to sexual violence, risk-reduction messaging to increase personal safety, and general education about the law with a particular emphasis on what constitutes consent (Berkowitz & O'Connor, 2014). RAINN asserts that elimination of rape may not be possible but that there are effective strategies to reduce people's risk of victimization and increase their confidence in becoming an active bystander to prevent a sexual assault—with the caveat that the most effective way to prevent rape is an effective criminal justice response, namely getting rapists off the streets (Berkowitz & O'Connor, 2014).

Beyond programs for students and those aimed specifically at athletes and military personnel, one specialized segment of bystander intervention training targets bartenders, servers, other hospitality workers, and rideshare drivers. Equipping these workers to recognize dangerous behavior and intervene safely widens the safety net available to college communities and engages workplaces, employers, and employees as valuable community members whose safety should be cared for.

Training specifically for bartenders and staff at bars, restaurants, breweries, and other alcohol-serving establishments is offered by BarTAB—Bar Training for Active Bystanders, Raise the Bar, and Safe Bar Collective (Safe Bar Collective, 2022). Workplaces generally receive a two-hour training for up to 20 participants on how to respond to sexual and race-based incidents, how to manage aggressive behaviors to ultimately prevent assaults and how to connect staff and patrons to resources if they experience harassment. As the Safe Bar Collective states on its website: "Alcohol doesn't cause violence. But it's used as a weapon or an excuse in 50% of physical and sexual assaults. This connection puts the staff of alcohol-serving establishments in a unique position to respond and work to prevent violence."

Men's Violence Prevention

A distinct outreach and training strategy toward SV prevention zeroes in on the importance of engaging men and boys. Since much violence against women is committed by men and arises out of sexist attitudes and masculine domination it makes sense that men can and should play a proactive and strategic role in ending that violence (Barker et al., 2007). Men's violence prevention (MVP) includes one-time events and trainings, in-person and online educational programs and larger social change activism and campaigns to raise men's awareness of violence against women, teach bystander intervention, and foster equitable intimate relationships. Below, I detail two examples of MVP efforts (MVP Strategies, 2022).

Tony Porter, co-founder of A Call to Men, has said: "If women could end violence against women and girls by themselves, they would have done it already" (A Call to Men, 2022a). He argues that we must continue to center the voices of women, but since we know that most gender-based violence is committed by men, men have to be active and essential components of the solution. A Call to Men promotes healthy manhood in a Training Institute for Gender and Racial Justice, using the Man Box to reveal how "expectations are taught to men – sometimes unconsciously – and reinforced by society." A Call to Men teaches that "the principles of healthy, respectful manhood" include expressing emotion, repudiating fearlessness and control, valuing women's lives and equality of all and renouncing denigrating, sexist language (A Call to Men, 2022b, para. 6). This program also extends training and educational resources to businesses, schools, faith communities, coaches and government agencies including awareness of LBGQ, Trans, Non-binary and racial issues. "By breaking out of the Man Box," says the website, "male-identified people become healthier and help to build and sustain more equitable communities" (A Call to Men, 2022c, para. 2).

Mentors in Violence Prevention (MVP) is a gender violence prevention, education, and training organization founded in 1994 by Jackson Katz (1994). MVP was the first large-scale initiative in the world to leverage the influence and social power of sports culture in the struggle against all forms of gender violence and also the first system-wide gender violence prevention program in the US Armed Services—the Marine Corps. MVP's cadre of staff trainers and consultants "explicitly discuss the gender, sexual and racial norms and structures of power that often underlie abusive acts and affect the likelihood of interventions" (MVP Strategies, 2022).

Trainings incorporate Act Like a Man/Woman Box and Sexual Assault in the Daily Routine, which reveals women's actions to stay safe from sexual violence. MVP has trained thousands of male and female student-athletes, coaches, and administrators in NCAA college programs and dozens of professional teams as well as small and large companies (Katz, 2018).

Multiple outreach programs for men use sports teams as the venue and coaches as the facilitators. A collaboration called RALIANCE maintains an online database of more than 100 prevention programs for the sports pipeline of athletes from children through professionals (McCray, 2015). RALIANCE has a goal "to end sexual violence in one generation" (RALIANCE, 2022). Additionally, RALIANCE Business advises employers on how to incorporate prevention of sexual harassment, misconduct, and abuse as they instill diversity, equity, and inclusion within their workplaces (RALIANCE Business, 2022).

The Memphis Approach to Prevention: Men as Primary Audience

Reaching and engaging men in the work of prevention is an ongoing priority of Memphis Says NO MORE. For example, the male police director and mayor were among the first faces and voices in the Memphis Says NO MORE poster and video series along with a male survivor of family domestic violence, a member of Congress, a leading black minister, a retired Navy commander, a male survivor of intimate partner violence, and a well-known male Hispanic minister. Just as the national NO MORE campaign partnered with the NFL, Memphis Says NO MORE partnered with the NBA Memphis Grizzlies. Four different star players, the manager and the coach posed for posters, and the team hosted a rollout of the new images during a game, with a half-time program and a screening of the images on the arena jumbotron. Memphis Says NO MORE t-shirts were "shot" into the audience and volunteers distributed thousands of palm cards, wristbands, and posters. The star players were featured on the backs and interior walls of 20 Memphis Area Transit Authority buses saying "NO MORE It's Not My Problem," extending the messaging throughout Memphis neighborhoods for nearly a year. The bus signs also guided viewers to www.memphissaysnomore.com where local help for victims/survivors is found along with other campaign materials and videos. The Grizzlies' messages also looped on overhead screens at the Memphis International Airport baggage area.

Memphis Says NO MORE also continues to sponsor the annual Memphis Walk a Mile in Her Shoes, a rally to engage men and boys in allyship with women and girls to end rape, stalking, domestic violence, and harassment. The 10th public in-person rally in September 2021 drew more than 280 walkers to the University of Memphis, even during a COVID surge and amidst extensive health protocols. Local founders of the Walk shared local crime numbers and the toll of gender violence. Students including athletes, Memphis police officers and men from various professions walked a one-mile circuit on city streets, in women's shoes and not, with signs proclaiming their commitment to valuing women and ending gender violence, see Figure 23.1.

Figure 23.1 Image of Memphis' Walk a Mile in Her Shoes

Figure 23.2 Image of NO MORE Campaign on Memphis Bus

As depicted in Figure 23.2, the latest series of Memphis Says NO MORE bus signs focus on men and youth with faces of a well-known local civil rights leader, a Hispanic teen boy, and an African-American woman. Messaging in English and Spanish declares, "Memphis Says NO MORE Not My Problem, Memphis Says NO MORE Why Didn't She Leave? Memphis Says NO MORE She Asked for It." Collaborations with Task Force partners and other community allies help carry the Memphis Says NO MORE campaign across important communities to reach men and boys in various settings. The University of Memphis leads Safe Bars training for university-area businesses, and Shelby County Crime Victims & Rape Crisis Center advocates train the Coaching Boys into Men curriculum in local schools. Memphis Says NO MORE hosts presentations such as the 2018 Roll Red Roll film and panel at area colleges. And Memphis Says NO MORE partners with Bridge Builders local youth organizers and their Memphis Against Sexual Harassment and Assault (MASHA) program for speakers and campaign champions from diverse race and gender identities to enact SV awareness and protections for students.

Strategy Three: Social Media and Technology

Social media has given perpetrators of gender violence new tools for abuse—to demean, harass, stalk, and threaten. Future prevention programs must pay attention to social media's role in perpetuating sexual violence. Sexual abusers have been known to gain access to their victims via online forums and websites. Conversely, some training programs have begun to consider how social media can be used to interrupt and challenge abusive behaviors, give victims/survivors a voice and help advocates and law enforcement respond to sexual violence.

One technology that was quickly adapted for violence prevention was mobile phone apps. A multitude of both free and paid apps are available for smartphone users. Most offered to date are considered more useful for intimate partner violence and domestic violence than for sexual violence (Sinha et al., 2020). For example, emergency assistance apps can serve as an intervention tool to provide a degree of safety against street violence (Sinha et al., 2020). BSafe, Guard My Angel, ReactMobile, and StaySafe are all apps that allow users to notify emergency contacts in the event of violence or danger. As smartphones become increasingly common worldwide, even among adolescents, additional development of the apps could extend their usability regarding sexual violence prevention, with attention to non-English languages and improved and appropriate linkage to police or other emergency services (Sinha et al., 2020).

myPlan is a smartphone app that helps women assess the danger of their relationships, find resources, and make a safety plan (Scarlett, 2016). The app was tested in multiple randomized controlled trials and incorporates the Danger Assessment validated risk assessment tool (myPlan: Our Story, 2022). The app provides immediate feedback on next steps such as moving out or seeking a restraining order, but the objective is not only about staying or leaving (Glass et al., 2015, 2021). It is well known that survivors of IPV are most at risk when attempting to leave violent relationships. "Safety is the ultimate outcome," says developer Dr. Nancy Glass. The app emphasizes how to take action "as safely as possible" (Scarlett, 2016). Though created in response to the needs of domestic violence victims, myPlan could be applicable to sexual violence prevention given that most rapes in the United States are by acquaintances and that between 40% and 45% of women in abusive relationships will also be sexually assaulted during the relationship (NCDAV).

Other new technologies that put information and communication at our fingertips hold promise for future innovation in the realm of sexual violence prevention and safety. A QR code on bar napkins or tabletops could in the future instantly call bar staff or police if swiped by a threatened customer, for example (Guarino, 2021). Social media content could update hot spots or share alerts about violent incidents. The ever-evolving landscape of online platforms such as TikTok and Instagram has changed the meaning of bystander, as all social media users may become bystanders if witnessing cyber abuse. While social media has led to new types of abuse—cyber-bullying, stalking, online harassment, and revenge porn—social media also could be useful in interrupting or calling out abusive behaviors (Fairbairn, 2020). Thus, creators of future sexual violence prevention initiatives must be alert to new developments and ready to adapt to ever-changing social norms and technology. This is the direction that Memphis is heading.

The Memphis Approach—Pivoting with Social Media Technology

The Memphis Says NO MORE website is loaded with videos, posters, and other material available to download for schools, workplaces, or teams. An interactive map on the Memphis Says NO MORE website locates victim resources. Memphis Says NO MORE and the Memphis Area Women's Council use Facebook, Instagram, and Twitter to share upcoming events and updated data on crimes, victim services, highlights from research, and other messaging. During the COVID era, outreach sessions on domestic violence and sexual assault were held online with sororities and other women's groups, the Memphis Veterans Affairs Medical Center, and other workplaces. The printed resource information card was updated to reflect the availability of counselors and advocates even during times of closed offices or staggered hours. The update was posted on social media sites, distributed thru email and news media, as well as at the few in-person client distribution events by partner agencies, such as a series of community walks against gun violence. "White papers" on men and gender violence, consent, and other topics written by local researchers were posted on websites and previewed in email newsletters.

The Memphis Approach: Assessing Campaign's Impact

Since most sexual and intimate partner violence is not reported to authorities (see Chapter 3), the Memphis Says NO MORE messaging and awareness campaign is aimed at encouraging increased reporting of these crimes so that more survivors get help and more perpetrators are brought to justice for their crimes. Memphis Says NO MORE has been evaluated three times—once before campaign materials and ads were spread across the city, once five months later, and then six years later, in the spring of 2021.

The Themis Center for Justice Policy, Practice and Research at the University of Memphis in conjunction with marketing experts at Splash Creative evaluated community attitudes before and after Memphis Says NO MORE launch through the use of six focus groups (some single-gender, some mixed) and 450 scale-ranking surveys that were available online and in hard copy. Survey responders were 80% female and 20% male, 60% White non-Hispanic, and 35% Black non-Hispanic. Respondent ages ranged from 17 to 82 years.

Before the campaign, focus group respondents reported a high awareness of domestic violence and sexual assault problems and considerable awareness of an ongoing rape kit testing issue in Memphis, but the details were sparse. After the launch period, more participants were familiar with Memphis Says NO MORE as compared to participants in the pre-launch phase (72% vs. 21%). Thirty of the 32 people knew about the local rape kit issue, and some could explain it well. Several also knew a task force was working on it.

Results from the 2017 evaluation were even more impressive. After the campaign, victim-blaming lessened. Higher numbers of people indicated that women do not bring domestic violence and rape on themselves, they are not asking for trouble when wearing sexy clothes, staying out late, or drinking too much. However, this research also indicated that between 23% and 43% of respondents did not disagree with these statements. Meanwhile, awareness of the Memphis Says NO MORE campaign increased from 43% to 76% of participants, indicating that the campaign was on the right track and needed to continue.

In spring 2021, an online survey was created by criminal justice researcher Larisa McKinnerney at the University of Memphis to assess community members' beliefs and attitudes after six years of the Memphis Says NO MORE campaign. A total of 209 responses to 14 items were obtained and analyzed. Among respondents, 87% self-identified as female, 65% as White, and 32% as Black with 0.01% as either Hispanic or Native American. Responses showed strong disagreement with statements that blamed victim behavior as a cause of sexual violence. Three in four respondents knew about local sexual assault and domestic violence resources if needed. However, an area needing increased messaging was distrust of law enforcement to assist with these crimes. To the statement, "If I reported being a victim of sexual assault and/ or rape, I would feel confident in law enforcement taking action," only 23% Agreed ($n = 49$), 39% Disagreed ($n = 81$), and 38% were Neutral ($n = 79$). To the statement, "If I reported being a victim of domestic violence, I would feel confident in law enforcement taking action," again, only 24% Agreed ($n = 51$), 34% Disagreed ($n = 70$), and 41% were Neutral ($n = 86$). With only one-fourth of respondents reporting confidence in law enforcement's sexual assault or domestic violence response, Memphis Says NO MORE campaign strategies and collaborations are being adapted to further encourage survivors to seek help and healing along the community care continuum while ensuring that all victims have access to safety and justice.

Conclusion

Despite the increasing social and mass media presence of sexual violence awareness, including the #MeToo movement, public awareness is not enough to prevent gender violence. As RALIANCE co-founder Sandra Henriquez states, "Our cultural institutions, our government, leading corporations, have yet to do enough to really take responsibility for addressing sexual harassment, assault, and abuse. We have to recognize that sexual abuse is not inevitable. We need to establish a cultural consensus that sexual violence is preventable" (RALIANCE, 2021, para. 11).

Men's violence against women is learned, which means it can be unlearned. So said the posters and banners created by Coaching Boys into Men 20 years ago. Prevention is possible—over time, with diligence, with collaboration and allyship between all persons and when paired with changes in culture to assure safety, justice, and equity for everyone, everywhere. Prevention is possible when children understand consent. Prevention is possible when each of us is equipped and united within and across our agencies and systems to provide early education about consent and healthy relationships. Prevention is possible when each of us is willing to step in to intervene and assist. A future without rape is possible; helping communities adopt a sustainable, multilevel public health response to the problem is an important avenue to prevention.

Key Points

- A public health approach to sexual violence prevention that incorporates consistent messaging, in conjunction with targeted training and awareness activities, works to change attitudes, influence a public system response, and foster community learning around the topic.
- Technology and public media messaging play a growing role in changing community attitudes toward domestic violence and sexual assault.
- Engaging with influential community leaders is an important way to distribute messaging around violence prevention.
- Several public programs have demonstrated research efficacy around sexual violence prevention and choosing a strategy may be highly dependent on the community context in which this work is situated.
- Public messaging and campaigns work to increase awareness of the pervasive nature of sexual violence. They also encourage community members to enact change.

Discussion Questions

1 How could some of the aforementioned programs to prevent domestic violence and sexual assault function in your community? Do you see any barriers to their implementation?

2 What is the importance of public advocacy movements in the prevention of sexual violence? How does public marketing play a role in cultural change around sexual assault?

3 Based on what you have read in this chapter, including the case example from Memphis, what would be important action items if starting a sexual violence prevention initiative in a new city? Is there anything else that you believe needs to be considered that was not mentioned in this chapter?

Further Reading

Armstrong, C. L., & Mahone, J. (2017). "It's on us." The role of social media and rape culture in individual willingness to mobilize against sexual assault. *Mass Communication and Society, 20*(1), 92–115. https://doi.org/10.1080/15205436.2016.1185127

Carlyle, K. E., Guidry, J. P. D., Dougherty, S. A., & Burton, C. W. (2019). Intimate partner violence on Instagram: Visualizing a public health approach to prevention. *Health Education & Behavior, 46*(2_suppl), 90S–96S. https://doi.org/10.1177/1090198119873917

Culture of Respect. (2002). *Ending campus sexual violence*. https://cultureofrespect.org/

Dills, J., Fowler, D., & Payne, G. (2016). *Sexual violence on campus: Strategies for prevention*. National Center for Injury Prevention and Control, Centers for Disease Control and Prevention.

McMahon, S., & Banyard, V. L. (2012). When can I help? A conceptual framework for the prevention of sexual violence through bystander intervention. *Trauma, Violence, & Abuse, 13*(1), 3–14. https://doi.org/10.1177/1524838011426015

References

A Call to Men. (2022a). https://www.acalltomen.org/healthy-manhood/

A Call to Men. (2022b). A call to men: FAQs. https://www.acalltomen.org/about/faqs/

A Call to Men. (2022c). Video: What is the man box? https://www.acalltomen.org/resources/video-what-is-the-man-box/

Barker, G., Ricardo, C., Nascimento, M., & World Health Organization. (2007). *Engaging men and boys in changing gender-based inequity in health: Evidence from programme interventions*. World Health Organization.

Berkowitz, S., & O'Connor, R. (2014, February 28). *RAINN comments and recommendations to the White House Task Force to protect students from sexual assault*. https://gendertruce.files.wordpress.com/2014/08/rainn-wh-task-force-rainn-recommendations.pdf

Centers for Disease Control and Prevention. (2021). *Prevention strategies*. https://www.cdc.gov/violenceprevention/sexualviolence/prevention.html

Centers for Disease Control and Prevention. (2022). *The social-ecological model: A framework for prevention*. https://www.cdc.gov/violenceprevention/about/social-ecologicalmodel.html

Culture of Respect. (2022). *Prevention programming matrix: Bringing in the bystander*. https://cultureofrespect.org/program/bringing-in-the-bystander/

DeGue, S., Valle, L. A., Holt, M. K., Massetti, G. M., Matjasko, J. L., & Tharp, A. T. (2014). A systematic review of primary prevention strategies for sexual violence perpetration. *Aggression and Violent Behavior, 19*(4), 346–362.

Dills, J., Fowler, D., & Payne, G. (2016). *Sexual violence on campus: Strategies for prevention*. National Center for Injury Prevention and Control, Centers for Disease Control and Prevention.

Fairbairn, J. (2020). Before #MeToo: Violence against women social media work, bystander intervention, and social change. *Societies*, *10*(3), 51–72.

Fielding, J. E., Teutsch, S., & Breslow, L. A. (2010). Framework for public health in the United States. *Public Health Review*, *32*, 174–189. https://doi.org/10.1007/BF03391597

Foshee, V. A., Linder, G. F., Bauman, K. E., Langwick, S. A., Arriaga, X. B., Heath, J. L., McMahon, P. M., & Bangdiwala, S. (1996). The safe dates project: Theoretical basis, evaluation design, and selected baseline findings. *American Journal of Preventive Medicine*, *12*(5), 39–47. https://doi.org/10.1016/S0749-3797(18)30235-6

Glass, N., Clough, A., Case, J., Hanson, G., Barnes-Hoyt, J., Waterbury, A., Alhusen, J., Ehrensaft, M., Grace, K. T., & Perrin, N. (2015). A safety app to respond to dating violence for college women and their friends: The myPlan study randomized controlled trial protocol. *BMC Public Health*, *15*(1), 1–13. https://doi.org/10.1186/s12889-015-2191-6

Glass, N. E., Clough, A., Messing, J. T., Bloom, T., Brown, M. L., Eden, K. B., Campbell, J. C., Gielen, A., Laughon, K., Grace, K. T., Turner, R. M., Alvarez, C., Case, J., Barnes-Hoyt, J., Alhusen, J., Hanson, G. C., & Perrin, N. A. (2021). Longitudinal impact of the myPlan app on health and safety among college women experiencing partner violence. *Journal of Interpersonal Violence*. https://doi.org/10.1177/0886260521991880

Guarino, J. C. (2021). Innovative strategies to facilitate safe assessment and intervention for intimate partner violence during a pandemic and beyond. *Nursing for Women's Health*, *25*(5), 395–399.

Joyful Heart Foundation. (2022). *NOMORE PSA Campaign*. https://www.joyfulheartfoundation.org/programs/no-more-psa-campaign

Katz, J. (1994). *Mentors in Violence Prevention (MVP) trainer's guide*. Center for the Study of Sport in Society.

Katz, J. (2018). Bystander training as leadership training: Notes on the origins, philosophy, and pedagogy of the mentors in violence prevention model. *Violence Against Women*, *24*(15), 1755–1776. https://doi.org/10.1177/1077801217753322

McCray, K. L. (2015). Intercollegiate athletes and sexual violence: A review of literature and recommendations for future study. *Trauma, Violence, & Abuse*, *16*(4), 438–443. https://doi.org/10.1177/1524838014537907

Melnick, R. S. (2020, June 11). Analyzing the Department of Education's final Title IX rules on sexual misconduct. *Brookings*. https://www.brookings.edu/research/analyzing-the-department-of-educations-final-title-ix-rules-on-sexual-misconduct/

Moracco, K. E., Runyan, C. W., Bowling, J. M., & Earp, J. A. L. (2007). Women's experiences with violence: A national study. *Women's Health Issues*, *17*(1), 3–12.

MVP Strategies. (2022). https://mvpstrat.com/about/accomplishments/

myPlan: Our Story. (2022). https://www.myplanapp.org/en/our-story

No More Blog. (2022). *Tony Porter: A call to men*. https://nomore.org/tony-porter-a-call-to-men/

NOMORE.Org. (2022). *Together we can end domestic violence and sexual assault*. https://nomore.org/about/our-story/

RAINN. (2022). *RAINN: Statistics*. https://www.rainn.org/statistics/perpetrators-sexual-violence

RALIANCE. (2021). *RALIANCE Co-founder Sandra Henriquez: We need to establish a cultural consensus that sexual violence is preventable*. https://www.raliance.org/raliance-co-founder-sandra-henriquez-we-need-to-establish-a-cultural-consensus-that-sexual-violence-is-preventable/

RALIANCE. (2022). *RALIANCE*. https://www.raliance.org

RALIANCE Business. (2022). *RALIANCE Business*. https://www.raliance.org/business/

Safe Bar Collective. (2022). https://safebarcollective.org/home/

Scarlett, K. (2016, September 7). *Interactive app provides help for domestic violence victims*. The Hub. https://hub.jhu.edu/magazine/2016/fall/domestic-violence-app-nursing/

Sinha, S., Shrivastava, A., & Paradis, C. (2020). A survey of the mobile phone-based interventions for violence prevention among women. *Advances in Social Work, 19*(2), 493–517. https://doi.org/10.18060/22526

Taylor, B. G., Stein, N. D., Mumford, E. A., & Woods, D. (2013). Shifting boundaries: An experimental evaluation of a dating violence prevention program in middle schools. *Prevention Science, 14*(1), 64–76. https://doi.org/10.1007/s11121-012-0293-2

World Health Organization. (2018). *Violence against women prevalence estimates, 2018— Executive summary.* https://www.who.int/publications-detail-redirect/9789240026681

World Health Organization. (2021). *About the violence prevention alliance.* https://www.who.int/groups/violence-prevention-alliance/about

24 Envisioning a better victim response

Survivor-centered advocacy, destigmatization, collaboration, and accountability

Margaret J. McGuire, Danielle B. Sabo, and Joanna Klingenstein

In 1972, the first official rape crisis center in the United States was established in Washington, DC. This marked a significant achievement for the anti-rape movement and acknowledged that formal support was needed to address the trauma uniquely suffered by survivors of sexual violence (Loney-Howes, 2020). Over time, the services available to survivors expanded from volunteer-run hotlines and crisis services to providing ongoing counseling, advocacy, outreach, and education. Engagement between community agencies and the criminal justice system has also evolved into various collaborative, multidisciplinary teams (MDTs) and task forces working together to improve our overall response to sexual violence. These improvements developed alongside a similar growth in services for domestic violence and child abuse survivors. The victim services field includes those working in law enforcement (e.g., police officers and prosecutors), health-care providers (e.g., mental health counselors, sexual assault nurse examiners), and advocacy professionals (e.g., personnel working for rape crisis, domestic violence, and child advocacy organizations) (Greeson & Campbell, 2012; Melton, 2020). Building upon these accomplishments, the field of victim services has evolved into a web of intersecting agencies and professionals who seek to support survivors throughout their healing journey in the aftermath of sexual violence.

Technological advancement in how services are provided has increased access to services, improved societal recognition of sexual violence, and enhanced relationships between law enforcement and community-based agencies. These advancements serve to strengthen victim services while increasing communication and coordination in ways that improve victims' willingness to remain in the process (Luminais et al., 2020). However, a comprehensive reformed response also entails reducing negative interpersonal interactions that survivors can have with victim services providers—termed **secondary victimization (or secondary trauma)** (Campbell, 1998). **Secondary victimization** is the additional harm(s) or sense of injustice victims may experience in the wake of a traumatic event when the response services they receive fall short of being empowering or affirming (Laing, 2017). As highlighted in Chapter 3, negative interactions—especially those that occur very early in the process—profoundly impact the degree to which a survivor remains engaged with the criminal justice system and processes trauma from the sexual assault. In addition to secondary trauma, survivors can be retraumatized by inadequate treatment within the criminal justice system, the medical field, and even community-based victim services (Campbell, 1998; Laing, 2017). What has been termed **institutional betrayal** encapsulates the gravity

DOI: 10.4324/9781003186816-28

that negative institutional action or lack of expected positive protective action (i.e., inaction) in response to traumatic experiences has. It can significantly impact survivors and deter others from coming forward (Smith & Freyd, 2014).

This chapter is also informed by the professional experiences related to victim service delivery of each author. All three authors worked as research team members under Dr Rachel Lovell on the Sexual Assault Kit Initiative in Cuyahoga County. Prior to Margaret McGuire's research role, she worked in the anti-sexual violence field with Ohio's statewide coalition, the Ohio Alliance to End Sexual Violence. Her research focuses on systems advocacy and increasing access to both victim and health services by underserved populations. Danielle Sabo previously served as the Campus Survivor Confidential Advocate at Case Western Reserve University and as Associate Director for Violence Prevention & Response out of the Flora Stone Mather Center for Women. Danielle's mixed-methods research focuses on the lived experience of trauma for marginalized (LGBTQ+, BIPOC, Neurodiverse) survivors of sexual violence and its impact on health outcomes over the life course. Finally, Joanna Klingenstein has worked in various social work settings including foster care, children services, and residential treatment for juvenile sexual offenders. In these positions, she focused on crisis intervention, risk and safety assessment, and familial and kinship reconciliation. In her research position, she concentrates on gender-based violence and urban violent crime.

In the context of a reformed response to sexual assault, in this chapter we explore *how victim services could better serve survivors*. What themes exist among survivors' demands for change in the system and what services are research-supported? Lessons from the past indicate that the future of victim services must prioritize empowering, trauma-informed, intersectional and culturally responsive, and accessible services for all survivors of sexual violence. Recognizing that trauma impacts all aspects of a survivor's life, **trauma-informed care** means intentionally structuring both interpersonal interactions and organizational responses to promote healing and avoid causing further harm or distress (Palmieri & Valentine, 2021).

There are four essential principles derived from past reforms in the victim-services field. Framed as tenets to signify their lasting importance, these values are (1) survivor-centered advocacy, (2) the destigmatization of sexual violence, (3) victim services collaboration, and (4) trauma-informed accountability. In this chapter, we discuss these four tenets and demonstrate how and why each tenet is necessary for the victim services field to be able to accomplish each of victim services' goals, that is, providing victim-centered experiences, successful outcomes, and improving public safety, while continuously building and enacting reforms for the benefit of all survivors of sexual violence.

Tenet 1: Survivor-Centered Advocacy

Survivor-centered advocacy is the first and most essential tenet due to the robust evidence demonstrating that this model greatly impacts survivors' well-being and the chance for successful outcomes when utilizing victim services. **Survivor-centered advocacy,** also known as **survivor-defined advocacy,** is guided by the premise that survivors gain individual autonomy, empowerment, and protection from further trauma or abuse by being granted the power to control their own choices in the healing and justice process (Cattaneo et al., 2020; Herman, 1997; Nichols, 2013).

Survivor-centered advocacy services afford victims autonomy and control in the justice process, which is essential in developing quality wraparound services. A **wraparound model** occurs when community service partners and criminal justice agencies coordinate to focus the service plan on the survivor's priorities (Koss et al., 2017). As supported by research, the future of survivor advocacy services moves toward comprehensive, survivor-first service models for a better and more empowered future for all survivors.

Advocacy that is survivor-defined and empowering

Survivors of sexual violence deserve advocacy and wraparound victim services that are empowering, trauma-informed, individualized, intersectional, and accessible to all members of the community in need. To accomplish this, victim services for survivors of sexual assault and their families should actively move toward trauma-informed paradigms that prioritize the survivor's needs. Survivor-centered victim services assume that survivors' individual lived experiences and violence narratives vary and actively disengage from systemic racist, patriarchal, homophobic, xenophobic, and transphobic practices. Therefore, survivor-driven advocacy is tailored to each unique victim and puts full decision-making power and control in their hands at each step of the healing, investigation, and criminal justice process (Nichols, 2013).

Notably, survivor-centered advocacy can reduce secondary victimization. The revictimization stems from victims' expectations that they will be believed and affirmed but are instead blamed or dismissed (Laing, 2017; Smith & Freyd, 2014). Research indicates that victim perception of successful advocacy emphasizes reducing victim-blaming and secondary victimization, utilizing available services, and diminishing post-traumatic stress following criminal justice system engagement (Brooks & Burman, 2017; Campbell, 2006; Zweig & Burt, 2007). Most importantly, by implementing more survivor-driven advocacy services and paradigms within the justice process, victims may come to define their healing journey as successful. Additionally, survivor-centered approaches are necessary to meet all the overarching goals of victim services, including community safety and perpetrator accountability. Improving survivors' experiences within the justice process leads to increased victim engagement, and research continues to demonstrate that this increased participation strengthens sexual assault investigations and prosecutions (Gaines & Wells, 2015; Lovell et al., 2021).

Current issues impeding the implementation of survivor-centered advocacy

While centering survivors in advocacy is primarily a goal of community-based programs or wraparound services, current issues within the criminal justice system and the medical field complicate this objective. Conventional criminal justice systems are designed to focus on protecting the rights of the accused and the safety of its collective citizenry, which often results in failing to protect and support the needs and interests of survivors of sexual violence (Brooks & Burman, 2017; McGlynn et al., 2017).

Moreover, the traditional defendant and incarceration-focused criminal justice practices often further disenfranchise and silence survivors with marginalized identities (including Black Indigenous survivors of color, international survivors, and members of the LGBTQIA+ community) who are already less likely to report sexual assault (Brubaker, 2019, see also Chapter 3 on disclosure). Incarceration-focused criminal justice processes assume that survivors are typically seeking out punishment against their perpetrator as opposed to pursuing other empowering services such as medical care, therapy, and support groups for healing. Brubaker (2019) maintains that "because marginalized communities (…) are often small and close-knit, members often rely on one another for support and may be reluctant to report, especially when the perpetrator is a member of their community" (p. 314). When identity, community, and intersectionality are not considered or advocated for—survivors are silenced, and violence is pervasive, making survivor-driven advocacy even more important to prioritize.

Examples of innovative approaches to centering survivors

Restorative justice alternatives

Restorative justice approaches for victims of sexual violence often can be considered trauma-informed and survivor-driven. **Restorative justice** is "a process whereby all parties with a stake in a particular offence come together to resolve collectively how to deal with the aftermath of the offence and its implications for the future" (Marshall, 1999, p. 5). Upon speaking with survivors, Herman (2005) and Jülich (2006) found that many expressed a desire for restorative justice approaches which go beyond current criminal justice services. For example, a pilot program named RESTORE offered sexual violence victims restorative justice approaches (Wemmers, 2017). RESTORE gave victims the opportunity to engage in conversations with their offenders with the purpose of reducing the number of cases that drop out of the criminal justice process (Koss, 2014).

The RESTORE program is separated into four stages: (1) prosecutorial case referral and informed consent, (2) addressing safety concerns and ground rules for participation, (3) meeting with all parties as a team (including victim advocates and professionals) for a highly moderated dialogue, and (4) sustaining accountability and reintegration through more than a year of meetings, conferences, financial obligations, and formal apologies. Both parties are offered free legal counsel and the choice to remain in the criminal justice system, explore civil justice options, or remain in the program (Koss, 2014). The RESTORE program found PTSD decreased from 82% to 66% among survivors after the moderated dialogue, over 90% of RESTORE participants felt satisfied with the process, and 91% of the cases completed the entire process. Importantly, survivors reported this restorative justice approach led to both substantial stress reduction and the ability to "take back control" through the moderated dialogues (Wemmers, 2017).

The restorative justice process may not be a suitable option for all victim-survivors or perpetrators. Extant research suggests that certain types of perpetrators should be deemed unfit for the RJ process. These include perpetrators who have been identified as repeat offenders, those that are a danger to the community, those that lack actual accountability that is genuine for their crime(s), and/or those that have certain psychological characteristics (Burns & Sinko, 2021). Additionally, while restorative justice may not be a solution for all survivors, particularly in cases where gratuitous violence was involved, or there is no relationship between the survivor and offender (Burns & Sinko, 2021), the RESTORE program demonstrates the potential opportunities for survivor healing and accountability that may be more accessible, trauma-informed, and successful as compared to the criminal justice process.

Smartphone technology

Recent technological advancements can increase access to support and ensure a more survivor-centered experience. Anonymous smartphone applications, such as JDoe, Circle of Six, and Callisto, can connect survivors who have a shared perpetrator, offer safe and convenient support, and provide the option to share information with law enforcement anonymously. Technology such as this, paired with victim-centered wraparound services that work in tandem with both the criminal justice process and restorative approaches, can allow survivors to experience genuine autonomy in the healing process (see Figure 24.1).

Envisioning the future of survivor-centered victim services

Survivor-driven advocacy must consider a victim's intersection of identities, the community in which their identities exist, and their goals regarding their healing journey. A fundamental way the future of victim services can deliver survivor-driven advocacy is by encouraging medical care teams and criminal justice units to utilize more convenient, accessible, and trauma-informed options through ever-evolving technological developments and offer a range of both criminal and

Figure 24.1 Anonymous Smartphone Applications Offer Innovative Support

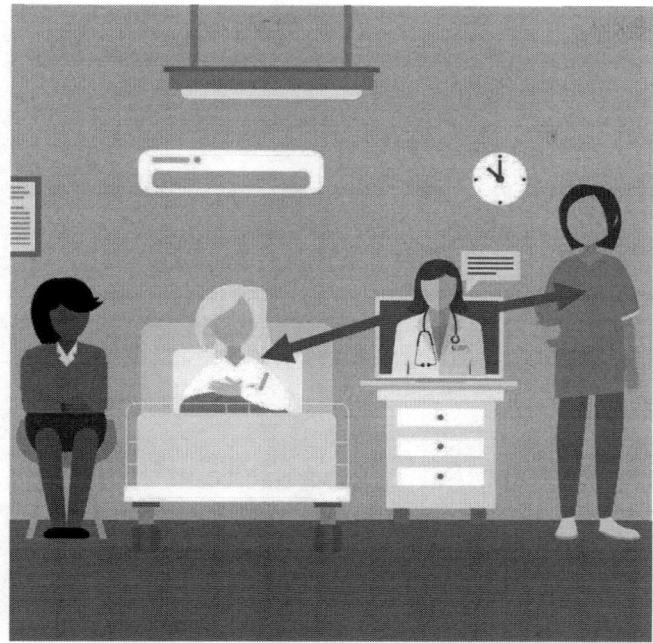

Figure 24.2 Photo Illustration Shows How teleSANE Services Work. Video Conferencing Equipment Is Placed in the Patient's Room, Allowing a Sexual Assault Nurse Examiner to Communicate with the Patient and Nurses at the Hospital Caring for Them. A Rape Crisis Advocate Can Be in the Room to Support the Patient Too

Source: Photo courtesy of the Massachusetts Department of Public Health (Corpuz, 2020).

restorative justice options, made available 24/7, which allow for anonymous reporting from the privacy of a survivor's own home. Convenient and effective tele-advocacy options for police, SANE units, and advocates could be made available via web platforms, which have already seen promising results (see Highlight on Tele-advocacy SANE Units in Figure 24.2; Walsh et al., 2019). Small changes like these that are trauma-informed, intersectional, and survivor-driven, can make a profound difference to those impacted by sexual violence.

Tenet 2: Destigmatization of Sexual Violence

The stigma associated with sexual violence impedes victim services from providing adequate support and can deter survivors from coming forward to seek out medical treatment, police intervention, or support of any kind in the wake of their trauma. The term **stigma** refers to an attribute of the self that society deems as profoundly discrediting. Stigma can also refer to some aspect of the self that conveys a character flaw or a feature devalued by society (Goffman, 1963). Cultural tropes as to what constitutes a credible, "good" or "real" victim of sexual violence are often not encompassing the multitude of possible trauma narratives and may ultimately encourage survivors to conceal their identities (Campbell, 1998). The future of survivor advocacy services must prioritize the destigmatization of sexual violence from within the criminal justice system and even from victim service providers (Campbell, 1998).

How stigma continues to impact victim services

Internalized stigma deterring help-seeking

Overstreet and Quinn's (2013) Intimate Partner Violence (IPV) Stigmatization Model maintains that the combination of three types of stigma—anticipated, internalized, and cultural—operate in unison to deter survivors from seeking support or speaking out about their experiences. *Anticipated stigma* for sexual assault survivors is the feeling that others will not believe their trauma narrative or the assumption that medical professionals will discriminate against them during an exam (Overstreet & Quinn, 2013). *Stigma internalization* is the feeling of guilt, fault, low self-worth, and humiliation (Murray et al., 2016; Overstreet & Quinn, 2013). Finally, *cultural stigma* is societal attitudes which contribute to rape joke culture, the minimization of sexual violence as a problem, myths surrounding the types of individuals who experience sexual violence, and widespread victim-blaming discourse (Overstreet & Quinn, 2013).

Discriminatory treatment of marginalized populations

These three stigmas are experienced in diverse ways but may be characterized by survivors feeling dismissed, blamed, denied from services, or discriminated against by others when seeking support (Murray et al., 2016). Despite advocate support, survivors who do not fit the narrative of a "good" victim are more likely to have negative experiences within the legal, medical, and mental health systems (Campbell, 1998). Furthermore, males, LGBTQIA+, and other marginalized populations of survivors may experience this stigma in different and more pervasive ways (Murray et al., 2016). Within the criminal justice system, stigma impacts perceptions of victim credibility in sexual assault investigations and prosecutions, which in turn play a vital role in the experiences, services received, and outcomes of victims (Lovell et al., 2021).

The impacts of this type of stigmatization are multifaceted and serve to turn helping professionals into "gatekeepers" who, guided by extant discriminatory practices, biased attitudes, and a dearth of accurate knowledge about sexual assault victimology, continue to act as barriers for survivors seeking support and justice. Historically, many wraparound victim services were tailored for cis-gender, female, heterosexual victims of sexual violence. The unique needs of male, transgender, and queer survivors are still too often disregarded in professionals' training and education requirements (Murray et al., 2016), and stigmatizing practices by medical experts, criminal justice professionals, and advocates may make the justice and healing process for male, LGBTQIA+, and other marginalized survivors retraumatizing and sometimes even life-threatening (Palmieri & Valentine, 2021). The intersection of multiple stigmatized survivor identities, such as male, queer, trans, BIPOC (Black, Indigenous, People of Color) identified survivors must be considered when building future wraparound victim services that are accessible to all survivors. Additionally, there must be a consideration for the impact of language barriers, immigrant status, sex workers, fringe religious values, and ability status on access to victim services.

Envisioning a future free from stigma for survivors

If significant progress toward survivor-centered, affirming, accessible victim service response is to be realized, future victim services should actively work to destigmatize the experience of sexual violence and dispel dangerous rape myths. Future continued education and prevention efforts for those in victim services, health care, and the criminal justice process must prioritize diversity training on a range of intersectional victim narratives and identities, which seek to dispel the "perfect rape victim" trope.

Additionally, report and case note writing classes are needed to reduce biased and discriminatory language in official documentation of crimes and services and instead to embed affirming and validating language into all interactions with survivors and their families. Survivor-centered advocacy can also benefit from anti-rape culture social norming campaigns, which promote accurate information about sexual violence and survivors of it. (See Figure 24.3 as an example.) Future destigmatizing practices among professional victim support services must continuously dispel harmful sexual violence myths and encourage victims with an intersection of identities and with a range of trauma narratives to come forward, be believed, and expect unbiased justice and support.

Tenet 3: Victim Services Collaboration

Collaboration is the third essential tenet for improving victim services for sexual violence survivors. In this context, **collaboration** refers to the intentional forming of multidisciplinary task forces or teams of differing professionals working together around an investigative case or more extensive issue. Coordination and communication within collaborative agencies are vital components to accomplish each of victim

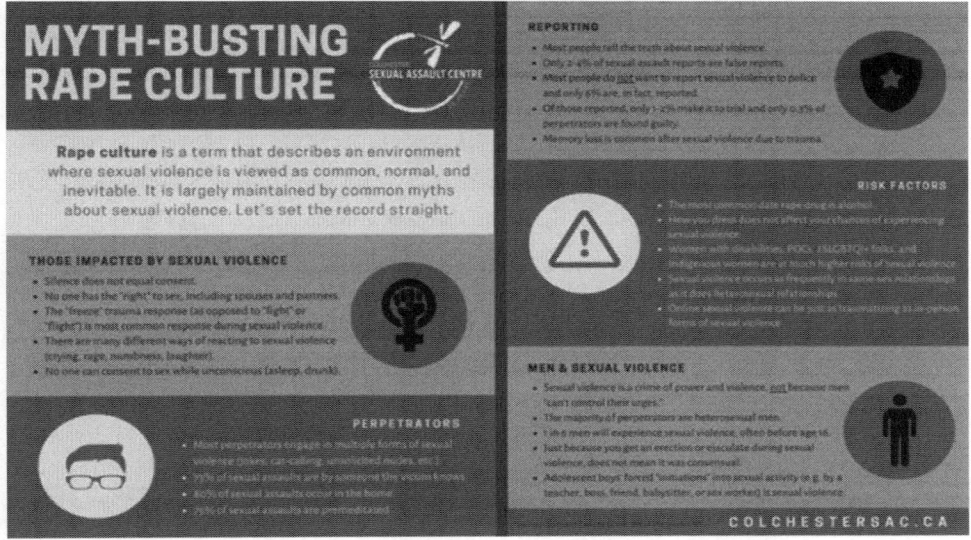

Figure 24.3 Myth Busting Rape Culture

services' goals, that is providing victim-centered experiences, successful outcomes, and improving public safety. Expanding and improving upon existing collaborative models shows promise toward improving victim outcomes (Herbert & Bromfield, 2019; Melton, 2020).

These collaborations often consist of advocates, social workers, investigators, prosecutors, and health and human service professionals. Standard collaboration methods between victim service agencies are MDTs, Sexual Assault Response Teams (SARTs), task forces, and/or wraparound services. MDTs are state or local-level teams created to identify or improve victim services to be survivor-centered and trauma-informed. SARTs provide local-level support through coordinating victim services and improving response through multidisciplinary case reviews (Melton, 2020). Similar collaboration models also exist in the child abuse, domestic violence, elder abuse, and human trafficking fields.

Collaboration within victim services

Research demonstrates that collaboration improves the quality of services and promotes access to criminal justice and victim service agencies (Herbert & Bromfield, 2019). MDTs are particularly beneficial for complex types of victimization where survivors require multiple agencies to support them (Campbell, 2008). As stated in the first tenet, wraparound services are an effective mode of collaboration because they center on and elevate the priorities of the survivor (Koss et al., 2017). Collaborative services can also alleviate issues in victim service delivery due to common pitfalls many agencies and law enforcement offices face due to a lack of resources. For example, insufficient resources at the Cleveland Division of Police's Sex Crimes Unit partially accounted for why so many sexual assault kits (SAKs) had not been tested. An understaffed department led to investigators moving quickly through problematic cases, such as those where the victim could not be located or missed appointments, or where the suspect was unidentified (Luminais et al., 2017). A study of multidisciplinary collaboration around commercial sexual exploitation of children found that the MDTs improved victim identification, agency information sharing, and collaboration among participating members (Farrell et al., 2020). Sharing information and resources within an MDT can alleviate burdens placed on individual departments and improve the overall quality of service.

Examples of successful reforms through collaboration

Cuyahoga County sexual assault kit task force

The Cuyahoga County Sexual Assault Kit Task Force (Task Force) is an example of how a collaborative MTD can both address a sizeable systemic issue and propel victim services forward with innovative strategies. The Task Force brought together county prosecutors, victim advocates, law enforcement, and the state forensic testing agency to address the investigative and prosecutorial workload resulting from the DNA testing of nearly 7,000 untested SAKs between 1993 and 2011 in Cuyahoga County, Ohio. The Task Force was innovative for its inclusion and integration of victim advocates, whose contributions and positive influence on the Task Force were documented by their research partners (Luminais et al., 2020). Specifically, this collaboration was made more robust through intentional efforts to address the common pitfalls that MDTs and task forces face: integration across different disciplines. Task Force members frequently cross-trained each other and recognized how victim advocates improved the communication and retention of victims throughout the process (Luminais et al., 2020). Similarly, a process evaluation of the Task Force found that intentionally arranging for a shared workspace for the Task Force members from different agencies improved their communication, collaboration, and full use of each member's expertise (Luminais et al., 2017).

Persisting issues around collaboration

Though collaboration improves service quality, collaborative team efficacy is still influenced by systemic discrimination, multiprofessional discrepancies, and confidentiality concerns (Lonsway & Archambault, 2020; Luminais et al., 2020). Survivor race, age, previous mental health or addiction treatment, insurance status, partner status, gender identity, socioeconomic status, and disability status continue to impact whether a victim will seek services or even have access to services (Amstadter et al., 2008; McCauley et al., 2019; Price et al., 2014). As stated in the second tenet, common tropes about victimology can lead many MDTs to focus on stranger rapes or prioritize victims with visible injuries. Because systemic discrimination is present within legal, medical, and social systems responding to sexual assault survivors, research and collaborative focus must continue to observe and improve the help-seeking experiences of traditionally underserved sexual assault survivors (Campbell, 2008).

Additionally, the strength of a collaborative relationship hinges on the quality of communication between agencies. Re-traumatization is still commonly experienced by survivors who must repeatedly retell the events and who experience inter-agency disconnections (Greeson & Campbell, 2012). MDTs must work diligently to combine their skills when appropriate and respect the different roles each professional plays in the progression of the case (Luminais et al., 2020). Competing priorities and role confusion are noted barriers to collaboration across medical, legal, and social service disciplines (Gaines & Wells, 2015; Greeson & Campbell, 2012; Payne, 2007). To state simply, survivors are negatively impacted when teams do not collaborate successfully and when they fail to acknowledge systemic inequalities.

Finally, variations in confidentiality guidelines continue to present major obstacles for collaborative partnerships through causing confusion, hampering detailed case discussion, and causing conflict between professionals. Confidentiality guidelines differ between fields and service agencies, even state to state, making collaborating professionals uneasy about what case information can be shared across agencies or in the presence of advocates (Koss et al., 2017; Lonsway & Archambault, 2020). In many states, both community and system-based advocates do not have client confidentiality protection, often referred to as *client-privilege*, that other professionals on the MDT would have, such as lawyers, social workers, and counselors. Additionally, the differences in proximity to the criminal justice system between community and system-based advocates can add additional obstacles to communication and trust between professionals from different agencies (Lonsway & Archambault, 2020). Cole's (2011) study of a SART highlights a similar problem;

medical and criminal justice professionals did not understand the breadth and depth of victim advocate-victim confidentiality, and that in many cases, victims needed to sign a waiver before the advocate could discuss case information with other professionals. Because these hesitations can negatively impact the victim's experience and case outcomes, there is a continued need to prioritize interprofessional training to achieve a thorough understanding of different confidentiality statutes within collaborative teams and to develop strategies to navigate confidentiality obstacles to ensure positive outcomes for survivors.

Envisioning the future of services regarding collaboration

A future strengthened victim services field capitalizes on and further integrates collaboration into every facet of service delivery. Through expanding the use of MDTs, wraparound models, and task forces, survivors will be afforded more opportunities to receive trauma-informed care that is also capable of holding their perpetrators accountable. As successful collaborations thus far have demonstrated, these collaborative bodies act as conduits to reach expanding circles of professionals with both formal and informal training on trauma-informed care, intersectionality, and systemic oppression. These trainings are necessary to reduce survivors' negative experiences with service providers or law enforcement (Campbell, 2008; Leung & Williams, 2019; Lovell et al., 2021). For example, a survivor undergoing a sexual assault exam conducted by a SANE nurse with specialized training is likely to also interact and be affected by many professionals without training in trauma-informed care throughout their journey through health and criminal justice systems (Campbell, 2008; Herbert & Bromfield, 2019). Additionally, growing support for more data sharing systems, improving client confidentiality protection, and clarifying professional confidentiality protocols generate optimism that collaborative teams and case management will be more able to deliver survivor-centered and successful outcomes for both the survivor and the community (see Figure 24.4).

Tenet 4: Trauma-Informed Accountability

Accountability is the fourth essential tenet necessary to ensure better victim services for survivors of sexual violence. In the context of this chapter, **accountability** is defined as actions intended to ensure any reforms or changes to victim services are continuously enacted and enforced. Accountability related to victim services most often occurs through the intentional codification of changes to policies or procedures, external or internal case review, and increased transparency about the process with the survivor, the public, or both (Smith & Freyd, 2014; Women's Law Project, 2013). **Trauma-informed accountability** prioritizes reducing trauma, respecting autonomy, and understanding the myriad of ways trauma may impact the needs of survivors interacting with any service provider or system. In victim services, accountability is crucial to ensure improvements "stick" in criminal investigations, interactions with providers, and systemic procedures. Most importantly, accountability is about ensuring all services, reforms, and policies are survivor-centered, trauma-informed, and culturally responsive.

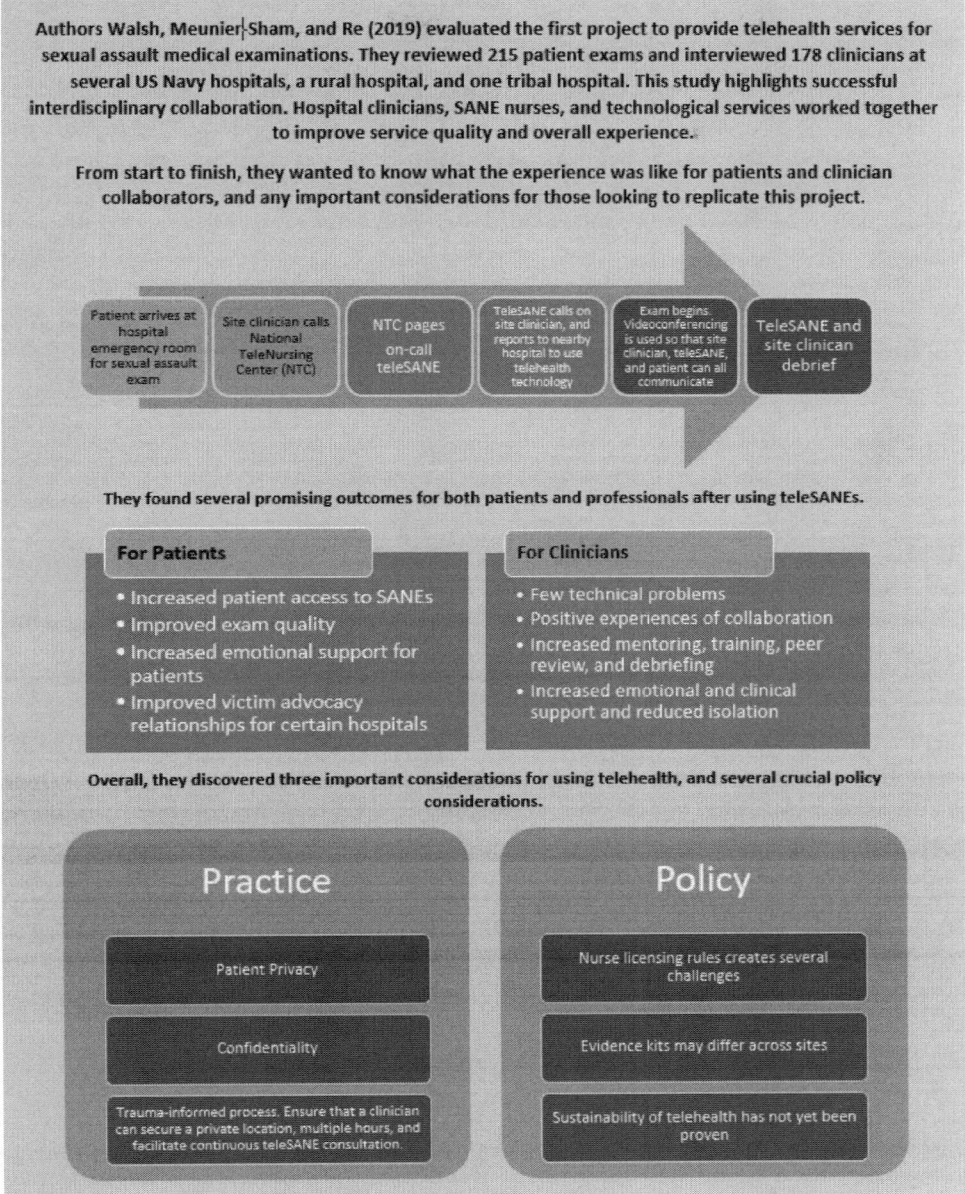

Authors Walsh, Meunier-Sham, and Re (2019) evaluated the first project to provide telehealth services for sexual assault medical examinations. They reviewed 215 patient exams and interviewed 178 clinicians at several US Navy hospitals, a rural hospital, and one tribal hospital. This study highlights successful interdisciplinary collaboration. Hospital clinicians, SANE nurses, and technological services worked together to improve service quality and overall experience.

From start to finish, they wanted to know what the experience was like for patients and clinician collaborators, and any important considerations for those looking to replicate this project.

| Patient arrives at hospital emergency room for sexual assault exam | Site clinician calls National TeleNursing Center (NTC) | NTC pages on-call teleSANE | TeleSANE calls on site clinician, and reports to nearby hospital to use telehealth technology | Exam begins. Videoconferencing is used so that site clinician, teleSANE, and patient can all communicate | TeleSANE and site clinican debrief |

They found several promising outcomes for both patients and professionals after using teleSANEs.

For Patients
- Increased patient access to SANEs
- Improved exam quality
- Increased emotional support for patients
- Improved victim advocacy relationships for certain hospitals

For Clinicians
- Few technical problems
- Positive experiences of collaboration
- Increased mentoring, training, peer review, and debriefing
- Increased emotional and clinical support and reduced isolation

Overall, they discovered three important considerations for using telehealth, and several crucial policy considerations.

Practice
- Patient Privacy
- Confidentiality
- Trauma-informed process. Ensure that a clinician can secure a private location, multiple hours, and facilitate continuous teleSANE consultation.

Policy
- Nurse licensing rules creates several challenges
- Evidence kits may differ across sites
- Sustainability of telehealth has not yet been proven

Figure 24.4 Collaborative Innovation: Telehealth and Sexual Assault Nurse Examiners

Incorporating trauma-informed accountability into victim service reform

Ongoing accountability is crucial for the future of victim services. Accountability in victim services can be implemented differently depending on the provider or system and the authority available to enforce the changes. Examples would include requiring comprehensive training and routine program evaluation, elevating survivors' feedback, and updating agency policies and procedures to require survivor-centered, trauma-informed practices by their providers (Melton, 2020). Accountability can also occur in informal ways, such as through MDT and SART meetings and group training (Melton, 2020). However, ensuring these growth opportunities are prioritized and enforced by leadership is a vital component of accountability (Luminais et al., 2017; 2020), as is the codification of trauma-informed practices and the training of law enforcement, health-care providers, and health and human service providers. When survivors seek support, they should do so without fear of blame, disbelief, or being retraumatized (Campbell et al., 2021; Lonsway & Archambault, 2020; Smith & Freyd, 2014).

Accountability enforces each of the tenets

Tying accountability to each of the first three tenets—survivor-centered advocacy, destigmatization, and collaboration—is essential for the long-term incorporation of these values. Enforcing survivor-defined advocacy means ensuring all current and future victim service models prioritize survivor-centeredness in their development and outcomes through frequent program evaluation and routinely collecting survivor feedback (Nichols, 2013). Destigmatizing sexual assault requires holding all victim service providers and their collaborative partners accountable to ensure all survivors can access services and feel welcomed and celebrated while minimizing gatekeeping behavior and practices. Destigmatizing sexual violence can only truly be successful if there are mechanisms in place to ensure that these efforts are developed in collaboration with the communities they seek to address. Finally, one of the key benefits of MDTs and other collaborative partnerships is the opportunity to increase transparency, cross-training, internal policy changes, and education on trauma-informed care (Luminais et al., 2020). Oversight and evaluation of different victim services are necessary to root out and address any discriminatory or inadequate services. Collaborative teams often already incorporate these types of accountability activities, which further demonstrates the value in expanding their use across all victim services.

Examples of accountability in action

External pressure and lasting reform

Successful transformations of victim services have often been propelled by external pressure. External pressure by national advocacy groups can effectively bring public awareness to areas still in need of improvement. For example, the organization End The Backlog created the Accountability Project as a centralized, national tracking of still-existing SAK backlogs throughout the United States (End the Backlog, 2016). In Ohio, an investigative journalist, Rachel Dissell, used a team of volunteers to survey jurisdictions throughout the state to inquire if investigations associated with now tested SAKs were reopened. After discovering that police departments throughout Ohio were still not investigating the tested SAKs, the project demonstrated that public attention was still necessary to reform the handling of SAKs (Lovell & Dissell, 2021). SAK tracking systems ensure survivors had access to their SAK test's progression. Portland, Oregon police created their own tracking system in 2018. Many states now have their own systems as well (End the

Backlog, 2016). (See Chapter 22 for how Washington legislated accountability via mandated case reviews.) As each of these examples demonstrates, accountability has been a necessary component in the successful reforms to result from the national movement to test SAKs.

Multidisciplinary oversight

Increasing oversight and transparency is necessary to ensure SAKs, investigations, and the treatment of survivors who choose to report continues to be prioritized. In New York, sex offender management courts have been created to centralize sex offense case oversight and resources. Sex offender management courts are focused on the offender and therefore are not inherently survivor-centered. However, there is innovation in this alternative court design that allows for survivor-centered advocacy to occur readily. By centralizing resources and personnel, sex offender management courts have been found to increase victims' access to services, simplify communication, and improve offender compliance which supports victims' safety (Thomforde-Hauser & Grant, 2010).

MDTs and other collaborative teams often perform more formal approaches to accountability, such as case reviews. The process of case review, often performed by MDTS and SARTs, provides necessary oversight and opportunity to address gaps and failings within victim service delivery. Informally, cross-training and informal discussion within MDTs, especially enhanced by embedding advocates onto investigative teams, can ensure participating professionals are educated in intersectionality and the impact of systemic oppression on the survivors they serve (Luminais et al., 2020). See Box 24.1 for another in-depth example of what an external case review by an advocacy organization with law enforcement entails, referred to as the Philadelphia Model. Accountability in collaborative teams and partnership are essential because of how negatively impacted survivors are when service providers do not communicate and coordinate effectively (Campbell, 2008; Lovell et al., 2021).

Common obstacles to incorporating accountability

Significant obstacles remain to ensure future victim service reform is accountable and survivor-centered. There is often limited ability to enforce change, and holding multisystemic services accountable can be complex. Measuring progress and conducting evaluations are crucial to accountability, and accountability within non-profit organizations is often enforced by funding agencies. However, research has shown that too much pressure on data collection as part of accountability enforced by funding agencies can lead to employee burnout and less time to work with clients (Ullman & Townsend, 2007; Wiley, 2020).

There continues to be a need to increase access to services by increasing gender inclusivity, promoting accessibility for disabled survivors, and addressing the marginalization of women of color (Weist et al., 2014). Both criminal justice and health-care systems are large and addressing the impact of systemic oppression throughout their many services is complex and ongoing. Additionally, primary care is a common pathway for survivors to disclose. As research has shown, there is a need to improve how primary care physicians screen, discuss, and support survivors of sexual violence (Palmieri & Valentine, 2021). Addressing the treatment of survivors beyond SANE programs would require the buy-in of a wide range of partners outside of victim services.

Improvements are needed in the reporting process to reduce poor treatment by professionals in health care or police departments (McCauley et al., 2019; Nichols, 2013).

Envisioning a future of accountable victim services for survivors

An improved future victim service field would understand that the longevity of any reform must include accountability, namely transparency, oversight, or evaluation to ensure priority is placed on implementing survivor-centered, trauma-informed approaches, as discussed in Chapters 19 and 21. So much progress has been made toward ensuring greater accessibility and enhanced quality of victim services. However, sustained pressure and political will are needed to ensure survivor-driven improvements remain in use and are updated across time, e.g., SAK tracking systems (End the Backlog, 2016). Continued pressure is needed to incorporate accountability into medical services, which are often a gateway into other victim services but traumatizing interactions with untrained professionals can deter seeking help (Palmieri & Valentine, 2021).

Discussion

This chapter has laid out four major tenets for the field of victim services to move toward a more just future in terms of survivor advocacy and response by summarizing existing research-informed improvements, expanding on current obstacles in implementing change, especially in the context of intersectionality with marginalized populations, and providing examples to demonstrate progress.

Box 24.1

The Philadelphia model: Accountability through external review

Accountability is an essential component for improved investigations, regaining public trust, and improving multidisciplinary collaboration. The Philadelphia Model is an external review process of Philadelphia's sex crimes unit by the Women's Law Project. Starting in 1999, in response to the discovery that the Philadelphia Police Department was failing to investigate sexual assault cases, the Women's Law Project established a yearly case review model. Because this approach to the accountability of law enforcement was both unprecedented and effective, this yearly case review is now referred to as a best practice model. This approach to case review is an example of how external audits can detect bias or systematic failings, which encourages public accountability and improves community relations (Police Executive Research Forum, 2018; Women's Law Project, 2013). In this model, advocates work with the sex crimes unit to assess random selections of sex crime cases together, and the advocates provide feedback. Because this model was in response to a breach of public trust, this model relies on a more public approach to case review to keep the department accountable. However, many case review models, often conducted by MDTs, are intentionally internal, held more frequently throughout the year, and approached collaboratively with multiple agencies involved. This approach to accountability can be more effective in encouraging year-round improvements and identifying gaps not just in law enforcement but with other victim service agencies at the table as well.

These four tenets were chosen to simplify and centralize the many essential gains in the victim services field since their inception in the 1970s. These tenets were once considered aspirational yet often unachievable goals for victim service programs. However, by looking closely at recent changes made in the victim service field, we see that implementing these tenets is possible and necessary. Survivor-centered advocacy, destigmatizing sexual violence, collaboration, and accountability have lasting value to survivors and should be required components for all aspects of victim services moving forward. A sustainability plan is recommended to incorporate these values directly into agency strategic planning so that survivor-centered, trauma-informed approaches are prioritized.

Destigmatizing sexual violence requires an intersectional approach directed specifically at reaching traditionally underserved populations within victim services. Specifically, male survivors, sex workers, the LGBTQIA+ community, and individuals with physical or developmental disabilities deserve services that go beyond just welcoming them. Prioritizing centering survivors in advocacy will require difficult conversations about how internal and external biases continue to be held against various survivors and that ongoing and significant changes to policies and procedures are needed (Ullman & Townsend, 2007; Weist et al., 2014).

Collaboration continues to serve the victim services field well in expanding the reach of where victim-centeredness and trauma-informed care education are needed. Healthcare professionals, social workers, government health and human service agencies, detention centers, addiction recovery, Title IX and campus service providers, and childcare professionals can act as gatekeepers or retraumatize survivors who disclose to them. Incorporating trauma-informed accountability into each profession is necessary to reduce secondary trauma and center survivors through codifying policies or procedures, mandating internal or external review, and promoting transparency with the public.

In terms of limitations, due to the prevalence of research focused on the criminal justice aspects of victim services and response, this chapter includes more examples of criminal justice-based services, such as MDTs and law enforcement reform. As stated, survivors are not just interested in criminal justice solutions (Herman, 2005; Jülich, 2006). There is a continued need for research and emphasis on improving community-based victim services (McGlynn et al., 2017). Additionally, a deeper examination is needed of what barriers and stigma still impede survivors from seeking support and how to enact enduring change most effectively in different fields of victim services.

The path forward for a better victim service field is clear. Future technology, policy, legislation, funding, and/or other victim service reforms must do more than just aspire to meet each of these tenets, but instead require a survivor-centered, trauma-informed structure in all future reforms. The future of victim services must continue listening to all survivors and holding themselves accountable to ensure hard-fought progress is not undone.

Key Points

- Survivor-centered advocacy ensures that all victim services prioritize the right of survivors to make choices about their healing journey or what defines success to them. Advocacy efforts need to center on survivors to prevent future marginalization by services or systems not designed to prioritize or recognize their unique needs.

- Stigma interferes with a survivor's access to services and the quality of their interactions with providers of victim services. Destigmatizing sexual violence requires an intersectional approach to ensure intentional inclusion and support for all survivors, especially those that continue to be excluded from traditionally accepted groups of survivors.
- Prioritizing and expanding collaboration within victim services will improve the efficacy of multidisciplinary partnerships, reduce secondary trauma, and increase survivor engagement.
- Trauma-informed accountability can be implemented in many ways to ensure victim services continue to build upon past progress while always putting survivors' needs first.

Discussion Questions

1 Considering each of the stated four tenets necessary for improved victim services, what would be a fifth tenet based on the needs and priorities stated in the research and input given by survivors?
2 Collaborating professionals from different fields must consider how to ethically discuss the needs of their clients without violating confidentiality or ethical guidelines specific to their profession. What are some concerns victim advocates might have about safeguarding their client's information? How are these concerns similar or different from a police detective's concerns? Suggest some ways these professionals can communicate these concerns productively.
3 A recommendation to reduce retraumatizing experiences for survivors is to provide trauma-informed care training to more professionals involved in victim services. Why would the authors recommend expanding training to other professionals not traditionally viewed as related to victim services? What would be some obstacles to carrying out this recommendation?

Funding Acknowledgment

This project was supported by Grant No. 2018 AK-BX-0001 awarded by the Bureau of Justice Assistance. The Bureau of Justice Assistance is a component of the US Department of Justice's Office of Justice Programs, which also includes the Bureau of Justice Statistics, the National Institute of Justice, the Office of Juvenile Justice and Delinquency Prevention, the Office for Victims of Crime, and the SMART Office. Points of view or opinions in this document are those of the authors and do not necessarily represent the official position or policies of the US Department of Justice.

Conflict of Interest

The authors have no conflicts of interest to disclose.

Further Reading

Guckenheimer, D. (2021). "What are we going to do with a penis in the room?": Rape crisis centers and treatment of transgender survivors. In A. J. LeBlanc & B. L. Perry (Eds.), *Advances in medical sociology* (pp. 299–319). Emerald Publishing Limited. https://doi.org/10.1108/S1057-629020210000021018

Mulla, S. (2014). *Violence of care: Rape victims, forensic nurses, and sexual assault intervention.* NYU Press.

Sprankle, E., Bloomquist, K., Butcher, C., Gleason, N., & Schaefer, Z. (2018). The role of sex work stigma in victim blaming and empathy of sexual assault survivors. *Sexuality Research and Social Policy, 15*(3), 242–248. https://doi.org/10.1007/s13178-017-0282-0

References

Amstadter, A. B., McCauley, J. L., Ruggiero, K. J., Resnick, H. S., & Kilpatrick, D. G. (2008). Service utilization and help seeking in a national sample of female rape victims. *Psychiatric Services, 59*(12), 1450–1457. https://doi.org/10.1176/ps.2008.59.12.1450

Brooks, O., & Burman, M. (2017). Reporting rape: Victim perspectives on advocacy support in the criminal justice process. *Criminology & Criminal Justice, 17*(2), 209–225. https://doi.org/10.1177/1748895816667996

Brubaker, S. J. (2019). Campus-based sexual assault victim advocacy and Title IX: Revisiting tensions between grassroots activism and the criminal justice system. *Feminist Criminology, 14*(3), 307–329. https://doi.org/10.1177/1557085118772087

Burns, C. J., & Sinko, L. (2021). Restorative justice for survivors of sexual violence experienced in adulthood: A scoping review. *Trauma, Violence, & Abuse.* https://doi.org/10.1177/15248380211029408

Campbell, R. (1998). The community response to rape: Victims' experiences with the legal, medical, and mental health systems. *American Journal of Community Psychology, 26*(3), 355–379. https://doi.org/10.1023/A:1022155003633

Campbell, R. (2006). Rape survivors' experiences with the legal and medical systems: Do rape victim advocates make a difference? *Violence Against Women, 12*(1), 30–45. https://doi.org/10.1177/1077801205277539

Campbell, R. (2008). The psychological impact of rape victims. *American Psychologist, 63*(8), 702–717. https://doi.org/10.1037/0003-066X.63.8.702

Campbell, R., Fehler-Cabral, G., Pierce, S. J., Sharma, D. B., Shaw, J., Horsford, S., & Feeney, H. (2021). Changing the criminal justice system response to sexual assault: An empirical study of a participatory action research project. *American Journal of Community Psychology, 67*(1–2), 166–178. https://doi.org/10.1002/ajcp.12428

Cattaneo, L. B., Stylianou, A. M., Hargrove, S., Goodman, L. A., Gebhard, K. T., & Curby, T. W. (2020). Survivor-centered practice and survivor empowerment: Evidence from a research–practitioner partnership. *Violence Against Women, 27*(9), 1252–1272. https://doi.org/10.1177/1077801220935196

Cole, J. (2011). Victim confidentiality on sexual assault response teams (SART). *Journal of Interpersonal Violence, 26*(2), 360–376. https://doi.org/10.1177/0886260510362895

Corpuz, M. (2020, Mar 4). *Brockton hospital connects rape survivors with sexual assault nurse examiners.* https://www.enterprisenews.com/news/20200304/brockton-hospital-connects-rape-survivors-with-sexual-assault-nurse-examiners

End the Backlog. (2016). Accountability project. *Joyful Heart Foundation.* http://endthebacklog.org/backlog-where-it/accountability-project

Farrell, A., Wills, C., & Nicolas, C. (2020). Police engagement in multidisciplinary team approaches to commercial sexual exploitation of children. In B. Fox, J. A. Reid, & A. J. Masys (Eds.), *Science informed policing* (pp. 195–214). Springer International Publishing. https://doi.org/10.1007/978-3-030-41287-6_10

Gaines, D. C., & Wells, W. (2015). Investigators' and prosecutors' perceptions of collaborating with victim advocates on sexual assault casework. *Criminal Justice Policy Review, 28*(6), 555–569. https://doi.org/10.1177/0887403415592176

Goffman, E. (1963). *Stigma: Notes on the management of spoiled identity.* Prentice-Hall.

Greeson, M. R., & Campbell, R. (2012). Sexual assault response teams (SARTs): An empirical review of their effectiveness and challenges to successful implementation. *Trauma, Violence, & Abuse, 14*(2), 83–95. https://doi.org/10.1177/1524838012470035

Herbert, J. L., & Bromfield, L. (2019). Better together? A review of evidence for multidisciplinary teams responding to physical and sexual child abuse. *Trauma, Violence & Abuse, 20*(2), 214. https://doi.org/10.1177/1524838017697268

Herman, J. (1997). *Trauma and recovery*. Basic Books.

Herman, J. L. (2005). Justice from the victim's perspective. *Violence Against Women, 11*(5), 571–602. https://doi.org/10.1177/1077801205274450

Jülich, S. (2006). Views of justice among survivors of historical child sexual abuse: Implications for restorative justice in New Zealand. *Theoretical Criminology, 10*(1), 125–138. https://doi.org/10.1177/1362480606059988

Koss, M. P. (2014). The RESTORE program of restorative justice for sex crimes: Vision, process, and outcomes. *Journal of Interpersonal Violence, 29*(9), 1623–1660. https://doi.org/10.1177/0886260513511537

Koss, M. P., White, J. W., & Lopez, E. C. (2017). Victim voice in reenvisioning responses to sexual and physical violence nationally and internationally. *American Psychologist, 72*(9), 1019–1030. https://doi.org/10.1037/amp0000233

Laing, L. (2017). Secondary victimization: Domestic violence survivors navigating the family law system. *Violence Against Women, 23*(11), 1314–1335. https://doi.org/10.1177/1077801216659942

Leung, R., & Williams, R. (2019). #MeToo and intersectionality: An examination of the #MeToo movement through the R. Kelly Scandal. *Journal of Communication Inquiry, 43*(4), 349–371. https://doi.org/10.1177/0196859919874138

Loney-Howes, R. (2020). The contours and critiques of antirape activism: A brief history. *Online antirape activism: Exploring the politics of the personal in the age of digital media* (pp. 17–32). Emerald Publishing Limited. https://doi.org/10.1108/978-1-83867-439-720201004

Lonsway, K. A., Archambault, J. (2020). Advocates and law enforcement: Oil and water? Part 1: Role of advocates in the criminal justice system. *End Violence Against Women International.* https://evawintl.org/wp-content/uploads/TB-Oil-Water-1-3-Combined.pdf

Lovell, R. E., & Dissell, R. (2021). Dissemination and impact amplified: How a researcher–reporter collaboration helped improve the criminal justice response to victims with untested sexual assault kits. *Journal of Contemporary Criminal Justice, 37*(2), 257–275. https://doi.org/10.1177/1043986221999880

Lovell, R., Overman, L., Huang, D., & Flannery, D. J. (2021). The bureaucratic burden of identifying your rapist and remaining "cooperative": What the sexual assault kit initiative tells us about sexual assault case attrition and outcomes. *American Journal of Criminal Justice, 46*(3), 528–553. https://doi.org/10.1007/s12103-020-09573-x

Luminais, M., Lovell, R., & Flannery, D. J. (2017). *Changing culture through sharing space: A case study of the Cuyahoga County sexual assault kit task force.* Begun Center for Violence Prevention Research and Education at the Jack, Joseph and Morton Mandel School of Applied Social Sciences at Case Western Reserve University. http://hdl.handle.net/2186/ksl:2006061456

Luminais, M., Lovell, R., McGuire, M., Klingenstein, J., Kavadas, A., & Overman, L. (2020). *Victim advocates and cold case investigations: Impact of integration on the Cuyahoga County sexual assault kit task force.* The Begun Center for Violence Prevention Education and Research at the Jack, Joseph and Morton Mandel School of Applied Social Sciences at Case Western Reserve University. http://hdl.handle.net/2186/ksl:2006061588

Marshall, T. F. (1999). *Restorative justice: An overview*. Home Office.

McCauley, H. L., Campbell, R., Buchanan, N. T., & Moylan, C. A. (2019). Advancing theory, methods, and dissemination in sexual violence research to build a more equitable future: An intersectional, community-engaged approach. *Violence Against Women*, 25(16), 1906–1931. https://doi.org/10.1177/1077801219875823

McGlynn, C., Downes, J., & Westmarland, N. (2017). Seeking justice for survivors of sexual violence: Recognition, voice and consequences. In E. Zinsstag & M. Keenan (Eds.), *Restorative responses to sexual violence.* (pp. 179–191). Routledge. https://doi.org/10.4324/9781315630595

Melton, P. A. (2020). *Enacting an improved response to sexual assault: A criminal justice practitioner's guide.* RTI Press. https://doi.org/10.3768/rtipress.2020.op.006.2007

Murray, C., Crowe, A., & Akers, W. (2016). How can we end the stigma surrounding domestic and sexual violence? A modified Delphi study with national advocacy leaders. *Journal of Family Violence*, 31(3), 271–287. https://doi.org/10.1007/s10896-015-9768-9

Nichols, A. J. (2013). Survivor-defined practices to mitigate revictimization of battered women in the protective order process. *Journal of Interpersonal Violence*, 28(7), 1403–1423. https://doi.org/10.1177/0886260512468243

Overstreet, N. M., & Quinn, D. M. (2013). The intimate partner violence stigmatization model and barriers to help seeking. *Basic and Applied Social Psychology*, 35(1), 109–122. https://doi.org/10.1080/01973533.2012.746599

Palmieri, J., & Valentine, J. L. (2021). Using trauma-informed care to address sexual assault and intimate partner violence in primary care. *The Journal for Nurse Practitioners*, 17(1), 44–48. https://doi.org/10.1016/j.nurpra.2020.08.028

Payne, B. K. (2007). Victim advocates' perceptions of the role of health care workers in sexual assault cases. *Criminal Justice Policy Review*, 18(1), 81–94. https://doi.org/10.1177/0887403406294900

Police Executive Research Forum. (2018). Executive guidebook: Practical approaches for strengthening law enforcement's response to sexual assault. *Police Executive Research Forum*. https://www.policeforum.org/assets/SexualAssaultResponseExecutiveGuidebook.pdf

Price, M., Davidson, T. M., Ruggiero, K. J., Acierno, R., & Resnick, H. S. (2014). Predictors of using mental health services after sexual assault. *Journal of Traumatic Stress*, 27(3), 331–337. https://doi.org/10.1002/jts.21915

Smith, C. P., & Freyd, J. J. (2014). Institutional betrayal. *American Psychologist*, 69(6), 575–587. https://doi.org/10.1037/a0037564

Thomforde-Hauser, R., & Grant, J. A. (2010). Sex offense courts: Supporting victim and community safety through collaboration. *Center for Court Innovation*. https://www.courtinnovation.org/publications/sex-offense-courts

Ullman, S. E., & Townsend, S. M. (2007). Barriers to working with sexual assault survivors: A qualitative study of rape crisis center worker. *Violence Against Women*, 13(4), 412–443. https://doi.org/10.1177/1077801207299191

Walsh, W. A., Meunier-Sham, J., & Re, C. (2019). Using telehealth for sexual assault forensic examinations: A process evaluation of a national pilot project. *Journal of Forensic Nursing*, 15(3), 152–162. https://doi.org/10.1097/jfn.0000000000000254

Weist, M. D., Kinney, L., Taylor, L. K., Pollitt-Hill, J., Bryant, Y., Anthony, L., & Wilkerson, J. (2014). African American and White women's experience of sexual assault and services for sexual assault. *Journal of Aggression, Maltreatment & Trauma*, 23(9), 901–916. https://doi.org/10.1080/10926771.2014.953715

Wemmers, J. A. (2017). Judging victims: Restorative choices for victims of sexual violence. Victims of Crime, 12.

Wiley, K. (2020). Implementing domestic violence policy: When accountability trumps mission. *Affilia*, 35(4), 533–551. https://doi.org/10.1177/0886109919894649

Women's Law Project. (2013). *Policy brief: Advocacy to improve police response to sex crimes*. http://www.womenslawproject.org/wp-content/uploads/2017/02/Policy_Brief_Improving_Police_Response_to_Sexual_Assault.pdf

Zweig, J. M., & Burt, M. R. (2007). Predicting women's perceptions of domestic violence and sexual assault agency helpfulness: What matters to program clients? *Violence Against Women, 13*(11), 1149–1178. https://doi.org/10.1177/1077801207307799

25 Making progress

Putting the past, present, and future together to promote needed reform

Jennifer Langhinrichsen-Rohling,
Rachel E. Lovell, and Bridget Jules

Author Note

The opinions or points of view expressed in this chapter are solely those of the authors and do not reflect the official positions of any participating organization or the US Department of Justice.

The Discovery of Thousands of Untested Sexual Assault Kits: Pulling the Past, Present, and Future Together to Make Progress Toward Needed Reform

As editors of this book, we (JLR, RL) sought to curate the paradigm-shifting knowledge emerging from the U.S. Department of Justice's (DOJ) Sexual Assault Kit Initiative, otherwise known as SAKI. DOJ's SAKI provided police departments, prosecutors' offices, crime labs, and rape crisis centers with the resources and technical assistance necessary to address hundreds of thousands of previously untested sexual assault kits (SAKs) from across the United States. Many funded SAKI sites have paired with action-oriented researchers (e.g., sexual assault nurse examiners (SANEs), criminologists, sociologists, psychologists, economists) to determine the context in which their backlog accumulated, study rapists' behaviors and patterns, and consult and promote evidence-based training, practice, and adoption of policy across the justice system. SAKI sites constituted multidisciplinary teams to tackle their current "backlog" of kits and prevent the recurrence of future backlogs. Consequently, the tragic discovery of these untested kits—many of which were shelved and shamefully forgotten—has resulted in at least one key silver lining. *These kits have provided a gateway to transforming our collective and systemically inadequate response to sexual violence.* It is not hyperbole to say that as a direct result of DOJ's SAKI, there has been monumental progress with regard to our understanding of:

- Factors influencing the accumulation of kits and case attrition for rape (Chapters 1 and 2);
- Trauma responses among survivors as well as factors influencing victim disclosure and reporting processes (Chapters 3, 5, and 8);
- The essential role of advocates when enacting a trauma-sensitive, victim-centered, cooperative, multidisciplinary response to rape (Chapters 4 and 24);

DOI: 10.4324/9781003186816-29

- The usefulness of multidisciplinary response teams, special victim units, and family justice centers (Chapters 6 and 21) to promote accountability, transparency, and victim-centered justice responses;
- The latest information about rapists and their offending patterns (Chapter 7);
- Needed changes in hospital, police, forensic lab, prosecutor, campus, and political policies, laws, and practices in response to rape (Chapters 10, 13, 16, 18, 19, and 22);
- More effective and specialized prosecution of rapists (Chapter 11);
- The influential role of SANEs in the rape response process (Chapters 12, 14, and 15);
- The importance of thoughtful trauma-sensitive victim notification processes (Chapter 9 and 20);
- The economics of forensic and kit testing decisions (Chapter 17);
- The continued need for effective implementation of comprehensive, community-wide, multimedia rape and violence prevention efforts (Chapter 23).

Used wisely, this collection of information can change practice and policy to promote needed reform of our collective response to rape. For example, less than a decade ago, prior to DOJ's SAKI, most US jurisdictions saw little value in efforts to test all currently collected kits. They were even less likely to attach value to testing "old" stored kits. Now, as cogently argued in Chapter 17, we can show there is an economic benefit to testing all kits. A demonstrated return on investment is also associated with testing all swabs contained within the submitted kits.

Similarly, as little as ten years ago, the United States had little appetite for a public reckoning around sexual violence. However, as demonstrated by the recent #Metoo and #TimesUp viral social movements, numerous long-standing rape stereotypes, entrenched cultural biases toward rape survivors, and prevailing rape myths have been questioned (Chapter 3). Consent conversations are now being routinely modeled across college campuses, and formerly untouchable celebrity predators are being brought to justice (Chapter 15). We have learned that to prevent the miscarriage of justice and/or the long history of horrific neglect for thousands of rape survivors (Chapter 1) and to resist the retraumatization of victims, advocates, and other professionals working in this field, all components of the rape response process need to be examined under the bright light of reform.

SAK initiatives from across the United States have played a vital role in illuminating important transformational processes. We have learned that testing is not the solution but a starting point. We also need to enact evidence-based multimedia prevention strategies in conjunction with the universal adoption of trauma-centered responses to assault disclosures if our collective response to rape is to advance. Hopefully, as readers moved through this book, they were encouraged to affirm and/or reaffirm their commitment to the health and well-being of survivors. Commitment to survivors is accomplished through effective and evidence-based responses to rape disclosure and trauma-sensitive care throughout their journey.

In that spirit, *we highlight the multidimensional value of each victim's kit.* As detailed in many chapters included in this book, prior to rape kit reform efforts, most jurisdictions only tested certain kits—primarily those in which the perpetrator was a stranger and the victim was prosecution-oriented and endorsed by the justice system. This has proven to be short-sighted. Testing a kit provides so much more than just a potential lead in one particular case or trial information in another. Testing should not be reserved only for cases judged from the outset as likely to go to trial and result in a conviction. Instead, testing all kits provides an equitable response and supportive signal to all victims. It also sends an important accountability signal to perpetrators. Testing also provides a wealth of information. It can confirm a suspect's identity. It can link an offender from one kit to another and to evidence collected from numerous other types of crimes. It can help delineate sexual offending patterns and behaviors while populating the federal DNA database in a manner that can potentially solve a host of past, current, and future crimes. Importantly, a "test all kits" policy can also exonerate innocent suspects.

This book describes economic analyses that demonstrate that "test-all kits" practices are economically sound; this equitable practice is therefore being mandated into law in many states. Training law enforcement to routinely conduct and document rape investigations that include: visiting and collecting evidence at the assault site, looking for and interviewing potential witnesses, and testing all available evidence, is a prime pathway toward a safer world in which offenders are held fully accountable for their assaults. Meanwhile, hearing the voices of survivors and listening to the wisdom of change agents has solidified public support for kit testing as the morally right thing to do for victims.

Unfortunately, SAKI comes with an explicit acknowledgment that, as a culture, we have not done right by rape victims and their loved ones. These wrongs have contributed to negative psychological outcomes for survivors, including deleterious mental and physical health effects, institutional mistrust and betrayal, and for some, an increased risk for revictimization. We have allowed perpetrators to escape the consequences of their crimes and given them the freedom to re-offend. Across DOJ's SAKI and with the production of this book, we have striven to the right some wrongs, disseminate important knowledge, and promote transformative and trauma-informed accountability. We hope this book will facilitate the many ongoing efforts to reform our informal, formal, and systemic responses to rape.

To accomplish this goal, we have chosen to highlight many different types of change agents, each of whom is key to this transformational effort. While this book contains many essential research findings and a variety of important recommendations for multidisciplinary policy and practice changes, it also pays homage to these reform champions who are nested within government, law, non-profit, university, media, forensic, and criminal justice settings. These chapters are written by survivors and scientists, prosecutors, and policy makers. As these disparate voices are woven together, it is clear that multiple systems intersect in response to each victim's rape. To that end, we hope that emerging and practicing professionals from an array of disciplines (e.g., nurses, police officers, lawyers, detectives, crime analysts, psychologists, criminologists, politicians, economists, advocates, policy makers, consultants, researchers, and members of the media) will use this work to find the motivation to do more and better within their part of the response system. We are also heartened that there are specific best-practice recommendations for prosecutors (Chapter 11), advocates (Chapter 24), police departments (Chapters 7, 10, and 21), forensic analysts (Chapter 16), sexual assault medical examiners (Chapter 12), policy makers (Chapter 18), officer training programs (Chapter 19), multidisciplinary teams (Chapter 21), case review programs (Chapter 22), and preventionists (Chapter 23) contained in this book.

We also affirm many of the conclusions reached by contributors in this book. For example, there continue to be unacceptable attrition levels in rape cases; less than 5% of reported cases result in a conviction (Chapter 2). There also continues to be an unacceptable level of variability in how rape cases are investigated and a lack of adoption of recommended best practices and standards related to rape response. One of the themes linking chapters in this book is the call for greater accountability (Chapters 21, 22, and 24). There is a need to establish, monitor, and reinforce core standards for law enforcement, nurse examiners, and prosecutors. Likewise, routine partnering with crime analysts and researchers promotes greater adherence to protocols and provides the data to monitor compliance and promote transparency. At the same time, several chapter contributors describe how the traditional reliance on arrest and conviction rates has not fully aligned with a victim-centered approach. In conjunction with the quality, efficiency, and timeliness of service delivery, routine monitoring of victim satisfaction with services is an important next step. We highlight the wisdom of developing a SAKI training and technical assistance program. As described in Chapter 6, the SAKI TTA program, led by RTI International, has been instrumental in disseminating information, training programs/webinars, and resources to facilitate the ability of jurisdictions to establish practices that are: trauma-informed, victim-centered, evidence-based, and sustainable. They were also foundational in supporting a community of practice among SAKI researchers, crime analysts, police officers, advocates, and change agents; this book largely developed from TTA efforts.

Additionally, we note the repeated theme, expressed across the book, that creating a just and more equitable society requires us all to participate fully in the prevention of sexual violence (Chapter 23). Consideration needs to be given to the finding that perpetrators disproportionately target vulnerable and marginalized victims to evade being caught and escape justice. We continue to argue that these victims deserve increased societal support. We assert that this support can be enacted by creating a system designed to #StartByBelieving, that is transparent and trauma-informed, and performs effectively and with accountability to investigate and obtain justice for reported crimes.

We would also like to spotlight several other emergent take-away points from the information presented in this book. *First*, given what we now know about sexual assault offending, it is even more vital that we create response processes that are victim-centered and supportive. We now know that it is unlikely that any given perpetrator perpetrates one and only one rape. Correspondingly, we also know that the cost of victim disengagement is high. Yet, the justice system continues to ask a lot from victims. They are expected to survive their assault and function as a key asset within the criminal justice system, a process that may take years to fully unfold and often starts on the worst night of a person's life. Knowing this, we must turn the question from *Is this victim credible and likely to be believed by a jury if this case ever comes to trial?* to this, *Are we doing all we can do to make each victim continue to choose to remain involved in the justice process from start to finish?*

Second, it is clear that forensic testing is advancing rapidly; we must be ready to reexamine case files for additional evidence and/or retest evidence, as warranted, across time as these advances materialize. Evidence storage spaces require maintenance, ongoing accountability, and ready access across time. We must also continue to lawfully expand CODIS with offender and crime DNA. The utility of CODIS will only grow as it is more heavily populated. We now know there are widespread problems with collecting lawfully "owed" DNA from perpetrators who should be in CODIS because of a qualifying offense but are not. Testing all kits, uploading eligible profiles, and collecting and submitting owed DNA are important pathways to solving already committed crimes. Making these pathways robust may also deter perpetrators from additional future assaults.

Third, commonly held but erroneous rape supportive attitudes and stereotypical rape scripts are challenged with new and emerging evidence. We now know that false accusations of rape are relatively uncommon. Humans, including police officers and detectives, are not accurate lie detectors. Trauma can result in fragmented memories. Freezing is a common reaction to highly traumatic events. Blaming victims for their trauma is a common human reaction that comes from our desire to feel safe (i.e., *Bad things happen to bad people; I am not a bad person, therefore that cannot and will not happen to me*). We also know that perpetrators use these same beliefs and common challenges to victim credibility to their advantage by targeting vulnerable and/ or marginalized victims. Continued education of potential jurors, prosecutors, police officers, and others who interact with victims or who respond to rape disclosures is essential.

Fourth, changing our response to rape requires effort from all stakeholders. SAKI has revealed that the backlog of untested kits is not just law enforcement or prosecution problem; *it is a public problem.* Thus, transformative change requires us all to hold systems—and the professionals working within those systems—accountable. Members of the general public should take note as well. We must support those doing the reform work so they can continue their efforts without burning out or succumbing to vicarious trauma. Further, while the change agents in this book are inspirational, their efforts can serve as a guide to others. As shown in this book, light is being brought into dark spaces; shame and stigma are being replaced with science and support.

Finally, at the outset of this effort, we envisioned this book as an opportunity to take stock of where we were, where we are now, and where we want to be. This book is also an enduring record of this journey and, hopefully, an inspirational guide for jurisdictions that have yet to face their backlog or embrace the practice and policy changes from SAKI. *The lessons learned and best practice recommendations shared in this book are not the end but a significant jumping-off point for the journey to continue.* We hope to continue to advance our knowledge while creating a culture that is even less tolerant of sexual misconduct and violence. We envision a world that provides better support for all survivors while holding more offenders accountable. We hope to see comprehensive, integrated, transparent, multisystem rape responses occurring within communities that are implementing innovative and effective violence prevention strategies in partnership with a long and inclusive list of allies.

While the transformation is ongoing, through it all, we must continue to center the voices of survivors. To a large extent, the story of untested kits is a story of forgotten victims of rape whose kits remained shelved and whose perpetrators remained free. Those forgotten kits were too often considered only as insufficient evidence from uncertain events. More often than not, the victims of these events were female and/or from marginalized communities. Some were children. Many were not believed nor supported. And it is their pain and evidence from their bodies that have been shelved and forgotten. It is a paradigm shift to remember that each SAK represents a person. That kit is a valuable contribution, intimately collected from a survivor's body through their brave expression of choice and voice in the face of considerable vulnerability. To this end, we will continue to use our collective voices to advance the work, test all kits, and demand change. Thus, we hope this book serves as both a curation of information and a continued call to action.

Index

Note: Page references in *italics* denote figures, in **bold** tables and with "n" endnotes.

9781032033396